COMMENTARY ON THE GOSPEL OF SAINT JOHN
Part I

St. Thomas Aquinas

The frontispiece is from the rare *Vita D. Thomae Aquinatis.* Othonis Vaeni ingenio et manu delineata. Antverpiae Sumptibus Othonis Vaeni, 1610. The caption reads: *After an important discussion about the holy sacrament of the Eucharist, Thomas wrote out his opinion and placed it on the altar before an image of the Crucified, and prayed that Christ would confirm it by some sign. Suddenly he was raised from the ground and clearly heard the crucified Christ saying to him: "Thomas! You have written well about me. What reward will you accept?" And Thomas answered: "Only yourself, Lord."*

Cùm graui disceptatione de Ven. Sacramento Eucharistiæ orta, Thomas sententiam
suam scripto consignasset, eamque in altari coram Crucifixo posuisset, orans vt eam
Christus signo aliquo confirmaret; ecce tibi subitò Thomam à terra sublimem, Cruci-
fixumque ad eum clara voce dicentem: Benè scripsisti de me, Thoma,
quam ergo mercedem accipies? Cui ille, Non aliam nisi te, Domine.

AQUINAS SCRIPTURE SERIES VOL. 4

COMMENTARY ON
THE GOSPEL OF ST. JOHN

St. Thomas Aquinas

James A. Weisheipl, O.P., S.T.M.
General Director and Consultant
Pontifical Institute of Mediaeval Studies, Toronto
and
Fabian R. Larcher, O.P.

Part I

MAGI BOOKS, INC. 33 BUCKINGHAM DR. ALBANY, N.Y. 12208

Other works by James A. Weisheipl
DEVELOPMENT OF PHYSICAL THEORY IN THE MIDDLE AGES
FRIAR THOMAS D'AQUINO: HIS LIFE, THOUGHT AND WORKS

Composition in Press Roman by Magi Books, Inc., Albany, N.Y.

Library of Congress Cataloging in Publication Data (Revised)

Thomas Aquinas, Saint, 1225? - 1274.
    Aquinas Scripture series.

    Includes bibliographical references and indexes.
    CONTENTS: v. 1. Commentary on Saint Paul's Epistle
to the Galatians, translated by F. R. Larcher. — —v. 2.
Commentary on Saint Paul's Epistle to the Ephesians;
translation and introd. by M. L. Lamb. — —[etc.] — —v. 4.
Commentary on the Gospel of Saint John, translation of
J. A. Weisheipl with F. R. Larcher. v.
    1. Bible — — Commentaries. I. Title.
BS491.2.T5   220.7   66-19306

ISBN 0—87343—031—X

CONTENTS

AN INTRODUCTION TO THE COMMENTARY ON THE GOSPEL OF SAINT JOHN OF ST. THOMAS AQUINAS

by

James A. Weisheipl, O.P., S.T.M.

St. Thomas' commentary on the Gospel of St. John is unique among his many writings on Sacred Scripture. It is the work of a master theologian, delivered at the University of Paris, then the intellectual center in Christendom, when Thomas was at the height of his fame and apostolic zeal for souls. A fourteenth-century list of Thomas' writings notes that this commentary is a *reportatio* by Reginald of Piperno and adds "better than which none can be found."(1)   A *reportatio* is a verbal report of an actual lecture taken down by a scribe or student in the course of actual delivery. In this case the scribe was the faithful Friar Reginald of Piperno, who had been the "constant companion," or *socius,* for the last fifteen years of Thomas' short but busy life. The Italian Province of Dominicans wisely provided Thomas with this kind of personal secretary and general factotum after he returned from Paris as a Master in Sacred Theology in 1260.(2)

A *reportatio* is not exactly a dictation in our sense of the term; it is more like a student's notebook in shorthand containing basically the gist of what is being said, but usually with varying numbers of verbal omissions and inaccuracies. But this commentary is more than a mere scribal report. It was in fact "corrected" by Thomas himself – if we are to believe Tolomeo of Lucca, one of Thomas' early biographers and confreres – before the commentary went into circulation through copies made by hand, the customary mode of publication before the era of the printing press. More than that: according to Bernard Gui, another confrere and early biographer, Thomas himself wrote out in full the commentary on the first five chapters of John (and hence this section ought to be considered an authentic *expositio,* or authoritative version), while the rest of it survived in the hand of Reginald, corrected by Thomas.

This commentary was very popular in the Middle Ages, and it ranks among the best of Thomas' work as a master theologian and saintly man of faith. It was read not only by theologians searching for the truth, but also by preachers and pious men and women desiring solid food for meditation and fervent prayer. Scattered throughout the world there still exist thirty-three complete and thirteen incomplete manuscript copies of this work, attesting to its considerable popularity before the age of printing. Innumerable copies of this work have no doubt been lost or destroyed in the tumult of centuries following the Middle Ages.

This detailed commentary is St. Thomas' personal response to the Word of God Incarnate as described in the sublime words of John "the Divine." For St. Thomas, the God of Abraham, Isaac, and Jacob spoke to his chosen people through the mouth of prophets in the long course of salvation history. "But when the appointed time came, God sent his Son, born of a woman, born a subject of the Law, to redeem the subjects of the Law and to enable us to be adopted as sons" (Gal 4:4-5). This Incarnate Son, Jesus Christ, is the total manifestation of the Father, the Eternal Word made flesh. There is nothing left unsaid in the Word; the Father's love is complete in the love the Son bears for the Father and for us. Christ's whole life, his passion, death, and resurrection, are the praise and glory of the Father "through the working of the Holy Spirit." "You must believe me when I say that I am in the Father and the Father is in me" (Jn 14:11). "Whatever you ask for in my name I will do, so that the Father may be glorified in the Son" (Jn 14:13). Christ's "food" was to do the will of his Father in all things, thus glorifying the Father in Jesus.

One of St. Thomas' basic theological principles is that everything Jesus Christ did and said was for our instruction and imitation. Thus the sanctity of our lives is the on-going praise and glory of the Father, through the Son, by the working of the Holy Spirit. The very being of the Father is the unqualified affirmation of love for the Son and *for us* in the Son. "God is love" (1 Jn 4:8). This love elicits from us an unreserved affirmation of love for God and neighbor, by which God is glorified and resplendent in us. The whole of our happiness is this eternal "glory" in tasting and seeing that the Lord is good (see Ps 34:8). This commentary is St. Thomas' tasting and seeing the goodness of Jesus, the Word Incarnate, embodied in the tender words of St. John, the "beloved disciple," who leaned on the breast of the Savior at the Last Supper.

Thomas brought to his writing of this commentary on John all the resources at his disposal — which were considerable — especially the riches of the whole Patristic teaching of the "Saints" (the *sancti Doctores),* the wealth of a living tradition in the Roman Church contained in its teaching, laws, liturgy, and the living Spirit, as well as fidelity to the infallible norms of the Holy See.

In an address to students and professors of the "Angelicum" (now the Pontifical University of St. Thomas in Rome) given on January 14, 1958, Pope Pius XII extolled the virtues of its patron, the Angelic Doctor, who serves as a divinely inspired guide in both philosophy and theology.(3) Pope Pius spoke especially of St. Thomas' own studies as a norm for every student of the religious disciplines. Just as St. Thomas diligently explored and studied the Bible as the font and life-spring of all theological studies, so too should the modern student find in biblical studies the source of his theological development. As St. Thomas himself assures us, "[sacred doctrine] uses the authority of the canonical Scriptures properly and of necessity in its investigations . . . for our faith is founded on the Revelation made to the Apostles and Prophets, who wrote the canonical books, but not on revelation (if such there be) made to other teachers."(4) In this conviction Thomas developed all his own theology. That is to say, the "complement" to Thomas' speculations and synthesis are to be found in his commentaries on the books of the Old and New Testaments, especially those on the Epistles of St. Paul.

In the opinion of those most expert to judge, Thomas' commentaries on Scripture "shine with such solidity, subtlety, and precision that they can be numbered among his greatest theological works," and are to be esteemed as such. "Wherefore, if anyone should neglect them, he is scarcely to be said to clearly and fully enjoy a familiarity and knowledge of the holy Angelic Doctor." The significant fact is not that Pius XII emphasized the importance of studying Thomas' biblical commentaries to Dominicans, who had made their special prerogative the teaching of "speculative Thomistic theology" and the pursuit of contemplative prayer. The significant fact is that Pius XII expressed these sentiments shortly before his death and fifteen years after one of his most important encyclicals, *Divino afflante spiritu* (30 Sept. 1943), the basic charter of all Catholic biblical studies in our day, leading to the Dogmatic Constitution on Divine Revelation, *Dei verbum,* of the Second Vatican Council (18 Nov. 1965). In other words, the enormous advances of modern biblical studies do not automatically nullify the importance of St. Thomas' commentaries on the Sacred Text.

St. Thomas' commentaries on the Sacred Text are typically *medieval,* that is, they lack the unction, colloquialism, and engaging informality of Patristic commentaries (which were largely homilies), and the technical and sometimes journalistic resources of modern commentaries, explanations, and paraphrases. In other words, it is easier to read St. Augustine's commentary on John than it is to read St. Thomas' or that of any other medieval writer addressing students in the "schools" of Paris and elsewhere. The big difference is between Patristic and Monastic commentaries, which were largely homiletic, pastoral, personal, and mystical, on the one hand, and

Scholastic commentaries aimed at teaching students in the university or *studium* the literal meaning of the text. The style of medieval Scholastic commentaries is rather formal, literal, student-orientated, and bookish. This style often makes such commentaries difficult for a modern reader to follow, and to some extent hinders him from deriving the greatest benefit for his mind and heart. At first glance, such a "commentary" — with its definitions, divisions, arguments, footnotes and concern for the orthodox meaning of the sacred message — may seem like searching for a needle in a haystack. But in the case of Thomas' commentaries the reader may be confident that his efforts at discovering that needle will prove to be both intellectually and spiritually rewarding; once discovered, it will be valued as "the pearl of great price" (Mt 13:46).

In this introduction I hope to show the historical context of this particular commentary and to indicate some aids to a fruitful study of it.

First of all, this work is a biblical commentary by a master in a medieval university. In the Middle Ages, the Bible and the Bible alone was the official basis for the teaching of theology by fully qualified masters in the major universities of Europe. In fact, one could say with some justification that the ultimate goal of all medieval education was an understanding of the Bible for those who pursued the full course in the Faculty of Theology. Such an understanding was the nature of sacred theology (*fides quaerens intellectum,* "faith seeking understanding"). It was the source of all preaching of the Word of God, and it was the inexhaustible font of living water for the spiritual life. In order to reach such a lofty goal, much preparation was required. First, tools had to be acquired as a means of such study. This was the role of a good liberal arts education and the acquisition of philosophy, "the handmaid of theology." The study of the liberal arts and the acquisition of philosophy were functions of the Arts Faculty in the university or *studium.* Approximately eight years were devoted by medieval students to acquiring these tools — roughly equivalent to our four years of high school and four years of college. After the full course had been completed in "the humanities," the young man, generally in his mid-twenties, would begin his study of the Sacred Text, having already heard many sermons in Church and having received much instruction at home. His study of the Sacred Text began with *listening* and *reading.*

In the Middle Ages, a personal copy of the Bible was relatively rare, certainly outside university circles. Every copy of the Bible was written out by hand on parchment, a writing surface made from carefully treated skins of sheep. Such a copy was extremely expensive and hard to come by. Although every student of theology tried desperately to obtain a personal copy, most people had to rely on hearing the Word read to them and recollecting from memory the actual words of the Bible. For that reason the beginner in theology would *listen* to older students and the master (professor). One of the older students, the bachelor of theology, read aloud and paraphrased a particular book of the Bible. This bachelor was called a "Cursor Biblicus," a "runner through" the actual words of the Bible, who did this to acquaint himself and his hearers with the inspired words.

A splendid example of the work of such a "runner" is St. Thomas' commentary on Isaiah; it is the work of a *cursor* and not that of a master. Only a master could expound the text with authority and confidence; the bachelor merely skimmed through it as a runner would skim over the course in a race. A higher ranking bachelor devoted his energies mainly to explaining the official theological handbook, the *Sentences* of Peter Lombard (d. 1160). These *Sentences* were a systematic collection of Patristic teachings, arranged in four books following the order of the Apostles' Creed. This bachelor was called the *bachalarius Sententiarum,* a "Bachelor of the *Sentences.*" After listenting to others for about four years, the young student of theology would himself become a bachelor and perform certain duties under a particular master, his main professor of theology.

Every university in the Middle Ages had a limited number of chairs, or professorships, for the masters to occupy. At the time of St. Thomas, there were twelve chairs of theology at the University of Paris, the Dominicans having two of them. Before occupying one of these chairs, the student had to have devoted many long years to study and actual discussions, or "disputations," in the university. He had to be at least thirty-five years old before meriting the title of "Master of the Sacred Page" and the right to expound the Bible in an authoritative manner as a true theologian, professionally qualified.

St. Thomas was twice professor of theology at Paris — a fact most unusual in itself. There were very few such cases where a fully fledged master would return to his old chair, thus preventing a new master from occupying it. But the intellectual, social, and religious climate in Paris at that time demanded the return of Thomas to the center of all theological learning in Europe. The new mendicant Orders (mainly Dominicans and Franciscans) were again being attacked by secular (i.e., diocesan) masters of theology, and their right to teach, preach, and beg was challenged by some of the most powerful voices in Europe. The center of this controversy was the University of Paris, where the very existence of Dominicans and Franciscans was under fire. At the climax of this renewed attack, the second in the history of the Dominican Order, St. Thomas was recalled to Paris by the Master General of the Dominican Order, Blessed John of Vercelli. Thomas arrived in Paris with his companion Reginald in the cold winter of 1269 after the academic term had begun. Immediately Thomas took upon himself the duties of a master in theology, namely, lecturing on a carefully chosen book of the Bible, presiding at academic "disputations" and resolving the question under discussion, and preaching to the university crowd. At the same time, he was composing the Second Part of his *Summa theologiae,* which he had begun in Rome two years earlier, and dictating a number of literal commentaries on various works of Aristotle for young masters in arts, that is, teachers in the Faculty of Arts, whose duty it was to expound the text of Aristotle. During the two and a half years Thomas spent at Paris the second time, he successfully defended the rights of mendicants to teach, preach, and flourish. During this same Parisian regency he lectured on the Gospel of St. John.

These lectures on John would have been lost to posterity had not the faithful Reginald taken notes, which were later "corrected" by Thomas himself. The reason Thomas "corrected" Reginald's transcription was that a wealthy secular (i.e., diocesan) student wanted a copy for himself. This student was Adenulf of Anagni, an Italian cleric, provost of Saint-Omer (since 1264), later master in theology (1282–85), and canon of Notre Dame Cathedral in Paris. Adenulf, a student of Thomas during the years 1269–72, offered a considerable amount of money to have a professional scribe make a copy of this remarkable commentary for himself. Without Adenulf's enthusiasm and money, the "lectures" (*lecturae*) on John would have remained a simple report, or *reportatio.* If it had not been for Reginald, apparently, these lectures would have gone completely from history. But the fact is that we do have at hand the acute mind of Thomas Aquinas, a master theologian and saint, on the Gospel of St. John. This commentary reflects the mind of Thomas at its peak, but before he composed the Third Part of the *Summa* dealing with Christ, the Sacraments, and the Church. It is a scholastic analysis of St. John's remarkable testimony of the Good News of Salvation, namely, that the Word became flesh, died for our salvation, and is now risen from the dead to come again as our merciful judge.

Earlier, at the request of his intimate friend Pope Urban IV,

Thomas had compiled a continuous gloss on all four Gospels, which he had collated from the Latin and Greek Fathers of the Church. Frequently he even instigated new translations of Greek sources, as he himself confessed in the prologue. This continuous gloss, popularly called the *Catena Aurea,* or "Golden Chain," was not finished when Urban died in 1264. But Thomas continued his labors on the gloss, which he completed in 1267 and dedicated to Cardinal Annibaldo d'Annibaldi, Thomas' close friend and former pupil at Paris. The intense labor on the Gospel of John for the *Catena* molded the mind of Thomas in his personal understanding of the Sacred Text of John. St. John's Gospel is very difficult to understand. Unlike the Synoptic writers, Matthew, Mark, and Luke, St. John's Gospel is a carefully devised presentation of his personal understanding of the sacred doctrine taught by Jesus, on whose breast he reclined at the Last Supper. John was always known as "the disciple whom Jesus loved." For St. Thomas, John, the Son of Zebedee, the author of this Gospel, was a virgin, whose appropriate symbol is the eagle soaring in the heights of contemplation. Thomas' detailed study of the Latin and Greek Fathers, needed to complete his Gloss on John, prepared him to shed his own light on the text when the opportune moment arrived. That moment arrived when Thomas returned to Paris for the second time (1269–72) at the age of about forty-four, full of strength and vigor.

But his is a typical medieval commentary because, unlike Patristic, monastic, and modern commentaries on John, it utilizes certain techniques familiar to all in the Middle Ages, but strange to us today. First of all, it is a theological commentary concerned with penetrating the literal sense of the words recorded, and seeing through the literal sense to the spiritual. The medieval university theologian was primarily concerned with the literal sense of scripture, that is, with the sacred message intended by the human and divine author. It is therefore primarily concerned with "the theological teaching" of the Bible. St. Thomas did not have at his disposal the infinitely varied techniques of modern biblical scholarship. He knew almost nothing about biblical and near-eastern languages, archeology, philology, comparative religion, and the historical method. If he had, he would most certainly have used them. In the Encyclical *Divino afflante Spiritu* (30 Sept. 1943), Pope Pius XII urged the importance of textual criticism, biblical and oriental languages, archeology, profane and sacred history, as well as form criticism and the demands of a sound historical method.(5) He noted with the Angelic Doctor that "in Scripture divine things are presented to us in the manner which is in common use amongst men."(6) The Bible is the Word of God in the words of men, and this manner of speaking in various ages to various people must be carefully studied with all the auxiliary sciences. But even after all this has been tended to, there is still "the theological doctrine" contained in the Sacred Books. The modern exegete should use every means available to discover and explain "the literal sense and especially the theological."(7) It is this "theological sense" (*sensus theologicus*), expounded by St. Thomas in his commentary, that is most fruitful for our meditation, prayer, and preaching the Word of God today.

The literal sense, as St. Thomas teaches, is the objective, formal, and direct meaning intended by the words in the sacred and inspired text.(8) The author of these words is both God and man, since the Bible is "the inspired Word of God." Modern biblical techniques, of course, were unknown to Thomas. All he had was his personal copy of the Latin Vulgate (which was not a critical edition), the familiar teaching of all the Latin and Greek Fathers known to him, his own prayerful reflection on the text, and his native genius attentive to the Spirit of God and to the text. Among the human means Thomas had at his disposal were grammar, logic, and Aristotelian philosophy. The literal (or historical) sense was in principle the only basis of theological thought and discussion. The spiritual sense only enlarged, or extended, the basic literal sense. By "spiritual sense" we do not mean the pious, personal, private, and subjective sense a reader might derive from a prayerful reading of the text. Rather, the "spiritual sense" is the enlarged reality "intended" by person, place, or thing signified in the literal, as when the brazen serpent raised by Moses in the desert is taken to signify Christ's crucifixion as the divine means of healing mankind, or when the paschal lamb is taken to signify Christ who was sacrificed for our sins. The "spiritual sense" is the enlarged sense "intended" by a given symbol in the plan of divine providence.

Since only God as the author of all things can make one symbol significative of another reality, the Bible is the only book that can contain a "spiritual sense" as it was understood by medieval theologians. Consequently only the sacred author himself can inform us of the existence of such a sense. We could never know that one reality is to be taken as a symbol of another reality unless the Sacred Author so informs us in the literal sense. For example, the author of the Book of Numbers (21:19) explains how Moses was directed to make a brazen "serpent" and set it up as a sign; whoever was bitten by one of the fiery serpents and "looked at the sign" that Moses had set up was saved from death. But it is John (3:14–15) who explains that "as Moses lifted up the serpent in the desert, so must the Son of man be lifted up that whoever believes in him may not perish, but may have life everlasting." The significance of Old Testament texts is declared by the sacred writer when he explains Christ's actions as being "in fulfillment of the Scriptures." Similarly St. Paul frequently reveals the "spiritual sense" of the Law and Prophets by declaring the Christian fulfillment in Jesus.

There were three kinds of spiritual sense recognized by medieval theologians: the allegorical, the moral, and the anagogical.(9). When anything in the Old Testament was taken to signify something in the New Testament, this sense was called allegorical. Under this sense would be included all those figures, persons, and events as symbolic of Jesus and his life and death on earth. When anything in the life of Jesus is taken as a model for our life, we call this the moral sense. Under this sense would be included all those virtues presented to us for our imitation of Christ. When anything in the Scriptures is taken to signify something in the eternal kingdom hereafter, for example, "the new Jerusalem," we call this the anagogical sense. Thus the "spiritual sense" of a passage was taken to be an objective meaning intended by the sacred author, the Holy Spirit. This, of course, presupposes that the authors of the New Testament were inspired by the Holy Spirit.

Whatever personal message one may derive from reading the Bible prayerfully and thoughtfully is purely personal and beyond the science of theology as the study of God's message to mankind. The personal message is most significant for the reader, but this personal significance must be carefully controlled by objective theological norms such as the Christian faith, sacred doctrine, the constant teaching of the Church, and a prayerful listening to the Holy Spirit.

The most difficult technique of medieval commentators for us to comprehend is the use of logic and the "scholastic method." Aristotelian logic is the most significant technique contained in the scholastic method. The purpose of the scholastic method was to instill "scientific" knowledge through 1. definition, 2. division, and 3. demonstration, or demonstrative proof. These techniques (or *modi sciendi*) were taken for granted by every medieval theologian as the best means of learning the truth about anything. It was a method of teaching, the *via docendi*, which was an imitation of the "way of discovery" (*via inveniendi* or *inventionis*). The goal of all education is truth. The goal of theological education is an understanding of the doctrines of revelation, the *sacra doctrina*.(10) It is faith seeking understanding (*fides quaerens intellectum*), as St. Anselm puts it. The scholastic method, in a sense, is artificial and humanly contrived by means of logic. In the Middle Ages the scho-

lastic method was thought to be the best way of learning everything from A to Z. An example of this method of learning is em-
bedded in Thomas' commentary on John's Gospel. It cannot be
eliminated. Therefore it depends on us moderns to bend a little by
trying to see through it, and not be put off by it. Always one will
find definitions, divisions, and proofs in all medieval commentaries,
whether they be on Aristotle, Boethius, or the Bible.

The Scholastics had a penchant for *order*; where none existed,
one was imposed. Heeding the words of Aristotle that "it belongs to
the wise man to order," they thought the prerogative of a good
teacher was to order all things well, setting out the message, or
truth to be conveyed, in an orderely and fitting way.(11) This is
why the first thing one notices when reading a medieval commentary
is the *division*, or the ordering of the whole into parts. The least
one can perceive is a beginning, a middle, and an end. But more
than not, one can usually perceive some orderly procedure in the
middle.

Modern biblical scholars usually see in St. John's Gospel a
prologue (1:1-14), a middle (cc. 1-20), and an epilogue (c. 21).
They then proceed to divide the middle into the Book of Signs
(cc. 1-12) and the Book of Glory (cc. 13-20). St. Thomas also
divides the Gospel into roughly these two parts, but he considers
chapter 12 as belonging to the Book of Glory, because the chapter
opens "six days before Passover" with the anointing of the feet
of Jesus for his burial (12:1-11), continues on to the triumphal
entry into Jerusalem (12:12-19), builds to the coming of the Greeks
(12:20-22), and the long discourse of Jesus in which he cries out,
"Father, glorify your name" (12:28). In any case, it is particularly
in this second part that Thomas had to use his ingenuity to resolve
the discrepancies between John and the Synoptics. The Synoptics
compress the public life of Jesus into one year with the one tragic
journey of Jesus up to Jerusalem, where he is crucified and dies,
to be raised up on the third day. John extends the public life of
Jesus into three years with the final year ending in his passion,
death, and resurrection. St. Thomas is very much concerned with
the literal, or historical, sense of the narrative, especially as concerns
the passion, death, and resurrection of the Lord. Throughout the
whole exposition of the narrative, Thomas relied heavily on the
interpretation of the Fathers of the Church, both Latin and Greek.
He quotes the authority of St. Augustine 373 times, St. John Chrysostom 217 times, and Origen 95 times. It is an exposition that
relies heavily on the tradition of the Church and on his own prayerful theological reflections.

In the commentary on St. John's Gospel, Thomas is concerned not only with the literal sense, which for him is of prime importance and concern, but also with the spiritual sense, as explained above. More than the other Evangelists, John reveals the "fulfillment of the Scriptures," that is, concern with the prophecies and symbols of the Old Law. Christ's own prophetic words and actions are seen by John to be a foreshadowing of the passion, death, and resurrection of the Lord by which we are all saved. Above all, for St. Thomas, John is the Evangelist of the divinity of Jesus, "the Word made flesh." He says, "While the other Evangelists treat principally of the mysteries of the humanity of Christ, John, especially and above all, makes known the divinity of Christ in his Gospel" (Prologue). Thomas, following the lead of St. Jerome, thought that John wrote his Gospel after the other three Gospels had been written, in order to refute new heresies that had arisen concerning the divinity of Christ. Following Jerome, Thomas singled out the Ebionites (whose founder Thomas erroneously thought to have been "Ebion") and Cerinthus, a Gnostic heretic who flourished around 100 A.D., as among those who denied the divinity of Christ. Even St. Irenaeus (*Adv. haer.*, III, 11) asserts that St. John wrote his Gospel to refute Cerinthus. Thus, St. Thomas observes in his Prologue, while John did not pass over the mysteries of Christ's humanity, he especially conveys the divinity of Christ in his Gospel. In this commentary, therefore, Thomas repeatedly refutes the heresies of Apollinaris, Arius, the Arians, Ebionites, Eutyches, the Manichees, Nestorius, Pelagius, the Pelagians, and Sabellius — all of which plagued the Church in the first five centuries of its existence. For Thomas these heresies were not merely false doctrines irrelevant to the modern Christian, but vital guidelines to the purity of the Christian faith, the orthodox teaching of the living Church.

Earlier in his career, Thomas had been asked by the archbishop of Palermo to write a short work that could be memorized, dealing with the articles of faith "from the Creed of the Fathers" (i.e., the Apostles' Creed) and also the basic errors concerning them; the archbishop apparently asked also for the same presentation for all the sacraments of the Church.(12) Thomas complied with this request in a most remarkable treatise in two parts: *De articulis fidei* and *De ecclesiae sacramentis*.(13) The wide popularity of this treatise is attested to by the 277 extant manuscripts of this work. The six articles pertaining to the divinity of Christ and the six pertaining to his humanity are set forth, and all the errors concerning the twelve articles of the Creed are briefly named and refuted. Although the sacraments of the Church are implicit in the fourth article of the Creed, they are discussed separately in the second part of the treatise, because the archbishop explicitly asked for a special discussion of the sacraments and the heresies concerning them. Thomas' knowledge of the various heresies in the history of the Church is most remarkable. All of these same heresies are again discussed in his commentary on John's Gospel. That is why St. Thomas says in the Prologue, "[This Gospel] refutes all heresies." The numerous heresies of the past ought to be of great concern to the modern Christian so that he may avoid all taint of them in his own, personal belief. A conscious affirmation of belief in the truth of revealed teaching that developed in the living Church guided by the Spirit of Christ can bring us into a deeper and more meaningful awareness of being united with the Eternal Truth. In this commentary, Thomas is concerned above all with bolstering the faith of the hearer or reader, or, as he put it, "to confirm the Catholic Truth."

In other words, there are four goals Thomas aimed to achieve in his commentary on St. John:

1. determination of the literal, or historical, sense of the narrative;
2. explanation of the spiritual sense as found in the Old Testament (allegorical sense), the goals of our own life in imitating Jesus (moral sense), and life of the "'kingdom" here and hereafter (anagogical sense);
3. refutation of all error through the testimony of the inspired Word of God;
4. confirmation of the true Catholic Faith given to us by God through his Church, the Body of Christ.

These are the same goals Thomas had set for himself in composing the *Catena Aurea,* particularly in the *Catena* on John's Gospel, which was composed only four or five years earlier.(14)

There are four outstanding features that will be noticed as one studies the commentary of Thomas on the Gospel of John. First, Thomas had an extraordinary knowledge of the whole Bible. It has been said, not without likelihood, that Thomas memorized the entire Bible during the year he was confined to his family castle at Roccasecca, 1244–45. This is not at all difficult to believe. His memory was far superior to any man-made concordance of the Bible. Thomas always saw the *unity* of divine revelation. It was the unity of *sacra doctrina* as a single "science."(15) The "orthodox" teaching of Christ, Son of the Living God, cannot be anything but *one*. Because of this unity, Thomas could use any one part of Sacred Scripture to explain and illumine any other part. Thus Thomas could use the teaching of St. Paul and the Psalms to explain the text of John. This use of one part of revelation to illumine another has been aptly called "the analogy of faith" (*secundum rationem fidei,* as St. Paul says in Romans 12:6).(16)

Second, Thomas had an unusual knowledge of the Latin and Greek Fathers of the Church. This knowledge, no doubt aided by his work on the *Catena Aurea,* is brought to bear on every difficult question or obscure passage in John, even when it is a question of chronology, geography, Jewish customs, or language. The medieval mind associated words, quotations, and parallels with uncanny facility, always trying to find the best pertinent quotation from the proper authorities (*auctoritates*). Great weight, sometimes of pro- bative value, was always given to the recognized *auctoritates,* which, in theology were always the Bible and the *sancti,* meaning recognized or canonized Doctors of the Church, who were the *regula fidei* ("the rule of faith"), the "norms" of Christian belief. Thomas' knowledge of these Doctors was prodigious. The contemporaries of Thomas relied heavily on all available works of the Latin Fathers, especially those of St. Augustine. But, as has been pointed out earlier, Thomas not only accepted the eminent authority of St. Augustine, but also had a wealth of Greek sources from which to draw, including the early Ecumenical Councils of the Church, whose *Acts* were largely neglected or forgotten in the Latin Middle Ages.(17)

Third, Thomas was, after all, an outstanding theologian for any season. His theology was not only biblical and patristic, but also logical and philosophical. While he absorbed and refined the phil- osophy of Aristotle, newly translated from the Greek, he never put this philosophy ahead of his Catholic faith. Rather he used that philosophy *in obsequium fidei* (Phil 2:17), as a "handmaid of theo- logy." His comprehension of Aristotle and his use of the scholastic method are among the glories of the Middle Ages. In St. Thomas we find an exceptionally gifted mind carefully honed to human per- fection by self-dicipline, long study, and clear thinking. This was natural talent, ranked by many as a true genius, brought to the highest human perfection by the grace of God.

Finally, Friar Thomas d'Aquino was a saint, one of the great saints in the Latin Church. A basic principle of Thomas' theology is that "grace perfects nature"; that is, the grace of God never destroys or replaces nature, but builds upon it. For St. Thomas, there is in divine providence a certain kind of proportion between God's gifts of nature and his gifts of grace. Even when we accept this principle with all the necessary qualifications needed, we can readily see that in the mind and heart of St. Thomas, God's grace abundant- ly perfected an already great man. Not only did Thomas meditate prayerfully on the Sacred Scriptures, but he drew from them substantial nourishment for his soul. This process of enrichment can be seen conspicuously in the commentary on John, particularly the section dealing with the "Last Discourse" of Jesus to his disciples at the Last Supper, collected in "the sayings of Jesus" in chapters 14 to 17. Here Thomas' discussion of the Son's procession from the Father while being consubstantially one with the Father, is precise, illuminating, and brilliant; the mission of the Holy Spirit from the Father *and* from the Son (*Filioque*) is clearly demonstrated against the Greek Orthodox who used this question as one of the many issues that separated them from Rome, initially in the ninth, and decisively in the eleventh century. But above all, the indwelling of the Holy Trinity in the hearts of the faithful is alive and vital; the extraordinary love Jesus had for his faithful disciples is movingly real and dynamic. In this commentary on John we have all the elements of a real masterpiece of its kind in medieval literature.

St. Thomas was very much impressed by the force and absolute veracity of the Gospel proclaimed by John: "This disciple is the one who vouches for these things and has written them down, and we know that his testimony is true" (Jn 21:24). St. Thomas comments that the Evangelist makes this statement "in the person of the whole Church (*in persona totius Ecclesiae*) from whom this Gospel is received [by us]." The Evangelist himself knows the veracity of his narrative, and even St. Paul condemns those who would preach a gospel other than the one he had received (see Gal 1:9). The firmness and stability of our Christian faith is the authority of God speaking through Evangelists, Apostles and other authors of the canonical Books of Scripture. Their testimony leaves us without any doubt as to our faith, because "the Canonical Scriptures alone are the rule of faith."(18) This *sola scriptura* of which St. Thomas speaks is far different from the *sola scriptura* ("only the Bible") of the Reformers. This battle cry was made famous by Luther, who insisted that what is not contained in the Bible is not "of faith." But Luther and Thomas (or any other medieval theologian) meant two different things by the word *Bible*, or *Sacred Scriptures*. For Luther and the Reformers the Bible was thought of as a finished, edited, and (by then) printed collection, while Thomas and the medieval theologians meant the Sacred Word *together with* the gloss of the Fathers, liturgy, and the living Church. The Reformers thought of "The Bible" completely devoid of a history and a historical context, devoid of transmission and development; in short, they thought of "The Bible" distinct from the Church. Thus in the face of this misunderstanding, the Council of Trent spoke *as though* there were two sources of our faith: "the written books and the unwritten traditions."(19) But even this manner of speaking was a concession to a false dichotomy that was historically conditioned. The Second Vatican Council, however, described these two "sources" more traditionally as a single mirror (*veluti speculum sunt*) reflecting both sacred tradition and Sacred Scripture.(20)

Historically speaking, the revelation given by God and received by the chosen people was prior to any scriptural document. Abraham, Isaac, and Jacob were given the message of salvation long before there was any question of a written Torah. Christ's message of salvation was accepted by the Apostles, disciples, and early Christians for a quarter of a century before the first fraction of the New Testament was written — and this by St. Paul (1 Thessalonians, probably at the beginning of 52 A.D.). We must always remember that the Canon of the New Testament was not established as an inspired unit until 382 A.D., at the earliest. That is, the living Church existed long before the New Testament was "written," and it existed for 350 years before the present books were collected into an exclusive and canonical unity. For this reason, St. Thomas could speak of the "whole Church from whom this Gospel is received."

Finally, a word should be said in aid of a fruitful reading of St. Thomas' commentary on John. Although the pericope or section commented upon in every "Lecture" is printed in full at the head of the commentary, it would be best to procure a second copy of the whole text and read the particular chapter in full before proceeding to the comment. It is of utmost importance to follow the *divisions* of the text made by St. Thomas and always keep the context well in view. The lemmata, or phrases commented upon, are clearly set off from the comment by the printer. Unless the particular lemma is constantly related to the context as a whole, one can easily get lost in the forest of words, cross references, and quotations. Since *order* and *division* are such important elements in the scholastic method, these must be continuously related to the *whole*, whether it be a collection of chapters, an individual chapter, part of a chapter, a parable, narrative, pericope, or sentence. Those who wish to obtain the greatest understanding of the Sacred Text might well augment the study of St. Thomas' "theological sense" of John with a modern commentary, such as the outstanding commentary by Father Raymond Brown in the Anchor Bible (2 vols.).

For the fruitful reading of St. Thomas' commentary on John, we should further note that throughout the long history of the Church, listeners and readers of the Sacred Text have always been encouraged to prepare their minds and souls for a fruitful reception of the Word. The Word of God, like the seed in the parable (Lk 8:15), needs to be received in "good ground" in order to yield fruit a hundredfold. The reception of anything, according to the ancient philosophers, depends on the condition of the receiver. The Word of God is Spirit (Jn 6:63), and only the Holy Spirit can prepare the soul for fruitful reception of the Word. In the solemn proclamation of the Gospel in the Liturgy of the Word, the Church prays for the Deacon that the Lord be in his heart and on his lips in order to announce the Holy Gospel of Peace.(21) Preparing one's mind and heart by prayer and recollection is of greatest importance for the reception of God's message for us. This message is directed primarily to us as God's chosen people, the pilgrim Church on earth, and through the Church to us as individuals beloved by God and "purchased at a great price" (1 Cor 6:20). The message of salvation is addressed to us individually and collectively, and we both individually and collectively must attune our minds and hearts to the Spirit. "The Advocate, the Holy Spirit, whom the Father will send in my name, will teach you everything and remind you of all I have said to you" (Jn 14:26). The Holy Spirit speaks to our hearts through the Scriptures, inspired and animated by him. The Scriptures as a spiritual resource cannot be dissociated from personal prayer and cultivation of our sacramental life in the Church. Being receptive is the important thing as we begin our study.

Finally, the power of reading or hearing the Sacred Scriptures is so great that it actually forgives sins. Apart from "the Sacraments of the faith" (*sacramenta fidei*), it is one of the many ways by which our many sins are forgiven. The Fathers of the Church have always listed — along with almsgiving, contrition, and good works — the special efficacy of reading the Scriptures for the forgiveness of sins. The new liturgy of the Mass prompted by the Second Vatican Council still retains the ancient prayer: "May the words of the Gospel wipe away our sins." The humble and contrite reading of any part of the Scriptures wipes away sin because the power of the Word is the power of God, who alone can forgive sins. Thus we should always approach the Scriptures with a "humble and contrite heart." The Psalmist declares, "A contrite and humbled heart, O God, you will not despise" (Ps 50:19). God always answers a humble and contrite heart in order to glorify himself in us, just as the Father is always glorified in the Son. "Whatever you ask for in my name I will do, so that the Father may be glorified in the Son" (Jn 14:13). This "glory" of the Father through the Son in the Holy Spirit is sometimes called the indwelling of the Trinity within our souls. It is the "conformity" of our whole being to the Father through the Word animated by the Spirit. In this conformity of our innermost being with the splendor of God lies the whole perfection of the

Christian life. In this pefection consists the glory and splendor of God himself. This union of one's deepest self and the innermost being of God is the answer to the prayer of Jesus to the Father: "That they may be one, as we also are one" (Jn 17:11).

From this it follows that the study of St. Thomas' commentary on St. John's Gospel is richly rewarding in healing our wounds and leading us to greater union with the Father of our Lord Jesus Christ, whose message of salvation is here proclaimed by "the disciple whom Jesus loved" (Jn 20:2). For our guide we can have none better than the Angelic Doctor, whom Jesus loved.

James A. Weisheipl, O.P.

Pontifical Institute of Mediaeval Studies
Toronto, Canada

[References will be found on page 444]

PROLOGUE

TO THE

GOSPEL OF SAINT JOHN

St. Thomas Aquinas

I saw the Lord seated on a high and lofty throne, and the whole house was full of his majesty, and the things that were under him filled the temple. (Is 6:1)

1 These are the words of a contemplative, and if we regard them as spoken by John the Evangelist they apply quite well to showing the nature of this Gospel. For as Augustine says in his work, *On the Agreement of the Evangelists*: "The other Evangelists instruct us in their Gospels on the active life; but John in his Gospel instructs us also on the contemplative life."

The contemplation of John is described above in three ways, in keeping with the threefold manner in which he contemplated the Lord Jesus. It is described as high, full, and perfect. It is high: **I saw the Lord seated on a high and lofty throne**; it is full: **and the whole house was full of his majesty**; and it was perfect: **and the things that were under him filled the temple.**

2 As to the first, we must understand that the height and suulimity of contemplation consists most of all in the contemplation and knowledge of God. "Lift up your eyes on high, and see who has created these things" (Is 40:26). A man lifts up his eyes on high when he sees and contemplates the Creator of all things. Now since John rose above whatever had been created — mountains, heavens, angels — and reached the Creator of all, as Augustine says, it is clear that his contemplation was most high. Thus, **I saw the Lord**. And because, as John himself says below (12:41), "Isaiah said this because he had seen his glory," that is, the glory of Christ, "and spoke of him," the Lord **seated on a high and lofty throne** is Christ.

Now a fourfold height is indicated in this contemplation of John. A height of authority; hence he says, **I saw the Lord**. A height of eternity; when he says, **seated**. One of dignity, or nobility of nature; so he says, **on a high throne**. And a height of incomprehensible truth; when he says, **lofty**. It is in these four ways that the early philosophers arrived at the knowledge of God.

3 Some attained to a knowledge of God through his authority, and this is the most efficacious way. For we see the things in nature acting for an end, and attaining to ends which are both useful and certain. And since they lack intelligence, they are unable to direct themselves, but must be directed and moved by one directing them, and who possesses an intellect. Thus it is that the movement of the things of nature toward a certain end indicates the existence of something higher by which the things of nature are directed to an end and governed. And so, since the whole course of nature advances to an end in an orderly way and is directed, we have to posit something higher which directs and governs them as Lord; and this is God.

This authority in governing is shown to be in the Word of God when he says, **Lord**. Thus the Psalm (88:10) says: "You rule the power of the sea, and you still the swelling of its waves," as though saying: You are the Lord and govern all things. John shows that he knows this about the Word when he says below (1:11), "He came unto his own," i.e., to the world, since the whole universe is his own.

4   Others came to a knowledge of God from his eternity. They saw that whatever was in things was changeable, and that the more noble something is in the grades of being, so much the less it has of mutability. For example, the lower bodies are mutable both as to their substance and to place, while the heavenly bodies, which are more noble, are immutable in substance and change only with respect to place. We can clearly conclude from this that the first principle of all things, which is supreme and more noble, is changeless and eternal. The prophet suggests this eternity of the Word when he says, **seated**, i.e., presiding without any change and eternally. "Your throne, O God, is forever and ever" (Ps 44:7); "Jesus Christ is the same yesterday, today, and forever" (Heb 13:8). John points to this eternity when he says below (1:1), "In the beginning was the Word."

5   Still others came to a knowledge of God from the dignity of God; and these were the Platonists. They noted that everything which is something by participation is reduced to what is the same thing by essence, as to the first and highest. Thus, all things which are fiery by participation are reduced to fire, which is such by its essence. And so since all things which exist participate in existence (*esse*) and are beings by participation, there must necessarily be at the summit of all things something which is existence (*esse*) by its essence, i.e., whose essence is its existence. And this is God, who is the most sufficient, the most eminent, and the most perfect cause of the whole of existence, from whom all things that are participate existence (*esse*). This dignity is shown in the words, **on a high throne**, which, according to Denis, refer to the divine nature. "The Lord is high above all nations" (Ps 112:4). John shows us this dignity when he says below (1:1), "the Word was God," with "Word" as subject and "God" as the predicate.

6   Yet others arrived at a knowledge of God from the incomprehensibility of truth. All the truth which our intellect is able to grasp is finite, since according to Augustine, "everything that is known is bounded by the comprehension of the one knowing"; and if it is bounded, it is determined and particularized. Therefore, the first and supreme Truth, which surpasses every intellect, must necessarily be incomprehensible and infinite; and this is God. Hence the Psalm (8:2) says, "Your greatness is above the heavens," i.e.,

above every created intellect, angelic and human. The Apostle says this in the words, "He dwells in unapproachable light" (1 Tim 6:16). This incomprehensibility of Truth is shown to us in the word, **lofty**, that is, above all the knowledge of the created intellect. John implies this incomprehensibility to us when he says below (1:18), "No one has ever seen God."

Thus, the contemplation of John was high as regards authority, eternity, dignity, and the incomprehensibility of the Word. And John has passed on this contemplation to us in his Gospel.

7 John's contemplation was also full. Now contemplation is full when someone is able to consider all the effects of a cause in the cause itself, that is, when he knows not only the essence of the cause, but also its power, according as it can extend out to many things. Of this flowing outward we read, "It overflows with wisdom, like the Pishon, and like the Tigris in the days of the new fruits" (Sir 25:35); "The river of God is full with water," since the divine wisdom has depth in relation to its knowledge of all things (Ps 65:9). "With you from the beginning is wisdom, who knows your works" (Wis 9:9).

Since John the Evangelist was raised up to the contemplation of the nature of the divine Word and of his essence when he said, "In the beginning was the Word; and the Word was with God," he immediately tells us of the power of the Word as it extends to all things, saying, "Through him all things came into being." Thus his contemplation was full. And so after the prophet had said, **I saw the Lord seated**, he added something about his power, **and the whole house was full of his majesty**, that is, the whole fullness of things and of the universe is from the majesty and power of God, through whom all things were made, and by whose light all the men coming into this world are enlightened. "The earth and its fullness are the Lord's" (Ps 23:1).

8 The contemplation of John was also perfect. For contemplation is perfect when the one contemplating is led and raised to the height of the thing contemplated. Should he remain at a lower level, then no matter how high the things which he might contemplate, the contemplation would not be perfect. So in order that it be perfect it is necessary that it rise and attain the end of the thing contemplated, adhering and assenting by affection and understanding to the truth contemplated. Job (37:16) says, "Do you not know the path of the clouds," that is, the contemplation of those preaching, "how perfect they are?" inasmuch as they adhere firmly by affection and understanding to contemplating the highest truth.

Since John not only taught how Christ Jesus, the Word of God, is God, raised above all things, and how all things were made through him, but also that we are sanctified by him, and adhere to him by the grace which he pours into us, he says below (1:16), "Of his fullness we have all received — indeed, grace in return for grace." It is therefore apparent that his contemplation is perfect. This perfection is shown in the addition, **and the things that were under him filled the temple.** For "the head of Christ is God" (1 Cor 11:3). The things that are under Christ are the sacraments of his humanity, through which the faithful are filled with the fullness of grace. In this way, then, **the things that were under him filled the temple,** i.e., the faithful, who are the holy temple of God (1 Cor 3:17) insofar as through the sacraments of his humanity all the faithful of Christ receive from the fullness of his grace.

The contemplation of John was thus full, high, and perfect.

9   We should note, however, that these three characteristics of contemplation belong to the different sciences in different ways. The perfection of contemplation is found in Moral Science, which is concerned with the ultimate end. The fullness of contemplation is possessed by Natural Science, which considers things as proceeding from God. Among the physical [natural] sciences, the height of contemplation is found in Metaphysics. But the Gospel of John contains all together what the above sciences have in a divided way, and so it is most perfect.

10   In this way then, from what has been said, we can understand the matter of this Gospel. For while the other Evangelists treat principally of the mysteries of the humanity of Christ, John, especially and above all, makes known the divinity of Christ in his Gospel, as we saw above. Still, he does not ignore the mysteries of his humanity. He did this because, after the other Evangelists had written their Gospels, heresies had arisen concerning the divinity of Christ, to the effect that Christ was purely and simply a man, as Ebion and Cerinthus falsely thought. And so John the Evangelist, who had drawn the truth about the divinity of the Word from the very fountain-head of the divine breast, wrote this Gospel at the request of the faithful. And in it he gives us the doctrine of the divinity of Christ and refutes all heresies.

The order of this Gospel is clear from the above. For John first shows us **the Lord seated on a high and lofty throne,** when he says below (1:1), "In the beginning was the Word." He shows secondly how **the house was full of his majesty,** when he says, "through him all things came into being" (1:3). Thirdly, he shows how the **things that were under him filled the temple,** when he says, "the Word was made flesh" (1:14). The end of this Gospel is also clear, and it is that the faithful become the temple of God, and become filled with the majesty of God; and so John says below (20:31), "These things are written so that you may believe that

Jesus is the Christ, the Son of God."

The matter of this Gospel, the knowledge of the divinity of the Word, is clear, as well as its order and end.

11 Then follows the condition of the author, who is described above in four ways: as to his name, his virtue, his symbol, and his privilege. He is described as to name as John, the author of this Gospel. "John" is interpreted as "in whom is grace," since the secrets of the divinity cannot be seen except by those who have the grace of God within themselves. "No one knows the deep things of God but the Spirit of God" (1 Cor 2:11).

As concerns his virtue, John **saw the Lord seated**, because he was a virgin; for it is fitting that such persons see the Lord: "Blessed are the pure in heart" (Mt 5:8).

He is described as to his symbol, for John is symbolized by an eagle. The other three Evangelists, concerned with those things which Christ did in his flesh, are symbolized by animals which walk on the earth, namely, by a man, a bull calf, and a lion. But John flies like an eagle above the cloud of human weakness and looks upon the light of unchanging truth with the most lofty and firm eyes of the heart. And gazing on the very deity of our Lord Jesus Christ, by which he is equal to the Father, he has striven in this Gospel to confide this above all, to the extent that he believed was sufficient for all. Concerning this flight of John it says in Job (39:27): "Will the eagle," that is, John, "fly up at your command?" And further on it says, "His eyes look far away," because the Word of God is seen in the bosom of the Father by the eye of the mind.

John is described as to privilege since, among the other disciples of the Lord, John was more loved by Christ. Without mentioning his own name John refers to himself below (21:20) as "the disciple whom Jesus loved." And because secrets are revealed to friends, "I have called you friends because everything I have heard from my father I have made known to you" (below 15:15), Jesus confided his secrets in a special way to that disciple who was specially loved. Thus it says in Job (36:32): "From the savage," that is, the proud, "he hides his light," that is, Christ hides the truth of his divinity, "and shows his friend," that is, John, "that it belongs to him," since it is John who sees the light of the Incarnate Word more excellently and expresses it to us, saying "He was the true light" (below 1:19).

Now the matter, order, end and author of this Gospel of the blessed John are clear.

1

LECTURE I

1 In the beginning was the Word;
and the Word was with God;
and the Word was God.
2 He was in the beginning with God.

23　John the Evangelist, as already indicated, makes it his principal object to show the divinity of the Incarnate Word. Accordingly, his Gospel is divided into two parts. In the first he states the divinity of Christ; in the second he shows it by the things Christ did in the flesh (2:1). In regard to the first, he does two things. First he shows the divinity of Christ; secondly he sets forth the manner in which Christ's divinity is made known to us (1:14). Concerning the first he does two things. First he treats of the divinity of Christ; secondly of the incarnation of the Word of God (1:6).

Because there are two items to be considered in each thing, namely, its existence and its operation or power, first he treats the existence of the Word as to his divine nature; secondly of his power or operation (1:3). In regard to the first he does four things. First he shows when the Word was: **In the beginning was the Word**; secondly where he was: **and the Word was with God**; thirdly what he was: **and the Word was God**; fourthly, in what way he was: **He was in the beginning with God.** The first two pertain to the inquiry "whether something exists"; the second two pertain to the inquiry "what something is."

24　With respect to the first of these four we must examine the meaning of the statement, **In the beginning was the Word.** And here three things present themselves for careful study according to the three parts of this statement. First it is necessary to investigate the name **Word**; secondly the phrase **in the beginning**; thirdly the meaning of the Word **was in the beginning.**

25　To understand the name **Word** we should note that according to the Philosopher [*On Interpretation* 16a3] vocal sounds are signs of the affections that exist in our soul. It is customary in Scripture for the things signified to be themselves called by the names of their signs, as in the statement, "And the rock was Christ" (1 Cor 10:4). It is fitting that what is within our soul, and which is signified by our external word, be called a "word." But whether the name "word" belongs first to the exterior vocal sound or to the conception in our mind, is not our concern at present. However, it is obvious that what is signified by the vocal sound, as existing interiorly in the soul, exists prior to the vocal expression inasmuch as it is its actual cause. Therefore if we wish to grasp the meaning of the interior word, we must first look at the meaning of that which is exteriorly expressed in words.

Now there are three things in our intellect: the intellectual power itself, the species of the thing understood (and this species is its form, being to the intellect what the species of a color is to the eye), and thirdly the very activity of the intellect, which is to understand. But none of these is what is signified by the exterior vocal word: for the name "stone" does not signify the substance of the intellect because this is not what the one naming intends; nor does it signify the species, which is that by which the intellect understands, since this also is not the intention of the one naming; nor does it signify the act itself of understanding since to understand is not an action proceeding to the exterior from the one understanding, but an action remaining within. Therefore, that is properly called an interior word which the one understanding forms when understanding.

Now the intellect forms two things, according to its two operations. According to its operation which is called "the understanding of indivisibles," it forms a definition; while according to its operation by which it unites and separates, it forms an enunciation or something of that sort. Hence, what is thus formed and expressed by the operation of the intellect, whether by defining or enunciating, is what the exterior vocal sound signifies. So the Philosopher says that the notion (*ratio*) which a name signifies is a definition. Hence, what is thus expressed, i.e., formed in the soul, is called an interior word. Consequently it is compared to the intellect, not as that by which the intellect understands, but as that in which it understands, because it is in what is thus expressed and formed that it sees the nature of the thing understood. Thus we have the meaning of the name "word."

Secondly, from what has been said we are able to understand that a word is always something that proceeds from an intellect existing in act; and furthermore, that a word is always a notion (*ratio*) and likeness of the thing understood. So if the one understanding and the thing understood are the same, then the word is a notion and likeness of the intellect from which it proceeds. On the other hand, if the one understanding is other than the thing understood, then the word is not a likeness and notion of the one understanding but of the thing understood, as the conception which one has of a stone is a likeness of only the stone. But when the intellect understands itself, its word is a likeness and notion of the intellect. And so Augustine (*On the Trinity* IX, 5) sees a likeness of the Trinity in the soul insofar as the mind understands itself, but not insofar as it understands other things.

It is clear then that it is necessary to have a word in any intellectual nature, for it is of the very nature of understanding that the intellect in understanding should form something. Now what is formed is called a word, and so it follows that in every being which understands there must be a word.

However, intellectual natures are of three kinds: human, angelic and divine; and so there are three kinds of words. The human word, about which it is said in the Psalm (13:1): "The fool said in his heart, 'There is no God.' " The angelic word, about which it is said in Zechariah (1:9), and in many places in Sacred Scripture, "And the angel said to me." The third is the divine word, of which Genesis (1:3) says, "And God said, 'Let there be light.' " So when the Evangelist says, **In the beginning was the Word**, we cannot understand this as a human or angelic word, because both these words have been made since man and angel have a cause and principle of their existence and operation, and the word of a man or an angel cannot exist before they do. The word the Evangelist had in mind he shows by saying that this word was not made, since all things were made by it. Therefore, the word about which John speaks here is the Word of God.

26 We should note that this Word differs from our own word in three ways. The first difference, according to Augustine, is that our word is formable before being formed, for when I wish to conceive the notion of a stone, I must arrive at it by reasoning. And so it is in all other things that are understood by us, with the sole possible exception of the first principles which, since they are known in a simple manner, are known at once without any discourse of reason. So as long as the intellect, in so reasoning, casts about this way and that, the formation is not yet complete. It is only when it has conceived the notion of the thing perfectly that for the first time it has the notion of the complete thing and a word. Thus in our mind there is both a "cogitation," meaning the discourse involved in an investigation, and a word, which is formed according to a perfect contemplation of the truth. So our word is first in potency before it is in act. But the Word of God is always in act. In consequence, the term "cogitation" does not properly speaking apply to the Word of God. For Augustine says (*On the Trinity* XV): "The Word of God is spoken of in such a way that cogitation is not included, lest anything changeable be supposed in God." Anselm was speaking improperly when he said: "For the supreme Spirit to speak is for him to look at something while cogitating."

27   The second difference is that our word is imperfect, but
the divine Word is most perfect. For since we cannot express all our
conceptions in one word, we must form many imperfect words
through which we separately express all that is in our knowledge.
But it is not that way with God. For since he understands both himself and everything else through his essence, by one act, the single
divine Word is expressive of all that is in God, not only of the
Persons but also of creatures; otherwise it would be imperfect. So
Augustine says: "If there were less in the Word than is contained in
the knowledge of the One speaking it, the Word would be imperfect;
but it is obvious that it is most perfect; therefore, it is only one."
"God speaks once" (Jb 33:14).

28   The third difference is that our word is not of the same
nature as we; but the divine Word is of the same nature as God. And
therefore it is something that subsists in the divine nature. For the
understood notion which the intellect is seen to form about some
thing has only an intelligible existence in our soul. Now in our soul,
to understand is not the same as the nature of the soul, because our
soul is not its own operation. Consequently, the word which our intellect forms is not of the essence of our soul, but is an accident of
it. But in God, to understand and to be are the same; and so the
Word of the divine intellect is not an accident but belongs to its
nature. Thus it must be subsistent, because whatever is in the nature
of God is God. Thus Damascene says that God is a substantial Word,
and a hypostasis, but our words are concepts in our mind.

29   From the above it is clear that the Word, properly speaking,
is always understood as a Person in the Divinity, since it implies only
something expressed by the one understanding; also, that in the
Divinity the Word is the likeness of that from which it issues; and
that it is co-eternal with that from which it issues, since it was not
first formable before being formed, but was always in act; and that
it is equal to the Father, since it is perfect and expressive of the
whole being of the Father; and that it is co-essential and consubstantial with the Father, since it is his substance.

It is also clear that since in every nature that which issues forth
and has a likeness to the nature from which it issues is called a son,
and since this Word issues forth in a likeness and identity to the
nature from which it issues, it is suitably and appropriately called a
"Son," and its production is called a generation.

So now the first point is clear, the meaning of the term **Word**.

30   There are four questions on this point, two of them from
Chrysostom. The first is: Why did John the Evangelist omit the
Father and begin at once with the Son, saying, **In the beginning was**

the Word?

There are two answers to this. One is that the Father was known to everyone in the Old Testament, although not under the aspect of Father, but as God; but the Son was not known. And so in the New Testament, which is concerned with our knowledge of the Word, he begins with the Word or Son.

The other answer is that we are brought to know the Father through the Son: "Father, I have manifested your name to the men whom you have given to me" (below 17:6). And so wishing to lead the faithful to a knowledge of the Father, the Evangelist fittingly began with the Son, at once adding something about the Father when he says, **and the Word was with God**.

31 The second question is also from Chrysostom. Why did he say **Word** and not "Son," since, as we have said, the Word proceeds as Son?

There are also two answers to this. First, because "son" means something begotten, and when we hear of the generation of the Son, someone might suppose that this generation is the kind he can comprehend, that is, a material and changeable generation. Thus he did not say "Son," but **Word**, which signifies an intelligible proceeding, so that it would not be understood as a material and changeable generation. And so in showing that the Son is born of the Father in an unchangeable way, he eliminates a faulty conjecture by using the name **Word**.

The second answer is this. The Evangelist was about to consider the Word as having come to manifest the Father. But since the idea of manifesting is implied better in the name "Word" than in the name "Son," he preferred to use the name **Word**.

32 The third question is raised by Augustine in his book *Eighty-three Questions*; and it is this. In Greek, where we have "Word," they have "Logos"; now since "Logos" signifies in Latin both "notion" and "word" [i.e., *ratio et verbum*], why did the translators render it as "word" and not "notion," since a notion is something interior just as a word is?

I answer that "notion" [*ratio*], properly speaking, names a conception of the mind precisely as in the mind, even if through it nothing exterior comes to be; but "word" signifies a reference to something exterior. And so because the Evangelist, when he said "Logos," intended to signify not only a reference to the Son's existence in the Father, but also the operative power of the Son, by which, through him, all things were made, our predecessors preferred to translate it "Word," which implies a reference to something exterior, rather than "notion," which implies merely a concept of the mind.

33 The fourth question is from Origen, and is this. In many
passages, Scripture, when speaking of the Word of God, does not
simply call him the Word, but adds "of God," saying, "the Word of
God," or "of the Lord": "The Word of God on high is the foundation of wisdom" (Sir 1:5); "His name is the Word of God" (Rv
19:13). Why then did the Evangelist, when speaking here of the
Word of God, not say, "In the beginning was the Word of God," but
said **In the beginning was the Word**?

I answer that although there are many participated truths,
there is just one absolute Truth, which is Truth by its very essence,
that is, the divine act of being (*esse*); and by this Truth all words are
words. Similarly, there is one absolute Wisdom elevated above all
things, that is, the divine Wisdom, by participating in which all wise
persons are wise. Further, there is one absolute Word, by participating in which all persons having a word are called speakers. Now this
is the divine Word which of itself is the Word elevated above all
words. So in order that the Evangelist might signify this super-
eminence of the divine Word, he pointed out this Word to us absolutely without any addition.

And because the Greeks, when they wished to signify something
separate and elevated above everything else, did this by affixing the
article to the name (as the Platonists, wishing to signify the separated
substances, such as the separated good or the separated man, called
them the good *per se*, or man *per se*), so the Evangelist, wishing to
signify the separation and elevation of that Word above all things,
affixed an article to the name "Logos," so that if it were stated in
Latin we would have "*the* Word."

34 Secondly, we must consider the meaning of the phrase,
In the beginning. We must note that according to Origen, the word
principium has many meanings [such as "principle," "source," or
"beginning"]. Since the word *principium* implies a certain order of
one thing to another, one can find a *principium* in all those things
which have an order. First of all, order is found in quantified things;
and so there is a principle of number and lengths, as for example,
a line. Second, order is found in time; and so we speak of a "beginning" of time, or of duration. Third, order is found in learning;
and this in two ways: as to nature, and as to ourselves, and in both
cases we can speak of a "beginning": "By this time you ought to
be teachers" (Heb 5:12). As to nature, in Christian doctrine the
beginning and principle of our wisdom is Christ, inasmuch as he is
the Wisdom and Word of God, i.e., in his divinity. But as to ourselves, the beginning is Christ himself inasmuch as the Word has become flesh, i.e., by his incarnation. Fourth, an order is found in

the production of a thing. In this perspective there can be a *principium* on the part of the thing generated, that is, the first part of the thing generated or made; as we say that the foundation is the beginning of a house. Another *principium* is on the part of the generator, and in this perspective there are three "principles": of intention, which is the purpose, which motivates the agent; of reason, which is the idea in the mind of the maker; and of execution, which is the operative faculty. Considering these various ways of using the term, we now ask how *principium* is used here when it says, **In the beginning was the Word**.

35 We should note that this word can be taken in three ways. In one way so that *principium* is understood as the Person of the Son, who is the principle of creatures by reason of his active power acting with wisdom, which is the conception of the things that are brought into existence. Hence we read: "Christ the power of God and the wisdom of God" (1 Cor 1:24). And so the Lord said about himself: "I am the *principium* who also speaks to you" (below 8:25). Taking *principium* in this way, we should understand the statement, **In the beginning was the Word**, as though he were saying, "The Word was in the Son," so that the sense would be: The Word himself is the *principium*, principle, in the sense in which life is said to be "in" God, when this life is not something other than God. And this is the explanation of Origen. And so the Evangelist says **In the beginning** here in order, as Chrysostom says, to show at the very outset the divinity of the Word by asserting that he is a principle because, as determining all, a principle is most honored.

36 In a second way *principium* can be understood as the Person of the Father, who is the principle not only of creatures, but of every divine process. It is taken this way in, "Yours is princely power (*principium*) in the day of your birth" (Ps 110:3). In this second way one reads **In the beginning was the Word** as though it means, "The Son was in the Father." This is Augustine's understanding of it, as well as Origen's. The Son, however, is said to be in the Father because both have the same essence. Since the Son is his own essence, then the Son is in whomsoever the Son's essence is. Since, therefore, the essence of the Son is in the Father by consubstantiality, it is fitting that the Son be in the Father. Hence it says below (14:10): "I am in the Father and the Father is in me."

37 In a third way, *principium* can be taken for the beginning of duration, so that the sense of **In the beginning was the Word** is that the Word was before all things, as Augustine explains it. According to Basil and Hilary, this phrase shows the eternity of the Word.

The phrase **In the beginning was the Word** shows that no

matter which beginning of duration is taken, whether of temporal things which is time, or of aeviternal things which is the aeon, or of the whole world or any imagined span of time reaching back for many ages, at that beginning the Word already was. Hence Hilary says (*On the Trinity* VII): "Go back season by season, skip over the centuries, take away ages. Set down whatever you want as the beginning in your opinion: the Word already was." And this is what Proverbs (8:23) says: "The Lord possessed me in the beginning of his ways, before he made anything." But what is prior to the beginning of duration is eternal.

38   And thus the first explanation asserts the causality of the Word; the second explanation affirms the consubstantiality of the Word with the Father, who utters the Word; and the third explanation affirms the co-eternity of the Word.

39   Now we should consider that it says that the Word **was** (*erat*), which is stated in the past imperfect tense. This tense is most appropriate for designating eternal things if we consider the nature of time and of the things that exist in time. For what is future is not yet in act; but what is at present is in act, and by the fact that it is in act what is present is not described as having been. Now the past perfect tense indicates that something has existed, has already come to an end, and has now ceased to be. The past imperfect tense, on the other hand, indicates that something has been, has not yet come to an end, nor has ceased to be, but still endures. Thus, whenever John mentions eternal things he expressly says "was" (*erat*, past imperfect tense), but when he refers to anything temporal he says "has been" (*fuit*, past perfect tense), as will be clear later.

But so far as concerns the notion of the present, the best way to designate eternity is the present tense, which indicates that something is in act, and this is always the characteristic of eternal things. And so it says in Exodus (3:14): "I am who am." And Augustine says: "He alone truly is whose being does not know a past and a future."

40   We should also note that this verb **was**, according to the Gloss, is not understood here as indicating temporal changes, as other verbs do, but as signifying the existence of a thing. Thus it is also called a substantive verb.

41   Someone may ask how the Word can be co-eternal with the Father since he is begotten by the Father: for a human son, born from a human father, is subsequent to his father.

I answer that there are three reasons why an originative principle is prior in duration to that which derives from that principle.

First of all, if the originative principle of anything precedes in time the action by which it produces the thing of which it is the principle; thus a man does not begin to write as soon as he exists, and so he precedes his writing in time. Secondly, if an action is successive; consequently, even if the action should happen to begin at the same time as the agent, the termination of the action is nevertheless subsequent to the agent. Thus, as soon as fire has been generated in a lower region, it begins to ascend; but the fire exists before it has ascended, because the motion by which it tends upward requires some time. Thirdly, by the fact that sometimes the beginning of a thing depends on the will of its principle, just as the beginning of a creature's coming-to-be depends on the will of God, such that God existed before any creature.

Yet none of these three is found in the generation of the divine Word. God did not first exist and then begin to generate the Word: for since the generation of the Word is nothing other than an intelligible conception, it would follow that God would be understanding in potency before understanding in act, which is impossible. Again, it is impossible that the generation of the Word involve succession: for then the divine Word would be unformed before it was formed (as happens in us who form words by "cogitating"), which is false, as was said. Again, we cannot say that the Father pre-established a beginning of duration for his Son by his own will, because God the Father does not generate the Son by his will, as the Arians held, but naturally: for God the Father, understanding himself, conceives the Word; and so God the Father did not exist prior to the Son.

An example of this, to a limited degree, appears in fire and in the brightness issuing from it: for this brightness issues naturally and without succession from the fire. Again, if the fire were eternal, its brightness would be coeternal with it. This is why the Son is called the brightness of the Father: "the brightness of his glory" (Heb 1:3). But this example lacks an illustration of the identity of nature. And so we call him Son, although in human sonship we do not find coeternity: for we must attain our knowledge of divine things from many likenesses in material things, for one likeness is not enough. The Council of Ephesus says that the Son always coexists with the Father: for "brightness" indicates his unchangeability, "birth" points to the Word himself, but the name "Son" suggests his consubstantiality.

42 And so we give the Son various names to express his perfection, which cannot be expressed by one name. We call him "Son" to show that he is of the same nature as the Father; we call him "image" to show that he is not unlike the Father in any way; we call

him "brightness" to show that he is coeternal; and he is called the "Word" to show that he is begotten in an immaterial manner.

43   Then the Evangelist says, **and the Word was with God**, which is the second clause in his account. The first thing to consider is the meaning of the two words which did not appear in the first clause, that is, **God**, and **with**; for we have already explained the meanings of "Word," and "beginning."Let us continue carefully by examining these two new words, and to better understand the explanation of this second clause, we must say something about the meaning of each so far as it is relevant to our purpose.

44   At the outset, we should note that the name "God" signifies the divinity concretely and as inherent in a subject, while the name "deity" signifies the divinity in the abstract and absolutely. Thus the name "deity" cannot naturally and by its mode of signifying stand for a [divine] person, but only for the [divine] nature. But the name "God" can, by its natural mode of signifying, stand for any one of the [divine] persons, just as the name "man" stands for any individual (*suppositum*) possessing humanity. Therefore, whenever the truth of a statement or its predicate require that the name "God" stand for the person, then it stands for the person, as when we say, "God begets God." Thus, when it says here that **the Word was with God**, it is necessary that **God** stand for the person of the Father, because the preposition **with** signifies the distinction of the Word, which is said to be **with God**. And although this preposition signifies a distinction in person, it does not signify a distinction in nature, since the nature of the Father and of the Son is the same. Consequently, the Evangelist wished to signify the person of the Father when he said **God**.

45   Here we should note that the preposition **with** signifies a certain union of the thing signified by its grammatical antecedent to the thing signified by its grammatical object, just as the preposition "in" does. However, there is a difference, because the preposition "in" signifies a certain intrinsic union, whereas the preposition **with** implies in a certain way an extrinsic union. And we state both in divine matters, namely, that the Son is *in* the Father and *with* the Father. Here the intrinsic union pertains to consubstantiality, but the extrinsic union (if we may use such an expression, since "extrinsic" is improperly employed in divine matters) refers only to a personal distinction, because the Son is distinguished from the Father by origin alone. And so these two words designate both a consubstantiality in nature and distinction in person: consubstantiality inasmuch as a certain union is implied; but distinction, inasmuch as a certain otherness is signified as was said above.

The preposition "in," as was said, principally signifies consubstantiality, as implying an intrinsic union and, by way of consequence, a distinction of persons, inasmuch as every preposition is transitive. The preposition "with" principally signifies a personal distinction, but also a consubstantiality inasmuch as it signifies a certain extrinsic, so to speak, union. For these reasons the Evangelist specifically used here the preposition "with" in order to express the distinction of the person of the Son from the Father, saying, **and the Word was with God**, that is, the Son was with the Father as one person with another.

46 We should note further that this preposition **with** has four meanings, and these eliminate four objections. First, the preposition **with** signifies the subsistence of its antecedent, because things that do not subsist of themselves are not properly said to be "with" another; thus we do not say that a color is with a body, and the same applies to other things that do not subsist of themselves. But things that do subsist of themselves are properly said to be "with" another; thus we say that a man is with a man, and a stone with a stone.

Secondly, it signifies authority in its grammatical object. For we do not, properly speaking, say that a king is with a soldier, but that the soldier is with the king. Thirdly, it asserts a distinction. For it is not proper to say that a person is with himself, but rather that one man is with another. Fourthly, it signifies a certain union and fellowship. For when some person is said to be with another, it suggests to us that there is some social union between them.

Considering these four conditions implied in the meaning of this preposition **with**, the Evangelist quite appropriately joins to the first clause, **In the beginning was the Word**, this second clause, **and the Word was with God**. For if we omit one of the three explanations of, **In the beginning was the Word** (namely, the one in which *principium* was understood as the Son), certain heretics make a twofold objection against each of the other explanations (namely, the one in which *principium* means the same as "before all things," and the one in which it is understood as the Father). Thus there are four objections, and we can answer these by the four conditions indicated by this preposition **with**.

47 The first of these objections is this. You say that the Word was in the beginning, i.e., before all things. But before all things there was nothing. So if before all things there was nothing, where then was the Word? This objection arises due to the imaginings of those who think that whatever exists is somewhere and in some place. But this is rejected by John when he says, **with God**, which indicates the union mentioned in the last of the four conditions. So, according to

Basil, the meaning is this: Where was the Word? The answer is: **with God**; not in some place, since he is unsurroundable, but he is with the Father, who is not enclosed by any place.

48   The second objection against the same explanation is this. You say that the Word was in the beginning, i.e., before all things. But whatever exists before all things appears to proceed from no one, since that from which something proceeds seems to be prior to that which proceeds from it. Therefore, the Word does not proceed from another. This objection is rejected when he says, **the Word was with God**, taking "with" according to its second condition, as implying authority in what is causing. So the meaning, according to Hilary, is this: From whom is the Word if he exists before all things? The Evangelist answers: **the Word was with God**, i.e., although the Word has no beginning of duration, still he does not lack a *principium* or author, for he was with God as his author.

49   The third objection, directed to the explanation in which *principium* is understood as the Father, is this. You say that **In the beginning was the Word**, i.e., the Son was in the Father. But that which is in something does not seem to be subsistent, as a hypostasis; just as the whiteness in a body does not subsist. This objection is solved by the statement, **the Word was with God**, taking "with" in its first condition, as implying the subsistence of its grammatical antecedent. So according to Chrysostom, the meaning is this: **In the beginning was the Word**, not as an accident, but he was **with God**, as subsisting, and a divine hypostasis.

50   The fourth objection, against the same explanation, is this. You say that the Word was in the beginning, i.,e., in the Father. But whatever is in something is not distinct from it. So the Son is not distinct from the Father. This objection is answered by the statement, **and the Word was with God**, taking "with" in its third condition, as indicating distinction. Thus the meaning, according to Alcuin and Bede, is this: **The Word was with God**, and he was "in" the Father by a consubstantiality of nature, while still being "with" him through a distinction in person.

51   And so, **and the Word was with God**, indicates: the union of the Word with the Father in nature, according to Basil; their distinction in person, according to Alcuin and Bede; the subsistence of the Word in the divine nature, according to Chrysostom; and the authorship of the Father in relation to the Word, according to Hilary.

52   We should also note, according to Origen, that **the Word was with God** shows that the Son has always been with the Father. For in the Old Testament it says that the word of the Lord "came" to Jeremiah or to someone else, as is plain in many passages of sacred Scripture. But it does not say that the word of the Lord was "with"

Jeremiah or anyone else, because the word "comes" to those who begin to have the word after not having it. Thus the Evangelist did not say that the Word "came" to the Father, but was "with" the Father, because, given the Father, the Word was with him.

53   Then he says, **and the Word was God**. This is the third clause in John's account, and it follows most appropriately considering the order of teaching. For since John had said both *when* and *where* the Word was, it remained to inquire *what* the Word was, that is, **the Word was God**, taking "Word" as the subject, and "God" as the predicate.

54   But since one should first inquire what a thing is before investigating where and when it is, it seems that John violated this order by discussing these latter first.

Origen answers this by saying that the Word of God is with man and with God in different ways. The Word is with man as perfecting him, because it is through him that man becomes wise and good: "She makes friends of God and prophets" (Wis 7:27). But the Word is not with God as though the Father were perfected and enlightened by him. Rather, the Word is with God as receiving natural divinity from him, who utters the Word, and from whom he has it that he is the same God with him. And so, since the Word was with God by origin, it was necessary to show first that the Word was in the Father and with the Father before showing that the Word was God.

55   This clause also enables us to answer two objections which arise from the foregoing. The first is based on the name "Word," and is this. You say that **In the beginning was the Word**, and that the Word was **with God**. Now it is obvious that "word" is generally understood to signify a vocal sound and the statement of something necessary, a manifesting of thoughts. But these words pass away and do not subsist. Accordingly, someone could think that the Evangelist was speaking of a word like these.

According to Hilary and Augustine, this question is sufficiently answered by the above account. Augustine says (Homily 1 *On John*) that it is obvious that in this passage "Word" cannot be understood as a statement because, since a statement is in motion and passes away, it could not be said that **In the beginning was the Word**, if this Word were something passing away and in motion. The same thing is clear from **and the Word was with God**: for to be "in" another is not the same as to be "with" another. Our word, since it does not subsist, is not "with" us, but "in" us; but the Word of God is subsistent, and therefore "with" God. And so the Evangelist expressly says, **and the Word was with God**. To entirely remove the ground of the objection, he adds the nature and being of the Word, saying, **and the Word was God.**

56   The other question comes from his saying, **with God.** For since "with" indicates a distinction, it could be thought that **the Word was with God,** i.e., the Father, as distinct from him in nature. So to exclude this he adds at once the consubstantiality of the Word with the Father, saying, **and the Word was God.** As if to say: the Word is not separated from the Father by a diversity of nature, because the Word itself is God.

57   Note also the special way of signifying, since he says, **the Word was God,** using "God" absolutely to show that he is not God in the same way in which the name of the deity is given to a creature in Sacred Scripture. For a creature sometimes shares this name with some added qualification, as when it says, "I have appointed you the God of Pharaoh" (Ex 7:1), in order to indicate that he was not God absolutely or by nature, because he was appointed the god of someone in a qualified sense. Again, it says in the Psalm (81:6): "I said, 'You are gods.' " − as if to say: in my opinion, but not in reality. Thus the Word is called God absolutely because he is God by his own essence, and not by participation, as men and angels are.

58   We should note that Origen disgracefully misunderstood this clause, led astray by the Greek manner of speaking. It is the custom among the Greeks to put the article before every name in order to indicate a distinction. In the Greek version of John's Gospel the name "Word" in the statement, **In the beginning was the Word,** and also the name "God" in the statement, **and the Word was with God,** are prefixed by the article, so as to read "the Word" and "the God," in order to indicate the eminence and distinction of the Word from other words, and the principality of the Father in the divinity. But in the statement, **the Word was God,** the article is not prefixed to the noun "God," which stands for the person of the Son. Because of this Origen blasphemed that the Word, although he was Word by essence, was not God by essence, but is called God by participation; while the Father alone is God by essence. And so he held that the Son is inferior to the Father.

59   Chrysostom proves that this is not true, because if the article used with the name "God" implied the superiority of the Father in respect to the Son, it would never be used with the name "God" when it is used as a predicate of another, but only when it is predicated of the Father. Further, whenever said of the Father, it would be accompanied by the article. However, we find the opposite to be the case in two statements of the Apostle, who calls Christ "God," using the article. For in Titus (2:13) he says, "the

coming of the glory of the great God and our Savior Jesus Christ," where "God" stands for the Son, and in the Greek the article is used. Therefore, Christ is the great God. Again he says (Rom 9:5): "Christ, who is God over all things, blessed forever," and again the article is used with "God" in the Greek. Further, in 1 John (5:20) it says: "That we may be in his true Son, Jesus Christ; he is the true God and eternal life." Thus, Christ is not God by participation, but truly God. And so the theory of Origen is clearly false.

Chrysostom gives us the reason why the Evangelist did not use the article with the name "God," namely, because he had already mentioned God twice using the article, and so it was not necessary to repeat it a third time, but it was implied. Or, a better reason would be that "God" is used here as the predicate and is taken formally. And it is not the custom for the article to accompany names used as predicates, since the article indicates separation. But if "God" were used here as the subject, it could stand for any of the persons, as the Son or the Holy Spirit; then, no doubt, the article would be used in the Greek.

60 Then he says, **He was in the beginning with God.** This is the fourth clause and is introduced because of the preceding clause. For from the Evangelist's statement that **the Word was God**, two false interpretations could be held by those who misunderstand. One of these is by the pagans, who acknowledge many and different gods, and say that their wills are in opposition. For example, those who put out the fable of Jupiter fighting with Saturn; or as the Manicheans, who have two contrary principles of nature. The Lord said against this error (Dt 6:4): "Hear O Israel: The Lord our God is one Lord."

Since the Evangelist had said, **the Word was with God; and the Word was God**, they could adduce this in support of their error by understanding the God with whom the Word is to be one [God],and the Word to be another, having another, or contrary, will to the former; and this is against the law of the Gospel. And so to exclude this he says, **He was in the beginning with God,** as if to say, according to Hilary: I say that the Word is God, not as if he has a distinct divinity, but he is with God, that is, in the one same nature in which he is. Further, lest his statement, **and the Word was God**, be taken to mean that the Word has an opposed will, he added that the Word **was in the beginning with God,** namely, the Father; not as divided from him or opposed, but having an identity of nature with him and a harmony of will. This union comes about by the sharing of the divine nature in the three persons, and by the bond of the natural love of the Father and the Son.

61   The Arians were able to draw out another error from the above. They think that the Son is less than the Father because it says below (14:28): "The Father is greater than I." And they say the Father is greater than the Son both as to eternity and as to divinity of nature. And so to exclude this the Evangelist added: **He was in the beginning with God.** For Arius admits the first clause, **In the beginning was the Word,** but he will not admit that *principium* should be taken for the Father, but rather for the beginning of creatures. So he says that the Word was in the beginning of creatures, and consequently is in no sense coeternal with the Father. But this is excluded, according to Chrysostom, by this clause, **He was in the beginning,** not of creatures, but **in the beginning with God,** i.e., whenever God existed. For the Father was never alone without the Son or Word, but **He,** that is, the Word, was always **with God.**

62   Again, Arius admits that the Word was God, but nevertheless inferior to the Father. This is excluded by what follows. For there are two attributes proper to the great God which Arius attributed solely to God the Father, that is, eternity and omnipotence. So in whomever these two attributes are found, he is the great God, than whom none is greater. But the Evangelist attributes these two to the Word. Therefore, the Word is the great God, and not inferior. He says the Word is eternal when he states, **He was in the beginning with God,** i.e., the Word was with God from eternity, and not only in the beginning of creatures (as Arius held) , but with God, receiving being and divinity from him. Further, he attributes omnipotence to the Word when he adds, **Through him all things came into being.**

63   Origen gives a rather beautiful explanation of this clause, **He was in the beginning with God,** when he says that it is not separate from the first three, but is in a certain sense their epilogue. For the Evangelist, after he had indicated that truth was the Son's and was about to describe his power, in a way gathers together in a summary form, in this fourth clause, what he had said in the first three. For in saying **He,** he understands the third clause; by adding **was in the beginning,** he recalls the first clause; and by adding **with God,** he recalls the second, so that we do not think that the Word which was in the beginning is different than the Word which was God; but this Word which was God **was in the beginning with God.**

64   If one considers these four propositions well, he will find that they clearly destroy all the errors of the heretics and of the philosophers. For some heretics, as Ebion and Cerinthus, said that Christ did not exist before the Blessed Virgin, but took from her the beginning of his being and duration; for they held that he was a mere man, who had merited divinity by his good works. Photinus

and Paul of Samosata, following them, said the same thing. But the Evangelist excludes their errors saying, **In the beginning was the Word**, i.e., before all things, and in the Father from eternity. Thus he did not derive his beginning from the Virgin.

Sabellius, on the other hand, although he admitted that the God who took flesh did not receive his beginning from the Virgin, but existed from eternity, still said that the person of the Father, who existed from eternity, was not distinct from the person of the Son, who took flesh from the Virgin. He maintained that the Father and Son were the same person; and so he failed to distinguish the trinity of persons in the deity. The Evangelist says against this error, **and the Word was with God**, i.e., the Son was with the Father, as one person with another.

Eunomius declared that the Son is entirely unlike the Father. The Evangelist rejects this when he says, **and the Word was God**. Finally, Arius said that the Son was less than the Father. The Evangelist excludes this by saying, **He was in the beginning with God**, as was explained above.

65 These words also exclude the errors of the philosophers. For some of the ancient philosophers, namely, the natural philosophers, maintained that the world did not come from any intellect or through some purpose, but by chance. Consequently, they did not place at the beginning as the cause of things a reason or intellect, but only matter in flux; for example, atoms, as Democritus thought, or other material principles of this kind as different philosophers maintained. Against these the Evangelist says, **In the beginning was the Word**, from whom, and not from chance, things derive their beginning.

Plato, however, thought that the Ideas of all the things that were made were subsistent, i.e., existing separately in their own natures; and material things exist by participating in these. For example, he thought men existed through the separated Idea of man, which he called Man *per se*. So lest you suppose, as did Plato, that this Idea through which all things were made be Ideas separated from God, the Evangelist adds, **and the Word was with God**.

Other Platonists, as Chrysostom relates, maintained that God the Father was most eminent and first, but under him they placed a certain mind in which there were the likenesses and ideas of all things. So lest you think that the Word was with the Father in such a way as to be under him and less than he, the Evangelist adds, **and the Word was God**.

Aristotle, however, thought that the ideas of all things are in God, and that in God, the intellect, the one understanding, and what is understood, are the same. Nevertheless, he thought that the world is coeternal with him. Against this the Evangelist says, **He**, the Word alone, **was in the beginning with God**, in such a way that **He** does not exclude another person, but only another coeternal nature.

66 Note the difference in what has been said between John and the other Evangelists: how he began his Gospel on a loftier plane than they. They announced Christ the Son of God born in time: "When Jesus was born in Bethlehem" (Mt 2:1); but John presents him existing from eternity: **In the beginning was the Word**. They show him suddenly appearing among men: "Now you dismiss your servant, O Lord, in peace, according to your word; because my eyes have seen your salvation" (Lk 2:29); but John says that he always existed with the Father: **and the Word was with God**. The others show him as a man: "They gave glory to God who had given such authority to men" (Mt 9:8); but John says that he is God: **and the Word was God**. The others say he lives with men: "While living in Galilee, Jesus said to them" (Mt 17:21); but John says that he has always been with the Father: **He was in the beginning with God**.

67 Note also how the Evangelist designedly uses the word **was** (*erat*) to show that the Word of God transcends all times: present, past and future. It is as though he were saying: He was beyond time: present, past and future, as the Gloss says.

LECTURE 2

3 All things were made through him,
and without him nothing was made.
What was made 4a in him was life.

68 After the Evangelist has told of the existence and nature of the Divine Word, so far as it can be told by man, he then shows the might of his power. First, he shows his power with respect to all things that come into existence. Secondly, with respect to man. As to the first, he uses three clauses; and we will not distinguish these at present because they will be distinguished in different ways according to the different explanations given by the saints.

69 The first clause, **All things were made through him**, is used to show three things concerning the Word. First, according to Chrysostom, to show the equality of the Word to the Father. For as stated earlier, the error of Arius was rejected by the Evangelist when he showed the coeternity of the Son with the Father by saying, "He was in the beginning with God." Here he excludes the same error when he shows the omnipotence of the Son, saying, **All things were made**

through him. For to be the principle of all the things that are made is proper to the great omnipotent God, as the Psalm (134:6) says, "Whatever the Lord wills he does, in heaven and on earth."Thus the Word, through whom all things were made, is God, great and coequal to the Father.

70 Secondly, according to Hilary, this clause is used to show the coeternity of the Word with the Father. For since someone might understand the earlier statement, "In the beginning was the Word," as referring to the beginning of creatures, i.e., that before there were any creatures there was a time in which the Word did not exist, the Evangelist rejects this by saying, **All things were made through him**. For if all things were made through the Word, then time was also. From this we can form the following argument: If all time was made through him, there was no time before him or with him, because before all these, he was. Therefore they [the Son and the Father] are eternally coeternal.

71 Thirdly, according to Augustine, this clause is used to show the consubstantiality of the Word with the Father. For if all things were made through the Word, the Word himself cannot be said to have been made; because, if made, he was made through some Word, since all things were made through the Word. Consequently, there would have been another Word through whom was made the Word of whom the Evangelist is speaking. This Word, through whom all things are made, we call the only begotten Son of God, because he is neither made nor is he a creature. And if he is not a creature, it is necessary to say that he is of the same substance with the Father, since every substance other than the divine essence is made. But a substance that is not a creature is God. And so the Word, through whom all things were made, is consubstantial with the Father, since he is neither made, nor is he a creature.

72 And so in saying **All things were made through him**, you have, according to Chrysostom, the equality of the Word with the Father; the coeternity of the Word with the Father, according to Hilary; and the consubstantiality of the Word with the Father, according to Augustine.

73 Here we must guard against three errors. First, the error of Valentine. He understood **All things were made through him** to mean that the Word proferred to the Creator the cause of his creating the world; so that all things were made through the Word as if the Father's creating the world came from the Word. This leads to the position of those who said that God created the world because of some exterior cause; and this is contrary to Proverbs (16:4), "The Lord made all things for himself." The reason this is an error

is that, as Origen says, if the Word had been a cause to the Creator by offering him the material for making things, he would not have said, **All things were made through him**, but on the contrary, that all things were made through the Creator by the Word.

74   Secondly, we must avoid the error of Origen. He said that the Holy Spirit was included among all the things made through the Word; from which it follows that he is a creature. And this is what Origen thought. This is heretical and blasphemous, since the Holy Spirit has the same glory and substance and dignity as the Father and the Son, according to the words of Matthew (28:19), "Make disciples of all the nations, baptizing them in the name of the Father, and of the Son, and of the Holy Spirit." And, "There are three who give testimony in heaven, the Father, the Word, and the Holy Spirit; and these three are one" (1 Jn 5:7). Thus when the Evangelist says, **All things were made through him**, one should not understand "all things" absolutely, but in the realm of creatures and of things made. As if to say: All things that were made, were made through him. Otherwise, if "all things" were taken absolutely, it would follow that the Father and the Holy Spirit were made through him; and this is blasphemous. Consequently, neither the Father nor anything substantial with the Father was made through the Word.

75   Thirdly, we must avoid another of Origen's errors. For he said that all things were made through the Word as something is made by a greater through a lesser, as if the Son were inferior to, and an instrument of, the Father. But it is clear from many places in Scripture that the preposition "through" (*per*) does not signify inferiority in the thing which is its grammatical object, i.e., in the Son or Word. For the Apostle says, "God is faithful, through whom you were called into the fellowship of his Son" (1 Cor 1:9). If he "through" whom something is done has a superior, then the Father has a superior. But this is false. Therefore, the preposition "through" does not signify any inferiority in the Son when all things are said to have been made through him.

76   To explain this point further, we should note that when something is said to be made through someone, the preposition "through" (*per*) denotes some sort of causality in its object with respect to an operation; but not always the same kind of causality. For since an operation, according to our manner of signifying, is considered to be medial between the one acting and the thing produced, the operation itself can be regarded in two ways. In one way, as issuing from the one operating, who is the cause of the action itself; in another way, as terminated in the thing produced. Accordingly, the preposition "through" sometimes signifies the cause of the operation insofar as it issues from the one operating; but

sometimes as terminated in the thing which is produced. It signifies the cause of the operation as issuing from the one operating when the object of the preposition is either the efficient or formal cause why the one operating is operating. For example, we have a formal cause when fire is heating through heat; for heat is the formal cause of the fire's heating. We have a movent or efficient cause in cases where secondary agents act through primary agents; as when I say that the bailiff acts through the king, because the king is the efficient cause of the bailiff's acting. This is the way Valentine understood that all things were made through the Word: as though the Word were the cause of the maker's production of all things. The preposition "through" implies the causality of the operation as terminated in the thing produced when what is signified through that causality is not the cause which operates, but the cause of the operation precisely as terminated in the thing produced. So when I say, "The carpenter is making a bench through [by means of] a hatchet," the hatchet is not the cause of the carpenter's operating; but we do say that it is the cause of the bench's being made by the one acting.

And so when it says that **All things were made through him**, if the "through" denotes the efficient or movent cause, causing the Father to act, then in this sense the Father does nothing through the Son, but he does all things through himself, as has been said. But if the "through" denotes a formal cause, as when the Father operates through his widsom, which is his essence, he operates through his wisdom as he operates through his essence. And because the wisdom and power of the Father are attributed to the Son, as when we say, "Christ, the power of God and the wisdom of God" (1 Cor 1:24), then by appropriation we say that the Father does all things through the Son, i.e., through his wisdom. And so Augustine says that the phrase "from whom all things," is appropriated to the Father; "through whom all things," is appropriated to the Son; and "in whom all things," is appropriated to the Holy Spirit. But if the "through" denotes causality from the standpoint of the thing produced, then the statement, "The Father does all things through the Son," is not [mere] appropriation but proper to the Word, because the fact that he is a cause of creatures is had from someone else, namely the Father, from whom he has being.

However, it does not follow from this that the Word is the instrument of the Father, although whatever is moved by another to effect something partakes of the nature of an instrument. For when I say that someone works through a power received from another, this can be understood in two ways. In one way, as meaning that the power of the giver and of the receiver is numerically one and the same power; and in this way the one operating through a power received from another is not inferior but equal to the one from whom he receives it. Therefore, since the same power which the Father has he gives to the Son, through which the Son works, when it is said that "the Father works through the Son," one should not on that account say that the Son is inferior to the Father or is his instrument. This would be the case, rather, in those who receive from another not the same power, but another and created one. And so it is plain that neither the Holy Spirit nor the Son are causes of the Father's working, and that neither is the minister or instrument of the Father, as Origen raved.

77   If we carefully consider the words, **All things were made through him**, we can clearly see that the Evangelist spoke with the utmost exactitude. For whoever makes something must preconceive it in his wisdom, which is the form and pattern of the thing made: as the form preconceived in the mind of an artisan is the pattern of the cabinet to be made. So, God makes nothing except through the conception of his intellect, which is an eternally conceived wisdom, that is, the Word of God, and the Son of God. Accordingly, it is impossible that he should make anything except through the Son. And so Augustine says, in *The Trinity*, that the Word is the art full of the living patterns of all things. Thus it is clear that all things which the Father makes, he makes through him.

78   It should be remarked that, according to Chrysostom, all the things which Moses enumerates individually in God's production of things, saying, "And God said, 'Let there be light' " (Gn 1:3) and so forth, all these the Evangelist transcends and embraces in one phrase, saying, **All things were made through him**. The reason is that Moses wished to teach the emanation of creatures from God; hence he enumerated them one by one. But John, hastening toward loftier things, intends in this book to lead us specifically to a knowledge of the Creator himself.

79   Then he says, **and without him nothing was made**. This is the second clause which some have distorted, as Augustine says in his work, *The Nature of the Good*. Because of John's manner of speaking here, they believed that he was using "nothing" in an affirmative sense; as though nothing was something which was made without the Word. And so they claimed that this clause was added by the Evangelist in order to exclude something which was not made by the Word. They say that the Evangelist, having said that **All things were made through him**, added **and without him nothing was made**. It was as if to say: I say that all things were made through him in such a way that still something was made without him, that is, the "nothing."

80 Three heresies came from this. First, that of Valentine. He affirmed, as Origen says, a multitude of principles, and taught that from them came thirty eras. The first principles he postulates are two: the Deep, which he calls God the Father, and Silence. And from these proceed ten eras. But from the Deep and from Silence, he says, there are two other principles, Mind and Truth; and from these issued eight eras. Then from Mind and Truth, there are two other principles, Word and Life; and from these issued twelve eras; thus making a total of thirty. Finally, from the Word and Life there proceeded in time, the man Christ and the Church. In this way Valentine affirmed many eras previous to the issuing forth of the Word. And so he said that because the Evangelist had stated that **all things were made through him**, then, lest anyone think that those previous eras had been effected through the Word, he added, **and without him nothing was made**, i.e., all the preceding eras and all that had existed in them. All of these John calls "nothing," because they transcend human reason and cannot be grasped by the mind.

81 The second error to arise from this was that of Manichaeus, who affirmed two opposing principles: one is the source of incorruptible things, and the other of corruptible things. He said that after John had stated that **All things were made through him**, then, lest it be thought that the Word is the cause of corruptible things, he immediately added, **and without him nothing was made**, i.e., things subject to corruption, which are called "nothing" because their being consists in being continually transformed into nothing.

82 The third error is that of those who claim that by "nothing" we should understand the devil, according to Job (18:15), "May the companions of him who is not dwell in his house." And so they say that all things except the devil were made through the Word. In this way they explain, **without him nothing was made**, that is, the devil.

83 All these three errors, arising as they do from the same source, namely, taking "nothing" in a positive sense, are excluded by the fact that "nothing" in not used here in an affirmative, but in a merely negative sense: the sense being that all things were made through the Word in such a way that there is nothing participating in existence that was not made through him.

84 Perhaps someone will object and say that it was superflous to add this clause, if it is to be understood negatively, on the ground that the Evangelist, in stating that **All things were made through him**, seems to have already said adequately enough that there is not something that was not made through the Word.

The answer to this is that, according to many expositors, this clause was added in many ways for a number of reasons. One of these reasons is, according to Chrysostom, so that no one reading the

Old Testament and finding only visible things listed by Moses in the creation of things, would think that these were the only things made through the Word. And so after he had said, **All things were made through him**, namely, those that Moses listed, the Evangelist then added, **and without him nothing was made**, as though he were saying: None of the things which exist, whether visible or invisible, was made without the Word. Indeed, the Apostle also speaks in this way (Col 1:16), saying that all things, visible and invisible, were created in Christ; and here the Apostle makes specific mention of invisible things because Moses had made no express mention of them on account of the lack of erudition of that people, who could not be raised above the things of sense.

Chrysostom also gives another reason why this clause was added. For someone reading in the Gospels of the many signs and miracles worked by Christ, such as, "The blind see, the lame walk, lepers are cleansed" (Mt 11:5), might believe that in saying, **All things were made through him**, John meant that only the things mentioned in those Gospels, and nothing else, were made through him. So lest anyone suspect this, the Evangelist adds, **and without him nothing was made**. As if to say: Not only all the things contained in the Gospels were made through him, but none of the things that were made, was made without him. And so, according to Chrysostom, this clause is added to bring out his total causality, and serves, as it were, to complete his previous statement.

85   According to Hilary, however, this clause is introduced to show that the Word has operative power from another. For since the Evangelist had said, **All things were made through him**, it might be supposed that the Father is excluded from all causality. For that reason he added, **and without him nothing was made**. As if to say: All things were made through him, but in such a way that the Father made all things with him. For "without him" is equivalent to saying, "not alone," so that the meaning is: It is not he alone through whom all things were made, but he is the other one without whom nothing was made. It is as if he said: **Without him**, with another working, i.e., with the Father, **nothing was made**, as it says, "I was with him forming all things" (Prv 8:30).

86   In a certain homily attributed to Origen, and which begins, "The spiritual voice of the eagle," we find another rather beautiful exposition. It says there that the Greek has *thoris* where the Latin has *sine* (without). Now *thoris* is the same as "outside" or "outside of." It is as if he had said: **All things were made through him** in such a way that outside him **nothing was made**. And so he says this to show that all things are conserved through the Word and in the Word, as stated in Hebrews (1:3), "He sustains all things by his powerful

word." Now there are certain things that do not need their producer except to bring them into existence, since after they have been produced they are able to subsist without any further activity on the part of the producer. For example, a house needs a builder if it is to come into existence, but it continues to exist without any further action on the part of the builder. So lest anyone suppose that all things were made through the Word in such a way that he is merely the cause of their production and not of their continuation in existence, the Evangelist added, **and without him nothing was made**, i.e., nothing was made outside of him, because he encompasses all things, preserving them.

87 This clause is also explained by Augustine and Origen and several others in such a way that "nothing" indicates sin. Accordingly, because **All things were made through him** might be interpreted as including evil and sin, he added, **and without him nothing**, i.e., sin, **was made**. For just as art is not the principle or cause of the defects in its products, but is through itself the cause of their perfection and form, so the Word, who is the art of the Father, full of living archetypes, is not the cause of any evil or disarrangement in things, particularly of the evil of sin, which carries the full notion of evil. The *per se* cause of this evil is the will of the creature, either a man or an angel, freely declining from the end to which it is ordained by its nature. One who can act in virtue of his art but purposely violates it, is the cause of the defects occurring in his works, not by reason of his art, but by reason of his will. So in such cases, his art is not the source or cause of the defects, but his will is. Consequently, evil is a defect of the will and not of any art. And so to the extent that it is such [i.e., a defect], it is nothing.

88 So then, this clause is added to show the universal causality of the Word, according to Chrysostom; his association with the Father, according to Hilary; the power of the Word in the preserving of things, according to Origen; and finally, the purity of his causality, because he is so the cause of good as not to be the cause of sin, according to Augustine, Origen, and a number of others.

89 Then he says, **What was made in him was life**; and this is the third clause. Here we must avoid the false interpretation of Manichaeus, who was led by this to maintain that everything that exists is alive: for example, stones, wood, men, and anything else in the world. He understood the clause this way: **What was made in him**, comma, **was life**. But it was not life unless alive. Therefore, whatever was made in him is alive. He also claimed that **in him** is the same as saying "through him," since very often in Scripture "in him" and "through him" are interchangeable, as in "In him and through him

all things were created" (Col 1:16). However, our present explanation shows that this interpretation is false.

90 There are, nevertheless, a number of ways to explain it without error. In that homily, "The spiritual voice," we find this explanation: **What was made in him**, i.e., through him, **was life**, not in each thing itself, but in its cause. For in the case of all things that are caused, it is always true that effects, whether produced by nature or by will, exist in their causes, not according to their own existence, but according to the power of their appropriate cause. Thus, lower effects are in the sun as in their cause, not according to their respective existences but according to the power of the sun. Therefore, since the cause of all effects produced by God is a certain life and an art full of living archetypes, for this reason **What was made in him**, i.e., through him, **was life**, in its cause, i.e., in God.

91 Augustine reads this another way, as: **What was made**, comma, **in him was life**. For things can be considered in two ways: as they are in themselves, and as they are in the Word. If they are considered as they are in themselves, then it is not true that all things are life or even alive, but some lack life and some are alive. For example, the earth was made and metals were made, but none is life, none is living; animals and men were made, and these, considered in themselves, are not life, but merely living. Yet considered as they are in the Word, they are not merely living, but also life. For the archetypes which exist spiritually in the wisdom of God, and through which things were made by the Word, are life, just as a chest made by an artisan is in itself neither alive nor life, yet the exemplar of the chest in the artisan's mind prior to the existence of the chest is in some sense living, insofar as it has an intellectual existence in the mind of the artisan. Nevertheless it is not life, because it is neither in his essence nor is it his existence through the act of understanding of the artisan. But in God, his act of understanding is his life and his essence. And so whatever is in God is not only living, but is life itself, because whatever is in God is his essence. Hence the creature in God is the creating essence. Thus, if things are considered as they are in the Word, they are life. This is explained in another place.

92 Origen, commenting on John, gives another reading, thus: **That which was made in him**; and then, **was life**. Here we should note that some things are said of the Son of God as such; for example, that he is God, omnipotent, and the like. And some things are said of him in relation to ourselves; for example, we say he is Savior and Redeemer. Some things are said in both ways, such as wisdom and justice. Now in all things said absolutely and of the Son as such, it is not said that he was "made"; for example, we do not say that the Son was made God or omnipotent. But in things said in reference to

us, or in both ways, the notion of being made can be used, as in, "God made him [Jesus Christ] our wisdom, our justice, our sanctification and redemption" (1 Cor 1:30). And so, although he was always wisdom and justice in himself, yet it can be said that he was newly made justice and wisdom for us.

And so Origen, explaining it along these lines, says that although in himself the Son is life, yet he was made life for us by the fact that he gave us life, as is said, "Just as in Adam all die, so in Christ all will come to life" (1 Cor 15:22). And so he says "the Word that was made" life for us **in himself was life**, so that after a time he could become life for us; and so he immediately adds, **and that life was the light of men.**

93 Hilary reads the clause differently, thus: **And without him was made nothing, which was made in him**, and later it says, **he was life.** For he says (*The Trinity* II) that when the Evangelist says **without him nothing was made**, one might be perplexed and ask whether there are still other things made by him that were not made through him, although not without him, but with respect to which he was associated with the maker; and this clause is added to correct the aforesaid error. Therefore lest this be so understood, when the Evangelist says, **All things were made through him**, he adds, **and without him nothing was made**, which was made, **in him**, that is, through him; and the reason for this is that **he was life.**

For it is plain that all things are said to have been made through the Word inasmuch as the Word, who proceeds from the Father, is God. But let us suppose that some father has a son who does not perfectly exercise the operations of a man, but reaches such a state gradually. In that case the father will do many things, not through the son, yet not without [having] him. Since, therefore, the Son of God has from all eternity the same life that the Father has — "Just as the Father possesses life in himself, so has he granted it to the Son to have life in himself" (below 5:26) — one cannot say that God the Father, although he made nothing without the Son, nevertheless made some things not through him, because he was life. For in living things which participate life, it can happen that imperfect life precedes perfect life; but in *per se* life, which does not participate life but is simply and absolutely life, there can be no imperfection at all. Accordingly, because the Word is *per se* life, there was never imperfect life in him, but always perfect life. And so in such a way that nothing was made without him that was not also made in him, i.e., through him.

94 Chrysostom has a different reading and punctuation, thus: **And without him was made nothing that was made.** The reason for this is that someone might believe that the Holy Spirit was made

through the Word. So to exclude this, the Evangelist says, **that was made**, because the Holy Spirit is not something that is made. And afterward follows, **In him was life**, which is introduced for two reasons. First, to show that after the creation of all things his causality was indefectible not only with respect to the things already produced, but also with respect to things yet to be produced. As if to say: **In him was life**, by which he could not only produce all things, but which has an unfailing flow and a causality for producing things continually without undergoing any change, being a living fountain which is not diminished in spite of its continuous outflow; whereas collected water, that is not living [i.e., running] water, is diminished when it flows out, and is used up. So the Psalm (35:10) says, "With you is the fountain of life." The second reason is to show that things are governed by the Word. For since **In him was life**, this shows that he produced things by his intellect and will, not by a necessity of his nature, and that he governs the things he made. "The Word of God is living" (Heb 4:12).

Chrysostom is held in such esteem by the Greeks in his explanations that they admit no other where he expounded anything in Holy Scripture. For this reason, this passage in all the Greek works is found to be punctuated exactly as Chrysostom did, namely, **And without him was made nothing that was made**.

LECTURE 3

4b And that life was the light of men.
5 And the light shines in the darkness,
and the darkness did not overcome it.

95   Above, the Evangelist described the power of the Word insofar as he brought all things into existence; here he describes his power as it is related to men, saying that this Word is a light to men. First, he introduces a certain light to us (v 4b); secondly, the light's irradiation (v 5a); thirdly, participation in the light (v 5b). This whole section may be explained in two ways: first, according to the influx of natural knowledge; secondly, according to participation in grace.

As to the first point he says, **And that life was the light of men**.

96   Here we should note first that, according to Augustine and many others, light is more properly said of spiritual things than of sensible things. Ambrose, however, thinks that brightness is said metaphorically of God. But this is not a great issue, for in whatever

way the name "light" is used, it implies a manifestation, whether that manifesting concerns intelligible or sensible things. If we compare sensible and intelligible manifestation, then, according to the nature of things, light is found first in spiritual things. But for us, who give names to things on the basis of their properties as known to us, light is discovered first in sensible things, because we first used this name to signify sensible light before intelligible light; although as to power, light belongs to spiritual things in a prior and truer way than to sensible things.

97 To clarify the statement, **And that life was the light of men**, we should remark that there are many grades of life. For some things live, but do so without light, because they have no knowledge; for example, plants. Hence their life is not light. Other things both live and know, but their knowledge, since it is on the sense level, is concerned only with individual and material things, as is the case with the brutes. So they have both life and a certain light. But they do not have the light of men, who live, and know, not only truths, but also the very nature of truth itself. Such are rational creatures, to whom not only this or that are made manifest, but truth itself, which can be manifested and is manifestive to all.

And so the Evangelist, speaking of the Word, not only says that he is life but also **light**, lest anyone suppose he means life without knowledge. And he says that he is the **light of men**, lest anyone suppose he meant only sensible knowledge, such as exists in the brutes.

98 But since he is also the light of angels, why did he say, **of men**? Two answers have been given to this. Chrysostom says that the Evangelist intended in this Gospel to give us a knowledge of the Word precisely as directed to the salvation of men, and therefore refers, in keeping with his aim, more to men than to angels. Origen, however, says that participation in this light pertains to men insofar as they have a rational nature; accordingly, when the Evangelist says, **the light of men**, he wants us to understand every rational nature.

99 We also see from this the perfection and dignity of this life, because it is intellectual or rational. For whereas all things that in some way move themselves are called living, only those that perfectly move themselves are said to have perfect life; and among lower creatures only man moves himself, properly speaking, and perfectly. For although other things are moved by themselves by some inner principle, that inner principle is nevertheless not open to opposite alternatives; hence they are not moved freely but from necessity. As a result, those things that are moved by such a principle are more truly made to act than act themselves. But man, since he is master of his act, moves himself freely to all that he wills.

Consequently, man has perfect life, as does every intellectual nature. And so the life of the Word, which is the light of men, is perfect life.

100 We find a fitting order in the above. For in the natural order of things, existence is first; and the Evangelist implies this in his first statement, **In the beginning was the Word**. Secondly, comes life; and this is mentioned next, **In him was life**. Thirdly comes understanding; and that is mentioned next; **And that life was the light of men**. And, according to Origen, he fittingly attributes light to life because light can be attributed only to the living.

101 We should note that light can be related in two ways to what is living: as an object and as something in which they participate, as is clear in external sight. For the eyes know external light as an object, but if they are to see it, they must participate in an inner light by which the eyes are adapted and disposed for seeing the external light. And so his statement, **And that life was the light of men**, can be understood in two ways. First, that the **light of men** is taken as an object that man alone can look upon, because the rational creature alone can see it, since he alone is capable of the vision of God who "teaches us more than the beasts of the earth, and enlightens us more than the birds of the air" (Jb 35:11); for although other animals may know certain things that are true, nevertheless, man alone knows the nature itself of truth.

The **light of men** can also be taken as a light in which we participate. For we would never be able to look upon the Word and light itself except through a participation in it; and this participation is in man and is the superior part of our soul, i.e., the intellectual light, about which the Psalm (4:7) says, "The light of your countenance, O Lord, is marked upon us," i.e., of your Son, who is your face, by whom you are manifested.

102   Having introduced a certain light, the Evangelist now considers its irradiation, saying, **And the light shines in the darkness**. This can be explained in two ways, according to the two meanings of "darkness."

First, we might take "darkness" as a natural defect, that of the created mind. For the mind is to that light of which the Evangelist speaks here as air is to the light of the sun; because, although air is receptive of the light of the sun, considered in itself it is a darkness. According to this the meaning is: **the light**, i.e., that life which is the light of men, **shines in the darkness**, i.e., in created souls and minds, by always shedding its light on all. "On a man from whom the light is hidden" (Jb 3:23).

And the darkness did not overcome it, i.e., enclose it [i.e., intellectually]. For to overcome something [*comprehendere*, to overcome, to comprehend, to seize or apprehend, and so forth], is to enclose and understand its boundaries. As Augustine says, to reach God with the mind is a great happiness; but to overcome [comprehend] him is impossible. And so, **the darkness did not overcome it**. "Behold, God is great, exceeding our knowledge" (Jb 36:26); "Great in counsel, incomprehensible in thought" as Jeremiah (32:19) says. This explanation is found in that homily which begins, "The spiritual voice of the eagle."

103   We can explain this passage in another way by taking "darkness" as Augustine does, for the natural lack of wisdom in man, which is called a darkness. "And I saw that wisdom excells folly as much as light excells knowledge" (Ecc 2:13). Someone is without wisdom, therefore, because he lacks the light of divine wisdom. Consequently, just as the minds of the wise are lucid by reason of a participation in that divine light and wisdom, so by the lack of it they are darkness. Now the fact that some are darkness is not due to a defect in that light, since on its part it shines in the darkness and radiates upon all. Rather, the foolish are without that light because **the darkness did not overcome it**, i.e., they did not apprehend it, not being able to attain a participation in it due to their foolishness; after having been lifted up, they did not persevere. "From the savage," i.e., from the proud, "he hides his light," i.e., the light of wisdom, "and shows his friend that it belongs to him, and that he may approach it" (Jb 36:32); "They did not know the way to wisdom, nor did they remember her paths" (Bar 3:23).

Although some minds are darkness, i.e., they lack savory and lucid wisdom, nevertheless no man is in such darkness as to be completely devoid of divine light, because whatever truth is know by anyone is due to a participation in that light which shines in the darkness; for every truth, no matter by whom it is spoken, comes from the Holy Spirit. Yet **the darkness**, i.e., men in darkness, **did not overcome it**, apprehend it in truth. This is the way, [i.e., with respect to the natural influx of knowledge] that Origen and Augustine explain this clause.

104   Starting from **And that life was the light of men**, we can explain this in another way, according to the influx of grace, since we are illuminated by Christ.

After he had considered the creation of things through the Word, the Evangelist considers here the restoration of the rational creature through Christ, saying, **And that life**, of the Word, **was the light of men**, i.e., of all men in general, and not only of the Jews. For the Son of God assumed flesh and came into the world to illumine all men with grace and truth. "I came into the world for this, to testify to the truth" (below 18:37); "As long as I am in the world I am the light of the world" (below 9:5). So he does not say, "the light of the Jews," because although previously he had been known only in Judea, he later became known to the world. "I have given you as a light to the nations, that you might be my salvation to the ends of the earth" (Is 49:6).

It was fitting to join light and life by saying, **And that life was the light of men**, in order to show that these two have come to us through Christ: life, through a participation in grace, "Grace and truth have come through Jesus Christ" (below 1:17); and light, by a knowledge of truth and wisdom.

105   According to this explanation, **the light shines in the darkness**, can be expounded in three ways, in the light of the three meanings of "darkness."

In one way, we can take "darkness" for punishment. For any sadness and suffering of heart can be called a darkness, just as any joy can be called a light. "When I sit in darkness and in suffering the Lord is my light," i.e., my joy and consolation (Mi 7:8). And so Origen says: In this explanation, **the light shines in the darkness**, is Christ coming into the world, having a body capable of suffering and without sin, but "in the likeness of sinful flesh" (Rom 8:3). The light is in the flesh, that is, the flesh of Christ, which is called a darkness insofar as it has a likeness to sinful flesh. As if to say: The light, i.e., the Word of God, veiled about by the darkness of the flesh, shines on the world; "I will cover the sun with a cloud" (Ez 32:7).

106   Secondly, we can take "darkness" to mean the devils, as in Ephesians (6:12), "Our struggle is not against flesh and blood; but against principalities and powers, against the rulers of the world of this darkness." Looked at this way he says, **the light**, i.e., the Son of God, **shines in the darkness**, i.e., has descended into the world where darkness, i.e., the devils, hold sway: "Now the prince of this world will be cast out" (below 12:31). **And the darkness**, i.e., the devils, **did not overcome it**, i.e., were unable to obscure him by their temptations, as is plain in Matthew (c 4)

107   Thirdly, we can take "darkness" for the error or ignorance which filled the whole world before the coming of Christ, "You were at one time darkness" (Eph 5:8). And so he says that **the light**, i.e., the incarnate Word of God, **shines in the darkness**, i.e., upon the men of the world, who are blinded by the darkness or error and ignorance. "To enlighten those who sit in darkness and in the shadow of death" (Lk 1:79); "The people who were sitting in darkness saw a great light" (Is 9:2).

And the darkness did not overcome it, i.e., did not overcome him. For in spite of the number of men darkened by sin, blinded by envy, shadowed over by pride, who have struggled against Christ (as is plain from the Gospel) by upbraiding him, heaping insults and calumnies upon him, and finally killing him, nevertheless they **did not overcome it**, i.e., gain the victory of so obscuring him that his brightness would not shine throughout the whole world. Wisdom (7:30) says, "Compared to light, she takes precedence, for night supplants it, but wisdom," that is, the incarnate Son of God, "is not overcome by wickedness," that is, of the Jews and of heretics, because it says, "She gave him the prize for his stern struggle that he might know that wisdom is mightier than all else" (Wis 10:12).

LECTURE 4

6 There was a man sent by God, whose name was John.
7 He came as a witness, that he might bear witness to the light,
so that through him all men might believe. 8 He was not the light,
but [he came] in order to bear witness to the light.

108   Above, the Evangelist considered the divinity of the Word; here he begins to consider the incarnation of the Word. And he does two things concerning this: first, he treats of the witness to the incarnate Word, or the precursor; secondly, of the coming of the Word (1:9). As to the first, he does two things: first, he describes the precursor who comes to bear witness; secondly, he shows that he was incapable of the work of our salvation (1:8).

He describes the precursor in four ways. First, according to his nature, **There was a man**. Secondly, as to his authority, **sent by God**. Thirdly, as to his suitability for the office, **whose name was John**. Fourthly, as to the dignity of his office, **He came as a witness**.

109   We should note with respect to the first that, as soon as the Evangelist begins speaking of something temporal, he changes his manner of speech. When speaking above of eternal things, he used the word "was" (*erat*), which is the past imperfect tense; and this indicates that eternal things are without end. But now, when he is speaking of temporal things, he uses "was" (*fuit*, i.e., "has been"); this indicates temporal things as having taken place in the past and coming to an end there.

110   And so he says, **There was a man** (*Fuit homo*). This excludes at the very start the incorrect opinion of certain heretics who were in error on the condition or nature of John. They believed

that John was an angel in nature, basing themselves on the words of
the Lord, "I send my messenger [in Greek, *angelos*] before you, who
will prepare your way" (Mt 11:10); and the same thing is found in
Mark (1:2). But the Evangelist rejects this, saying, **There was a man**
by nature, not an angel. "The nature of man is known, and that he
cannot contend in judgment with one who is stronger than himself"
(Ecc 6:10).

Now it is fitting that a man be sent to men, for men are more
easily drawn to a man, since he is like themselves. So in Hebrews
(7:28) it says, "The law appoints men, who have weakness, priests."
God could have governed men through angels, but he preferred men
so that we could be more instructed by their example. And so John
was a man, and not an angel.

111   John is described by his authority when it says, **sent by
God**. Indeed, although John was not an angel in nature, he was so
by his office, because he was **sent by God**. For the distinctive office
of angels is that they are sent by God and are messengers of God.
"All are ministering spirits, sent to serve" (Heb 1:14). Hence it is
that "angel" means "messenger." And so men who are sent by God
to announce something can be called angels. "Haggai the messenger
of the Lord" (Hg 1:13).

If someone is to bear witness to God, it is necessary that he
be sent by God. "How can they preach unless they are sent?" as is
said in Romans (10:15). And since they are sent by God, they seek
the things of Jesus Christ, not their own. "We do not preach ourselves, but Jesus Christ" (2 Cor 4:5). On the other hand, one who
sends himself, and is not sent by God, seeks his own things or those
of man, and not the things of Christ. And so he says here, **There was
a man sent by God**, so that we would understand that John proclaimed something divine, not human.

112   Note that there are three ways in which we see men sent
by God. First, by an inward inspiration. "And now the Lord God
has sent me, and his spirit" (Is 48:16). As if to say: I have been sent
by God through an inward inspiration of the spirit. Secondly, by an
expressed and clear command, perceived by the bodily senses or the
imagination. Isaiah was also sent in this way; and so he says, "And I
heard the voice of the Lord saying, 'Whom shall I send, and who will
go for us?' Then I said, 'Here I am! Send me' " (Is 6:8). Thirdly, by
the order of a prelate, who acts in the place of God in this matter.
"I have pardoned in the person of Christ for your sake" as it says
in 2 Corinthians (2:10). This is why those who are sent by a prelate
are sent by God, as Barnabas and Timothy were sent by the Apostle.

When it is said here, **There was a man sent by God**, we should understand that he was sent by God through an inward inspiration, or perhaps even by an outward command. "He who sent me to baptize with water had said to me: 'The man on whom you see the Spirit come down and rest is the one who is to baptize with the Holy Spirit' " (below 1:33).

113 We should not understand, **There was a man sent by God,** as some heretics did, who believed that from the very beginning human souls were created without bodies along with the angels, and that one's soul is sent into the body when he is born, and that John was sent to life, i.e., his soul was sent to a body. Rather, we should understand that he was sent by God to baptize and preach.

114 John's fitness is given when he says, **whose name was John.** One must be qualified for the office of bearing witness, because unless a witness is qualified, then no matter in what way he is sent by another, his testimony is not acceptable. Now a man becomes qualified by the grace of God. "By the grace of God I am what I am" (1 Cor 15:10); "who has made us fit ministers of a new covenant" (2 Cor 3:6). So, the Evangelist appropriately implies the precursor's fitness from his name when he says, **whose name was John,** which is interpreted, "in whom is grace."

This name was not given to him meaninglessly, but by divine preordination and before he was born, as is clear from Luke (1:13), "You will name him John," as the angel said to Zechariah. Hence he can say what is said in Isaiah (49:1), "The Lord called me from the womb"; "He who will be, his name is already called" (Ecc 6:10). The Evangelist also indicates this from his manner of speaking, when he says **was,** as to God's preordination.

115 Then he is described by the dignity of his office. First, his office is mentioned. Secondly, the reason for his office, **to bear witness to the light.**

116 Now his office is to bear witness; hence he says, **He came as a witness.**

Here it should be remarked that God makes men, and everything else he makes, for himself. "The Lord made all things for himself" (Prv 16:4). Not, indeed, to add anything to himself, since he has no need of our good, but so that his goodness might be made manifest in all of the things made by him, in that "his eternal power and divinity are clearly seen, being understood through the things that are made"(Rom 1:20). Thus, each creature is made as a witness to God in so far as each creature is a certain witness of the divine goodness. So, the vastness of creation is a witness to God's power and omnipotence; and its beauty is a witness to the divine wisdom. But certain men are ordained by God in a special way, so that they bear witness to God not only naturally by their existence, but also spiritually by their good works. Hence all holy men are witnesses to God inasmuch as God is glorified among men by their good works. "Let your light so shine before men, that they may see your good works, and glorify your Father who is in heaven" (Mt 5:16). But those who not only share in God's gifts in themselves by acting well through the grace of God, but also spread them to others by their teaching, influencing and encouraging others, are in a more special way witnesses to God. "Everyone who calls upon my name, I have created for my glory" (Is 43:7). And so John came as a witness in order to spread to others the gifts of God and to proclaim his praise.

117 This office of John, that of bearing witness, is very great, because no one can testify about something except in the manner in which he has shared in it. "We know of what we speak, and we bear witness of what we see" (below 3:11). Hence, to bear witness to divine truth indicates a knowledge of that truth. So Christ also had this office: "I have come into the world for this, to testify to the truth" (below 18:37). But Christ testifies in one way and John in another. Christ bears witness as the light who comprehends all things, indeed, as the existing light itself. John bears witness only as participating in that light. And so Christ gives testimony in a perfect manner and perfectly manifests the truth, while John and other holy men give testimony in so far as they have a share of divine truth. John's office, therefore, is great both because of his participation in the divine light and because of a likeness to Christ, who carried out this office. "I made him a witness to the peoples, a leader and a commander of the nations" (Is 55:4).

118 The purpose of this office is given when he says, **that he might bear witness to the light**. Here we should understand that there are two reasons for bearing witness about something. One reason can be on the part of the thing with which the witness is concerned; for example, if there is some doubt or uncertainty about that thing. The other is on the part of those who hear it; if they are hard of heart and slow to believe. John came as a witness, not because of the thing about which he bore witness, for it was light. Hence he says, **bear witness to the light**, i.e., not to something obscure, but to something clear. He came, therefore, to bear witness on account of those to whom he testified, **so that through him** (i.e., John) **all men might believe**. For as light is not only visible in itself and of itself, but through it all else can be seen, so the Word of God is not only light in himself, but he makes known all things that are known. For since a thing is made known and understood through its form, and all forms exist through the Word, who is the art full of living forms, the Word is light not only in himself, but as making known all things; "all that appears is light" (Eph 5:13).

And so it was fitting for the Evangelist to call the Son "light," because he came as "a revealing light to the Gentiles" (Lk 2:32). Above, he called the Son of God the Word, by which the Father expresses himself and every creature. Now since he is, properly speaking, the light of men, and the Evangelist is considering him here as coming to accomplish the salvation of men, he fittingly interrupts the use of the name "Word" when speaking of the Son, and says, "light."

119 But if that light is adequate of itself to make known all things, and not only itself, what need does it have of any witness? This was the objection of the Manichaeans, who wanted to destroy the Old Testament. Consequently, the saints gave many reasons, against their opinion, why Christ wanted to have the testimony of the prophets.

Origen gives three reasons. The first is that God wanted to have certain witnesses, not because he needed their testimony, but to ennoble those whom he appointed witnesses. Thus we see in the order of the universe that God produces certain effects by means of intermediate causes, not because he himself is unable to produce them without these intermediaries, but he deigns to confer on them the dignity of causality because he wishes to ennoble these intermediate causes. Similarly, even though God could have enlightened all men by himself and lead them to a knowledge of himself, yet to preserve due order in things and to ennoble certain men, he willed that divine knowledge reach men through certain other men. " 'You are my witnesses,' says the Lord" (Is 43:10).

A second reason is that Christ was a light to the world through his miracles. Yet, because they were performed in time, they passed away with time and did not reach everyone. But the words of the prophets, preserved in Scripture, could reach not only those present, but could also reach those to come after. Hence the Lord willed that men come to a knowledge of the Word through the testimony of the prophets, in order that not only those present, but also men yet to come, might be enlightened about him. So it says expressly, **so that through him all men might believe**, i.e., not only those present, but also future generations.

The third reason is that not all men are in the same condition, and all are not led or disposed to a knowledge of the truth in the same way. For some are brought to a knowledge of the truth by signs and miracles; others are brought more by wisdom. "The Jews require signs, and the Greeks seek wisdom" (1 Cor 1:22). And so the Lord, in order to show the path of salvation to all, willed both ways to be open, i.e., the way of signs and the way of wisdom, so that those who would not be brought to the path of salvation by the miracles of the Old and New Testaments, might be brought to a knowledge of the truth by the path of wisdom, as in the prophets and other books of Sacred Scripture.

A fourth reason, given by Chrysostom, is that certain men of weak understanding are unable to grasp the truth and knowledge of God by themselves. And so the Lord chose to come down to them and to enlighten certain men before others about divine matters, so that these others might obtain from them in a human way the knowledge of divine things they could not reach by themselves. And so he says, **that through him all men might believe.** As if to say: **he came as a witness,** not for the sake of the light, but for the sake of men, **so that through him all men might believe.** And so it is plain that the testimonies of the prophets are fitting and proper, and should be received as something needed by us for the knowledge of the truth.

120   He says **believe,** because there are two ways of participating in the divine light. One is the perfect participation which is present in glory, "In your light, we shall see the light" (Ps 35:10). The other in imperfect and is acquired through faith, since **he came as a witness.** Of these two ways it is said, "Now we see through a mirror, in an obscure manner, but then we shall see face to face" (1 Cor 13:12). And in the same place we find, "Now I know in part, but then I shall know even as I am known." Among these two ways, the first is the way of participation through faith, because through it we are brought to vision. So in Isaiah (7:9) where our version has, "If you do not believe, you will not persist," another version has, "If you do not believe, you will not understand." "All of us, gazing on the Lord's glory with unveiled faces, are being transformed from glory to glory into his very image," which we have lost (2 Cor 3:18). "From the glory of faith to the glory of vision," as a Gloss says.

And so he says, **that through him all men might believe,** not as though all would see him perfectly at once, but first they would believe through faith, and later enjoy him through vision in heaven.

121   He says **through him,** to show that John is different than Christ. For Christ came so that all might believe in him. "He who believes in me, as Scripture says, 'Out of his heart shall flow rivers of living water' " (below 7:38). John, on the other hand, came **that all men might believe,** not in him, but in Christ **through him.**

One may object that not all have believed. So if John came to that all might believe through him, he failed. I answer that both on the part of God, who sent John, and of John, who came, the method used is adequate to bring all to the truth. But on the part of those "who have fixed their eyes on the ground" (Ps 16:11), and refused to see the light, there was a failure, because all did not believe.

122   Now although John, of whom so much has been said,
even including that he was sent by God, is an eminent person, his
coming is not sufficient to save men, because the salvation of man
lies in participating in the light. If John had been the light, his
coming would have sufficed to save men; but he was not the light.
So he says, **he was not the light.** Consequently, a light was needed
that would suffice to save men.

Or, we could look at it another way. John came to bear witness
to the light. Now it is the custom that the one who testifies is of
greater authority than the one for whom he bears witness. So, lest
John be considered to have greater authority than Christ, the Evangelist says, **he was not the light, but he came in order to bear witness
to the light.** For he bears witness not because he is greater, but because he is better known, even though he is not as great.

123   There is a difficulty about his saying, **he was not the light.**
Conflicting with this is, "You were at one time darkness, but now
you are light in the Lord" (Eph 5:8); and "You are the light of the
world" (Mt 5:14). Therefore, John and the apostles and all good men
are a light.

I answer that some say that John was not the light, because this
belongs to God alone. But if "light" is taken without the article,
then John and all holy men were made lights. The meaning is this:
the Son of God is light by his very essence; but John and all the
saints are light by participation. So, because John participated in
the true light, it was fitting that he bear witness to the light; for
fire is better exhibited by something afire than by anything else,
and color by something colored.

LECTURE 5

9 He [the Word] was the true light,
which enlightens every man coming into this world.
10 He was in the world, and through him the world was made,
and the world did not know him.

124   Above, the Evangelist considered the precursor and his
witness to the incarnate Word; in the present section he considers
the incarnate Word himself. As to this he does three things. First,
he shows why it was necessary for the Word to come. Secondly,
the benefit we received from the coming of the Word (1:11). And
thirdly, the way he came (1:14).

The necessity for the Word's coming is seen to be the lack of divine knowledge in the world. He points out this need for his coming when he says, "For this was I born, and I came into the world for this, to testify to the truth" (below 18:37). To indicate this lack of divine knowledge, the Evangelist does two things. First, he shows that this lack does not pertain to God or the Word. Secondly, that it does pertain to men (v 10b).

He shows in three ways that there was no defect in God or in the Word that prevented men from knowing God and from being enlightened by the Word. First, from the efficacy of the divine light itself, because **He was the true light, which enlightens every man coming into this world.** Secondly, from the presence of the divine light, because **He was in the world.** Thirdly, from the obviousness of the light, because **through him the world was made.** So the lack of divine knowledge in the world was not due to the Word, because it is sufficient. First, he shows the nature of this efficiency, that is, **He was the true light.** Secondly, its very efficiency, **which enlightens every man.**

125   The divine Word is efficacious in enlightening because **He was the true light.** How the Word is light, and how he is the light of men need not be discussed again, because it was sufficiently explained above. What we must discuss at present is how he is the true light. To explain this, we should note that in Scripture the "true" is contrasted with three things. Sometimes it is contrasted with the false, as in "Put an end to lying, and let everyone speak the truth" (Eph 4:25). Sometimes it is contrasted with what is figurative, as in "The law was given through Moses; grace and truth have come through Jesus Christ" (below 1:17), because the truth of the figures contained in the law was fulfilled by Christ. Sometimes it is contrasted with what is something by participation, as in "that we may be in his true Son" (1 Jn 5:20), who is not his Son by participation.

Before the Word came there was in the world a certain light which the philosophers prided themselves on having; but this was a false light, because as is said, "They became stultified in their speculations, and their foolish hearts were darkened; claiming to be wise, they became fools" (Rom 1:21); "Every man is made foolish by his knowledge" (Jer 10:14). There was another light from the teaching of the law which the Jews boasted of having; but this was a symbolic light, "The law has a shadow of the good things to come, not the image itself of them" (Heb 10:1). There was also a certain light in the angels and in holy men in so far as they knew God in a more special way by grace; but this was a participated light, "Upon whom does his light not shine?" (Jb 25:3), which is like saying: Whoever shine, shine to the extent that they participate in his light, i.e., God's light.

But the Word of God was not a false light, nor a symbolic light, nor a participated light, but the true light, i.e., light by his essence. Therefore he says, **He was the true light**.

126   This excludes two errors. First, that of Photinus, who believed that Christ derived his beginning from the Virgin. So, lest anyone suppose this, the Evangelist, speaking of the incarnation of the Word, says, **He was the true light**, i.e., eternally, not only before the Virgin, but before every creature. This also excludes the error of Arius and Origen; they said that Christ was not true God, but God by participation. If this were so, he could not be the true light, as the Evangelist says here, and as in "God is light" (1 Jn 1:5), i.e., not by participation, but **the true light**. So if the Word was the true light, it is plain that he is true God. Now it is clear how the divine Word is effective in causing divine knowledge.

127   The effectiveness or efficiency of the Word lies in the fact that he **enlightens every man coming into this world**. For everything which is what it is by participation is derived from that which is such by its essence; just as everything afire is so by participation in fire, which is fire by its very essence. Then since the Word is the true light by his very essence, then everything that shines must do so through him, insofar as it participates in him. And so he **enlightens every man coming into this world**.

128   To understand this, we should know that "world" is taken in three ways in Scripture. Sometimes, from the point of view of its creation, as when the Evangelist says here, "through him the world was made" (v 10). Sometimes, from the point of view of its perfection, which it reaches through Christ, as in "God was, in Christ, reconciling the world to himself" (2 Cor 5:19). And sometimes it is taken from the point of view of its perversity, as in "The whole world lies under the power of the evil one" (1 Jn 5:19).

On the other hand, "enlightenment" or "being enlightened" by the Word is taken in two ways. First, in relation to the light of natural knowledge, as in "The light of your countenance, O Lord, is marked upon us" (Ps 4:7). Secondly, as the light of grace, "Be enlightened, O Jerusalem" (Is 60:1).

129   With these two sets of distinctions in mind, it is easy to solve a difficulty which arises here. For when the Evangelist says, he **enlightens every man**, this seems to be false, because there are still many in darkness in the world. However, if we bear in mind these distinctions and take "world" from the standpoint of its creation, and "enlighten" as referring to the light of natural reason, the statement of the Evangelist is beyond reproach. For all men coming into this visible world are enlightened by the light of natural knowl-

edge through participating in this true light, which is the source of all the light of natural knowledge participated in by men.

When the Evangelist speaks of **man coming into this world**, he does not mean that men had lived for a certain time outside the world and then came into the world, since this is contrary to the teaching of the Apostle in Romans (9:11), "When the children were not yet born nor had they done anything good or evil." Therefore, since they had done nothing before they were born, it is plain that the soul does not exist prior to its union with the body. He refers to **every man coming into this world**, to show that men are enlightened by God with respect to that according to which they came into the world, i.e., with respect to the intellect, which is something external [to the world]. For man is constituted of a twofold nature, bodily and intellectual. According to his bodily or sensible nature, man is enlightened by a bodily and sensible light; but according to his soul and intellectual nature, he is enlightened by an intellectual and spiritual light. Now man does not come into this world according to his bodily nature, but under this aspect, he is from the world. His intellectual nature is derived from a source external to the world, as has been said, i.e., from God through creation; as in "Until all flesh returns to its origin, and the spirit is directed to God, who made it" (Ecc 12:7). For these reasons, when the Evangelist speaks of **every man coming into this world**, he is showing that this enlightenment refers to what is from without, that is, the intellect.

130   If we understand "enlightenment" with respect to the light of grace, then he **enlightens every man** may be explained in three ways. The first way is by Origen in his homily, "The great eagle," and is this. "World" is understood from the point of view of its perfection, which man attains by his reconciliation through Christ. And so we have, he **enlightens every man coming**, by faith, **into this world**, i.e., this spiritual world, that is, the Church, which has been enlightened by the light of grace.

Chrysostom explains it another way. He takes "world" under the aspect of creation. Then the sense is: He **enlightens**, i.e., the Word does, in so far as it depends on him, because he fails no one, but rather "wants all men to be saved, and to come to the knowledge of the truth" (1 Tim 2:4); **every man coming**, i.e., who is born into this sensible world. If anyone is not enlightened, it is due to himself, because he turns from the light that enlightens.

Augustine explains it a third way. For him, "every" has a restricted application, so that the sense is: He **enlightens every man coming into this world**, not every man universally, but every man who is enlightened, since no one is enlightened except by the Word. According to Augustine, the Evangelist says, **coming into this world**, in order to give the reason why man needs to be enlightened, and he is taking "world" from the point of view of its perversity and defect. It is as though he were saying: Man needs to be enlightened because he is coming into this world which is darkened by perversity and defects and is full of ignorance. (This followed the spiritual world of the first man.) As Luke says (1:79), "To enlighten those who sit in darkness and in the shadow of death."

131 The above statement refutes the error of the Manichaeans, who think than men were created in the world from an opposing principle, i.e., the devil. For if man were a creature of the devil when coming into this world, he would not be enlightened by God or by the Word, for "Christ came into the world to destroy the works of the devil" (1 Jn 3:8).

132 So it is clear, from the efficacy of the divine Word, that the lack of knowledge in men is not due to the Word, because he is effective in enlightening all, being **the true light, which enlightens every man coming into this world.**

But so you do not suppose this lack arose from the withdrawal or absence of the true light, the Evangelist rules this out adding, **He was in the world.** A comparable statement is found in "He is not far from any one of us," that is, God, "for in him we live, and move, and are" (Acts 17:28). It is as though the Evangelist were saying: The divine Word is effective and is at hand in order to enlighten us.

133 We should remark that something is said to be "in the world" in three ways. In one way, by being contained, as a thing in place exists in a place: "They are in the world" (below 17:11). In another way, as a part in a whole; for a part of the world is said to be in the world even though it is not in a place. For example, supernatural substances, although not in the world as in a place, are nevertheless in it as parts: "God ... who made heaven and earth, the sea, and all things that are in them" (Ps 145:6). But the true light was not in the world in either of these ways, because that light is neither localized nor is it a part of the universe. Indeed, if we can speak this way, the entire universe is in a certain sense a part, since it participates in a partial way in his goodness.

Accordingly, the true light was in the world in a third way, i.e., as an efficient and preserving cause: "I fill heaven and earth" as said in Jeremiah (23:24). However, there is a difference between the way the Word acts and causes all things and the way in which other agents act. For other agents act as existing externally: since they do not act except by moving and altering a thing qualitatively in some way with respect to its exterior, they work from without. But God acts in all things from within, because he acts by creating. Now to create is to give existence (*esse*) to the thing created. So, since *esse* is innermost in each thing, God, who by acting gives *esse* acts in things from within. Hence God was in the world as one giving *esse* to the world.

134 It is customary to say that God is in all things by his essence, presence and power. To understand what this means, we should know that someone is said to be by his power in all the things that are subject to his power; as a king is said to be in the entire kingdom subject to him, by his power. He is not there, however, by presence or essence. Someone is said to be by presence in all the things that are within his range of vision; as a king is said to be in his house by presence. And someone is said to be by essence in those things in which his substance is; as a king is in one determinate place.

Now we say that God is everywhere by his power, since all things are subject to his power: "If I ascend into heaven, you are there.... If I take my wings early in the morning, and dwell in the furthest part of the sea, even there your hand will lead me, and your right hand will hold me" (Ps 138:8). He is also everywhere by his presence, because "all things are bare and open to his eyes," as is said in Hebrews (4:13). He is present everywhere by his essence, because his essence is innermost in all things. For every agent, as acting, has to be immediately joined to its effect, because mover and moved must be together. Now God is the maker and preserver of all things, with respect to the *esse* of each. Hence, since the *esse* of a thing is innermost in that thing, it is plain that God, by his essence, through which he creates all things, is in all things.

135 It should be noted that the Evangelist significantly uses the word "was," when he says, **He was in the world**, showing that from the beginning of creation he was always in the world, causing and preserving all things; because if God for even a moment were to withold his power from the things he established, all would return to nothing and cease to be. Hence Origen uses an apt example to show this, when he says that as a human vocal sound is to a human word conceived in the mind, so is the creature to the divine Word; for as our vocal sound is the effect of the word conceived in our mind, so the creature is the effect of the Word conceived in the divine mind. "For he spoke, and they were created" (Ps 148:5). Hence, just as we notice that as soon as our inner word vanishes, the sensible vocal sound also ceases, so, if the power of the divine Word were withdrawn from things, all of them would immediately cease to be at that moment. And this is because he is "sustaining all things by his powerful word" (Heb 1:3).

136 So it is plain that a lack of divine knowledge in minds is not due to the absence of the Word, because **He was in the world**; nor is it due to the invisibility or concealment of the Word, because he has produced a work in which his likeness is clearly reflected, that

is, the world: "For from the greatness and beauty of creatures, their creator can be seen accordingly" (Wis 13:5), and "The invisible things of God are clearly seen, being understood through the things that are made" (Rom 1:20). And so the Evangelist at once adds, **and through him the world was made**, in order that that light might be manifested in it. For as a work of art manifests the art of the artisan, so the whole world is nothing else than a certain representation of the divine wisdom conceived within the mind of the Father, "He poured her [wisdom] out upon all his works," as is said in Sirach (1:10).

Now it is clear that the lack of divine knowledge is not due to the Word, because he is efficacious, being **the true light**; and he is at hand, since he **was in the world**; and he is knowable, since **through him the world was made**.

137 The Evangelist indicates the source of this lack when he says, **and the world did not know him**. As if to say: It is not due to him, but to the world, who did not know him.

He says **him** in the singular, because earlier he had called the Word not only the "light of men," but also "God"; and so when he says **him**, he means God. Again, he uses "world" for man. For the angels knew him by their understanding, and the elements by their obeying him; but **the world**, i.e., man, who lives in the world, **did not know him**.

138 We attribute this lack of divine knowledge either to the nature of man or to his guilt. To his nature, indeed, because although all the aforesaid aids were given to man to lead him to the knowledge of God, human reason in itself lacks this knowledge. "Man beholds him from afar" (Jb 36:25), and immediately after, "God is great beyond our knowledge." But if some have known him, this was not insofar as they were in the world, but above the world; and the kind for whom the world was not worthy, because **the world did not know him**. Hence if they mentally perceived anything eternal, that was insofar as they were not of this world.

But if this lack is attributed to man's guilt, then the phrase, **the world did not know him**, is a kind of reason why God was not known by man; in this sense **world** is taken for inordinate lovers of the world. It is as though it said, **The world did not know him**, because they were lovers of the world. For the love of the world, as Augustine says, is what chiefly withdraws us from the knowledge of God, because "Love of the world makes one an enemy to God" (Jas 4:4); "The sensual man does not perceive the things that pertain to the Spirit of God" (1 Cor 2:14).

139 From this we can answer the question of the Gentiles who

futilely ask this: If it is only recently that the Son of God is set before the world as the Savior of men, does it not seem that before that time he scorned human nature? We should say to them that he did not scorn the world but was always in the world, and on his part is knowable by men; but it was due to their own fault that some have not known him, because they were lovers of the world.

140 We should also note that the Evangelist speaks of the incarnation of the Word to show that the incarnate Word and that which "was in the beginning with God," and God, are the same. He repeats what he had said of him earlier. For above he had said he [the Word] "was the light of men"; here he says he was **the true light.** Above, he said that "all things were made through him"; here he says that **through him the world was made.** Earlier he had said, "without him nothing was made," i.e., according to one explanation, he conserves all things; here he says, **he was in the world,** creating and conserving the world and all things. There he had said, "the darkness did not overcome it"; here he says, **the world did not know him.** And so, all he says after **he was the true light,** is an explanation of what he had said before.

141   We can gather three reasons from the above why God willed to become incarnate. One is because of the perversity of human nature which, because of its own malice, had been darkened by vices and the obscurity of its own ignorance. And so he said before, **the darkness did not overcome it.** Therefore, God came in the flesh so that the darkness might apprehend the light, i.e., obtain a knowledge of it. "The people who walked in darkness saw a great light" (Is 9:2).

The second reason is that the testimony of the prophets was not enough. For the prophets came and John had come; but they were not able to give sufficient enlightenment, because **he was not the light.** And so, after the prophecies of the prophets and the coming of John, it was necessary that the light itself come and give the world a knowledge of itself. And this is what the Apostle says: "In past times, God spoke in many ways and degrees to our fathers through the prophets; in these days he has spoken to us in his Son" as we find in Hebrews (1:1). "We have the prophetic message, to which you do well to give attention, until the day dawns" (2 Pt 1:19).

The third reason is because of the shortcomings of creatures. For creatures were not sufficient to lead to a knowledge of the Creator; hence he says, **through him the world was made, and the world did not know him.** Thus it was necessary that the Creator himself come into the world in the flesh, and be known through himself. And this is what the Apostle says: "Since in the wisdom of God the world did not know God by its wisdom, it pleased God to save those who believe by the foolishness of our preaching" (1 Cor 1:21).

LECTURE 6

11 He came unto his own, and his own did not receive him;
12 but whoever received him, he gave them power to become
the sons of God, to all who believe in his name,
13 who are born not from blood, nor from the desiers of the flesh,
nor from man's willing it, but from God.

142   Having given the necessity for the incarnation of the Word, the Evangelist then shows the advantage men gained from that incarnation. First, he shows the coming of the light (v 11); secondly, its reception by men (v 11b); thirdly, the fruit brought by the coming of the light (v 12).

143   He shows that the light which was present in the world and evident, i.e., disclosed by its effect, was nevertheless not known by the world. Hence, **he came unto his own,** in order to be known. The Evangelist says, **unto his own,** i.e., to things that were his own, which he had made. And he says this so that you do not think that when he says, **he came,** he means a local motion in the sense that he came as though ceasing to be where he previously was and newly beginning to be where he formerly had not been. He came where he already was. "I came forth from the Father, and have come into the world," as said below (16:28).

He came, I say, **unto his own,** i.e., to Judea, according to some, because it was in a special way his own. "In Judea God is known" (Ps 75:1); "The vineyard of the Lord of hosts is the house of Israel" (Is 5:7). But it is better to say, **unto his own,** i.e., into the world created by him. "The earth is the Lord's" (Ps 23:1).

144   But if he was previously in the world, how could he come into the world? I answer that "coming to some place" is understood in two ways. First, that someone comes where he absolutely had not been before. Or, secondly, that someone begins to be in a new way where he was before. For example, a king, who up to a certain time was in a city of his kingdom by his power and later visits it in person, is said to have come where he previously was: for he comes by his substance where previously he was present only by his power. It was in this way that the Son of God came into the world and yet was in the world. For he was there, indeed, by his essence, power and presence, but he came by assuming flesh. He was there invisibly, and he came in order to be visible.

145   Then when he says, **and his own did not receive him,** we have the reception given him by men, who reacted in different ways.

For some did receive him, but these were not his own; hence he says, **his own did not receive him.** "His own" are men, because they were formed by him. "The Lord God formed man" (Gn 2:7); "Know that the Lord is God: he made us" (Ps 99:3). And he made them to his own image, "Let us make man to our image" (Gn 1:26).

But it is better to say, **his own,** i.e., the Jews, **did not receive him,** through faith by believing, and by showing honor to him. "I have come in the name of my Father, and you do not receive me" (below 5:43), and "I honor my Father and you have dishonored me" (below 8:49). Now the Jews are his own because they were chosen by him to be his special people. "The Lord chose you to be his special people" (Dt 26:18). They are his own because related according to the flesh, "from whom is Christ, according to the flesh," as said in Romans (9:3). They are also his own because enriched by his kindness, "I have reared and brought up sons" (Is 1:2). But although the Jews were his own, they did not receive him.

146 However, there were not lacking those who did receive him. Hence he adds, **but whoever received him.** The Evangelist uses this manner of speaking, saying, **but whoever,** to indicate that the deliverance would be more extensive than the promise, which had been made only to his own, i.e., to the Jews. "The Lord is our law giver, the Lord is our king; he will save us" (Is 33:22). But this deliverance was not only for his own, but for **whoever received him,** i.e., whoever believe in him. "For I say that Christ was a minister to the circumcised, for the sake of God's truth, to confirm the promises made to the fathers" (Rom 15:8). The Gentiles, however, [are delivered] by his mercy, because they were received through his mercy.

147 He says, **whoever,** to show that God's grace is given without distinction to all who receive Christ. "The grace of the Holy Spirit has been poured out upon the Gentiles"(Acts 10:45). And not only to free men, but to slaves as well; not only to men, but to women also. "In Christ Jesus there is neither male nor female, Jew or Greek, the circumcised or uncircumcised" (Gal 3:28).

148 Then when he says, **he gave them power to become the sons of God,** we have the fruit of his coming. First, he mentions the grandeur of the fruit, for **he gave them power.** Secondly, he shows to whom it is given, **to all who believe.** Thirdly, he indicates the way it is given, **not from blood,** and so forth.

149 The fruit of the coming of the Son of God is great, because by it men are made sons of God. "God sent his Son made from a woman ... so that we might receive our adoption as sons" (Gal 4:5). And it was fitting that we, who are sons of God by the fact that we are made like the Son, should be reformed through the Son.

150 So he says, **he gave them power to become the sons of God**. To understand this we should remark that men become sons of God by being made like God. Hence men are sons of God according to a threefold likeness to God. First, by the infusion of grace; hence anyone having sanctifying grace is made a son of God. "You did not receive the spirit of slavery ... but the spirit of adoption as sons," as said in Romans (8:15). "Because you are sons of God, God sent the Spirit of his Son into your hearts" (Gal 4:6).

Secondly, we are like God by the perfection of our actions, because one who acts justly is a son: "Love your enemies ... so that you may be the children of your Father" (Mt 5:44).

Thirdly, we are made like God by the attainment of glory. The glory of the soul by the light of glory, "When he appears we shall be like him" (1 Jn 3:2); and the glory of the body, "He will reform our lowly body" (Phil 3:21). Of these two it is said in Romans (8:23), "We are waiting for our adoption as sons of God."

151 If we take the power to become the sons of God as referring to the perfection of our actions and the attainment of glory, the statement offers no difficulty. For then when he says, **he gave them power**, he is referring to the power of grace; and when a man possesses this, he can perform works of perfection and attain glory, since "The grace of God is eternal life" (Rom 6:23). According to this way we have, **he gave them**, to those who received him, **power**, i.e., the infusion of grace, **to become the sons of God**, by acting well and acquiring glory.

152 But if this statement refers to the infusion of grace, then his saying, **he gave them power**, gives rise to a difficulty. And this is because it is not in our power to be made sons of God, since it is not in our power to possess grace. We can understand, **he gave them power**, as a power of nature; but this does not seem to be true since the infusion of grace is above our nature. Or we can understand it as the power of grace, and then to have grace is to have **power to become the sons of God**. And in this sense he did not give them power to become sons of God, but to be sons of God.

153 The answer to this is that when grace is given to an adult, his justification requires an act of consent by a movement of his free will. So, because it is in the power of men to consent and not to consent, **he gave them power**. However, he gives this power of accepting grace in two ways: by preparing it, and by offering it to him. For just as one who writes a book and offers it to a man to read is said to give the power to read it, so Christ, through whom grace was produced (as will be said below), and who "accomplished salvation on the earth" (Ps 73:12), **gave us power to become the sons of God** by offering grace.

154   Yet this is not sufficient since even free will, if it is to be moved to receive grace, needs the help of divine grace, not indeed habitual grace, but movent grace. For this reason, secondly, he gives power by moving the free will of man to consent to the reception of grace, as in "Convert us to yourself, O Lord," by moving our will to your love, "and we will be converted" (Lam 5:21). And in this sense we speak of an interior call, of which it is said, "Those whom he called," by inwardly moving the will to consent to grace, "he justified," by infusing grace (Rom 8:3).

155   Since by this grace man has the power of maintaining himself in the divine sonship, one may read these words in another way. He gave them, i.e., those who receive him, **power to become the sons of God**, i.e., the grace by which they are able to be maintained in the divine sonship. "Every one who is born from God does not sin, but the grace of God," through which we are reborn as children of God, "preserves him" (1 Jn 5:18).

156   Thus, **he gave them power to become the sons of God**, through sanctifying grace, through the perfection of their actions, and through the attainment of glory; and he did this by preparing this grace, moving their wills, and preserving this grace.

157   Then when he says, **to all who believe in his name**, he shows those on whom the fruit of his coming is conferred. We can understand this in two ways: either as explaining what was said before, or as qualifying it. We can regard it as explaining as the Evangelist had said, **whoever received him**, and now to show what it is to receive him, he adds by way of explanation, **who believe in his name**. It is as though he were saying: To receive him is to believe in him, because it is through faith that Christ dwells in your hearts, as in "that Christ may dwell in your hearts through faith" (Eph 3:17). Therefore, they **received him, who believe in his name**.

158   Origen regards this as a qualifying statement, in his homily, "The spiritual voice." In this sense, many receive Christ, declaring that they are Christians, but they are not sons of God, because they do not truly believe in his name; for they propose false dogmas about Christ by taking away something from his divinity or humanity, as in "Every spirit that denies Christ is not from God" (1 Jn 4:3). And so the Evangelist says, as though contracting his meaning, **he gave them**, i.e., those who receive him by faith, **power to become the sons of God**, to those, however, **who believe in his name**, i.e., who keep the name of Christ whole, in such a way as not to lessen anything of the divinity or humanity of Christ.

159   We can also refer this to formed faith, in the sense that **to all**, that is, **he gave power to become the sons of God, who believe in**

his name, i.e., those who do the works of salvation through a faith formed by charity. For those who have only an unformed faith do not believe in his name because they do not work unto salvation.

However, the first exposition, which is taken as explaining what preceded, is better.

160 Then when he says, **who are born not from blood**, he shows the way in which so great a fruit is conferred on men. For since he had said that the fruit of the light's coming is the power given to men to become the sons of God, then to forestall the supposition that they are born through a material generation he says, **not from blood**. And although the word "blood" (*sanguis*) has no plural in Latin, but does in Greek, the translator [from Greek into Latin] ignored a rule of grammar in order to teach the truth more perfectly. So he does not say, "from blood," in the Latin manner, but "from bloods" (*ex sanguinibus*). This indicates whatever is generated from blood, serving as the matter in carnal generation. According to the Philosopher [*On the Generation of Animals*, I, c 18, 726a26-8], "semen is a residue derived from useful nourishment in its final form." So "blood" indicates either the seed of the male or the menses of the female.

The cause moving to the carnal act is the will of those coming together, the man and the woman. For although the act of the generative power as such is not subject to the will, the preliminaries to it are subject to the will. So he says, **nor from the desires of the flesh**, referring to the woman; **nor from man's willing it**, as from an efficient cause; **but from God**. It is as though he were saying: They became sons of God, not carnally, but spiritually.

According to Augustine, "flesh" is taken here for the woman, because as the flesh obeys the spirit, so woman should obey man. Adam (Gn 2:23) said of the woman, "This, at last, is bone of my bones." And note, according to Augustine, that just as the possessions of a household are wasted away if the woman rules and the man is subject, so a man is wasted away when the flesh rules the spirit. For this reason the Apostle says, "We are not debtors to the flesh, so that we should live according to the flesh" (Rom 8:12). Concerning the manner of this carnal generation, we read, "In the womb of my mother I was molded into flesh" (Wis 7:1).

161 Or, we might say that the moving force to carnal generation is twofold: the intellectual appetite on the one hand, that is, the will; and on the other hand, the sense appetite, which is concupiscence. So, to indicate the material cause he says, **not from blood**. To indicate the efficient cause, in respect to concupiscence, he says, **nor from the desires of the flesh** [*ex voluntate carnis*, literally, "from the

will of the flesh"], even though the concupiscence of the flesh is improperly called a "will" in the sense of Galatians (5:17), "The flesh lusts against the spirit." Finally, to indicate the intellectual appetite he says, **nor from man's willing it.** So, the generation of the sons of God is not carnal but spiritual, because they were born **from God.** "Every one who is born from God conquers the world" (1 Jn 5:4).

162 Note, however, that this preposition *de* ("of," or "from"), always signifies a material cause as well as an efficient and even a consubstantial cause. Thus we say a blacksmith makes a knife *de ferro* ("from" iron), and a father generates his son *de seipso* ("from" himself), because something of his concurs somehow in begetting. But the preposition *a* ("by") always signifies a moving cause. The preposition *ex* ("from," or "by") – [in the sense of "out of" or "by reason of"] – is taken as something common, since it implies an efficient as well as a material cause, although not a consubstantial cause.

Consequently, since only the Son of God, who is the Word, is "of" (*de*) the substance of the Father and indeed is one substance with the Father, while the saints, who are adopted sons, are not of his substance, the Evangelist uses the preposition *ex*, saying of others that they are born **from God** (*ex Deo*), but of the natural Son, he says that he is born of the Father (*de Patre*).

163 Note also that in the light of our last exposition of carnal generation, we can discern the difference between carnal and spiritual generation. For since the former is from blood, it is carnal; but the latter, because it is not from blood, is spiritual. "What is born from flesh is itself flesh; and what is born from Spirit is itself spirit" (below 3:6). Again, because material generation is from the desires of the flesh, i.e., from concupiscence, it is unclean and begets children who are sinners: "We were by nature children of wrath" as it says in Ephesians (2:3). Again, because the former is **from man's willing it,** that is, from man, it makes children of men; but the latter, because it is from God, makes children of God.

164 But if he intends to refer his statement, **he gave them power,** to baptism, in virtue of which we are reborn as sons of God, we can detect in his words the order of baptism: that is, the first thing required is faith, as shown in the case of catechumens, who must first be instructed about the faith so that they may believe in his name; then through baptism they are reborn, not carnally from blood, but spiritually from God.

LECTURE 7

14a And the Word was made flesh, and made his dwelling among us.

165 Having explained the necessity for the Word's coming in the flesh as well as the benefits this conferred, the Evangelist now shows the way he came (v 14a). He thus resumes the thread with his earlier statement, **he came unto his own.** As if to say: The Word of God came unto his own. But lest anyone suppose that he came by changing his location, he shows the manner in which he came, that is, by an incarnation. For he came in the manner in which he was sent by the Father, by whom he was sent, i.e., he was made flesh. "God sent his Son made from a woman" (Gal 4:4). And Augustine says about this that "He was sent in the manner in which he was made."

According to Chrysostom, however, he is here continuing the earlier statement, **he gave them power to become the sons of God.** As if to say: If you wonder how he was able to give this power to men, i.e., that they become sons of God, the Evangelist answers: because **the Word was made flesh**, he made it possible for us to be made sons of God. "God sent his Son ... so that we might receive our adoption as sons" (Gal 4:5).

But according to Augustine, he is continuing the earlier statement, **who are born from God.** For since it seemed a hard saying that men be born from God, then, as though arguing in support of this and to produce belief in the existence of the Word, the Evangelist adds something which seems less seemly, namely, that **the Word was made flesh.** As if to say: Do not wonder if men are born from God, because **the Word was made flesh**, i.e., God became man.

166 It should be noted that this statement, **the Word was made flesh**, has been misinterpreted by some and made the occasion of error. For certain ones have presumed that the Word became flesh in the sense that he or something of him was turned into flesh, as when flour is made into bread, and air becomes fire. One of these was Eutyches, who postulated a mixture of natures in Christ, saying that in him the nature of God and of man was the same. We can clearly see that this is false because, as was said above, "the Word was God." Now God is immutable, as is said, "I am the Lord, and I do not change" (Mal 3:6). Hence in no way can it be said that he was turned into another nature. Therefore, one must say in opposition to Eutyches, **the Word was made flesh**, i.e., the Word assumed flesh, but not in the sense that the Word himself is that flesh. It is as if we were to say: "The man became white," not that he is that whiteness, but that he assumed whiteness.

167   There were others who, although they believed that the
Word was not changed into flesh but assumed it, nevertheless said
that he assumed flesh without a soul; for if he had assumed flesh
with a soul, the Evangelist would have said, "the Word was made
flesh with a soul." This was the error of Arius, who said that there
was no soul in Christ, but that the Word of God was there in place of
a soul.

The falsity of this opinion is obvious, both because it is in conflict with Sacred Scripture, which often mentions the soul of Christ,
as: "My soul is sad, even to the point of death" (Mt 26:38), and because certain affections of the soul are observed in Christ which can
not possibly exist in the Word of God or in flesh alone: "He began to
be sorrowful and troubled" (Mt 26:37). Also, God cannot be the
form of a body. Nor can an angel be united to a body as its form,
since an angel, according to its very nature, is separated from body,
whereas a soul is united to a body as its form. Consequently, the
Word of God cannot be the form of a body.

Furthermore, it is plain that flesh does not acquire the specific
nature of flesh except through its soul. This is shown by the fact that
when the soul has withdrawn from the body of a man or a cow, the
flesh of the man or the cow is called flesh only in an equivocal sense.
So if the Word did not assume flesh with a soul, it is obvious that he
did not assume flesh. But **the Word was made flesh**; therefore, he
assumed flesh with a soul.

168   And there were others who, influenced by this, said that
the Word did indeed assume flesh with a soul, but this soul was only
a sensitive soul, not an intellectual one; the Word took the place of
the intellectual soul in Christ's body. This was the error of Apollinaris. He followed Arius for a time, but later in the face of the [scrip-
tural] authorities cited above, was forced to admit a soul in Christ
which could be the subject of these emotions. But he said this soul
lacked reason and intellect, and that in the man Christ their place
was taken by the Word.

This too is obviously false, because it conflicts with the authority of Sacred Scripture in which certain things are said of Christ that
cannot be found in his divinity, nor in a sensitive soul, nor in flesh
alone; for example, that Christ marvelled, as in Matthew (8:10). For
to marvel or wonder is a state which arises in a rational and intellectual soul when a desire arises to know the hidden cause of an
observed effect. Therefore, just as sadness compels one to place a
sensitive element in the soul of Christ, against Arius, so marvelling or
amazement forces one to admit, against Apollinaris, an intellectual
element in Christ.

The same conclusion can be reached by reason. For as there is no flesh without a soul, so there is no human flesh without a human soul, which is an intellectual soul. So if the Word assumed flesh which was animated with a merely sensitive soul to the exclusion of a rational soul, he did not assume human flesh; consequently, one could not say: "God became man."

Besides, the Word assumed human nature in order to repair it. Therefore, he repaired what he assumed. But if he did not assume a rational soul, he would not have repaired it. Consequently, no fruit would have accrued to us from the incarnation of the Word; and this is false. Therefore, **the Word was made flesh**, i.e., assumed flesh which was animated by a rational soul.

169 But you may say: If the Word did assume flesh with such a soul, why did the Evangelist not mention "rational soul," instead of only "flesh," saying, **the Word was made flesh**? I answer that the Evangelist had four reasons for doing this.

First, to show the truth of the incarnation against the Manichaeans, who said that the Word did not assume true flesh, but only imaginary flesh, since it would not have been becoming for the Word of the good God to assume flesh, which they regarded as a creature of the devil. And so to exclude this the Evangelist made special mention of the flesh, just as Christ showed the truth of the resurrection to the disciples when they took him for a spirit, saying: "A spirit does not have flesh and bones, as you see that I have" (Lk 24:39).

Secondly, to show the greatness of God's kindness to us. For it is evident that the rational soul has a greater conformity to God than does flesh, and that it would have been a great sign of compassion if the Word had assumed a human soul, as being conformed to himself. But to assume flesh too, which is something far removed from the simplicity of his nature, was a sign of a much greater, indeed, of an incomprehensible compassion. As the Apostle says (1 Tim 3:16): "Obviously great is the mystery of godliness which appeared in the flesh." And so to indicate this, the Evangelist mentioned only flesh.

Thirdly, to demonstrate the truth and uniqueness of the union in Christ. For God is indeed united to other holy men, but only with respect to their soul; so it is said: "She [wisdom] passes into holy souls, making them friends of God and prophets" (Wis 7:27). But that the Word of God is united to flesh is unique to Christ, according to the Psalmist: "I am alone until I pass" (Ps 140:10). "Gold cannot equal it" (Jb 28:17). So the Evangelist, wishing to show the uniqueness of the union in Christ, mentioned only the flesh, saying, **the Word was made flesh**.

Fourthly, to suggest its relevance to man's restoration For man was weak because of the flesh. And thus the Evangelist, wishing to suggest that the coming of the Word was suited to the task of our restoration, made special mention of the flesh in order to show that the weak flesh was repaired by the flesh of the Word. And this is what the Apostle says: "The law was powerless because it was weakened by the flesh. God, sending his Son in the likeness of sinful flesh and in reparation for sin, condemned sin in his flesh" (Rom 8.3).

170 A question arises as to why the Evangelist did not say that the Word assumed flesh, but rather that **the Word was made flesh.** I answer that he did this to exclude the error of Nestorius. He said that in Christ there were two persons and two sons, [one being the Son of God] the other being the son of the Virgin. Thus he did not admit that the Blessed Virgin was the mother of God.

But if this were so, it would mean that God did not become man, for one particular *suppositum* cannot be predicated of another. Accordingly, if the person or *suppositum* of the Word is different than the person or *suppositum* of the man, in Christ, then what the Evangelist says is not true, namely, **the Word was made flesh.** For a thing is made or becomes something in order to be it; if, then, the Word is not man, it could not be said that the Word became man. And so the Evangelist expressly said **was made,** and not "assumed," to show that the union of the Word to flesh is not such as was the "lifting up" of the prophets, who were not "taken up" into a unity of person, but for the prophetic act. This union is such as would truly make God man and man God, i.e., that God would be man.

171 There were some, too, who, misunderstanding the manner of the incarnation, did indeed admit that the aforesaid assumption was terminated at a oneness of person, acknowledging in God one person of God and man. But they said that in him there were two hypostases, i.e., two *supposita*; one of a human nature, created and non-eternal, and the other of the divine nature, non-created and eternal. This is the first opinion presented in the *Sentences* (III, d6).

According to this opinion the proposition, "God was made man and man was made God," is not true. Consequently, this opinion was condemned as heretical by the Fifth Council, where it is said: "If anyone shall assert one person and two hypostases in the Lord Jesus Christ, let him be anathema." And so the Evangelist, to exclude any assumption not terminated at a oneness of person, says, **was made.**

172 If you ask how the Word is man, it must be said that he is man in the way that anyone is man, namely, as having human nature. Not that the Word is human nature itself, but he is a divine *suppositum* united to a human nature. The statement, **the Word was made flesh,** does not indicate any change in the Word, but only in the nature newly assumed into the oneness of a divine person. **And the Word was made flesh** through a union to flesh. Now a union is a re-

lation. And relations newly said of God with respect to creatures do not imply a change on the side of God, but on the side of the creature relating in a new way to God.

173 Now follows, **and made his dwelling among us.** This is distinguished in two ways from what went before. The first consists in stating that above the Evangelist dealt with the incarnation of the Word when he said, **the Word was made flesh**; but now he touches on the manner of the incarnation, saying, **and made his dwelling among us.** For according to Chrysostom and Hilary, by the Evangelist saying **the Word was made flesh**, someone might think that he was converted into flesh and that there are not two distinct natures in Christ, but only one nature compounded from the human and divine natures. And so the Evangelist, excluding this, added, **and made his dwelling among us,** i.e., in our nature, yet so as to remain distinct in his own. For what is converted into something does not remain distinct in its nature from that into which it is converted.

Furthermore, something which is not distinct from another does not dwell in it, because to dwell implies a distinction between the dweller and that in which it dwells. But the Word dwelt in our nature; therefore, he is distinct in nature from it. And so, inasmuch as human nature was distinct from the nature of the Word in Christ, the former is called the dwelling place and temple of the divinity, according to John (2:21): "But he spoke of the temple of his body."

174 Now although what is said here by these holy men is orthodox, care must be taken to avoid the reproach which some receive for this. For the early doctors and saints were so intent upon refuting the emerging errors concerning the faith that they seemed meanwhile to fall into the opppsite ones. For example, Augustine, speaking against the Manichaeans, who destroyed the freedom of the will, disputed in such terms that he seemed to have fallen into the heresy of Pelagius. Along these lines, John the Evangelist added, **and made his dwelling among us,** so that we would not think there was a mingling or transformation of natures in Christ because he had said, **the Word was made flesh.**

Nestorius misunderstood this phrase, **and made his dwelling among us,** and said that the Son of God was united to man in such a way that there was not one person of God and of man. For he held that the Word was united to human nature only by an indwelling through grace. From this, however, it follows that the Son of God is not man.

175 To clarify this we should know that we can consider two things in Christ: his nature and person. In Christ there is a distinction in nature, but not in person, which is one and the same in the two

natures, since the human nature in Christ was assumed into a oneness of person. Therefore, the indwelling which the saints speak of must be referred to the nature, so as to say, he **made his dwelling among us,** i.e., the nature of the Word inhabited our nature; not according to the hypostasis or person, which is the same for both natures in Christ.

176 The blasphemy of Nestorius is further refuted by the authority of Sacred Scripture. For the Apostle calls the union of God and man an emptying, saying of the Son of God: "He, being in the form of God ... emptied himself, taking the form of a servant" (Phil 2:6). Clearly, God is not said to empty himself insofar as he dwells in the rational creature by grace, because then the Father and the Holy Spirit would be emptying themselves, since they too are said to dwell in man through grace: for Christ, speaking of himself and of the Father says, "We will come to him and make our home with him" (below 14:23); and of the Holy Spirit the Apostle says: "The Spirit of God dwells in us" (1 Cor 3:16).

Furthermore, if Christ was not God as to his person, he would have been most presumptuous to say: "I and the Father are one" (below 10:30), and "Before Abraham came to be, I am," as is said below (8:58). Now "I" refers to the person of the speaker. And the one who was speaking was a man, who, as one with the Father, existed before Abraham.

177 However, another connection [besides that given in 173] with what went before is possible, by saying that above he dealt with the incarnation of the Word, but that now he is treating the manner of life of the incarnate Word, saying, he **made his dwelling among us,** i.e., he lived on familiar terms with us apostles. Peter alludes to this when he says, "During all the time that the Lord Jesus came and went among us" (Acts 1:21). "Afterwards, he was seen on earth" (Bar 3:38).

178 The Evangelist added this for two reasons. First, to show the marvelous likeness of the Word to men, among whom he lived in such a way as to seem one of them. For he not only willed to be like men in nature, but also in living with them on close terms without sin, in order to draw to himself men won over by the charm of his way of life.

Secondly, to show the truthfulness of his [the Evangelist's] statements. For the Evangelist had already said many great things about the Word, and was yet to mention more wonderful things about him; and so that his testimony would be more credible he took as a proof of his truthfulness the fact that he had lived with Christ, saying, he **made his dwelling among us.** As if to say: I can well bear witness to him, because I lived on close terms with him.

"We tell you ... what we have heard, what we have seen with our eyes" (1 Jn 1:1); "God raised him up on the third day, and granted that he be seen, not by all the people, but by witnesses preordained by God," that is, "to us who ate and drank with him" (Acts 10:40).

LECTURE 8

14b And we have seen his glory,
the glory as of the Only Begotten of the Father,
full of grace and truth.

179 Having set forth the incarnation of the Word, the Evangelist then begins to give the evidence for the incarnate Word. He does two things about this. First, he shows the ways in which the incarnate Word was made known. Secondly, he clarifies each way, below (1:16). Now the incarnate Word was made known to the apostles in two ways: first of all, they obtained knowledge of him by what they saw; secondly, by what they heard of the testimony of John the Baptist. So first, he states what they saw about the Word; secondly, what they heard from John (v 15).

He states three things about the Word. First, the manifestation of his glory; hence he says, **we have seen his glory**. Secondly, the uniqueness of his glory, when he adds, **as of the Only Begotten**. Thirdly, the precise nature of this glory, because **full of grace and truth**.

180 **And we have seen his glory**, can be connected in three ways with what went before. First, it can be taken as an argument for his having said, **the Word was made flesh**. As if to say: I hold and know that the Word of God was incarnate because I and the other apostles **have seen his glory**. "We know of what we speak, and we bear witness of what we see" (below 3:11). "We tell you ... what we have heard, what we have seen with our eyes" (1 Jn 1:1).

181 Secondly, according to Chrysostom, the connection is made by taking this statement as expressing many benefits. As if to say: The incarnation of the Word not only conferred on us the benefit of becoming sons of God, but also the good of seeing his glory. For dull and feeble eyes cannot see the light of the sun; but they can see it when it shines in a cloud or on some opaque body. Now before the incarnation of the Word, human minds were incapable of seeing the divine light in itself, the light which enlightens every rational nature. And so, in order that it might be more easily seen and contemplated by us, he covered it with the cloud of our flesh: "They

looked towards the desert, and saw the glory of the Lord in a cloud" (Ex 16:10), i.e., the Word of God in the flesh.

182 According to Augustine, however, the connection refers to the gift of grace. For the failure of the spiritual eyes of men to contemplate the divine light is due not only to their natural limitations but also to the defects incurred by sin: "Fire," that is, of concupiscence, "fell on them, and they did not see the sun," of justice (Ps 57:9). Hence in order that the divine light might be seen by us, he healed our eyes, making an eye salve of his flesh, so that with the salve of his flesh the Word might heal our eyes, weakened by the concupiscence of the flesh. And this is why just after saying, **the Word was made flesh,** he says, **we have seen his glory.** To indicate this the Lord made clay from his saliva and spread the clay upon the eyes of the man born blind (below 9:6). For clay is from the earth, but saliva comes from the head. Similarly, in the person of Christ, his human nature was assumed from the earth; but the incarnate Word is from the head, i.e., from God the Father. So, when this clay was spread on the eyes of men, **we saw his glory.**

183 This is the glory of the Word Moses longed to see, saying, "Show me your glory" (Ex 32:18). But he did not deserve to see it; indeed, he was answered by the Lord: "You shall see my back" (Ex 33:23), i.e., shadows and figures. But the apostles saw his brightness: "All of us, gazing on the Lord's glory with unveiled faces, are being transformed from glory to glory into his very image" (2 Cor 3:18). For Moses and the other prophets saw in an obscure manner and in figures the glory of the Word that was to be manifested to the world at the end of their times; hence the Apostle says: "Now we see through a mirror, in an obscure manner, but then face to face" in 1 Corinthians (13:12); and below (12:41), "Isaiah said this when he saw his glory." But the apostles saw the very brilliance of the Word through his bodily presence: "All of us, gazing on the Lord's glory," and so forth (2 Cor 3:18); "Blessed are the eyes which see what you see. For many kings and prophets desired to see what you see, and did not see it" (Lk 10:23).

184 Then when he says, **the glory as of the Only Begotten,** he shows the uniqueness of his glory. For since it is written of certain men that they were in glory, as of Moses it says that "his face shone" (Ex 34:29), or was "horned," according to another text, someone might say that from the fact that they saw him [Jesus] in glory, it should not be said that the Word of God was made flesh. But the Evangelist excludes this when he says, **the glory as of the Only Begotten of the Father.** As if to say: His glory is not like the glory of an angel, or of Moses, or Elijah, or Elisha, or anything like that; but

the glory as of the Only Begotten; for as it is said, "He [Jesus] was counted worthy of more glory than Moses" (Heb 3:3); "Who among the sons of God is like God?" (Ps 88:7).

185 The word **as**, according to Gregory, is used to express the fact. But according to Chrysostom, it expresses the manner of the fact: as if someone were to see a king approaching in great glory and being asked by another to describe the king he saw, he could, if he wanted to be brief, express the grandeur of his glory in one word, and say that he approached "as" a king, i.e., as became a king. So too, here, the Evangelist, as though asked by someone to describe the glory of the Word which he had seen, and being unable to fully express it, said that it was "as" of the Only Begotten of the Father, i.e., such as became the Only Begotten of God.

186 The uniqueness of the glory of the Word is brought out in four ways. First, in the testimony which the Father gave to the Son. For John was one of the three who had seen Christ transfigured on the mountain and heard the voice of the Father saying: "This is my beloved Son, with whom I am well pleased" (Mt 17:5). Of this glory it is said, "He received honor and glory from God the Father ... 'This is my beloved Son' " (2 Pt 1:17)

Secondly, it is brought out by the service of the angels. For prior to the incarnation of Christ, men were subject to the angels. But after it, angels ministered, as subjects, to Christ. "Angels came and ministered to him" (Mt 4:11).

Thirdly, it is brought out by the submission of nature. For all nature obeyed Christ and heeded his slightest command, as something established by him, because "All things were made through him" (above 1:3). This is something granted neither to angels nor to any creature, but to the incarnate Word alone. And this is what we read, "What kind of man is this, for the winds and the sea obey him?" (Mt 8:27).

Fourthly, we see it in the way he taught and acted. For Moses and the other prophets gave commands to men and taught them not on their own authority, but on the authority of God. So they said: "The Lord says this"; and "The Lord spoke to Moses." But Christ speaks as the Lord, and as one having power, i.e., by reason of his own power. Hence he says, "I say to you" (Mt 5:22). This is the reason why, at the end of the Sermon on the Mountain, it is said that he taught as one "having authority" (Mt 7:29). Furthermore, other holy men worked miracles, but not by their own power. But Christ worked them by his own power. In these ways, then, the glory of the Word is unique.

187 Note that sometimes in Scripture we call Christ the Only Begotten, as here, and below (1:18): "It is the Only Begotten Son,

who is in the bosom of the Father, who has made him known." At other times we call him the First-born: "When he brings the First-born into the world, he says, 'Let all the angels of God adore him' " (Heb 1:6). The reason for this is that just as it belongs to the whole Blessed Trinity to be God, so it belongs to the Word of God to be God Begotten. Sometimes, too, he is called God according to what he is in himself; and in this way he alone is uniquely God by his own essence. It is in this way that we say there is but one God: "Hear, O Israel: the Lord your God is one" (Dt 6:4). At times, we even apply the name of deity to others, insofar as a certain likeness of the divinity is given to men; in this sense we speak of many gods: "Indeed, there are many gods and many lords" (1 Cor 8:5).

Along these lines, if we consider what is proper to the Son as Begotten, and consider the way in which this sonship is attributed to him, that is, through nature, we say that he is the Only Begotten of God: because, since he alone is naturally begotten by the Father, the Begotten of the Father is one only. But if we consider the Son, insofar as sonship is conferred on others through a likeness to him, then there are many sons of God through participation. And because they are called sons of God by a likeness to him, he is called the First-born of all. "Those whom he foreknew, he predestined to become conformed to the image of his Son, so that he might be the First-born of many brothers" (Rom 8:29).

So, Christ is called the Only Begotten of God by nature; but he is called the First-born insofar as from his natural sonship, by means of a certain likeness and participation, a sonship is granted to many.

188   Then when he says, **full of grace and truth**, he determines the glory of the Word. As if to say: His glory is such that he is full of grace and divinity. Now these words can be applied to Christ in three ways.

First, from the point of view of union. For grace is given to someone so that he might be united to God through it. So he who is most perfectly united to God is full of grace. Now some are joined to God by participating in a natural likeness: "Let us make man to our image and likeness" (Gn 1:26). Some are joined by faith: "That Christ may dwell in your hearts through faith" (Eph 3:17). And others are united by charity, because "He who abides in love abides in God" (1 Jn 4:16). But all these ways are partial: because one is not perfectly united to God by participating a natural likeness; nor is God seen as he is by faith; nor is he loved to the extent that he is lovable by charity − for since he is the infinite Good, his lovableness is infinite, and the love of no creature is able to love this infinitely. And so these unions are not full.

But in Christ, in whom human nature is united to the divinity in the unity of a *suppositum*, we find a full and perfect union with God. The reason for this is that this union was such that all the acts not only of his divine but also of his human nature were acts of the *suppositum* [or person]. So he was **full of grace** insofar he he did not receive any special gratuitous gift from God, but that he should be God himself. "He gave him," i.e., God the Father gave to the Son, "a name which is above every name" (Phil 2:9). "He was foreordained to be the Son of God in power" (Rom 1:4). He was also **full of truth**, because the human nature in Christ attained to the divine truth itself, that is, that this man should be the divine Truth itself. In other men we find many participated truths, insofar as the First Truth gleams back into their minds through many likenesses; but Christ is Truth itself. Thus it is said: "In whom all the treasures of wisdom are hidden" (Col 2:3).

189 Secondly, these words can be applied in relation to the perfection of his soul. Then he is said to be **full of grace and truth** inasmuch as in his soul there was the fulness of all graces without measure: "God does not bestow the Spirit in fractions," as we read below (3:34). Yet it was given in fractions to all rational creatures, both angels and men. For according to Augustine, just as there is one sense common to all the parts of the body, namely, the sense of touch, while all the senses are found in the head, so in Christ, who is the head of every rational creature (and in a special way of the saints who are united to him by faith and charity), all virtues and graces and gifts are found superabundantly; but in others, i.e., the saints, we find participations of the graces and gifts, although there is a gift common to all the saints, and that is charity. We read about this fulness of Christ's grace: "There shall come forth a shoot out of the root of Jesse, and a flower shall spring up out of his root. And the spirit of the Lord shall rest upon him: the spirit of wisdom and of understanding, the spirit of counsel and of fortitude, the spirit of knowledge and of piety" (Is 11:1).

Further, Christ was also **full of truth** because his precious and blessed soul knew every truth, human and divine, from the instant of his conception. And so Peter said to him, "You know all things" (below 21:17). And the Psalm (88:25) says: "My truth," i.e., the knowledge of every truth, "and my mercy," i.e., the fulness of all graces, "shall be with him."

190 In a third way these words can be explained in relation to his dignity as head, i.e., inasmuch as Christ is the head of the Church. In this way it is his prerogative to communicate grace to others, both by producing virtue in the minds of men through the inpouring of grace and by meriting, through his teaching and works

and the sufferings of his death, superabundant grace for an infinite number of worlds, if there were such. Therefore, he is **full of grace** insofar as he conferred perfect justice upon us. We could not acquire this perfect justice through the law, which was infirm and could make no one just or bring anyone to perfection. As we read: "The law was powerless because it was weakened by the flesh. God, sending his Son in the likeness of sinful flesh and in reparation for sin, condemned sin in his flesh" (Rom 8:3).

Again, he was **full of truth** insofar as he fulfilled the figures of the Old Law and the promises made to the fathers. "Christ was a minister to the circumcised to confirm the promises made to the fathers" (Rom 15:8); "All the promises of God are fulfilled in him" (2 Cor 1:20).

Further, he is said to be **full of grace** because his teaching and manner of life were most gracious. "Grace is poured out upon your lips" (Ps 44:3). And so it is said, "All the people came to him early in the morning," i.e., in the morning they were eager to come (Lk 21:38). He was **full of truth**, because he did not teach in enigmas and figures, nor gloss over the vices of men, but preached the truth to all, openly and without deception. As it says below: "Now you are speaking plainly" (16:29).

LECTURE 9

15 John bore witness to him, and he cried out saying:
"This is the one of whom I said:
'He who comes after me, ranks ahead of me,
because he existed before me.'"

191   Having given the evidence by which the Word was made known to the apostles by sight, the Evangelist then presents the evidence by which the Word was made known to persons other than the apostles by their hearing the testimony of John. He does three things about this. First, the witness is presented. Secondly, his manner of testifying is indicated. Thirdly, his testimony is given.

192   So he says: We indeed have seen his glory, the glory as of the Only Begotten of the Father. But we are not believed, perhaps because we are held in suspicion. So let his witness come forth, that is, John the Baptist, who bears witness to Christ. He is a faithful witness who will not lie: "A faithful witness will not lie" (Prv 14:5); "You sent [messengers] to John; and he bore witness to the truth" (below 5:33). John gives his testimony here and fulfills his office

with perseverance because he came as a witness. As Proverbs (12:19) says, "Truthful lips endure forever."

193 Then when he says, **John bore witness to him, and he cried out**, he describes the way he bore witness, that is, it was with a cry. So he says, **he cried out**, i.e., freely without fear. "Cry out in a loud voice.... Say to the cities of Judah: Here is your God" (Is 40:9). He cried out ardently and with great fervor, because it is said, "His word burned like a torch" (Si 48:1); "Seraphim cried one to another" (Is 6:3), which is expressive of a more interior eagerness of spirit. The use of a cry shows that the statements of the witness are not made to a few in figurative language or secretly, but that a truth is being declared openly and publicly, and told not to a few but to many. "Cry out, and do not stop" (Is 58:1).

194 Then he adds his testimony. And he does two things. First, he shows that his testimony was continuous. Secondly, he describes the person to whom he bore witness.
195 The testimony of the Baptist was continuous because he bore witness to him not only once but many times, and even before Christ had come to him. And so he says, **This is the one of whom I said**, i.e., before I saw him in the flesh I bore witness to him. "And you, child, shall be called the prophet of the Most High" (Lk 1:76). He pointed him out both as present and when about to come. And his testimony is certain because he not only predicted that he would come, but pointed him out when he was present, saying, **Look! There is the Lamb of God**. This implies that Christ was physically present to John; for he had often come to John before being baptized.

196 Then he describes the one to whom he bore witness, saying, **He who comes after me, ranks ahead of me**. Here we should note that John does not at once preach to his disciples that Christ is the Son of God, but he draws them little by little to higher things: first, by preferring Christ to himself, even though John had such a great reputation and authority as to be considered the Christ or one of the great prophets. Now he compares Christ to himself: first, with regard to the order of their preaching; secondly, as to the order of dignity; and thirdly, as to the time of their existence.
197 With respect to the order of their preaching, John preceded Christ as a servant precedes his master, and as a soldier his king, or as the morning star the sun: "See, I am sending my messenger, and he will prepare the way before me" (Mal 3:1). So, **He comes after me**, in being known to men, through my preaching. Observe that **comes** is in the present tense, because in Greek the present participle is used.

Now John preceded Christ for two reasons. First, according to Chrysostom, because John was a blood relation of Christ according to the flesh: "your relative, Elizabeth" (Lk 1:36). Therefore, had he borne witness to Christ after knowing him, his testimony might have been open to question; accordingly, John came preaching before he was acquainted with Christ, in order that his testimony might have more force. Hence he says, "And I did not know him! And yet it was to reveal him to Israel that I came baptizing with water" (below 1:31).

Secondly, John preceded Christ because in things that pass into act from potency, the imperfect is naturally prior to the perfect; hence it is said in 1 Corinthians (15:46): "The spiritual is not first, but the animal." Accordingly, the perfect doctrine of Christ should have been preceded by the less perfect teaching of John, which was in a certain manner midway between the doctrine of the law and the prophets (which announced the coming of Christ from afar), and the doctrine of Christ, which was clear and plainly made Christ known.

198 He [John] compares him to himself with respect to dignity when he says, he **ranks ahead of me** [*ante me factus est*, literally, he "was made before me"]. It should be noted that it is from this text that the Arians took occasion for their error. For they said that "He who comes after me," is to be understood of Christ as to the flesh he assumed, but what follows, "was made before me," can only be understood of the Word of God, who existed before the flesh; and for this reason Christ as the Word was made, and was not coeternal with the Father.

According to Chrysostom, however, this exposition is stupid, because if it were true, the Baptist would not have said, he "was made before me, because he existed before me," since no one is unaware that if he was before him, he was made before him. He rather would have said the opposite: "He was before me, because he was made before me." And so, according to Chrysostom, these words should be taken as referring to his [Christ's] dignity, that is, he was preferred to me and placed ahead of me. It is as though he said: Although Jesus came to preach after me, he was made more worthy than I both in eminence of authority and in the repute of men: "Gold will not be equal to it" (Jb 28:17). Or alternatively: he is preferred **ahead of me**, that is, before my eyes, as the Gloss says and as the Greek text reads. As if to say: Before my eyes, i.e., in my sight, because he came into my view and was recognized.

199 He compares him to himself with respect to their duration, saying, **because he existed before me**. As if to say: He was God from all eternity, I am a frail man of time. And therefore, even though I came to preach ahead of him, yet it was fitting that he rank before

me in the reputation and opinion of men, because he preceded all things by his eternity: "Jesus Christ is the same yesterday, today, and forever" (Heb 13:8). "Before Abraham came to be, I am," as we read below (8:58).

If we understand this passage as saying that he "was made before me," it can be explained as referring to the order of time according to the flesh. For in the instant of his conception Christ was perfect God and perfect man, having a rational soul perfected by the virtues, and a body possessed of all its distinctive features, except that it lacked perfect size: "A woman shall enclose a man," i.e., a perfect man (Jer 31:22). Now it is evident that Christ was conceived as a perfect man before John was born; consequently he says that he "was made before me," because he was a perfect man before I came forth from the womb.

LECTURE 10

16 Of his fullness we have all received — indeed, grace upon grace;
17 because, while the law was given through Moses,
grace and truth have come through Jesus Christ.

200   He follows with, **Of his fullness we have all received**. These words and those that follow to (v 19), "This is the testimony of John," are taken in two ways. According to Origen, these are the words of John the Baptist and are added by him to support what he had said previously. It is as though he said: Truly, **he existed before me**, because **of his fullness**, i.e., of his grace, not only I but **all**, including the prophets and patriarchs, **have received**, because all had the grace they possessed by faith in the incarnate Word. According to this explanation, John the Baptist began weaving the story of the incarnation at, "John bore witness to him" (v 15).

But according to Augustine and Chrysostom, the words from "John bore witness to him" (v 15), are those of John the Evangelist. And they are connected with the previous words, "full of grace and truth," as though he were saying: Above, the Evangelist gave the evidence for the Word which was learned through sight and by hearing; but here he explains each. First, how he was made known to the apostles through sight, which was tantamount to receiving the evidence from Christ. Secondly, how John bore witness to him, at "This is the testimony of John" (v 19). As to the first he does two things. First, he shows that Christ is the origin, as a fountain, of

every spiritual grace. Secondly, he shows that grace is dispensed to
us through him and from him.

201   He says first of all: We know from our own experience
that we have seen him full of grace and truth, because **of his fullness
we have all received.** Now one fullness is that of sufficiency, by
which one is able to perform acts that are meritorious and excellent,
as in the case of Stephen. Again, there is a fullness of superabun-
dance, by which the Blessed Virgin excels all the saints because of
the eminence and abundance of her merits. Further, there is a fullness of efficiency and overflow, which belongs only to the man
Christ as the author of grace. For although the Blessed Virgin super-
abounds her grace into us, it is never as authoress of grace. But grace
flowed over from her soul into her body: for through the grace of
the Holy Spirit, not only was the mind of the Virgin perfectly united
to God by love, but her womb was supernaturally impregnated by
the Holy Spirit. And so after Gabriel said, "Hail, full of grace," he
refers at once to the fullness of her womb, adding, "the Lord is with
you" (Lk 1:28). And so the Evangelist, in order to show this unique
fullness of efficiency and overflow in Christ, said, **Of his fullness we
have all received,** i.e., all the apostles and patriarchs and prophets and
just men who have existed, do now exist, and will exist, and even all
the angels.

202   Note that the preposition *de* [of, from] sometimes signifies efficiency, i.e., an originative cause, as when it is said that a ray
is or proceeds "from" the sun. In this way it signifies the efficiency
of grace in Christ, i.e., authorship, because the fullness of grace in
Christ is the cause of all graces that are in intellectual creatures.
"Come to me, all you who desire me, and be filled with my fruits,"
that is to say, share in the fullness of those fruits which come from
me (Si 24:26).

But sometimes this preposition *de* signifies consubstantiality,
as when it is said that the Son is "of" the Father [*de Patre*]. In this
usage, the fullness of Christ is the Holy Spirit, who proceeds from
him, consubstantial with him in nature, in power and in majesty.
For although the habitual gifts in the soul of Christ are other than
those in us, nevertheless it is one and the same Holy Spirit who is in
him and who fills all those to be sanctified. "One and the same Spirit
produces all these" (1 Cor 12:11); "I will pour out my Spirit upon
all flesh" (Jl 2:28); "If anyone does not have the Spirit of Christ, he
does not belong to him" (Rom 8:9). For the unity of the Holy Spirit
produces unity in the Church: "The Spirit of the Lord filled the
whole world" (Wis 1:7).

In a third way, the preposition *de* [of, from] can signify a portion, as when we say "take 'from' this bread or wine [*de hoc pane,*

vel vino]," i.e., take a portion and not the whole. Taken in this way it signifies that those who take a part derive it from the fullness. For he [Christ] received all the gifts of the Holy Spirit without measure, according to a perfect fullness; but we participate through him some portion of his fullness; and this is according to the measure which God grants to each. "Grace has been given to each of us according to the degree to which Christ gives it" (Eph 4:7).

203 Then when he says, **grace upon grace**, he shows the distribution of graces into us through Christ. Here he does two things. First, he shows that we receive grace from Christ, as its author. Secondly, that we receive wisdom from him (1:18). As to the first he does two things. First, he shows that we have received of his fullness. Secondly, our need to receive it.

204 First, he says that we have received of the fullness of Christ what is described as **grace upon grace**. In the light of what is said, we are forced to understand that of his fullness we have received grace, and that upon that grace we have received another. Accordingly, we must see what that first grace is upon which we have received a second one, and also what that second grace is.

According to Chrysostom, the first grace, which was received by the whole human race, was the grace of the Old Testament received in the law. And this was indeed a great grace: "I will give you a good gift" (Prv 4:2). For it was a great benefit for idolatrous men to receive precepts from God, and a true knowledge of the one true God. "What is the advantage of being a Jew, or the benefit of circumcision? It is great in every way. First indeed, because the words of God were entrusted to them" (Rom 3:1). Upon that grace, then, which was first, we have received a second far better. "He will follow grace with grace" (Zec 4:7).

But was not the first grace sufficient? I answer that it was not, because the law gives only a knowledge of sin, but does not take it away. "The law brought nothing to perfection" (Heb 7:19). Hence it was necessary that another grace come that would take away sin and reconcile one with God.

205 And so he says, **because, while the law was given through Moses, grace and truth have come through Jesus Christ**. Here the Evangelist ranks Christ above Moses the lawgiver, whom the Baptist ranked above himself. Now Moses was regarded as the greatest of the prophets: "There did not arise again in Israel a prophet like Moses" (Dt 34:10). But he ranks Christ above Moses in excellence and in dignity of works, **because the law was given through Moses**; and between these two, the One excels the other as the reality excels

the symbol and the truth the shadow: "The law had a shadow of the good things to come" (Heb 10:1). Further, Christ excels him in the way he works, because the law was given by Moses as by one proclaiming it, but not originating it; for "The Lord alone is our lawgiver" (Is 33:22). But **grace and truth have come through Jesus Christ**, as through the Lord and Author of truth and grace, as was explained above.

206 According to Augustine, however, the first grace is justifying and prevenient grace, which is not given to us because of our works: "If it is by grace, it is not now by works" (Rom 11:6). Upon that grace, then, which is imperfect, we have received another grace which is perfect, i.e., the grace of eternal life. And although eternal life is in some way acquired by merits, nevertheless, because the principle of meriting in everyone is prevenient grace, eternal life is called a grace: "The grace of God is eternal life" (Rom 6:23). To be brief, whatever grace is added to prevenient grace, the whole is called **grace upon grace**.

The need for this second grace arises from the insufficiency of the law, which showed what was to be done and what avoided; but it gave no help to fulfill what was commanded. Indeed, what seemed to have been directed to life was the occasion for producing death. Hence the Apostle says that the law was a minister of death: "If the ministry that condemned had glory, the ministry that justifies has much more glory" (2 Cor 3:9). Also, it promised the help of grace but did not fulfill, because "The law brought nothing to perfection" (Heb 7:19). Again, it prefigured the truth of the new grace by its sacrifices and ceremonies; indeed, its very rites proclaimed that it was a figure. Hence is was necessary that Christ come, who by his own death would destroy other deaths and grant the help of new grace, in order that we might both fulfill his precepts with ease and joy, and die to our sins and our old way of life: "Our old self was crucified with him" (Rom 6:6), and in order that the truth of the figures contained in the law might be revealed and the promises made to the fathers be fulfilled.

This can be explained in another way: **truth has come through Jesus Christ**, as to the wisdom and truth which was hidden for centuries, and which he openly taught when he came into the world: "I came into the world for this, to testify to the truth," as we read below (18:37).

207 But if Christ is the Truth, as it says below (14:6), how did truth come [i.e., come to be, be made] through him, because nothing can make itself? I answer that by his essence he is the uncreated Truth, which is eternal and not made, but is begotten of the Father;

but all created truths were made through him, and these are certain participations and reflections of the first Truth, which shines out in those souls who are holy.

LECTURE 11

18 No one has ever seen God;
it is the Only Begotten Son,
who is in the bosom of the Father,
who has made him known.

208   Above, the Evangelist showed how the apostles received grace from Christ as its author; here he shows how they received it from him as a teacher. About this he does three things. First, he shows the need for this teaching. Secondly, the competency of the teacher. Thirdly, the teaching itself.

209   The need for this teaching arose from the lack of wisdom among men, which the Evangelist implies by alluding to the ignorance concerning God which prevailed among men, saying: **No one has ever seen God**. And he does this fittingly, for wisdom consists properly in the knowledge of God and of divine things. Hence Augustine says that wisdom is the knowledge of divine things, as science is the knowledge of human things.

210   But this statement of the Evangelist, **No one has ever seen God**, seems to contradict many passages of divine Scripture. For it is said in Isaiah (6:1): "I saw the Lord seated on a high and lofty throne." And about the same is found in 2 Samuel (6:2). Again in Matthew (5:8), the Lord says: "Blessed are the pure in heart, for they shall see God." If someone were to answer this last statement by saying that it is true that in the past no one has seen God, but will see him in the future, as the Lord promises, the Apostle would exclude this, saying, "He dwells in unapproachable light, whom no man has seen or can see" (1 Tim 6:16).

Because the Apostle says, "no man has seen," someone might say that if he cannot be seen by men, then at least he can be seen by angels; especially since God says, "Their angels in heaven always see the face of my Father" (Mt 18:10). But it cannot be taken in this way either, because it is said, "The sons of the resurrection will be like the angels of God in heaven" (Mt 22:30). If, therefore, the angels see God in heaven, then it is plain that the sons of the resurrection also see him: "When he appears we shall be like him, and we shall see him as he is" (1 Jn 3:2).

211   How then are we to understand what the Evangelist says: **No one has ever seen God**? To understand it we must know that God

is said to be seen in three ways. First, through a created substitute presented to the bodily sight; as Abraham is believed to have seen God when he saw three [men] and adored one (Gn 1). He adored one because he recognized the mystery of the Trinity in the three, whom he first thought to be men, and later believed to be angels. In a second way, through a representation in the imagination; and in this way Isaiah saw the Lord seated on a high and lofty throne. Many visions of this sort are recorded in the Scriptures. In a third way, he is seen through an intelligible species abstracted from material things; and in this way he is seen by those who, considering the greatness of creatures, see with their intellect the greatness of the Creator, as it is said: "From the greatness and beauty of creatures, their Creator can be seen accordingly" (Wis 13:5); "The invisible things of God are clearly seen, being understood through the things that are made," as found in Romans (1:20). In another way, God is seen through a certain spiritual light infused by God into spiritual minds during contemplation; and this is the way Jacob saw God face to face, as it says in Genesis (32:30). According to Gregory, this vision came about through his lofty contemplation.

But the vision of the divine essence is not attained by any of the above visions: for no created species, whether it be that by which an external sense is informed, or by which the imagination is informed, or by which the intellect is informed, is representative of the divine essence as it is. Now man knows as to its essence only what the species he has in his intellect represents as it is. Therefore, the vision of the divine essence is not attained through any species.

The reason why no created species can represent the divine essence is plain: for nothing finite can represent the infinite as it is; but every created species is finite; therefore [it cannot represent the infinite as it is]. Further, God is his own *esse*; and therefore his wisdom and greatness and anything else are the same. But all those cannot be represented through one created thing. Therefore, the knowledge by which God is seen through creatures is not a knowledge of his essence, but a knowledge that is dark and mirrored, and from afar. "Everyone sees him," in one of the above ways, "from afar" (Jb 36:25), because we do not know what God is by all these acts of knowing, but what he is not, or that he is. Hence Denis says, in his *Mystical Theology*, that the perfect way in which God is known in this present life is by taking away all creatures and every thing understood by us.

212 There have been some who said that the divine essence will never by seen by any created intellect, and that it is seen neither by the angels nor by the blessed. But this statement is shown to be false and heretical in three ways. First, because it is contrary to the au-

thority of divine Scripture: "We shall see him as he is" (1 Jn 3:2); "This is eternal life, that they know you, the only true God, and Jesus Christ whom you have sent" (below 17:3). Secondly, because the brightness of God is the same as his substance; for he does not give forth light by participating in light, but through himself. And thirdly, because it is impossible for anyone to attain perfect happiness except in the vision of the divine essence. This is because the natural desire of the intellect is to understand and know the causes of all the effects that it knows; but this desire cannot be fulfilled unless it understands and knows the first universal cause of all things, which is a cause that is not composed of cause and effect, as second causes are. Therefore, to take away the possibility of the vision of the divine essence by man is to take away happiness itself. Therefore, in order for the created intellect to be happy, it is necessary that the divine essence be seen. "Blessed are the pure in heart, for they shall see God" (Mt 5:8).

213 Three things should be noted about the vision of the divine essence. First, it will never be seen with a bodily eye, either by sense or imagination, since only sensate bodily things are perceived by the senses, and God is not bodily: "God is spirit" (below 4:24). Secondly, that as long as the human intellect is in the body it cannot see God, because it is weighed down by the body so that it cannot attain the summit of contemplation. So it is that the more a soul is free of passions and is purged from affections for earthly things, the higher it rises in the contemplation of truth and tastes how sweet the Lord is. Now the highest degree of contemplation is to see God through his essence; and so as long as a man lives in a body which is necessarily subject to many passions, he cannot see God through his essence. "Man will not see me and live" (Ex 33:20). Therefore, if the human intellect is to see the divine essence it must wholly depart from the body: either by death, as the Apostle says, "We would prefer to be absent from the body and present with the Lord" (2 Cor 5:8); or by being wholly abstracted by rapture from the senses of the body, as is mentioned of Paul in 2 Corinthians (12:3).

Thirdly, no created intellect (however abstracted, either by death, or separated from the body) which does see the divine essence, can comprehend it in any way. And so it is commonly said that although the whole divine essence is seen by the blessed, since it is most simple and has no parts, yet it is not wholly seen, because this would be to comprehend it. For "wholly" implies a certain mode. But any mode of God is the divine essence. Hence one who does not see him wholly does not comprehend him. For one is properly said to comprehend a thing through knowledge when he

knows that thing to the extent that it is knowable in itself; otherwise, although he may know it, he does not comprehend it. For
example, one who knows this proposition, "A triangle has three
angles equal to two right angles," by a dialectical syllogism, does not
know it as well as it is knowable in itself; thus he does not know it
wholly. But one who knows this by a demonstrative syllogism does
know it wholly. For each thing is knowable to the extent that it has
being and truth; while one is a knower according to his amount of
cognitive power. Now a created intellectual substance is finite; hence
it knows in a finite way. And since God is infinite in power and
being, and as a consequence is infinitely knowable, he cannot be
known by any created intellect to the degree that he is knowable.
And thus he remains incomprehensible to every created intellect.
"Behold, God is great, exceeding our knowledge" (Jb 36:26). He
alone contemplates himself comprehensively, because his power to
know is as great as his entity in being. "O most mighty, great, powerful, your name is Lord of hosts, great in counsel, incomprehensible in
thought" (Jer 32:18).

214 Using the above explanations, we can understand, **No one
has ever seen God**. First, **No one**, i.e, no man, has seen God, that is,
the divine essence, with the eye of the body of or the imagination.
Secondly, **No one**, living in this mortal life, has seen the divine
essence in itself. Thirdly, **No one**, man or angel, has seen God by a
vision of comprehension. So when it is said that certain ones have
seen God with their eyes or while living in the body, he is not seen
through his essence, but through a creature acting as a substitute, as
was said.
     And thus it was necessary for us to receive wisdom, because
No one has ever seen God.

215 The Evangelist mentions the competent teacher of this
wisdom when he adds, **it is the Only Begotten Son, who is in the
bosom of the Father**. He shows the competence of this teacher in
three ways: by a natural likeness, by a singular excellence, and by a
most perfect consubstantiality.
216 By natural likeness, because a son is naturally like his
father. Wherefore it also follows that one is called a son of God
insofar as he shares in the likeness of his natural son; and one knows
him insofar he he has a likeness to him, since knowledge is attained
through assimilation [or "likeness to"]. Hence 1 John (3:2) says,
"Now we are sons of God," and he immediately adds, "when he
comes, we will be like him, and we will see him as he is." Therefore,
when the Evangelist says **Son**, he implies a likeness as well as an
aptitude for knowing God.

217 Because this teacher knows God in a more special way than other sons do, the Evangelist suggests this by his singular excellence, saying, **the Only Begotten**. As if to say: He knows God more than other sons do. Hence, because he is the natural Son, having the same nature and knowledge as the Father, he is called **the Only Begotten**. "The Lord said to me: 'You are my Son' " (Ps 2:7).

218 Although he may know in a unique way, he would be lacking the ability to teach if he were not to know wholly. Hence he adds a third point, namely, his consubstantiality to the Father, when he says, **who is in the bosom of the Father**. "Bosom" is not to be taken here as referring to men in their garments, but it indicates the secret things of the Father. For what we carry in our bosom we do in secret. The secret things of the Father refer to his unsurpassed power and knowledge, since the divine essence is infinite. Therefore, in that bosom, i.e., in the most secret things of the paternal nature and essence, which transcends all the power of the creature, is **the Only Begotten Son**; and so he is consubstantial with the Father.

What the Evangelist signifies by "bosom," David expressed by "womb," saying: "From the womb, before the daystar," i.e., from the inmost secret things of my essence, incomprehensible to every created intellect, "I begot you" (Ps 109:3), consubstantial with me, and of the same nature and power, and virtue and knowledge. "What man knows the things of a man except the spirit of the man that is in him? So also, no one knows the things of God except the Spirit of God" (1 Cor 2:11). Therefore, he comprehends the divine essence, which is his own.

219 But the soul of Christ, which knows God, does not comprehend him, because this is attributed only to the Only Begotten Son who is in the bosom of the Father. So the Lord also says: "No one knows the Father except the Son, and any to whom the Son wishes to reveal him"(Mt 11:27); we should understand this as referring to the knowledge of comprehension, about which the Evangelist seems to be speaking here. For no one comprehends the divine essence except the Father, the Son, and the Holy Spirit. And so we have shown the competence of the teacher.

220 We should note that the phrase, **who is in the bosom of the Father**, rejects the error of those who say that the Father is invisible, but the Son is visible, though he was not seen in the Old Testament. For from the fact that he is among the hidden things of the Father, it is plain that he is naturally invisible, as is the Father. So it is said of him: "Truly, you are a hidden God" (Is 45:15). And so Scripture mentions the incomprehensibility of the Son: "No one knows the Son except the Father, and no one knows the Father except the Son" (Mt 11:27), "What is the name of his son, if you know?" as we read in Proverbs (30:4).

221 Then the Evangelist indicates the way in which this teaching is handed down, saying that it is the Only Begotten Son **who has made him known**. For in the past, the Only Begotten Son revealed knowledge of God through the prophets, who made him known to the extent that they shared in the eternal Word. Hence they said things like, "The Word of the Lord came to me." But now the Only Begotten Son **has made him known** to the faithful: "It is I who spoke; here I am" (Is 52:6); "God, who in many and varied ways, spoke to the fathers in past times through the prophets, has spoken to us in these days in his Son" (Heb 1:1).

And this teaching surpasses all other teachings in dignity, authority and usefulness, because it was handed on immediately by the Only Begotten Son, who is the first Wisdom. "It was first announced by the Lord, and confirmed to us by those who heard him" (Heb 2:3).

222 But what did he make known except the one God? And even Moses did this: "Hear, O Israel: the Lord your God is one" (Dt 6:4). What did this add to Moses? It added the mystery of the Trinity, and many other things that neither Moses nor any of the prophets made known.

LECTURE 12

19 This is the testimony of John, when the Jews sent priests and Levites from Jerusalem to him, to ask him: "Who are you?" 20 He declared openly, and did not deny, and stated clearly, "I am not the Messiah." 21 And they questioned him, "Who then? Are you Elijah?" And he said, "I am not." "Are you the Prophet?" And he responded, "No." 22 They therefore said to him, "Who are you? We must take back an answer to those who sent us. What have you to say about yourself?" 23 He said, quoting the prophet Isaiah, "I am 'a voice that cries in the wilderness: Make a straight way for the Lord' " [Is 40:3].

223 Above, the Evangelist showed how Christ was made known to the apostles through the testimony of John; here he develops this testimony more fully. First, he presents John's testimony to the people. Secondly, the testimony he gave of Christ to his own disciples (below 1:35). If we carefully consider what was said, we discover a twofold testimony of John to Christ: one which he gave to Christ in his presence, the other in his absence. For he would not have said,

"It is he" (below 1:30), unless he had given testimony in Christ's presence; and he would not have said, "of whom I said," unless he gave testimony to him in his absence. So first, the Evangelist develops the testimony John gave to Christ in his absence; secondly, that he gave in his presence (v 29).

Now these two testimonies differ, because the first was given when he was questioned; the other was spontaneous. So in the first instance, we are given not only his testimony, but also the questions. First, he was asked about himself; secondly, about his office (v 24). First we are shown how John stated that he was not what he really was not; secondly, that he did not deny what he was.

224 As to the first, there are three questions and three answers, as is plain from the text. In the first question there is great respect for John shown by the Jews. They had sent certain ones to him to ask about his testimony. The greatness of their respect is gathered from four facts. First, from the dignity of those who sent the questioners; for they were not sent by Galileans, but by those who were first in rank among the people of Israel, namely, Judeans, of the tribe of Juda, who lived about Jerusalem. It was from Juda that God chose the princes of the people.

Secondly, from the preeminence of the place, that is, from Jerusalem, which is the city of the priesthood, the city dedicated to divine worship: "You people claim that Jerusalem is the place where men must worship God" (below 4:20); "They will worship him with sacrifices and offerings" (Is 19:21). Thirdly, from the authority of the messengers, who were religious and from among the holier of the people, namely, priests and Levites; "You will be called the priests of the Lord" (Is 61:6).

Fourthly, from the fact that they sent them so that John might bear witness to himself, indicating that they put such trust in his words as to believe John even when giving testimony about himself. Hence he says they were sent to ask him, **Who are you?** They did not do this to Christ; in fact they said to him: "You are bearing witness to yourself; your testimony is not true" (below 8:13).

225 Then when he says, **He declared openly, and did not deny**, John's answer is given. The Evangelist twice mentioned that John spoke forth to show his humility; for although he was held in such high esteem among the Jews that they believed he might be the Messiah, he, on his part, usurped no honor what was not due him; indeed, he stated clearly, **I am not the Messiah.**

226 What of the statement, **He declared openly, and did not deny?** For it seems that he did deny, because he said that he was not the Messiah. It must be answered that he did not deny the truth, for

he said he was not the Messiah; otherwise he would have denied the truth. "A very great iniquity, and a denial of the most high God" (Jb 31:28). Thus he did not deny the truth, because however great he might have been considered, he did not become proud, usurping for himself the honor of another. He stated clearly, **I am not the Messiah**; because in truth he was not. "He was not the light," as was said above (1:8).

227   Why did John answer, **I am not the Messiah**, since those who had been sent did not ask if he was the Messiah, but who he himself was? I answer that John directed his answer more to the mind of the questioners than to their question. And we can understand this in two ways. According to Origen, the priests and Levites came to John with a good intention. For they knew from the Scriptures, and particularly from the prophecy of Daniel, that the time for the coming of the Messiah had arrived. So, seeing John's holiness, they suspected that he might be the Messiah. So they sent to John, wishing to learn by their question, **Who are you?** whether John would admit that he was the Messiah. And so he directs his answer to their thoughts: **I am not the Messiah.**

Chrysostom, however, says that they questioned him as a stratagem. For John was related to priests, being the son of a chief priest, and he was holy. Yet, he bore witness to Christ, whose family seemed lowly; for that reason they even said, "Is not this the son of the carpenter?"; and they did not know him. So, preferring to have John as their master, not Christ, they sent to him, intending to entice him by flattery and persuade him to take this honor for himself, and to state that he was the Messiah. But John, seeing their evil intent, said, **I am not the Messiah.**

228   The second question is stated when they ask him, **Who then? Are you Elijah?** Here we should note that just as the Jews a-waited the Lord who was to come, so to they waited for Elijah, who would precede the Messiah: "I will send you Elijah, the prophet" (Mal 4:5). And so those who were sent, seeing that John did not say that he was the Messiah, pressed him that at least he state if he were Elijah. And this is what they ask: **Who then? Are you Elijah?**

229   There are certain heretics who say that souls migrate from one body to another. And this belief was current among the Jews of that time. For this reason they believed that the soul of Elijah was in John's body, because of the similarity of John's actions to those of Elijah. And they say that these messengers asked John whether he was Elijah, i.e., whether the soul of Elijah was in John. They support this with Christ's statement, "He is Elijah who is to come," as is found in Matthew (11:14). But John's answer conflicts with their opinion, as he says, **I am not**, i.e., Elijah.

They counter this by saying that John answered in ignorance, not knowing whether his soul was the soul of Elijah. But Origen says in answer to this that it seems most unreasonable that John, a prophet enlightened by the Spirit, and telling such things about the Only Begotten Son of God, should be ignorant of himself, and not know whether his soul had been in Elijah.

230 So this was not the reason John was asked, **Are you Elijah?** Rather it was because they took it from Scripture (2 Kings 2:11) that Elijah did not die, but had been carried alive by a whirlwind into heaven. Accordingly, they believed that he had suddenly appeared among them.

But against this opinion is the fact that John was born from parents who were known, and his birth had been known to everyone. So it says in Luke (1:66) that all said, "What do you think this child will be?" One might say to this that it is not incredible that they should regard John in the manner described. For a similar situation in found in Matthew (14:1): for Herod thought that Christ was John, whom he had beheaded, even though Christ had been preaching and was known for some time before John had been beheaded. And so from a similar stupidity and madness the Jews asked John whether he was Elijah.

231 Why does John say, **I am not** Elijah, while Christ said, "He is Elijah" (Mt 11:14). The angel gives us the answer: "He will go before him in the spirit and power of Elijah" (Lk 1:17), i.e., in his works. Thus he was not Elijah in person, but in spirit and power, i.e., because he showed a similarity to Elijah in his works.

232 This likeness can be found in three matters. First, in their office: because as Elijah will precede the second coming of Christ, so John preceded the first. Thus the angel said, "He will go before him." Secondly, in their manner of living. For Elijah lived in desert places, ate little food and wore coarse clothing, as recorded in 1 and 2 Kings. John, also, lived in the desert, his food was locusts and wild honey, and he wore clothing of camel's hair. Thirdly, in their zeal. For Elijah was filled with zeal; thus it was said, "I have been very zealous for the Lord" (1 Kgs 19:10). So, also, John died because of his zeal for the truth, as is clear from Matthew (14:6).

233 Then when he says, **Are you the Prophet?** the third question is presented. Here there is a difficulty, for since it is said in Luke (1:76), "And you, child, shall be called the prophet of the Most High," why does John, when asked if he is a prophet, answer that he is not a prophet?

There are three ways of answering this. One is that John is not just a prophet, but more than a prophet. For the other prophets only predicted future things from afar: "If there is a delay, wait for it"

(Hb 2:2). But John proclaimed that the Messiah was present, pointing him out with his finger: "Look, there is the Lamb of God," as it says below (1:36). And so the Lord says that he is more than a prophet (Mt 11:9).

Again, in another way, according to Origen, because through a misunderstanding the Jews associated three great personages with the coming of Christ: Christ himself, Elijah, and some other person, the greatest of the prophets, about whom Deuteronomy (18:15) says: "The Lord your God will raise up a prophet for you." And although this greatest of the prophets is in fact none other than Christ, according to the Jews he is someone other than Christ. And so they do not ask simply whether he is a prophet, but whether he is that "greatest of the prophets." And this is clear from the order of their questions. For they first ask whether he is the Messiah; secondly, whether he is Elijah; thirdly, whether he is that prophet. Accordingly, in Greek, the article is used here as signifying *the* prophet, as it were, antonomastically.

In a third way, because the Pharisees were indignant at John for assuming the office of baptizing outside the order of the law and their tradition. For the Old Testament mentions three persons to whom this office could belong. First, to the Messiah, since "I will pour clean water upon you, and you will be cleansed" (Ez 36:25), are words considered as spoken by the person of the Messiah. Secondly, to Elijah, of whom it says in 2 Kings that he divided the water of the Jordan, and crossing over, was taken up. Finally, to Elisha, who made Naaman the Syrian wash seven times in the Jordan so as to be cured of leprosy, as mentioned in 2 Kings (c 5). And so when the Jews saw that John was baptizing, they believed that he was one of those three: the Messiah, or Elijah, or Elisha. Accordingly, when they ask here, **Are you the Prophet?** they are asking whether he is Elisha, who is called "prophet" in a special way because of the many miracles he had performed; hence he himself says, "Let him come to me, so that he may know that there is a prophet in Israel" (2 Kgs 5:8). And to this John answers, **No**, I am not Elisha.

234   Then he shows how he declared who he was. First, the question of the messengers is given; secondly, his answer (v 23).

235   They said, **Who are you? We must take back an answer to those who sent us.** As if to say: We were sent to learn who you are; so tell us, **What have you to say about yourself?**

Notice John's devotion. He has already fulfilled what the Apostle says, "It is not I who now live, but Christ lives in me" (Gal 2:20). And so he does not answer, "I am the son of Zachary," or this or that, but only the way in which he followed Christ.

236 So he says, **I am a voice that cries in the wilderness.** And he says that he is a voice because from the point of view of origin, a voice comes after the [mental, interior] word, but before the knowledge it causes. For we know a [mental, interior] word conceived in the heart by means of the voice which speaks it, since it is its sign. But God the Father sent the precursor John, who came to be in time, in order to make known his Word, which was conceived from eternity. And so he fittingly says, **I am a voice.**

237 The addition, **that cries,** can be understood in two ways: as referring to John, crying and preaching in the wilderness; or to Christ crying in him, according to, "Do you want proof that Christ is speaking in me" (2 Cor 13:3).

Now he cries for four reasons. First of all, a cry implies a showing; and so he cries in order to show that Christ is clearly speaking in John and in himself: "Now on the last, the great day of the feast, Jesus stood and cried out, saying, 'If any one thirsts, let him come to me and drink' " (below 7:37). But he did not cry out in the prophets because prophecies were given in enigmas and figures; so it is said that he was "wrapped in dark rain-clouds" (Ps 17:12). Secondly, because a cry is made to those who are at a distance; and the Jews were far from God. Thus it was necessary that he cry: "You have taken my friends and neighbors away from me" (Ps 88:19). He cries, in the third place, because they were deaf: "Who is deaf, but my servant?" (Is 42:19). He cries, fourthly, because he speaks with indignation, for they deserved God's wrath: "He will speak to them in his anger" (Ps 2:5).

238 Note that he cries **in the wilderness,** because "The word of the Lord came to John, the son of Zechariah, in the desert," as we read in Luke (3:2). There can be both a literal and a mystical reason for this. The literal reason is that by living in the desert he would be immune from all sin, and so be more worthy to bear witness to Christ, and his testimony would be more credible to men because of his life.

The mystical reason is twofold. For the wilderness or desert designates paganism, according to Isaiah (54:1); "She who is deserted has more children than she who has a husband." Accordingly, in order to show that God's teaching would from now on not be in Jerusalem alone, but also among the pagans, he cried **in the wilderness.** "The kingdom of God will be taken away from you, and given to a people that will produce its fruits" (Mt 21:43). Again, the desert can indicate Judea, which was already deserted: "Your house will be left to you, deserted" (Mt 23:38). And so he cried in the desert, **in the wilderness,** i.e., in Judea, to indicate that the people to whom he was preaching had already been deserted by God: "In a desert land, where there is no way or water, so I have come to your sanctuary" (Ps 62:3).

239 Why does he cry, **Make a straight way for the Lord?** Because this is the task for which he was sent. "And you, child, will be called the prophet of the Most High, for you will go before the face of the Lord to prepare his way" (Lk 1:76). The way, prepared and straight, for receiving the Lord is the way of justice, according to Isaiah (26:7): "The way of the just is straight." For the way of the just is straight when the whole man is subject to God, i.e., the intellect through faith, the will through love, and actions through obedience, are all subject to God.

And this was spoken, i.e., predicted, by **the prophet Isaiah.** As if to say: I am the one in whom these things are fulfilled.

LECTURE 13

24 Now these men had been sent from the Pharisees, 25 and they put this further question to him: "Why then do you baptize, if you are not the Messiah, nor Elijah, nor the Prophet?" 26 John replied, "I baptize with water. But there is one standing in your midst whom you do not recognize − 27 the one who is to come after me, who ranks ahead of me − the strap of whose sandal I am not worthy to unfasten." 28 This happened at Bethany, on the far side of the Jordan, where John was baptizing.

240 Above, we saw John bear witness to Christ as he was being questioned on matters concerning himself; here, on matters concerning his office. Four things are set forth: first, those who question him; secondly, their questions; thirdly, his answer, in which he bore witness; and fourthly, the place where all this happened.

241 His interrogators were Pharisees. Hence he says, **Now these men had been sent from the Pharisees.** According to Origen, what is being said from this point on describes a different testimony given by John; and further, those who were sent from the Pharisees are not the same as those priests and Levites sent by the generality of the Jews, but others who were specifically sent by the Pharisees. And according to this it says: **Now these men had been sent,** not by the Jews, as the priests and Levites had been, but were others, **from the Pharisees.** So he says about this that because the priests and Levites were educated and respectful, they ask John humbly and respectfully whether he is the Messiah, or Elijah, or the Prophet. But these others,

who were from the Pharisees, according to their name "separated" and importunate, used disdainful language. Thus they asked him, **Why then do you baptize, if you are not the Messiah, nor Elijah, nor the Prophet?**

But according to others, such as Gregory, Chrysostom, and Augustine, these Pharisees are the same priests and Levites who had been sent by the Jews. For there was among the Jews a certain sect which was separated from the others by reason of its external cult; and for this reason its members were called Pharisees, i.e., "divided." In this sect there were some priests and Levites, and some of the people. And so, in order that the delegates [to John] might possess a greater authority, they sent priests and Levites, who were Pharisees, thus furnishing them with the dignity of a priestly caste and with religious authority.

242   The Evangelist adds, **these men had been sent from the Pharisees,** to disclose, first, the reason why they asked about John's baptizing, which was not why they were sent. It is as though he were saying: They were sent to ask John who he was. But they asked, **Why do you baptize?** because they were from the Pharisees, whose religion was being challenged. Secondly, as Gregory says, in order to show with what intention they asked John, "Who are you?" (1:19). For the Pharisees, more than all the others, showed themselves crafty and insulting to Christ. Thus they said of him: "He casts out devils by Beelzebub, the prince of devils" (Mt 12:24). Further, they consulted with the Herodians on how to trap Jesus in his speech (Mt 22:15). And so in saying that **these men had been sent from the Pharisees,** he shows that they were disrespectful and were questioning him out of envy.

243   Their questions concerned his office of baptizing. Hence he says that they asked him, **Why then do you baptize?** Here we should note that they are asking not to learn, but to obstruct. For since they saw many people coming to John because of the new rite of baptism, foreign both to the rite of the Pharisees and of the law, they became envious of John and tried all they could to hinder his baptism. But being unable to contain themselves any longer, they reveal their envy and say, **Why then do you baptize if you are not the Messiah, nor Elijah, nor the Prophet?** As if to say: You should not baptize, since you deny that you are any of those three persons in whom baptism was prefigured, as was said above. In other words, **if you are not the Messiah,** who will possess the fountain by which sins are washed away, **nor Elijah, nor the Prophet,** i.e., Elisha, who made a dry passageway through the Jordan (2 Kgs 2:8), how do you dare baptize? They are like envious persons who hinder the progress of souls, "who say to the seers, 'See no visions' " (Is 30:10).

244   His answer is true: and so he says that John answered, **I baptize with water**. As if to say: You should not be disturbed, if I, who am not the Messiah, nor Elijah, nor the Prophet, baptize; because my baptism is not completive but imperfect. For the perfection of baptism requires the washing of the body and of the soul; and the body, by its nature, is indeed washed by water, but the soul is washed by the Spirit alone. So, **I baptize with water**, i.e., I wash the body with something bodily; but another will come who will baptize perfectly, namely, with water and with the Holy Spirit; God and man, who will wash the body with water and the spirit with the Spirit, in such a way that the sanctification of the spirit will be distributed throughout the body. "For John indeed baptized with water but you will be baptized with the Holy Spirit not many days from now" (Acts 1:5).

245   Then he bears witness to Christ. First, in relation to the Jews. Secondly, in relation to himself (v 27).

246   He relates him to the Jews when he says, **But there is one standing in your midst**. As if to say: I have done an incomplete work, but there is another who will complete my work, and he is **standing in your midst**.

This is explained in a number of ways. First, according to Gregory, Chrysostom and Augustine, it refers to the ordinary way Christ lived among men, because according to his human nature he appeared to be like other men: "He, being in the form of God ... emptied himself, taking the form of a servant" (Phil 2:6). And according to this he says, **there is one standing in your midst**, i.e., in many ways he lived as one of you: "I am in your midst" (Lk 22:27), **whom you do not recognize**, i.e., you cannot grasp the fact that God was made man. Likewise, **you do not recognize** how great he is according to the divine nature which is concealed in him: "God is great, and exceeds our knowledge" (Jb 36:26). And so, as Augustine says, "The lantern was lighted," namely, John, "so that Christ might be found." "I have prepared a lamp for my anointed" (Ps 131:17).

It is explained differently by Origen; and in two ways. First, as referring to the divinity of Christ: and according to this, **there is one standing**, namely, Christ, **in your midst**, that is, in the midst of all things; because he, as Word, has filled all from the beginning of creation: "I fill heaven and earth" (Jer 23:24). **Whom you do not recognize**, because, as was said above (1:10), "He was in the world ... and the world did not know him."

It is explained another way as referring to his causality of human wisdom. **But there is one standing in your midst**, i.e., he shines in everyone's understanding; because whatever light and whatever wisdom exists in men has come to them from participating in the Word. And he says, **in your midst**, because in the midst of man's body lies the heart, to which is attributed a certain widsom and understanding; hence, although the intellect has no bodily organ, yet because the heart is our chief organ, it is the custom to take it for the intellect. So he is said to stand among men because of this likeness, insofar as he "enlightens every man coming into this world" (1:9). **Whom you do not recognize**, because, as was said above (1:5), "The light shines in the darkness, and the darkness did not overcome it."

In a fourth way, it is explained as referring to the prophetic foretelling of the Messiah. In this sense the answer is directed chiefly to the Pharisees, who continually searched the writings of the Old Testament in which the Messiah was foretold; and yet they did not recognize him. And according to this it says, **there is one standing in your midst**, i.e., in the Sacred Scriptures which you are always considering: "Search the Scriptures" (below 5:39); **whom you do not recognize**, because your heart is hardened by unbelief, and your eyes blinded, so that you do not recognize as present the person you believe is to come.

247   Then John compares Christ to himself. First, he states the superiority of Christ as compared to himself. Secondly, he shows the greatness of this superiority.

248   He shows the superiority of Christ in comparison to himself both in preaching and in dignity. Now, as to the order of preaching, John was the first to become known. Thus he says, **the one who is to come after me**, to preach, to baptize and to die; because as was said in Luke (1:76): "You will go before the face of the Lord to prepare his way." John preceded Christ as the imperfect the perfect, and as the disposition the form; for as is said, "The spiritual is not first, but the animal" (1 Cor 15:46). For the entire life of John was a preparation for Christ; so he said above, that he was "a voice that cries in the wilderness."

But Christ preceded John and all of us as the perfect precedes the imperfect and the exemplar precedes the copy: "If any one wishes to come after me, let him deny himself, and take up his cross, and follow me" (Mt 16:24); "Christ suffered for us, leaving you an example" (1 Pt 2:21).

Then he compares Christ to himself as to dignity, saying, **who ranks ahead of me**, i.e., he has been placed above me and is above me in dignity, because as he says (below 3:30), "He must increase, and I must decrease."

249   He touches on the greatness of his superiority when he says, **the strap of whose sandal I am not worthy to unfasten**. As if

to say: You must not suppose that he ranks ahead of me in dignity in the way that one man is placed ahead of another, rather he is ranked so far above me that I am nothing in comparison to him. And this is clear from the fact that it is he **the strap of whose sandal I am not worthy to unfasten**, which is the least service that can be done for men. It is clear from this that John had made great progress in the knowledge of God, so far that from the consideration of God's infinite greatness, he completely lowered himself and said that he himself was nothing. So did Abraham, when he recognized God, and said (Gn 18:27), "I will speak to my Lord, although I am but dust and ashes." And so also did Job, saying, "Now I see you, and so I reprove myself, and do penance in dust and ashes" (Jb 42:5). Isaiah also said, after he had seen the glory of God, "Before him all the nations are as if they are not" (Is 40:17). And this is the literal explanation.

250 This is also explained mystically. Gregory explains it so that the sandal, made from the hides of dead animals, indicates our mortal human nature, which Christ assumed: "I will stretch out my sandal to Edom" (Ps 59:10). The strap of Christ's sandal is the union of his divinity and humanity, which neither John nor anyone can unfasten or fully investigate, since it is this which made God man and made man God. And so he says, **the strap of whose sandal I am not worthy to unfasten**, i.e., to explain the mystery of the incarnation perfectly and fully. For John and other preachers unfasten the strap of Christ's sandal in some way, although imperfectly.

It is explained in another way by recalling that it was ordered in the Old Law that when a man died without children, his brother was obligated to marry the wife of the dead man and raise up children from her as his brother's. And if he refused to marry her, then a close relative of the dead man, if willing to marry her, was to remove the sandals of the dead man as a sign of this willingness and marry her; and his home was then to be called the home of the man whose sandals were removed (Dt 25:5). And so according to this he says, **the strap of whose sandal I am not worthy to unfasten**, i.e., I am not worthy to have the bride, that is, the Church, to which Christ has a right. As if to say: I am not worthy to be called the bridegroom of the Church, which is consecrated to Christ in the baptism of the Spirit; but I baptize only in water. As it says below (3:29): "It is the groom who has the bride."

251 The place where these events happened is mentioned when he says, **This happened at Bethany, on the far side of the Jordan.** A question arises on this: Since Bethany is on the Mount of Olives, which is near Jerusalem, as is said in John (11:1) and also in Matthew (26:6), how can he say that these things happened beyond the

Jordan, which is quite far from Jerusalem? Origen and Chrysostom answer that it should be called Bethabora, not Bethany, which is a village on the far side of the Jordan; and that the reading "Bethany" is due to a copyist's error. However, since both the Greek and Latin versions have Bethany, one should rather say that there are two places called Bethany: one is near Jerusalem on the side of the Mount of Olives, and the other is on the far side of the Jordan where John was baptizing.

252 The fact that he mentions the place has both a literal and a mystical reason. The literal reason, according to Chrysostom, is that John wrote this Gospel for certain ones, perhaps still alive, who would recall the time and who saw the place where these things happened. And so, to lead us to a greater certitude, he makes them witnesses of the things they had seen.

The mystical reason is that these places are appropriate for baptism. For in saying "Bethany," which is interpreted as "house of obedience," he indicates that one must come to be baptized through obedience to the faith. "To bring all the nations to have obedience to the faith" (Rom 1:5). But if the name of the place is "Bethabora," which is interpreted as "house of preparation," it signifies that a man is prepared for eternal life through baptism.

There is also a mystery in the fact that this happened on the far side of the Jordan. For "Jordan" is interpreted as "the descent of them"; and according to Origen it signifies Christ, who descended from heaven, as he himself says that he descended from heaven to do the will of his Father (below 6:38).

Further, the river Jordan aptly signifies baptism. For it is the border line between those who received their inheritance from Moses on one side of the Jordan, and those who received it from Josue on the other side. Thus baptism is a kind of border between Jews and Gentiles, who journey to this place to wash themselves by coming to Christ so that they might put off the debasement of sin. For just as the Jews had to cross the Jordan to enter the promised land, so one must pass through baptism to enter into the heavenly land. And he says, **on the far side of the Jordan**, to show that John preached the baptism of repentance even to those who trangressed the law and sinners; and so the Lord also says, "I did not come to call the righteous, but sinners" (Mt 9:13).

LECTURE 14

29 The next day John saw Jesus coming toward him and he said, "Look! There is the Lamb of God who takes away the sins of the world. 30 It is he of whom I said:
'After me is to come a man, who ranks ahead of me, because he existed before me.'
31 And I did not know him! And yet it was to reveal him to Israel that I came baptizing with water." 32 John gave this testimony also:
"I saw the Spirit coming down on him from heaven like a dove, and resting on him. 33 And I did not know him, but he who sent me to baptize with water had said to me: 'The man on whom you see the Spirit come down and rest is the one who is to baptize with the Holy Spirit.' 34 Now I have seen for myself and have given testimony that he is the Son of God."

253   Above, John had given testimony to Christ when he was questioned. Here, he gives testimony to him on his own initiative. First, he gives the testimony; secondly, he confirms it (v 32). As to the first: first, the circumstances of the testimony are given; and secondly, the testimony itself is given (v 29); thirdly, suspicion is removed from the witness (v 31).

254   The circumstances are first described as to the time. Hence he says, **The next day.** This gives credit to John for his steadfastness, because he bore witness to Christ not for just one day or once, but on many days and frequently: "Every day I will bless you" (Ps 144:2). His progress, too, is cited, because one day should not be just like the day before, but the succeeding day should be different, i.e., better: "They will go from strength to strength" (Ps 83:8).

Another circumstance mentioned is his manner of testifying, because **John saw Jesus.** This shows his certitude, for testimony based on sight is most certain. The last circumstance he mentions is about the one to whom he bore witness. Hence he says that he saw **Jesus coming toward him,** i.e., from Galilee, as it says, "Jesus came from Galilee" (Mt 3:13). We should not understand this as referring to the time when he came to be baptized, of which Matthew is here speaking, but of another time, i.e., a time when he came to John after he had already been baptized and was staying near the Jordan. Otherwise, he would not have said, " 'The man on whom you see the Spirit come down and rest is the one who is to baptize with the Holy Spirit.' Now I have seen" (v 33). Therefore, he had already seen him and the Spirit come down as a dove upon him.

255 One reason why Christ now came to John was to confirm the testimony of John. For John had spoken of Christ as "the one who is to come after me" (v 27). But since Christ was now present, some might not understand who it was that was to come. So Christ came to John to be pointed out by him, with John saying, **Look! There is the Lamb of God**. Another reason Christ came was to correct an error. For some might believe that the first time Christ came, i.e., to be baptized, he came to John to be cleansed from his sins. So, in order to preclude this, Christ came to him even after his baptism. Accordingly, John clearly says, **There is the Lamb of God who takes away the sins of the world**. He committed no sin, but came to take away sin. He also came to give us an example of humility, because as it is said, "The greater you are the more humble you should be in all matters" (Sir 3:20).

Note that after the conception of Christ, when his mother, the Virgin, went in haste to the mountainous country to visit John's mother, Elizabeth, that John, still in his mother's womb and unable to speak, leaped in her womb as though performing a religious dance out of reverence for Christ. And as then, so even now; for when Christ comes to John out of humility, John offers his testimony and reverence and breaks out saying, **Look! There is the Lamb of God**.

256 With these words John gives his testimony showing the power of Christ. Then Christ's dignity is shown (v 30). He shows the power of Christ in two ways: first, by means of a symbol; secondly, by explaining it (v 29).

257 As to the first, we should note, as Origen says, that it was customary in the Old Law for five animals to be offered in the temple: three land animals, namely, the heifer, goat and sheep (although the sheep might be a ram, a sheep or a lamb) and two birds, namely, the turtle-dove and the dove. All of these prefigured the true sacrifice, which is Christ, who "gave himself for us as an offering to God," as is said in Ephesians (5:2).

Why then did the Baptist, when giving witness to Christ, specifically call him a Lamb? The reason for this is that, as stated in Numbers (28:3), although there were other sacrifices in the temple at other times, yet each day there was a time in which a lamb was offered every morning, and another was offered in the evening. This never varied, but was regarded as the principal offering, and the other offerings were in the form of additions. And so the lamb, which was the principal sacrifice, signified Christ, who is the principal sacrifice. For although all the saints who suffered for the faith of Christ contribute something to the salvation of the faithful, they do this only inasmuch as they are immolated upon the oblation of the Lamb, they being, as it were, an oblation added to the principal sacrifice. The lamb is offered in the morning and in the evening because it is through Christ that the way is opened to the contemplation and enjoyment of the intelligible things of God, and this pertains to "morning knowledge"; and we are instructed how to use earthly things without staining ourselves, and this pertains to "evening knowledge." And so he says, **Look! There is the Lamb of God**, i.e., the one signified by the lamb.

He says, **of God**, because there are two natures in Christ, a human nature and a divine nature. And it is due to the power of the divinity that this sacrifice has the power to cleanse and sanctify us from our sins, inasmuch as "God was, in Christ, reconciling the world to himself" (2 Cor 5:19). Or, he is called **the Lamb of God**, because offered by God, i.e., by Christ himself, who is God; just as we call what a man offers the offering of the man. Or, he is called **the Lamb of God**, that is, of the Father, because the Father provided man with an oblation to offer that satisfied for sins, which man could not have through himself. So when Isaac asked Abraham, "Where is the victim for the holocaust?" he answered, "God himself will provide a victim for the holocaust" (Gn 22:7); "God did not spare his own Son, but delivered him up for all of us" (Rom 8:32).

258 Christ is called a **Lamb**, first, because of his purity: "Your lamb will be without blemish" (Ex 12:5); "You were not redeemed by perishable gold or silver" (1 Pt 1:18). Secondly, because of his gentleness: "Like a lamb before the shearer, he will not open his mouth" (Is 53:7). Thirdly, because of his fruit; both with respect to what we put on: "Lambs will be your clothing" (Prv 27:26), "Put on the Lord Jesus Christ" (Rom 13:14); and with respect to food: "My flesh is for the life of the world" (below 6:52). And so Isaiah said (16:1): "Send forth, O Lord, the lamb, the ruler of the earth."

259 Then when he says, **who takes away the sins of the world**, he explains the symbol he used. In the law, sin could not be taken away either by a lamb or by any other sacrifice, because as is said in Hebrews (10:4), "It is impossible that sins be taken away by the blood of bulls and goats." This blood **takes away**, i.e., removes, **the sins of the world**. "Take away all iniquity" (Hos 14:3). Or, **takes away**, i.e., he takes upon himself the **sins of the** whole **world**, as is said, "He bore our sins in his own body" (1 Pt 2:24); "It was our infirmities that he bore, our sufferings that he endured," as we read in Isaiah (53:4).

However, according to a Gloss, he says **sin**, and not "sins," in order to show in a universal way that he has taken away every kind of sin: "He is the offering for our sins" (1 Jn 2:2); or because he died for one sin, that is, original sin: "Sin entered into this world through one man" (Rom 5:12).

260 Above, the Baptist bore witness to the power of Christ; now he bears witness to his dignity, comparing Christ to himself in three respects. First, with respect to their office and order of preaching. So he says, **It is he**, pointing him out, that is, the Lamb, **of whom I said**, i.e., in his absence, **After me is to come a man**, to preach and baptize, who in birth came after me.

Christ is called a man by reason of his perfect age, because when he began to teach, after his baptism, he had already reached a perfect age: "Jesus was now about thirty years of age" (Lk 3:23). He is also called a man because of the perfection of all the virtues that were in him: "Seven women," i.e., the virtues, "will take hold of one man," the perfect Christ (Is 4:1); "Look, a man! His name is the Orient," because he is the origin of all the virtues found in others (Zec 6:12). He is also called a man because of his espousal, since he is the spouse of the Church: "You will call me 'my husband' " (Hos 2:16); "I espoused you to one husband" (2 Cor 11:2).

261 Secondly, he compares himself to Christ with respect to dignity when he says, **who ranks ahead of me**. As if to say: Although he comes to preach after me, yet he ranks before me in dignity. "See, he comes, leaping upon the mountains, skipping over the hills" (Sg 2:8). One such hill was John the Baptist, who was passed over by Christ, because as is said below (3:30), "He must increase, and I must decrease."

262 Thirdly, he compares himself to Christ with respect to duration, saying, **because he existed before me**. As if to say: It is not strange if he ranks ahead of me in dignity; because although he is after me in time, he is before me in eternity, **because he existed before me.**

This statement refutes a twofold error. First, that of Arius, for John does not say that "he was made before me," as though he were a creature, but **he existed before me**, from eternity, before every creature: "The Lord brought me forth before all the hills," as is said in Proverbs (8:25). The second error refuted is that of Paul of Samosata: for John said, **he existed before me**, in order to show that he did not take his beginning from Mary. For if he had taken the beginning of his existence from the Virgin, he would not have existed before the precursor, who, in the order of human generation, preceded Christ by six months.

263 Next (v 31), he precludes an erroneous conjecture from his testimony. For someone might say that John bore witness to Christ because of his affection for him, coming from a special friendship. And so, excluding this, John says, **And I did not know him!**; for John had lived in the desert from boyhood. And although many mir-

acles happened during the birth of Christ, such as the Magi and the star and so on, they were not known to John: both because he was an infant at the time, and because, after withdrawing to the desert, he had no association with Christ. In the interim between his birth and baptism, Christ did not perform any miracles, but led a life similar to any other person, and his power remained unknown to all.

264   It is clear that he worked no miracles in the interim until he was thirty years old from what is said below (2:11): "This beginning of signs Jesus worked in Cana of Galilee." This shows the error of the book, *The Infancy of the Savior.* The reason he performed no miracles during this period was that if his life had not been like that of other infants, the mystery of the circumcision and incarnation might have been regarded as pure fancy. Accordingly, he postponed showing his knowledge and power to another time, corresponding to the age when other men reach the fulness of their knowledge and power. About this we read, "And Jesus increased in grace and wisdom" (Lk 2:52); not that he acquired a power and wisdom that he previously lacked, for in this respect he was perfect from the instant of his conception, but because his power and wisdom were becoming known to men: "Indeed, you are a hidden God" (Is 45:15).

265   The reason why John did not know him was that he had so far seen no signs, and no one else had known Christ through signs. Hence he adds: **It was to reveal him to Israel that I came baptizing with water.** As if to say: My entire ministry is to reveal: "He was not the light, but he came in order to bear witness to the light," as was said above (1:8).

266   He says, **I came baptizing with water,** to distinguish his baptism from that of Christ. For Christ baptized not just in water, but in the Spirit, conferring grace; and so the baptism of John was merely a sign, and not causative.

John's baptism made Christ known in three ways. First, by the preaching of John. For although John could have prepared the way for the Lord and led the people to Christ without baptizing, yet because of the novelty of the service many more came to him than would have come if his preaching were done without baptism. Secondly, John's baptism was useful because of Christ's humility, which he showed by willing to be baptized by John: "Christ came to John, to be baptized by him" (Mt 3:13). This example of humility he gives us here is that no one, however great, should disdain to receive the sacraments from any person ordained for this purpose. Thirdly, because it was during Christ's baptism by John that the power of the Father was present in the voice, and the Holy Spirit was present in the dove, by which the power and dignity of Christ were all the more shown: "And the voice of the Father was heard: 'This is my beloved Son' " (Lk 3:22).

267 Then when he says, **John gave this testimony also**, he confirms by the authority of God the great things he testified to about Christ, that Christ alone would take away the sins of the whole world. As to this he does three things. First, he presents a vision. Secondly, he tells us the meaning of the vision (v 33). Thirdly, he shows what he learned from this vision (v 34).

268 He presents the vision when he says, **I saw the Spirit coming down on him from heaven**. When this actually happened John the Evangelist does not tell us, but Matthew and Luke say that it took place when Christ was being baptized by John. And it was indeed fitting for the Holy Spirit to be present at this baptism and to the person being baptized. It was appropriate for the one baptized, for as the Son, existing by the Father, manifests the Father, "Father, I have manifested your name" (below 17:6), so the Holy Spirit, existing by the Son, manifests the Son, "He will glorify me, because he will receive from me" (below 16:14). It was appropriate for this baptism because the baptism of Christ begins and consecrates our baptism. Now our baptism is consecrated by invoking the whole Trinity: "Baptizing them in the name of the Father, and of the Son, and of the Holy Spirit" (Mt 28:19). Thus, the ones we invoke in our baptism were present at the baptism of Christ: the Father in the voice, the Holy Spirit in the dove, and the Son in his human nature.

269 He says, **coming down**, because descent, since it has two termini, the start, which is from above, and the end, which is below, suits baptism in both respects. For there is a twofold spirit: one of the world and the other of God. The spirit of the world is the love of the world, which is not from above; rather, it comes up to man from below and makes him descend. But the spirit of God, i.e., the love of God, comes down to man from above and makes him ascend: "We have not received the spirit of this world, but the spirit of God," as is said in 1 Corinthians (2:12). And so, because that spirit is from above, he says, **coming down**.

Similarly, because it is impossible for the creature to receive God's goodness in the fulness in which it is present in God, the communication of this goodness to us is in a way a certain coming down: "Every perfect gift is from above, coming down from the Father of lights" (Jas 1:17).

270 The Evangelist, in describing the manner of the vision and of the coming down, says that the Holy Spirit did not appear in the spirit, i.e., in his nature, but in the form of a dove, saying, that he came like a dove. The reason for this is that the Holy Spirit cannot

be seen in his nature, as is said, "The Spirit blows where it wills, and you hear its sound, but you do not know where it comes from or where it goes" (below 3:8), and because a spirit does not come down but goes up, "The spirit lifted me up" (Ez 8:3).

It was appropriate that the Son of God, who was made visible through flesh, should be made known by the Holy Spirit in the visible form of a dove. However, the Holy Spirit did not assume the dove into a unity of person, as the Son of God assumed human nature. The reason for this is that the Son did not appear as a manifester but as a Savior. And so, according to Pope Leo, it was appropriate that he be God and man: God, in order to provide a remedy; and man, in order to offer an example. But the Holy Spirit appeared only to make known, and for this it was sufficient merely to assume a visible form which was suitable for this purpose.

271 As to whether this dove was a real animal and whether it existed prior to its appearance, it seems reasonable to say that it was a real dove. For the Holy Spirit came to manifest Christ, who, being the Truth, ought to have been manifested only by the truth. As to the other part of the question, it would seem that the dove did not exist prior to its appearance, but was formed at the time by the divine power, without any parental union, as the body of Christ was conceived by the power of the Holy Spirit, and not from a man's seed. Yet it was a real dove, for as Augustine says in his work, *The Christian Combat*: "It was not difficult for the omnipotent God, who produced the entire universe of creatures from nothing, to form a real body for the dove without the aid of other doves, just as it was not difficult to form the true body of Christ in the womb of the Blessed Virgin without natural semen."

Cyprian, in his *The Unity of the Church*, says: "It is said that the Holy Spirit appeared in the form of a dove because the dove is a simple harmless animal, not bitter with gall, not savage with its bites, not fierce with rending talons; it loves the dwellings of men, is able to live together in one nest, together it raises its young, they remain together when they fly, spend their life in mutual association, signify the concord of peace with the kiss of their bill, and fulfill the law of harmony in all things."

272 Many reasons are given why the Holy Spirit appeared as a dove rather than in some other form. First, because of its simplicity, for the dove is simple: "Be wise as serpents, and simple as doves" (Mt 10:16). And the Holy Spirit, because he inclines souls to gaze on one thing, that is, God, makes them simple; and so he appeared in the form of a dove. Further, according to Augustine, the Holy Spirit also appeared in the form of fire over the heads of the assembled apostles. This was done because some are simple, but

lukewarm; while others are fervent but guileful. And so in order that those sanctified by the Spirit may have no guile, the Spirit is shown in the form of a dove; and in order that their simplicity may not grow tepid, the Spirit is shown in fire.

A dove was used, secondly, because of the unity of charity; for the dove is much aglow with love: "One is my dove" (Sg 6:9). So, in order to show the unity of the Church, the Holy Spirit appears in the form of a dove. Nor should it disturb you that when the Holy Spirit rested on each of the disciples, there appeared separate tongues of fire; for although the Spirit appears to be different according to the different functions of his gifts, he nevertheless unites us through charity. And so, because of the first he appeared in separate tongues of fire, as is said, "There are different kinds of gifts" (1 Cor 12:4); but he appears in the form of a dove because of the second.

A dove was used, thirdly,because of its groaning, for the dove has a groaning chant; so also the Holy Spirit "pleads for us with indescribable groanings" (Rom 8:26); "Her maidens, groaning like doves" (Na 2:7). Fourthly, because of the doves fertility, for the dove is a very prolific animal. And so in order to signify the fecundity of spiritual grace in the Church, the Holy Spirit appeared in the form of a dove. This is why the Lord commanded an offering of two doves (Lv 5:7).

A dove was used, fifthly, because of its cautiousness. For it rests upon watery brooks, and gazing into them can see the hawk flying overhead and so save itself: "His eyes are like doves beside brooks of water" (Sg 5:12). And so, because our refuge and defense is found in baptism, the Holy Spirit appropriately appeared in the form of a dove.

The dove also corresponds to a figure in the Old Testament. For as the dove bearing the green olive branch was a sign of God's mercy to those who survived the waters of the deluge, so too in baptism, the Holy Spirit, coming in the form of a dove, is a sign of the divine mercy which takes away the sins of those baptized and confers grace.

273 He says that the Holy Spirit was **resting on him**. If the Holy Spirit does not rest on someone, it is due to two causes. One is sin. For all men except Christ are either suffering from the wound of mortal sin, which banishes the Holy Spirit, or are darkened with the stain of venial sin, which hinders some of the works of the Holy Spirit. But in Christ there was neither mortal nor venial sin; so, the Holy Spirit in him was never disquieted, but was **resting on him**.

The other reason concerns charismatic graces, for the other saints do not always possess their power. For example, the power to work miracles is not always present in the saints, nor is the spirit of prophecy always in the prophets. But Christ always possessed the power to accomplish any work of the virtues and the graces. So to indicate this, he says, **resting on him**. Hence this was the characteristic sign for recognizing Christ, as the Gloss says. "The Spirit of the Lord will rest on him" (Is 11:2), which we should understand of Christ as man, according to which he is less than the Father and the Holy Spirit.

274 Then when he says, **I did not know him**, he teaches us how this vision should be understood. For certain heretics, as the Ebionites, said that Christ was neither the Christ nor the Son of God from the time he was born, but only began to be the Son of God and the Christ when he was anointed with the oil of the Holy Spirit at his baptism. But this is false, because at the very hour of his birth the angel said to the shepherds: "This day a Savior has been born for you in the city of David, Christ the Lord" (Lk 2:11). Therefore, so that we do not believe that the Holy Spirit descended upon Christ in his baptism as though Christ needed to receive the Spirit anew for his sanctification, the Baptist gives the reason for the Spirit's coming down. He says that the Spirit descended not for the benefit of Christ, but for our benefit, that is, so that the grace of Christ might be made known to us. And so he says, **And I did not know him! And yet it was to reveal him to Israel that I came baptizing with water.**

275 There is a problem here. For he says, **he who sent me to baptize**. If he is saying that the Father sent him, it is true. Also, if he is saying that the Son sent him, it is even more clear, since it is said that both the Father and the Son sent him, because John is not one of those referred to in Jeremiah (23:21), "I did not send the prophets, yet they ran." But if the Son did send him, how can he then say, **I did not know him**? If it is said that although he knew Christ according to his divinity, yet he did not know him according to his humanity until after he saw the Spirit coming down upon him, one might counter that the Holy Spirit descended upon Christ when he was being baptized, and John had already known Christ before he was baptized, otherwise he would not have said: "I ought to be baptized by you, and you come to me?" (Mt 3:14).

So we must say that this problem can be resolved in three ways. In one way, according to Chrysostom, so that the meaning is to know familiarly; the sense being that **I did not know him**, i.e., in a familiar way. And if the objection is raised that John says, "I ought to be baptized by you," it can be answered that two different times are being discussed: so that **I did not know him**, refers to a time long before baptism, when he was not yet familiar with Christ; but when he says, "I ought to be baptized by you," he is referring to the time when Christ was being baptized, when he was now familiar with

Christ because of his frequent visits. In another way, according to Jerome, it could be said that Christ was the Son of God and the Savior of the world, and that John did in fact know this; but it was not through the baptism that he knew that he was the Savior of the world. And so to remedy this ignorance he adds, he **is the one who is to baptize with the Holy Spirit**. But it is better to say with Augustine that John knew certain things and was ignorant of others. Explaining what he did not know, he adds that the power of baptizing, which Christ could have shared with his faithful followers, would be reserved for himself alone. And this is what he says, **he who sent me to baptize with water ... is the one**, exclusively and solely, **who is to baptize with the Holy Spirit**, i.e., he and no one else, because this power he reserved for himself alone.

276 We should note that a threefold power of Christ is found in baptism. One is the power of efficiency, by which he interiorly cleanses the soul from the stain of sin. Christ has this power as God, but not as man, and it cannot be communicated to any other. Another is the power of ministry, which he does share with the faithful: "Baptizing them in the name of the Father, and of the Son, and of the Holy Spirit" (Mt 28:19). Therefore priests have the power to baptize as ministers. Christ too, as man, is called a minister, as the Apostle says. But he is also the head of all the ministers of the Church.

Because of this he alone has the power of excellence in the sacraments. And this excellence shows itself in four things. First, in the institution of the sacraments, because no mere man or even the entire Church could institute sacraments, or change the sacraments, or dispense with the sacraments. For by their institution the sacraments give invisible grace, which only God can give. Therefore, only one who is true God can institute sacraments. The second lies in the efficacy of Christ's merits, for the sacraments have their power from the merit of Christ's passion: "All of us who have been baptized into Christ Jesus, have been baptized into his death" (Rom 6:3). The third is that Christ can confer the effect of baptism without the sacrament; and this is peculiar to Christ. Fourthly, because at one time baptism was conferred in the name of Christ, although this is no longer done.

Now he did not communicate these four things to anyone; although he could have communicated some of them, for example, that baptism be conferred in the name of Peter or of someone else, and perhaps one of the remaining three. But this was not done lest schisms arise in the Church by men putting their trust in those in whose name they were baptized.

And so John, in stating that the Holy Spirit came down upon Christ, teaches that it is Christ alone who baptizes interiorly by his own power.

277 One might also say that when John said, "I ought to be baptized by you," he recognized Christ through an interior revelation, but that when he saw the Holy Spirit coming down upon him, he knew him through an exterior sign. And so he mentions both of these ways of knowing. The first when he says, **he who sent me to baptize with water had said to me**, i.e., revealed something in an interior way. The second when he adds, **The man on whom you see the Spirit come down and rest is the one who is to baptize with the Holy Spirit.**

278   Then he shows what the Baptist understood from this vision, that is, that Christ is the Son of God. And this is what he says, **Now I have seen for myself**, that is, the Spirit coming down on him, **and have given testimony that he**, that is, Christ, **is the Son of God**, that is, the true and natural Son. For there were adopted sons of the Father who had a likeness to the natural Son of God: "Conformed to the image of his Son" (Rom 8:29). So he who baptizes in the Holy Spirit, through whom we are adopted as sons, ought to fashion sons of God. "You did not receive the spirit of slavery ... but the spirit of adoption" (Rom 8:15). Therefore, because Christ is the one who baptizes in the Holy Spirit, the Baptist correctly concludes that he is the true and pure Son of God: "that we may be in his true Son" (1 Jn 5:20).

279   But if there were others who saw the Holy Spirit coming down upon Christ, why did they not also believe? I answer that they had not been so disposed for this. Or perhaps, this vision was seen only by the Baptist.

LECTURE 15

35 On the following day John was standing there again with two of his disciples. 36 And seeing Jesus walking by, he said, "Look! There is the Lamb of God." 37 Hearing this, the two disciples followed Jesus. 38 Jesus turned around, and seeing them following him said, "What are you looking for?" They replied, "Rabbi (which means Teacher), where do you live?" 39 "Come and see," he replied. They went and saw where he lived, and they stayed with him the rest of that day. It was about the tenth hour.
40 One of the two who had followed him after hearing John was Simon Peter's brother, Andrew. 41 The first thing he did was to look for his brother Simon, and say to him, "We have found the Messiah" (which means the Christ), 42 and he brought him to Jesus. Looking at him intently Jesus said, "You are Simon, son of John; you are to be called Cephas" (which is translated Peter).

280 Above, the Evangelist presented the Baptist's testimony to the people; here he presents his testimony to John's disciples. First, his testimony is given; secondly, the fruit of this testimony (v 37). As to the first he does three things: first, the one giving the testimony is described; secondly, his way of testifying is given (v 36); and thirdly, his testimony itself, **Look! There is the Lamb of God.**

281 The witness is described when he says, **On the following day John was standing there again with two of his disciples.** In saying **standing**, three things are noted about John. First, his manner of teaching, which was different from that of Christ and his disciples. For Christ went about teaching; hence it is said: "Jesus traveled over all Galilee" (Mt 4:23). The apostles also traveled the world teaching: "Go to the whole world, and preach the good news to every creature" (Mk 16:15). But John taught in one place; hence he says, **standing**, that is, in one place, on the far side of the Jordan. And John spoke of Christ to all who came to him.

The reason why Christ and his disciples taught going about is that the preaching of Christ was made credible by miracles, and so they went to various places in order that the miracles and powers of Christ might be made known. But the preaching of John was not confirmed by miracles, so that is is written, "John performed no sign" (below 10:41), but by the merit and sanctity of his life. And so he was **standing** in one place so that various people might stream to him and be led to Christ by his holiness. Furthermore, if John had gone from place to place to announce Christ without performing any miracles, his testimony would have been quite unbelievable, since it would seem to be inopportune and he would seem to be forcing himself upon the people.

Secondly, John's perseverence in the truth is noted, because John was not a reed shaken by the wind, but was firm in the faith; "Let him who thinks that he stands, take heed so he will not fall" (1 Cor 10:12); "I will stand my watch" (Hb 2:1).

Thirdly, and allegorically, it is noted that to stand is, in an allegorical sense, the same as to fail or cease: "The oil stood," i.e., failed (2 Kgs 4:6). So when Christ came John was standing, because when the truth comes the figure ceases. John stands because the law passes away.

282 The manner of his testifying is presented as being certain, because based on sight. So he says, **seeing Jesus walking by.** Here it should be remarked that the prophets bore witness to Christ: "All the prophets bear witness to him" (Acts 10:43). So did the apostles as they traveled the world: "You will be my witnesses in Jerusalem and in all of Judea and Samaria, and to the remotest parts of the world" (Acts 1:8). However, their testimony was not about a

person then visible or present, but on one who was absent. In the case of the prophets about one who was to come; in the case of the apostles, about one who was now gone. But John bore witness when Christ was present and seen by him; and so he says, **seeing Jesus**, with the eyes of his body and of his mind: "Look on the face of your Christ" (Ps 83:10); "They will see eye to eye" (Is 52:8).

He says, **walking**, to point out the mystery of the incarnation, in which the Word of God assumed a changeable nature: "I came forth from the Father, and have come into the world," as it says below (16:28).

283 Then he gives John's testimony in saying, **Look! There is the Lamb of God**. He says this not just to point out the power of Christ, but also in admiration of it: "His name will be called Wonderful" (Is 9:6). And this Lamb did possess truly wonderful power, because being slain, it killed the lion – that lion, I say, of which it says: "Your enemy, the devil, goes about like a roaring lion, seeking whom he can devour" (1 Pt 5:8). And so this Lamb, victorius and glorious, deserved to be called a lion: "Look! The Lion of the tribe of Judah has conquered" (Rv 5:5).

The testimony he bears is brief, **Look! There is the Lamb of God**. It is brief both because the disciples before whom he testified had already been sufficiently instructed about Christ from the things they had heard from John, and also because this is sufficient for John's intention, whose only aim was to lead them to Christ. Yet he does not say, "Go to him," so that the disciples would not seem to be doing Christ a favor by following him. But he does praise the grace of Christ so that they would regard it as of benefit to themselves if they followed Christ. And so he says, **Look! There is the Lamb of God**, i.e., here is the One in whom is found the grace and the power which cleanses from sin; for the lamb was offered for sins, as we have said.

284 The fruit of his testimony is given when he says, **Hearing this, the two disciples followed Jesus**. First, the fruit resulting from the testimony of John and his disciples is given. Secondly, the fruit resulting from the preaching of Christ (v 43). In relation to the first: first, the fruit arising from John's testimony is given; secondly, the fruit coming from the preaching of one of his disciples (v 40). With respect to the first he does two things. First, he shows the very beginning of the fruit coming from John's testimony. Secondly, its consummation as accomplished by Christ (v 38).

285 He says, **Hearing this**, John saying, "Look! There is the Lamb of God," **the two disciples**, who were with him, **followed Jesus**, literally, going with him.

We can note four points in this, according to Chrysostom.

First, the fact that it is John who speaks while Christ is silent, and that disciples gather to Christ through the words of John, all this points out a mystery. For Christ is the groom of the Church, and John, the friend and groomsman of the groom. Now the function of the groomsman is to present the bride to the groom, and verbally make known the agreements; the role of the groom is to be silent, from modesty, and to make arrangements for his new bride as he wills. Thus, the disciples are presented by John to Christ and espoused in faith. John speaks, Christ is silent; yet after Christ accepts them, he carefully instructs them.

We can note, secondly, that no one was converted when John praised the dignity of Christ, saying, he "ranks ahead of me," and "I am not worthy to unfasten the strap of his sandal." But the disciples followed Christ when John revealed Christ's humility and about the mystery of the incarnation; and this is because we are more moved by Christ's humility and the sufferings he endured for us. So it is said: "Your name is like oil poured out," i.e., mercy, by which you have obtained salvation for all; and the text immediately follows with, "young maidens have greatly loved you" (Sg 1:2).

We can note, thirdly, that the words of a preacher are like seed falling on different kinds of ground: on one they bear fruit, and on another they do not. So too, John, when he preaches, does not convert all his disciples to Christ, but only two, those who were well disposed. The others are envious of Christ, and they even question him, as mentioned in Matthew (9:14).

Fourthly, we may note that John's disciples, after hearing his witness to Christ, did not at once thrust themselves forward to speak with him hastily; rather, seriously and with a certain modesty, they tried to speak to Christ alone and in a private place: "There is a time and fitness for everything" (Ecc 8:6).

286   The consummation of this fruit is now set forth (v 38), for what John began is completed by Christ, since "the law brought nothing to perfection" (Heb 7:19). And Christ does two things. First, he questions the disciples who were following him. Secondly, he teaches them (v 39). As to the first we have: first, the question of Christ is given; secondly, the answer of the disciples.

287   He says, **Jesus turned around, and seeing them following him said.** According to the literal sense we should understand that Christ was walking in front of them, and these two disciples, following him, did not see his face at all; and so Christ turns to them to bolster their confidence. This lets us know that Christ gives confidence and hope to all who begin to follow him with a pure heart: "She goes to meet those who desire her" (Wis 6:14). Now Jesus turns

to us in order that we may see him; this will happen in that blessed vision when he will show us his face, as is said: "Show us your face, and we will be saved" (Ps 79:4). For as long as we are in this world we see his back, because it is through his effects that we acquire a knowledge of him; so it is said, "You will see my back" (Ex 33:23). Again, he turns to give us the riches of his mercy. This is requested in Psalm 89 (13): "Turn to us, O Lord." For as long as Christ withholds the help of his mercy he seems to be turned away from us. And so Jesus turned to the disciples of John who were following him in order to show them his face and to pour his grace upon them.

288 Christ examines them specifically about their intention. For all who follow Christ do not have the same intention: some follow him for the sake of temporal goods, and others for spiritual goods. And so the Lord asks their intention, saying, **What are you looking for?**; not in order to learn their intention, but so that, after they showed a proper intention, he might make them more intimate friends and show that they are worthy to hear him.

289 It may be remarked that these are the first words which Christ speaks in this Gospel. And this is appropriate, because the first thing that God asks of a man is a proper intention. And, according to Origen, after the six words that John had spoken, Christ spoke the seventh. The first words spoken by John were when, bearing witness to Christ, he cried out, saying, "This is the one of whom I said." The second is when he said, "I am not worthy to unfasten the strap of his sandal." The third is, "I baptize with water. But there is one standing in your midst whom you do not recognize." The fourth is, "Look! There is the Lamb of God." The fifth, "I saw the Spirit coming down on him from heaven like a dove." The sixth, when he says here, "Look! There is the Lamb of God." But it is Christ who speaks the seventh words so that we may understand, in a mystical sense, that rest, which is signified by the seventh day, will come to us through Christ, and that in him is found the fulness of the seven gifts of the Holy Spirit.

290 The disciples answer; and although there was one question, they gave two answers. First, why they are following Christ, namely, to learn; thus they call him Teacher, **Rabbi (which means Teacher).** As if to say: We ask you to teach us. For they already knew what is stated in Matthew (23:10): "You have one Teacher, the Christ." The second answer is what they want in following him, that is, **Where do you live?** And literally, it can be said that in truth they were looking for the home of Christ. For because of the great and wonderful things they had heard about him from John, they were not satisfied with questioning him only once and in a superficial way, but wanted to do so frequently and seriously. And so they wanted to know

where his home was so that they might visit him often, according to the advice of the wise man: "If you see a man of understanding, go to him early" (Sir 6:36), and "Happy is the man who hears me, who watches daily at my gates" (Prv 8:34).

In the allegorical sense, God's home is in heaven, according to the Psalm (122:1): "I have lifted up my eyes to you, who live in heaven." So they asked where Christ was living because our purpose in following him should be that Christ leads us to heaven, i.e., to heavenly glory.

Finally, in the moral sense, they ask, **Where do you live?** as though desiring to learn what qualities men should possess in order to be worthy to have Christ dwell in them. Concerning this dwelling Ephesians (2:22) says: "You are being built into a dwelling place for God." And the Song (1:6) says: "Show me, you whom my soul loves, where you graze your flock, where you rest at midday."

291 Then when he says, **Come and see**, Christ's instruction of the disciples is given. First we have the instruction of the disciples by Christ; secondly, their obedience is cited; and thirdly, the time is given.

292 First he says, **Come and see**, that is, where I live. There is a difficulty here: for since the Lord says, "The Son of Man does not have any place to lay his head" (Mt 8:20), why does he tell them to **Come and see** where he lives? I answer, according to Chrysostom, that when the Lord says, "The Son of Man does not have any place to lay his head," he showed that he had no home of his own, but not that he did not remain in someone else's home. And such was the home he invited them to see, saying, **Come and see**.

In the mystical sense, he says, **Come and see**, because the dwelling of God, whether of glory or grace, cannot be known except by experience: for it cannot be explained in words: "I will give him a white stone upon which is written a new name, which no one knows but he who receives it" (Rv 2:17). And so he says, **Come and see**: **Come**, by believing and working; **and see**, by experiencing and understanding.

293 It should be noted that we can attain to this knowledge in four ways. First, by doing good works; so he says, **Come**: "When shall I come and appear before the face of God" (Ps 41:3). Secondly, by the rest or stillness of the mind: "Be still and see" (Ps 45:10). Thirdly, by tasting the divine sweetness: "Taste and see that the Lord is sweet" (Ps 33:9). Fourthly, by acts of devotion: "Let us lift up our hearts and hands in prayer" (Lam 3:41). And so the Lord says: "It is I myself. Feel and see" (Lk 24:39).

294   Next the obedience of the disciples is mentioned; for immediately **they went and saw**, because by coming they saw him, and seeing they did not leave him. Thus it says, **and they stayed with him the rest of that day**, for as stated below (6:45): "Every one who hears the Father, and has learned, comes to me." For those who leave Christ have not yet seen him as they should. But those who have seen him by perfectly believing **stayed with him the rest of that day**; hearing and seeing that blessed day, they spent a blessed night: "Happy are your men, and happy are your servants, who always stand before you" (1 Kgs 8:10). And as Augustine says: "Let us also build a dwelling in our heart and fashion a home where he may come and teach us."

And he says, **that day**, because there can be no night where the light of Christ is present, where there is the Sun of justice.

295   The time is given when he says, **It was about the tenth hour**. The Evangelist mentions this in order that, considering the literal sense, he might give credit to Christ and the disciples. For the tenth hour is near the end of the day. And this praises Christ who was so eager to teach that not even the lateness of the hour induced him to postpone teaching them; but he taught them at the tenth hour. "In the morning sow your seed, and in the evening do not let your hands be idle" (Ecc 11:6).

296   The moderation of the disciples is also praised, because even at the tenth hour, when men usually have eaten and are less self-possessed for receiving wisdom, they were both self-possessed and prepared to hear wisdom and were not hindered because of food or wine. But this is not unexpected, for they had been disciples of John, whose drink was water and whose food was the locust and wild honey.

297   According to Augustine, however, the tenth hour signifies the law, which was given in ten precepts. And so the disciples came to Christ at the tenth hour and remained with him to be taught so that the law might be fulfilled by Christ, since it could not be fulfilled by the Jews. And so at that hour he is called Rabbi, that is, Teacher.

298   Then (v 40), he sets forth the fruit produced by the disciple of John who was converted to Christ. First, the disciple is described; secondly, the fruit begun by him (v 41); thirdly, the consummation of this fruit by Christ (v 42).

299   The disciple is described by name when he says, **Andrew**, i.e., "manly". "Act manfully, and let your heart be strong," as it says in Psalm 30 (v 25). He mentions his name in order to show his

privilege: he was not only the first to be perfectly converted to Christ, but he also preached Christ. So, as Stephen was the first martyr after Christ, so Andrew was the first Christian.

He is described, secondly, by his relationship, that is, as **Simon Peter's brother**, for he was the younger. And this is mentioned to commend him, for although younger in age, he became first in faith.

He is described, thirdly, by his discipleship, because he was **one of the two who had followed him**. His name is mentioned in order to show that Andrew's privilege was remarkable. For the name of the other disciple is not mentioned: either because it was John the Evangelist himself, who through humility followed the practice in his Gospel of not mentioning his own name when he was involved in some event; or, according to Chrysostom, because the other one was not a notable person, nor had he done anything great, and so there was no need to mention his name. Luke does the same in his Gospel (10:1), where he does not mention the names of the seventy-two disciples sent out by the Lord, because they were not the outstanding and important persons that the apostles were. Or, according to Alcuin, this other disciple was Philip: for the Evangelist, after discussing Andrew, begins at once with Philip, saying: "On the following day Jesus wanted to go to Galilee, and coming upon Philip" (below 1:43).

He is commended, fourthly, for the zeal of his devotion; hence he says that Andrew **followed him**, i.e., Jesus: "My foot has followed in his steps" (Jb 23:11).

300 The fruit begun by Andrew is mentioned when he says, **The first thing he did was to look for his brother Simon**. He first mentions the one for whom he bore fruit, that is, his brother, in order to mark the perfection of his conversion. For as Peter says, in the *Itinerary of Clement*, the evident sign of a perfect conversion of anyone is that, once converted, the closer one is to him the more he tries to convert him to Christ. And so Andrew, being now perfectly converted, does not keep the treasure he found to himself, but hurries and quickly runs to his brother to share with him the good things he has received. And so he says the **first thing he**, that is, Andrew, **did was to look for his brother Simon**, so that related in blood he might make him related in faith: "A brother that is helped by his brother is like a strong city" (Prv 18:19); "Let him who hears say, 'Come' " (Rv 22:17).

301 Secondly, he mentions the words spoken by Andrew, **We have found the Messiah (which means the Christ)**. Here, according to Chrysostom, he is tacitly answering a certain question: namely, that if someone were to ask what they had been instructed

about by Christ, they would have the ready answer that through the testimony of the Scriptures he instructed him in such a way that he knew he was the Christ. And so he says, **We have found the Messiah.** He implies by this that he had previously sought him by desire for a long time: "Happy is the man who finds wisdom" (Prv 3:13).

"Messiah," which is Hebrew, is translated as "Christos" in Greek, and in Latin as "Unctus" (anointed), because he was anointed in a special way with invisible oil, the oil of the Holy Spirit. So Andrew explicitly designates him by this title: "Your God has anointed you with the oil of gladness above your fellows," i.e., above all the saints. For all the saints are anointed with that oil, but Christ was singularly anointed and is singularly holy. So, as Chrysostom says, he does not simply call him "Messiah," but **the Messiah.**

302 Thirdly, he mentions the fruit he produced, because **he brought him**, that is, Peter, **to Jesus.** This gives recognition to Peter's obedience, for he came at once, without delay. And consider the devotion of Andrew: for he brought him to Jesus and not to himself (for he knew that he himself was weak); and so he leads him to Christ to be instructed by him. This shows us that the efforts and the aim of preachers should not be to win for themselves the fruits of their preaching, i.e., to turn them to their own private benefit and honor, but to bring them to Jesus, i.e., to refer them to his glory and honor: "What we preach is not ourselves, but Jesus Christ," as is said in 2 Corinthians (4:5).

303 The consummation of this fruit is given when he says, **Looking at him intently Jesus said.** Here Christ, wishing to raise him up to faith in his divinity, begins to perform works of divinity, making know things that are hidden. First of all, things which are hidden in the present: so **looking at him**, i.e, as soon as Jesus saw him, he considered him by the power of his divinity and called him by name, saying, **You are Simon.** This is not surprising, for as it is said: "Man sees the appearances, but the Lord sees the heart" (1 Sm 16:7). This name is appropriate for the mystery. For "Simon" means "obedient," to indicate that obedience is necessary for one who has been converted to Christ through faith: "He gives the Holy Spirit to all who obey him" (Acts 5:32).

304 Secondly, he reveals things hidden in the past. Hence he says, **son of John**, because that was the name of Simon's father; or he says, "son of Jonah," as we find in Matthew (16:17), "Simon Bar-Jonah." And each name is appropriate to this mystery. For "John" means "grace," to indicate that it is through grace that men come to the faith of Christ: "You are saved by his grace" (Eph 2:5). And "Jonah" means "dove," to indicate that it is by the Holy Spirit,

who has been given to us, that we are made strong in our love for God: "The love of God is poured out into our hearts by the Holy Spirit" (Rom 5:5).

305 Thirdly, he reveals things hidden in the future. So he says, **you are to be called Cephas (which is translated Peter)**, and in Greek, "head." And this is appropriate to this mystery, which is that he who was to be the head of the others and the vicar of Christ should remain firm. As Matthew (16:18) says: "You are Peter, and upon this rock I will build my church."

306 There is a question here about the literal meaning. First, why did Christ give Simon a name at the beginning of his conversion, rather than will that he have this name from the time of his birth? Two different answers have been given for this. The first, according to Chrysostom, is that divinely given names indicate a certain eminence in spiritual grace. Now when God confers a special grace upon anyone, the name indicating that grace is given at one's brith: as in the case of John the Baptist, who was named before he was born, because he had been sanctified in his mother's womb. But sometimes a special grace is given during the course of one's life: then such names are divinely given at that time and not at birth: as in the case of Abraham and Sarah, whose names were changed when they received the promise that their posterity would multiply. Likewise, Peter is named in a divine way when he is called to the faith of Christ and to the grace of apostleship, and particularly because he was appointed Prince of the apostles of the entire Church — which was not done with the other apostles.

But, according to Augustine, if he had been called Cephas from birth, this mystery would not have been apparent. And so the Lord willed that he should have one name at birth, so that by changing his name the mystery of the Church, which was built on his confession of faith, would be apparent. Now "Peter" (*Petrus*) is derived from "rock" (*petra*). But the rock was Christ. Thus, the name "Peter" signifies the Church, which was built upon that solid and immovable rock which is Christ.

307 The second question is whether this name was given to Peter at this time, or at the time mentioned by Matthew (16:18). Augustine answers that this name was given to Simon at this time; and at the event reported by Matthew the Lord is not giving this name but reminding him of the name that was given, so that Christ is using this name as already given. But others think that this name was given when the Lord said, "You are Peter, and upon this rock I will build my church" (Mt 16:18); and in this passage in the Gospel of John, Christ is not giving this name, but foretelling what will be given later.

308   The third question is about the calling of Peter and Andrew: for here it says that they were called near the Jordan, because they were John's disciples; but in Matthew (4:18) it says that Christ called them by the Sea of Galilee. The answer to this is that there was a triple calling of the apostles. The first was a call to knowledge or friendship and faith; and this is the one recorded here. The second consisted in the prediction of their office: "From now on you will be catching men" (Lk 5:10). The third call was to their apostleship, which is mentioned by Matthew (4:18). This was the perfect call because after this they were not to return to their own pursuits.

LECTURE 16

43 On the following day Jesus wanted to go to Galilee, and coming upon Philip, he said, "Follow me." 44 Now Philip came from Bethsaida, the same town as Andrew and Peter. 45 Philip sought out Nathanael, and said to him, "We have found the one Moses spoke of in the law – the prophets too – Jesus, son of Joseph, from Nazareth." 46 "From Nazareth!" Nathanael replied, "What good can come from that place?" Philip said, "Come and see." 47 When Jesus saw Nathanael coming toward him, he said of him: "Here is a true Israelite, in whom there is no guile." 48 Nathanael asked him, "How do you know me?" Jesus replied and said, "Before Philip called you, I saw you when you were sitting under the fig tree." 49 "Rabbi," said Nathanael, "you are the Son of God; you are the King of Israel." 50 Jesus responded and said, "You believed just because I said to you that I saw you sitting under the fig tree! You will see greater things than this." 51 He went on to say, "Amen, amen, I say to you, you will see the heavens opened and the angels of God ascending and descending on the Son of Man."

309   After having shown the fruit produced by John's preaching and that of his disciples, the Evangelist now shows the fruit obtained from the preaching of Christ. First, he deals with the conversion of one disciple as the result of Christ's preaching. Secondly, the conversion of others due to the preaching of the disciple just converted to Christ (v 45). As to the first he does three things: first, the occasion when the disciple is called is given; secondly, his calling is described; thirdly, his situation.
310   The occasion of his calling was the departure of Jesus

from Judea. So he says, **On the following day Jesus wanted to go to Galilee, and coming upon Philip**. There are three reasons why Jesus left for Galilee, two of which are literal. One of these is that after being baptized by John and desiring to shed honor on the Baptist, he left Judea for Galilee so that his presence would not obscure and lessen John's teaching authority (while he still retained that state); and this teaches us to show honor to one another, as is said in Romans (12:10).

The second reason is that there are no distinguished persons in Galilee: "No prophet is to rise from Galilee" (below 7:52). And so, to show the greatness of his power, Christ wished to go there and choose there the princes of the earth, who are greater than the prophets: "He has turned the desert into pools of water," as we read in Psalm 106 (v 35).

The third reason is mystical: for "Galilee" means "passage." So Christ desired to go from Judea into Galilee in order to indicate that on "on the following day," i.e., on the day of grace, that is, the day of the Good News, he would pass from Judea into Galilee, i.e., to save the Gentiles: "Is he going to go to those who are dispersed among the Gentiles, and teach the Gentiles?" (below 7:35).

311 A disciple's vocation is to follow: hence he says that after Christ found Philip he said, **Follow me**. Note that sometimes man finds God, but without knowing it, as it were: "He who finds me will find life, and will have salvation from the Lord" (Prv 8:35). And at other times God finds the man, in order to bestow honor and greatness upon him: "I have found David, my servant" (Ps 88:21). Christ found Philip in this way, that is, to call him to the faith and to grace. And so he says at once, **Follow me**.

312 There is a question here: Why did not Jesus call his disciples at the very beginning? Chrysostom answers that he did not wish to call anyone before someone clung to him spontaneoulsy because of John's preaching, for men are drawn by example more than by words.

313 One might also ask why Philip followed Christ immediately after only a word, while Andrew followed Christ after hearing about him from John, and Peter after hearing from Andrew.

Three answers can be given. One is that Philip had already been instructed by John: for according to one of the explanations given above, Philip was that other disciple who followed Christ along with Andrew. Another is that Christ's voice had power not only to act on one's hearing from without, but also on the heart from within: "My words are like fire" (Jer 23:29). For the voice of Christ was spoken not only to the exterior, but it enkindled the interior of the faithful to love him. The third answer is that Philip had perhaps already been instructed about Christ by Andrew and Peter, since they were from the same town. In fact, this is what the Evangelist seems to imply by adding, **Now Philip came from Bethsaida, the same town as Andrew and Peter.**

314   This gives us the situation of the disciples he called: for they were from Bethsaida. And this is appropriate to this mystery. For "Bethsaida" means "house of hunters," to show the attitude of Philip, Peter and Andrew at that time, and because it was fitting to call, from the house of hunters, hunters who were to capture souls for life: "I will send my hunters" (Jer 16:16).

315   Now the fruit produced by the disciple who was converted to Christ is given. First, the beginning of the fruit, coming from this disciple. Secondly, its consummation by Christ (v 47). As to the first, he does three things: first, the statement of Philip is given; secondly, Nathanael's response; and thirdly, Philip's ensuing advice.

316   As to the first, note that just as Andrew, after having been perfectly converted, was eager to lead his brother to Christ, so too Philip with regard to his brother, Nathanael. And so he says that Philip found Nathanael, whom he probably looked for as Andrew did for Peter; and this was a sign of a perfect conversion. The word "Nathanael" means "gift of God"; and it is God's gift if anyone is converted to Christ.

He tells him that all the prophecies and the law have been fulfilled, and that the desires of their holy forefathers are not in vain, but have been guaranteed, and that what God has promised was now accomplished. **We have found the one Moses spoke of in the law – the prophets too – Jesus.** We understand by this that Nathanael was fairly learned in the law, and that Philip, now having learned about Christ, wished to lead Nathanael to Christ through the things he himself knew, that is, from the law and the prophets. So he says, **the one Moses spoke of in the law.** For Moses wrote of Christ: "If you believed Moses, you would perhaps believe me, for he wrote of me" (below 5:46). **The prophets too** wrote of Christ: "All the prophets bear witness to him" (Acts 10:43).

317   Note that Philip says three things about Christ that are in agreement with the law and the prophets. First, the name: for he says, **We have found Jesus.** And this agrees with the prophets: "I will send them a Savior" (Is 19:20); "I will rejoice in God, my Jesus" (Hb 3:18).

Secondly, the family from which Christ took his human origin, when he says, **son of Joseph,** i.e., who was of the house and family of David. And although Jesus did not derive his origin from him, yet he did derive it from the Virgin, who was of the same line as Joseph. He calls him the **son of Joseph**, because Jesus was considered to be the son of the one to whom his mother was married. So it is said: "the son of Joseph (as was supposed)" (Lk 3:23). Nor is it strange that Philip called him the son of Joseph, since his own mother, who was aware of his divine incarnation, called him his son: "Your father and I have been looking for you in sorrow" (Lk 2:48). Indeed, if one is called the son of another because he is supported by him, this is more reason why Joseph should be called the father of Jesus, even though he was not so according to the flesh: for he not only supported him, but was the husband of his virgin mother. However, Philip calls him the son of Joseph (not as though he was born from the union of Joseph and the Virgin) because he knew that Christ would be born from the line of David; and this was the house and family of Joseph, to whom Mary was married. And this also is in agreement with the prophets: "I will raise up a just branch for David" (Jer 23:5).

Thirdly, he mentions his native land, saying, **from Nazareth**; not because he had been born there, but because he was brought up there; but he had been born in Bethlehem. Philip omits to mention Bethlehem but not Nazareth because, while the birth of Christ was not known to many, the place where he was brought up was. And this also agrees with the prophets: "A shoot will arise from the root of Jesse, and a flower (or Nazarene, according to another version) will rise up from his roots" (Is 11:1).

318   Then when he says, **Nathanael replied**, the answer of Nathanael is given. His answer can be interpreted as an assertion or as a question; and in either way it is suitable to Philip's affirmation. If it is taken as an assertion, as Augustine does, the meaning is: "Some good can come from Nazareth." In other words, from a city with that name it is possible that there come forth to us some very excellent grace or some outstanding teacher to preach to us about the flower of the virtues and the purity of sanctity; for "Nazareth" means "flower." We can understand from this that Nathanael, being quite learned in the law and a student of the Scriptures, knew that the Savior was expected to come from Nazareth — something that was not so clear even to the Scribes and Pharisees. And so when Philip said, **We have found Jesus from Nazareth**, his hopes were lifted and he answered: "Indeed, some good can come from Nazareth."

But if we take his answer as a question, as Chrysostom does, then the sense is: **From Nazareth! What good can come from that place?** As if to say: Everything else you say seems credible, because his name and his lineage are consistent with the prophecies; but your statement that he is **from Nazareth** does not seem possible. For Nathanael understood from the Scriptures that the Christ was to come from Bethlehem, according to: "And you, Bethlehem, land of Judah, are not the least among the princes of Judah: for out of you a ruler will come forth, who will rule my people Israel," as we read in Matthew (2:6). And so, not finding Philip's statement in agreement with the prophecy, he prudently and moderately inquires about its truth, **What good can come from that place?**

319   Then Philip's advice is given, **Come and see.** And this advice suits either interpretation of Nathanael's answer. To the assertive interpretation it is as though he says: You say that something good can come from Nazareth, but I say that the good I state to you is of such a nature and so marvelous that I am unable to express it in words, so **Come and see.** To the interpretation that makes it a question, it as as though he says: You wonder and say: **What good can come from that place?**, thinking that this is impossible according to the Scriptures. But if you are willing to experience what I experienced, you will understand that what I say is true, so **Come and see.**

Then, not discouraged by his questions, Philip brings Nathanael to Christ. He knew that he would no longer argue with him if he tasted the words and teaching of Christ. And in this, Philip was imitating Christ who earlier answered those who had asked about the place where he lived: "Come and see." "Come to him, and be enlightened" (Ps 33:6).

320   Then when he says, **When Jesus saw Nathanael,** the consummation of this fruit by Christ is described. We should note that there are two ways in which men are converted to Christ: some by miracles they have seen and things experienced in themselves or in others; others are converted through internal insights, through prophecy and the foreknowledge of what is hidden in the future. The second way is more efficacious than the first: for devils and certain men who receive their help can simulate marvels; but to predict the future can only be done by divine power. "Tell us what is to come, and we will say that you are gods" (Is 41:23); "Prophecies are for those who believe." And so our Lord draws Nathanael to the faith not by miracles but by making known things which are hidden. And so he says of him, **Here is a true Israelite, in whom there is no guile.**

321   Christ mentions three hidden matters: things hidden in the present, in the heart; past facts; and future heavenly matters. To know these three things is not a human but a divine achievement.

He mentions things hidden in the present when he says, **Here is a true Israelite, in whom there is no guile.** Here we have, first, the prior revelation of Christ; secondly, Nathanael's question, **How do you know me?**

322 First he says, **When Jesus saw Nathanael coming toward him.** As if to say: Before Nathanael reached him, Jesus said, **Here is a true Israelite.** He said this about him before he came to him, because had he said it after he came, Nathanael might have believed that Jesus had heard it from Philip.

Christ said, **Here is a true Israelite, in whom there is no guile.** Now "Israel" has two meanings. One of these, as the Gloss says, is "most righteous". "Do not fear, my most righteous servant, whom I have chosen" (Is 44:2). Its second meaning is "the man who sees God." And according to each meaning Nathanael is a true Israelite. For since one in whom there is no guile is called righteous, Nathanael is said to be **a true Israelite, in whom there is no guile.** As if to say: You truly represent your race because you are righteous and without guile. Further, because man sees God through cleanness of heart and simplicity, Christ said, **a true Israelite**, i.e., you are a man who truly sees God because you are simple and without guile.

Further, he said, **in whom there is no guile**, so that we do not think that it was with malice that Nathanael asked: **What good can come from that place?**

323 Augustine has a different explanation of this passage. It is clear that all are born under sin. Now those who have sin in their hearts but outwardly pretend to be just are called guileful. But a sinner who admits that he is a sinner is not guileful. So Christ said, **Here is a true Israelite, in whom there is no guile**, not because Nathanael was without sin, or because he had no need of a physician, for no one is born in such a way as not to need a physician; but he was praised by Christ because he admitted his sins.

324 Then when he says, **How do you know me?**, we have Nathanael's question. For Nathanael, in wonder at the divine power in this revelation of what is hidden, because this can only be from God — "The heart is depraved and inscrutable, and who is able to know it? I the Lord search the heart and probe the loins" (Jer 17:9); "Man sees the appearances, but the Lord sees the heart" (1 Sm 16:7) — asks, **How do you know me?** Here we can recognize Nathanael's humility, because, although he had been praised, he did not become elated, but held this praise of himself suspect. "My people, who call you blessed, they are deceiving you" (Is 3:12).

325 Then he touches on matters in the past, saying, **Before Philip called you, I saw you when you were sitting under the fig tree.** First we have the statement of Christ; secondly, the confession of Nathanael.

326 As to the first, we should note that Nathanael might have had two misgivings about Christ. One, that Christ said this in order to win his friendship by flattery; the other, that Christ had learned what he knew from others. So, to remove Nathanael's suspicions and raise him to higher things, Christ reveals certain hidden matters that no one could know except in a divine way, that is, things that related only to Nathanael. He refers to these when he says, **Before Philip called you, I saw you when you were sitting under the fig tree.** In the literal sense, this means that Nathanael was under a fig tree when he was called by Philip — which Christ knew by divine power, for "The eyes of the Lord are far brighter than the sun" (Sir 23:28).

In the mystical sense, the fig tree signifies sin: both because we find a fig tree, bearing only leaves but no fruit, being cursed, as a symbol of sin (Mt 11:19); and because Adam and Eve, after they had sinned, made clothes from fig leaves. So he says here, **when you were sitting under the fig tree**, i.e., under the shadow of sin, before you were called to grace, **I saw you**, with the eye of mercy; for God's predestination looks upon the predestined, who are living under sin, with an eye of pity, for as Ephesians (1:4) says, " He chose us before the foundation of the world." And he speaks of this eye here: **I saw you**, by predestining you from eternity.

Or, the meaning is, according to Gregory: **I saw you when you were sitting under the fig tree**, i.e., under the shadow of the law. "The law has only a shadow of the good things to come" (Heb 10:1).

327 Hearing this, Nathanael is immediately converted, and, seeing the power of the divinity in Christ, breaks out in words of conversion and praise, saying, **Rabbi, you are the Son of God.** Here he considers three things about Christ. First, the fullness of his knowledge, when he says, **Rabbi**, which is translated as Teacher. As if to say: You are perfect in knowledge. For he had already realized what is said in Matthew (23:10): "You have one Teacher, the Christ." Secondly, the excellence of his singular grace, when he says, **you are the Son of God.** For it is due to grace alone that one becomes a son of God by adoption. And it is also through grace that one is a son of God through union; and this is exclusive to the man Christ, because that man is the Son of God not due to any preceding merit, but through the grace of union. Thirdly, he considers the greatness of his power when he says, **you are the King of Israel**, i.e., awaited by Israel as its king and defender: "His power is everlasting" (Dn 7:14).

328 A question comes up at this point, according to Chrysostom. For since Peter, who after many miracles and much teaching, confessed what Nathanael confesses here about Christ, that is, **you**

are the Son of God, merited a blessing, as the Lord said: "Blessed are you, Simon Bar-Jona" (Mt 16:17), why not the same for Nathanael, who said the same thing before seeing any miracles or receiving any teaching? Chrysostom answers that the reason for this is that even though Nathanael and Peter spoke the same words, the meaning of the two was not the same. For Peter acknowledged that Christ was the true Son of God by nature, i.e., he was man, and yet truly God; but Nathanael acknowledged that Christ was the Son of God by means of adoption, in the sense of, "I said: You are gods, and all of you the sons of the Most High"(Ps 81:6). This is clear from what Nathanael said next: for if he had understood that Christ was the Son of God by nature, he would not have said, **you are the King of Israel**, but "of the whole world." It is also clear from the fact that Christ added nothing to the faith of Peter, since it was perfect, but stated that he would build the Church on that profession. But he raises Nathanael to greater things, since the greater part of his profession was deficient; to greater things, i.e., to a knowledge of his divinity.

329   And so he said, **You will see greater things than this**. Here we have, thirdly, an allusion to the future. As if to say: Because I have revealed the past to you, you believe that I am the Son of God only by adoption, and the King of Israel; but I will bring you to greater knowledge, so that you may believe that I am the natural Son of God, and the King of all ages. And accordingly he says, **Amen, amen, I say to you, you will see the heavens opened and the angels of God ascending and descending on the Son of Man**. By this, according to Chrysostom, the Lord wishes to prove that he is the true Son of God, and God. For the peculiar task of angels is to minister and be subject: "Bless the Lord, all of you, his angels, his ministers, who do his will" (Ps 102:20). So when you see angels minister to me, you will be certain that I am the true Son of God. "When he leads his First-Begotten into the world, he says: 'Let all the angels of God adore him' " (Heb 1:6).

330   When did the apostles see this? They saw it, I say, during the passion, when an angel stood by to comfort Christ (Lk 22:13); again, at the resurrection, when the apostles found two angels who were standing over the tomb. Again, at the ascension, when the angels said to the apostles: "Men of Galilee, why are you standing here looking up to heaven? This Jesus, who has been taken from you into heaven, will come in the same way as you have seen him going into heaven" (Acts 1:11).

331   Because Christ spoke the truth about the past, it was easier for Nathanael to believe what he foretells about the future, saying, **you will see**. For one who has revealed the truth about things hidden

in the past, has an evident argument that what he is saying about the future is true. He says, **the angels of God ascending and descending on the Son of Man**, because, in his mortal flesh, he was a little less than the angels; and from this point of view, angels ascend and descend upon him. But insofar as he is the Son of God, he is above the angels, as was said.

332 According to Augustine, Christ is here revealing his divinity in a beautiful way. For it is recorded that Jacob dreamed of a ladder, standing on the ground, with "the angels of God ascending and descending on it" (Gn 28:16). Then Jacob arose and poured oil on a stone and said, "Truly, the Lord is in this place" (Gn 28:16). Now that stone is Christ, whom the builders rejected; and the invisible oil of the Holy Spirit was poured on him. He is set up as a pillar, because he was to be the foundation of the Church: "No one can lay another foundation except that which has been laid" (1 Cor 3:11). The angels are ascending and descending inasmuch as they are ministering and serving before him. So he said, **Amen, amen, I say to you, you will see the heavens opened**, and so forth, as if to say: Because you are truly an Israelite, give heed to what Israel saw, so that you many believe that I am the one signified by the stone anointed by Jacob, for you also will see angels ascending and descending upon him [viz. Jesus].

333 Or, the angels are, according to Augustine, the preachers of Christ: "Go, swift angels, to a nation rent and torn to pieces," as it says in Isaiah (18:2). They ascend through contemplation, just as Paul had ascended even to the third heaven (2 Cor 12:2); and they descend by instructing their neighbor. **On the Son of Man**, i.e., for the honor of Christ, because "what we preach is not ourselves, but Jesus Christ" (2 Cor 4:5). In order that they might ascend and descend, the heavens were opened, because heavenly graces must be given to preachers if they are to ascend and descend. "The heavens broke at the presence of God" (Ps 67:9); "I saw the heavens open" (Rv 4:1).

334 Now the reason why Nathanael was not chosen to be an apostle after such a profession of faith is that Christ did not want the conversion of the world to the faith to be attributed to human wisdom, but solely to the power of God. And so he did not choose Nathanael as an apostle, since he was very learned in the law; he rather chose simple and uneducated men. "Not many of you are learned," and "God chose the simple of the world" (1 Cor 1:26).

2

LECTURE 1

1 On the third day there was a wedding at Cana in Galilee, and the mother of Jesus was there. 2 Jesus and his disciples were also invited to the feast. 3 When the wine ran out, the mother of Jesus said to him, "They have no more wine." 4 Jesus then said to her, "Woman, what does that have to do with me and you? My time has not yet come." 5 His mother said to the servants, "Do whatever he tells you." 6 Now there were six stone water jars near by for purifications according to Jewish customs, each holding two or three metretes. 7 Jesus said to them, "Fill those jars with water." And they filled them to the top. 8 Then Jesus said to them, "Now pour out a drink and take it to the head waiter." They did as he instructed them. 9 Now when the head waiter tasted the water made wine, and not knowing where it came from (although the servants knew, since they had drawn the water), he called the groom over 10 and said to him, "People usually serve the choice wines first, and when the guests have had their fill, then they bring out inferior wine; but you have saved the best wine until now." 11 This beginning of signs Jesus worked in Cana of Galilee; and Jesus revealed his glory, and his disciples believed in him.

335 Above, the Evangelist showed the dignity of the incarnate Word and gave various evidence for it. Now he begins to relate the effects and actions by which the divinity of the incarnate Word was made known to the world. First, he tells the things Christ did, while living in the world, that show his divinity. Secondly, he tells how Christ showed his divinity while dying; and this from chapter twelve on.
As to the first he does two things. First, he shows the divinity of Christ in relation to the power he had over nature. Secondly, in relation to the effects of grace; and this from chapter three on. Christ's power over nature is pointed out to us by the fact that he changed a nature. And this change was accomplished by Christ as a sign: first, to his disciples, to strengthen them; secondly, to the people, to lead them to believe (2:12). This transformation of a nature, in order to strengthen the disciples, was accomplished at a marriage, when he turned water into wine. First, the marriage is described. Secondly, those present. Thirdly, the miracle performed by Christ.

336 In describing the marriage, the time is first mentioned. Hence he says, **On the third day there was a wedding**, i.e., after the

calling of the disciples mentioned earlier. For, after being made known by the testimony of John, Christ also wanted to make himself known. Secondly, the place is mentioned; hence he says, **at Cana in Galilee**. Galilee is a province, and Cana a small village located in that province.

337 As far as the literal meaning is concerned, we should note that there are two opinions about the time of Christ's preaching. Some say that there were two and a half years from Christ's baptism until his death. According to them, the events at this wedding took place in the same year that Christ was baptized. However, both the teaching and practice of the Church are opposed to this. For three miracles are commemorated on the feast of the Epiphany: the adoration of the Magi, which took place in the first year of the Lord's birth; secondly, the baptism of Christ, which implies that he was baptized on the same day thirty years later; thirdly, this marriage, which took place on the same day one year later. It follows from this that at least one year elapsed between his baptism and this marriage. In that year the only things recorded to have been done by the Lord are found in the sixth chapter of Matthew: the fasting in the desert, and the temptation by the devil; and what John tells us in this Gospel of the testimony by the Baptist and the conversion of the disciples. After this wedding, Christ began to preach publicly and to perform miracles up to the time of his passion, so that he preached publicly for two and one half years.

338 In the mystical sense, marriage signifies the union of Christ with his Church, because as the Apostle says: "This is a great mystery: I am speaking of Christ and his Church" (Eph 5:32). And this marriage was begun in the womb of the Virgin, when God the Father united a human nature to his Son in a unity of person. So, the chamber of this union was the womb of the Virgin: "He established a chamber for the sun" (Ps 18:6). Of this marriage it is said: "The kingdom of heaven is like a king who married his son" (Mt 22:2), that is, when God the Father joined a human nature to his Word in the womb of the Virgin. It was made public when the Chruch was joined to him by faith: "I will bind you to myself in faith" (Hos 2:20). We read of this marriage: "Blessed are they who are called to the marriage supper of the Lamb" (Rv 19:9). It will be consummated when the bride, i.e., the Church, is led into the resting place of the groom, i.e., into the glory of heaven.

The fact that this marriage took place on the third day is not without it own mystery. For the first day is the time of the law of nature; the second day is the time of the written law; but the third day is the time of grace, when the incarnate Lord celebrated the marriage: "He will revive us after two days; on the third day he will raise us up" (Hos 6:3).

The place too is appropriate. For "Cana" means "zeal," and "Galilee" means "passage." So this marriage was celebrated in the zeal of a passage, to suggest that those persons are most worthy of union with Christ who, burning with the zeal of a conscientious devotion, pass over from the state of guilt to the grace of the Church. "Pass over to me, all who desire me" (Sir 24:26). And they pass from death to life, i.e., from the state of mortality and misery to the state of immortality and glory: "I make all things new" (Rv 21:5).

339 Then the persons invited are described. Mention is made of three: the mother of Jesus, Jesus himself, and the disciples.

340 The mother of Jesus is mentioned when he says, **the mother of Jesus was there**. She is mentioned first to indicate that Jesus was still unknown and not invited to the wedding as a famous person, but merely as one acquaintance among others; for as they invited the mother, so also her son. Or, perhaps his mother is invited first because they were uncertain whether Jesus would come to a wedding if invited, because of the unusual piety they noticed in him and because they had not seen him at other social gatherings. So I think that they first asked his mother whether Jesus should be invited. That is why the Evangelist expressly said first that his mother was at the wedding, and that later Jesus was invited.

341 And this is what comes next: **Jesus was invited**. Christ decided to attend this wedding, first of all, to give us an example of humility. For he did not look to his own dignity, but "just as he condescended to accept the form of a servant, so he did not hesitate to come to the marriage of servants," as Chrysostom says. And as Augustine says: "Let man blush to be proud, for God became humble." For among his other acts of humility, the Son of the Virgin came to a marriage, which he had already instituted in paradise when he was with his Father. Of this example it is said: "Learn from me, for I am gentle and humble of heart" (Mt 11:29).

He came, secondly, to reject the error of those who condemn marriage, for as Bede says: "If there were sin in a holy marriage bed and in a marriage carried out with due purity, the Lord would not have come to the marriage." But because he did come, he implies that the baseness of those who denounce marriage deserves to be condemned. "If she marries, it is not a sin" (1 Cor 7:36).

342 The disciples are mentioned when he says, **and his disciples**.

343 In its mystical meaning, the mother of Jesus, the Blessed Virgin, is present in spiritual marriages as the one who arranges the marriage, because it is through her intercession that one is joined to Christ through grace: "In me is every hope of life and of strength"

(Sir 24:25). Christ is present as the true groom of the soul, as is said below (3:29): "It is the groom who has the bride." The disciples are the groomsmen uniting the Church to Christ, the one of whom it is said: "I betrothed you to one husband, to present you as a chaste virgin to Christ" (2 Cor 11:2).

344 At this physical marriage some role in the miracle belongs to the mother of Christ, some to Christ, and some to the disciples. When he says, **When the wine ran out**, he indicates the part of each. The role of Christ's mother was to superintend the miracle; the role of Christ to perform it; and the disciples were to bear witness to it. As to the first, Christ's mother assumed the role of a mediatrix. Hence she does two things. First, she intercedes with her Son. In the second place, she instructs the servants. As to the first, two things are mentioned. First, his mother's intercession; secondly, the answer of her Son.

345 In Mary's intercession, note first her kindness and mercy. For it is a quality of mercy to regard another's distress as one's own, because to be merciful is to have a heart distressed at the distress of another: "Who is weak, and I am not weak?" (2 Cor 11:29). And so because the Blessed Virgin was full of mercy, she desired to relieve the distress of others. So he says, **When the wine ran out, the mother of Jesus said to him**.

Note, secondly, her reverence for Christ: for because of the reverence we have for God it is sufficient for us merely to express our needs: "Lord, all my desires are known by you" (Ps 37:10). But it is not our business to wonder about the way in which God will help us, for as it is said: "We do not know what we should pray for as we ought" (Rom 8:26). And so his mother merely told him of their need, saying, **They have no more wine**.

Thirdly, note the Virgin's concern and care. For she did not wait until they were in extreme need, but **When the wine ran out**, that is, immediately. This is similar to what is said of God: "A helper in times of trouble" (Ps 9:10).

346 Chrysostom asks: Why did Mary never encourage Christ to perform any miracles before this time? For she had been told of his power by the angel, whose work had been confirmed by the many things she had seen happening in his regard, all of which she remembered, thinking them over in her heart (Lk 2:51). The reason is that before this time he lived like any other person. So, because the time was not appropriate, she put off asking him. But now, after John's witness to him and after the conversion of his disciples, she trustingly prompted Christ to perform miracles. In this she was true to the symbol of the synagogue, which is the mother of Christ: for it was

customary for the Jews to require miracles: "The Jews require signs" (1 Cor 1:22).

347 She says to him, **They have no more wine.** Here we should note that before the incarnation of Christ three wines were running out: the wine of justice, of wisdom, and of charity or grace. Wine stings, and in this respect it is a symbol of justice. The Samaritan poured wine and oil into the wounds of the injured man, that is, he mingled the severity of justice with the sweetness of mercy. "You have made us drink the wine of sorrow" (Ps 59:5). But wine also delights the heart, "Wine cheers the heart of man" (Ps 103:15). And in this respect wine is a symbol of wisdom, the meditation of which is enjoyable in the highest degree: "Her companionship has no bitterness" (Wis 8:16). Further, wine intoxicates: "Drink, friends, and be intoxicated, my dearly beloved" (Sg 5:1). And in this respect wine is a symbol of charity: "I have drunk my wine with my milk" (Sg 5:1). It is also a symbol of charity because of charity's fervor: "Wine makes the virgins flourish" (Zec 9:17).

The wine of justice was indeed running out in the old law, in which justice was imperfect. But Christ brought it to perfection: "Unless your justice is greater than that of the scribes and of the Pharisees, you will not enter into the kingdom of heaven" (Mt 5:20). The wine of wisdom was also running out, for it was hidden and symbolic, because as it says in 1 Corinthians (10:11): "All these things happened to them in symbol." But Christ plainly brought wisdom to light: "He was teaching them as one having authority" (Mt 7:29). The wine of charity was also running out, because they had received a spirit of serving only in fear. But Christ converted the water of fear into the wine of charity when he gave "the spirit of adoption as sons, by which we cry: 'Abba, Father' "(Rom 8:15), and when "the charity of God was poured out into our hearts," as Romans (5:5) says.

348 Then when he says, **Jesus said to her,** the answer of Christ is given. This answer has been the occasion for three heresies.

349 The Manicheans claim that Christ had only an imaginary body, not a real one. Valentinus maintained that Christ assumed a celestial body and that, as far as his body was concerned, Christ was not related to the Virgin at all. The source of this error was that he understood, **Woman, what does that have to do with me and you?** as if it meant: "I have received nothing from you." But this is contrary to the authority of Sacred Scripture. For the Apostle says: "God sent his Son, made from a woman" (Gal 4:4). Now Christ could not be said to have been made from her, unless he had taken something from her. Further, Augustine argues against them: "How do you

know that our Lord said, **What does that have to do with me and you?** You reply that it is because John says so. But he also says that the Virgin was the mother of Christ. So, if you believe the Evangelist when he states that Jesus said this to his mother, you should also belive him when he says, **and the mother of Jesus was there.**"

350 Then there was Ebion who said that Christ was conceived from a man's seed, and Elvidius, who said that the Virgin did not remain a virgin after childbirth. They were deceived by the fact that he said, **Woman**, which seems to imply the loss of virginity. But this is false, for in Sacred Scripture the word "woman" sometimes refers merely to the female sex, as it does in "made from a woman" (Gal 4:4). This is obvious also by the fact that Adam, speaking to God about Eve, said: "The woman whom you gave me as a companion, gave me fruit from the tree, and I ate it" (Gn 3:12); for Eve was still a virgin in Paradise, where Adam had not know her. Hence the fact that the mother of Christ is here called "woman" in this Gospel does not imply a loss of virginity, but refers to her sex.

351 The Priscillianists, however, erred by misunderstanding the words of Christ, **My time has not yet come.** They claimed that all things happen by fate, and that the actions of men, including those of Christ, are subject to predetermined times. And that is why, according to them, Christ said, **My time has not yet come.**

But this is false for any man. For since man has free choice, and this is because he has reason and will, both of which are spiritual, then obviously, as far as choice is concerned, man, so far from being subject to bodies, is really their master. For spiritual things are superior to material things, so much so that the Philosopher says that the wise man is master of the stars. Further, their heresy is even less true of Christ, who is the Lord and Creator of the stars. Thus when he says, **My time has not yet come**, he is referring to the time of his passion, which was fixed for him, not by necessity, according to divine providence. What is said in Sirach (33:7) is also contrary to their opinion: "Why is one day better than another?" And the answer is: "They have been differentiated by the knowledge of the Lord," i.e., they were differentiated from one another not by chance, but by God's providence.

352 Since we have eliminated the above opinions, let us look for the reason why our Lord answered, **Woman, what does that have to do with me and you?** For Augustine, Christ has two natures, the divine and the human. And although the same Christ exists in each, nevertheless things appropriate to him according to his human nature are distinct from what is appropriate to him according to his divine nature. Now to perform miracles is appropriate to him according to

his divine nature, which he received from the Father; while to suffer is according to his human nature, which he received from his mother. So when his mother requests this miracle, he answers, **Woman, what does that have to do with me and you?** as if saying: I did not receive from you that in me which enables me to perform miracles, but that which enables me to suffer, i.e., that which makes it appropriate for me to suffer, i.e., I have received a human nature from you. And so I will recognize you when this weakness hangs on the cross. And so he continues with, **My time has not yet come.** As if to say: I will recognize you as my mother when the time of my passion arrives. And so it was that on the cross he entrusted his mother to the disciple.

353   Chrysostom explains this differently. He says that the Blessed Virgin, burning with zeal for the honor of her Son, wanted Christ to perform miracles at once, before it was opportune; but that Christ, being much wiser than his mother, restrained her. For he was unwilling to perform the miracle before the need for it was known; otherwise, it would have been less appreciated and less credible. And so he says, **Woman, what does that have to do with me and you?** As if to say: Why bother me? **My time has not yet come,** i.e., I am not yet known to those present. Nor do they know that the wine ran out; and they must first know this, because when they know their need they will have a greater appreciation of the benefit they will receive.

354   Now although his mother was refused, she did not lose hope in her Son's mercy. So she instructs the servants, **Do whatever he tells you,** in which, indeed, consists the perfection of all justice. For perfect justice consists in obeying Christ in all things: "We will do all that the Lord commanded us" (Ex 29:35). **Do whatever he tells you,** is fittingly said of God alone, for man can err now and then. Hence in matters that are against God, we are not held to obey men: "We ought to obey God rather than men" (Acts 5:29). We ought to obey God, who does not err and cannot be deceived, in all things.

355   Now Christ's completion of the miracle is set forth. First, the vessels in which the miracle was performed are described. Secondly, the matter of the miracle is stated (v 7). Thirdly, we have how the miracle was made known and approved (v 8).

356   The miracle was performed in six vessels; **Now there were six stone water jars near by.** Here we should note, that as mentioned in Mark (7:2), the Jews observed many bodily washings and the cleansing of their cups and dishes. So, because they were in Palestine where there was a shortage of water, they had vessels in which they

kept the purest water to be used for washing themselves and their utensils. Hence he says, **there were six stone water jars near by**, i.e., vessels for holding water, **for purifications according to Jewish customs**, i.e., to use for purification, **each holding two or three metretes** of liquid, that is, two or three measures; for the Greek "metrete" is the same as the Latin "mensura."

These jars were standing there, as Chrysostom says, in order to eliminate any suspicion about the miracle: both on account of their cleanliness, lest anyone suspect that the water had acquired the taste of wine from the dregs of wine previously stored in them, for these jars were standing there **for purifications according to Jewish customs**, and so had to be very pure; and also on account of the capacity of the jars, so that it would be abundantly clear that the water in such jars could be changed into wine only by divine power.

357 In the mystical sense, the six water jars signify the six eras of the Old Testament during which the hearts of men were prepared and made receptive of God's Scriptures, and put forward as an example for our lives.

The term **metretes**, according to Augustine, refers to the Trinity of persons. And they are described as **two or three** because at times in Scripture three persons in the Trinity are distinctly mentioned: "Baptizing them in the name of the Father, and of the Son, and of the Holy Spirit" (Mt 28:19), and at other times only two, the Father and the Son, in whom the Holy Spirit, who is the union of the two, is implied: "If anyone loves me, he will keep my word, and my Father will love him, and we will come to him" (below 14:23). Or they are described as two on account of the two states of mankind from which the Church arose, that is, Jews and Gentiles. Or three on account of the three son of Noe, from whom the human race arose after the deluge.

358 Then when he says that Jesus instructed them, **Fill those jars with water**, he gives the material of the miracle. Here we might ask why this miracle was performed with already existing material, and not from nothing. There are three reasons for this. The first reason is literal, and is given by Chrysostom: to make something from nothing is much greater and more marvelous than to make something from material already existing; but it is not so evident and believable to many. And so, wishing to make what he did more believable, Christ made wine from water, thus condescending to man's capacity.

Another reason was to refute wrong dogmas. For there are some (as the Marcionists and Manicheans) who said that the founder of the world was someone other than God, and that all visible things were established by such a one, that is, the devil. And so the Lord performed many miracles using created and visible substances in order to show that these substances are good and were created by God.

The third reason is mystical. Christ made the wine from water, and not from nothing, in order to show that he was not laying down an entirely new doctrine and rejecting the old, but was fulfilling the old: "I have not come to destroy the law, but to fulfill it" (Mt 5:17). In other words, what was prefigured and promised in the old law, was disclosed and revealed by Christ: "Then he opened their minds so they could understand the Scriptures" (Lk 24:45).

Finally, he had the servants fill the jars with water so that he might have witnesses to what he did; so it is said, **the servants knew, since they had drawn the water.**

359 Then, the miracle is made known. For as soon as the jars were filled, the water was turned into wine. So the Lord reveals the miracle at once, saying: **Now pour out a drink and take it to the head waiter.** First, we have the command of Christ selecting who is to test the wine; secondly, the judgment of the head waiter who tasted it.

360 **Then Jesus said to them**, i.e., to the servants, **Now pour out a drink**, that is, of wine, from the jars, **and take it to the head waiter** (*architriclinus*). Here we should note that a *triclinium* is a place where there are three rows of tables, and it is called a *triclinium* from its three rows of dining couches: for *cline* in Greek means couch. For the ancients were accustomed to eat reclining on couches, as Maximus Valerius recounts. This is the reason why the Scriptures speak of lying next to and lying down. Thus the *architriclinus* was the first and chief among those dining. Or, according to Chrysostom, the *architriclinus* was the one in charge of the whole banquet. And because he had been busy and had not tasted anything, the Lord wanted him, and not the guests, to be the judge of what had been done, so some could not detract from the miracle by saying the guests were drunk and, their senses dulled, could not tell wine from water. For Augustine, the *architriclinus* was the chief guest, as was mentioned; and Christ wanted to have the opinion of this person in high position so it would be more acceptable.

361 In the mystical sense, those who pour out the water are preachers: "With joy you will draw water from the springs of the Savior" (Is 12:3). And the *architriclinus* is someone skilled in the law, as Nicodemus, Gamaliel or Paul. So, when the word of the Gospel, which was hidden under the letter of the law, is entrusted to such persons, it is as though wine made from water is poured out for the *architriclinus*, who, when he tastes it, gives his assent to the faith of Christ.

362   Then the judgment of the one examining the wine is given. First, he inquires into the truth of the fact; secondly, he gives his opinion.

He says, **Now when the head waiter tasted the water made wine, and not knowing where it came from**, because he did not know that the water had miraculously been made wine by Christ, **although the servants knew**, the reason being, **since they had drawn the water, he called the groom over**, in order to learn the truth and give his opinion of the wine. Hence he adds: **People usually serve the choice wines first, and when the guests have had their fill, then they bring out inferior wine.**

Here we should consider, according to Chrysostom, that everything is most perfect in the miracles of Christ. Thus, he restored most complete health to Peter's mother-in-law, so that she arose at once and waited on them, as we read in Mark (1:30) and Matthew (7:14). Again, he restored the paralytic to health so perfectly that he also arose immediately, took up his mat, and went home, as we read below (5:9). And this is also evident in this miracle, because Christ did not make mediocre wine from the water, but the very best possible. And so the head waiter says, **People usually serve the choice wines first, and when the guests have had their fill, then they bring out inferior wine**, because they drink less, and because good wine consumed in quantity along with a qunatity of food causes greater discomfort. It is as though he were saying: Where did this very good wine come from which, contrary to custom, you saved until now?

363   This is appropriate to a mystery. For in the mystical sense, he serves good wine first who, with an intent to deceive others, does not first mention the error he intends, but other things that entice his hearers, so that he can disclose his evil plans after they have been intoxicated and enticed to consent. We read of such wine: "It goes down pleasantly, but finally it will bite like a serpent" (Prv 23:31). Again, he serves good wine first who begins to live in a saintly and spiritual manner at the start of his conversion, but later sinks into a carnal life: "Are you so foolish as, having begun in the Spirit, to end in the flesh?" (Gal 3:3).

Christ, however, does not serve the good wine first, for at the very outset he proposes things that are bitter and hard: "Narrow is the way that leads to life" (Mt 7:14). Yet the more progress a person makes in his faith and teaching, the more pleasant it becomes and he becomes aware of a greater sweetness: "I will lead you by the path of justice, and when you walk you will not be hindered" (Prv 4:11). Likewise, all those who desire to live conscientiously in Christ suffer bitterness and troubles in this world: "You will weep and mourn" (below 16:20). But later they will experience delights and joys. So he goes on: "but your sorrow will be turned into joy." "I consider that the sufferings of this present time are not worthy to be compared with the glory to come, which will be revealed in us," as is said in Romans (8:18).

364 Then when he says, **This beginning of signs Jesus worked in Cana of Galilee**, he gives the disciples' acknowledgment of the miracle. We can see from this the falsity of the *History of the Infancy of the Savior*, which recounts many miracles worked by Christ as a boy. For if these accounts were true, the Evangelist would not have said, **This beginning of signs Jesus worked**. We have already given the reason why Christ worked no miracles during his childhood, that is, lest men regard them as illusions.

It was for the reason given above, then, that Jesus performed this miracle of turning water into wine at Cana of Galilee; and this was the first of the signs he did. **And Jesus revealed his glory**, i.e., the power by which he is glorious: "The Lord of hosts, he is the King of glory" (Ps 23:10).

365 **And his disciples believed in him**. But how did they believe? For they already were his disciples and had believed before this. I answer that sometimes a thing is described not according to what it is at the time, but according to what it will be. For example, we say that the apostle Paul was born at Tarsus, in Cilicia; not that an actual apostle was born there, but a future one was. Similarly, it says here that **his disciples believed in him**, i.e., those who would be his disciples. Or, one might answer that previously they had believed in him as a good man, preaching what was right and just; but now they believed in him as God.

LECTURE 2

12 After this he went down to Capernaum together with his mother, his brethren and his disciples; but they did not remain there many days. 13 The Jewish Passover was near at hand, and Jesus went up to Jerusalem. 14 In the temple precincts he came upon merchants selling oxen, sheep and doves, and moneychangers seated at tables. 15 And when he had made a kind of whip from cords, he drove everyone, including sheep and oxen, out of the temple, swept away the gold of the moneychangers, and knocked over their tables. 16 To those selling doves he said, "Get out of here! And stop making my Father's house into a marketplace." 17 His disciples then remembered that it is written: "Zeal for your house consumes me."

366 Above, the Evangelist presented the sign Christ worked in order to confirm his disciples; and this sign pertained to his power to change nature. Now he deals with the sign of his resurrection; a sign pertaining to the same power, but proposed by Christ to convert the people.

The Evangelist does two things as to this miracle. First, he mentions its occasion. Secondly, the prediction of the miracle (v 18). As to the first he does two things. First, he describes the place. Secondly, he tells of the incident which was the occasion for proposing this miracle (v 14). Now the place where this happened was Jerusalem. And so the Evangelist recounts step by step how the Lord had come to Jerusalem. First, then, he shows how he went down to Capernaum. Secondly, how he then went up to Jerusalem. As to the first he does three things. First, he mentions the place to which he went down. Secondly, he describes his company. Thirdly, he mentions the length of his stay.

367 The place to which Christ went down was Capernaum; and so he says, **After this**, i.e., the miracle of the wine, **he went down to Capernaum**. Now as far as the historical truth is concerned, this seems to conflict with Matthew's account that the Lord went down to Capernaum after John had been thrown into prison (Mt 4:12), while the entire series of events the Evangelist refers to here took place before John's imprisonment.

I answer that in order to settle this question we should bear in mind what is learned from the *Ecclesiastical History*, that is, that the other Evangelists, Matthew, Mark and Luke, began their account of the public life of Christ from the time that John was thrown into prison. Thus Matthew (4:12), after describing the baptism, fast and temptation of Christ, began at once to weave his story after John's imprisonment, saying: "When Jesus heard that John had been arrested." And Mark (1:14) says the same: "After John had been arrested, Jesus came into Galilee." John, who outlived the other three Evangelists, approved the accuracy and truth of their accounts when they came to his notice. Yet he saw that certain things had been left unsaid, namely, things which the Lord had done in the very first days of his preaching before John's imprisonment. And so, at the request of the faithful, John,* after he began his own Gospel in a loftier manner, recorded events that took place during the first year in which Christ was baptized before John's imprisonment, as is plain from the order of the events in his Gospel. According to this, then, the Evangelists are not in disagreement. Rather, the Lord went down to Capernaum twice: once before John's imprisonment (which is the one dealt with here), and once after his imprisonment, which is dealt with in Matthew (4:13) and Luke (4:31).

368   Now "Capernaum" means "very pretty village," and signifies this world, which has its beauty from the order and disposition of divine wisdom: "The beauty of the land is mine" (Ps 49:2). So the Lord went down to Capernaum, i.e., this world, with his mother and brethren and disciples. For in heaven the Lord has a Father without a mother; and on earth a mother without a father. Thus, he significantly mentions only his mother. In heaven he does not have brothers either, but is "the Only Begotten Son, who is in the bosom of the Father" (above 1:18). But on earth he is "the First-born of many brothers" (Rom 8:29). And on earth he has disciples, to whom he can teach the mysteries of the divinity, which were not known to men before: "In these days he has spoken to us in his Son" as we read in Hebrews (1:1).

Or, "Capernaum" means "the field of consolation"; and this signifies every man who bears good fruit: "The odor of my son is like the odor of a fruitful field" (Gn 27:27). Such a person is called a field of consolation because the Lord is consoled and rejoices in his achievement: "God will rejoice over you" (Is 62:5), and because the angels rejoice over his good: "There is joy in the angels of God over one repentant sinner" (Lk 15:10).

369   His companions were, first of all, his mother. So he says, **with his mother**, for because she had come to the wedding and had brought about the miracle, the Lord accompanied her back to the village of Nazareth. Nazareth was a village in Galilee, whose chief town was Capernaum.

370   Secondly, his companions were his brethren; and so he says, **his brethren** (*fratres*, brothers, brethren). We must avoid two errors here. First, that of Elvidius, who said that the Blessed Virgin had other sons after Christ; and he called these the brothers of the Lord. This is heretical, because our faith maintains that just as the mother of Christ was a virgin before giving birth, so in giving birth and after giving birth, she remained a virgin. We must also avoid the error of those who say that Joseph fathered sons with another wife, and that these are called the brothers of the Lord; for the Church does not admit this.

Jerome refutes this opinion: for on the cross the Lord entrusted his virgin mother to the care of his virgin disciple. Therefore, since Joseph was the special guardian of the Virgin, and of the Savior too, in his childhood, one may believe that he was a virgin. Consequently, it is a reasonable interpretation to say that the brothers of the Lord were those related to his virgin mother in some degree of consanguinity, or even to Joseph, who was the reputed father. And this conforms to the custom of Scripture which generally refers to relatives as brothers. Thus we read: "Let us not quarrel, for we are brothers"

(Gn 13:8), as Abram said to Lot, who was his nephew. And note that he distinguishes between relatives and disciples, because not all of Christ's relatives were his disciples; hence we read: "Even his brethren did not believe in him" (below 7:5).

371 Thirdly, his disciples were his companions; hence he says, **and his disciples.** But who were his disciples? For it seems, according to Matthew, that the first ones to be converted to Christ were Peter and Andrew, John and James; but they were called after John's imprisonment, as is clear from Matthew (4:18). Thus it does not seem that they went down to Capernaum with Christ, as it says here, since this was before John's imprisonment.

There are two answers to this. One is from Augustine, in his *De Consensu Evangelistarum*, namely, that Matthew does not follow the historical order, but in summarizing what he omitted, relates events that occurred before John's imprisonment as though they happened after. So, without any suggestion of a time lapse he says, "As Jesus was walking by the Sea of Galilee, he saw two brothers" (Mt 4:18), without adding "after this" or "at that time." The other answer, also by Augustine, is that in the Gospel not only the twelve whom the Lord chose and named apostles are called disciples of the Lord (Lk 6:13), but also all who believed in him and were instructed for the kingdom of heaven by his teaching. Therefore, it is possible that although those twelve did not yet follow him, others who adhered to him are called disciples here. But the first answer is better.

372 His stay there was short; hence he says, **but they did not remain there many days.** The reason for this was that the citizens of Capernaum were not eager to accept the teachings of Christ, being very corrupt, so that in Matthew (11:23)the Lord rebukes them for not doing penance in spite of the miracles done there and of Christ's teaching: "And you Capernaum, will you be lifted up to heaven? You will go down to hell. For if the mighty works that were done in you had been performed in Sodom, it would have stood until this day." But although they were evil, he went there to accompany his mother, and to stay there for a few days for her consolation and honor.

373 As for its mystical sense, this signifies that some cannot remain long with the many words spoken by Christ; a few of these words are enough for them, to enlighten them, because of the weakness of their understanding. Hence as Origen said, Christ reveals few things to such persons, according to "I have many things to tell you, but you cannot bear them now" (Jn 16:12).

374 Then when he says, **The Jewish Passover was near at hand,** he mentions the place to which he went up. And concerning this he does two things. First, the occasion is given. Secondly, the going up.

375 Now the occasion for his going up was the Jewish Passover. For in Exodus (13:17) it is commanded that every male be presented to the Lord three times a year; and one of these times was the Jewish Passover. So, since the Lord came to teach everyone by his example of humility and perfection, he wished to observe the law as long as it was in force. For he did not come to destroy the law, but to fulfill it (Mt 5:17). And so, because the Passover of the Jews was at hand, he went up to Jerusalem. So we, after his example, should carefully observe the divine precepts. For if the Son of God fulfilled the decrees of a law he himself had given, and celebrated the great feasts, with what zeal for good works ought we both to prepare for them and observe them?

376 It should be noted that in John's Gospel mention is made of the Passover in three passages: here, and in (6:4), when he worked the miracle of the loaves, where it is said: "Now the Jewish Passover was near at hand", and again in (13:1), where it says: "Before the feast day of the Passover." So, according to this Gospel, we understand that after the miracle of the wine Christ preached for two years plus the interval between his baptism and this Passover. For what he did here occurred near the Passover, as it says here, and then a year later, near the time of another Passover, he performed the miracle of the loaves, and in the same year John was beheaded. Thus John was beheaded near the time of the Passover, because we read in Matthew (14:13) that immediately after John was beheaded Christ withdrew to the desert, where he worked the miracle of the loaves; and this miracle took place near Passover time, as stated below (6:4). Nevertheless, the feast of this beheading of John is celebrated on the day his head was found. It was later, during another Passover, that Christ suffered.

So, according to the opinion of those who say that the miracle worked at the wedding and the events being discussed here occurred in the same year in which Christ was baptized, there was an interval of two and one half years between Christ's baptism and his passion. So, according to them, the Evangelist says, **The Jewish Passover was near at hand**, in order to show that Christ had been baptized just a few days before.

But the Church holds the opposite. For we believe that Christ worked the miracle of the wine on the first anniversary of the day of his baptism; then a year later, near Passover time, John was beheaded; and then there was another year between the Passover near which John was beheaded and the Passover during which Christ suffered. So between the baptsim of Christ and the miracle of the wine there had to be another Passover which the Evangelist does not mention. And so, according to what the Church holds, Christ preached for three and one half years.

377 He says, **the Jewish Passover**, not as though the people of other nations celebrated a Passover, but for two reasons. One, because when people celebrate a feast in a holy and pure way, it is said that they celebrate it for the Lord; but when they celebrate it in neither of those ways, they do not celebrate it for the Lord, but for themselves: "My soul hates your new moons and your feasts" (Is 1:14). It is as though he said: Those who celebrate for themselves and not for me, do not please me: "When you fasted, did you fast for me?" (Zec 7:5), as if to say: You did not do it for me, but for yourselves. And so because these Jews were corrupt and celebrated their Passover in an unbecoming manner, the Evangelist does not say, "the Passover of the Lord," but **the Jewish Passover** was at hand.

Or, he says this to differentiate it from our Passover. For the Passover of the Jews was symbolic, being celebrated by the immolation of a lamb which was a symbol. But our Passover is true, in which we recall the true passing [passion] of the Immaculate Lamb: "Christ, our Passover, has been sacrificed" (1 Cor 5:7).

378 The journey was to Jerusalem, and so he says, **and Jesus went up to Jerusalem**. Note here that according to the historical order, Jesus went up to Jerusalem near the time of the Passover and expelled the merchants from the temple on two occasions. The first, before John's imprisonment, is the one the Evangelist mentions here; the other is mentioned by Matthew (21:13) as occurring when the Passover and the hour of his passion were at hand. For the Lord frequently repeated works that were similar. For example, the two cases of giving sight to the blind: one in Matthew (9:28) and another in Mark (10:46). In like manner he twice cast merchants from the temple.

379 In the mystical sense, **Jesus went up to Jerusalem**, which is translated as the "vision of peace," and signifies eternal happiness. It is to here that Jesus ascended, and he took his own with him. There is no lack of mystery in the fact that he went down to Capernaum and later went up to Jerusalem. For if he did not first go down, he would not have been suited to go up, because, as it is said: "He who descended is the same as he who ascended" (Eph 4:10). Further, no mention is made of the disciples in the ascent to Jerusalem because the ascent of the disciples comes from the ascent of Christ: "No one has gone up to heaven except the one who came down from heaven, the Son of Man, who lives in heaven" (below 3:13).

380 Then when he says, **In the temple precincts he came upon merchants selling oxen, sheep and doves**, the Evangelist sets down what moved Christ to propose the sign of the resurrection. He does

three things with this. First, he exposes the faulty behavior of the Jews. Secondly, he discloses Christ's remedy (v 15). Thirdly, he gives the announcement of the prophecy (v 22).

381 With respect to the first, we should note that the devil plots against the things of God and strives to destroy them. Now among the means by which he destroys holy things, the chief is avarice; hence it is said: "The shepherds have no understanding. All have turned aside to their own way; everyone after his own gain, from the first one to the last" (Is 56:11). And the devil has done this from the earliest times. For the priests of the Old Testament, who had been established to care for divine matters, gave free rein to avarice. God commanded, in the law, that animals should be sacrificed to the Lord on certain feasts. And in order to fulfill this command, those who lived nearby brought the animals with them. But those who came a long distance were unable to bring animals from their own homes. And so because offerings of this kind resulted in profit for the priests, and so animals to offer would not be lacking to those who came from a distance, the priests themselves saw to it that animals were sold in the temple. And so they had them shown for sale in the temple, i.e., in the atrium of the temple. And this is what he says: **In the temple precincts he came upon merchants selling oxen, sheep and doves.**

Mention is first made of two land animals, which according to the law could be offered to the Lord: the ox and the sheep. The third land animal offered, the goat, is implied when he says "sheep", similarly, the turtle-dove is included when he says "doves."

382 It sometimes happened that some came to the temple not only without animals, but also without money to buy them. And so the priests found another avenue for their avarice; they set up moneychangers who would lend money to those who came without it. And although they would not accept a usurious gain, because this was forbidden in the law, nevertheless in place of this they accepted certain "collibia," i.e., trifles and small gifts. So this also was turned to the profit of the priests. And this is what he says, **moneychangers seated at tables**, i.e., in the temple, ready to lend money.

383 This can be understood mystically in three ways. First of all, the merchants signify those who sell or buy the things of the Church: for the oxen, sheep and doves signify the spiritual goods of the Church and the things connected with them. These goods have been consecrated and authenticated by the teachings of the apostles and doctors, signified by the oxen: "When there is an abundant harvest the strength of the ox is evident" (Prv 14:4); and by the blood of the martyrs, who are signified by the sheep: so it is said for them: "We are regarded as sheep for the slaughter" (Rom 8:36); and

by the gifts of the Holy Spirit, signified by the doves, for as stated above, the Holy Spirit appeared in the form of a dove. Therefore, those who presume to sell the spiritual goods of the Church and the goods connected with them are selling the teachings of the apostles, the blood of the martyrs, and the gifts of the Holy Spirit.

Secondly, it happens that certain prelates or heads of churches sell these oxen, sheep and doves, not overtly by simony, but covertly by negligence; that is, when they are so eager for and occupied with temporal gain that they neglect the spiritual welfare of their subjects. And this is the way they sell the oxen, sheep and doves, i.e., the three classes of people subject to them. First of all, they sell the preachers and laborers, who are signified by the oxen: "Happy are you who sow beside all the streams, letting the ox and the donkey range free" (Is 32:20); because prelates ought to arrange the oxen, i.e., teachers and wise men, with the donkeys, i.e., the simple and uneducated. They also sell those in the active life, and those occupied with ministering, signified by the sheep: "My sheep hear my voice" (below 10:27); and as is said in 2 Samuel (24:17): "But these, who are the sheep, what have they done?" They also sell the contemplatives, signified by the doves: "Who will give me wings like a dove, and I will fly?" (Ps 54:7).

Thirdly, by the temple of God we can understand the spiritual soul, as it says: "The temple of God is holy, and that is what you are" (1 Cor 3:17). Thus a man sells oxen, sheep and doves in the temple when he harbors bestial movements in his soul, for which he sells himself to the devil. For oxen, which are used for cultivating the earth, signify earthly desires; sheep, which are stupid animals, signify man's obstinacy; and the doves signify man's instability. It is God who drives these things out of men's hearts.

384   The Lord's remedy is at once set forth (v 15). Here the Lord's remedy consisted in action and in words, in order to instruct those who have charge of the Church that they must correct their subjects in deed and in word. And he does two things with respect to this. First, he gives the remedy Christ applied by his action. Secondly, the remedy he applied by word (v 16).

385   As to the first he does three things. First, he drives the men out. Secondly, the oxen and sheep. Thirdly, he sweeps away the money.

He drives the men out with a whip; and this is what he says, **when he had made a kind of whip from cords.** This is something that could be done only by divine power. For as Origen says, the divine power of Jesus was as able, when he willed, to quench the swelling anger of men as to still the storms of minds: "The Lord brings to nought the thoughts of men" (Ps 32:10). He makes the whip from cords because, as Augustine says, it is from our own sins that he forms the matter with which he punishes us: for a series of sins, in which sins are added to sins, is called a cord: "He is bound fast by the cords of his own sins" (Prv 5:22); "Woe to you who haul wickedness with cords" (Is 5:18). Then, just as he drove the merchants from the temple, so he swept away the gold of the moneychangers and knocked over their tables.

386 And mark well that if he expelled from the temple things that seemed somehow licit, in the sense that they were ordained to the worship of God, how much more if he comes upon unlawful things? The reason he cast them out was because in this matter the priests did not intend God's glory, but their own profit. Hence it is said: "It is for yourselves that you placed guardians of my service in my sancturay" (Ez 44:8)

Further, our Lord showed zeal for the things of the law so that he might by this answer the chief priests and the priests who were later to bring a charge against him on this very point. Again, by casting things of this kind out of the temple he let it be understood that the time was coming in which the sacrifices of the law were due to cease, and the true worship of God transferred to the Gentiles: "The kingdom of God will be taken away from you" (Mt 21:43). Also, this shows us the condemnation of those who sell spiritual things: "May your money perish together with you" (Acts 8:20).

387 Then when he says, **To those selling doves he said**, he records the treatment which the Lord applied by word. Here it should be noted that those who engage in simony should, of course, first be expelled from the Church. But because as long as they are alive, they can change themselves by free will and by the help of God return to the state of grace, they should not be given up as hopeless. If, however, they are not converted, then they are not merely to be expelled, but handed over to those to whom it is said: "Bind him hand and foot, and cast him into outer darkness" (Mt 22:13). And so the Lord, attending to this, first warns them, and then gives the reason for his warning, saying, **stop making my Father's house into a marketplace**.

388 He warns those selling the doves by reproaching them, for they signify those who sell the gifts of the Holy Spirit, i.e., those who engage in simony.

389 He gives his reason for this when he says, **stop making my Father's house into a marketplace**. "Take away your evil from my sight" (Is 1:16). Note that Matthew (21:13) says: "Do not make my

house a den of thieves," while here he says, **a marketplace**. Now the Lord does this because, as a good physician, he begins first with the gentler things; later on, he would propose harsher things. Now the action recorded here was the first of the two; hence in the beginning he does not call them thieves but merchants. But because they did not stop such business out of obstinacy, the Lord, when driving them out the second time (as mentioned in Mark 11:15), rebukes them more severely, calling robbery what he had first called business.

He says, **my Father's house**, to exclude the error of Manicheus, who said that while the God of the New Testament was the Father of Christ, the God of the Old Testament was not. But if this were true, then since the temple was the house of the Old Testament, Christ would not have referred to the temple as **my Father's house**.

390 Why were the Jews not disturbed here when he called God his Father, for as is said below (5:18), this is why they persecuted him? I answer that God is the Father of certain men through adoption; for example, he is the Father of the just in this way. This was not a new idea for the Jews: "You will call me Father, and you will not cease to walk after me" (Jer 3:19). However, by nature he is the Father of Christ alone: "The Lord said to me: 'You are my Son' " (Ps 2:7), i.e., the true and natural Son. It is this that was unheard of among the Jews. And so the Jews persecuted him because he called himself the true Son of God: "the Jews tried all the harder to kill him, because he not only broke the Sabbath rest, but even called God his own Father, making himself equal to God" (below 5:18). But when he called God his Father on this occasion, they said it was by adoption.

391 That the house of God shall not be made a marketplace is taken from Zechariah (14:21): "On that day there will no longer be any merchants in the house of the Lord of hosts"; and from the Psalm (70:16), where one version has the reading: "Because I was not part of the marketplace, I will enter into the strength of the Lord."

392 Then when he says, **His disciples then remembered**, he sets down a prophecy which was written in Psalm 69 (v 9): "Zeal for your house consumes me." Here we should remark that zeal, properly speaking, signifies an intensity of love, whereby the one who loves intensely does not tolerate anything which is repugnant to his love. So it is that men who love their wives intensely and cannot endure their being in the company of other men, as this conflicts with their own love, are called "zelotypes." Thus, properly speaking, one is said to have zeal for God who cannot patiently endure anything contrary to the honor of God, whom he loves above all else: "I have

been very zealous for the Lord God of hosts" (1 Kgs 19:10). Now we should love the house of the Lord, according to the Psalm (25:8): "O Lord, I have loved the beauty of your house." Indeed, we should love it so much that our zeal consumes us, so that if we notice anything amiss being done, we should try to eliminate it, no matter how dear to us are those who are doing it; nor should we fear any evils that we might have to endure as a result. So the Gloss says: "Good zeal is a fervor of spirit, by which, scorning the fear of death, one is on fire for the defense of the truth. He is consumed by it who takes steps to correct any perversity he sees; and if he cannot, he tolerates it with sadness."

LECTURE 3

18 At this the Jews responded and said, "What sign can you show us authorizing you to do these things?" 19 Jesus replied, "Destroy this temple, and in three days I will raise it up again." 20 The Jews then retorted, "This temple took forty-six years to build, and you are going to raise it up again in three days!" 21 He was speaking, however, of the temple of his body. 22 When, therefore, he had risen from the dead, his disciples recalled that he had said this; they then believed the Scriptures and the statement Jesus had made. 23 While he was in Jerusalem during the Passover feast, many people, seeing the signs he was working, believed in his name. 24 But Jesus did not trust himself to them, for he knew all men, 25 and he did not need anyone to give him testimony about men. He was well aware of what was in man's heart.

393 Having set forth the occasion for showing the sign, the Evangelist then states the sign which would be given. First, he gives the sign. Secondly, he mentions the fruit of the signs Christ performed (v 23). As to the first he does three things. First, the request for the sign is given. Secondly, the sign itself (v 19). Thirdly, the way the sign was understood (v 20).

394 The Jews ask for a sign; and this is what he says: **What sign can you show us authorizing you to do these things?**

395 Here we should note that when Jesus drove the merchants out of the temple, two things could be considered in Christ: his rectitude and zeal, which pertain to virtue; and his power or authority. It was not appropriate to require a sign from Christ concerning the virtue and zeal with which he did the above action, since every-

one may lawfully act according to virtue. But he could be required to give a sign concerning his authority for driving them out of the temple, since it is not lawful for anyone to do this unless he has the authority.

And so the Jews, not questioning his zeal and virtue, ask for a sign of his authority; and so they say, **What sign can you show us authorizing you to do these things?** i.e., Why do you drive us out with such power and authority, for this does not seem to be your office? They say the same thing in Matthew (21:23): "By what authority are you doing these things?"

396 The reason they ask for a sign is that it was the usual thing for Jews to require a sign, seeing that they were called to the law by signs: "There did not arise again in Israel a prophet like Moses, whom the Lord knew face to face, with all his signs and wonders," as is said in Deuteronomy (34:10), and "The Jews require signs," as we find in 1 Corinthians (1:22). Hence David complains for the Jews saying: "We have not seen our signs" (Ps 73:9). However, they asked him for a sign not in order to believe, but in the hope that he would not be able to provide the sign, and then they could obstruct and restrain him. And so, because they asked in an evil manner, he did not give them an evident sign, but a sign clothed in a symbol, a sign concerning the resurrection.

397 Hence he says, **Jesus replied**, and he gives the sign for which they asked. He gives them the sign of his future resurrection because this shows most strikingly the power of his divinity. For it is not within the power of mere man to raise himself from the dead. Christ alone, who was free among the dead, did this by the power of his divinity. He shows them a similar sign in Matthew (12:30): "An evil and adulterous generation asks for a sign. And a sign will not be given it, except the sign of Jonah the prophet." And although he gave a hidden and symbolic sign on both occasions, the first was stated more clearly, and the second more obscurely.

398 We should note that before the incarnation, God gave a sign of the incarnation to come: "The Lord himself will give you a sign. A virgin will conceive, and give birth to a son" (Is 7:14). And in like manner, before the resurrection he gave a sign of the resurrection to come. And he did this because it is especially by these two events that the power of the divinity in Christ is evidenced. For nothing more marvelous could be done than that God become man and that Christ's humanity should become a partaker of divine immortality after his resurrection: "Christ, rising from the dead, will not die again ... his life is life with God" (Rom 6:9), i.e., in a likeness to God.

399   We should note the words Christ used in giving this sign. For Christ calls his body a temple, because a temple is something in which God dwells, according to "The Lord is in his holy temple" (Ps 10:5). And so a holy soul, in which God dwells, is also called a temple of God: "The temple of God is holy, and that is what you are" (1 Cor 3:17). Therefore, because the divinity dwells in the body of Christ, the body of Christ is the temple of God, not only according to the soul but also according to the body: "In him all the fulness of the divinity dwells bodily" (Col 2:9). God dwells in us by grace, i.e., according to an act of the intellect and will, neither of which is an act of the body, but of the soul alone. But he dwells in Christ according to a union in the person; and this union includes not only the soul, but the body as well. And so the very body of Christ is God's temple.

400   But Nestorius, using this text in support of his error, claims that the Word of God was joined to human nature only by an indwelling, from which it follows that the person of God is distinct from that of man in Christ. Therefore it is important to insist that God's indwelling in Christ refers to the nature, since in Christ human nature is distinct from the divine, and not to the person, which in the case of Christ is the same for both God and man, that is, the person of the Word, as was said above.

401   Therefore, granting this, the Lord does two things with respect to this sign. First, he foretells his future death. Secondly, his resurrection.

402   Christ foretells his own death when he says, **Destroy this temple**. For Christ died and was killed by others: "And they will kill him" (Mt 17:22), yet with him willing it: because as is said: "He was offered because it was his own will" (Is 53:7). And so he says, **Destroy this temple**, i.e., my body. He does not say, "it will be destroyed," lest you suppose he killed himself. He says, **Destroy**, which is not a command but a prediction and a permission. A prediction, so that the sense is, **Destroy this temple**, i.e., you will destroy. And a permission, so that the sense is, **Destroy this temple**, i.e., do with my body what you will, I submit it to you. As he said to Judas: "What you are going to do, do quickly" (below 13:27), not as commanding him, but as abandoning himself to his decision.

He says **Destroy**, because the death of Christ is the dissolution of his body, but in a way different from that of other men. For the bodies of other men are destroyed by death even to the point of the body's returning to dust and ashes. But such a dissolution did not take place in Christ, for as it is said: "You will not allow your Holy One to see corruption" (Ps 15:10). Nevertheless, death did bring a dissolution to Christ, because his soul was separated from his body as a form from matter, and because his blood was separated from his body, and because his body was pierced with nails and a lance.

403   He foretells his resurrection when he says, **and in three days I will raise it up again**, that is, his body; i.e., I will raise it from the dead. He does not say, "I will be raised up," or "The Father will raise it up," but **I will raise it up**, to show that he would rise from the dead by his own power. Yet we do not deny that the Father raised him from the dead, because as it is said: "Who raised Jesus from the dead" (Rom 8:11); and "O Lord, have pity on me, and raise me up" (Ps 40:10). And so God the Father raised Christ from the dead, and Christ arose by his own power: "I have slept and have taken my rest, and I have risen, because the Lord has taken me" (Ps 3:6). There is no contradiction in this, because the power of both is the same; hence "whatever the Father does, the Son does likewise" (below 5:19). For if the Father raised him up, so too did the Son: "Although he was crucified through weakness, he lives through the power of God" (2 Cor 13:4).

404   He says, **and in three days**, and not "after three days," because he did not remain in the tomb for three complete days; but, as Augustine says, he is employing synecdoche, in which a part is taken for the whole.

Origen, however, assigns a mystical reason for this expression, and says: The true body of Christ is the temple of God, and this body symbolizes the mystical body, i.e., the Church: "You are the body of Christ" (1 Cor 12:27). And as the divinity dwells in the body of Christ through the grace of union, so too he dwells in the Church through the grace of adoption. Although that body may seem to be destroyed mystically by the adversities of persecutions with which it is afflicted, nevertheless it is raised up in "three days," namely, in the "day" of the law of nature, the "day" of the written law, and the "day" of the law of grace; because in those days a part of that body was destroyed, while another still lived. And so he says, **in three days**, because the spiritual resurrection of this body is accomplished in three days. But after those three days we will be perfectly risen, not only as to the first resurrection, but also as to the second: "Happy are they who share in the second [*sic*] resurrection" (Rv 20:6).

405   Then when he says, **The Jews then retorted**, we have the interpretation of the sign he gave. First, the false interpretation of the Jews. Secondly, its true understanding by the apostles (v 21).

406   The interpretation of the Jews was false, because they believed that Christ was saying this of the material temple in which

he then was; consequently, they answer according to this interpretation and say: **This temple took forty-six years to build**, i.e., this material temple in which we are standing, **and you are going to raise it up again in three days!**

407 There is a literal objection against this. For the temple in Jerusalem was built by Solomon, and it is recorded in 2 Chronicles (6:1) that it was completed by Solomon in seven years. How then can it be said that this temple took forty-six years to build? I answer that according to some this is not to be understood of the very first temple, which was completed by Solomon in seven years: for that temple built by Solomon was destroyed by Nebuchadnezzar. But it is to be understood of the temple rebuilt under Zerubbabel, after they returned from captivity, as recorded in the book of Ezra (5:2). However, this rebuilding was so hindered and delayed by the frequent attacks of their enemies on all sides, that the temple was not finished until forty-six years had passed.

408 Or it could be said, according to Origen, that they were speaking of Solomon's temple: and it did take forty-six years to build if the time be reckoned from the day when David first spoke of building a temple and discussed it with Nathan the prophet, as we find in 2 Samuel (7:2), until its final completion under Solomon. For from that first day onward David began preparing the material and the things necessary for building the temple. Accordingly, if the time in question is carefully calculated, it will come to forty-six years.

409 But although the Jews referred their interpretation to the material temple, nevertheless, according to Augustine, it can be referred to the temple of Christ's body. As he says in *The Book of Eighty-tnree Questions*, the conception and formation of the human body is completed in forty-five days in the following manner. During the first six days, the conception of a human body has a likeness to milk; during the next nine days it is converted into blood; then in the next twelve days, it is hardened into flesh; then the remaining eighteen days, it is formed into a perfect outlining of all the mem--bers. But if we add six, nine, twelve and eighteen, we get forty-five; and if we add "one" for the sacrament of unity, we get forty-six.

410 However a question arises about this: because this process of formation does not seem to have taken place in Christ, who was formed and animated at the very instant of conception. But one may answer that although in the formation of Christ's body there was something unique, in that Christ's body was perfect at that instant as to the outlining of its members, it was not perfect as to the quantity due the body; and so he remained in the Virgin's womb until he attained the due quantity.

However, let us take the above numbers and select six, which was the first, and forty-six, which was the last, and let us multiply one by the other. The result is two hundred seventy-six. Now if we assemble these days into months, allotting thirty days to a month, we get nine months and six days. Thus it was correct to say that it took forty-six years to build the temple, which signifies the body of Christ; the suggestion being that there were as many years in building the temple as there were days in perfecting the body of Christ. For from March twenty-five, when Christ was conceived, and (as is believed) when he suffered, to December twenty-five, there are this number of days, namely, two hundred seventy-six, a number that is the result of multiplying forty-six by six.

411 Augustine (as is plain from the Gloss) has another mystical interpretation of this number. For he says that if one adds the letters in the name "Adam," using for each the number it represented for the Greeks, the result is forty-six. For in Greek, A represents the number one, since it is the first letter of the alphabet. And according to this order, D is four. Adding to the sum of these another one for the second A and forty for the letter M, we have forty-six. This signifies that the body of Christ was derived from the body of Adam.

Again, according to the Greeks, the name "Adam" is composed of the first letters of the names of the four directions of the world: namely, Anathole, which is the east; Disis, which is the west; Arctos, which is the north; and Mensembria, the south. This signifies that Christ derived his flesh from Adam in order to gather his elect from the four parts of the world: "He will gather his elect from the four winds" (Mt 24:31).

412 Then, the true interpretation of this sign as understood by the apostles is given (v 21). First, the way they understood it is given. Secondly, the time when they understood it (v 22).

413 He says therefore: The Jews said this out of ignorance. But Christ did not understand it in their way; in fact, he meant the temple of his body, and this is what he says: **He was speaking, however, of the temple of his body**. We have already explained why the body of Christ could be called a temple.

Apollinaris misunderstood this and said that the body of Christ was inanimate matter because the temple was inanimate. He was mistaken in this for when it is said that the body of Christ is a temple, one is speaking metaphorically. And in this way of speaking a likeness does not exist in all respects, but only in some respect, namely, as to indwelling, which is referred to the nature, as was explained. Further, this is evident from the authority of Sacred Scripture, when Christ himself said: "I have the power to lay down my life," as we read below (10:18).

414 The time when the apostles acquired this true understanding is then shown by the Evangelist when he says, **When,
therefore, he had risen from the dead, his disciples recalled that he
had said this.** Prior to the resurrection it was difficult to understand
this. First, because this statement asserted that the true divinity was
in the body of Christ; otherwise it could not be called a temple. And
to understand this at that time was above human ability. Secondly,
because in this statement mention is made of the passion and resurrection, when he says, **I will raise it up again**; and this is something
none of the disciples had heard mentioned before. Consequently,
when Christ spoke of his resurrection and passion to the apostles,
Peter was scandalized when he heard it, saying, "God forbid, Lord"
(Mt 16:22). But after the resurrection, when they now clearly understood that Christ was God, through what he had shown in regard to
his passion and resurrection, and when they had learned of the mystery of his resurrection, **his disciples recalled that he had said this** of
his body, and **they then believed the Scriptures**, i.e., the prophets:
"He will revive us after two days; on the third day he will raise us
up" (Hos 6:3), and "Jonah was in the belly of the fish three days and
three nights" (Jon 2:1). So it is that on the very day of the resurrection he opened their understanding so that they might understand
the Scriptures **and the statement Jesus had made**, namely, **Destroy
this temple, and in three days I will raise it up again.**

415 In the anagogical sense, according to Origen, we understand by this that in the final resurrection of nature we will be
disciples of Christ, when in the great resurrection the entire body of
Jesus, that is, his Church, will be made certain of the things we now
hold through faith in a dark manner. Then we shall receive the fulfillment of faith, seeing in actual fact what we now observe through
a mirror.

416 Then (v 23) he sets forth the fruit which resulted from the
signs, namely, the conversion of certain believers. Concerning this he
does three things. First, he mentions those who believed on account
of the miracles. Secondly, he shows the attitude of Christ to them
(v 24). Thirdly, he gives the reason for this (v 25).

417 The fruit which developed from the signs of Jesus was
abundant, because many believed and were converted to him; and
this is what he says, **While he was in Jerusalem during the Passover
feast, many people, seeing the signs he was working, believed in his
name**, i.e., in him.

418 Note that they believed in two ways: some on account of
the miracles they saw, and some on account of the revelation and
prophecy of hidden things. Now those who believe on account of

doctrine are more commendable, because they are more spiritual than those who believe on account of signs, which are grosser and on the level of sense. Those who were converted are shown to be more on the level of sense by the fact that they did not believe on account of the doctrine, as the disciples did, but **seeing the signs he was working**: "Prophecies are for those who believe" (1 Cor 14:22).

419 One might ask which signs woked by Jesus they saw, for we do not read of any sign worked by him in Jerusalem at that time. According to Origen, there are two answers to this. First, Jesus did work many miracles there at that time, which are not recorded here; for the Evangelist purposely omitted many of Christ's miracles, since he worked so many that they could not easily be recorded: "Jesus did many other signs, and if every one was written, the world itself, I think, would not be able to contain the books that would be written" (below 21:25). And the Evangelist expressly shows this when he says, **seeing the signs he was working**, without mentioning them, because it was not the intention of the Evangelist to record all the signs of Jesus, but as many as were needed to instruct the Church of the faithful. The second answer is that among the miracles the greatest could be the sign in which Jesus by himself drove from the temple a crowd of men with a whip of small cords.

420 The attitude of Jesus to those who believed in him is shown when he says, **But Jesus did not trust himself to them**, i.e., those who had believed in him. What is this, men entrust themselves to God, and Jesus himself does not entrust himself to them? Could they kill him against his will? Some will say that he did not trust himself to them because he knew that their belief was not genuine. But if this were true, the Evangelist would surely not have said that many believed in his name, and yet he did not trust himself to them. According to Chrysostom, the reason is that they did believe in him, but imperfectly, because they were not yet able to attain to the profound mysteries of Christ, and so **Jesus did not trust himself to them**, i.e., he did not yet reveal his secret mysteries to them; for there were many things he would not reveal even to the apostles: "I still have many things to say to you, but you cannot bear them now" (below 16:12), and "I could not speak to you as spiritual persons, but as sensual" (1 Cor 3:1). And so it is significant that in order to show that they believed imperfectly, the Evangelist does not say that they believed "in him," because they did not yet believe in his divinity, but he says, **in his name**, i.e., they believed what was said about him, nominally, i.e., that he was just, or something of that sort.

Or, according to Augustine, these people represent the catechumens in the Chruch, who, although they believe in the name of

Christ, Jesus does not trust himself to them, because the Church does not give them the body of Christ. For just as no priest except one ordained in the priesthood can consecrate that body, so no one but a baptized person may receive it.

421 The reason Jesus did not trust himself to them arises from his perfect knowledge; hence he says, **for he knew all men**. For although one must ordinarily presume good of everyone, yet after the truth about certain people is known, one should act according to their condition. Now because nothing in man was unknown to Christ and since he knew that they believed imperfectly, he did not trust himself to them.

422 The universal knowledge of Christ is then described: for he knew not only those who were on close terms with him, but strangers too. And therefore he says, **for he knew all men**; and this by the power of his divinity: "The eyes of the Lord are far brighter than the sun" (Sir 23:28). Now a man, although he may know other people, cannot have a sure knowledge of them, because he sees only what appears; consequently, he must rely on the testimony of others. But Christ knows with the greatest certainty, because he beholds the heart; and so **he did not need anyone to give testimony about men**. In fact, he is the one who gives testimony: "Look, my witness is in heaven" (Jb 16:20)

His knowledge was perfect, because it extended not only to what was exterior, but even to the interior; thus he says, **He was well aware of what was in man's heart**, i.e., the secrets of the heart: "Hell and destruction are open to the Lord: how much more the hearts of the children of men" (Prv 15:11).

3

LECTURE 1

1 There was a certain Pharisee named Nicodemus, a member of the Sanhedrin. 2 He came to Jesus at night and said to him, "Rabbi, we know that you are a teacher come from God, for no one could perform the signs you perform, unless he had God with him." 3 Jesus responded and said to him,

"Amen, amen, I say to you,
unless one is born again,
he cannot see the kingdom of God."

4 Nicodemus said to him, "How can a man be born again when he is already an old man? Is it possible for him to return to his mother's womb and be born all over again?" 5 Jesus replied,

"Amen, amen, I say to you,
unless one is born again of water and the Holy Spirit,
he cannot enter the kingdom of God.
6 What is born of flesh is itself flesh;
and what is born of Spirit is itself spirit."

423   Above, the Evangelist showed Christ's power in relation to changes affecting nature; here he shows it in relation to our reformation by grace, which is his principal subject. Reformation by grace comes about through spiritual generation and by the conferring of benefits on those regenerated. First, then, he treats of spiritual generation. Secondly, of the spiritual benefits divinely conferred on the regenerated, and this in chapter five.

As to the first he does two things. First, he treats of spiritual regeneration in relation to the Jews. Secondly, of the spreading of the fruits of this regeneration even to foreign peoples, and this in chapter four. Concerning the first he does two things. First, he explains spiritual regeneration with words. Secondly, he completes it with deeds (3:22).

As to the first he does three things. First, he shows the need for a spiritual regeneration. Secondly, its quality (3:4). Thirdly, its mode and nature (3:9). As to the first he does two things. First, he mentions the occasion for showing this need. Secondly, the need itself for this regeneration (3:3).

The occasion was presented by Nicodemus; hence he says, **There was a certain Pharisee named Nicodemus.** And he describes him as to his person, from the time, and from his statements.

424   He describes his person in three ways. First, as to his religion, because he was a Pharisee; hence he says, **There was a certain Pharisee.** For there were two sects among the Jews: the Pharisees

181

and the Sadducees. The Pharisees were closer to us in their beliefs, for they believed in the resurrection, and admitted the existence of spiritual creatures. The Sadducees, on the other hand, disagree more with us, for they believed neither in the resurrection to come nor in the existence of spirits. The former were called Pharisees, as being separated from the others. And because their opinion was the more credible and nearer to the truth, it was easier for Nicodemus to be converted to Christ. "I lived as a Pharisee, according to the strictest sect of our religion" (Acts 26:5).

425   As to his name he says, **named Nicodemus,** which means "victor," or "the victory of the people." This signifies those who overcame the world through faith by being converted to Christ from Judaism. "This is the victory that overcomes the world, our faith" (1 Jn 5:4).

426   Thirdly, as to his rank he says, **a member of the Sanhedrin.** For although our Lord did not choose the wise or powerful or those of high birth at the beginning, lest the power of the faith be attributed to human widsom and power − "Not many of you are learned in the worldly sense, not many powerful, not many of high birth. But God chose the simple ones of the world" (1 Cor 1:26) − still he willed to convert some of the wise and powerful to himself at the very beginning. And he did this so that his doctrine would not be held in contempt, as being accepted exclusively by the lowly and uneducated, and so that the number of believers would not be attributed to the rusticity and ignorance of the converts rather than to the power of the faith. However, he did not will that a large number of those converted to him be powerful and of high birth, lest, as has been said, it should be ascribed to human power and wisdom. And so it says, "many of those in authority believed in him" (below 12:42), among whom was this Nicodemus. "The rulers of the people have come together" (Ps 46:10).

427   Then he describes him as to the time, saying, **he came to Jesus at night.** In regard to this, it might be noted that in Scripture the quality of the time is mentioned as to certain persons in order to indicate their knowledge or the condition of their actions. Here an obscure time is mentioned, **at night.** For the night is obscure and suited to the state of mind of Nicodemus, who did not come to Jesus free of care and anxiety, but in fear; for he was one of those of whom it is said that they "believed in him; but they did not admit it because of the Pharisees, so that they would not be expelled from the synagogue" (below 12:42). For their love was not perfect, so it continues, "For they loved the glory of men more than the glory of God."

Further, night was appropriate to his ignorance and the imperfect understanding he had of Christ: "The night has passed, and day is at hand. So let us cast off the works of darkness" (Rom 13:12); "They have not known or understood; they are walking in darkness" (Ps 81:5).

428 Then he is described from his statements, when he says that Nicodemus said to Jesus: **Rabbi, we know that you are a teacher come from God.** Here he affirms Christ's office as teacher when he says, **Rabbi,** and his power of acting, saying, **for no one could perform the signs you perform, unles he had God with him.** And in both remarks he says what is true, but he does not affirm enough.

He is right is calling Jesus **Rabbi,** i.e., Teacher, because, "You call me Teacher and Lord; and you do well, for so I am," as we read below (13:13). For Nicodemus had read what was written in Joel (2:23): "Children of Sion, rejoice, and be joyful in the Lord your God, because he has given you a teacher of justice." But he says too little, because he says that Jesus came as a teacher from God, but is silent on whether he is God. For to come as a teacher from God is common to all good prelates: "I will give you shepherds after my own heart, and they will feed you with knowledge and doctrine," as it says in Jeremiah (3:15). Therefore, this is not unique to Christ even though Christ taught in a manner unlike other men. For some teachers teach only from without, but Christ also instructs within, because "He was the true light, which enlightens every man" (above 1:9); thus he alone gives wisdom: "I will give you an eloquence and a wisdom" (Lk 21:15), and this is something that no mere man can say.

429 He affirms his power because of the signs he saw. As if to say: I believe that you have come as a teacher from God, **for no one could perform the signs you perform.** And he is speaking the truth, because the signs which Christ did cannot be worked except by God, and because God was with him: "He who sent me is with me" (below 8:29). But he says too little, because he believed that Christ did not perform these signs through his own power, but as relying on the power of another; as though God were not with him by a unity of essence but merely by an infusion of grace. But this is false, because Christ performed these signs not by an exterior power but by his own; for the power of God and of Christ is one and the same. It is similar to what the woman says to Elijah: "Because of this I know that you are a man of God" (1 Kgs 17:24).

430 Then when he says that Jesus answered, **Amen, amen, I say to you,** he sets down the necessity for spiritual regeneration,

because of the ignorance of Nicodemus. And so he says, **Amen, amen.** Here we should note that this word, **amen,** is a Hebrew word frequently employed by Christ; hence out of reverence for him no Greek or Latin translator wanted to translate it. Sometimes it means the same as "true" or "truly"; and sometimes the same as "so be it." Thus is the Psalms 71 (v 19), 88 (v 53), and 106, where we have, "So be it, so be it," the Hebrew has "Amen, amen." But John is the only Evangelist who duplicates or makes a twin use of this word. The reason for this is that the other Evangelists are concerned mainly with matters pertaining to the humanity of Christ, which, since they are easier to believe, need less reinforcement; but John deals chiefly with things pertaining to the divinity of Christ, and these, since they are hidden and remote from men's knowledge and experience, require greater formal declaration.

431 Next we should point out that at first glance this answer of Christ seems to be entirely foreign to Nicodemus' statement. For what connection is there between Nicodemus' statement, **Rabbi, we know that you are a teacher come from God,** and the Lord's reply, **unless one is born again, he cannot see the kingdom of God.**

But we should note, as has already been stated, that Nicodemus, having an imperfect opinion about Christ, affirmed that he was a teacher and performed these signs as a mere man. And so the Lord wishes to show Nicodemus how he might arrive at a deeper understanding of him. And as a matter of fact, the Lord might have done so with an argument, but because this might have resulted in a quarrel — the opposite of which was prophesied about him: "He will not quarrel" (Is 42:2) — he wished to lead him to a true understanding with gentleness. As if to say: It is not strange that you regard me as a mere man, because one cannot know these secrets of the divinity unless he has achieved a spiritual regeneration. And this is what he says: **unless one is born again, he cannot see the kingdom of God.**

432 Here we should point out that since vision is an act of life, then according to the diverse kinds of life there will be diversity of vision. For there is a sentient life which some living things share in common, and this life has a sentient vision or knowledge. And there is also a spiritual life, by which man is made like God and other holy spirits; and this life enjoys a spiritual vision. Now spiritual things cannot be seen by the sentient: "The sensual man does not perceive those things that pertain to the Spirit of God" (1 Cor 2:14), but they are perceived by the spiritual vision: "No one knows the things of God but the Spirit of God" (1 Cor 2:11). So the apostle says: "You did not receive the spirit of slavery, putting you in fear again, but the spirit of adoption" (Rom 8:15). And we receive this

spirit through a spiritual regenaration: "He saved us by the cleansing of regeneration in the Holy Spirit" (Ti 3:3). Therefore, if spiritual vision comes only through the Holy Spirit, and if the Holy Spirit is given through a cleansing of spiritual regeneration, then it is only by a cleansing of regeneration that we can see the kingdom of God. Thus he says, **unless one is born again of water and the Holy Spirit, he cannot enter the kingdom of God.** As if to say: It is not surprising if you do not see the kingdom of God, because no one can see it unless he receives the Holy Spirit, through whom one is reborn a son of God.

433 It is not only the royal throne that pertains to a kingdom, but also the things needed for governing the kingdom, such as the royal dignity, royal favors, and the way of justice by which the kingdom is consolidated. Hence he says, **he cannot see the kingdom of God,** i.e., the glory and dignity of God, i.e., the mysteries of eternal salvation which are seen through the justice of faith: "The kingdom of God is not food and drink" (Rom 14:17).

Now in the Old Law there was a spiritual regeneration; but it was imperfect and symbolic: "All were baptized into Moses, in the cloud and in the sea" (1 Cor 10:2), i.e., they received baptism in symbol. Accordingly, they did see the mysteries of the kingdom of God, but only symbolically: "seeing from afar" (Heb 11:13). But in the New Law there is an evident spiritual regeneration, although imperfect, because we are renewed only inwardly by grace, but not outwardly by incorruption: "Although our outward nature is wasting away, yet our inward nature is being renewed day by day" (2 Cor 4:16). And so we do see the kingdom of God and the mysteries of eternal salvation, but imperfectly, for as it says, "Now we see in a mirror, in an obscure manner" (1 Cor 13:12). But there is perfect regeneration in heaven, because we will be renewed both inwardly and outwardly. And therefore we shall see the kingdom of God in a most perfect way: "But then we will see face to face," as is said in 1 Corinthians (13:12); and "When he appears we will be like him, because we will see him as he is" (1 Jn 3:2).

434 It is clear, therefore, that just as one does not have bodily vision unless he is born, so one cannot have spiritual vision unless he is reborn. And according to the threefold regeneration, there is a threefold kind of vision.

435 Note that the Greek reading is not "again," but *anothe*, i.e., "from above," which Jerome translated as "again," in order to suggest addition. And this is the way Jerome understood the saying, **unless one is born again.** It is as if he were saying: Unless one is reborn once more through a fraternal generation.

Chrysostom, however, says that to be "born from above" is

peculiar to the Son of God, because he alone is born from above: "The one who came from above is above all things" (below 3:31). And Christ is said to be born from above both as to time (if we may speak thus), because he was begotten from eternity: "Before the daystar I begot you" (Ps 109:3), and as to the principle of his generation, because he proceeds from the heavenly Father: "I came down from heaven not to do my own will, but the will of him who sent me" (below 6:38). Therefore, because our regeneration is in the likeness of the Son of God, inasmuch as "Those whom he foreknew he predestined to become conformed to the image of his Son" (Rom 8:29), and because that generation is from above, our generation also is from above: both as to the time, because of our eternal predestination, "He chose us in him before the foundation of the world" (Eph 1:4), and as to its being a gift of God, as we read below (6:44), "No one can come to me unless the Father, who sent me, draws him"; and "You have been saved by the grace of God" (Eph 2:5).

436   Then when he says, **Nicodemus said to him**, he gives the manner of and the reason for this spiritual regeneration. First, the doubt of Nicodemus is set forth. Secondly, Christ's response (v 5).

437   As to the first we should note that as stated in 1 Corinthians (2:14): "The sensual man does not perceive those things that pertain to the Spirit of God." And so because Nicodemus was yet carnal and sensual, he was unable to grasp, except in a carnal manner, the things that were said to him. Consequently, what the Lord said to him about spiritual regeneration, he understood of carnal generation. And this is what he says: **How can a man be born again when he is already an old man?**

We should note here, according to Chrysostom, that Nicodemus wanted to object to what was said by the Savior. But his objection is foolish, because Christ was speaking of spiritual regeneration, and he is objecting in terms of carnal regeneration. In like manner, all the reasons brought forth to attack the things of faith are foolish, since they are not according to the meaning of Sacred Scripture.

438   Nicodemus objected to the Lord's statement that a man must be born again according to the two ways in which this seemed impossible. In one way, on account of the irreversibility of human life; for a man cannot return to infancy from old age. Hence we read, "I am walking on a path," namely, this present life, "by which I will not return" (Jb 16:23). And it is from this point of view that he says, **How can a man be born again when he is already an old man?** As if to say: Shall he become a child once more so that he can be reborn? "He will not return again to his home, and his place will not know him any more" (Jb 7:10). In the second way, regeneration

seemed impossible because of the mode of carnal generation. For in the beginning, when a man is generated, he is small in size, so that his mother's womb can contain him; but later, after he is born, he continues to grow and reaches such a size that he cannot be contained within his mother's womb. And so Nicodemus says, **Is it possible for him to return to his mother's womb and be born all over again?** As if to say: He cannot, because the womb cannot contain him.

439 But this does not apply to spiritual generation. For no matter how spiritually old a man might become through sin, according to the Psalm (31:3): "Because I kept silent, all my bones grew old," he can, with the help of divine grace, become new, according to the Psalm (102:5): "Your youth will be renewed like the eagle's." And no matter how enormous he is, he can enter the spiritual womb of the Church by the sacrament of baptism. And it is clear what that spiritual womb is; otherwise it would never have been said: "From the womb, before the daystar, I begot you" (Ps 109:3). Yet there is a sense in which his objection applies. For just as a man, once he is born according to nature, cannot be reborn, so once he is born in a spiritual way through baptism, he cannot be reborn, because he cannot be baptized again: "One Lord, one faith, one baptism," as we read in Ephesians (4:5).

440 Then we have the answer of Christ. Concerning this he does three things. First, he answers the arguments of Nicodemus by showing the nature of regeneration. Secondly, he explains this answer with a reason (v 6). Thirdly, he explains it with an example.

441 He answers the objections by showing that he is speaking of a spiritual regeneration, not a carnal one. And this is what he says: **unless one is born again of water and the Holy Spirit, he cannot enter the kingdom of God.** As if to say: You are thinking of a carnal generation, but I am speaking of a spiritual generation.

Note that above he had said, **he cannot see the kingdom of God,** while here he says, **he cannot enter the kingdom of God,** which is the same thing. For no one can see the things of the kingdom of God unless he enters it; and to the extent that he enters, he sees. "I will give him a white stone upon which is written a new name, which no one knows but he who receives it" (Rv 5:5).

442 Now there is a reason why spiritual generation comes from the Spirit. It is necessary that the one generated be generated in the likeness of the one generating; but we are regenerated as sons of God, in the likeness of his true Son. Therefore, it is necessary that our spiritual regeneration come about through that by which we are made like the true Son; and this comes about by our having his Spirit: "If

any one does not have the Spirit of Christ, he is not his" (Rom 8:9); "By this we know that we abide in him, and he in us: because he has given us of his Spirit" (1 Jn 4:13). Thus spiritual regeneration must come from the Holy Spirit. "You did not receive the spirit of slavery, putting you in fear again, but the spirit of adoption" (Rom 8:15); "It is the Spirit that gives life" (below 6:63).

443 Water, too, is necessary for this regeneration, and for three reasons. First, because of the condition of human nature. For man consists of soul and body, and if the Spirit alone were involved in his regeneration, this would indicate that only the spiritual part of man is regenerated. Hence in order that the flesh also be regenerated, it is necessary that, in addition to the Spirit through whom the soul is regenerated, something bodily be involved, through which the body is regenerated; and this is water.

Secondly, water is necessary for the sake of human knowledge. For, as Dionysius says, divine wisdom so disposes all things that it provides for each thing according to its nature. Now it is natural for man to know; and so it is fitting that spiritual things be conferred on men in such a way that he may know them: "so that we may know what God has given us" (1 Cor 2:12). But the natural manner of this knowledge is that man know spiritual things by means of sensible things, since all our knowledge begins in sense knowledge. Therefore, in order that we might understand what is spiritual in our regeneration, it was fitting that there be in it something sensible and material, that is, water, through which we understand that just as water washes and cleanses the exterior in a bodily way, so through baptism a man is washed and cleansed inwardly in a spiritual way.

Thirdly, water was necessary so that there might be a correspondence of causes. For the cause of our regeneration is the incarnate Word: "He gave them power to become the sons of God," as we saw above (1:12). Therefore it was fitting that in the sacraments, which have their efficacy from the power of the incarnate Word, there be something corresponding to the Word, and something corresponding to the flesh, or body. And spiritually speaking, this is water when the sacrament is baptism, so that through it we may be conformed to the death of Christ, since we are submerged in it during baptism as Christ was in the womb of the earth for three days: "We are buried with him by baptism" (Rom 6:4).

Further, this mystery was suggested in the first production of things, when the Spirit of God hovered over the waters (Gn 1:2). But a greater power was conferred on water by contact with the most pure flesh of Christ; because in the beginning water brought forth crawling creatures with living souls, but since Christ was baptized in the Jordan, water has yielded spiritual souls.

444 It is clear that the Holy Spirit is God, since he says, **unless one is born again of water and the Holy Spirit** (*ex aqua et Spiritu Sancto*). For above (1:13) he says: "who are born not from blood, nor from the desires of the flesh, nor from man's willing it, but from God (*ex Deo*)." From this we can form the following argument: He from whom men are spiritually reborn is God; but men are spiritually reborn through the Holy Spirit, as it is stated here; therefore, the Holy Spirit is God.

445 Two questions arise here. First, if no one enters the kingdom of God unless he is born again of water, and if the fathers of old were not born again of water (for they were not baptized), then they have not entered the kingdom of God. Secondly, since baptism is of three kinds, that is, of water, of desire, and of blood, and many have been baptized in the latter two ways (who we say have entered the kingdom of God immediately, even though they were not born again of water), it does not seem to be true to say that **unless one is born again of water and the Holy Spirit, he cannot enter the kingdom of God.**

The answer to the first is that rebirth or regeneration from water and the Holy Spirit takes place in two ways: in truth and in symbol. Now the fathers of old, although they were not reborn with a true rebirth, were nevertheless reborn with a symbolic rebirth, because they always had a sense perceptible sign in which true rebirth was prefigured. So according to this, thus reborn, they did enter the kingdom of God, after the ransom was paid.

The answer to the second is that those who are reborn by a baptism of blood and fire, although they do not have regeneration in deed, they do have it in desire. Otherwise neither would the baptism of blood mean anything nor could there be a baptism of the Spirit. Consequently, in order that man may enter the kingdom of heaven, it is necessary that there be a baptism of water in deed, as in the case of all baptized persons, or in desire, as in the case of the martyrs and catechumens, who are prevented by death from fulfilling their desire, or in symbol, as in the case of the fathers of old.

446 It might be remarked that it was from this statement, **unless one is born again of water and the Holy Spirit**, that the Pelagians derived their error that children are baptized not in order to be cleansed from sin, since they have none, but in order to be able to enter the kingdom of God. But this is false, because as Augustine says in his book, *The Baptism of Children*, it is not fitting for an image of God, namely, man, to be excluded from the kingdom of God except for some obstacle, which can be nothing but sin. Therefore, there must be some sin, namely, original sin, in children who are excluded from the kingdom.

447   Then when he says, **What is born of flesh is itself flesh,** he proves by reason that it is necessary to be born of water and the Holy Spirit. And the reasoning is this: No one can reach the kingdom unless he is made spiritual; but no one is made spiritual except by the Holy Spirit; therefore, no one can enter the kingdom of God unless he is born again of the Holy Spirit.

So he says, **what is born of flesh** (*ex carne*) **is itself flesh,** i.e., birth according to the flesh makes one be born into the life of the flesh: "The first man was from the earth, earthly" (1 Cor 15:47); **and what is born of Spirit** (*ex Spiritu*) , i.e., from the power of the Holy Spirit, **is itself spirit,** i.e., spiritual.

448   Note, however, that this preposition *ex* (from, of, by) sometines designates a material cause, as when I say: "A knife is made of (*ex*) iron"; sometimes it designates an efficient cause, as when I say: "The house was built by (*ex*) a carpenter." Accordingly, the phrase, **what is born of (*ex*) flesh is itself flesh,** can be understood according to either efficient or material causality. As efficient cause, indeed, because a power existing in flesh is productive of generation; and as material cause, because some carnal element in animals makes up the animal generated. But nothing is said to be made out of spirit (*ex spiritu*) in a material sense, since spirit is unchangeable, whereas matter is the subject of change; but it is said in the sense of efficient causality.

According to this, we can discern a threefold generation. One is materially and effectively from (*ex*) the flesh, and is common to all who exist according to the flesh. Another is according to the Spirit effectively, and according to it we are reborn as sons of God through the grace of the Holy Spirit, and are made spiritual. The third is midway, that is, only materially from the flesh but effectively from the Holy Spirit. And this is true in the singular case of Christ: because he was born deriving his flesh materially from the flesh of his mother, but effectively from the Holy Spirit: "What she has conceived is of the Holy Spirit" (Mt 1:20). Therefore, he was born holy: "The Holy Spirit will come upon you, and the power of the Most High will overshadow you. And so the Holy One who will be born from you, will be called the Son of God" (Lk 1:35).

7 "Do not be surprised that I said to you,
you must be born again.
8 The wind blows where it wills,
and you hear its sound, but you do not know
where it comes from or where it goes.
So it is with everyone who is born of the Spirit."
9 "How can all this happen?" asked Nicodemus. 10 Jesus
replied: "You are a teacher in Israel and you do not know these
things?
11 "Amen, amen I say to you,
that we know of what we speak,
and we bear witness of what we see;
but you do not accept our testimony.
12 If I spoke of earthly things,
and you did not believe me,
how will you believe if I tell you of heavenly things?
13 No one has gone up to heaven
except the One who came down from heaven,
the Son of Man, who lives in heaven.
14 Just as Moses lifted up the serpent in the desert,
so must the Son of Man be lifted up,
15 so that everyone who believes in him may not be lost,
but have eternal life."

449   Above, in his instruction on spiritual generation, the Lord
presented a reason; here he gives an example. For we are led to see
that Nicodemus was troubled when he heard that **what is born of
Spirit is itself spirit.** And so the Lord says to him, **Do not be surprised that I said to you, you must be born again.**

Here we should note that there are two kinds of surprise or
astonishment. One is the astonishment of devotion in the sense that
someone, considering the great things of God, sees that they are
incomprehensible to him; and so he is full of astonishment: "The
Lord on high is wonderful" (Ps 92:4), "Your testimonies are wonderful" (Ps 118:129). Men are to be encouraged, not discouraged,
to this kind of astonishment The other is the astonishment of disbelief, when someone does not believe what is said. So Matthew
(13:54) says: "They were astonished," and further on adds that
"They did not accept him." It is from this kind of astonishment that
the Lord diverts Nicodemus when he proposes an example and says:
The wind (*spiritus*, wind, spirit) **blows where it wills.** In the literal
sense, the same words can be explained in two ways.

450   In the first way, according to Chrysostom, *spiritus* is taken for the wind, as in Psalm 148 (v 8): "The winds of the storm that fulfill his word." According to this interpretation, he says four things about the wind. First, the power of the wind, when he says, **the wind blows where it wills**. And if you say that the wind has no will, one may answer that "will" is taken for a natural appetite, which is nothing more than a natural inclination, about which it is said: "He created the weight of the wind" (Jb 28:25). Secondly, he tells the evidence for the wind, when he says, **and you hear its sound**, where "sound" (*vox*, voice, sound) refers to the sound the wind makes when it strikes a body. Of this we read: "The sound (*vox*) of your thunder was in the whirlwind" (Ps 76:19).

Thirdly, he mentions the origin of the wind, which is unknown; so he says, **but you do not know where it comes from**, i.e., from where it starts: "He brings forth the winds out of his storehouse" (Ps 134:7). Fourthly, he mentions the wind's destination, which is also unknown; so he says, **or where it goes** you do not know, i.e., where it remains.

And he applies this similarity to the subject under discussion, saying, **So it is with everyone who is born of the Spirit**. As if to say: If the wind, which is corporeal, has an origin which is hidden and a course that is unknown, why are you surprised if you cannot understand the course of spiritual regeneration.

451   Augustine objects to this explanation and says that the Lord was not speaking here about the wind, for we know where each of the winds comes from and where it goes. For "Auster" comes from the south and goes to the north; "Boreas" comes from the north and goes to the south. Why, then, does the Lord say of this wind, **you do not know where it comes from or where it goes?**

One may answer that there are two ways in which the source of the wind might be unknown. In one way, in general: and in this way it is possible to know where it comes from, i.e., from which direction of the world, for example, that Auster comes from the south, and where it goes, that is, to the north. In another way, in particular: and in this sense it is not known where the wind comes from, i.e., at which precise place it originated, or where it goes, i.e., exactly where it stops. And almost all the Greek doctors agree with this exposition of Chrysostom.

452   In another way, *spiritus* is taken for the Holy Spirit. And according to this, he mentions four things about the Holy Spirit. First, his power, saying, **The Spirit blows where it wills**, because it is by the free use of his power that he breathes where he wills and when he wills, by instructing hearts: "One and the same Spirit does

all these things, distributing to each as he wills" (1 Cor 12:11). This refutes the error of Macedonius who thought that the Holy Spirit was the minister of the Father and the Son. But then he would not be breathing where he willed, but where he was commanded.

453 Secondly, he mentions the evidence for the Holy Spirit, when he says, **and you hear its voice**: "Today, if you hear his voice, do not harden your hearts" (Ps 94:8).

Chrysostom objects to this and says that this cannot pertain to the Holy Spirit. For the Lord was speaking to Nicodemus, who was still an unbeliever, and thus not fit to hear the voice of the Holy Spirit. We may answer to this, with Augustine, that there is a twofold voice of the Holy Spirit. One is that by which he speaks inwardly in man's heart; and only believers and the saints hear this voice, about which the Psalm (84:9) says: "I will hear what the Lord God says within me." The other voice is that by which the Holy Spirit speaks in the Scriptures or through those who preach, according to Matthew (10:20): "For it is not you who speak, but the Holy Spirit who is speaking through you." And this voice is heard by unbelievers and sinners.

454 Thirdly, he refers to the origin of the Holy Spirit, which is hidden; thus he says, **but you do not know where it comes from**, although you may hear its voice. And this is because the Holy Spirit comes from the Father and the Son: "When the Paraclete comes, whom I will send you from the Father, the Spirit of truth, who proceeds from the Father" (below 15:26). But the Father and the Son "dwell in inaccessible light, whom no man has seen or is able to see" (1 Tim 6:16).

455 Fourthly, he gives the destination of the Holy Spirit, which is also hidden; and so he says, you do not know **where it goes**, because the Spirit leads one to a hidden end, that is, eternal happiness. Thus it says in Ephesians (1:14) that the Holy Spirit is "the pledge of our inheritance." And again, "The eye has not seen, nor has the ear heard, nor has the heart of man conceived, what God has prepared for those who love him" (1 Cor 2:9).

Or, **you do not know where it comes from**, i.e., how the Spirit enters into a person, **or where it goes**, i.e., to what perfection he may lead him: "If he comes toward me, I will not see him" (Jb 9:11).

456 **So it is with everyone who is born of the Spirit**, i.e., they are like the Holy Spirit. And no wonder: for as he had said before, "What is born of Spirit is itself spirit," because the qualities of the Holy Spirit are present in the spiritual man, just as the qualities of fire are present in burning coal.

Therefore, the above four qualities of the Holy Spirit are found in one who has been born of the Holy Spirit. First of all, he has freedom: "Where the Spirit of the Lord is, there is freedom" (2 Cor 3:17), for the Holy Spirit leads us to what is right: "Your good Spirit will lead me to the right path" (Ps 142:10); and he frees us from the slavery of sin and of the law: "The law of the Spirit, of life in Christ, has set me free" (Rom 8:2). Secondly, we get an indication of him through the sound of his words; and when we hear them we know his spirituality, for it is out of the abundance of the heart that the mouth speaks.

Thirdly, he has an origin and an end that are hidden, because no one can judge one who is spiritual: "The spiritual man judges all things, and he himself is judged by no one" (1 Cor 2:15). Or, we do not know where such a person comes from, i.e., the source of his spiritual birth, which is baptismal grace; or where he goes, i.e., of what he is made worthy, that is, of eternal life, which remains concealed from us.

457   Then the cause and reason for spiritual regeneration are set forth. First, a question is asked by Nicodemus; secondly, the Lord's answer is given (v 10).

458   It is apparent from the first that Nicodemus, as yet dull, and remaining a Jew on the level of sense, was unable to understand the mysteries of Christ in spite of the examples and explanations that were given. And so he says, **How can all this happen?**

There are two reasons why one may question about something. Some question because of disbelief, as did Zechariah, saying: "How will I know this? For I am an old man, and my wife is advanced in age" (Lk 1:18); "He confounds those who search into mysteries" (Is 40:23). Others, on the other hand, question because of a desire to know, as the Blessed Virgin did when she said to the angel: "How shall this be, since I do not know man?" (Lk 1:34). It is the latter who are instructed. And so, because Nicodemus asked from a desire to learn, he deserved to be instructed.

459   And this is what follows: **Jesus replied.** First the Lord chides him for his slowness. Secondly, he answers his question (v 13).

460   He chides him for his slowness, basing himself on three things. First, the condition of the person to whom he is speaking, when he says, **You are a teacher in Israel.** And here the Lord did not chide him to insult him. Rather, because Nicodemus, presuming on his own knowledge, was still relying on his status as a teacher, the Lord wished to make him a temple of the Holy Spirit by humbling him: "For whom will I have regard? For he who is humble and of contrite spirit" (Is 66:2). And he says, **You are a teacher,** because

it is tolerable if a simple person cannot grasp profound truths, but in a teacher, it deserves rebuke. And so he says, **You are a teacher,** i.e., of the letter that kills (2 Cor 3:6), **and you do not know these things?** i.e., spiritual things. "For although you ought to be teachers by now, you yourselves need to be taught again" (Heb 5:12).

461 You might say that the Lord would have rebuked Nicodemus justly if he had spoken to him about matters of the Old Law and he did not understand them; but he spoke to him about the New Law. I answer that the things which the Lord says of spiritual generation are contained in the Old Law, although under a figure, as is said in 1 Corinthians (10:2): "All were baptized into Moses, in the cloud and in the sea." And the prophets also said this: "I will pour clean water upon you, and you will be cleansed from all your uncleanness" (Ez 36:25).

462 Secondly, he rebukes him for his slowness on account of the character of the person who is speaking. For it is tolerable if one does not acquiesce to the statements of an ignorant person; but it is reprehensible to reject the statements of a man who is wise and who possesses great authority. And so he says, **Amen, amen I say to you, that we know of what we speak, and we bear witness of what we see.** For a qualified witness must base his testimony on hearing or sight: "What we have seen and heard" (1 Jn 1:3). And so the Lord mentions both: **we know of what we speak, and we bear witness of what we see.** Indeed, the Lord as man knows all things: "Lord, you know all things" (below 21:17); "The Lord, whose knowledge is holy, knows clearly" (2 Mc 6:30). Further, he sees all things by his divine knowledge: "I speak of what I have seen with my Father," as we read below (8:38).

He speaks in the plural, **we know, we see,** in order to suggest the mystery of the Trinity: "The Father, who dwells in me, he does the works" (below 14:10). Or, **we know,** i.e., I, and others who have been made spiritual, because "No one knows the Father but the Son, and he to whom the Son wishes to reveal him" (Mt 11:27).

But you do not accept our testimony, so approved, so solid. "And his testimony no one accepts (below 3:32).

463 Thirdly, he rebukes him for his slowness because of the quality of the things under discussion. For it is not unusual when someone does not grasp difficult matters, but it is inexcusable not to grasp easy things. So he says, **If I spoke of earthly things, and you did not believe, how will you believe if I tell you of heavenly things?** As if to say: If you do not grasp these easy things, how will you be able to understand the progress of the Holy Spirit? "What is on earth we find difficult, and who will search out the things in heaven," as is said in Wisdom (9:16).

464   But one might object that the above does not show that the Lord spoke of earthly things to Nicodemus. I answer, according to Chrysostom, that the Lord's statement, **If I spoke of earthly things**, refers to the example of the wind. For the wind, being something which is generable and corruptible, is regarded as an earthly thing. Or one might say, again according to Chrysostom, that the spiritual generation which is given in baptism is heavenly as to its source, which sanctifies and regenerates; but it is earthly as to its subject, for the one regenerated, man, is of the earth.

Or one might answer, according to Augustine, that we must understand this in reference to what Christ said earlier: "Destroy this temple," which is earthly, because he said this about the temple of his body, which he had taken from the earth.

If I spoke of earthly things, and you did not believe, how will you believe if I tell you of heavenly things? As if to say: If you do not believe in a spiritual generation occurring in time, how will you believe in the eternal generation of the Son? Or, if you do not believe what I tell you about the power of my body, how will you believe what I tell you about the power of my divinity and about the power of the Holy Spirit?

465   **Jesus replied.** Here he answers the question. First, he lays down the causes of spiritual regeneration. Secondly, he explains what he says (3:16). Now there are two causes of spiritual regeneration, namely, the mystery of the incarnation of Christ, and his passion. So first, he treats of the incarnation; secondly, of the passion (3:14).

466   Here we should consider, first of all, how this answer of Christ is an adequate reply to the question of Nicodemus. For above, when the Lord was speaking of the Spirit, he said: **you do not know where it comes from or where it goes.** We understand by this that spiritual regeneration has a hidden source and a hidden end. Now the things in heaven are hidden from us: "Who will search out the things in heaven?" (Wis 9:16). Therefore, the sense of Nicodemus' question, **How can all this happen?** is this: How can something come from the secret things of heaven or go to the secret things of heaven? So before answering, the Lord expressed this interpretation of the question, saying, **how will you believe if I tell you of heavenly things?**

And immediately he begins to show whose prerogative it is to ascend into heaven, namely, anyone who came down from heaven, according to the statement of Ephesians (4:10): "He who descended is he who ascended." This is verified even in natural things, namely, that each body tends to a place according to its origin or nature. And so in this way it can come about that someone, through the Spirit, may go to a place which carnal persons do not know, i.e., by ascending into heaven, if this is done through the power of one who descended from heaven: because he descended in order that, in ascending, he might open a way for us: "He ascends, opening the way before them" (Mi 2:13).

467 Some have fallen into error because of his saying, **the One who came down from heaven, the Son of Man**. For since Son of Man designates human nature, which is composed of soul and body, then because he says that the Son descended from heaven, Valentinus wanted to maintain that he even took his body from heaven and thus passed through the Virgin without receiving anything from her, as water passes through a pipe; so that his body was neither of an earthly substance nor taken from the Virgin. But this is contrary to the statement of the Apostle, writing to the Romans (1:3): "who was made from the seed of David according to the flesh."

On the other hand, Origen said that he descended from heaven as to his soul, which, he says, had been created along with the angels from the very beginning, and that later this soul descended from heaven and took flesh from the Virgin. But this also conflicts with the Catholic faith, which teaches that souls do not exist before their bodies.

468 Therefore, we should not understand that the Son of Man descended from heaven according to his human nature, but only according to his divine nature. For since in Christ there is one suppositum, or hypostasis, or person of the two natures, the divine and human natures, then no matter from which of these two natures this suppositum is named, divine and human things can be attributed to him. For we can say that the Son of Man created the stars and that the Son of God was crucified. But the Son of God was crucified, not according to his divine nature, but according to his human nature; and the Son of Man created the stars according to his divine nature. And so in things that are said of Christ, the distinction is not to be taken with respect to that about which they are said, because divine and human things are said of God and man indifferently; but a distinction must be made with respect to that according to which they are said, because divine things are said of Christ according to his divine nature, but human things according to his human nature. Thus, to descend from heaven is said of the Son of Man, not according to his human nature, but according to his divine nature, according to which it was appropriate to him to have been from heaven before the incarnation, as is said, "Heaven belongs to the Lord" (Ps 113:16).

469 He is said to have come down, but not by local motion, because then he would not have remained in heaven; for nothing which moves locally remains in the place from which it comes down. And so to exclude local motion, he adds, **who lives in heaven**. As if

to say: He descended from heaven in such a way as yet to be in heaven. For he came down from heaven without ceasing to be above, yet assuming a nature which is from below. And because he is not enclosed or held fast by his body which exists on earth, he was, according to his divinity, in heaven and everywhere. And therefore to indicate that he is said to have come down in this way, because he assumed a [human] nature, he said, **the Son of Man** came down, i.e., insofar as he became Son of Man.

470 Or it can be said, as Hilary does, that he came down from heaven as to his body: not that the material of Christ's body came down from heaven, but that the power which formed it was from heaven.

471 But why does he say, **No one has gone up to heaven except the Son of Man, who lives in heaven**? For have not Paul and Peter and the other saints gone up, according to 2 Corinthians (5:1): "We have a house in the heavens." I answer that no one goes up into heaven except Christ and his members, i.e., those believers who are just. Accordingly, the Son of God came down from heaven in order that, by making us his members, he might prepare us to ascend into heaven: now, indeed, in hope, but later in reality. "He has raised us up, and has given us a place in heaven in Christ Jesus" (Eph 2:6).

472 Here he mentions the mystery of the passion, in virtue of which baptism has its efficacy: "We who have been baptized into Christ Jesus, have been baptized into his death" (Rom 6:3). And with regard to this he does three things. First, he gives a symbol for the passion. Secondly, the manner of the passion. Thirdly, the fruit of the passion.

473 He takes the symbol from the old law, in order to adapt to the understanding of Nicodemus; so he says, **Just as Moses lifted up the serpent in the desert**. This refers to Numbers (21:5) when the Lord, faced with the Jewish people saying, "We are sick of this useless food," sent serpents to punish them; and when the people came to Moses and he interceded with the Lord, the Lord commanded that for a remedy they make a serpent of bronze; and this was to serve both as a remedy against those serpents and as a symbol of the Lord's passion. Hence it says that this bronze serpent was lifted up as a sign (Nm 21:9).

Now it is characteristic of serpents that they are poisonous, but not so the serpent of bronze, although it was a symbol of a poisonous serpent. So, too, Christ did not have sin, which is also a poison: "Sin, when it is fully developed, brings forth death" (Jas 1:15); but he had the likeness of sin: "God sent his own Son, in the likeness of sinful flesh" (Rom 8:3). And thus Christ had the effect of the serpent against the insurgence of inflamed concupiscences.

474   He shows the manner of the passion when he says, **so must the Son of Man be lifted up**: and this refers to the lifting up of the cross. So below (12:34) when it says, "The Son of Man must be lifted up," it also has, "He said this to indicate the manner of his death."

He willed to die lifted up, first of all, to cleanse the heavens: for since he had cleansed the things on earth by the sanctity of his life, the things of the air were left to be cleansed by his death: "through him he should reconcile all things to himself, whether on earth or in the heavens, making peace through his blood" (Col 1:20). Secondly, to triumph over the demons who prepare for war in the air: "the prince of the power of the air" (Eph 2:2). Thirdly, he wished to die lifted up to draw our hearts to himself: "I, if I am lifted up from the earth, will draw all to myself" (below 12:32). And fourthly, because in the death of the cross he was lifted up in the sense that there he triumphed over his enemies; so it is not called a death, but a lifting up: "He will drink from the stream on the way, therefore he will lift up his head" (Ps 109:7). Fifthly, he willed to die lifted up because the cross was the reason for his being lifted up, i.e., exalted: "He became obedient to the Father even to death, the death of the cross; on account of which God has exalted him" (Phil 2:8).

475   Now the fruit of Christ's passion is eternal life; hence he says, **so that everyone who believes in him**, performing good works, **may not be lost, but have eternal life**. And this fruit corresponds to the fruit of the symbolic serpent. For whoever looked upon the serpent of bronze was freed from poison and his life was preserved. But he who looks upon the lifted up Son of Man, and believes in the crucified Christ, he is freed from poison and sin: "Whoever believes in me will never die" (below 11:26), and is preserved for eternal life. "These things are written that you may believe ... and that believing you may have life in his name" (below 20:31).

LECTURE 3

16 "For God so loved the world
that he gave his Only Begotten Son,
so that whoever believes in him should not perish,
but have eternal life.
17 God did not send his Son into the world
to judge the world,
but that the world might be saved through him.

18 Whoever believes in him is not judged;
but whoever does not believe is already judged,
since he does not believe in the name of the
Only Begotten Son of God.
19 The judgment of condemnation is this:
the light came into the world,
and men loved darkness more than the light,
because their deeds were evil.
20 Everyone who practices evil hates the light,
and does not approach the light
for fear that his deeds might be exposed.
21 But everyone who practices the truth
comes to the light, to make clear
that his deeds are done in God."

476   Above, the Lord assigned as the cause of spiritual regeneration the coming down of the Son and the lifting up of the Son of Man; and he set forth its fruit, which is eternal life. But this fruit seemed unbelievable to men laboring under the necessity of dying. And so now the Lord explains this. First, he proves the greatness of the fruit from the greatness of God's love. Secondly, he rejects a certain reply (v 17).

477   Here we should note that the cause of all our good is the Lord and divine love. For to love is, properly speaking, to will good to someone. Therefore, since the will of God is the cause of things, good comes to us because God loves us. And God's love is the cause of the good of nature: "You love everything which exists" (Wis 11:25). It is also the cause of the good which is grace: "I have loved you with an everlasting love, and so I have drawn you" i.e., through grace (Jer 31:3). But it is because of his great love that he gives us the good of glory. So he shows us here, from four standpoints, that this love of God is the greatest.

First, from the person of the one loving, because it is God who loves, and immeasurably. So he says, **For God so loved**: "He has loved the people; all the holy ones are in his hand" (Dt 33:3). Secondly, from the condition of the one who is loved, because it is man, a bodily creature of the world, i.e., existing in sin: "God shows his love for us, because while we were still his enemies, we were reconciled to God by the death of his Son" (Rom 5:8). Thus he says, **the world**. Thirdly, from the greatness of his gifts, for love is shown by a gift; as Gregory says: "The proof of love is given by action." But God has given us the greatest of gifts, his Only Begotten Son; and so he says, **that he gave his Only Begotten Son**. "God did not spare his own Son, but delivered him up for all of us" (Rom 8:32).

He says **his** Son, i.e., his natural Son, consubstantial, not an adopted son, i.e., not those sons of which the Psalmist says: "I said: You are gods" (Ps 81:6). This shows that the opinion of Arius is false: for if the Son of God were a creature, as he said, the immensity of God's love through the taking on of infinite goodness, which no creature can receive, could not have been revealed in him. He further says **Only Begotten**, to show that God does not have a love divided among many sons, but all of it is for that Son whom he gave to prove the immensity of his love: "For the Father loves the Son, and shows him everything that he does" (below 5:20).

Fourthly, from the greatness of its fruit, because through him we have eternal life. Hence he says, **so that whoever believes in him should not perish, but have eternal life**, which he obtained for us through the death of the cross.

478 But did God give his Son with the intention that he should die on the cross? He did indeed give him for the death of the cross inasmuch as he gave him the will to suffer on it. And he did this in two ways. First, because as the Son of God he willed from eternity to assume flesh and to suffer for us; and this will he had from the Father. Secondly, because the will to suffer was infused into the soul of Christ by God.

479 Note that above, when the Lord was speaking about the coming down which belongs to Christ according to his divinity, he called him the Son of God; and this because of the one suppositum of the two natures, as was explained above. And so divine things can be said about the suppositum of the human nature, and human things can be said about the suppositum of the divine nature, but not with reference to the same nature. Rather, divine things are said with reference to the divine nature, and human things with reference to the human nature. Now the specific reason why he here calls him the Son of God is that he set forth that gift as a sign of the divine love, through which the fruit of eternal life comes to us. And so, he should have been called by that name which indicates the power that produces eternal life; and this power is not in Christ as Son of Man but as Son of God: "This is the true God and eternal life," as we read in 1 John (5:20); "In him was life" (above 1:4).

480 Note also that he says, **should not perish**. Someone is said to be perishing when he is hindered from arriving at the end to which he is ordained. But the end to which man is ordained is eternal life, and as long as he sins, he turns himself from that end. And although while he is living he cannot entirely perish in the sense that he cannot be restored, yet when he dies in sin, then he entirely perishes: "The way of the wicked will perish" (Ps 1:7).

He indicates the immensity of God's love in saying, **have eternal life**: for by giving eternal life, he gives himself. For eternal life is nothing else than enjoying God. But to give oneself is a sign of great love: "But God, who is rich in mercy, has brought us to life in Christ" (Eph 2:5), i.e., he gave us eternal life.

481   Here the Lord excludes an objection that might be made. For in the old law it was promised that the Lord would come to judge: "The Lord will come to judge" (Is 3:14). So someone might say that the Son of God had not come to give eternal life but in order to judge the world. The Lord rejects this. First, he shows that he has not come to judge. Secondly, he proves it (v 18).

482   So he says: The Son of God has not come to judge, because **God did not send his Son,** referring to his first coming, **into the world to judge the world, but that the world might be saved through him**. The same thing is found below (12:47): "I did not come to judge the world, but to save the world."

Now man's salvation is to attain to God: "My salvation is in God" (Ps 61:8). And to attain to God is to obtain eternal life; hence to be saved is the same as to have eternal life. However, because the Lord says, "I did not come to judge the world," men should not be lazy or abuse God's mercy, or give themselves over to sin: because although in his first coming he did not come to judge but to forgive, yet in his second coming, as Chrysostom says, he will come to judge but not to forgive. "At the appointed time I will judge with rigor" (Ps 74:3).

483   However, this seems to conflict with what is said below (9:39): "I came into this world to judge." I answer that there are two kinds of judgment. One is the judgment of distinction, and the Son has come for this in his first coming; because with his coming men are distinguished, some by blindness and some by the light of grace. The other is the judgment of condemnation; and he did not come for this as such.

484   Now he proves what he had said, as though by a process of elimination, in the following way: Whoever will be judged will be either a believer or an unbeliever. But I have not come to judge unbelievers, because they are already judged. Therefore, from the outset, God did not send his Son to judge the world. So first he shows that believers are not judged. Secondly, that unbelievers are not judged (v 18).

485   He says therefore: I have not come to judge the world: because he did not come to judge believers, for **Whoever believes in him is not judged**, with the judgment of condemnation, with which

no one who believes in him with faith informed by love is judged: "Whoever believes ... will not encounter judgment, but will pass from death to life" (below 5:24). But he is judged with the judgment of reward and approval, of which the Apostle says: "It is the Lord who judges me" (1 Cor 4:4).

486   But will there be many believing sinners who will not be damned? I reply that some heretics [e.g., Origen] have said that no believer, however great a sinner he may be, will be damned, but he will be saved by reason of his foundation of salvation, namely, his faith, although he may suffer some [temporary] punishment. They take as the basis of their error the statement of the Apostle: "No one can lay a foundation other that the one that has been laid, that is, Jesus Christ" (1 Cor 3:11); and further on: "If a man's building burns ... he himself will be saved as one fleeing through fire" (3:15).

But this view is clearly contrary to what the Apostle says in Galatians (5:1): "It is obvious what proceeds from the flesh: lewd conduct, impurity, licentiousness ... Those who do such things will not inherit the kingdom of God." Therefore we must say that the foundation of salvation is not faith without charity (unformed faith), but faith informed by charity. Significantly therefore the Lord did not say, "whoever believes him," but **whoever believes in him**, that is, whoever by believing tends toward him through love **is not judged**, because he does not sin mortally, thereby removing the foundation.

Or one could say, following Chrysostom, that everyone who acts sinfully is not a believer: "They profess to know God, but they deny him by their actions" (Ti 1:16); but only one who acts worthily: "Show me your faith by your works" (Jas 2:18). It is only such a one who is not judged and not condemned for unbelief.

487   Here [the Lord] shows that unbelievers are not judged. First he makes the statement; secondly, he explains it (v 19).

488   Concerning the first we should note, according to Augustine, that Christ does not say, "whoever does not believe is judged," but rather **is not judged**. This can be explained in three ways. For, according to Augustine, whoever does not believe is not judged, because he is already judged, not in fact, but in God's foreknowledge, that is, it is already known to God that he will be condemned: "The Lord knows who are his" (2 Tim 2:19). In another way: according to Chrysostom, **whoever does not believe is already judged**, that is, the very fact that he does not believe is for him a condemnation: for not to believe is not to adhere to the light — which is to live in darkness, and this is a momentous condemnation: "All were bound with one chain of darkness" (Wis 17:17). "What kind of joy can I have; I who sit in darkness and do not see the light

of heaven?" (Tb 5:12). In a third way: also according to Chrysostom, **whoever does not believe is not judged**, that is, being already condemned, he displays the obvious reason for his condemnation. This is like saying that a person who is proven guilty of death is already dead, even before the sentence of death has been passed on him, because he is as good as dead.

Hence Gregory says that in passing judgments there is a twofold order. Some will be sentenced by a trial; such are the ones who have something not deserving of condemnation, namely, the good of faith, that is, sinners who believe. But unbelievers, whose reason for condemnation is manifest, are sentenced without trial; and of these it is said, **whoever does not believe is already judged.** "In judgment the wicked will not stand" (Ps 1:6), that is, stand in trial.

489 It should be noted that to be judged is the same as to be condemned; and to be condemned is to be shut out from salvation, to which only one road leads, that is, the name of the Son of God: "There is no other name under heaven given to men, by which we are saved" (Acts 4:12); "O God, save me by your name" (Ps 53:3). Therefore, those who do not believe in the Son of God are cut off from salvation, and the cause of their damnation is evident.

490 Here the Lord explains his statement that unbelievers have an evident cause for their condemnation. First, he sets forth the sign which shows this. Secondly, the fittingness of this sign (v 20).

491 In the sign he sets forth he does three things. First, he mentions the gift of God. Secondly, the perversity of mind in unbelievers. Thirdly, the cause of this perversity.

So he says: It is abundantly clear that **whoever does not believe is already judged**, because **the light came into the world.** For men were in the darkness of ignorance, and God destroyed this darkness by sending a light into the world so that men might know the truth: "I am the light of the world. He who follows me does not walk in darkness, but will have the light of life" (below 8:12); "To enlighten those who sit in darkness and in the shadow of death" (Lk 1:78). Now the light came into the world because men could not come to it: for "He dwells in inaccessible light, whom no man has seen or is able to see" (1 Tim 6:16).

It is also clear from the perversity of mind in unbelievers who **loved darkness more than the light,** i.e., they preferred to remain in the darkness of ignorance rather than be instructed by Christ: "They have rebelled against the light" (Jb 24:13); "Woe to you who substitute darkness for light, and light for darkness" (Is 5:20).

And the cause of this perversity is that **their deeds were evil**: and such deeds do not conform to the light but seek the darkness:

"Let us cast off the works of darkness" (Rom 13:12), i.e., sins, which seek the darkness; "Those who sleep, sleep at night" (1 Thes 5:7); "The eye of the adulterer watches for the darkness," as we read in Job (24:15). Now it is by withdrawing from the light,which is unpleasant to him, that one does not believe the light.

492   But do all unbelievers produce evil works? It seems not: for many Gentiles have acted with virtue; for example, Cato, and many others. I answer, with Chrysostom, that is it one thing to work by reason of virtue, and another by reason of a natural aptitude or disposition. For some act well because of their natural disposition, because their temperament is not inclined in a contrary way. And even unbelievers can act well in this way. For example, one may live chastely because he is not assailed by concupiscence; and the same for the other virtues. But those who act well by reason of virtue do not depart from virute, in spite of inclinations to the contrary vice, because of the rightness of their reason and the goodness of their will; and this is proper to believers.

Or, one might answer that although unbelievers may have done good things, they do not do them for love of virute but out of vainglory. Further, they did not do all things well; for they failed to render to God the worship due him.

493   Then when he says, **Everyone who practices evil hates the light**, he shows the appropriateness of the sign he used. First, with respect to those who are evil. Secondly, with respect to the good.

494   So he says: The reason why they did not love the light is that their works were evil. And this is plain because **Everyone who practices evil hates the light**. He does not say, "practiced," but rather **practices**: because if someone has acted in an evil way, but has repented and is sorry,seeing that he has done wrong, such a person does not hate the light but comes to the light. But **Everyone who practices evil**, i.e., persists in evil, is not sorry, nor does he come to the light, but he hates it; not because it reveals truth, but because it reveals a person's sins. For an evil person still wants to know the light and the truth; but he hates to be unmasked by it. "If the dawn suddenly appears, they regard it as the shadow of death" (Jb 24:17). And so he **does not approach the light**; and this **for fear that his deeds might be exposed**. For no one who is unwilling to desert evil wants to be rebuked; this is fled from and hated. "They hate the one who rebukes at the city gate" (Am 5:10); "A corrupt man does not love the one who rebukes him" (Prv 15:12).

495   Now he shows the same things with respect to the good, who practice the truth, i.e., perform good works. For truth is found not only in thought and words, but also in deeds. Everyone of these **comes to the light**.

But did anyone practice the truth before Christ? It seems not, for to practice the truth is not to sin; and "before Christ all have sinned" (Rom 3:23). I answer, according to Augustine, that he practices the truth in himself who is displeased at the evil he has done; and after leaving the darkness, keeps himself from sin, and repenting of the past, **comes to the light**, with the special intention of making his actions known.

496 But this conflicts with the teaching that no one should make public the good he has done; and this was a reason why the Lord rebuked the Pharisees. I answer that it is lawful to want one's works to be seen by God so that they may be approved: "It is not the one who commends himself who is approved, but the one whom God commends" (2 Cor 10:18); "My witness is in heaven," as is said in Job (16:20). It is also lawful to want them to be seen by one's own conscience, so that one may rejoice: "Our glory is this: the testimony of our conscience" (2 Cor 1:12). But it is reprehensible to want them to be seen by men in order to be praised or for one's own glory. Yet, holy persons desire that their good works be known to men for the sake of God's glory and for the good of the faith: "Let your light so shine before men that they may see your good works, and glorify your Father in heaven" (Mt 5:16). Such a person **comes to the light to make clear that his deeds are done in God**, that is, according to God's commandment or through the grace of God. For whatever good we do, whether it be avoiding sin, repenting of what has been done, or doing good works, it is all from God: "You have accomplished all our works" (Is 26:12).

LECTURE 4

22 After this Jesus and his disciples came to Judean territory; he stayed there with his disciples and was baptizing. 23 But John also was baptizing at Aenon near Salim, where the water was plentiful, and people kept coming and were baptized. 24 John, of course, had not yet been thrown into prison. 25 A controversy arose between the disciples of John and the Jews concerning purification. 26 They went to John and said to him, "Rabbi, the man who was with you across the Jordan, the one of whom you have given testimony, he is here baptizing, and all the people are flocking to him."

497 Above, the Lord gave us his teaching on spiritual regeneration in words; here he completes his teaching through action,

by baptizing. First, two kinds of baptism are mentioned. Secondly, a question about their relationship is raised (v 25). As to the first, two things are done. Mention is first made of the baptism of Christ. Secondly, of the baptism of John.

498 He says first, **After this**, i.e., the teaching on spiritual regeneration, **Jesus and his disciples came to Judean territory**. There is a question here about the literal meaning. For above, the Evangelist had said that the Lord had come from Galilee to Jerusalem, which is in Judean territory, where he taught Nicodemus. So how, after teaching Nicodemus, can he come into Judea, since he was already there?

Two answers are given to this. According to Bede, after his discussion with Nicodemus, Christ went to Galilee, and after remaining there for a time, returned to Judea. And so **After this Jesus and his disciples came to Judean territory**, should not be understood to mean that he came into Judea immediately after his talk with Nicodemus. Another explanation, given by Chrysostom, is that he did come into the territory of Judea immediately after this discussion: for Christ wanted to preach where the people gathered, so that many might be converted: "I have declared your justice in the great assembly" (Ps 39:10); "I have spoken openly to the world" (below 18:20). Now there were two places in Judea where the Jewish people gathered: Jerusalem, where they went for their feasts, and the Jordan, where they gathered on account of John's preaching and his baptism. And so the Lord used to visit both places; and after the feast days were over in Jerusalem, which is in one part of Judea, he went to another part, to the Jordan, where John was baptizing.

499 As for the moral sense, Judea means "confession," to which Jesus came, for Christ visits those who confess their sins or speak in praise of God: "Judea became his sanctuary" (Ps 113:2). **He stayed there**, because he did not make a merely temporary visit: "We will come to him, and make our abode with him," as it says below (14:23). **And was baptizing**, i.e., cleansing from sin; because unless one confesses his sins he does not obtain forgiveness: "He who hides his sins will not prosper" (Prv 28:13).

500 Then when he says, **But John also was baptizing**, the Evangelist presents the baptism of John. And in regard to this he does four things. First, he presents the person who is baptizing. Secondly, the place of the baptism. Thirdly, its fruit. Fourthly, the time.

501 John is the person who is baptizing; so he says, **John also was baptizing**. There is a question about this: Since John's baptism was ordained to the baptism of Christ, it seems that John should

have stopped baptizing when Christ started to baptize, just as the symbol does not continue when the truth comes. Three reasons are given for this. The first is in relation to Christ, for John baptized in order that Christ might be baptized by him. But it was not fitting that John baptize just Christ; otherwise, on this point alone, it might seem that John's baptism was superior to Christ's. Accordingly, it was expedient that John baptize others before Christ, because before Christ's teaching was to be made public it was necessary that men be prepared for Christ by John's baptism. In this way, the baptism of John is related to the baptism of Christ as the catechesis or religious instruction given to prospects to teach and prepare them for baptism is related to the true baptism. It was likewise important that John baptize others after he had baptized Christ, so that John's baptism would not seem to be worthless. For the same reason, the practice of the ceremonies of the old law was not abolished as soon as the truth came, but as Augustine says, the Jews could lawfully observe them for a time.

The second reason relates to John. For if John had stopped baptizing at once after Christ began baptizing, it might have been thought that he stopped out of envy or anger. And because, as the Apostle says, "We ought to look after what is good, not only before God, but also before all men" (Rom 12:17), this is the reason why John did not stop at once.

The third reason relates to John's disciples, who were already beginning to act like zealots toward Christ and his disciples, because they were baptizing. So if John had entirely stopped from baptizing, it would have provoked his disciples to an even greater zeal and opposition to Christ and his disciples. For even while John continued baptizing, they were hostile to Christ's baptism, as later events showed. And so John did not stop at once: "Take care that your freedom does not become a hindrance to those who are weak," as is said in 1 Corinthians (8:9).

502 The place of his baptism was **at Aenon near Salim, where the water was plentiful.** Another name for Salim is Salem, which is the village from which the king Melchizedek came. It is called Salim here because among the Jews a reader may use any vowel he chooses in the middle of his words; hence it made no difference to the Jews whether it was pronounced Salim or Salem. He added, **where the water was plentiful,** to explain the name of this place, i.e., **Aenon,** which is the same as "water."

503 The fruit of his baptism is the remission of sins; thus he says, **people kept coming and were baptized,** i.e., cleansed: for as is stated in Matthew (3:5) and in Luke (3:7), great crowds came to John.

504 The time is indicated when he says, **John had not yet been thrown into prison.** He says this so that we may know that he began his narrative of Christ's life before the other Evangelists. For the others began their account only from the time of John's imprisonment. So Matthew (4:12) says: "When Jesus heard that John had been arrested, he withdrew into Galilee." And so, because they had passed over the things that Christ did before John's imprisonment, John, who was the last to write a Gospel, supplied these omissions. He suggests this when he says: **John had not yet been thrown into prison.**

505 Note that by divine arrangement it came about that when Christ began to baptize, John did not continue his own baptizing and preaching for very long, in order not to create disunion among the people. But he was granted a little time so that it would not seem that he deserved to be repudiated, as was mentioned before. Again, by God's arrangement, it came about that after the faith had been preached and the faithful converted, the temple was utterly destroyed, in order that all the devotion and hope of the faithful could be directed to Christ.

506 Then when he says, **A controversy arose,** he brings in the issue of the two baptisms. First, the issue is mentioned. Secondly, it is brought to John's attention (v 26). Thirdly, the issue is resolved.

507 Because both John and Christ were baptizing, the disciples of John, out of zeal for their teacher, started a controversy over this. And this is what he says, **A controversy arose,** i.e., a dispute, **between the disciples of John,** who were the first to raise the issue, **and the Jews,** whom the disciples of John had rebuked for preferring Christ, because of the miracles he did, to John, who did not do any miracles. The issue was **concerning purification,** i.e., baptizing. The cause of their envy and the reason why they started the controversy was the fact that John sent those he baptized to Christ, but Christ did not send those he baptized to John. It seemed from this, and perhaps the Jews even said so, that Christ was greater than John. Thus, the disciples of John, having not yet become spiritual, quarreled with the Jews over the baptisms. "While there is envy and fighting among you, are you not carnal?" (1 Cor 3:3).

508 They referred this issue to John; hence he says, **They went to John.** If we examine this closely, we see that they were trying to incite John against Christ. Indeed, they are like the gossip and the double-tongued: "Those who gossip and are double-tongued are accursed, for they disturb many who are at peace" (Sir 28:15).

So they bring up four things calculated to set John against Christ. First, they recall the previous unimportant status of Christ.

Secondly, the good John did for him. Thirdly, the role which Christ took on. Fourthly, the loss to John because of Christ's new role.

509   They recall Christ's unimportance when they say, **the man who was with you**, as one of your disciples; and not the one you were with as your teacher. For there is no good reason for envy if honor is shown to one who is greater; rather, envy is aroused when honor is given to an inferior: "I have seen slaves on horses, and princes walking like slaves" (Ecc 10:7); "I called my servant, and he did not answer me" (Jb 19:16). For a master is more disturbed at the rebellion of a servant and a subject than of anyone else.

510   Secondly, they remind John of the good he did Christ. Thus they do not say, "the one whom you baptized," because they would then be admitting the greatness of Christ which was shown during his baptism when the Holy Spirit came upon him in the form of a dove and in the voice of the Father speaking to him. So they say, **the one of whom you have given testimony**, i.e., we are very angry that the one you made famous and admired dares to repay you in this way: "The one who ate my bread has lifted his heel against me" (Ps 40:10). They said this because those who seek their own glory and personal profit from their office become dejected if their office is taken over by someone else

511   And so thirdly, they even add that Christ took over John's office for himself, when they say, **he is here baptizing**, i.e., he is exercising your office; and this also distrubed them very much. For we generally see that men of the same craft are envious and under-handed with respect to one another; a potter envies another potter, but does not envy a carpenter. So, even teachers, who are seeking their own honor, become sad if another teaches the truth. In opposition to them, Gregory says: "The mind of a holy pastor wishes that others teach the truth which he cannot teach all by himself." So also Moses: "Would that all the people might prophesy," as we read in Numbers (11:29).

512   Yet they were not satisfied with merely disturbing John, rather they report something that should really excite him, that is, the loss that John seemed to be having because of the office Christ took over. They give this when they say: **and all the people are flock-ing to him**, i.e., the ones who used to come to you. In other words, they have rejected and disowned you, and now are all going to his baptism. It is clear from Matthew (11:7) that they used to go to John: "What did you go into the desert to see?" The same envy affected the Pharisees against Christ; so they said: "Look, the whole world has gone after him" (below 12:19). However, all this did not set John againt Christ, for he was not a reed swaying in the wind; and this is clear from John's answer to their question.

LECTURE 5

27 John replied and said:
"No one can lay hold of anything
unless it is given to him from heaven.
28 "You yourselves are witnesses to the fact that I said: I am not
the Christ, but the one sent before him.
29 "It is the groom who has the bride.
The groom's friend waits there and listens to him,
rejoicing at hearing his voice.
Therefore in this case my joy is complete.
30 He must increase,
and I must decrease.
31 The One who came from above
is above all things.
He who is of earth is earthly,
and speaks of earthly things.
32a The One who comes from heaven
is above all things,
and he testifies to what he sees,
and to what he hears.

513 Here we have John's answer to the question presented to
him by his disciples. Their question contained two points: a complaint about the office Christ took on, and so they said, **he is here
baptizing**; and about Christ's increasing fame and reputation among
the people, and so they said, **all the people are flocking to him**. Accordingly, John directs his answer to these two complaints. First he
answers the complaint about the office Christ took on. Secondly, the
complaint about Christ's increasing reputation (v 30). As to the first
he does two things. First, he shows the source of Christ's office and
of his own. Secondly, their difference (v 28). Thirdly, how Christ
and he are related to these offices.

514 As to the first, note that although John's disciples broach
their question maliciously, and so deserve to be rebuked, John nevertheless does not sharply reprove them; and this because of their
imperfection. For he feared that they might be provoked by a
rebuke, leave him, and, joining forces with the Pharisees, publicly
harass Christ. In acting this way he was putting into practice what
is said of the Lord: "The burised reed he will not break" (Is 42:3).
Again, we should also note that he begins his answer not by telling
them what is great and wonderful about Christ, but what is common
and obvious; and he did this on account of their envy. For since the

211

excellence of a person provokes others to envy, if John had stressed
Christ's excellence at once, he would have fed the fire of their envy.

515 Thus he states something unpretentious, and says, **No one
can lay hold of anything unless it is given to him from heaven**; and he
said this to them in order to inspire them with reverence. As if to
say: If all men are going to him, it is God's doing, because **no one can
lay hold of anything**, in the order of perfection and goodness, **unless
it is given to him from heaven**. Therefore, if you oppose him, you
oppose God. "If this plan or work is from men, it will fail," as is
said in Acts (5:38). This is the way Chrysostom explains it, applying
these words to Christ.

Augustine, on the other hand, does much better when he refers
them to John. **No one can lay hold of anything unless it is given to
him from heaven**: as if to say: You are zealous on my behalf and you
want me to be greater than Christ; but that has not been given to me,
and I do not wish to usurp it: "No one takes this honor on himself"
(Heb 5:4). This is the origin of their offices.

516 Then follows the difference of their offices, when he says,
You yourselves are witnesses. As if to say: From the testimony
which I bore to him, you can know the office committed to me by
Christ: for **You yourselves are witnesses**, i.e., you can testify, **to the
fact that I said: I am not the Christ** — "He declared openly and did
not deny" (above 1:20) — **but the one sent before him**, as a herald
before a judge. And so from my own testimony you can know my
office, which is to go before Christ and prepare the way for him:
"There was a man sent by God, whose name was John" (above 1:6).
But the office of Christ is to judge and to preside. If we look at this
closely we can see that John, like a skilful disputant, answers them
with their own arguments: "I judge you out of your own mouth,"
as said in Luke (19:22).

517 He shows how John is related to his own office when he
says: **It is the groom who has the bride**. First, he gives a simile.
Secondly, he applies it to his own situation. With respect to the
first he does two things. First, he gives a simile which applies to
Christ; and secondly, to himself.

518 As to the first, we should note that on the human level
it is the groom who regulates, governs and has the bride. Hence he
says, **It is the groom who has the bride**. Now the groom is Christ:
"Like a bridegroom coming out of his bridal chamber" (Ps 18:6).
His bride is the Church, which is joined to him by faith: "I will
espouse you to myself in faith" (Hos 2:20). In keeping with this
figure, Zipporah said to Moses: "You are a spouse of blood to me"

(Ex 4:25). We read of the marriage: "The marriage of the Lamb has come" (Rv 19:7). So, because Christ is the groom, he has the bride, that is, the Church; but my part is only to rejoice in the fact that he has the bride.

519 Consequently he says, **The groom's friend waits there and listens to him, rejoicing at hearing his voice.** Although John had said earlier that he was not worthy to unfasten the strap of Jesus' sandal, he here calls himself the friend of Jesus in order to bring out the faithfulness of his love for Christ. For a servant does not act in the spirit of love in regard to the things that pertain to his master, but in a spirit of servitude; while a friend, on the other hand, seeks his friend's interests out of love and faithfulness. Hence a faithful servant is like a friend to his master: "If you have a faithful servant, treat him like yourself" (Sir 33:31). Indeed, it is proof of a servant's faithfulness when he rejoices in the prosperity of his master, and when he obtains various goods, not for himself, but for his master. And so because John did not keep the bride entrusted to his care for himself, but for the groom, we can see that he was a faithful servant and a friend of the groom. It is to suggest this that he calls himself **the groom's friend.**

Those who are friends of the truth should act in the same way, not turning the bride entrusted to their care to their own advantage and glory, but treating her honorably for the honor and glory of the groom; otherwise they would not be friends of the groom but adulterers. This is why Gregory says that a servant who is sent by the groom with gifts for the bride is guilty of adulterous thoughts if he himself desires to please the bride. This is not what the Apostle did: "I espoused you to one husband in order to present you to Christ as a chaste virgin" (2 Cor 11:2). And John did the same, because he did not keep the bride, i.e., the faithful, for himself, but brought them to the groom, that is, to Christ.

520 And so by saying, **the groom's friend**, he suggests the faithfulness of his love. Further, he suggests his constancy when he says, **waits**, firm in friendship and faithfulness, not extolling himself above what he really is: "I will stand my watch" (Hb 2:1); "Be steadfast and unchanging" (1 Cor 15:58); "A faithful friend, if he is constant, is like another self" (Sir 6:11).

He suggests his attention when he says, **and listens to him**, i.e., attentively considers the way in which the groom is united to the bride. For according to Chrysostom, these words explain the manner of this marriage, for it is accomplished through faith, and "faith comes through hearing" (Rom 10:17). Or, he **listens to him**, i.e., reverently obeys him, by caring for the bride according to the commands of the groom: "I will listen to him as my master," as is said in Isaiah (50:4). This is in opposition to those evil prelates who do not follow Christ's command in governing the Church.

Likewise, he hints at his spiritual joy when he says, **rejoicing at hearing his voice**, that is, when the groom talks to his bride. And he says, **rejoicing** (literally, "rejoicing with joy"), to show the truth and perfection of his joy. For one whose rejoicing is not over the good, does not rejoice with true joy. And so, if it made me sad that Christ, who is the true groom, preaches to the bride, i.e., the Church, I would not be a friend of the groom; but I am not sad.

521   **Therefore in this case my joy is complete**, namely, in seeing what I have so long desired, that is, the groom speaking to his bride. Or, **my joy is complete**, i.e., brought to its perfect and due measure, when the bride is united to the groom, because I now have my grace and I have completed my work: "I will rejoice in the Lord, and I will take joy in God, my Jesus" (Hb 3:18).

522   Then when he says, **He must increase, and I must decrease**, he answers their question as to their complaint about the increasing esteem given to Christ. First, he notes that such an increase is fitting. Secondly, he gives the reason for it (v 31).

523   So he says: You say that all the people are flocking to him, i.e., to Christ, and therefore that he is growing in honor and esteem among the people. But I say that this is not unbecoming, because **He must increase**, not in himself, but in relation to others, in the sense that his power become more and more known. **And I must decrease**, in the reverence and esteem of the people: for esteem and reverence are not due to me as if I were a principal; but they are due to Christ. And therefore since he has come, the signs of honor are diminishing in my regard, but increasing in regard to Christ, just as with the coming of the prince, the office of the ambassador ceases: "When the perfect comes, what is imperfect will pass away" (1 Cor 13:10). And just as in the heavens the morning star appears and gives light before the sun, only to cease giving light when the sun appears, so John went before Christ and is compared to the morning star: "Can you bring out the morning star?" (Jb 38:32).

This is also signified in John's birth and in his death. In his birth, because John was born at a time when the days are getting shorter; Christ, however, was born when the days are growing longer, on the twenty-fifth of December. In his death, because John dies shortened by decapitation; but Christ died raised up by the lifting up of the cross.

524   In the moral sense, this should take place in each one of us. Christ **must increase** in you, i.e., you should grow in the knowledge and love of Christ, because the more you are able to grasp him by knowledge and love, the more Christ increases in you; just as the more one improves in seeing one and the same light, the more that light seems to increase. Consequently, as men advance in this way, their self-esteem decreases; because the more one knows of the divine greatness, the less he thinks of his human smallness. As we read in Proverbs (30:1): "The revelation spoken by the man close to God"; and then there follows: "I am the most foolish of men, and the wisdom of men is not in me." "I have heard you, but now I see you, and so I reprove myself, and do penance in dust and ashes," as we read in Job (42:5).

525   Then when he says, **The One who came from above is above all things**, he gives the reason for what he has just said. And he does this in two ways. First, on the basis of Christ's origin. And secondly, by considering Christ's teaching.

526   Regarding the first, we should note that in order for a thing to be perfect, it must reach the goal fixed for it by its origin; for example, if one is born from a king, he should continue to progress until he becomes a king. Now Christ has an origin that is most excellent and eternal; therefore he must increase by the manifestation of his power, in relation to others, until it is recognized that he is above all things. Thus he says, **The One who came from above**, that is, Christ, according to his divinity. "No one has gone up to heaven except the One who came down from heaven" (above 3:13); "You are from below, I am from above" (below 8:23).

527   Or, he **came from above**, as to his human nature, i.e., from the "highest" condition of human nature, by assuming it according to what was predominant in it in each of its states. For human nature is considered in three states. First, is the state of human nature before sin; and from this state he took his purity by assuming a flesh unmarked by the stain of original sin: "A lamb without blemish" (Ex 12:5). The second state is after sin; and from this he took his capability to suffer and die by assuming the likeness of sinful flesh as regards its punishment, but not in its guilt: "God sent his own Son in the likeness of sinful flesh" (Rom 8:3). The third state is that of resurrection and glory; and from this he took his impossibility of sinning and his joy of soul.

528   Here we must be on guard against the error of those who say that there was left in Adam something materially unmarked by the original stain, and this was passed on to his descendants; for example, to the Blessed Virgin, and that Christ's body was formed

from this. This is heretical, because whatever existed in Adam in a material way was marked by the stain of original sin. Further, the matter from which the body of Christ was formed was purified by the power of the Holy Spirit when he sanctified the Blessed Virgin.

529 **The One who came from above**, according to his divinity as well as his human nature, **is above all things**, both by eminence of rank: "The Lord is high above all nations" (Ps 112:4), and by his authority and power: "He has made him the head of the Church," as is said in Ephesians (1:22).

530 Now he gives the reason for what he had said above (v 30), by considering the teaching of Christ. First, he describes the doctrine of Christ and its grandeur. Secondly, the difference in those who receive or reject this doctrine (v 32b). He does two things with respect to the first. First, he describes John's doctrine. Secondly, he describes the doctrine of Christ (v 32).

531 As to the first we should note that a man is known mainly by what he says: "Your accent gives you away" (Mt 26:73); "Out of the abundance of the heart the mouth speaks" (Mt 12:34). This is why the quality of a teaching or doctrine is considered according to the quality of its origin. Accordingly, in order to understand the quality of John's doctrine, we should first consider his origin. So he says, **He who is of earth**, that is John, not only as to the matter from which he was made, but also in his efficient cause: because the body of John was formed by a created power: "They dwell in houses of clay, and have a foundation of earth" (Jb 4:19). Secondly, we should consider the quality of John himself, which is earthly; and so he says, **is earthly**. Thirdly, the quality of his teaching is described: he **speaks of earthly things**. "You will speak of the earth" (Is 29:4).

532 But since John was full of the Holy Spirit while still in his mother's womb, how can he be said to speak of earthly things? I answer that, according to Chrysostom, John says he speaks of earthly things by comparison with the teaching of Christ. As if to say: The things I speak of are slight and inferior as becomes one of an earthly nature, in comparison to him "in whom are hidden all the treasures of wisdom and knowledge" (Col 2:3); "As the heavens are high above the earth, so my ways are high above your ways" (Is 55:9).

Or we could say according to Augustine, and this is a better explanation, that we can consider what any person has of himself and what he has received from another. Now John and every mere human of himself is of the earth. Therefore, from this standpoint, he has nothing to speak of except earthly things. And if he does speak of divine things, it is due to a divine enlightenment: "Your heart has visions, but unless they come from the Almighty, ignore them" (Sir 34:6). So the Apostle says, "It is not I, but the grace of God which is with me" (1 Cor 15:10); "For it is not you who speak, but the Holy Spirit who is speaking through you" (Mt 10:20). Accordingly, as regards John, he **is earthly and speaks of earthly things**. And if there was anything divine in him, it did not come from him, as he was the recipient, but from the one enlightening him.

533 Now he describes the doctrine of Christ. And he does three things. First, he shows its origin, which is heavenly; hence he says, **The One who comes from heaven is above all things.** For although the body of Christ was of the earth as regards the matter of which it was made, yet it came from heaven as to its efficient cause, inasmuch as his body was formed by divine power. It also came from heaven because the eternal and uncreated person of the Son came from heaven by assuming a body. "No one has gone up to heaven except the One who came down from heaven, the Son of Man, who lives in heaven" (above 3:13).

Secondly, he shows the dignity of Christ, which is very great; so he says, **is above all things.** This was explained above.

Thirdly, he infers the dignity of Christ's doctrine, which is most certain, because **he testifies to what he sees and to what he hears.** For Christ, as God, is truth itself; but as man, he is its witness: "For this was I born, and for this I came into the world: to testify to the truth" (below 18:37). Therefore, he gives testimony to himself: "You testify to yourself" (below 8:13). And he testifies to what is certain, because his testimony is about what he has heard with the Father: "I speak to the world what I have heard from my Father" (below 8:26); "What we have seen and heard" (1 Jn 1:3).

534 Note that knowledge of a thing is acquired in one way through sight and in another way through hearing. For by sight, a knowledge of a thing in acquired by means of the very thing seen; but by hearing, a thing is not made known by the very voice that is heard, but by means of the understanding of the one speaking. And so, because the Lord has knowledge which he has received from the Father, he says, **to what he sees**, insofar as he proceeds from the essence of the Father; **and to what he hears**, insofar as he proceeds as the Word of the Father's intellect. Now because among intellectual beings, their act of being is other than their act of understanding, their knowledge through sight is other than their knowledge through hearing. But in God the Father, the act of being (*esse*) and the act of understanding (*intelligere*) are the same. Thus in the Son, to see and hear are the same thing. Moreover, since even in one who sees there is

not the essence of the thing seen in itself but only its similitude, as also in the hearer there is not the actual thought of the speaker but only an indication of it, so the one who sees is not the essence of the thing in itself, nor is the listener the very thought expressed. In the Son, however, the very essence of the Father is received by generation, and he himself is the Word; and so in him to see and to hear are the same.

And so John concludes that since the doctrine of Christ has more grandeur and is more certain than his, one must listen to Christ rather than to him.

LECTURE 6

32b "And his testimony no one accepts.
33 But whoever accepts his testimony
has given a sign [*or* certifies]
that God is true.
34 For the One whom God sends
speaks the words of God,
for God does not bestow the Spirit in fractions.
35 The Father loves the Son,
and has put everything into his hands.
36 Whoever believes in the Son
has eternal life.
But whoever is unbelieving in the Son
will not see life;
rather, the anger of God rests on him."

535   Above, John the Baptist commended the teaching of Christ; here, however, he considers the difference in those who receive it. Thus, he treats of the faith that must be given to this teaching. And he does three things. First, he shows the scarcity of those who believe. Secondly, the obligation to believe (v 33). Lastly, the reward for belief (v 36).

536   He says therefore: I say that Christ has certain knowledge and that he speaks the truth. Yet although few accept his testimony, that is no reflection on his teaching, because it is not the fault of the teaching but of those who do not accept it: namely, the disciples of John, who did not yet believe, and the Pharisees, who slandered his teaching. Thus he says, **And his testimony no one accepts**.

537 **No one** can be explained in two ways. First, so that it implies a few; and so some did accept his testimony. He shows that some did accept it when he adds, "But whoever accepts his testimony." The Evangelist used this way of speaking before when he said: "He came unto his own, and his own did not receive him" (above 1:11): because a few did receive him.

In another way, to accept his testimony is understood as to believe in God. But no one can believe of himself, but only due to God: "You are saved by grace" (Eph 2:8). And so he says, **his testimony no one accepts**, i.e., of himself, but it is given to him by God.

This can be explained in another way by realizing that Scripture refers to people in two ways. As long as we are in this world the wicked are mingled with the good; and so Scripture sometimes speaks of "the people," or "they," meaning those who are good; while at other times, the same words can refer to the wicked. We can see this in Jeremiah (26): for first it says that all the people and the priests sought to kill Jeremiah, and this referred to those who were evil; then at once it says that all the people sought to free him, and this referred to those who were good. In the same way, John the Baptist says, looking to the left, i.e., toward those who are evil, **And his testimony no one accepts**; and later, referring to those on the right, i.e., to the good, he says, **But whoever accepts his testimony**.

538 **But whoever accepts his testimony.** Here he speaks of the obligation to believe, i.e., to submit oneself to divine truth. As to this he does four things. First, he presents the divine truth. Secondly, he speaks of the proclamation of the divine truth (v 34). Thirdly, of the ability to proclaim it (v 34b). Fourthly, he gives the reason for this ability (v 35).

539 Man's obligation to the faith is to submit himself to divine truth, and so he says that if few accept his testimony that means that some do. Hence he says, **whoever accepts his testimony**, i.e., whoever he may be, **has given a sign**, i.e., he ought to affix a certain sign or has in fact placed a seal in his own heart, that Christ is God. And he [Christ] **is true**, because he said that he is God. If he were not, he would not be true, but it is written: "God is true" (Rom 3:4). Concerning this seal it is said: "Set me as a seal on your heart" (Sg 8:6), and "The foundation of God stands firm, bearing a seal, etc." as we read in 2 Timothy (2:19).

Or, following Chrysostom, he **has given a sign**, i.e., he has shown **that God**, that is, the Father, **is true**, because he sent his Son whom he promised to send. The Evangelist says this to show that those who do not believe Christ deny the truthfulness of the Father.

540   Then immediately he adds a commendation of divine truth, saying, **For the One whom God sends speaks the words of God**. As if to say: He has given this as a sign, namely, that Christ, whose testimony he accepts, **the One whom God sends speaks the words of God**. Consequently, one who believes Christ believes the Father: "I speak to the world what I have heard from the Father" (below 8:26). So he expressed verbally nothing but the Father and the words of the Father, because he has been sent by the Father, and because he is the Word of the Father. Hence, he says that he even bespeaks the Father.

Or, if the statement **God is true** refers to Christ, we understand the distinction of persons; for since the Father is true God, and Christ is true God, it follows that the true God sent the true God, who is distinct from him in person, but not in nature.

541   The ability to proclaim divine truth is present in Christ in the highest degree, because he does not receive the Spirit in a partial way; and so he says, **for God does not bestow the Spirit in fractions.**

You might say that although God sent Christ, yet not all that Christ says is from God, but only some of the things; for even the prophets spoke at times from their own spirit, and at other times from the Spirit of God. For example, we read that the prophet Nathan (2 Sm 7:3), speaking out of his own spirit, advised David to build a temple, but that later, under the influence of the Spirit of God, he retracted this. However, the Baptist shows that such is not the case with Christ. For the prophets receive the Spirit of God only fractionally, i.e., in reference to some things, but not as to all things. Consequently, not all they say are the words of God. But Christ, who received the Spirit fully and in regards to all things, speaks the words of God as to all things.

542   But how can the Holy Spirit be given in fractions, since he is immense or infinite, according to the Creed of Athanasius: "Immense is the Father, immense the Son, immense the Holy Spirit"? I answer that the Holy Spirit is given in fractions, not in respect to his essence or power, according to which he is infinite, but as to his gifts, which are given fractionally: "Grace has been given to each of us according to degree" (Eph 4:7).

543   We should note that we can understand in two ways what is said here, namely, that God the Father did not give the Spirit to Christ in a partial way. We can understand it as applying to Christ as God, and, in another way, as applying to Christ as man. Something is given to someone in order that he may have it: and it is appropriate to Christ to have the Spirit, both as God and as man. And so

he has the Holy Spirit with respect to both. As man, Christ has the Holy Spirit as Sanctifier: "The Spirit of the Lord is upon me, because the Lord has anointed me" (Is 61:1), namely, as man. But as God, he has the Holy Spirit only as manifesting himself, inasmuch as the Spirit proceeds from him: "He will give glory to me," that is, make known, "because he will have received from me," as is said below (16:14).

Therefore, both as God and as man, Christ has the Holy Spirit beyond measure. For God the Father is said to give the Holy Spirit without measure to Christ as God, because he gives to Christ the power and might to bring forth (*spirandi*) the Holy Spirit, who, since he is infinite, was infinitely given to him by the Father: for the Father gives it just as he himself has it, so that the Holy Spirit proceeds from him as much as from the Son. And he gave him this by an everlasting generation. Similarly, Christ as man has the Holy Spirit without measure, for the Holy Spirit is given to different men in differing degrees, because grace is given to each "by measure" [cf., e.g., Mk 4:24; Mt 7:2]. But Christ as man did not receive a certain amount of grace; and so he did not receive the Holy Spirit in any limited degree.

544 It should be noted, however, that there are three kinds of grace in Christ: the grace of [the hypostatic] union, the grace of a singular person, which is habitual, and the grace of headship, which animates all the members. And Christ received each of these graces without measure.

The grace of union, which is not habitual grace, but a certain gratuitous gift, is given to Christ in order that in his human nature he be the true Son of God, not by participation, but by nature, insofar as the human nature of Christ is united to the Son of God in person. This union is called a grace because he had it without any preceding merits. Now the divine nature is infinite; hence from that union he received an infinite gift. Thus it was not by degree or measure that he received the Holy Spirit, i.e., the gift and grace of union which, as gratuitous, is attributed to the Holy Spirit.

His grace is termed habitual insofar as the soul of Christ was full of grace and wisdom: "the Only Begotten of the Father, full of grace and truth" (above 1:14). We might wonder if Christ did receive this grace without measure. For since such grace is a created gift, we must admit that it has a finite essence. Therefore, as far as its essence is concerned, since it is something created, this habitual grace was finite. Yet Christ is not said to have received this in a limited degree for three reasons.

First, because of the one who is receiving the grace. For it is plain that each thing's nature has a finite capacity, because even though one might receive an infinite good by knowing, loving and enjoying it, nevertheless one receives it by enjoying it in a finite way. Further, each creature has, according to its species and nature, a finite amount of capacity. But this does not make it impossible for the divine power to make another creature possessing a greater capacity; but then such a creature would not be of a nature which is specifically the same, just as when one is added to three, there is another species of number. Therefore, when some nature is not given as much of the divine goodness as its natural capacity is able to contain, then it is seen to be given to it by measure; but when its total natural capacity is filled, it is not given to it by measure, because even though there is a measure on the part of the one receiving, there is none on the part of the one giving, who is prepared to give all. Thus, if someone takes a pail to a river, he sees water present without measure, although he takes the water by measure on account of the limited dimensions of the pail. Thus, the habitual grace of Christ is indeed finite according to its essence, but it is said to be given in an infinite way and not by measure or partially, because as much was given to him as created nature was able to hold.

Secondly, Christ did not receive habitual grace in a limited way by considering the gift which is received. For every form or act, considered in its very nature, is not finite in the way in which it is made finite by the subject in which it is received. Nevertheless, there is nothing to prevent it from being finite in its essence, insofar as its existence (*esse*) is received in some subject. For that is infinite according to its essence which has the entire fulness of being (*essendi*): and this is true of God alone, who is the supreme *esse*. But if we consider some "spiritual" form as not existing in a subject, for example, whiteness or color, it would not be infinite in essence, because its essence would be confined to some genus or species; nevertheless it would still possess the entire fulness of that species. Thus, considering the nature of the species, it would be without limit or measure, since it would have everything that can pertain to that species. But if whiteness or color should be received into some subject, it does not always have everything that pertains necessarily and always to the nature of this form, but only when the subject has it as perfectly as it is capable of being possessed, i.e., when the way the subject possesses it is equivalent to the power of the thing possessed. Thus, Christ's habitual grace was   finite according to its essence; yet it is said to have been in him without a limit or measure because he received everything that could pertain to the nature of grace. Others, however, do not receive all this; but one receives in one way, and another in another way: "There are different graces" (1 Cor 12:4).

The third reason for saying that the habitual grace of Christ was not received in a limited way is based on its cause. For an effect is in some way present in its cause. Therefore, if someone has an infinite power to produce something, he is said to have what can be produced without measure and, in a way, infinitely. For example, if someone has a fountain which could produce an infinite amount of water, he would be said to have water in an infinite way and without measure. Thus, the soul of Christ has infinite grace and grace without measure from the fact that he has united to himself the Word, which is the infinite and unfailing source of the entire emanation of all created things.

From what has been said, it is clear that the grace of Christ which is called capital grace, insofar as he is head of the Church, is infinite in its influence. For from the fact that he possessed that from which the gifts of the Spirit could flow out without measure, he received the power to pour them out without measure, so that the grace of Christ is sufficient not merely for the salvation of some men, but for all the people of the entire world: "He is the offering for our sins; and not for ours only, but also for those of the entire world" (1 Jn 2:2), and even for many worlds, if they exsited.

545 Christ also had the ability appropriate for declaring divine truth, because all things are in his power; hence he says, **The Father loves the Son, and has put everything into his hands**. This can refer to Christ both as man and as God, but in different ways. If it refers to Christ according to his divine nature, then **loves** does not indicate a principle but a sign: for we cannot say that the Father gives all things to the Son because he loves him. There are two reasons for this. First, because to love is an act of the will; but to give a nature to the Son is to generate him. Therefore, if the Father gave a nature to the Son by his will, the will of the Father would be the principle of the generation of the Son; and then it would follow that the Father generated the Son by will, and not by nature; and this is the Arian heresy.

Secondly, because the love of the Father for the Son is the Holy Spirit. So, if the love of the Father for the Son were the reason why the Father put everything into his hands, it would follow that the Holy Spirit would be the principle of the generation of the Son; and this is not acceptable. Therefore, we should say that **loves** implies only a sign. As if to say: The perfect love with which **the Father loves the Son**, is a sign that the Father **has put everything into his hands**, i.e., everything which the Father has: "All things have been given to me by my Father" (Mt 11:27); "Jesus, knowing that the Father had given all things into his hands" (below 13:3).

But if **loves** refers to Christ as man, then it implies the notion of
a principle, so that the Father is said to have put everything into the
hands of the Son, everything, that is, that is in heaven and on earth:
"All authority has been given to me, in heaven and on earth," as
he says in Matthew (28:18); "He has appointed him [the Son] the
heir of all things" (Heb 1:2). And the reason why the Father gives
to the Son is because he loves the Son; hence he says, **The Father
loves the Son**, for the Father's love is the reason for creating each
creature: "You love everything which exists, and hate nothing which
you have made" (Wis 11:25). Concerning his love for the Son we
read in Matthew (3:17): "This is my beloved Son, in whom I am well
pleased"; "He has brought us into the kingdom of the Son of his
love," that is, i.e., of his beloved Son (Col 1:13).

546   Then when he says, **Whoever believes in the Son has
eternal life**, he shows the fruit of faith. First, he sets forth the
reward for faith. Secondly, the penalty for unbelief (v 36b).

547   The reward for faith is beyond our comprehension, because it is eternal life. Hence he says, **Whoever believes in the Son has
eternal life**. And this is shown from what has already been said. For
if the Father has given everything he has to the Son, and the Father
has eternal life, then he has given to the Son to be eternal life: "Just
as the Father possesses life in himself, so he has given it to the Son to
have life in himself" (below 5:26): and this belongs to Christ insofar
as he is the true and natural Son of God. "That you may be in his
true Son, Christ. This is the true God and eternal life" (1 Jn 5:20).
Whoever believes in the Son has that toward which he tends, that is,
the Son, in whom he believes. But the Son is eternal life; therefore,
whoever believes in him has eternal life. As it says below (10:27):
"My sheep hear my voice . . . and I give them eternal life."

548   The penalty for unbelief is unendurable, both as to the
punishment of loss and as to the punishment of sense. As to the
punishment of loss, because it deprives one of life; hence he says,
whoever is unbelieving in the Son will not see life. He does not
say, "will not have," but **will not see**, because eternal life consists
in the vision of the true life: "This is eternal life: that they may
know you, the only true God, and Jesus Christ, whom you have
sent" (below 17:3): and unbelievers will not have this vision and this
knowledge: "Let him not see the brooks of honey" (Jb 4:19), that
is, the sweetness of eternal life. And he says, **will not see**, because to
see life itself is the proper reward for faith united with love.

The punishment of sense is unendurable because one is severely
punished; so he says: **the anger of God rests on him**. For in the

Scriptures anger indicates the pain with which God punishes those who are evil. So when he says, **the anger of God**, the Father, **rests on him**, it is the same as saying: They will feel punishment from God the Father.

Although the Father "has given all judgment to the Son," as we read below (5:22), the Baptist refers this to the Father in order to lead the Jews to believe in the Son. It is written about this judgment: "It is a terrible thing to fall into the hands of the living God" (Heb 10:31). He says, **rests on him**, because this punishment will never be absent from the unbelieving, and because all who are born into this mortal life are the objects of God's anger, which was first felt by Adam: "We were by nature," that is, through birth, "children of anger" (Eph 2:3). And we are freed from this anger only by faith in Christ; and so the anger of God rests on those who do not believe in Christ, the Son of God.

4

1 When, therefore, Jesus learned that the Pharisees had heard that he was making more disciples and baptizing more than John 2 (although Jesus did not himself baptize, but his disciples did), 3 he left Judea, and went again to Galilee. 4 He had, however, to pass through Samaria. 5 He came therefore to a city of Samaria, called Sychar, near the plot of land which Jacob had given to his son Joseph. 6 This was the site of Jacob's well. Jesus, tired from his journey, rested there at the well. It was about the sixth hour. 7 When a Samaritan woman came to draw water, Jesus said to her, "Give me a drink." 8 (His disciples had gone to the town to buy some food.) 9 So the Samaritan woman said to him, "How is it that you, being a Jew, ask me, a woman of Samaria, for a drink?" (Recall that the Jews had nothing to do with the Samaritans.)

549   Having set forth the teaching of Christ on spiritual regeneration, and that Christ had given this grace of spiritual regeneration to the Jews, he now shows how Christ gave this grace to the Gentiles. Now the salutary grace of Christ had been dispensed in two ways to the Gentiles: through teaching and through miracles. "Going forth, they preached everywhere": this is the teaching; "the Lord cooperated with them, and confirmed the word with signs": these are the miracles (Mk 16:20).

First, he shows the future conversion of the Gentiles through teaching. Secondly, their future conversion through miracles (v 43). As to the first, he does two things. First, he sets down certain matters preliminary to the teaching. Secondly, he presents the teaching and its effect (v 10). As to the first, he sets down three preliminary facts. First, what relates to the one teaching. Secondly, something about the matter taught. Thirdly, something about who received the instruction (v 7). As to the person teaching, the preliminary remark is about his journey to the place where he taught. Here he does three things. First, he gives the place which he left, that is, from Judea. Secondly, the place where he was going, to Galilee. Thirdly, the place through which he passed, Samaria. As to the first, he does three things. First, he gives the reason for his leaving Judea. Secondly, he explains certain facts included in this reason. Thirdly, he describes Christ's departure from Judea (v 3).

550   The Evangelist says, **When, therefore, Jesus learned that the Pharisees had heard**, because he wished to show that after the Baptist had calmed the envy of his disciples, Jesus avoided the ill will of the Pharisees.

551   Since we read: "All things were known to the Lord God
before they were created" (Sir 23:29), and "All things are naked and
open to his eyes" (Heb 4:13), it seems that we should ask why Jesus
is said to acquire new knowledge. We must answer that Jesus, in
virtue of his divinity, knew from eternity all things, past, present and
to come, as the scriptural passages cited above indicate. Nevertheless,
as man, he did begin to know certain things through experiential
knowledge. And it is this experiential knowledge that is indicated
when it says here, **When Jesus learned**, after the news was brought to
him, **that the Pharisees had heard**. And Christ willed to acquire this
knowledge anew as a concession, to show the reality of his human
nature, just as he willed to do and endure many other things characteristic of human nature.

552   Why does he say: **the Pharisees had heard that he was
making more disciples and baptizing more than John**, when this
would seem to be of no concern to them? For they persecuted John
and did not believe in him: for as Matthew says (21:25), when the
Lord questioned them about the source of John's baptism, they said:
" 'If we say from heaven, he will say to us, "Why then did you not
believe him?" ' " Thus they did not believe in John.

There are two answers to this. One is that those disciples of
John who had spoken against Christ were either Pharisees or allies
of the Pharisees. For we see in Matthew (9:11, 14), that the Pharisees
along with the disciples of John raised questions against the disciples
of Christ. And so according to this explanation, then, the Evangelist
says that **When, therefore, Jesus learned that the Pharisees had heard**,
that is, after he learned that John's disciples, who were Pharisees or
allied with the Pharisees, had raised questions and had been disturbed
about his baptism and that of his disciples, **he left Judea**.

Or, we might say that the Pharisees were disturbed at John's
preaching due to their envy, and for this reason they persuaded
Herod to arrest him. This is plain from Matthew (17:12), where
Christ, speaking of John, says, "Elijah has already come ... and they
did with him whatever they wanted," and then he adds, "so also
will the Son of Man suffer from them." The Gloss comments on
this that it was the Pharisees who incited Herod to arrest John and
put him to death. Thus it seems probable that they felt the same way
toward Christ because of what he was preaching. And this is what
it says, that is, the envious Pharisees and persecutors of Christ **had
heard**, with the intention of persecuting him, **that he was making
more disciples and baptizing more than John**.

553   This kind of hearing is described by Job (28:22): "Death
and destruction have said: We have heard of his deeds." The good,
on the other hand, hear in order to obey: "We have heard him in

Ephrathah" (Ps 131:6), followed by, "We will adore at his footstool."

The Pharisees heard two things. First, that Christ made more disciples than John. This was right and reasonable, for as we read above (3:30), Christ must increase and John must decrease. The second thing was that Christ baptized; and rightly so, because he cleanses: "Wash me from my injustice" (Ps 50:4), and again in Psalm (7:7): "Rise up, O Lord," by baptizing, "in the command you have given," concerning baptism, "and a congregation of people," united through baptism, "will surrond you."

554 Then when he says, **although Jesus did not himself baptize**, he explains what he has just said about Christ's baptizing. Augustine says that there is an apparent inconsistency here: for he had stated that Jesus was baptizing, whereas now he says, as though correcting himself, **Jesus did not himself baptize**.

There are two ways to understand this. This first way is that of Chrysostom. What the Evangelist now says is true, i.e., that Christ did not baptize. When he said above that Jesus was baptizing, this was the report received by the Pharisees. For certain people came to the Pharisees and said: You are envious of John because he has disciples and is baptizing. But Jesus is making more disciples than John and is also baptizing. Why do you put up with him? So the Evangelist is not himself saying that Jesus was baptizing, but only that the Pharisees heard that he was. It is with the intention of correcting this false rumor that the Evangelist says: It is true that the Pharisees heard that Christ was baptizing, but this is not true. So he adds: **although Jesus did not himself baptize, but his disciples did**. And so for Chrysostom, Christ did not baptize, because the Holy Spirit was not given at any time before the passion of Christ in the baptism of John and his disciples. The purpose of John's baptism was to accustom men to the baptism of Christ and to gather people in order to instruct them, as he says. Moreover, it would not have been fitting for Christ to baptize if the Holy Spirit were not given in his baptism; but the Spirit was not given until after the passion of Christ, as we read below (7:39): "The Spirit had not yet been given, because Jesus had not yet been glorified."

According to Augustine, however, one should say, and this is the preferable, way, that the disciples did baptize with the baptism of Christ, that is, in water and the Spirit, and the Spirit was given in this baptism, and also that Christ did and did not baptize. Christ did baptize because he performed the interior cleansing; but he did not baptize because he did not wash them externally with the water. It was the office of the disciples to wash the body, while Christ gave the Spirit which cleansed within. So in the proper sense Christ did baptize, according to: "The man on whom you see the Spirit come down and rest is the one who is to baptize with the Holy Spirit," as was said above (1:33).

With respect to the opinion of Chrysostom that the Holy Spirit was not yet given and so on, we might say that the Spirit was not yet given in visible signs, as he was given to the disciples after the resurrection; nevertheless, the Spirit had been given and was being given to believers through an interior sanctification.

The fact that Christ was not always baptizing gives an example to us that the major prelates of the churches should not occupy themselves with things that can be performed by others, but should allow them to be done by those of lesser rank: "Christ did not send me to baptize, but to preach the Gospel" (1 Cor 1:17).

555 If someone should ask whether Christ's disciples had been baptized, it could be said, as Augustine answered Stelentius, that they had been baptized with the baptism of John, because some of Christ's disciples had been disciples of John. Or, which is more likely, they were baptized with the baptism of Christ, in order that Christ might have baptized servants through whom he would baptize others. This is the meaning of what is said below (13:10): "He who has bathed does not need to wash, except his feet," and then follows, "and you are clean, but not all."

556 He then mentions Christ's going away, **he left Judea**. He left for three reasons. First, to get away from the envy of the Pharisees, who were disturbed because of what they had heard about Christ, and were preparing to harass him. By this he gives us the example that we should, with gentleness, yield ground to evil for a time: "Do not pile wood on his fire" (Sir 8:4). Another reason was to show us that it is not sinful to flee from persecution: "If they persecute you in one town, flee to another" (Mt 10:23). The third reason was that the time of his passion had not yet come: "My time has not yet come" (above 2:4). And there is an additional reason, a mystical one: he indicated by his leaving that because of persecution the disciples were destined to abandon the Jews and go to the Gentiles.

557 Then when he says, **and went again to Galilee**, he shows where he was going. He says, **again**, because above (2:12) he had mentioned another time when Christ went to Galilee: when he went to Capernaum after the miracle at the wedding. Since the other three evangelists did not mention this first trip, the Evangelist says **again** to let us know that the other evangelists had mentioned none of the

matters he mentions up to this point, and that he is now beginning to give his account contemporaneous with theirs. According to one interpretation, Galilee is understood to signify the Gentile world, to which Christ passed from the Jews; for Galilee means "passage." According to another interpretation, Galilee signifies the glory of heaven, for Galilee also means "revelation."

558 Then he describes the intermediate place through which Christ passed; first in a general way, then specifically.
559 On his way to Galilee, Christ passes through Samaria; hence he says, **He had to pass through Samaria.** He says, **had to pass**, lest he seem to be acting contrary to his own teaching, for Christ says in Matthew (10:5): "Do not go on the roads of the Gentiles." Now since Samaria was Gentile territory, he shows that he went there of necessity and not by choice. Thus he says, **had to pass**, the reason being that Samaria was between Judea and Galilee.

It was Amri, the king of Israel, who bought the hill of Samaria from a certain Somer (1 Kgs 16:24); and it was there he built the city which he called Samaria, after the name of the person from whom he bought the land. After that, the kings of Israel used it as their royal city, and the entire region surrounding this city was called Samaria. When we read here that Christ **had to pass through Samaria,** we should understand the region rather than the city.

560 Describing it in more detail, he adds, **He came therefore to a city of Samaria,** i.e., of the region of Samaria, **called Sychar.** This Sychar is the same as Shechem. Genesis (33:18) says that Jacob camped near here and that two of his sons, enraged at the rape of Dinah, Jacob's daughter, by the son of the king of Shechem, killed all the males in that city. And so Jacob took possession of the city, and he lived there and dug many wells. Later, as he lay dying, he gave the land to his son Joseph: "I am giving you a portion more than your brothers" (Gn 48:22). And this is what he says: **near the plot of land which Jacob had given to his son Joseph.**

The Evangelist is so careful to record all these matters in order to show us that all the things which happened to the patriarchs were leading up to Christ, and that they pointed to Christ, and that he descended from them according to the flesh.

561 Then when he says, **This was the site of Jacob's well,** the Evangelist gives the material setting for the spiritual doctrine about to be taught. And this was most fitting: for the doctrine about to be taught was about water and a spiritual font, and so he mentions the material well, thus giving rise to a discussion of the spiritual font, which is Christ: "For with you is the fountain of life" (Ps 35:10),

namely, the Holy Spirit, who is the spirit of life. Likewise, the well symbolizes baptism: "On that day a fountain will be open to the house of David, to cleanse the sinner and the unclean" (Zec 13:1).

He does three things here. First, he describes the well. Secondly, Christ's rest at the well. Thirdly, the time.

562 He describes the water source saying, **the site of Jacob's well**. Here one might object that further on (v 11) he says this source is deep; thus it did not gush water like a fountain. I answer, as does Augustine, that it was both a well and gushed water like a fountain. For every well is a fountain, although the converse is not true. For when water gushes from the earth we have a fountain; and if this happens just on the surface, the source is only a fountain. But if the water gushes both on the surface and below, we have a well; although it is also still called a fountain. It is called Jacob's well because he had dug this well there due to a shortage of water, as we read in Genesis (c 34).

563 **Jesus, tired from his journey, rested there at the well.** Jesus reveals his weakness (even though his power was unlimited), not because of a lack of power, but to show us the reality of the [human] nature he assumed. According to Augustine, Jesus is strong, for "In the beginning was the Word" (above 1:1); but he is weak, for "the Word was made flesh" (above 1:14). And so Christ, wishing to show the truth of his human nature, allowed it to do and to endure things proper to men; and to show the truth of his divine nature, he worked and performed things proper to God. Hence when he checked the inflow of divine power to his body, he became hungry and tired; but when he let his divine power influence his body, he did not become hungry in spite of a lack of food, and he did not become tired in his labors. "He had fasted forty days and forty nights, and was hungry" (Mt 4:2).

564 Seeing Jesus becoming tired from his journey is an example to us not to shrink from our work for the salvation of others: "I am poor, and have labored since my youth" (Ps 87:16). We also have an example of poverty, as Jesus **rested there**, upon the bare earth.

In its mystical meaning, this resting [literally, a sitting] of Christ indicates the abasement of his passion: "You know when I sit down (i.e., the passion), and when I rise" (Ps 138:2). Also, it indicates the authority of his teaching, for he speaks as one having power; thus we read in Matthew (5:1) that Christ, "sitting down, taught them."

565 He indicates the time, saying, **It was about the sixth hour.** There are both literal and mystical reasons for fixing the time. The literal reason was to show the cause of his tiredness: for men are

more weary from work in the heat and at the sixth hour [at noon].
Again, it shows why Christ was resting: for men gladly rest near the
water in the heat of the day.

There are three mystical reasons for mentioning the time. First,
because Christ assumed flesh and came into the world in the sixth
age of the world. Another is that man was made on the sixth day,
and Christ was conceived in the sixth month. Third, at the sixth
hour the sun is at its highest, and there is nothing left for it but to
decline. In this context, the "sun" signifies temporal prosperity,
as suggested by Job (31:26): "If I had looked at the sun when it
shone, etc." Therefore Christ came when the prosperity of the world
was at its highest, that is, it flourished through love in the hearts of
men; but because of him natural love was bound to decline.

566 Next, we have a preliminary remark concerning the one
who listens to Christ. First, we are introduced to the person who is
taught. Secondly, we are given her preparation for his teaching.

567 The teaching is given to a Samaritan woman; so he says,
a Samaritan woman came to draw water. This woman signifies the
Church, not yet justified, of the Gentiles. It was then involved in
idolatry, but was destined to be justified by Christ. She **came** from
foreigners, i.e., from the Samaritans, who were foreigners, even
though they lived in the neighboring territory: because the Church
of the Gentiles, foreign to the Jewish race, would come to Christ:
"Many will come from the East and the West, and will sit down with
Abraham, and Isaac, and Jacob, in the kingdom of heaven," as we
find in Matthew (8:11).

568 Christ prepares this woman for his teaching when he says,
Give me a drink. First, we have the occasion for his asking her.
Secondly, the Evangelist suggests why it was opportune to make
this request (v 8).

569 The occasion and the preparation of the woman was
the request of Christ; thus he says, **Give me a drink**. He asks for
a drink both because he was thirsty for water on account of the
heat of the day, and because he thirsted for the salvation of man
on account of his love. Accordingly, while hanging on the cross
he cried out: "I thirst."

570 Christ had the opportunity to ask this of the woman
because his disciples, whom he would have asked for the water,
were not there; thus the Evangelist says, **His disciples had gone to
the town**.

Here we might notice three things about Christ. First, his
humility, because he was left alone. This is an example to his

disciples that they should suppress all pride. Someone might ask what need there was to train the disciples in humility, seeing that they had been but lowly fishermen and tentmakers. Those who say such things should remember that these very fishermen were suddenly made more deserving of respect than any king, more eloquent than philosophers and orators, and were the intimate companions of the Lord of creation. Persons of this kind, when they are suddenly promoted, ordinarily become proud, not being accustomed to such great honor.

Secondly, note Christ's temperance: for he was so little concerned about food that he did not bring anything to eat. Thirdly, note that he was also left alone on the cross: "I have trodden the wine press alone, and no one of the people was with me" (Is 63:3).

571   Our Lord prepared the woman to receive his spiritual teaching by giving her an occasion to question him. First, her question is given. Secondly, her reason for asking it (v 9).

572   Here we should point out that our Lord, when asking the woman for a drink, had in mind more a spiritual drink than a merely physical one. But the woman, not yet understanding about such a spiritual drink, though only of a physical drink. So she responds: **How is it that you, being a Jew, ask me, a woman of Samaria, for a drink?** For Christ was a Jew, because it was promised that he would be from Judah: "The scepter will not be taken away from Judah ... until he who is to be sent comes" (Gn 49:10); and he was born from Judah: "It is evident that our Lord came from Judah" (Heb 7:14). The woman knew that Christ was Jewish from the way he dressed: for as Numbers (15:37) says, the Lord commanded the Jews to wear tassels on the corners of their garments, and put a violet cord on each tassel, so that they could be distinguished from other people.

573   Then the reason for this question is given: either by the Evangelist, as the Gloss says, or by the woman herself, as Chrysostom says; the reason being, **the Jews had nothing to do with Samaritans**.

Apropos of this, we should note that, as mentioned in 2 Kings, it was on account of their sins that the people of Israel, i.e., of the ten tribes, who were worshipping idols, were captured by the king of the Assyrians, and led as captives into Babylonia. Then, so that Samaria would not remain unpopulated, the king gathered people from various nations and forced them to live there. While they were there, the Lord sent lions and other wild beasts to trouble them; he did this to show that he let the Jews be captured because of their sins, and not because of any lack in his own power. When news of their trouble reached the Assyrian king and he was informed that this was happening because these people were not observing the rites of the God of that territory, he sent them a priest of the Jews who would teach them God's law as found in the law of Moses. This is why, although these people were not Jewish, they came to observe the Mosaic law. However, along with their worship of the true God, they also worshipped idols, paid no attention to the prophets, and referred to themselves as Samaritans, from the city of Samaria which was built on a hill called Somer (1 Kgs 16:24). After the Jews returned to Jerusalem from their captivity, the Samaritans were a constant source of trouble, and as we read in Ezra, interfered with their building of the temple and the city. Although the Jews did not mix with other people, they especially avoided these Samaritans and would have nothing to do with them. And this is what we read: **Jews had nothing to do with the Samaritans**. He does not say that the Samaritans do not associate with Jews, for they would have gladly done so and have cooperated with them. But the Jews rebuffed them in keeping with what is said in Deuteronomy (7:2): "Do not make agreements with them."

574 If it was not lawful for the Jews to associate with Samaritans, why did God ask a Samaritan woman for a drink? One might answer, as Chrysostom does, that the Lord asked her because he knew that she would not give him the drink. But this is not an adequate answer, because one who asks what is not lawful is not free from sin — not to mention the scandal — even though what he asks for is not given to him. So we should say, as we find in Matthew (12:8): "The Son of Man is Lord even of the sabbath." Thus, as Lord of the law, he was able to use or not use the law and its observances and legalities as it seemed suitable to him. And because the time was near when the nations would be called to the faith, he associated with those nations.

LECTURE 2

10 Jesus replied and said:
   "If you knew the gift of God,
   and realized who it is who says to you,
   'Give me a drink,'
   you perhaps would have asked him
   that he give you living water."

11 The woman challenged him: "You, sir, have no bucket, and the well is deep. How then could you have living water? 12 Are you greater than our father Jacob, who gave us this well and drank from it with his sons and his flocks?" 13 Jesus replied and said:
"Whoever drinks this water
will be thirsty again,
but whoever drinks the water that I give,
will never be thirsty again.
14 The water that I give
will become a fountain within him,
leaping up to provide eternal life."
15 "Lord," the woman said, "Give me this water so that I shall not grow thirsty and have to keep coming here to draw water." 16 Jesus said to her: "Go, call your husband, and then come back here." 17 "I have no husband," replied the woman. Jesus said, "You are right in saying you have no husband, 18 for you have had five, and the man you are living with now is not your husband. What you said is true." 19 "Sir," said the woman, "I see that you are a prophet. 20 Our ancestors worshiped on this mountain, but you people claim that Jerusalem is the place where men must worship God." 21 Jesus said to her:
"Believe me, woman,
the hour is coming
when you will worship the Father
neither on this mountain nor in Jerusalem.
22 You people worship what
you do not understand,
while we understand what we worship,
since salvation is from the Jews.
23 But the hour is coming, and is now here,
when true worshipers will worship the Father
in spirit and in truth.
Indeed, it is just such worshipers the Father seeks.
24 God is spirit,
and those who worship him
ought to worship in spirit and truth."
25 The woman said to him: "I know that the Messiah is coming, the one called Christ; when he comes he will tell us everything." 26 Jesus replied:
"I who speak to you am he."

575   Now (v 10), the Evangelist gives us Christ's spiritual teaching. First, he gives the teaching itself. Secondly, the effect it had (v 27). As to the first, he does two things. First, a summary

of the entire instruction is given. Secondly, he unfolds it part by part (v 11).

576   He said therefore: You are amazed that I, a Jew, should ask you, a Samaritan woman, for water; but you should not be amazed, because I have come to give drink, even to the Gentiles. Thus he says: **If you knew the gift of God, and realized who it is who says to you, Give me a drink, you perhaps would have asked him.**

577   We may begin with what is last, and we should know first what is to be understood by water. And we should say that water signifies the grace of the Holy Spirit. Sometimes this grace is called fire, and at other times water, to show that it is neither one of these in its nature, but like them in the way it acts. It is called fire because it lifts up our hearts by its ardor and heat: "ardent in Spirit" (Rom 12:11), and because it burns up sins: "Its light is fire and flame" (Sg 8:6). Grace is called water because it cleanses: "I will pour clean water upon you, and you will be cleansed from all your uncleanness" (Ez 36:25), and because it brings a refreshing relief from the heat of temptations: "Water quenches a flaming fire" (Sir 3:33), and also because it satisfies our desires, in contrast to our thirst for earthly things and all temporal things whatever: "Come to the waters, all you who thirst" (Is 55:1).

Now water is of two kinds: living and non-living. Non-living water is water which is not connected or united with the source from which it springs, but is collected from the rain or in other ways into ponds and cisterns, and there it stands, separated from its source. But living water is connected with its source and flows from it. So according to this understanding, the grace of the Holy Spirit is correctly called living water, because the grace of the Holy Spirit is given to man in such a way that the source itself of the grace is also given, that is, the Holy Spirit. Indeed, grace is given by the Holy Spirit: "The love of God is poured out into our hearts by the Holy Spirit, who has been given to us" (Rom 5:5). For the Holy Spirit is the unfailing fountain from whom all gifts of grace flow: "One and the same Spirit does all these things" (1 Cor 12:11). And so, if anyone has a gift of the Holy Spirit without having the Spirit, the water is not united with its source, and so is not living but dead: "Faith without works is dead" (Jas 2:20).

578   Then we are shown that in the case of adults, living water, i.e., grace, is obtained by desiring it, i.e., by asking. "The Lord has heard the desire of the poor" (Ps 9:17), for grace is not given to anyone without their asking and desiring it. Thus we say that in the justification of a sinner an act of free will is necessary to detest

sin and to desire grace, according to Matthew (7:7): "Ask and you
will receive." In fact, desire is so important that even the Son himself
is told to ask: "Ask me, and I will give to you" (Ps 2:8). Therefore,
no one who resists grace receives it, unless he first desires it; this is
clear is the case of Paul who, before he received grace, desired it,
saying: "Lord, what do you want me to do?" (Acts 9:6). Thus it is
significant that he says, **you perhaps would have asked him**. He says
perhaps on account of free will, with which a person sometimes
desires and asks for grace, and sometimes does not.

579   There are two things which lead a person to desire and
ask for grace: a knowledge of the good to be desired and a knowledge of the giver. So, Christ offers these two to her. First of all,
a knowledge of the gift itself; hence he says, **If you knew the gift
of God**, which is every desirable good which comes from the Holy
Spirit: "I know that I cannot control myself unless God grants it
to me" (Wis 8:21). And this is a gift of God, and so forth. Secondly,
he mentions the giver; and he says, **and realized who it is who says to
you**, i.e., if you knew the one who can give it, namely, that it is I:
"When the Paraclete comes, whom I will send you from the Father,
the Spirit of truth ... he will bear witness to me" (below 15:26);
"You have given gifts to men" (Ps 67:19).

Accordingly, this teaching concerns three things: the gift of
living water, asking for this gift, and the giver himself.

580   When he says, **The woman challenged him**, he treats
these three things explicitly. First, the gift; secondly, asking for
the gift (v 19); and thirdly, the giver (v 25). He does two things
about the first. First, he explains the gift by showing its power.
Secondly, he considers the perfection of the gift (v 15). About
the first he does two things. First, he gives the woman's request.
Secondly, Christ's answer (v 13).

581   We should note, with respect to the first, that this Samaritan woman, because she was sensual, understood in a worldly sense
what the Lord understood in a spiritual sense: "The sensual man
does not perceive those things that pertain to the Spirit of God"
(1 Cor 2:14). Consequently, she tried to reject what our Lord said
as unreasonable and impossible with the following argument: You
promise me living water; and it must come either from this well
or from another one. But it cannot come from this well because
You, sir, have no bucket, and the well is deep; and it does not seem
probable that you can get if from some other well, because you are
not **greater than our father Jacob, who gave us this well**.

582   Let us first examine what she says, **You, sir, have no
bucket**, i.e., no pail to use to draw water from the well, **and the**

well is deep, so you cannot reach the water by hand without a bucket.

The depth of the well signifies the depth of Sacred Scripture and of divine wisdom: "It has great depth. Who can find it out?" (Ecc 7:25). The bucket with which the water of wisdom is drawn out is prayer: "If any of you lack wisdom, ask God" (Jas 1:5).

583 The second point is given at, **Are you greater than our father Jacob, who gave us this well?** As if to say: Have you better water to give us than Jacob? She calls Jacob her father not because the Samaritans were descendants of the Jews, as is clear from what was said before, but because the Samaritans had the Mosaic law, and because they occupied the land promised to the descendants of Jacob.

The woman praised this well on three counts. First, on the authority of the one who gave it; so she says: **our father Jacob, who gave us this well.** Secondly, on account of the freshness of its water, saying: **Jacob drank from it with his sons:** for they would not drink it if it were not fresh, but only give it to their cattle. Thirdly, she praises its abundance, saying, **and his flocks:** for since the water was fresh, they would not have given it to their flocks unless it were also abundant.

So, too, Sacred Scripture has great authority: for it was given by the Holy Spirit. It is delightfully fresh: "How sweet are your words to my palate" (Ps 118:103). Finally, it is exceedingly abundant, for it is given not only to the wise, but also to the unwise.

584 Then when he says, **Jesus replied and said**, he sets down the Lord's response, in which he explains the power of his doctrine. First, with respect to the fact that he had called it water. Secondly, with respect to the fact that he called it living water (v 14).

585 He shows that his doctrine is the best water because it has the effect of water, that is, it takes away thirst much more than does that natural water. He shows by this that he is greater than Jacob. So he says, **Jesus replied and said**, as if to say: You say that Jacob gave you a well; but I will give you better water, because **whoever drinks this water**, that is, natural water, or the water of sensual desire and concupiscence, although it may satisfy his appetite for a while, **will be thirsty again**, because the desire for pleasure is insatiable: "When will I wake up and find wine again?" (Prv 23:35). **But whoever drinks the water**, that is, spiritual water, **that I give, will never be thirsty again.** "My servants will drink, and you will be thirsty," as said in Isaiah (65:13).

586 Since we read in Sirach (24:29): "Those who drink me will still thirst," how is it possible that we will never be thirsty if

we drink this water of divine wisdom, since this Wisdom itself says we will still thirst? I answer that both are true: because he who drinks the water that Christ gives still thirsts and does not thirst. But whoever drinks natural water will become thirsty again for two reasons. First, because material and natural water is not eternal, and it does not have an eternal cause, but an impermanent one; therefore its effects must also cease: "All these things have passed away like a shadow" (Wis 5:9). But spiritual water has an eternal cause, that is, the Holy Spirit, who is the unfailing fountain of life. Accordingly, he who drinks of this will never thirst; just as someone who had within himself a fountain of living water would never thirst.

The other reason is that there is a difference between a spiritual and a temporal thing. For although each produces a thirst, they do so in different ways. When a temporal thing is possessed it causes us to be thirsty, not for the thing itself, but for something else; while a spiritual thing when possessed takes away the thirst for other things, and causes us to thirst for it. The reason for this is that before temporal things are possessed, they are highly regarded and thought satisfying; but after they are possessed, they are found to be neither so great as thought nor sufficient to satisfy our desires, and so our desires are not satisfied but move on to something else. On the other hand, a spiritual thing in not known unless it is possessed: "No one knows but he who receives it" (Rv 2:17). So, when it is not possessed, it does not produce a desire; but once it is possessed and known, then it brings pleasure and produces desire, but not to possess something else. Yet, because it is imperfectly known on account of the deficiency of the one receiving it, it produces a desire in us to possess it perfectly. We read of this thirst: "My soul thirsted for God, the living fountain" (Ps 41:2). This thirst is not completely taken away in this world because in this life we cannot understand spiritual things; consequently, one who drinks this water will still thirst for its completion. But he will not always be thirsty, as though the water will run out, for we read (Ps 35:9): "They will be intoxicated from the richness of your house." In the life of glory, where the blessed drink perfectly the water of divine grace, they will never be thirsty again: "Blessed are they who hunger and thirst for what is right," that is, in this world, "for they will be satisfied," in the life of glory" (Mt 5:6).

587   Then when he says, **The water that I give will become a fountain within him, leaping up to provide eternal life**, he shows from the movement of the water that his doctrine is living water; thus he says that it is a leaping fountain: "The streams of the river bring joy to the city of God" (Ps 45:4).

The course of material water is downward, and this is different from the course of spiritual water, which is upward. Thus he says: I say that material water is such that it does not slake your thirst; but the water that I give not only quenches your thirst, but it is a living water because it is united with its source. Hence he says that this water **will become a fountain within** one: a fountain leading, through good works, to eternal life. So he says, **leaping up**, that is, making us leap up, **to eternal life**, where there is no thirst: "He who believes in me, out of his heart there will flow rivers ," that is, of good desires, "of living water" (below 7:38); "With you is the fountain of life" (Ps 35:10).

588 Then when he says, **The woman said**, he states her request for the gift. First, her understanding of the gift is noted. Secondly, the woman is found guilty (v 17). As was said, the way to obtain this gift is by prayer and request. And so first, we have the woman's request. Secondly, Christ's answer (v 16).

589 We should note with respect to the first that at the beginning of this conversation the woman did not refer to Christ as "Lord," but simply as a Jew, for she said: "How is it that you, being a Jew, ask me, a woman of Samaria, for a drink?" But now as soon as she hears that he can be of use to her and give her water, she calls him "Lord": **Lord, give me this water.** For she was thinking of natural water, and was subject to the two natural necessities of thirst and labor, that is, of going to the well and of carrying the water. So she mentions these two things when asking for the water: saying in reference to the first, **so that I shall not grow thirsty**; and in reference to the second, **and have to keep coming here to draw water**, for man naturally shrinks from labor: "They do not labor as other men" (Ps 72:5).

590 Then (v 16), the answer of Jesus is given. Here we should note that our Lord answered her in a spiritual way, but she understood in a sensual way. Accordingly, this can be explained in two ways. One way is that of Chrysostom, who says that our Lord intended to give the water of spiritual instruction not only to her, but especially to her husband, for as is said, "Man is the head of woman" (1 Cor 11:3), so that Christ wanted God's precepts to reach women through men, and "If the wife wishes to learn anything, let her ask her husband at home" (1 Cor 14:35). So he says, **Go, call your husband, and then come back here**; and then I will give it to you with him and through him.

Augustine explains it another way, mystically. For as Christ spoke symbolically of water, he did the same of her husband. Her husband, according to Augustine, is the intellect: for the will brings forth and conceives because of the cognitive power that moves it; thus the will is like a woman, while the reason, which moves the will, is like her husband. Here the woman, i.e., the will, was ready to receive, but was not moved by the intellect and reason to a correct understanding, but was still detained on the level of sense. For this reason the Lord said to her, **Go**, you who are still sensual, **call your husband**, call in the reasoning intellect so you can understand in a spiritual and intellectual way what you now perceive in a sensual way; **and then come back here**, by understanding under the guidance of reason.

591   Here (v 17), the woman is found guilty by Christ. First, her answer is set down. Secondly, the encounter in which she is found guilty by Christ.

592   As to the first, we should note that the woman, desiring to hide her wrongdoing, and regarding Christ as only a mere man, did answer Christ truthfully, although she keep silent about her sin, for as we read, "A fornicating woman will be walked on like dung in the road" (Sir 9:10). She said, **I have no husband**. This was true; for although she previously had a number of husbands, five of them, she did not now have a lawful husband, but was just living with a man; and it is for this that the Lord judges her.

593   Then the Evangelist reports that Jesus said to her: **You are right in saying you have no husband**, a legitimate husband; **for you have had five**, before this one, **and the man you are living with now**, using as a husband, **is not your husband. What you said is true**, because you do not have a husband. The reason our Lord spoke to her about these things he had not learned from her and which were her secrets, was to bring her to a spiritual understanding so that she might believe there was something divine about Christ.

594   In the mystical sense, her five husbands are the five books of Moses: for, as was said, the Samaritans accepted these. And so Christ says, **you have had five**, and then follows [understanding Christ's words in a slightly different sense, as meaning:] **and he whom you now have**, i.e., he to whom you are now listening, i.e., Christ, **is not your husband**, because you do not believe.

This explanation, as Augustine says, is not very good. For this woman came to her present "husband" after having left the other five, whereas those who come to Christ do not put aside the five books of Moses. We should rather say, **you have had five**, i.e., the five senses, which you have used up to this time; but **the man you are living with now**, i.e., an erring reason, with which you still understand spiritual things in a sensual way, **is not your** lawful **husband**, but an adulterer who is corrupting you. **Call your husband**, i.e., your intellect, so that you may really understand me.

595 Now the Evangelist treats of the request by which the gift is obtained, which is prayer. First there is the woman's inquiry about prayer. Secondly, Christ's answer (v 21). Concerning the first the woman does two things. First, she admits that Christ is qualified to answer her question. Secondly, she asks the question (v 20).

596 And so this woman, hearing what Christ had told her about things that were secret, admits that the one who up to now she believed was a mere man, is a prophet, and capable of settling her doubts. For it is characteristic of prophets to reveal what is not present, and hidden: "He who is now called a prophet was formerly called a seer" (1 Sm 9:9). And so she says, **Sir, I see that you are a prophet.** As if to say: You show that you are a prophet by revealing hidden things to me. It is clear from this, as Augustine says, that her husband was beginning to return to her. But he did not return completely because she regarded Christ as a prophet: for although he was a prophet, "A prophet is not without honor except in his own country" (Mt 13:57), he was more than a prophet, because he produces prophets: "Wisdom produces friends of God and prophets" (Wis 7:27)

597 Then she asks her question about prayer, saying: **Our ancestors worshiped on this mountain, but you people claim that Jerusalem is the place where men must worship God.** Here we should admire the woman's diligence and attention: for women are considered curious and unproductive, and not only unproductive, but also lovers of ease (1 Tim 5), whereas she did not ask Christ about worldly affairs, or about the future, but about the things of God, in keeping with the advice, "Seek first the kingdom of God" (Mt 6:33)

She first asks a question about a matter frequently discussed in her country, that is, about the place to pray; this was the subject of argument between Jews and Samaritans. She says, **Our ancestors worshiped on this mountain, but you people say.** We should mention that the Samaritans, worshiping God according to the precepts of the law, built a temple in which to adore him; and they did not go to Jerusalem where the Jews interfered with them. They built their temple on Mount Gerizim, while the Jews built their temple on Mount Sion. The question they debated was which of these places was the more fitting place of prayer; and each presented reasons for its own side. The Samaritans said that Mount Gerizim was more fitting, because their ancestors worshiped the Lord there. So she says, **Our ancestors worshiped on this mountain.**

598   How can this woman say, **our ancestors**, since the Samaritans were not descended from Israel? The answer, according to Chrysostom, is that some claim that Abraham offered his son on that mountain; but others claim that is was on Mount Zion. Or, we could say that **our ancestors** means Jacob and his sons, who as stated in Genesis (33) and as mentioned before, lived in Shechem, which is near Mount Gerizim, and who probably worshiped the Lord there on that mountain. Or it could be said that the children of Israel worshiped on this mountain when Moses ordered them to ascend Mount Gerizim that he might bless those who observed God's precepts, as recorded in Deuteronomy (6). And she calls them her ancestors either because the Samaritains observed the law given to the children of Israel, or because the Samaritans were now living in the land of Israel, as said before.

The Jews said that the place to worship was in Jerusalem, by command of the Lord, who had said: "Take care not to offer your holocausts in every place, but offer them in the place the Lord will choose" (Dt 12:13). At first, this place of prayer was in Shiloh, and then after, on the authority of Solomon and the prophet Nathan, the arc was taken from Shiloh to Jerusalem, and it was there the temple was built: so we read: "He left the tabernacle in Shiloh," and a few verses later, "But he chose the tribe of Judah, Mount Zion, which he loved" (Ps 77:60). Thus the Samaritans appealed to the authority of the patriarchs, and the Jews appealed to the authority of the prophets, whom the Samaritans did not accept. This is the issue the woman raises. It is not surprising that she was taught about this, for it often happens in places where there are differences in beliefs that even the simple people are instructed about them. Because the Samaritans were continually arguing with the Jews over this, it came to the knowledge of the women and ordinary people.

599   Christ's answer is now set down (v 21). First he distinguishes three types of prayer. Secondly, he compares them to each other (v 22).

600   As to the first, he first of all gains the woman's attention, to indicate that he was about to say something important, saying, **Believe me**, and have faith, for faith is always necessary: "To come to God, one must believe" (Heb 11:6); "If you do not believe, you will not understand" (Is 7:9).

Secondly, he mentions the three kinds of worship: two of these were already being practiced, and the third was to come. Of the two that were current, one was practiced by the Samaritans, who worshiped on Mount Gerizim; he refers to this when he says, **the hour is coming when you will worship the Father neither on this moun-**

tain, of Gerizim. The other way was that of the Jews, who prayed on Mount Zion; and he refers to this when he says, **nor in Jerusalem**.

The third type of worship was to come, and it was different from the other two. Christ alludes to this by excluding the other two: for if the hour is coming when they will no longer worship on Mount Gerizim or in Jerusalem, then clearly the third type to which Christ refers will be a worship that does away with the other two. For if someone wishes to unite two people, it is necessary to eliminate that over which they disagree, and give them something in common on which they will agree. And so Christ, wishing to unite the Jews and Gentiles, eliminated the observances of the Jews and the idolatry of the Gentiles; for these two were like a wall separating the peoples. And he made the two people one: "He is our peace, he who has made the two of us one" (Eph 2:14). Thus the ritual observances [of the Jews] and the idolatry of the Gentiles were abolished, and the true worship of God established by Christ.

601 As for the mystical sense, and according to Origen, the three types of worship are three kinds of participation in divine wisdom. Some participate in it under a dark cloud of error, and these adore on the mountain: for every error springs from pride: "I am against you, destroying mountain" (Jer 51:25). Others participate in divine wisdom without error, but in an imperfect way, because they see in a mirror and in an obscure way; and these worship in Jerusalem, which signifies the present Church: "The Lord is building Jerusalem" (Ps 146:2). But the blessed and the saints participate in divine wisdom without error in a perfect way, for they see God as he is, as said in 1 John (3:2). And so Christ says, **the hour is coming**, i.e., is waited for, when you will participate in divine wisdom neither in error nor in a mirror in an obscure way, but as it is.

602 Then (v 22), he compares the different kinds of worship to each other. First, he compares the second to the first, Secondly, the third to the first and second (v 23). As to the first he does three things. First, he shows the shortcomings of the first type of worship. Secondly, the truth of the second (v 22b). Thirdly, the reason for each statement.

603 As to the first he says, **You people worship what you do not understand**.

Some might think that the Lord should have explained the truth of the matter and solve the woman's problem. But the Lord does not bother to do so because each of these kinds of worship was due to end.

As to his saying, **You people worship**, and so on, it should be pointed out that, as the Philosopher says, knowledge of complex things is different than knowledge of simple things. For something can be known about complex things in such a way that something else about them remains unknown; thus there can be false knowledge about them. For example, if someone has true knowledge of an animal as to its substance, he might be in error touching the knowledge of one of its accidents, such as whether it is black or white; or of a difference, such as whether it has wings or is four-footed. But there cannot be false knowledge of simple things: because they are either perfectly known inasmuch as their quiddity is known; or they are not known at all, if one cannot attain to a knowledge of them. Therefore, since God is absolutely simple, there cannot be false knowledge of him in the sense that something might be known about him and something remain unknown, but only in the sense that knowledge of him is not attained. Accordingly, anyone who believes that God is something that he is not, for example, a body, or something like that, does not adore God but something else, because he does not know him, but something else.

Now the Samaritans had a false idea of God in two ways. First of all, because they thought he was corporeal, so that they believed that he should be adored in only one definite corporeal place. Further, because they did not believe that he transcended all things, but was equal to certain creatures, they adored along with him certain idols, as if they were equal to him. Consequently, they did not know him, because they did not attain to a true knowledge of him. So the Lord says, **You people worship what you do not understand**, i.e., you do not adore God because you do not know him, but only some imaginary being you think is God, "as the Gentiles do, with their foolish ideas" (Eph 4:17).

604 As to the second, i.e., the truth of the worship of the Jews, he says, **we understand what we worship**. He includes himself among the Jews, because he was a Jew by race, and because the woman thought he was a prophet and a Jew. **We understand what we worship**, because through the law and the prophets the Jews acquired a true knowledge or opinion of God, in that they did not believe that he was corporeal nor in one definite place, as though his greatness could be enclosed in a place: "If the heavens, and the heavens of the heavens cannot contain you, how much less this house that I have built" (1 Kgs 8:27). And neither did they worship idols: "God is known in Judah" (Ps 75:2).

605 He gives the reason for this when he says, **since salvation is from the Jews**. As if to say: The true knowledge of God was possessed exclusively by the Jews, for it had been determined that

salvation would come from them. And as the source of health should itself be healthy, so the source of salvation, which is acquired by the true knowledge and the true worship of God, should possess the true knowledge of God. Thus, since the source of salvation and its cause, i.e., Christ, was to come from them, according to the promise in Genesis (22:18): "All the nations will be blessed in your descendents," it was fitting that God be known in Judah.

606   Salvation comes from the Jews in three ways. First in their teaching of the truth, for all other peoples were in error, while the Jews held fast to the truth, according to Romans (3:2): "What advantage do Jews have? First, they were entrusted with the words of God." Secondly, in their spiritual gifts: for prophecy and the other gifts of the Spirit were given to them first, and from them they reached others: "You," i.e., the Gentiles, "a wild olive branch, are ingrafted on them," i.e., on the Jews (Rom 11:17); "If the Gentiles have become sharers in their (i.e., the Jews') spiritual goods, they ought to help the Jews as to earthly goods" (Rom 15:27). Thirdly, since the very author of salvation is from the Jews, since "Christ came from then in the flesh" (Rom 9:5).

607   Now (v 23), he compares the third kind of worship to the first two. First, he mentions its superiority to the others. Secondly, how appropriate this kind of worship is (v 23b).

608   As to the first point, we should note, as Origen says, that when speaking above of the third kind of worship, the Lord said, **the hour is coming when you will worship the Father neither on this mountain nor in Jerusalem**; but he did not then add, **and is now here.** But now, in speaking of it, he does say, **the hour is coming, and is now here.** The reason is because the first time he was speaking of the worship found in heaven, when we will participate in the perfect knowledge of God, which is not possessed by those still living in this mortal life. But now he is speaking of the worship of this life, and which has now come through Christ.

609   So he says, **But the hour is coming, and is now here, when true worshipers will worship the Father in spirit and in truth.** We can understand this, as Chrysostom does, as showing the superiority of this worship to that of the Jews. So that the sense is: Just as the worship of the Jews is superior to that of the Samaritans, so the worship of the Christians is superior to that of the Jews. It is superior in two respects. First, because the worship of the Jews is in bodily rites: "Rites for the body, imposed only until the time they are reformed" (Heb 9:10); while the worship of the Christians is in spirit. Secondly, because the worship of the Jews is in symbols: for the Lord was not pleased with their sacrificial victims insofar as

they were things; so we read, "Shall I eat the flesh of bulls, or drink the blood of goats?" (Ps 49:13), and again, "You would not be pleased with a holocaust" (Ps 50:18), that is, as a particular thing; but such a sacrificial victim would be pleasing to the Lord as a symbol of the true victim and of the true sacrifice: "The law has only a shadow of the good things to come" (Heb 10:1). But the worship of the Christians is in truth, because it is pleasing to God in itself: "grace and truth have come through Jesus Christ," as we saw above (1:17). So he is saying here that **true worshipers will worship in spirit**, not in bodily rites, **and in truth**, not in symbols.

610   This passage can in interpreted in a second way, by saying that when our Lord says, **in spirit and in truth**, he wants to show the difference between the third kind of worship and not just that of the Jews, but also that of the Samaritans. In this case, **in truth**, refers to the Jews: for the Samaritans, as was said, were in error, because they worshiped what they did not understand. But the Jews worshiped with a true knowledge of God.

611   **In spirit and in truth** can be understood in a third way, as indicating the characteristics of true worship. For two things are necessary for a true worship: one is that the worship be spiritual; so he says, **in spirit**, i.e., with fervor of spirit: "I will pray with spirit, and I will pray with my mind" (1 Cor 14:15); "Singing to the Lord in your hearts" (Eph 5:19). Secondly, the worship should be **in truth**. First, in the truth of faith, because no fervent spiritual desire is meritorious unless united to the truth of faith, "Ask with faith, without any doubting" (Jas 1:6). Secondly, **in truth**, i.e., without pretense or hypocrisy; against such attitudes we read: "They like to pray at street corners, so people can see them" (Mt 6:5).

This prayer, then, requires three things: first, the fervor of love; secondly, the truth of faith; and thirdly, a correct intention.

He says, the true worshipers will worship **the Father** in spirit and in truth, because under the law, worship was not given to the Father, but to the Lord. We worship in love, as sons; whereas they worshiped in fear, as slaves.

612   He says **true** worshipers, in opposition to three things mentioned in the above interpretations. First, in opposition to the false worship of the Samaritans: "Put aside what is not true, and speak the truth" (Eph 4:25). Secondly, in opposition to the fruit-less and transitory character of bodily rites: "Why do you love what is without profit, and seek after lies" (Ps 4:3). Thirdly, it is opposed to what is symbolic: "Grace and truth have come through Jesus Christ" (above 1:17).

613   Then when he says, **Indeed, it is just such worshipers**

the **Father seeks**, he shows that this third kind of worship is appropriate for two reasons. First, because the One worshiped wills and accepts this worship. Secondly, because of the nature of the One worshiped (v 24).

614 Concerning the first, we should note that for a man to merit receiving what he asks, he should ask for things which are not in opposition to the will of the giver, and also ask for them in a way which is acceptable to the giver. And so when we pray to God, we ought to be such as God seeks. But God seeks those who will worship him in spirit and in truth, in the fervor of love and in the truth of faith; "And now, Israel, what does the Lord your God want from you, but that you fear the Lord your God, and walk in his ways, and love him, and serve the Lord your God with all your heart" (Dt 10:12); and in Micah (6:8): "I will show you, man, what is good, and what the Lord requires of you: to do what is right, and to love mercy, and to walk attentively with your God."

615 Then he shows that the third type of worship is appropriate from the very nature of God, saying, **God is spirit**. As is said in Sirach (13:19), "Every animal loves its like"; and so God loves us insofar as we are like him. But we are not like him by our body, because he is incorporeal, but in what is spiritual in us, for **God is spirit**: "Be renewed in the spirit," of your mind (Eph 4:23).

In saying, **God is spirit**, he means that God is incorporeal: "A spirit does not have flesh and bones" (Lk 24:39); and also that he is a life-giver, because our entire life is from God, as its creative source. God is also truth: "I am the way, and the truth, and the life" (below 14:6). Therefore, we should worship him in spirit and in truth.

616 When he says, **The woman said to him**, he mentions the one who gives the gift; and this corresponds to what our Lord said before, **If you knew the gift of God, and realized who it is who says to you, Give me a drink, you perhaps would have asked him**. First, we have the woman's profession. Secondly, the teaching of Christ (v 26). As to the first, he does two things. First, the woman professes her faith in the Christ to come. Secondly, in the fulness of his teaching, **he will tell us everything**.

617 The woman, wearied by the profound nature of what Christ was saying, was confused and unable to understand all this. She says: **I know that the Messiah is coming, the one called Christ**. As if to say: I do not understand what you are saying, but a time will come when the Messiah will arrive, and then we will understand all these things. For "Messiah" in Hebrew means the same as "Anointed One" in Latin, and "Christ" in Greek. She knew that the

Messiah was coming because she had been taught by the books of Moses, which foretell the coming of Christ: "The scepter will not be taken away from Judah ... until he who is to be sent comes" (Gn 49:10). As Augustine says, this is the first time the woman mentions the name "Christ": and we see by this that she is now beginning to return to her lawful husband.

618 When this Messiah comes, he will give us a complete teaching. Hence she says, **when he comes he will tell us everything**. This was foretold by Moses: "I will raise up a prophet for them, from among their own brothers, like them; and I will put my words in his mouth, and he will tell them all I command him" (Dt 18:18). Because this woman had now called her husband, i.e., intellect and reason, the Lord now offers her the water of spiritual teaching by revealing himself to her in a most excellent way.

619 And so Jesus says: **I who speak to you am he**, i.e., I am the Christ: "Wisdom goes to meet those who desire her, so she may first reveal herself to them" (Wis 6:14), and below (14:21): "I will love him, and reveal myself to him."

Our Lord did not reveal himself to this woman at once because it might have seemed to her that he was speaking out of vainglory. But now, having brought her step by step to a knowledge of himself, Christ revealed himself at the appropriate time: "Words appropriately spoken are like apples of gold on beds of silver" (Prv 25:11). In contrast, when he was asked by the Pharisees whether he was the Christ, "If you are the Christ, tell us clearly" (below 10:24), he did not reveal himself to them clearly, because they did not ask to learn but to test him. But this woman is speaking in all simplicity.

LECTURE 3

27 His disciples, returning at this point, were amazed that Jesus was speaking with a woman. But no one said, "What do you want?" or "Why are you talking to her?" 28 The woman then left her water jar and went off to the town. And she said to the people: 29 "Come, and see the man who told me everything that I have done. Could he not be the Christ?" 30 At that they set out from the town to meet him. 31 Meanwhile, his disciples asked him saying, "Rabbi, eat something." 32 But he said to them,
"I have food to eat of which you do not know."
33 At this the disciples said to one another, "Do you suppose that someone has brought him something to eat?"

620   After presenting the teaching on spiritual water, the Evangelist now deals with the effect of this teaching. First, he sets down the effect itself. Secondly, he elaborates on it (v 31). The effect of this teaching is its fruit for those who believe. And first we have its fruit which relates to the disciples, who were surprised at Christ's conduct. Secondly, its fruit in relation to the woman, who proclaimed Christ's power (v 28).

621   We are told three things about the disciples. First, their return to Christ: he says, **His disciples, returning at this point**. As Chrysostom reminds us, it was very convenient that the disciples returned after Christ had revealed himself to the woman, since this shows us that all events are regulated by divine providence: "He made the small and the great, and takes care for all alike" (Wis 6:8); "There is a time and fitness for everything" (Ecc 8:6).

622   Secondly, we see their surprise at what Christ was doing; he says, they **were amazed that Jesus was speaking with a woman**. They were amazed at what was good; and as Augustine says, they did not suspect any evil. They were amazed at two things. First, at the extraordinary gentleness and humility of Christ: for the Lord of the world stooped to speak with a poor woman, and for a long time, giving us an example of humility: "Be friendly to the poor" (Sir 4:7). Secondly, they were amazed that he was speaking with a Samaritan and a foreigner, for they did not know the mystery by which this woman was a symbol of the Church of the Gentiles; and Christ sought the Gentiles, for he came "to seek and to save what was lost" (Lk 19:10).

623   Thirdly, we see the disciples' reverence for Christ, shown by their silence. For we show our reverence for God when we do not presume to discuss his affairs: "It is to the glory of God to conceal things; and to the glory of kings to search things out" (Prv 25:2). So the Evangelist says that although his disciples were surprised, none of them said, **What do you want?** or asked him, **Why are you talking to her?** "Listen in silence" (Sir 32:9). Yet the disciples had been so trained to observe order, because of their reverence and filial fear toward Christ, that now and then they would question him about matters that concerned themselves, i.e., when Christ said things relating to them, but which were beyond their understanding: "Young men, speak if you have to" (Sir 32:10). At other times they did not question him; in those matters that were not their business, as here.

624   Then (v 28), we have the fruit which relates to the woman; by what she said to her people, she was taking on the role of an apostle. From what she says and does, we can learn three things. First,

her affective devotion; secondly, her way of preaching; thirdly, the effect her preaching had (v 30).

625   Her affection is revealed in two ways. First, because her devotion was so great that she forgot why she had come to the well, and left without the water and her water jar. So he says, **the woman then left her water jar and went off to the town**, to tell of the wonderful things Christ had done; and she was not now concerned for her own bodily comfort but for the welfare of others. In this respect she was like the apostles, who "leaving their nets, followed the Lord" (Mt 4:20). The water jar is a symbol of worldly desires, by which men draw out pleasures from the depths of darkness — symbolized by the well — i.e., from a worldly manner of life. Accordingly, those who abandon worldly desires for the sake of God leave their water jars: "No soldier of God becomes entangled in the business of this world" (2 Tim 2:4). Secondly, we see her affection from the great number of those to whom she brings the news: not to just one or two, but to the entire town; we read that she **went off to the town**. This signifies the duty Christ gave to the apostles: "Go, teach all nations" (Mt 28:19); and "I have chosen you to go and bring forth fruit" (below 15:16).

626   Next we see her manner of preaching (v 29). She first invites them to see Christ, saying, **Come and see the man**. Although she had heard Christ say that he was the Christ, she did not at once tell the people that they should come to the Christ, or believe, so as not to give them a reason for scoffing. So at first she mentions things that were believable and evident about Christ, as that he was a man: "made in the likeness of men" (Phil 2:7). Neither did she say, "believe," but **Come, and see**; for she was convinced that if they were to taste from that well by seeing him, they would be affected in the same way she was: "Come, and I will tell you the great things he has done for me" (Ps 65:16). In this she is imitating the example of a true preacher, not calling men to himself, but to Christ: "What we preach is not ourselves, but Jesus Christ" (2 Cor 4:5).

627   Secondly, she mentions a clue to Christ's divinity, saying, **who told me everything that I have done**, that is, how many husbands she had had. For it is the function and sign of the divinity to disclose hidden things and the secrets of hearts. Although the things she had done would cause her shame, she is still not ashamed to mention them; for as Chrysostom says: "When the soul is on fire with the divine fire, it no longer pays attention to earthly things, neither to glory nor to shame, but only to that flame that holds it fast."

628 Thirdly, she infers the greatness of Christ, saying, **Could he not be the Christ?** She did not dare to say that he was the Christ, lest she seem to be trying to teach them; they could have become angry at this and refuse to go with her. Yet she was not entirely silent on this point, but submitting it to their judgment, set it forth in the form of a question, saying, **Could he not be the Christ?** For this is an easier way to persuade someone.

629 This insignificant woman signifies the condition of the apostles, who were sent out to preach: "Not many of you are learned in the worldly sense, not many powerful ·... But God chose the simple ones of the world to embarrass the wise" (1 Cor 1:26). Thus in Proverbs (9:3) the apostles are called handmaids: "She," divine wisdom, i.e., the Son of God, "sent out her handmaids," the apostles, "to summon to the tower."

630 The fruit of her preaching is given when he says, **At that they set out from the town**, to where she had returned, **to meet him**, Christ. We see by this that if we desire to come to Christ, we must set out from the town, i.e., leave behind our carnal desires: "Let us go out to him outside the camp, bearing the abuse he took," as we read in Hebrews (13:13).

631 Now the effect of this spiritual teaching is elaborated. First, by what Christ said to his disciples; secondly, by the effect of all this on the Samaritans (v 39). Concerning the first he does two things. First, we have the situation in which Christ speaks to his disciples; secondly, what he said (v 32).

632 The situation is the insistence of the apostles that Christ eat. He says, **Meanwhile**, i.e., between the time that Christ and the woman spoke and the Samaritans came, **his disciples asked him**, that is, Christ, **Rabbi, eat something**: for they thought that then was a good time to eat, before the crowds came from the town. For the disciples did not usually offer Christ food in the presence of strangers: so we read in Mark (6:31), that so many people came to him that he did not even have time to eat.

633 After presenting the situation, he gives its fruit. First, it is given in figurative language. Secondly, we see the disciples are slow in understanding this. Thirdly, the Lord explains what he meant (v 34).

634 The fruit of his spiritual teaching is proposed under the symbols of food and nourishment; so the Lord says, **I have food to eat.** We should note that just as bodily nourishment is incomplete unless there is both food and drink, so also both should be found in spiritual nourishment: "The Lord fed him with the bread of life

and understanding," this is the food, "and gave him a drink of the water of saving wisdom," and this is the drink (Sir 15:3). So it was appropriate for Christ to speak of food after having given drink to the Samaritan woman. And just as water is a symbol for saving wisdom, so food is a symbol of good works.

The food that Christ had to eat is the salvation of men; this was what he desired. When he says that he has food to eat, he shows how great a desire he has for our salvation. For just as we desire to eat when we are hungry, so he desires to save us: "My delight is to be with the children of men" (Prv 8:31). So he says, **I have food to eat**, i.e., the conversion of the nations, **of which you do not know**; for they had no way of knowing beforehand about this conversion of the nations.

635 Origen explains this in a different way, as follows. Spiritual food is like bodily food. The same amount of bodily food is not enough for everyone; some need more, others less. Again, what is good for one is harmful to another. The same thing happens in spiritual nourishment: for the same kind and amount should not be given to everyone, but adjusted to what is appropriate to the disposition and capacity of each. "Like newborn babes, desire spiritual milk" (1 Pt 2:2). Solid food is for the perfect; thus Origen says that the man who understands the loftier doctrine, and who has charge of others in spiritual matters, can teach this doctrine to those who are weaker and have less understanding. Accordingly, the Apostle says in 1 Corinthians (3:2): "Being little ones in Christ, I gave you milk, not solid food." And Jesus could say this with much more truth: **I have food to eat**; and "I have many things to tell you, but you cannot bear them now" (below 16:12).

636 The slowness of the disciples to understand these matters is implied by the fact that what our Lord said about spiritual food, they understood as referring to bodily food. For even they were still without understanding, as we see from Matthew (15:16). It is not surprising that this Samaritan woman did not understand about spiritual water, for even the Jewish disciples did not understand about spiritual food.

In their saying to each other, **Do you suppose that someone has brought him something to eat?** we should note that it was customary for Christ to accept food from others; but not because he needs our goods: "He does not need our goods" (Ps 15:2), nor our food, because it is he who gives food to every living thing.

637 Then why did he desire and accept goods from others? For two reasons. First, so that those who give him these things might acquire merit. Secondly, in order to give us an example that those engrossed in spiritual matters should not be ashamed of their

poverty, nor regard it burdensome to be supported by others. For it is fitting that teachers have others provide their food so that, being free from such concerns, they may carefully pay attention to the ministry of the word, as Chrysostom says, and as we find in the Gloss. "Let the elders who rule well be regarded as worthy of a double compensation; especially those concerned with preaching and teaching (1 Tim 5:17).

LECTURE 4

34 Jesus explained to them,
    "My food is to do the will of him
    who sent me, to accomplish his work.
    35 Do you not have a saying:
    'There are still four months,
    and it will be harvest time'?
    So I say to you: Lift up your eyes,
    look at the fields, because they are
    already white for the harvest!
    36 He who reaps receives his wages
    and gathers fruit for eternal life,
    so that the sower can rejoice
    at the same time as the reaper.
    37 For here the saying is verified:
    'One man sows, another reaps.'
    38 I have sent you to reap
    what you have not worked for.
    Others have done the work,
    and you have entered into their labors."

638 Since the disciples were slow to understand the Lord's figure of speech, the Lord now explains it. First, we have its explanation; secondly, its application (v 35).

639 As to the first, we should note that just as Christ explained to the Samaritan woman what he had told her in figurative language about water, so he explains to his apostles what he told them in figurative language about food. But he does not do so in the same way in both cases. Since the apostles were able to understand these matters more easily, he explains to them at once and in few words; but to the Samaritan woman, since she could not understand as well, our Lord leads her to the truth with a longer explanation.

640 It is perfectly reasonable for Christ to say, **My food is**

to do the will of him who sent me, to accomplish his work. For as bodily food sustains a man and brings him to perfection, the spiritual food of the soul and of the rational creature is that by which he is sustained and perfected; and this consists in being joined to his end and following a higher rule. David, understanding this, said: "For me, to adhere to God is good" (Ps 72:28). Accordingly, Christ, as man, fittingly says that his food is to do the will of God, to accomplish his work.

641 These two expressions can be understood as meaning the same thing, in the sense that the second is explaining the first. Or, they can be understood in different ways.

If we understand them as meaning the same, the sense is this: **My food is**, i.e., in this is my strength and nourishment, **to do the will of him who sent me**; according to, "My God, I desired to do your will, and your law is in my heart" (Ps 39:9), and, "I came down from heaven not to do my own will, but the will of him who sent me" (below 6:38). But because "to do the will" (*facere voluntatem*) of another can be understood in two ways — one, by making him will it, and second, by fulfilling what I know he wills — therefore, explaining what it means to do the will of him who sent him, the Lord says, **to accomplish his work**, that is, that I might complete the work I know he wants: "I must do the works of him who sent me while it is day" (below 9:4).

If these two expressions are understood as different, then we should point out that Christ did two things in this world. First, he taught the truth, in inviting and calling us to the faith; and by this he fulfilled the will of the Father: "This is the will of my Father, who sent me: that everyone who sees the Son and believes in him should have eternal life" (below 6:40). Secondly, he accomplished the truth by opening in us, by his passion, the gate of life, and by giving us the power to arrive at complete truth: "I have accomplished the work which you gave me to do" (below 17:4). Thus he is saying: **My food is to do the will of him who sent me**, by calling men to the faith, **to accomplish his work**, by leading them to what is perfect.

642 Another interpretation, given by Origen, is that every man who does good works should direct his intention to two things: the honor of God and the good of his neighbor: for as it is said: "The end of the commandment is love" (1 Tim 1:5), and this love embraces both God and our neighbor. And so, when we do something for God's sake, the end of the commandment is God; but when it is for our neighbor's good, the end of the commandment is our neighbor. With this in mind, Christ is saying, **My food is to do the will of him who sent me**, God, i.e., to direct and regulate my inten-

tion to those matters that concern the honor of God, **to accomplish his work,** i.e., to do things for the benefit and perfection of man.

643   On the other hand, since the works of God are perfect, it does not seem proper to speak of accomplishing or completing them. I answer that among lower creatures, man is the special work of God, who made him to his own image and likeness (Gn 1:26). And in the beginning God made this a perfect work, because as we read in Ecclesiastes (7:30): "God made man upright." But later, man lost this perfection by sin, and abandoned what was right. And so, this work of the Lord needed to be repaired in order to become right again; and this was accomplished by Christ, for "Just as by the disobedience of one man, many were made sinners, so by the obedience of one man, many will be made just" (Rom 5:19). Thus Christ says, **to accomplish his work,** i.e., to bring man back to what is perfect

644   Then when he says, **Do you not have a saying: There are still four months, and it will be harvest time?** he makes use of a simile. Note that when Christ asked the Samaritan woman for a drink, "Give me a drink," he made use of a simile concerning water. But here, the the disciples are urging the Lord to eat, and now he makes use of a simile concerning spiritual food.

There are some persons whom God asks for a drink, as this Samaritan woman; and there are some who offer a drink to God. But no one offers food to God unless God first asks him for it: for we offer spiritual food to God when we ask him for our salvation, that is, when we ask, "Your will be done on earth as it is in heaven" (Mt 6:10). We cannot obtain salvation of ourselves, unless we are pre-moved by "prevenient grace," according to the statement in Lamentations (5:21): "Make us come back to you, O Lord, and we will come back" (Lam 5:21). The Lord himself, therefore, first asks for that which makes us ask through "prevenient grace."

In this simile, we have first, the harvest. Secondly, those who reap the harvest (v 36). He does two things concerning the first. First, he states the simile concerning the natural harvest; secondly, concerning the spiritual harvest (v 35b).

645   **Do you not have a saying: There are still four months, and it will be harvest time?**   We can see from this that, as stated in Matthew (4:12), Christ left Judea and traveled through Samaria right after John was arrested, and that all this happened during the winter. So, because the harvests ripen there more according to the season, there were four months from that time till the harvest. Thus he says, **Do you not have a saying,** about the natural harvest,

There are still four months that must pass, and it will be harvest time? i.e., the time for gathering up the harvest. So I say to you, speaking of the spiritual harvest, Lift up your eyes, look at the fields, because they are already white for the harvest.

646 Here we should point out that harvest time is the time when the fruit is gathered; and so whenever fruit is gathered can be regarded as a harvest time. Now fruit is gathered at two times: for both in temporal and in spiritual matters there is nothing to prevent what is fruit in relation to an earlier state from being seed in relation to something later. For example, good works are the fruit of spiritual instruction, as is faith and other such things; but these in turn are seeds of eternal life, because eternal life is acquired through them. So Sirach (24:23) says: "My blossoms," in relation to the fruit to follow, "bear the fruit of of honor and riches," in relation to what preceded.

With this in mind, there is a certain gathering of a spiritual harvest; and this concerns an eternal fruit, i.e., the gathering of the faithful into eternal life, of which we read: "The harvest is the end of the world" (Mt 13:39). We are not here concerned with this harvest. Another spiritual harvest is gathered in the present; and this is understood in two ways. In the first, the gathering of the fruit is the converting of the faithful to be assembled in the Church; in the second, the gathering is the very knowing of the truth, by which a person gathers the fruit of truth into his soul. And we are concerned with these two gatherings of the harvest, depending on the different expositions.

647 Augustine and Chrysostom understand the gathering of the harvest in the first way, as follows. You say that it is not yet the time for the natural harvest; but this is not true of the spiritual harvest. Indeed, I say to you: Lift up your eyes, i.e., the eyes of your mind, by thinking, or even your physical eyes, look at the fields, because they are already white for the harvest: because the entire countryside was full of Samaritans coming to Christ.

The statement that the fields are already white is metaphorical: for when sown fields are white, it is a sign that they are ready for harvest. And so he only means to say by this that the people were ready for salvation and to hear the word. He says, look at the fields, because not only the Jews, but the Gentiles as well, were ready for the faith: "The harvest is great, but the workers are few" (Mt 9:37). And just as harvests are made white by the presence of the burning heat of the summer sun, so by the coming of the Sun of justice, i.e., Christ, and his preaching and power, men are made ready for salvation. Malachi (4:2) says: "The sun of justice will rise on you who fear my name." Thus it is that the time of Christ's coming is called the time of plenitude or fulness: "When the fulness of time had come, God sent his Son" (Gal 4:4).

648   Origen deals with the second gathering of the harvest, i.e., the gathering of truth in the soul. He says that one gathers as much of the fruit of truth in the harvest as the truths he knows. And he says that everything said here (v 35) was presented as a parable. In this interpretation, the Lord does two things. First, he mentions a false doctrine held by some. Secondly, he rejects it, **I say to you.**

Some thought that man could not acquire any truth about anything. This opinion gave rise to the heresy of the Academicians, who maintained that nothing can be known as certain in this life; about which we read: "I tested all things by wisdom. I said: 'I will acquire wisdom,' and it became further from me" (Ecc 7:24). Our Lord mentions this opinion when he says, **Do you not have a saying: There are still four months and it will be harvest time?** i.e., this whole present life, in which man serves under the four elements, must end, so that after it truth may be gathered in another life.

Our Lord rejects this opinion when he says: This is not true, **I say to you: Lift up your eyes.** Sacred Scripture usually uses this expression when something subtle and profound is being presented; as, "Lift up your eyes on high, and see who has created these things" (Is 40:26). For when our eyes are not lifted away from earthly things or from the desires of the flesh, they are not fit to know spiritual fruit. For sometimes they are prevented from considering divine things because they have stooped to earthly things: "They have fixed their eyes on the earth" (Ps 16:11); sometimes they are blinded by concupiscence: "They have averted their eyes so as not to look at heaven or remember the judgments of God" (Dn 13:9).

649   So he says, **Lift up your eyes, look at the fields, because they are already white for the harvest,** i.e., they are such that the truth can be learned from them: for by the "fields" we specifically understand all those things from which truth can be acquired, especially the Scriptures: "Search the Scriptures ... they bear witness to me" (below 5:39). Indeed, these fields existed in the Old Testament, but they were not white for the harvest because men were not able to pick spiritual fruit from them until Christ came, who made them white by opening their understanding: "He opened their minds so they could understand the Scriptures" (Lk 24.45). Again, creatures are harvests from which the fruit of truth is gathered: "The invisible things of God are clearly known by the things that have been made" (Rom 1:20). None the less, the Gentiles who pursued a knowledge of these things gathered the fruits of error rather than of truth from them; because as we read, "they served the creature rather than the Creator" (Rom 1:25). So the harvests were not yet white; but they were made white for the harvest when Christ came.

650 Next (v 36), he deals with the reapers. First, he gives their reward. Secondly, he mentions a proverb. And thirdly, he explains it, i.e., applies it (v 38).

651 Concerning the first, we should note that when the Lord was explaining earlier about spiritual water, he mentioned the way in which spiritual water differs from natural water: a person who drinks natural water will become thirsty again, but one who drinks spiritual water will never be thirsty again. Here, too, in explaining about the harvest, he points out the difference between a natural and a spiritual harvest. Three things are mentioned.

First, the way in which the two harvests are similar: namely, in that the person who reaps either harvest receives a wage. But the one who reaps spiritually is the one who gathers the faithful into the Church, or who gathers the fruit of truth into his soul. Each of these will receive a wage, according to: "Each one will receive his own wage according to his work" (1 Cor 3:8).

The two other points he mentions concern the ways the two harvests are unlike each other. First, the fruit gathered from a natural harvest concerns the life of the body; but the fruit gathered by one who reaps a spiritual harvest concerns eternal life. So he says, he who reaps, i.e., he who reaps spiritually, **gathers fruit for eternal life**, that is, the faithful, who will obtain eternal life: "Your fruit is sanctification, your end is eternal life" (Rom 6:22). Or, this fruit is the very knowing and explaining of the truth by which man acquires eternal life: "Those who explain me will have eternal life," as we read in Sirach (24:31). Secondly, the two harvests are unlike because in a natural harvest it is considered a misfortune that one should sow and another reap; hence he who sows is saddened when another reaps. But it is not this way when the seed is spiritual, for **the sower can rejoice at the same time as the reaper**.

According to Chrysostom and Augustine, the ones who sow spiritual seed are the fathers and prophets of the Old Testament, for "The seed is the word of God" (Lk 8:11), which Moses and the prophets sowed in the land of Judah. But the apostles were the reapers, because the former were not able to accomplish what they wanted to do, i.e., to bring men to Christ; this was done by the apostles. And so both the apostles and the prophets rejoice together, in one mansion of glory, over the conversion of the faithful: "Joy and gladness will be found there, thanksgiving and the voice of praise" (Is 51:3). This refutes the heresy of the Manicheans who condemn the fathers of the Old Testament; for as the Lord says here, they will rejoice with the apostles.

According to Origen, however, the "sowers" in any faculty [of the soul] are those who confer the very first principles of that faculty; but the reapers are those who proceed from these principles to further truths. And this is all the more true of the science of all the sciences. The prophets are sowers, because they handed down many things concerning divine matters; but the apostles are the reapers, because in preaching and teaching they revealed many things which the prophets did not make known: "which was not made known to the sons of men in other generations as it has now been revealed to his holy apostles" (Eph 3:5).

652 Then when he says, **For here the saying is verified**, we are given a proverb. As if to say: **For here**, i.e., in this fact, **the saying is verified**, i.e., the proverb in current use among the Jews is fulfilled: **One man sows, another reaps**. This proverb seems to have grown out of a statement in Leviticus (26:16): "You will sow your seed in vain for it will be devoured by your enemies." As a result, the Jews used this proverb when one person labored on something, but another received the pleasure from it. This then is what our Lord says: The proverb is verified here because it was the prophets who sowed and labored, while you are the ones to reap and rejoice.

Another interpretation would be this. **For here the saying is verified**, i.e. what I am saying to you, **One man sows, another reaps**, because you will reap the fruits of the labor of the prophets. Now the prophets and the apostles are different, but not in faith, for they both had faith: "But now the justice of God has been manifested outside the law; the law and the prophets bore witness to it" (Rom 3:21). They are different in their manner of life, for the prophets lived under the ceremonies of the law, from which the apostles and Christians have been freed: "When we were children, we were slaves under the elements of this world. But when the fulness of time came, God sent his Son, made of a woman, made under the law, to redeem those who were under the law, so that we could receive adoption as sons" (Gal 4:3). And although the apostles and prophets labor at different times, nevertheless they will rejoice equally and receive wages **for eternal life, so that the sower can rejoice at the same time as the reaper**. This was prefigured in the transfiguration of Christ, where all had their own glory, both the fathers of the Old Testament, that is, Moses and Elijah, and the fathers of the New Testament, that is, Peter, John and James. We see from this that the just of the New and of the Old Testaments will rejoice together in the glory to come.

653 Then (v 38), he applies the proverb. First, he calls the apostles reapers. Secondly, he says they are laborers (v 38b).

654 He says concerning the first: I say that it is one who reaps,

because you are reapers, and another who sows, for **I have sent you to reap what you have not worked for.** He does not say, "I will send you," but **I have sent you.** He says this because he sent them twice. One time was before his passion, when he sent them to the Jews, saying: "Do not go on the roads of the Gentiles ... but go rather to the lost sheep of the house of Israel" (Mt 10:5). In this case, they were sent to reap that on which they did not work, that is, to convert the Jews, among whom the prophets worked. After the resurrection, Christ sent them to the Gentiles, saying: "Go to the whole world, and preach the good news to every creature," as we find in Mark (16:15). This time they were sent to sow for the first time; for as the Apostle says: "I have preached the good news, but not where Christ was already known, so as not to build on another's foundation. But as it is written: 'They to whom he was not proclaimed will see, and they who have not heard will understand.' " (Rom 15:20). And so Christ says, **I have sent you,** referring to the first time they were sent. This is the way, then, the apostles are reapers, and others, the prophets, are the sowers.

655 Accordingly, he says, **Others have done the work,** by sowing the beginnings of the doctrine of Christ, **and you have entered into their labors,** to collect the fruit: "The fruit of good labors is glorious" (Wis 3:15). The prophets labored, I say, to bring men to Christ: "If you believed Moses, you would perhaps believe me, for he wrote of me" (below 5:46). If you do not believe his written words, how will you believe my spoken words? But the prophets did not reap the fruit; so Isaiah said with this in mind: "I have labored for nothing and without reason; in vain I have exhausted my strength" (Is 49:4).

LECTURE 5

39 Many Samaritans of that town believed in him on the testimony of the woman who said, "He told me everything I ever did." 40 So when the Samaritans came to him, they begged him to stay with them awhile. So he stayed there two days. 41 And many more believed in him because of his own words. 42 And they said to the woman, "Now we believe not just because of your story, but because we have heard him ourselves, and we know that here is truly the Savior of the world."

656 Above, the Lord foretold to the apostles the fruit to be

produced among the Samaritans by the woman's witness. Now the Evangelist deals with this fruit. First, the fruit of the woman's witness is given. Secondly, the growth of this fruit produced by Christ (v 41). The fruit of the woman's witness is shown in three ways.

657 First, by the faith of the Samaritans, for they believed in Christ. Thus he says, **Many Samaritans of that town**, to which the woman had returned, **believed in him**, and this, **on the testimony of the woman**, from whom Christ asked for a drink of water, who said, **He told me everything I ever did**: for this testimony was sufficient inducement to believe Christ. For since Christ had disclosed her failures, she would not have mentioned them if she had not been brought to believe. And so the Samaritans believed as soon as they heard her. This indicates that faith comes by hearing.

658 Secondly, the fruit of her witness is shown in their coming to Christ: for faith gives rise to a desire for the thing believed. Accordingly, after they believed, they came to Christ, to be perfected by him. So he says, **So when the Samaritans came to him**. "Come to him, and be enlightened" (Ps 33:6); "Come to me, all you who labor and are burdened, and I will refresh you" (Mt 11:28).

659 Thirdly, the fruit of her witness is shown in their desire: for a believer must not only come to Christ, but desire that Christ remain with him. So he says, **they begged him to stay with them awhile. So he stayed there two days.**

The Lord remains with us through charity: "If anyone loves me, he will keep my word" (below 14:23), and further on he adds, "and we will make our abode with him." The Lord remains for two days because there are two precepts of charity: the love of God and the love of our neighbor, "On these two commandments all the law and the prophets depend" (Mt 22:40). But the third day is the day of glory: "He will revive us after two days; on the third day he will raise us up" (Hos 6:3). Christ did not remain there for that day because the Samaritans were not yet capable of glory.

660 Then (v 41), the Evangelist says that the fruit resulting from the witness of the woman was increased by the presence of Christ; and this in three ways. First, in the number of those who believed. Secondly, in their reason for believing. Thirdly, in the truth they believed.

661 The fruit was increased as to the number of those who believed because while many believed in Christ on account of the woman, **many more believed in him because of his own words**, i.e., Christ's own words. This signifies that although many believed because of the prophets, many more were converted to the faith

after Christ came, according to the Psalm (7:7): "Rise up, O Lord, in the command you have given, and a congregation of people will surround you."

662   Secondly, this fruit was increased because of the way in which they believed: for they say to the woman: **Now we believe not just because of your story.**

Here we should note that three things are necessary for the perfection of faith; and they are given here in order. First, faith should be right; secondly, it should be prompt; and thirdly, it should be certain.

Now faith is right when it obeys the truth not for some alien reason, but for the truth itself; and as to this he says that they said to the woman, **Now we believe**, the truth, **not just because of your story**, but because of the truth itself. Three things lead us to believe in Christ. First of all, natural reason: "Since the creation of the world the invisible things of God are clearly known by the things that have been made" (Rom 1:20). Secondly, the testimony of the law and the prophets: "But now justification from God has been manifested outside the law; the law and the prophets bore witness to it" (Rom 3:21). Thirdly, the preaching of the apostles and others: "How will they believe without someone to preach to them?" as Romans (10:14) says. Yet when a person, having been thus instructed, believes, he can then say that it is not for any of these reasons that he believes: i.e., neither on account of natural reason, nor the testimony of the law, nor the preaching of others, but solely on account of the truth itself: "Abram believed God, who regarded this as his justification" (Gn 15:6).

Faith is prompt if it believes quickly; and this was verified in these Samaritans because they were converted to God by merely hearing him; so they say: **we have heard him ourselves**, and believe in him, **and we know that here is truly the Savior of the world**, without seeing miracles, as the Jews saw. And although to believe men quickly is an indication of thoughtlessness, according to Sirach (19:4): "He who believes easily is frivolous," yet to believe God quickly is more praiseworthy: "When they heard me, they obeyed me" (Ps 17:45).

Faith should be certain, because one who doubts in the faith is an unbeliever: "Ask with faith, without any doubting" (Jas 1:6). And so their faith was certain; thus they say, **and we know**. Sometimes, one who believes is said to know (*scire*), as here, because *scientia* [science, knowledge in a more perfect state] and faith agree in that both are certain. For just as *scientia* is certain, so is faith; indeed, the latter is much more so, because the certainty of *scientia* rests on human reason, which can be decieved, while the certainty of faith rests on divine reason, which cannot be contradicted. However they differ in mode: because faith possesses its certainty due to a divinely infused light, while *scientia* possesses its certainty due to a natural light. For as the certitude of *scientia* rests on first principles naturally known, so the principles of faith are known from a light divinely infused: "You are saved by grace, through faith; and this is not due to yourselves, for it is the gift of God" (Eph 2:8).

663 Thirdly, the fruit was increased in the truth believed; so they say, **here is truly the Savior of the world**. Here they are affirming that Christ is the unique, true and universal Savior.

He is the unique Savior for they assert that he is different from others when they say, **here is**, i.e., here he alone is who has come to save: "Truly, you are a hidden God, the God of Israel, the Savior" (Is 45:15); "There is no other name under heaven given to men, by which we are saved" (Acts 4:12).

They affirm that Christ is the true Savior when they say, **truly**. For since salvation, as Dionysius says, is deliverance from evil and preservation in good, there are two kinds of salvation: one is true, and the other is not true. Salvation is true when we are freed from true evils and preserved in true goods. In the Old Testament, however, although certain saviors had been sent, they did not truly bring salvation, for they set men free from temporal evils, which are not truly evils, nor true goods, because they do not last. But Christ is truly the Savior, because he frees men from true evils, that is, sins: "He will save his people from their sins" (Mt 1:21), and he preserves them in true goods, that is, spiritual goods.

They affirm that he is the universal Savior because he is not just for some, i.e., for the Jews alone, but is the Savior **of the world**. "God did not send his Son into the world to judge the world, but that the world might be saved through him" (above 3:17).

LECTURE 6

43 After two days he left that place and went to Galilee. 44 Jesus himself had testified that a prophet has no honor in his own country. 45 When however he arrived in Galilee, the Galileans welcomed him, because they had seen all the things he had done in Jerusalem on the festive day, where they too had gone. 46a He therefore went to Cana in Galilee once more, where he had made the water wine.

664 Having described the conversion of the Gentiles due to teaching, their conversion due to miracles is now given. The Evan-

gelist mentions a miracle performed by Christ: first, giving the place; secondly, describing the miracle; and thirdly, its effect (v 53). He does two things about the first. First, he gives the general location of the miracle, that is, Christ's own homeland. Secondly, the specific place (v 46). With respect to the first he does two things. First, he mentions the general place. Secondly, he tells how Christ was received there (v 45). Concerning the first he does two things. First, he indicates the general place. Secondly, he gives a certain reason, at (v 44).

665　He says first of all: I say that Jesus remained with these Samaritans for two days, and **after two days he left that place**, i.e., Samaria, **and went to Galilee**, where he had been raised. This signifies that at the end of the world, when the Gentiles have been confirmed in the faith and in the truth, a return will be made to convert the Jews, according to: "until the full number of the Gentiles enters, and so all Israel will be saved" (Rom 11:25).

666　Then he gives a certain reason, saying: **Jesus himself had testified that a prophet has no honor in his own country**. There are two questions here: one is about the literal meaning; and the other about the continuity of this passage with the first.

The problem about the literal meaning is that it does not seem to be true, as stated here, that a prophet has no honor in his own country: for we read that other prophets were honored in their own land. Chrysostom answers this by saying that the Lord is speaking here about the majority of cases. So, although there might be an exception in some individual cases, what is said here should not be considered false: for in matters concerning nature and morals, that rule is true which is verified in most cases; and if a few cases are otherwise, the rule is not considered to be false.

Now what the Lord says was true with respect to most of the prophets, because in the Old Testament it is hard to find any prophet who did not suffer persecution, as stated in Acts (7:52): "Which of the prophets did your fathers not persecute?"; and in Matthew (23:37): "Jerusalem, Jerusalem, you kill the prophets and stone those who are sent to you." Further, this statement of our Lord holds true not only in the case of the prophets among the Jews, but also, as Origen says, with many among the Gentiles, because they were held in contempt by their fellow citizens and put to death: for living with men in the usual way, and too much familiarity, lessen respect and breed contempt. So it is that those with whom we are more familiar we come to reverence less, and those with whom we cannot become acquainted we regard more highly.

However, the opposite happens with God: for the more intimate we become with God through love and contemplation, realizing how superior he is, the more we respect him and the less do we
esteem ourselves. "I have heard you, but now I see you, and so I
reprove myself, and do penance in dust and ashes" (Jb 42:5). The
reason for this is that man's nature is weak and fragile; and when one
lives with another for a long time, he notices certain weaknesses in
him, and this results in a loss of respect for him. But since God is
infinitely perfect, the more a person knows him the more he admires
his superior perfection, and as a result the more he respects him.

667   But was Christ a prophet? At first glance it seems not,
because prophecy involves an obscure knowledge: "If there is a
prophet of the Lord among you, I will appear to him in a vision"
(Nm 12:6). Christ's knowledge, however, was not obscure. Yet he
was a prophet, as is clear from, "The Lord your God will raise up
a prophet for you, from your nation and your brothers; he will be
like me. You will listen to him" (Dt 18:15). This text is referred
to Christ.

I answer that a prophet has a twofold function. First, that
of seeing: "He who is now called a prophet was formerly called
a seer" (1 Sm 9:9). Secondly, he makes known, announces; Christ
was a prophet in this sense for he made known the truth about God:
"For this was I born, and for this I came into the world: to testify
to the truth" (below 18:37). As for the seeing function of a prophet,
we should note that Christ was at once both a "wayfarer" and a
"comprehensor," or blessed. He was a wayfarer in the sufferings
of his human nature and in all the things that relate to this. He
was a blessed in his union with the divinity, by which he enjoyed
God in the most perfect way. There are two things in the vision or
seeing of a prophet. First, the intellectual light of his mind; and as
regards this Christ was not a prophet, because his light was not at
all deficient; his light was that of the blessed. Secondly, an imaginary
vision is also involved; and with respect to this Christ did have a
likeness to the prophets insofar as he was a wayfarer and was able
to form various images with his imagination.

668   Secondly, there is the problem about continuity. For
the Evangelist does not seem to be right in connecting the fact that
After two days he left that place and went to Galilee, with the
statement of Jesus that **a prophet has no honor in his own country**.
It would seem that the Evangelist should have said that Christ did
not go into Galilee, for if he was not honored there, that would be
a reason for not going there.

Augustine answers this by suggesting that the Evangelist said this to answer a question that could have been raised, namely: Why did Christ return to Galilee since he had lived there for a long time, and the Galileans were still not converted to him; while the Samaritans were converted in two days? It is the same as saying: Even though the Galileans had not been converted, still Jesus went there, for **Jesus himself had testified that a prophet has no honor in his own country**.

Chrysostom explains this in a different way: **After two days he left**, not for Capernaum, which was his homeland because of his continuous residence there, nor for Bethlehem, where he was born, nor for Nazareth, where he was educated. Thus he did not go to Capernaum; hence in Matthew (11:23) he upbraids them, saying: "And you, Capernaum, will you be exalted to heaven? You will descend even to hell." He went rather to Cana in Galilee. And he gives the reason here [for not going to Capernaum]: because they were ill-disposed toward him. This is what he says: **Jesus himself had testified that a prophet has no honor in his own country**.

669 Was Christ seeking glory from men? It seems not, for he says: "I do not seek my own glory" (below 8:50). I answer that it is only God who seeks his own glory without sin. A man should not seek his own glory from men, but rather the glory of God. Christ, however, as God, fittingly sought his own glory, and as man, he sought the glory of God in himself.

670 Then he shows that Christ was received by the Galileans more respectfully than before, saying, **When however he arrived in Galilee, the Galileans welcomed him**, respectfully. The reason behind this was **because they had seen all the things he had done in Jerusalem on the festive day, where they too had gone**, as the law commanded.

This seems to conflict with the fact that we did not read above of any miracles being performed by Christ at Jerusalem. I answer, with the opinion of Origen, that the Jews thought it a great miracle that Christ drove the traders from the temple with such authority (above 2:14). Or, we could say that Christ performed many miracles which were not written down, according to, "Jesus did many other signs ... which are not written down in this book" (below 20:30).

671 In its mystical sense, this gives us an example that if we wish to receive Jesus Christ within ourselves, we should go up to Jerusalem on a festive day, that is, we should seek tranquility of mind, and examine everything which Jesus does there: "Look upon Zion, the city of our festive days" (Is 33:20); "I have meditated on all your works" (Ps 142:5).

672 Note that as men were lesser in dignity, they were better with respect to God. The Judeans were superior in dignity to the Galileans: "Look at the Scriptures and see that the Prophet will not come from Galilee" (below 7:52); and the Galileans were superior in dignity to the Samaritans: "The Jews had nothing to do with the Samaritans" (above 4:9). On the other hand, the Samaritans were better than the Galileans because more of them believed in Christ in two days without any miracles than the Galileans did in a long period of time and even with the miracle of the wine: for none of them believed in him except his disciples. Finally, the Judeans were worse than the Galileans, because none of them believed in Jesus, except perhaps Nicodemus.

673 Then he says, **He therefore went to Cana in Galilee**. According to Chrysostom, this is given as a conclusion from what went before; it is as though he were saying: Christ did not go to Capernaum because he was not held in honor there. But he was under an obligation to go to Cana in Galilee: for on the first occasion he had been invited to the wedding, and now he goes again without being invited. The two trips to Cana are mentioned by the Evangelist to show their hardness of heart: for at the first miracle of the wine, only his disciples believed in Christ; and at the second miracle, only the official and his household believed. On the other hand, the Samaritans believed on Christ's words alone.

674 In the mystical sense, the two visits to Cana signify the effect of God's words on our minds. First of all they cause delight, because they who hear the word "receive the word with joy" (Mt 13:20). This is signified in the miracle of the wine, which as the Psalm (103:15) says, "gladdens the heart of man." Secondly, the word of God heals: "It was neither a herb nor a poultice that healed them, but your word, O Lord, which heals all things" (Wis 16:12). And this is signified by the curing of the sick son.

Further, these two visits to Cana indicate the two comings of the Son of God. The first coming was in all gentleness to bring joy: "Rejoice and give praise, people of Zion, for he is great who is in your midst, the Holy One of Israel" (Is 12:6). So the angel said to the shepherds: "I bring you good news of great joy ... this day a Savior has been born to you" (Lk 2:10). This is signified by the wine. His second coming into the world will be in majesty, when he will come to take away our weaknesses and our punishments, and to make us like his radiant body. And this is signified in the cure of the sick son.

46b There happened to be a certain official, whose son lay sick at Capernaum. 47 When he heard that Jesus had come to Galilee from Judea, he went to him, and begged him to come down and heal his son, who was at the point of death. 48 But Jesus said to him, "Unless you see signs and wonders, you do not believe." 49 The official said to him, "Lord, come down before my child dies." 50 Jesus told him, "Go, your son lives." The man took Jesus at his word, and started for home. 51 While he was on his way down, his servants ran up to meet him with word that his son was going to live. 52 He asked them at what time his boy got better. And they told him that yesterday at the seventh hour the fever left him. 53 The father then realized that it was at that very hour when Jesus told him, "Your son lives." He and his whole household became believers. 54 This was the second sign Jesus had performed on returning from Judea to Galilee.

675 Having told us the place of this miracle, the Evangelist now describes the miracle itself: telling us of the person who was ill; the one who interceded for him; and the one who healed him. The one who was ill was the son of the official; his father interceded for him; and it was Christ who was to heal him.

676 About the person who was ill, he first tells us of his status, a **son** of an official; secondly, where he was, **at Capernaum**; thirdly, his illness, a **fever**.

He says about the first, **There happened to be a certain official, whose son lay sick**. Now one can be called an official for a variety of reasons. For example, if one is in charge of a small territory. This is not its meaning here for at this time there was no king in Judea: "We have no king but Caesar" (below 19:15). One is also called an official, as Chrysostom says, because he is from a royal family; and this is also not its meaning here. In a third way, an official is some officer of a king or ruler; and this is its meaning here.

Some think, as Chrysostom reports, that this official is the same as the centurion mentioned by Matthew (8:5). This is not so, for they differ in four ways. First, because the illness was not the same in each. The centurion was concerned with a paralytic, "My servant is lying paralyzed at home" (Mt 8:6); while this official's son is suffering from a fever, **yesterday at the seventh hour the fever left him**. Secondly, those who are sick are not the same. In the first case, it was a servant, "my servant"; but now we have a son, as it says, **whose son**. Thirdly, what is requested is different.

For when Christ wanted to go to the home of the centurion, the centurion discouraged him, and said: "Lord, I am not worthy to have you come under my roof; but only say the word and my servant will be healed" (Mt 8:8). But this official asked Christ to come to his house, **Lord, come down before my child dies.** Fourthly, the places are different. For the first healing took place at Capernaum, while this one is at Cana in Galilee. So this official is not the same as the centurion, but was from the household of Herod the Tetrarch, or some kind of a herald, or an official of the Emperor.

677   In its allegorical sense, this official is Abraham or one of the fathers of the Old Testament, in so far as he adheres by faith to the king, that is, to Christ, about which we read, "I was made king by him over Zion" (Ps 2:6). Abraham adhered to him, for as is said below (8:56): "Abraham, your father, rejoiced that he might see my day." The son of this official is the Jewish people: "We are the descendants of Abraham, and we have never been slaves to any one" (below 8:33). But they are sick from evil pleasures and incorrect doctrines. They are sick at Capernaum, i.e., in the abundance of goods which caused them to leave their God, according to, "The beloved grew fat and rebellious ... he deserted the God who made him, and left God his Savior" (Dt 32:15).

678   In the moral sense, in the kingdom of the soul, the king is reason itself: "The king, who sits on his throne of judgment" (Prv 20:8). But why is reason called the king? Because man's entire body is ruled by it: his affections are directed and informed by it, and the other powers of the soul follow it. But sometimes it is called an official [not the king], that is, when its knowledge is obscured, with the result that it follows inordinate passions and does not resist them: "They live with their foolish ideas, their understanding obscured by darkness" (Eph 4:17). Consequently, the son of this official, i.e., the affections, are sick, that is, they deviate from good and decline to what is evil. If reason were the king, that is, strong, its son would not be sick; but being only an official, its son is sick. This happens at Capernaum because a great many temporal goods are the cause of spiritual sickness: "This was the crime of your sister Sodom: richness, satiety in food, and idleness" (Ez 16:49).

679   Now we see the person making his request (v 47). First, we have the incentive for making his request. Secondly, the request itself. Thirdly, the need for the request.

680   The incentive for making the request was the arrival of Christ. So he says, **When he,** the official, **heard that Jesus had come to Galilee from Judea, he went to him.** For as long as the coming

of Christ was delayed, men's hope of being healed from their sins was that much fainter; but when it is reported that his coming is near, our hope of being healed rises, and then we go to him. For he came into this world to save sinners: "The Son of Man came to seek and to save what was lost" (Lk 19:22). Further, as Sirach says (18:23), we should prepare our soul by prayer, and we do this by going to God through our desires. And this is what the official did, as we read, **he went to him**. Amos (4:12) says, "Be prepared to meet your God, O Israel."

681 The request of the official was that Christ heal his son. So the Evangelist says that he **begged him to come down**, out of compassion: "O that you would rend the heavens, and come down" (Is 64:1), **and heal his son**. We, too, ought to ask to be healed from our sins: "Heal my soul, for I have sinned against you" (Ps 40:5). For no one of himself can return to the state of justice; rather, he has to be healed by God: "I cannot help myself" (Jb 6:13). The fathers of the Old Testament interceded for the people of Israel in the same way; for as we read of one: "He loves his brothers, because he prays much for the holy city and for the people of Israel, Jeremiah, the prophet of God" (2 Mc 15:14).

682 The need for this request was urgent, for the son **was at the point of death**. When a person is tempted, he is beginning to become sick; and as the temptation grows stronger and takes the upper hand, inclining him to consent, he is near death. But when he has consented, he is at the point of death and beginning to die. Finally, when he completes his sin, he dies; for as we read: "Sin, when it is completed, brings forth death" (Jas 1:15). The Psalm (33:22) says about this: "The death of sinners is the worst," because it begins here and continues into the future without end.

683 Now he deals with the request for Christ to heal the son of the official. First, our Lord's criticism is given. Secondly, the official's request. Thirdly, the granting of the request.

684 Our Lord criticizes him for his lack of faith, saying, **Unless you see signs and wonders, you do not believe**. This raises a question, for it does not seem right to say this to this official, for unless he had believed that Christ was the Savior, he would not have asked him to heal his son.

The answer to this is that this official did not yet believe perfectly; indeed, there were two defects in his faith. The first was that although he believed that Christ was a true man, he did not believe that he had divine power; otherwise he would have believed that Christ could heal one even while absent, since God is everywhere, as Jeremiah (23:24) says: "I fill heaven and earth." And so he would not have asked Christ to come down to his house, but simply give his command. The second defect in his faith, according to Chrysostom, was that he was not sure that Christ could heal his son: for had he been sure, he would not have waited for Christ to return to his homeland, but would have gone to Judea himself. But now, despairing of his son's health, and not wishing to overlook any possibility, he went to Christ like those parents who in their despair for the health of their children consult even unskilled doctors.

685   In the second place, it does not seem that he should have been criticized for looking for signs, for faith is proved by signs. The answer to this is that unbelievers are drawn to Christ in one way, and believers in another way. For unbelievers can not be drawn to Christ or convinced by the authority of Sacred Scripture, because they do not believe it; neither can they be drawn by natural reason, because faith is above reason. Consequently, they must be led by miracles: "Signs are given to unbelievers, not to believers" (1 Cor 14:22). Believers, on the other hand, should be led and directed to faith by the authority of Scripture, to which they are bound to assent. This is why the official is criticized: although he had been brought up among the Jews and instructed in the law, he wanted to believe through signs, and not by the authority of the Scripture. So the Lord reproaches him, saying, **Unless you see signs and wonders**, i.e., miracles, which sometimes are signs insofar as they bear witness to divine truth. Or **wonders** (*prodigia*), either because they indicate with utmost certitude, so that a prodigy is taken to be a "portent" or some "sure indication"; or because they portend something in the future, as if something were called a **wonder** as if showing at a great distance some future effect.

686   Now we see the official's persistence, for he does not give up after the Lord's criticism, but insists, saying. **Lord, come down before my child dies**: "We should pray always, and not lose heart" (Lk 18:1). This shows an improvement in his faith in one respect, that is, in that he calls him "Lord." But there is not a total improvement, for he still thought that Christ had to be physically present to heal his son; so he asked Christ to come.

687   His request is granted by the Lord, for persevering prayer is answered. Jesus said to him: **Go, your son lives**. Here we have first, the statement by Christ, who cured the boy, that the boy was cured. Secondly, we are told of the persons who witnessed the cure (v 51). Two things are mentioned concerning the first: the command of the

Lord and the obedience of the official (v 50b).

688 As to the first, the Lord does two things. First, he orders; secondly, he affirms. He orders the official to go: hence he says, **Go**, i.e., prepare to receive grace by a movement of your free will toward God: "Turn to me, and you will be saved" (Is 45:22); and by a movement of your free will against sin. For four things are required for the justification of an adult sinner: the infusion of grace, the remission of guilt, a movement of the free will toward God, which is faith, and a movement of the free will against sin, which is contrition.

Then the Lord says that his son is healed, which was the request of the official: **Your son lives**.

689 One may ask why Christ refused to go down to the home of this official as asked, while he promised to go see the servant of the centurion. There are two reasons for this. One, according to Gregory, is to blunt our pride; the pride of us who offer our services to great men, but refuse to help the insignificant: since the Lord of all offered to go to the servant of the centurion, but refused to go to the son of an official: "Be well-disposed to the poor" (Sir 4:7). The other reason, as Chrysostom says, was that the centurion was already confirmed in the faith of Christ, and believed that he could heal even while not present; and so our Lord promised to go to show approval of his faith and devotion. But this official was still imperfect, and did not yet clearly know that Christ could heal even while absent. And so our Lord does not go, in order that he may realize his imperfection.

690 The obedience of this official is pointed out in two ways. First, because he believed what Christ said; so he says, **The man took Jesus at his word**, that is, **Your son lives**. Secondly, because he did obey the order of Christ; so he says, he **started for home**, progressing in faith, although not yet fully or soundly, as Origen says. This signifies that we must be justified by faith: "Justified by faith, let us have peace with God, through our Lord Jesus Christ" (Rom 5:1). We also must go and start out by making progress: because he who stands still runs the risk of being unable to preserve the life of grace. For, along the road to God, if we do not go forward we fall back.

691 Next we see the servants bringing news of the healing. First, the news of the healing is given. Secondly, there is an inquiry about the time of the healing (v 52).

692 He says, **While he was on his way down**, from Cana of Galilee to his own home, **his servants ran up to meet him** – which shows that this official was wealthy and had many servants – **with**

word that his son was going to live: and they did this because they thought that Christ was coming, and his presence was no longer necessary as the boy was already cured.

693 In the mystical sense, the servants of the official, i.e., of reason, are a man's works, because man is master of his own acts and of the affections of his sense powers, for they obey the command and direction of reason. Now these servants announce that the son of the official, that is, of reason, lives, when a man's good works shine out, and his lower powers obey reason, according to: "A man's dress, and laughter, and his walk, show what he is" (Sir 19:27).

694 Because this official did not yet believe either fully or soundly, he still wanted to know whether his son had been cured by chance or by the command of Christ. Accordingly, he asks about the time of the cure. **He asked them,** the servants, **at what time his boy got better.** And he found that his son was cured at exactly the same hour that our Lord said, **Go, your son lives.** And no wonder, because Christ is the Word, through whom heaven and earth were made: "He spoke and they were made; he commanded and they were created" (Ps 148:5).

695 **And they,** his servants, **told him that yesterday at the seventh hour the fever left him.** In the mystical sense, the seventh hour, when the boy is cured of his fever, signifies the seven gifts of the Holy Spirit, through whom sins are forgiven, according to: "Receive the Holy Spirit; whose sins you forgive, are forgiven" (below 20:22), and through whom spiritual life is produced in the soul: "It is the Spirit that gives life" (below 6:64). Again, the seventh hour signifies the appropriate time for rest, for the Lord rested from all his work on the seventh day. This indicates that the spiritual life of man consists in spiritual rest or quiet, according to: "If you remain at rest, you will be saved" (Is 30:15). But of the evil we read: "The heart of the wicked is like the raging sea, which cannot rest" (Is 57:20).

696 Next, we are given the effect of this miracle (v 53). First, its fruit is mentioned. Secondly, this miracle is linked with another one (v 54).

697 He says, **The father then realized,** by comparing the hour mentioned by the servants with the hour of Christ's affirmation, **that it was at that very hour when Jesus told him, Your son lives.** Because of this he was converted to Christ, realizing that it was by his power that the miracle was accomplished. **He and his whole household became believers,** that is, his servants and his aides, because the attitude of servants depends on the condition, whether good or wicked, of their masters: "As the judge of the people is himself, so also are his ministers" (Sir 10:2); and in Genesis (18:19) we read: "I know that he will direct his sons."

This also shows that the faith of the official was constantly growing: for at the beginning, when he pleaded for his sick son, it was weak; then it began to grow more firm, when he called Jesus "Lord", then when he believed what the Lord said and started for home, it was more perfect, but not completely so, because he still doubted. But here, clearly realizing God's power in Christ, his faith is made perfect, for as Proverbs (4:18) says: "The way of the just goes forward like a shining light, increasing to the full light of day."

698 Finally, this miracle is linked with the previous one, **This was the second sign Jesus had performed on returning from Judea to Galilee**. We can understand this in two ways. In one way, that our Lord performed two miracles during this one trip from Judea to Galilee; but the first of these was not recorded, only the second. In the other way, we could say that Jesus worked two signs in Galilee at different times: the one of the wine, and this second one about the son of this official after he returned again to Galilee from Judea.

We also see from this that the Galileans were worse than the Samaritans. For the Samaritans expected no sign from the Lord, and many believed in his word alone; but as a result of this miracle, only this official and his whole household believed: for the Jews were converted to the faith little by little on account of their hardness, according to: "I have become as one who harvests in the summer time, like a gleaner at the vintage: not one cluster to eat, not one of the early figs I desire" (Mi 7:1).

5

LECTURE 1

1 After this there was a Jewish festival, and Jesus went up to Jerusalem. 2 Now at Jerusalem there is a Sheep Pool, called in Hebrew Bethsaida, having five porticoes. 3 In these porticoes lay a great number of people: feeble, blind, lame and withered, waiting for the movement of the water. 4 From time to time an angel of the Lord used to come down into the pool and the water was stirred up, and the first one into the pool after it was stirred was healed of whatever ailment he had. 5 There was one man lying there who had been sick for thirty-eight years with his infirmity. 6 Jesus, seeing him lying there and knowing that he had been sick a long time, said to him, "Do you wish to be healed?" 7 The sick man said, "Sir, I have no one to plunge me into the pool once the water is stirred up. By the time I get there, someone else has gone in before me." 8 Jesus said to him, "Stand up, pick up your mat and walk!" 9a The man was immediately cured; he picked up his mat, and walked.

699 Above, our Lord dealt with spiritual rebirth; here he deals with the benefits God gives to those who are spiritually reborn. Now we see that parents give three things to those who are physically born from them: life, nourishment, and instruction or discipline. And those who are spiritually reborn receive these three from Christ: spiritual life, spiritual nourishment, and spiritual teaching. And so these three things are considered here: first, the giving of spiritual life; secondly, the giving of spiritual food (c 6); and thirdly, spiritual teaching (c 7).

About the first he does three things. First, he sets forth a visible sign in which he shows Christ's power to produce and to restore life. This is the usual practice in this Gospel: to always join to the teaching of Christ some appropriate visible action, so that what is invisible can be made known through the visible. Secondly, the occasion for this teaching is given (v 9b). Thirdly, the teaching itself is given (v 19). As to the first he does three things. First, the place of the miracle is given. Secondly, the illness involved. Thirdly, the restoration of the sick person to health (v 8).

700 The place of this miracle is described in two ways: in general and in particular. The general place is Jerusalem; so he says, **After this**, i.e., after the miracle performed in Galilee, **there was a Jewish festival**, that is Pentecost, according to Chrysostom. For above, when Christ went to Jerusalem, it was the Passover that was mentioned; and now, on the following festival of Pentecost,

Jesus went up to Jerusalem again. For as we read in Exodus (23:17), the Lord commanded that all Jewish males be presented in the temple three times a year: on the festival days of the Passover, Pentecost, and the Dedication.

There were two reasons why our Lord went up to Jerusalem for these festivals. First, so that he would not seem to oppose the law, for he said himself: "I have not come to destroy the law, but to complete it" (Mt 5:17); and in order to draw the many people gathered there on the feast days to God by his signs and teaching: "I will praise him in the midst of the people" (Ps 108:30); and again, "I have declared your justice in the great assembly" (Ps 39:10). So Christ himself says, as we read below (18:20): "I have spoken openly to the world."

701 The specific place of the miracle was the pool called the Sheep Pool; so he says, **Now at Jerusalem there is a Sheep Pool**. This is described here in four ways: by its name, its structure, from its occupants, and from its power.

702 First, it is described from its name when he says, **there is a Sheep Pool** (*probatica piscina*), for *probaton* is Greek for "sheep." It was called the Sheep Pool for it was there that the priests washed the sacrificial animals; especially the sheep, who were used more than the other animals. And so in Hebrew it was called **Bethsaida**, that is, the "house of sheep." This pool was located near the temple, and formed from collected rain water.

703 In its mystical sense, this pool, according to Chrysostom, has prefigured Baptism. For the Lord, wishing to prefigure the grace of baptsim in different ways, first of all chose water: for this washes the body from the uncleanness which came from contact with what was legally unclean (Nm 19). Secondly, he gave this pool a power that expresses even more vividly than water the power of Baptism: for it not only cleansed the body from its uncleanness, but also healed it from its illness; for symbols are more expressive, the closer they approach the reality. Thus it signified the power of Baptism: for as this water when applied to the body had the power (not by its own nature, but from an angel) to heal its illness, so the water of Baptism has the power to heal and cleanse the soul from sins: "He loved us, and washed us from our sins" (Rv 1:5). This is the reason why the passion of Christ, prefigured by the sacrifices of the Old Law, is represented in Baptism: "All of us who have been baptized into Christ Jesus, have been baptized into his death" (Rom 6:3).

According to Augustine, the water in this pool signified the condition of the Jewish people, according to: "The waters are the peoples" (Rv 17:15). The Gentiles were not confined within the limits of the divine law, but each of them lived according to the vanity of his heart (Eph 4:17). But the Jews were confined under the worship of the one God: "We were kept under the law, confined, until the faith was revealed" (Gal 3:23). So this water, confined to the pool, signified the Jewish people. And it was called the Sheep Pool, for the Jews were the special sheep of God: "We are his people, his sheep" (Ps 94:7).

704 The pool is described in its structure as **having five porticoes**, i.e., round about, so that a number of the priests could stand and wash the animals without inconvenience. In the mystical sense these five porticoes, according to Chrysostom, signify the five wounds in the body of Christ; about which we read: "Put your hand into my side, and do not be unbelieving, but believe" (below 20:27). But according to Augustine, these five porticoes signify the five books of Moses.

705 The pool is also described from its occupants, for **in these porticoes lay a great number of people: feeble, blind, lame and withered.** The literal explanation of this is that since all the afflicted persons gathered because of the curative power of the water, which did not always cure nor cure many at the same time, it was inevitable that there be many hanging around waiting to be cured. The mystical meaning of this, for Augustine, was that the law was incapable of healing sins: "It is impossible that sins be taken away by the blood of bulls and goats" (Heb 10:4). The law merely shed light on them, for "The knowledge of sin comes from the law" (Rom 3:20).

706 And so, subject to various illnesses, these people lay there, unable to be cured. They are described in four ways. First, by their posture: for there they **lay**, i.e., clinging to earthly things by their sins; for one who is lying down is in direct contact with the earth: "He had compassion on them, for they were suffering, and lying like sheep without a shepherd" (Mt 9:36). But the just do not lie down, but stand upright, toward the things of heaven: "They," i.e., sinners, "are bound, and have fallen down; but we," the just, "have stood and are erect" (Ps 19:9).

Secondly, they are described as to their number, for there was **a great number** of them: "The evil are hard to correct, and the number of fools is infinite" (Ecc 1:15); and in Matthew (7:13): "The road that leads to destruction is wide, and many go this way."

Thirdly, these sick people are described as to their condition. And he mentions four things which a person brings on himself through sin. First, a person who is ruled by sinful passions is made listless or feeble; and so he says, **feeble.** So it is that Cicero calls certain passions of the soul, such as anger and concupiscence and the like, illnesses of the soul. And the Psalm says: "Have mercy on me, O Lord, for I am week" (Ps 6:3).

Secondly, due to the rule and victory of a man's passions, his reason is blinded by consent; and he says as to this, **blind**, that is, through sins. According to Wisdom (2:21): "Their own evil blinded them"; and in the Psalm (57:9): "Fire," that is the fire of anger and concupiscence, "fell on them, and they did not see the sun."

Thirdly, a person who is feeble and blind is inconstant in his works and is, in a way, lame. So we read in Proverbs (11:18): "The work of the wicked is unsteady." With respect to this the Evangelist says, **lame**. "How long will you be lame?" (1 Kgs 18:21).

Fourthly, a man who is thus feeble, blind in understanding, and lame in his exterior actions, becomes dry in his affections, in the sense that all the fatness of devotion withers within him. This devotion is sought in the Psalm (62:6): "May my soul be filled with fat and marrow." With respect to this the Evangelist says, **withered**. "My strength is dried up like baked clay" (Ps 21:16).

But there are some so afflicted by the lassitude of sin, who do not wait for the motion of the water, wallowing in their sins, according to Wisdom (14:22): "They live in a great strife of ignorance, and they call so many and great evils peace." We read of such people: "They are glad when they do evil, and rejoice in the worst of things" (Prv 2:14). The reason for this is that they do not hate their sins: they do not sin from ignorance or weakness, but from malice. But others, who do not sin from malice, do not wallow in their sins, but wait by desire for the motion of the water. So he says, **waiting**. "Every day of my service I wait for my relief to come" (Jb 14:14). This is the way those in the Old Testament waited for Christ: "I will wait for your salvation, O Lord" (Gn 49:18).

707 Finally, the power of the pool is described, for it healed all physical illnesses in virtue of an angel who came to it; so he says, **From time to time an angel of the Lord used to come down into the pool**. In certain ways, the power of this pool is like that of Baptism. It is like it, first, in the fact that its power was unperceived: for the power of the water in this pool did not come from its very nature, otherwise it would have healed at all times; its power was unseen, being from an angel. So he says, **From time to time an angel of the Lord used to come down into the pool**. The water of Baptism is like this in that precisely as water it does not have the power to cleanse souls, but this comes from the unseen power of the Holy Spirit, according to: "Unless one is born again of water and the Holy Spirit, he cannot enter the kingdom of God" (above 3:5). It is like

it, in a second way, in its effect: for as the water of Baptism heals, so also the water of that pool healed. So he says, **the first one into the pool was healed**. Further, God gave to that water the power to heal so that men by washing might learn through their bodily health to seek their spiritual health.

Yet the water of this pool differs from the water of Baptism in three ways. First, in the source of its power: for the water in the pool produced health because of an angel, but the water of Baptism produces its effect by the uncreated power not only of the Holy Spirit, but of the entire Trinity. Thus the entire Trinity was present at the baptism of Christ: the Father in the voice, the Son in person, and the Holy Spirit in the form of a dove. This is why we invoke the Trinity in our baptism.

Secondly, this water differs in its power: for the water in the pool did not have a continuous power to cure, but only **from time to time**; while the water of Baptism has a permanent power to cleanse, according to: "On that day a fountain will be open to the house of David, and to the inhabitants of Jerusalem, to cleanse the sinner and the unclean" (Zec 13:1).

Thirdly, this water differs as regards the number of people healed: for only one person was cured when the water of this pool was moved; but all are healed when the water of Baptism is moved. And no wonder: for the power of the water in the pool, since it is created, is finite and has a finite effect; but in the water of Baptism there is an infinite power capable of cleansing an infinite number of souls, if there were such: "I will pour clean water upon you, and you will be cleansed from all your uncleanness" (Ez 36:25).

708   According to Augustine, however, the angel signifies Christ, according to this reading of Isaiah (9:6): "He will be called the angel of the great counsel." Just as the angel descended at certain times into the pool, so Christ descended into the world at a time fixed by the Father: "The time is near" (Is 14:1); "When the fulness of time had come God sent his Son, made from a woman, made under the law" (Gal 4:4). Again, just as the angel was not seen except by the motion of the water, so Christ was not known as to his divinity, for "If they had known, they would never have crucified the Lord of glory" (1 Cor 2:8). For as Isaiah (45:15) says: "Truly, you are a hidden God." And so the motion of the water was seen, but not the one who set it in motion, because, seeing the weakness of Christ, the people did not know of his divinity. And just as the one who went into the pool was healed, so a person who humbly believes in God is healed by his passion: "Justified by faith, through the redemption which is in Christ, whom God put forward as an expiation" (Rom 3:24). Only one was healed, because no one can

be healed except in the oneness or unity of the Church: "One Lord, one faith, one baptism" (Eph 4:5). Therefore, woe to those who hate unity, and divide men into sects.

709   Then (v 5), the Evangelist mentions the disability of a man who lay by the pool. First, we are told how long he was disabled; and secondly, why it was so long (v 7).

710   He was disabled for a long time, for **There was one man lying there who had been sick for thirty-eight years with his infirmity**. This episode is very aptly mentioned: the man who could not be cured by the pool was to be cured by Christ, because those whom the law could not heal, Christ heals perfectly, according to: "God did what the law, weakened by the flesh, could not do: by sending his own Son in the likeness of sinful flesh, and as a sin-offering, he condemned sin in his flesh" (Rom 8:3); and in Sirach (36:6): "Perform new signs and wonders."

711   The number thirty-eight is well-suited to his infirmity, for we see it associated with sickness rather than with health. For, as Augustine says, the number forty signifies the perfection of justice, which consists in observing the law. But the law was given in ten precepts, and was to be preached to the four corners of the world, or be completed by the four Gospels, according to: "The end of the law is Christ" (Rom 10:4). So since ten times four is forty, this appropriately signifies perfect justice. Now if two is subtracted from forty, we get thirty-eight. This two is the two precepts of charity, which effects perfect justice. And so this man was sick because he had forty minus two, that is, his justice was imperfect, for "On these two commandments all the law and the prophets depend" (Mt 22:40).

712   Now the reason for the length of the man's illness is considered. First, we have the Lord's query; secondly, the sick man's answer (v 7).

713   John says, **Jesus, seeing him**, the man, **lying there**. Jesus saw him not only with his physical eyes, but also with the eyes of his mercy; this is the way David begged to be seen, saying: "Look at me, O Lord, and have mercy on me" (Ps 85:16). And Jesus **knowing that he had been sick a long time** — which was repugnant to the heart of Christ as well as to the sick man himself: "A long illness is a burden to the physician" (Sir 10:11) — said to him, **Do you wish to be healed?** He did not say this because he did not know the answer, for it was quite evident that the man wanted to be healed; he said it to arouse the sick man's desire, and to show his patience in waiting so many years to be cured of his sickness, and in not giving up. We see from this that he was all the worthier to be cured: "Act

bravely, and let your heart be strengthened, all you who hope in the Lord" (Ps 30:25). Jesus incites the man's desires because we keep more securely what we perceive with desire and more easily acquire. "Knock," by your desire, "and it will be opened to you," as we read in Matthew (7:7).

Note that in other situations the Lord requires faith: "Do you believe that I can do this for you" (Mt 9:28); but here he does not make any such demand. The reason is that the others had heard of the miracles of Jesus, of which this man knew nothing. And so Jesus does not ask faith from him until after the miracle has been performed.

714 Then (v 7), the answer of the sick man is given. Two reasons are given for the length of his illness: his poverty and his weakness. As he was poor, he could not afford a man to plunge him into the pool; so he says, **Sir, I have no one to plunge me into the pool.** Perhaps he thought, as Chrysostom says, that Christ might even help to put him into the water. Someone else always reached the pool before him because he was weak and not able to move fast; so he says, **By the time I get there, someone else has gone in before me.** He could say with Job: "I cannot help myself" (Jb 6:13). This signifies that no mere man could save the human race, for all had sinned and needed the grace of God. Mankind had to wait for the coming of Christ, God and man, by whom it would be healed.

715 Now we see the man restored to health, i.e., the working of the miracle. First, the Lord's command is given; secondly, the man's obedience (v 9).

716 The Lord commanded both the nature of the man and his will, for both are under the Lord's power. He commanded his nature when he said, **Stand up.** This command was not directed to the man's will, for this was not within the power of his will. But it was within the power of his nature, to which the Lord gave the power to stand by his command. He gave two commands to the man's will: **pick up your mat and walk!** The literal meaning for this is that these two things were commanded in order to show that the man had been restored to perfect health. For in all his miracles the Lord produced a perfect work, according to what was best in the nature of each case: "The works of God are perfect" (Dt 32:4). Now this man was lacking two things: first, his own energy, since he could not stand up by himself, thus our Lord found him lying by the pool. Secondly, he lacked the help of others; so he said, **I have no one.** So our Lord, in order that this man might recognize his perfect health, ordered him who could not help himself to pick up his mat, and him who could not walk to walk.

717   These are the three things which the Lord commands in the justification of a sinner. First, he should **stand up**, by leaving his sinful ways: "Rise up, you who sleep, and arise from the dead" (Eph 5:14). Secondly, he is commanded to **pick up your mat**, by making satisfaction for the sins he has committed. For the mat on which a man rests signifies his sins. And so a man takes up his mat when he begins to do the penance given to him for his sins. "I will bear the anger of God, because I have sinned against him" (Mi 7:9). Thirdly, he is commanded to **walk**, by advancing in what is good, according to: "They will go from strength to strength" (Ps 83:8).

718   According to Augustine, this sick man was lacking two things: the two precepts of charity. And so our Lord gives two commands to his will, which is perfected by charity: to take up his mat, and to walk. The first concerns the love of neighbor, which is first in the order of doing; the second concerns the love of God, which is first in the order of precept. Christ says, with respect to the first, **pick up you mat**. As if to say: When you are weak, your neighbor bears with you and, like a mat, patiently supports you: "We who are stronger ought to bear with the infirmities of the weak, and not seek to please ourselves" (Rom 15:1). Thus, after you have been cured, **pick up your mat**, i.e., bear and support your neighbor, who carried you when you were weak: "Carry each other's burdens" (Gal 6:2). About the second he says, **walk**, by drawing near God; so we read: "They will go from strength to strength" (Ps 83:8); "Walk while you have the light" (below 12:35).

719   Next we see the man's obedience. First, the obedience of his nature, because, **The man was immediately cured**. And no wonder, because Christ is the Word through whom heaven and earth were made: "He commanded and they were created" (Ps 148:5); "By the Word of the Lord the heavens were made" (Ps 32:6). Secondly, we see the obedience of the man's will: first, because **he picked up his mat**, and secondly, because he **walked**. "We will do everything that the Lord commands, and obey him" (Ex 24:7).

LECTURE 2

9b That day, however, was a Sabbath. 10 Therefore the Jews told the man who had been cured, "It is the Sabbath; it is not permitted for you to carry your mat." 11 He replied to them, "He who cured me said to me: 'Pick up your mat and walk.' " 12 They then asked him, "Who is this man who told you to pick up your mat and walk?" 13 But he who was cured had no idea who it was, for Jesus had slipped away from the crowd that had gathered in that place. 14 Later, Jesus found the man in the temple and said to him, "Remember, you have been made well; now do not sin again lest something worse happen to you." 15 The man went off and related to the Jews that it was Jesus who had cured him. 16 For reasons like this the Jews began to persecute Jesus, because he performed such works on the Sabbath. 17 But Jesus had a reply for them: "My Father works even until now, and so do I." 18 Consequently, the Jews tried all the harder to kill him, because he not only broke the Sabbath rest, but even called God his own Father, making himself equal to God.

720 Having seen a visible miracle which shows the power of Christ to restore spiritual life, we now see an opportunity given to him to teach. This opportunity was the persecution launched against him by the Jews. These Jews, who were envious of Christ, persecuted him for two reasons: first, the above act of his mercy; secondly, his teaching of the truth (v 17). As to the first, the Evangelist does three things. First, he gives the occasion for their persecution. Secondly, the false accusation against the man who was just cured (v 10). And thirdly, their attempt to belittle Christ (v 12).

721 Their opportunity to persecute Christ was the fact that he cured the man on the Sabbath; accordingly, the Evangelist says, **That day, however, was a Sabbath**, when Christ performed the miracle of commanding the man to pick up his mat.

Three reasons are given why our Lord began to work on the Sabbath. The first is given by Ambrose, in his commentary, *On Luke*. He says that Christ came to renovate the work of creation, that is, man, who had become deformed. And so he should have begun where the Creator had left off the work of creation, that is, on a Sabbath, as mentioned in Genesis (c 1). Thus Christ began to work on the Sabbath to show that he was the renovator of the whole creature.

Another reason was that the Sabbath day was celebrated by the Jews in memory of the first creation. But Christ came to make, in a way, a new creature, according to Galatians (6:15): "In Christ Jesus, neither circumcision nor the lack of circumcision is a benefit; what counts is a new creation," i.e., through grace, which comes through the Holy Spirit: ""You will send forth your Spirit, and they will be created; and you will renew the face of the earth" (Ps 103:30). And so Christ worked on the Sabbath to show that a new creation, a re-creation, was taking place through him: "that we might be the first-fruits of his creatures" (Jas 1:18).

The third reason was to show that he was about to do what the law could not do: "God did what the law, weakened by the flesh, could not do: by sending his own Son in the likeness of sinful flesh, he condemned sin in his flesh, in order that the requirements of the law might be accomplished in us" (Rom 8:3).

The Jews, however, did not do any work on the Sabbath, as a symbol that there were certain things pertaining to the Sabbath which were to be accomplished, but which the law could not do. This is clear in the four things which God ordained for the Sabbath: for he sanctified the Sabbath day, blessed it, completed his work on it, and then rested. These things the law was not able to do. It could not sanctify; so we read: "Save me, O Lord, for there are no holy people left" (Ps 11:1). Nor could it bless; rather, "Those who rely on the works of the law are under a curse" (Gal 3:10). Neither could it complete and perfect, because "the law brought nothing to perfection" (Heb 7:19). Nor could it bring perfect rest: "If Joshua had given them rest, God would not be speaking after of another day" (Heb 4:8).

These things, which the law could not do, Christ did. For he sanctified the people by his passion: "Jesus, in order to sanctify the people with his own blood, suffered outside the gate" (Heb 13:12). He blessed them by an inpouring of grace: "Blessed be God, the Father of our Lord Jesus Christ, who has blessed us with every spiritual blessing of heaven, in Christ" (Eph 1:3). He brought the people to perfection by instructing them in the ways of perfect justice: "Be perfect, as your heavenly Father is perfect" (Mt 5:48). He also led them to true rest: "We who have believed will find rest," as is said in Hebrews (4:3). Therefore, it is proper for him to work on the Sabbath, who is able to make perfect those things that pertain to the Sabbath, from which an impotent law rested.

722 Then (v 10), the Evangelist gives the accusation brought against the man who was healed. First, we have the accusation; and secondly, the explanation given by the man who was healed (v 11).

723 The man was accused for carrying his mat on the Sabbath, and not for being healed; so they say: **It is the Sabbath; it is not permitted for you to carry your mat**. There are several reasons for this. One is that the Jews, although frequently charging Christ with healing on the Sabbath, had been embarrassed by him on the ground that they themselves used to pull their cattle from ditches on the Sabbath in order to save them. For this reason the Jews did not mention his healing, as it was useful and necessary; but they charge him with carrying his mat, which did not seem to be necessary. As if to say: Although your cure need not have been post-

poned, there was no need for you to carry your mat, or for the order to carry it. Another reason was that the Lord had shown, contrary to their opinion, that it was lawful to do good on the Sabbath. And so, because being healed is not the same as doing good, but being done a good, they attack the one healed rather than the one healing. The third reason was that the Jews thought that they were forbidden by the law to do any work on the Sabbath; and it was the carrying of burdens that was especially forbidden on the Sabbath: "Do not carry a burden on the Sabbath" (Jer 17:21). Accordingly, they made a special point of being against the carrying of anything on the Sabbath, as being opposed to the teaching of the prophet. But this command of the prophet was mystical: for when he forbade them to carry burdens, he wanted to encourage them to rest from the burdens of their sins on the Sabbath. Of these sins it is said: "My iniquities are a heavy burden and have weighed me down" (Ps 37:5). Therefore, since the time had come to explain the meaning of obscure symbols, Christ commanded him to take up his mat, i.e, to help his neighbors in their weaknesses: "Bear one another's burdens, and so you will fulfil the law of Christ" (Gal 6:2).

724 Then (v 11), we see the man who was healed defending himself. His defense is wisely taken: for a doctrine is never so well proved to be divinely inspired as by miracles which can be accomplished only by divine power: "Going out, they preached everywhere, and the Lord worked with them and confirmed the word by the signs that followed" (Mk 16:20). Thus he argued with those who were defaming the one who healed him, saying: **He who cured me said to me.** As if to say: You say that I am forbidden to carry a burden on the Sabbath, and this on divine authority; but I was commanded by the same authority to pick up my mat. For, **he who cured me**, and by restoring my health showed that he had divine power, said to me, **Pick up your mat and walk.** Therefore, I was duty bound to obey the commands of one who has such power and who had done me such a favor. "I will never forget your precepts because you have brought me to life by them" (Ps 118:93).

725 Then, since they could not very well charge the man who was cured, they try to belittle Christ's cure, for this man defended himself through Christ. But since he did not indicate precisely who he was, they maliciously ask him who it was. With respect to this, first, the search for Christ is set down. Secondly, his discovery. And thirdly, his persecution (v 16).

726 Three things are mentioned about the first: the Jews' interrogation; the ignorance of the man who was cured; and the cause of that ignorance.

As to the first, we read: **They then asked him**, not with the good intention of making progress, but for the evil purpose of persecuting and destroying Christ: "You will seek me, and you will die in your sin" (below 8:21). Their very words show their malice: for while our Lord had commanded the man who was sick to become healed and to pick up his mat, they ignored the first, which is an undeniable sign of divine power, and harped on the second, which seemed to be against the law, saying, **Who is this man who told you to pick up you mat and walk?** "He lies in wait, and turns good into evil, and he will put blame," i.e., attempt to put blame, "on the elect" (Sir 11:33).

727   As to the second, the Evangelist says, **But he who was cured had no idea who it was**. This cured man signifies those who believe and have been healed by the grace of Christ: "You are saved by grace" (Eph 2:8). Indeed, they do not know who Christ is, but they know only his effects: "While we are in the body, we are absent from the Lord: for we walk by faith, and not by sight" (2 Cor 5:6). We will know who Christ is when "we shall see him as he is," as said in 1 John (3:2).

728   Next, the Evangelist gives the reason for the man's ignorance, saying, **for Jesus had slipped away from the crowd that had gathered in that place**. There are both literal and mystical reasons why Christ left. Of the two literal reasons, the first is to give us the example of concealing our good deeds and of not using them to seek the applause of men: "Take care not to perform your good actions in the sight of men, in order to be seen by them" (Mt 6:1). The second literal reason is to show us that, in all our actions, we should leave and avoid those who are envious, so as not to feed and increase their envy: "Do not be provoked by one who speaks evil of you, so he will not trap you by your own words" (Sir 8:14).

There are also two mystical reasons why Christ slipped away. First, it teaches us that Christ is not easy to find in the midst of men, or in the whirlwind of temporal cares; rather, he is found in spiritual seclusion: "I will lead her into the wilderness, and there I will speak to her heart" (Hos 2:14); and in Ecclesiastes (9.17): "The words of the wise are heard in silence." Secondly, this suggests to us that Christ was to leave the Jews for the Gentiles: "He hid his face for a while from the house of Jacob" (Is 8:17), i.e., he withdrew the knowledge of his truth from the Jewish people.

729   Then (v 14), the Evangelist tells us how Jesus was found. First, he says that he was found. Secondly, that after having been found, he taught. Thirdly, that after having taught, his identity was reported to the Jews.

730 The Evangelist tells us both where and the way in which Christ was found. The way in which he was found was remarkable, for Christ is not found unless he first finds; hence he says, **Later, after the above events, Jesus found the man.** For we cannot find Jesus by our own power unless Christ first presents himself to us; so we read: "Seek your servant" (Ps 118:176); and, "She [wisdom] goes to meet those who desire her" (Wis 6:14).

The place Christ was found was holy, **in the temple,** according to: "The Lord is in his holy temple" (Ps 10:5). For his mother had also found him in the temple (Lk 2:46); and he was there for he had to be concerned with his Father's affairs. We see from this that this man was not cured in vain, but having been converted to a religious way of life, he visited the temple and found Christ: because if we desire to come to a knowledge of the Creator, we must run from the tumult of sinful affections, leave the company of evil men, and flee to the temple of our heart, where God condescends to visit and live.

731 After Christ was found, he began to teach (v 14). First, Christ reminded the man of the gift he was given. Secondly, he offered him sound advice. And thirdly, he pointed out an imminent danger.

732 The gift was remarkable, for it was a sudden restoration to health; so he says, **Remember, you have been made well.** Therefore, you should always keep this in mind, according to: "I will remember the tender mercies of the Lord" (Is 63:7).

733 His advice, too, was useful, that is, **do not sin again.** "My son, you have sinned. Do not sin again" (Sir 21:1).

Why did our Lord mention sin to this paralytic and to certain others that he cured, and not to the rest? He did this to show that illness comes to certain people as a result of their previous sins, according to: "For this reason many of you are weak and sick, and many have died" (1 Cor 11:30). In this way he even showed himself to be God, pointing out sins and the hidden secrets of the heart: "Hell and destruction are open to the Lord; how much more the hearts of the children of men" (Prv 15:11). And so Christ mentioned sin only to some he cured and not to all, for not all infirmities are due to previous sins: some come from one's natural disposition, and some are permitted as a trial, as with Job. Or, Christ might have brought up sin to some because they were better prepared for his correction: "Do not rebuke one who mocks, lest he hate you; rebuke a wise man, and he will love you" (Prv 9:8). Or, we could say, in telling some not to sin, he intended his words for all the others.

734 The imminent danger was great; so he says, **lest something worse happen to you.** This can be understood in two ways, according

to the two events that preceded. For this man was first punished with a troublesome infirmity, and then received a marvelous favor. Accordingly, Christ's statement can refer to each. To the first, for when anyone is punished for his sin, and the punishment does not check him from sinning, it is just for him to be punished more severely. So Christ says, **do not sin again**, because if you do sin, something worse will happen to you: "I have struck your children in vain" (Jer 2:30). It can refer to the second, for one who falls into sin after receiving favors deserves a more severe punishment because of his ingratitude, as we see in 2 Peter (2:20): "It would be better for them not to know the way of truth, than to turn back after knowing it." Also, because after a man has once returned to sin, he sins more easily, according to Matthew (12:45): "The last state of that man becomes worse than the first"; and in Jeremiah (2:20): "You broke your yoke a long time ago, and snapped off your chains, and said: ' I will not serve.' "

735 Then when he says, **The man went off and related to the Jews**, we see Jesus identified. Some think, as Chrysostom reports, that this man identified Jesus out of malice. But this does not seem probable: that he would be so ungrateful after receiving such a favor. He **related to the Jews that it was Jesus who had cured him**, in order to make it clear that Christ had the power to heal: "Come ... and I will tell you what great things the Lord has done for me," as we read in the Psalm (65:16). This is obvious, for they had asked him who commanded him to pick up his mat, but he told them that **it was Jesus who had cured him**.

736 Next (v 16), we have the persecution of Christ, begun because he performed a work of mercy on the Sabbath. Thus the Evangelist says, **For reasons like this the Jews began to persecute Jesus, because he performed such works on the Sabbath**. "Princes have persecuted me without cause" (Ps 118:161).

737 Then (v 17), the second reason for his persecution is given: what he taught. First, we are given the truth he taught; and secondly, the perversity of his persecutors (v 18).

738 Our Lord taught the truth while justifying his breaking of the Sabbath. Here we should note that our Lord justified both himself and his disciples from breaking the Sabbath. He justified his disciples, since they were men, by comparing them to other men: as the priests who, although they worked in the temple on the Sabbath, did not break the Sabbath; and to David, who, while Ahimelech was priest, took the consecrated bread from the temple on the Sabbath when he was running from Saul (1 Sm 21:1).

Our Lord, who was both God and man, sometimes justified himself in breaking the Sabbath by comparing himself to men, as in Luke (14:5): "Which of you, if his donkey or ox falls into a pit, will not take him out on the Sabbath?" And sometimes he justified himself by comparing himself to God: particularly on this occasion, when he said: **My Father works even until now, and so do I.** As if to say: Do not think that my Father rested on the Sabbath in such a way that from that time he does not work; rather, just as he is working even now without laboring, so I also am working.

By saying this, Christ eliminated the misunderstanding of the Jews: for in their desire to imitate God, they did not do any work on the Sabbath, as if God entirely ceased from work on that day. In fact, although God rested on the Sabbath from producing new creatures, he is working always and continuously even till now, conserving creatures in existence. Hence it is significant that Moses used the word "rest," after recounting the works of God from which he rested: for this signifies, in its hidden meaning, the spiritual rest which God, by the example of his own rest, promised to the faithful, after they have done their own good works. So we may say that this command was a foreshadowing of something that lay in the future.

739 He expressly says, **works even until now**, and not "has worked," to indicate that God's work is continuous. For they might have thought that God is the cause of the world as a craftsman is the cause of a house, i.e., the craftsman is responsible only for the making or coming into existence of the house: in other words, just as the house continues in existence even when the craftsman has ceased working, so the world would exist if God's influence ceased. But according to Augustine, God is the cause of all creatures in such a way as to be the cause of their existing: for it his power were to cease even for a moment, all things in nature would at once cease to be, just as we may say that the air is illuminated only as long as the light of the sun remains in it. The reason for this is that things which depend on a cause only for their coming into existence, are able to exist when that cause ceases; but things that depend on a cause not only for their coming into existence but also to exist, need that cause for their continuous conservation in existence.

740 Further, in saying that **My Father works even until now**, he rejects the opinion of those who say that God creates through the instrumentality of secondary causes. This opinion conflicts with Isaiah (26:12): "O Lord, you have accomplished all our works for us." Therefore, just as **my Father**, who in the beginning created nature, **works even until now**, by preserving and conserving his creation by the same activity, **so do I** work, because I am the Word of the Father, through whom he accomplishes all things: "God said:

'Let there be light' " (Gn 1:3). Thus, just as he accomplished the first production of things through the Word, so also their conservation. Consequently, if he **works even until now, so do I**, because I am the Word of the Father, through whom all things are made and conserved.

741   Then (v 18), the Evangelist mentions the persecution of Christ, which resulted from his teaching: for it was because of his teaching that **the Jews tried all the harder**, i.e., with greater eagerness and a higher pitch of zeal, **to kill him**. For in the law two crimes were punished by death: the crime of breaking the Sabbath — thus anyone who gathered wood on the Sabbath was stoned, as we see from Numbers (15:32); and the crime of blashphemy — so we read: "Bring the blasphemer outside the camp ... and let all the children of Israel stone him" (Lv 24:14). Now they thought it was blasphemy for a man to claim that he was God: "We are not stoning you for any good work, but for blasphemy: because although you are a man, you make yourself God" (below 10:33). It was these two crimes they imputed to Christ: the first because he broke the Sabbath; the second because he said he was equal to God. So the Evangelist says that **the Jews tried all the harder to kill him, because he not only broke the Sabbath rest, but even called God his own Father**.

Because other just man had also called God their Father, as in "You will call me 'Father' " (Jer 3:19), they do not just say that he **called God his own Father**, but added what made it blasphemy, **making himself equal to God**, which they understood from his statement: **My Father works even until now, and so do I**. He said that God was his Father so that we might understand that God is his Father by nature, and the Father of others by adoption. He referred to both of these when he said: "I am going to my Father," by nature, "and to your Father," by grace (below 20:17). Again, he said that as the Father works, so he works. This answers the accusation of the Jews about his breaking the Sabbath: for this would not be a valid excuse unless he had equal authority with God in working. It was for this reason they said he made himself equal to God.

742   How great then is the blindness of the Arians when they say that Christ is less than God the Father: for they cannot understand in our Lord's words what the Jews were able to understand. For the Arians say that Christ did not make himself equal to God, while the Jews saw this. There is another way to settle this, from the very things mentioned in the text. For the Evangelist says that the Jews persecuted Christ because he broke the Sabbath, because he said God is his Father, and because he made himself equal to God. But Christ is either a liar or equal to God. But if he is equal to God, Christ is God by nature.

743 Finally, the Evangelist says, **making himself equal to God**, not as though he was making himself become equal to God, because he was equal to God through an eternal generation. Rather, the Evangelist is speaking according to the understanding of the Jews who, not believing that Christ was the Son of God by nature, understood him to say that he was the Son of God in the sense of wishing to make himself equal to God; but they could not believe he was such: "because although you are a man, you make yourself God" (below 10:33), i.e., you say that you are God, understanding this as you wish to make yourself God.

LECTURE 3

19 Jesus therefore replied and said to them:
"Amen, amen, I say to you,
the Son cannot do anything of himself,
but only what he sees the Father doing.
For whatever the Father does,
the Son does likewise.
20a For the Father loves the Son,
and shows him everything that he does."

744 Here we have Christ's teaching on his life-giving power. First, his teaching is presented. Secondly, it is confirmed (v 31). Two things are done with the first. First, Christ's teaching on his life-giving power in general is given. Secondly, it is presented in particular (v 20b). As to the first, three things are done. First, the origin of this power is mentioned. Secondly, the greatness of this power, at (v 19b). Thirdly, the reason for each is given (v 20).

745 We should point out, with respect to the first, that the Arians use what Christ said here, **the Son cannot do anything of himself**, to support their error that the Son is less than the Father. As the Evangelist said, the Jews persecuted Christ for making himself equal to God. But the Arians say that when our Lord saw that this disturbed the Jews, he tried to correct this by stating that he was not equal to the Father, saying, **Amen, amen, I say to you, the Son cannot do anything of himself, but only what he sees the Father doing**. As if to say: Do not interpret what I said, "My Father works even until now, and so do I," as meaning that I work as though I am equal to the Father, for I cannot do anything of myself. Therefore, they say, because the Son can do **only what he sees the Father doing**, he is

less than the Father. But this interpretation is false and erroneous. For if the Son were not equal to the Father, then the Son would not be the same as the Father; and this is contrary to: "I and the Father are one" (below 10:30). For equality is considered with respect to greatness, which in divine realities is the essence itself. Hence, if the Son were not equal to the Father, he would be different from him in essence.

746 To get the true meaning of Christ's statement, we should know that in those matters which seem to imply inferiority in the Son, it could be said, as some do, that they apply to Christ according to the nature he assumed; as when he said: "The Father is greater than I" (below 14:28). According to this, they would say that our Lord's statement, **the Son cannot do anything of himself**, should be understood of the Son in his assumed nature. However, this does not stand up, because then one would be forced to say that whatever the Son of God did in his assumed nature, the Father had done before him. For example, that the Father had walked upon the water as Christ did: otherwise, he would not have said, **but only what he sees the Father doing**.

And if we say that whatever Christ did in his flesh, God the Father also did in so far as the Father works in him, as said below (14:10): "The Father, who lives in me, he accomplishes the works," then Christ would be saying that **the Son cannot do anything of himself, but only what he sees the Father doing** in him, i.e., in the Son. But this cannot stand either, because Christ's next statement, **For whatever the Father does, the Son does likewise**, could not, in this interpretation, be applied to him, i.e., to Christ. For the Son, in his assumed nature, never created the world, as the Father did. Consequently, what we read here must not be understood as pertaining to Christ's assumed nature.

747 According to Augustine, however, there is another way of understanding statements which seem to, but do not, imply inferiority in the Son: namely, by referring them to the origin of the Son coming or begotten from the Father. For although the Son is equal to the Father in all things, he receives all these things from the Father in an eternal begetting. But the Father gets these from no one, for he is unbegotten. According to this explanation, the continuity of thought is the following: Why are you offended because I said that God is my Father, and because I made myself equal to the Father? **Amen, amen, I say to you, the Son can do nothing of himself.** As if to say: I am equal to the Father, but in such a way as to be from him, and not he from me; and whatever I may do, is in me from the Father.

748 According to this interpretation, mention is made of the power of the Son when he says, **can**, and of his activity when he says, **do**. Both can be understood here, so that, first of all, the derivation of the Son's power from the Father is shown, and secondly, the conformity of the Son's activity to that of the Father.

749 As to the first, Hilary explains it this way: Shortly above our Lord said that he is equal to the Father. Some heretics, basing themselves on certain scriptural texts which assert the unity and equality of the Son to the Father, claim that the Son is unbegotten. For example, the Sabellians, who say that the Son is identical in person with the Father. Therefore, so you do not understand this teaching in this way, he says, **the Son cannot do anything of himself**, for the Son's power is identical with his nature. Therefore the Son has his power from the same source as he has his being (*esse*); but he has his being (*esse*) from the Father: "I came forth from the Father, and I have come into the world" (Jn 16:28). He also has his nature from the Father, because he is God from God; therefore, it is from him that the Son has his power (*posse*).

So his statement, **the Son cannot do anything of himself, but only what he sees the Father doing**, is the same as saying: The Son, just as he does not have his being (*esse*) except from the Father, so he cannot do anything except from the Father. For in natural things, a thing receives its power to act from the very thing from which it receives its being: for example, fire receives its power to ascend from the very thing from which it receives its form and being. Further, in saying, **the Son cannot do anything of himself**, no inequality is implied, because this refers to a relation; while equality and inequality refer to quantity.

750 Someone might misunderstand his saying, **but only what he sees the Father doing**, and take it to mean that the Son works or acts in the way he sees the Father acting, i.e., that the Father acts first, and when the Son sees this, then the Son begins to act. It would be like two carpenters, a master and his apprentice, with the apprentice making a cabinet in the way he saw the master do. But this is not true for the Word, for it was said above (1:3): "All things were made through him." Therefore, the Father did not make something in such a way that the Son saw him doing it and so learned from it.

But this is said so that the communication of paternity to the Son might be designated in terms of begetting or generation, which is fittingly described by the verb **sees**, because knowledge is conveyed to us by another through seeing and hearing. For we receive our knowledge from things through seeing, and we receive knowledge from words through hearing. Now the Son is not other than Wisdom, as we read: "I came forth out of the mouth of the Most High, the first-born before all creatures" (Sir 24:5). Accordingly, the derivation of the Son from the Father is nothing other than the derivation of divine Wisdom. And so, because the act of seeing indicates the derivation of knowledge and wisdom from another, it is proper for the generation of the Son from the Father to be indicated by an act of seeing; so that for the Son to see the Father doing something is nothing other than to proceed by an intellectual procession from the acting Father.

Another possible explanation of this is given by Hilary. For him, the word **sees** eliminates all imperfection from the generation of the Son or Word. For in physical generation, what is generated changes little by little in the course of time from what is imperfect to what is perfect, for such a thing is not perfect when it is first generated. But this is not so in eternal generation, since this is the generation of what is perfect from what is perfect. And so he says, **but only what he sees the Father doing**. For since the act of seeing is the act of a perfect thing, it is plain that the Son was begotten as perfect at once, as seeing at once, and not as coming to perfection over a course of time.

751 Apropos of the second point, Chrysostom explains it as showing the conformity of the Father to the Son in operation. So that the sense is: I say that it is lawful for me to work on the Sabbath, because my Father, too, continues to work, and I cannot do anything opposed to him: and this is because **the Son cannot do anything of himself**. For one does something of himself when he does not conform himself to another in his actions. But whoever is from another sins, if he is opposed to him: "Whoever speaks on his own, seeks his own glory" (below 7:18). Therefore, whoever exists from another, but acts of himself, sins. Now the Son is from the Father; thus, if he acts of himself, he sins; and this is impossible. So by saying, **the Son cannot do anything of himself**, he means nothing more than that the Son cannot sin. As if to say: You are persecuting me unjustly for breaking the Sabbath, because I cannot sin, since I do not act in a way opposed to my Father.

Augustine makes use of both of these explanations, that of of Hilary and the one given by Chrysostom, but in different places.

752 Then when he says, **For whatever the Father does, the Son does likewise**, he affirms the greatness of Christ's power. He excludes three things in the power of Christ: limitation, difference, and imperfection.

First, limitation is excluded. Since there are diverse agents in the world, and the first universal agent has power over all other agents, but the other agents, which are from him, have a limited power in proportion to their rank in the order of causality, some might think that since the Son is not of himself, that he must have a power limited to certain existents, rather than a universal power over all, as the Father has. And so to exclude this he says, **whatever the Father does**, i.e., to all the things to which the Father's power extends, the Son's power also extends: "All things were made through him" (above 1:3).

Secondly, difference is excluded. For sometimes a thing that exists from another is able to do whatever that from which it exists does. And yet the things the former does are not the same as those done by that from which it is. For example, if one fire which exists from another can do whatever that other does, i.e., cause combustion, the act of causing combustion would be specifically the same in each, even though one fire ignites certain things and the other fire ignites different things. And so that you do not think that the Son's activity is different from the activity of the Father in this way, he says, **whatever** the Father does, the Son does, i.e., not different things, but the very same.

Thirdly, imperfection is excluded. Sometimes one and the same thing comes from two agents: from one as the principal and perfect agent, and from the other as an instrumental and imperfect agent. But it does not come in the same way, because the principal agent acts in a different way from the instrumental agent: for the instrumental agent acts imperfectly, and in virtue of the other. And so that no one thinks that this is the way the Son does whatever the Father does, he says that whatever the Father does, the Son does **likewise**, i.e., with the same power by which the Father acts, the Son also acts; because the same power and the same perfection are in the Father and the Son: "I was with him, forming all things" (Prv 8:30).

753 Then when he says, **For the Father loves the Son**, he gives the reason for each, i.e., for the origin of the Son's power and for its greatness. This reason is the love of the Father, who loves the Son. Thus he says, **For the Father loves the Son**.

In order to understand how the Father's love for the Son is the reason for the origin or communication of the Son's power, we should point out that a thing is loved in two ways. For since the good alone is loveable, a good can be related to love in two ways: as the cause of love, or as caused by love. Now in us, the good causes love: for the cause of our loving something is its goodness, the goodness in it. Therefore, it is not good because we love it, but rather we love it because it is good. Accordingly, in us, love is caused by what is good. But it is different with God, because God's love itself is the cause of the goodness in the things that are loved. For it is because God loves us that we are good, since to love is nothing else than to will a good to someone. Thus, since God's will is the cause of things, for "whatever he willed he made" (Ps 113:3), it is clear that God's love is the cause of the goodness in things. Hence Denis says in *The Divine Names* (c. 4) that the divine love did not allow itself to be without issue. So, if we wish to consider the origin of the Son, let us see whether the love with which the Father loves the Son, is the principle of his origin, so that he proceeds from it.

In divine realities, love is taken in two ways: essentially, so far as the Father and the Son and the Holy Spirit love; and notionally or personally, so far as the Holy Spirit proceeds as Love. But in neither of these ways of taking love can it be the principle of origin of the Son. For if is is taken essentially, it implies an act of the will; and if that were the sense in which it is the principle of origin of the Son, it would follow that the Father generated the Son, not by nature, but by will — and this is false. Again, love is not understood notionally, as pertaining to the Holy Spirit. For it would then follow that the Holy Spirit would be the principle of the Son — which is also false. Indeed, no heretic ever went so far as to say this. For although love, notionally taken, is the principle of all the gifts given to us by God, it is nevertheless not the principle of the Son; rather it proceeds from the Father and the Son.

Consequently, we must say that this explanation is not taken from love as from a principle (*ex principio*), but as from a sign (*ex signo*). For since likeness is a cause of love (for every animal loves its like), wherever a perfect likeness of God is found, there also is found a perfect love of God. But the perfect likeness of the Father is in the Son, as is said: "He is the image of the invisible God" (1:15); and "He is the brightness of the Father's glory, and the image of his substance" (Heb 1:3). Therefore, the Son is loved perfectly by the Father, and because the Father perfectly loves the Son, this is a sign that the Father has shown him everything and has communicated to him his very own [the Father's] power and nature. And it is of this love that we read above (3:5): "The Father loves the Son, and has put everything into his hands"; and, "This is my beloved Son" (Mt 3:17).

754 With respect to what follows, **and shows him everything that he does**, we should point out that someone can show another his works in two ways: either by sight, as an artisan shows his apprentice the things he has made; or by hearing, as when he verbally instructs him. In whatever of these ways **shows** is understood, there

can follow something which is not appropriate, that is, something that is not present when the Father shows things to the Son. For if we say the Father shows things to the Son by sight, then it follows, as with humans, that the Father first does something which he then shows to the Son; and that he does this by himself, without the Son. But the Father does not show the Son things which he did before, for the Son himself says: "The Lord possessed me at the beginning of his ways, before he made anything" (Prv 8:22). Nor does the Father show the Son things he has done without the Son, for the Father does all things through the Son: "All things were made through him" (above 1:3). If **shows** is understood as a kind of hearing, two things seem to follow. For the one who teaches by word first points out something to the one who is ignorant; again, the word is something intermediate between the one showing and the one being shown. But it is in neither of these ways that the Father shows things to the Son: for he does not do so to one who is ignorant, since the Son is the Wisdom of the Father: "Christ is the power of God, and the wisdom of God" (1 Cor 1:24); nor does the Father use some intermediate word, because the Son himself is the Word of the Father: "The Word was with God" (above 1:1).

Therefore, it is said that the Father **shows** all that he does to the Son, inasmuch as he gives the Son a knowledge of all of his works. For it is in this way that a master is said to show something to his disciple, inasmuch as he gives him a knowledge of the things he makes. Hence, according to Augustine, for the Father to show anything to the Son is nothing more than for the Father to beget or generate the Son. And for the Son to see what the Father does is nothing more than for the Son to receive his being (*esse*) and nature from the Father.

Nevertheless, this showing can be considered similar to seeing insofar as the Son is the brightness of the paternal vision, as we read in Hebrews (1:3): for the Father, seeing and understanding himself, conceives the Son, who is the concept of this vision. Again, it can be considered similar to hearing insofar as the Son proceeds from the Father as the Word. As if to say: **The Father shows him everything,** insofar he he generates him as the brightness and concept of his own wisdom, and as the Word. Thus the words, **The Father shows,** refer to what was said before: **the Son cannot do anything of himself, but only what he sees the Father doing.** And the word, **everything,** refers to, **For whatever the Father does, the Son does likewise.**

20b "Indeed, he will show him
even greater works than these,
such that you will be amazed.
21 For just as the Father raises the dead
and grants life, so the Son
grants life to those to whom he wishes.
22 The Father himself judges no one,
but he has given all judgment to the Son,
23 so that all men may honor the Son
as they honor the Father.
Whoever does not honor the Son
does not honor the Father who sent him.
24 Amen, amen, I say to you,
that whoever hears my voice
and believes in him who sent me,
possesses eternal life;
and he will not encounter judgment,
but has passed from death to life.
25 Amen, amen, I say to you,
the hour is coming, and is now here,
when the dead shall hear the voice
of the Son of God;
and those who hear it will live."

755   Having pointed out the power of the Son in general, he now shows it in more detail. First, the Lord discloses his life-giving power. Secondly, he clarifies what seemed obscure in what was said before (v 26). As to the first he does two things. First, he shows that the Son has life-giving power. Secondly, he teaches how life is received from the Son (v 24). Concerning the first he does three things. First, he presents the life-giving power of the Son. Secondly, he gives a reason for what he says (v 22). Thirdly, he shows the effect of this (v 23). With respect to the first he does two things. First, he sets forth this life-giving power in general. Secondly, he expands on it (v 21).

756   He says, to the first, **Indeed, he will show even greater works than these.** As if to say: You are astonished and affected by the power of the Son in his healing of the sick man, but the Father will show **even greater works than these**, as in raising the dead, **such that you will be amazed.**

757 This passage gives rise to two difficulties. First, about his saying, **he will show**. For the earlier statement that the Father shows everything to the Son (5:20) refers to his eternal generation. How, then, can he say here, **he will show**, if the Son is coeternal with him and eternity does not allow of a future? The second difficulty is over, **such that you will be amazed**. For if he intends to show something to amaze the Jews, then he will be showing it to the Son at the same time as to them; for they could not be amazed unless they saw it. And yet the Son saw all things from eternity with the Father.

758 We must say that this is explained in three ways. The first way is given by Augustine, and in it this future showing is referred to the disciples. For it is Christ's custom that now and then he says that what happens to his members happens to himself, as in Matthew (25:40): "As long as you did it to one of the least of my brethren, you did it to me." And then the meaning is this: You saw the Son do something great in healing the sick man, and you were amazed; but the Father **will show him even greater works than these**, in his members, that is, the disciples: "He will do greater things than these," as we read below (14:12). He then says, **such that you will be amazed**, for the miracles of the disciples so amazed the Jews that a great many of them were converted to the faith, as we see in the Acts.

759 The second explanation, also by Augustine, refers this showing to Christ according to his assumed nature. For in Christ there is both a divine nature and a human nature, and in each he has life-giving power from the Father, although not in the same way. According to his divinity he has the power to give life to souls; but according to his assumed nature, he gives life to bodies. Hence Augustine says: "The Word gives life to souls; but the Word made flesh gives life to bodies." For the resurrection of Christ and the mysteries which Christ fulfilled in his flesh are the cause of the future resurrection of bodies: "God, who is rich in mercy, has brought us to life in Christ" (Eph 2:5); "If it is preached that Christ rose from the dead, how can some of you say that there is no resurrection of the dead" (1 Cor 15:12). The first life-giving power he has from eternity; and he indicated this when he said: "The Father shows him everything that he does" (above 4:20), all of which he shows to his flesh.

The other life-giving power he has in time, and concerning this he says: **he will show him even greater works than these**, i.e., his power will be shown by the fact that he will do greater works, by raising the dead. He will raise some of the dead here: as Lazarus, the young girl, and the mother's only son; and finally he will raise all on the day of judgment.

760 A third explanation refers this showing to Christ in his divine nature, according to the custom of Scripture in saying that a thing is beginning to take place when it is beginning to be known. For example: "All power has been given to me, in heaven and on earth" (Mt 28:18); for although Christ had the complete fulness of power from eternity (because "whatever the Father does, the Son does likewise"), he still speaks of this power as being given to him after the resurrection, not because he was then receiving it for the first time, but because it was through the glory of the resurrection that it became most known. In this interpretation, then, he says that power is given to him insofar as he exercises it in some work. As if to say: **he will show him even greater works than these**, i.e., he will show by his works what has been given to him. And this will come about when you are amazed, i.e., when the one who seems to you to be a mere man is revealed to be a person of divine power and as God.

We could also take the word **show** as referring to an act of seeing, as was explained above [750].

761 Now he explains in more detail the life-giving power of the Son by indicating those greater works which the Father will show the Son (v 21). Here we should point out that in the Old Testament the divine power is particularly emphasized by the fact that God is the author of life: "The Lord kills, and brings to life" (1 Sm 2:6); "I will kill, and bring to life again" (Dt 32:39). Now just as the Father has this power, so also does the Son; hence he says, **For just as the Father raises the dead and grants life, so the Son grants life to those to whom he wishes**. As if to say: These are those greater works that the Father will show the Son, that is, he will give life to the dead. Such works are obviously greater, for it is greater to raise the dead than for a sick man to become well. Thus **the Son grants life to those to whom he wishes**, i.e., by giving initial life to the living, and by raising the dead.

We should not think that some are raised up by the Father and others by the Son. Rather, the same ones who are raised and vivified by the Father, are raised and vivified by the Son also: because just as the Father does all things through the Son, who is his power, so he also gives life to all through the Son, who is life, as he says below: "I am the way, and the truth, and the life" (14:6).

The Father does not raise up and give life through the Son as through an instrument, because then the Son would not have freedom of power. And so to exclude this he says, **the Son grants life to those to whom he wishes**, i.e., it lies in the freedom of his power to grant life to whom he wills. For the Son does not will anything different than the Father wills: for just as they are one substance, so they have one will; hence Matthew (20:15) says: "Is it not lawful for me to do as I will?"

762 Then when he says, **The Father himself judges no one**, he gives the reason for what was said above, and indicates his own power. It should be remarked that there are two expositions for the present passages: one is given by Augustine, and the other by Hilary and Chrysostom.

Augustine's explanation is this. The Lord had said that just as the Father raises the dead, so also does the Son. But so that we do not think that this refers only to those miracles the Son performs in raising the dead to this life, and not to the Son's raising to eternal life, he leads them to the deeper consideration of the resurrection to occur at the future judgment. Thus he refers explicitly to the judgment, saying, **The Father himself judges no one**.

Another explanation by Augustine, in which the same meaning is maintained, is that the earlier statement, **just as the Father raises the dead and grants life, so the Son**, should be referred to the resurrection of souls, which the Son causes inasmuch as he is the Word; but the text, **The Father himself judges no one**, should be referred to the resurrection of bodies, which the Son causes inasmuch as he is the Word made flesh. For the resurrection of souls is accomplished through the person of the Father and of the Son; and for this reason he mentions the Father and Son together, saying, **just as the Father raises the dead ... so the Son**. But the resurrection of bodies is accomplished through the humanity of the Son, according to which he is not coeternal with the Father. Consequently, he attributes judgment solely to the Son.

763 Note the wonderful variety of expressions. The Father is first presented as acting and the Son as resting, when it says: "the Son cannot do anything of himself, but only what he sees the Father doing" (5:19); but here, on the contrary, the Son is presented as acting and the Father as resting: **The Father himself judges no one, but he has given all judgment to the Son**. We can see from this that he is speaking from different points of view at different times. At first, he was speaking of an action which belongs to the Father and the Son; thus he says that "the Son cannot do anything of himself, but only what he sees the Father doing"; but here he is speaking of an action by which the Son, as man, judges, and the Father does not: thus he says that the Father **has given all judgment to the Son**. For the Father will not appear at the judgment because, in accord with what is just, God cannot appear in his divine nature before all who are to be judged: for since our happiness consists in the vision of

God, if the wicked were to see God in his own nature, they would be enjoying happiness. Therefore, only the Son will appear, who alone has an assumed nature. Therefore, he alone will judge who alone will appear to all. Yet he will judge with the authority of the Father: "He is the one appointed by God to be the judge of the living and of the dead" (Acts 10:42); and in the Psalm (71:1) we read: "O Lord, give your judgment to the king."

764 Then when he says, **so that all men may honor the Son,** he gives the effect which results from the power of the Son. First, he gives the effect. Secondly, he excludes an objection (v 23b).

765 He says that the Father has given all judgment to the Son, according to his human nature, because in the incarnation the Son emptied himself, taking the form of a servant, under which form he was dishonored by men, as is said below (8:49): "I honor my Father, and you have dishonored me." Therefore, judgment was given to the Son in his assumed nature in order **that all men may honor the Son as they honor the Father.** For on that day "they will see the Son of Man coming with great power and glory" (Lk 21:27); "They fell on their faces and worshipped, saying: 'Blessing and glory, and wisdom and thanks, and honor, power and strength, to our God' " (Rv 7:11).

766 Someone might say: I am willing to honor the Father, but do not care about the Son. This cannot be, because **Whoever does not honor the Son does not honor the Father who sent him.** For it is one thing to honor God precisely as God, and another to honor the Father. For someone may well honor God as the omnipotent and immutable Creator without honoring the Son. But no one can honor God as Father without honoring the Son; for he cannot be called Father if he does not have a Son. But if you dishonor the Son by diminishing his power, this also dishonors the Father; because where you give less to the Son, you are taking away from the power of the Father.

767 Another explanation, given by Augustine, is this. A twofold honor is due to Christ. One, according to his divinity, in regard to which he is owed an honor equal to that given the Father; and with respect to this he says, **that all men may honor the Son as they honor the Father.** Another honor is due the Son according to his humanity, but not one equal to that given the Father; and with respect to this he says, **Whoever does not honor the Son does not honor the Father who sent him.** Thus in the first case he significantly used "as"; but now, the second time, he does not say "as," but states absolutely that the Son should be honored: "He who rejects you, rejects me; and he who rejects me, rejects him who sent me," as we read in Luke (10:16).

768   Hilary and Chrysostom give a more literal explanation, but it is only slightly different. They explain it this way. Our Lord said above, **the Son grants life to those to whom he wishes.** Now whoever does anything according to the free decision of his will acts because of his own judgment. But it was stated above that "whatever the Father does, the Son does likewise" (5:19). Therefore, the Son enjoys a free decision of his own will in all things, since he acts because of his own judgment. Thus he immediately mentions judgment, saying that **the Father himself judges no one,** i.e., without or apart from the Son. Our Lord used this way of speaking below (12:47): "I do not judge him," i.e., I alone, "but the word that I have spoken will judge him on the last day." **But he has given all judgment to the Son,** as he has given all things to him. For as he has given him life and begotten him as living, so he has given him all judgment, i.e., begotten him as judge: "I judge only as I hear it" (below 5:30), i.e., just as I have being (*esse*) from the Father, so also judgment. The reason for this is that the Son is nothing other than the conception of the paternal wisdom, as was said. But each one judges by the concept of his wisdom. Hence, just as the Father does all things through the Son, so he judges all things through him. And the fruit of this is **that all men may honor the Son as they honor the Father,** i.e., that they may render to him the cult of "latria" as they do the Father. The rest does not change.

769   Hilary calls our attention to the remarkable relationship of the passages so that the errors concerning eternal generation can be refuted. Two heresies have arisen concerning this eternal generation. One was that of Arius, who said that the Son is less than the Father; and this is contrary to their equality and unity. The other was that of Sabellius, who said that that there is no distinction of persons in the divinity; and this is contrary to their origin.

So, whenever he mentions the unity and equality [of the Father and Son], he immediately also adds their distinction as persons according to origin, and conversely. Thus, because he mentions the origin of the persons when he says, "the Son cannot do anything of himself, but only what he sees the Father doing " (5:19),then, so we do not think this involves inequality, he at once adds: "for whatever the Father does, the Son does likewise." Conversely, when he states their equality by saying: **For just as the Father raises the dead and grants life, so the Son grants life to those to whom he wishes,** then, so that we do not deny that the Son has an origin and is begotten, he adds, **the Father himself judges no one, but he has given all judgment to the Son.** Similarly, when he mentions the equality of the persons by saying, **so that all men may honor the Son as they honor the Father,** he immediately adds something about a "mission," which indicates an origin, saying: **Whoever does not honor the Son does not honor the Father who sent him**, but not in such a way that involves a separation. Christ mentions such mission below (8:29) in saying: "He who sent me is with me, and he has not left me alone."

770   Above, our Lord showed that he had life-giving power; here he shows how someone can share in this life coming from him. First, he tells how one can share in this life through him. Secondly, he predicts its fulfillment (v 25).

771   With respect to the first, we should point out that there are four grades of life. One is found in plants, which take nourishment, grow, reproduce, and are reproduced. Another is in animals which only sense. Another in living things that move, that is, the perfect animals. Finally, there is another form of life which is present in those who understand. Now among those grades of life that exist, it is impossible that the foremost life be that found in plants, or in those with sensation, or even in those with motion. For the first and foremost life must be that which is *per se*, not that which is participated. This can be none other than intellectual life, for the other three forms are common to a corporal and spiritual creature [as man]. Indeed, a body that lives is not life itself, but one participating in life. Hence intellectual life is the first and foremost life, which is the spiritual life, that is immediately received from the first principle of life, whence it is called the life of wisdom. For this reason in the Scriptures life is attributed to wisdom: "He who finds me finds life, and has salvation from the Lord" (Prv 8:35). Therefore we share life from Christ, who is the Wisdom of God, insofar as our soul receives wisdom from him.

Now this intellectual life is made perfect by the true knowledge of divine Wisdom, which is eternal life: "This is eternal life: that they may know you, the only true God, and Jesus Christ, whom you have sent" (below 17:3). But no one can arrive at any wisdom except by faith. Hence it is that in the sciences, no one acquires wisdom unless he first believes what is said by his teacher. Therefore, if we wish to acquire this life of wisdom, we must believe through faith the things that are proposed to us by it. "He who comes to God must believe that he is and rewards those who seek him" (Heb 11:6); "If you do not believe, you will not understand," as we read in another version of Isaiah (28:16).

772   Thus, our Lord fittingly shows that the way of obtaining life is through faith, saying, **whoever hears my voice and believes in him who sent me, possesses eternal life**. First, he mentions the merit of faith. Secondly, the reward of faith, **eternal life**.

773   Concerning the merit of faith, he first indicates how faith is brought to us; and secondly, the foundation of faith, that on which it rests.

Faith comes to us through the words of men: "Faith comes through hearing, and hearing through the word of Christ" (Rom 10:17). But faith does not rest on man's word, but on God himself: "Abram believed God, who counted this as his justification" (Gn 15:6); "You who fear the Lord, believe in him" (Sir 2:8). Thus we are lead to believe through the words of men, not in the man himself who speaks, but in God, whose words he speaks: "When you heard the word we brought you as God's word, you did not receive it as the word of men, but, as what it really is, the word of God" (1 Thes 2:13). Our Lord mentions these two things. First, how faith is brought to us, when he says, **whoever hears my voice** [literally, **word**], which leads to faith. Secondly, he mentions that on which faith rests, saying, **and believes in him who sent me**, i.e., not in me, but in him in virtue of whom I speak.

This text can apply to Christ, as man, insofar as it is through Christ's human words that men were converted to the faith. And it can apply to Christ, as God, insofar as Christ is the Word of God. For since Christ is the Word of God, it is clear that those who heard Christ were hearing the Word of God, and as a consequence, were believing in God. And this is what he says: **whoever hears my word**, i.e., me, the Word of God, **and believes in him**, i.e., the Father, whose Word I am.

774   Then when he says, **possesses eternal life**, he mentions the reward of faith, and states three things we will possess in the state of glory; but they are mentioned in reverse order. First, there will be the resurrection from the dead. Secondly, we will have freedom from the future judgment. Thirdly, we will enjoy everlasting life, for as we read in Matthew (c 25), the just will enter into everlasting life. He mentions these three as belonging to the reward of faith; and the third was mentioned first since it is desired more than the others.

775   So he says, **whoever believes**, i.e., through faith, **possesses eternal life**, which consists in the full vision of God. And it is fitting that one who believes on account of God certain things that he does not see, should be brought to the full vision of these things: "These things are written that you may believe ... and that believing you may have life in his name" (below 20:31).

776   He mentions the second when he says, **and he will not encounter judgment**. But the Apostle says something which contradicts this: "We must all appear before the judgment seat of Christ" (2 Cor 5:10), even the apostles. Therefore, even one who

does believe will encounter judgment. I answer that there are two kinds of judgment. One is a judgment of condemnation, and no one encounters that judgment if he believes in God with a faith that is united with love [a "formed faith"]. We read about this judgment: "Do not enter into judgment with your servant, for no living man is just in your sight"; and it was said above (3:18): "Whoever believes is not judged." There is also a judgment of separation and examination; and, as the Apostle says, all must present themselves before the tribunal of Christ for this judgment. Of this judgment we read: "Judge me, O God, and distinguish my cause from those people who are not holy" (Ps 42:1).

777   Thirdly, he mentions a reward when he says, **but has passed from death to life**, or "will pass," as another version says. This statement can be explained in two ways. First, it can refer to the resurrection of the soul. In this case the obvious meaning is that he is saying: Through faith we attain not only to eternal life and freedom from judgment, but also to the forgiveness of our sins as well. Hence he says, **but has passed**, from unbelief to belief, from injustice to justice: "We know that we have passed from death to life" (1 Jn 3:14).

Secondly, this statement can be explained as referring to the resurrection of the body. Then it is an elaboration of the phrase, **possesses eternal life**. For some might think from what was said, that whoever believes in God will never die, but live forever. But this is impossible, because all men must pay the debt incurred by the first sin, according to: "Where is the man who lives, and will not see death?" (Ps 88:49). Consequently, we should not think that one who believes has eternal life in such a way as never to die; rather, he will pass from this life, through death, to life, i.e., through the death of the body he will be revived to eternal life.

Or, "will pass," might refer to the cause [of one's resurrection] : for when a person believes, he already has the merit for a glorious resurrection: "Your dead will live, your slain will rise" (Is 26:19). And then, once released from the death of the old man, we will receive the life of the new man, that is, Christ.

778   **Amen, amen, I say to you....** Since some might doubt if any would pass from death to life, our Lord predicts that this will happen, saying: I say that he [who believes] "will pass from death to life"; and I say it before it actually occurs. And this is what he states, saying: **Amen, amen, I say to you, the hour is coming**, not determined by a necessity of fate, but by God's decree: "It is the last hour" (1 Jn 2:18). And so that we do not think that it is far off, he adds, **and is now here** — "It is now the time for us to rise from sleep"

(Rom 13:11) – i.e., the hour is now here **when the dead shall hear the voice of the Son of God; and those who hear it will live.**

779 This can be explained in two ways. In one way as referring to the resurrection of the body, and so it is said that **the hour is coming, and is now here,** as if he had said: It is true that eventually all will rise, but even now is the hour when some, whom the Lord was about to resuscitate, **shall hear the voice of the Son of God.** This is the way Lazarus heard it when it was said to him, "Come forth," as we read below (11:43); and in this way the daughter of the leader of the synagogue heard it (Mt 9:18); and the widow's son (Lk 7:12). Therefore, he says significantly, **and is now here,** because through me the dead already are beginning to be raised.

Another explanation is given by Augustine, according to which **and is now here** refers to the resurrection of the soul. For as was said above, resurrection is of two kinds: the resurrection of bodies, which will happen in the future; this does not take place now, but will occur at the future judgment. The other is the resurrection of souls from the death of unbelief to the life of faith, and from the life of injustice to that of justice; and this **is now here.** Hence he says, **the hour is coming, and is now here, when the dead,** i.e., unbelievers and sinners, **shall hear the voice of the Son of God; and those who hear it will live,** according to the true faith.

780 This passage seems to imply two strange occurrences. One, when he says that the dead will hear. The other, when he adds that it is through hearing that they will come to life again, as though hearing comes before life, whereas hearing is a certain function of life. However, if we refer this to the resurrection, it is true that the dead will hear, i.e., obey the voice of the Son of God. For the voice expresses the interior concept. Now all nature obeys the slightest command of the divine will: "He calls into existence what does not exist" (Rom 4:17). According to this, then, wood, stones, all things, not just the dry bones but also the dust of dead bodies, **shall hear the voice of the Son of God** so far as they obey his slightest will. And this belongs to Christ, not insofar as he is the Son of Man, but insofar as he is the Son of God, because all things obey the Word of God. And so he significantly says, **of the Son of God;** "What kind of man is this, for the sea and winds obey him?" (Mt 8:27).

If this statement (25b) is understood as referring to the resurrection of souls, then the reason for it is this: the voice of the Son of God has a life-giving power, that voice by which he moves the hearts of the faithful interiorly by inspiration, or exteriorly by his preaching and that of others: "The words that I have spoken to you are spirit and life" (below 6:64). And so he gives life to the dead when he justifies the wicked. And since hearing is the way to life, either of nature through obedience, namely, by repairing nature, or the hearing of faith by repairing life and justice, he therefore says, **and those who hear it**, by obedience as to the resurrection of the body, or by faith as to the resurrection of souls, **will live**, in the body in eternal life, and in justice in the life of grace.

LECTURE 5

26 "Indeed, just as the Father possesses
life in himself,
so he has given it to the Son
to have life in himself.
27 And he [the Father] gave him
the power to pass judgment,
because he is the Son of Man.
28 Do not be surprised at this,
since the hour is coming when all those burried in tombs
will hear the voice of the Son of God.
29 And those who have done well will come forth
to a resurrection of life;
those who have done evil will come forth
to a resurrection of judgment [i.e., condemnation].
30 I cannot do anything of myself,
but I judge only as I hear it;
and my judgment is just,
because I am not seeking my own will,
but the will of him who sent me."

781 Above, our Lord showed that he had the power to give life and to judge; and he explained each by its effect. Here he shows how each of these powers belongs to him. First, he shows this with respect to his life-giving power. Secondly, with respect to his power to judge (v 27).

782 So he says, first: I say that as the Father raises the dead, so I do also; and anyone who hears my word has eternal life. And I possess this because, **just as the Father possesses life in himself, so he has given it to the Son to have life in himself.**

Apropos of this, we should note that some who live do not have life in themselves: as Paul, "I am living by faith in the Son of God" (Gal 2:20); and again in the same place: "It is not I who now live, but Christ lives in me." Thus he lived, yet not in himself, but in another through whom he lived: as a body lives, although it does not have life in itself, but in a soul through which it lives. So that has life in itself which has an essential, non-participated life, i.e., that which is itself life. Now in every genus of things, that which is something through its essence is the cause of those things that are it by participation, as fire is the cause of all things afire. And so, that which is life through its essence, is the cause and principle of all life in living things. Accordingly, if something is to be a principle of life, it must be life through its essence. And so our Lord fittingly shows that he is the principle of all life by saying that he has life in himself, i.e., through his essence, when he says: **just as the Father possesses life in himself**, i.e., as he is living through his essence, so does the Son. Therefore, as the Father is the cause of life, so also is his Son.

Further, he shows the equality of the Son to the Father when he says, **as the Father possesses life in himself**; and he shows their distinction when he says, **he has given it to the Son**. For the Father and the Son are equal in life; but they are distinct, because the Father gives, and the Son receives. However, we should not understand this to mean that the Son receives life from the Father as if the Son first existed without having life, as in lower things a first matter, already existing, receives a form, and as a subject receives accidents: because in the Son there is nothing that exists prior to the reception of life. For as Hilary says: "the Son has nothing unless it is begotten," i.e., nothing but what he receives through his birth. And since the Father is life itself, the meaning of, **he has given it to the Son to have life in himself**, is that the Father produced the Son as living. As if one were to say: the mind gives life to the word, not as though the word existed and then receives life, but because the mind produces the word in the same life by which it lives.

783 According to Hilary, this passage destroys three heresies. First, that of the Arians, who said that the Son is inferior to the Father. They were forced by what was stated earlier, that is, "For whatever the Father does, the Son does likewise" (5:19), to say that the Son is equal to the Father in power; but they still denied that the Son is equal to the Father in nature. But now, this too is refuted by this statement, namely, **just as the Father possesses life in himself, so he has given it to the Son to have life in himself**. For since life pertains to the nature, if the Son has life in himself as does the Father, it is clear that he has in himself, by his very origin, a nature indivisible from and equal to that of the Father.

The second error is also Arian: their denial that the Son is coeternal with the Father, when they say that the Son began to exist in time. This is destroyed when he says, **the Son has life in himself**. For in all living things whose generation occurs in time, it is always possible to find something that at some time or other was not living. But in the Son, whatever is, is life itself. Consequently, he so received life itself that he has life in himself, so as always to have been living.

Thirdly, by saying, **he has given**, he destroys the error of Sabellius, who denied the distinction of persons. For if the Father gave life to the Son, it is obvious that the Father, who gave it, is other than the Son, who received it.

784 Then (v 27), he makes it clear that he has the power to judge. First, he reveals his judiciary power. Secondly, he gives a reason for what he has said (v 30). As to the first he does two things. First, he indicates the origin of his judiciary power. Secondly, he shows that his judgment is just (v 29).

785 With regard to the first, we should note that his statement, **he [the Father] gave him the power**, can be understood in two ways. One way is that of Augustine; the other is that of Chrysostom.

786 If we understand it as Chrysostom does, then this section is divided into two parts. First, he reveals the origin of his judiciary power. Secondly, he settles a difficulty (v 27b).

Chrysostom punctuates this section in the following way. **He gave him the power to pass judgment**. And then a new sentence begins: **Because he is the Son of Man, do not be surprised at this**. The reason for this punctuation is that Paul of Samosata, an early heretic, who like Photius said that Christ was only a man and took his origin from the Virgin, punctuated it as: **He gave him the power to pass judgment because he is the Son of Man**. And then he began a new sentence: **Do not be surprised at this, since the hour is coming**. It was as if he thought that it was necessary for judiciary power to be given to Christ because he is the Son of Man, that is, a mere man, who, of himself, cannot judge men. And so, if Christ is to judge others, he must be given the power to judge.

But this, according to Chrysostom, cannot stand, because it is not at all in agreement with what is stated. For if it is because he is a man that he receives judiciary power, then for the same reason, since it would belong to every man to have judiciary power in virtue of his human nature, it would not belong to Christ any more than to other men. So we should not understand it this way. Rather, we should say that because Christ is the ineffable Son of God, he is on that account also judge. And this is what he says: The Father not only give him the power to give life, but also **he gave him the power**, through eternal generation, **to pass judgment**, just as he gave him, through eternal generation, to have life in himself: "He is the one appointed by God to be the judge of the living and of the dead," as we read in Acts (10:42).

He settles a difficulty when he says, **Do not be surprised at this.** First, he mentions the difficulty. Secondly, he clears it up.

787 The difficulty arose in the minds of the Jews and they were surprised because while they thought that Christ was no more than a man, he was saying things about himself that surpassed man and even the angels. So he says, **Do not be surprised at this,** that is, that I have said that the Son gives life to the dead and has the power to judge precisely **because he is the Son of Man.** They were surprised because, although they thought he was only a man, they saw that he accomplished divine effects: "What kind of man is this, for the sea and winds obey him?" (Mt 8:27). And he gives a reason why they should not be surprised, which is, because he who is the Son of Man is the Son of God. Although, as Chrysostom says, is it not said explicitly that the Son of Man is the Son of God, our Lord lays down the premises from which this statement necessarily follows: just as we notice that those who use syllogisms in their teaching do not express their main conclusion, but only that from which it follows with necessity. So our Lord does not say that he is the Son of God, but that the Son of Man is such that at his voice all the dead will rise. From this it necessarily follows that he is the Son of God: for it is a proper effect of God to raise the dead. Thus he says, **Do not be surprised at this, since the hour is coming when all those burried in tombs will hear the voice of the Son of God.** But he does not say of this hour, as he said above, "and is now here" (5:25). Again, here he says, **all,** which he did not say above: because at the first resurrection he raised only some, as Lazarus, the widow's son and the young girl; but at the future resurrection, at the time of judgment, **all will hear the voice of the Son of God,** and will rise. "I will open your graves, and lead you out of your tombs" (Ez 37:12).

788 Augustine punctuates this passage in the following way. **And he gave him the power to pass judgment because he is the Son of Man.** And then a new sentence follows: **Do not be surprised at this.** In this interpretation there are two parts. The first concerns the power to judge granted to the Son of Man. In the second, the granting of an even greater power is made clear, at **Do not be surprised at this.**

789 As to the first we should note that, according to the mind of Augustine, he spoke above of the resurrection of souls, which is accomplished through the Son of God; but here he is speaking of the resurrection of bodies, which is accomplished through the Son

of Man. And because the general resurrection of bodies will take place at the time of judgment, he mentions the judgment first, in saying, **And he [the Father] gave him**, i.e., Christ, **the power to pass judgment**, and this, **because he is the Son of Man**, i.e., according to his human nature. Thus it is also after the resurrection that he says in Matthew (28:18): "All power has been given to me, in heaven and on earth."

There are three reasons why judiciary power has been given to Christ as man. First, in order that he might be seen by all: for it is necessary that a judge be seen by all who are to be judged. Now both the good and the wicked will be judged. And the good will see Christ in his divinity and in his humanity; while the wicked will not be able to see him in his divinity, because this vision is the happiness of the saints and is seen only by the pure in heart: "Happy are the pure in heart, for they will see God" (Mt 5:8). And so, in order that Christ can be seen at the judgment not only by the good, but also by the wicked, he will judge in human form: "Every eye will see him, and all who pierced him" (Rv 1:7).

Secondly, the power to judge was given to Christ as man because by the self-abasement of his passion he merited the glory of an exaltation. Thus, just as he who died arose, so that [human] form which was judged, will judge, and he who stood before a human judge will preside at the judgment of men. He who was falsely found guilty will condemn the truly guilty, as Augustine remarks in his work, *The Sayings of the Lord*. "Your cause has been judged as that of the wicked; but cause and judgment you will recover" (Jb 36.17).

Thirdly, Christ as man was given judiciary power to suggest the compassion of the judge. For it is very terrifying for a man to be judged by God: "It is a terrible thing to fall into the hands of the living God" (Heb 10:31); but it produces confidence for a man to have another man as his judge. Accordingly, so you can experience the compassion of your judge, you will have a man as judge: "We do not have a high priest who cannot have compassion on our weakness" (Heb 4:15).

Thus, **he gave him**, Christ, **the power to pass judgment because he is the Son of Man**.

790 **Do not be surprised at this**, for he has given him a greater power, that is, the power to raise the dead. Thus he says, **since the hour is coming**, that is, the last hour at the end of the world: "The time has come, the day of slaughter is near" (Ez 7:7), **when all those burried in tombs will hear the voice of the Son of God**. Above he did not say "all," because there he was speaking of the spiritual resurrection, in which all did not rise at his first coming, for we read: "All do not have faith" (2 Thes 3:2). But here he is speaking of the

resurrection of the body, and all will rise in this way, as we read in 1 Corinthians (15:20). He adds, **those burried in tombs,** which he had not mentioned above, because only bodies, not souls, are in tombs, and it is the resurrection of bodies that will then take place.

All those burried in tombs will hear the voice of the Son of God. This voice will be a sense perceptible sign of the Son of God, at whose sound all will be raised: "The Lord will come with the cry of the archangel and with the trumpet of God" (1 Thes 4:15); we find the same in 1 Corinthians (15:52) and in Matthew (25:6): "There was a cry at midnight." This voice will derive its power from the divinity of Christ: "He will make his voice a powerful voice," as the Psalm (67:34) says.

791   As we saw, Augustine says that the resurrection of the body will be accomplished through the Word made flesh, but the resurrection of the soul is accomplished through the Word. One may wonder how to understand this: whether we are talking about a first cause or a meritorious cause. If we are referring to a first cause, then it is clear that the divinity of Christ is the cause of the corporal and spiritual resurrection, i.e., of the resurrection of bodies and of souls, according to: "I will kill, and I will bring to life again" (Dt 32:39). But if we are referring to a meritorious cause, then it is the humanity of Christ which is the cause of both resurrections: because through the mysteries accomplished in the flesh of Christ we are re-stored not only to an incorruptible life in our bodies, but also to a spiritual life in our souls: "He was put to death on account of our sins, and he rose for our justification" (Rom 4:25). Accordingly, what Augustine says does not seem to be true.

I answer that Augustine is speaking of the exemplary cause and of that cause by which that which is brought to life is made conformable to that which brings it to life: for everything that lives through another is conformed to that through which it lives. Now the resurrection of souls does not consist in souls being conformed to the humanity of Christ, but to the Word, because the life of the soul is through the Word alone; and so he says that the resurrection of souls takes place through the Word. But the resurrection of the body will consist in our bodies being conformed to the body of Christ through the life of glory, that is, through the glory of our bodies, according to: "He will change our lowly body so it is like his glorious body" (Phil 3:21). And it is from this point of view that he says that the resurrection of the body will take place through the Word made flesh.

792   Then (v 29), he shows the justness of his judgment: because the good will be rewarded, and so he says, **And those who have done well will come forth to a resurrection of life**, i.e., to living in eternal glory; but the wicked will be damned, and so he says, **those who have done evil will come forth to a resurrection of judgment [i.e., condemnation]**, i.e., they will rise for condemnation: "These," the wicked, "will go into everlasting punishment; but the just will go to eternal life" (Mt 25:46); "Many of those who sleep in the dust of the earth will awake: some to an everlasting life, and others to everlasting shame" (Dn 12:2).

793   Note than when he was speaking above of the resurrection of souls, he said, "those who hear it," the voice of the Son of God, "will live" (5:25); but here he says, **will come forth.** He says this because of the wicked, who will be condemned: for their life should not be called a life, but rather an eternal death. Again, above he mentioned only faith, saying, "Whoever hears my voice and believes in him who sent me, possesses eternal life; and he will not encounter judgment" (5:24). But here he mentions works, so that we do not think that faith alone, without works, is sufficient for salvation, saying: **And those who have done well will come forth to a resurrection of life.** As if to say: **Those will come forth to a resurrection of life** who do not just believe, but who have accomplished good works along with their faith: "Faith without works is dead," as we see from James (2:26).

794   Then when he says, **I cannot do anything of myself**, he gives the reason for what he has just said. Now he had spoken of two things: the origin of his power, and the justness of his judgment. Consequently, he mentions the reason for each.

795   The first point, when he says, **I cannot do anything of myself**, can be understood in two ways, even according to Augustine. First, as referring to the Son of Man in this manner: You say that you have the power to raise the dead because you are the Son of Man. But do you have this power precisely because you are the Son of Man? No, because **I cannot do anything of myself, but I judge only as I hear it**. He does not say, "as I see," as he said above: "The Son cannot do anything of himself, but only what he sees the Father doing" (5:19). But he does say, **as I hear it**: for in this context "to hear" is the same as "to obey." Now to obey belongs to one who receives a command, while to command pertains to one who is superior. Accordingly, because Christ, as man, is inferior to the Father, he says, **as I hear it**, i.e., as infused into my soul by God. We read of this kind of hearing in Psalm 84 (v 9): "I will hear what the Lord God says in me." But above he said "sees," because he was then speaking of himself as the Word of God.

796   Then when he says, **and my judgment is just**, he shows the justness of his judgment. For he had said: "Those who have done well will come forth to a resurrection of life." But some might say: Will he be partial and uneven when he punishes and rewards? So he answers: No, saying: **my judgment is just**; and the reason is **because I am not seeking my own will, but the will of him who sent me**. For there are two wills in our Lord Jesus Christ: one is a divine will, which is the same as the will of the Father; the other is a human will, which is proper to himself, just as it is proper to him to be a man. A human will is borne to its own good; but in Christ it was ruled and regulated by right reason, so that it would always be conformed in all things to the divine will. Accordingly he says: **I am not seeking my own will**, which as such is inclined to its own good, **but the will of him who sent me**, that is, the Father: "I have desired to do your will, my God" (Ps 39:9); "Not as I will, but as you will" (Mt 26:39).

If this is carefully considered, the Lord is assigning the true nature of a just judgment, saying: **because I am not seeking my own will**. For one's judgment is just when it is passed according to the norm of law. But the divine will is the norm and the law of the created will. And so, the created will, and the reason, which is regulated according to the norm of the divine will, is just, and its judgment is just.

797   Secondly, it is explained as referring to the Son of God; and then the aforesaid division still remains the same. Thus Christ, as the Divine Word showing the origin of his power, says: **I cannot do anything of myself**, in the way he said above, "the Son cannot do anything of himself" (5:19). For his very doing and his power are his being (*esse*); but being (*esse*) in him is from another, that is, from his Father. And so, just as he is not of himself (*a se*), so of himself he cannot do anything: "I do nothing of myself" (below 8:28).

His statement, **I judge only as I hear it**, is explained as his previous statement, "only what he sees the Father doing" (above 5:19). For we acquire science or any knowledge through sight and hearing (for these two senses are those most used in learing). But because sight and hearing are different is us, we acquire knowledge in one way through sight, that is, by discovering things, and in a different way through hearing, that is, by being taught. But in the Son of God, sight and hearing are the same; thus, when he says either "sees" or "hears," the meaning is the same so far as the acquisition of knowledge is concerned. And because judgment in any intellectual nature comes from knowledge, he says significantly, **I judge only as I hear it**, i.e., as I have acquired knowledge together with being from the Father, so I judge: "Everything I have heard from my Father I have made known to you" (below 15:15).

798   Showing the justness of his judgment he says: **and my judgment is just**: the reason being, **because I am not seeking my own will**. But do not the Father and the Son have the same will? I answer that the Father and the Son do have the same will, but the Father does not have his will from another, whereas the Son does have his will from another, i.e., from the Father. Thus the Son accomplishes his own will as from another, i.e., as having it from another; but the Father accomplishes his will as his own, i.e., not having it from another. Thus he says: **I am not seeking my own will**, that is, such as would be mine if it originated from myself, but my will, as being from another, that is from the Father.

LECTURE 6

31 "If I were to bear witness to myself,
my testimony would not be valid.
32 But there is someone else who testifies
on my behalf, and I know that the witness
he bears on my behalf is true.
33 You sent [messengers] to John;
and he bore witness to the truth.
34 I myself do not need proof from men;
but I say this in order that you may be saved.
35 He was a lamp, blazing and burning brightly.
And for a time you yourselves exulted in his light.
36 But I have testimony that is greater than that of John.
The very works which my Father has given me
to perform — those works that I myself perform —
they bear witness to me that the Father sent me.
37 Moreover, the Father who sent me has himself
given testimony on my behalf,
but you have neither heard his voice,
nor seen his image;
38 and you do not have his word abiding in your hearts,
for you do not believe in him whom he has sent.
39 Search the Scriptures,
since you think you have eternal life in them;
they too bear witness to me.
40 Yet you are unwilling to come to me
in order to possess that life."

799 Having given us the teaching on the life-giving power of the Son, he now confirms it. First, he confirms, with several testimonies, what he had said about the excellence of his power. In the second place, he reproves them because of their slowness to believe (v 41). He does two things about the first. First, he states why there was a need to resort to such testimonies. Secondly, he invokes the testimonies (v 32).

800 The need to appeal to testimony arose because the Jews did not believe in him; for this reason he says: **If I were to bear witness to myself, my testimony would not be valid** (*verum*, valid, true). Some may find this statement puzzling: for if our Lord says of himself, "I am the truth" (below 14:6), how can his testimony not be valid? If he is the truth, in whom shall one believe if the truth itself is not believed in? We may answer, according to Chrysostom, that our Lord is speaking here of himself from the point of view of the opinion of others, so that his meaning is: **If I were to bear witness to myself, my testimony would not be valid** so far as your outlook is concerned, because you do not accept what I say about myself unless it is confirmed by other testimony: "You are bearing witness to yourself; your testimony is not valid" (below 8:13).

801 Next, he presents these testimonies: first, a human testimony; secondly, a divine testimony. He does two things about the first. First, he mentions the testimony of John; secondly, he tells why this testimony was given (v 34). With respect to the first he does two things. First, he brings in the testimony; secondly, he commends it (v 32).

802 He brings on the witness when he says: **But there is someone else who testifies on my behalf.** This is, in the opinion of Chrysostom, John the Baptist, of whom we read above: "There was a man sent by God, whose name was John. He came as a witness, that he might bear witness to the light" (1:6).

803 He commends John's testimony on two grounds: first, because of its truth; secondly, because of its authority, for the Jews had sought it (v 33).

804 He commends his testimony because of its truth, saying: **And I know,** from certain experience, **that the witness he,** that is, John, **bears on my behalf is true.** His father, Zechariah, had prophesied this of him: "You will go before the face of the Lord to prepare his way, to give his people a knowledge of salvation" (Lk 1:76). Now it is obvious that false testimony is not a testimony that saves, because lying is a cause of death: "A lying mouth kills the soul" (Wis 1:11). Therefore, if John's testimony was for the purpose of giving knowledge of salvation to his people, his testimony is true.

805 The Gloss has a different explanation of this: **If I were to bear witness to myself, my testimony would not be valid**. For above, Christ was referring to himself as God, but here he is referring to himself as a man. And the meaning is: **If I**, namely, a man, **were to bear witness to myself**, i.e., apart from God, that is, which God the Father does not certify, then it follows that **my testimony would not be valid**, for human speech has no truth unless it is supported by God, according to: "God is true, but every man is a liar" (Rom 3:4). Thus, if we take Christ as a man separated from the Deity and not in conformity with it, we find a lie both in his essence and in his words: "Although I bear witness to myself, my testimony is true" (below 8:14); "I am not alone, because the Father is with me" (below 16:32). And so, because he was not alone but with the Father, his testimony is true.

Accordingly, to show that his testimony is true, not in virute of his humanity considered in itself, but in so far as it is united to his divinity and to the Word of God, he says, **But there is someone else who testifies on my behalf**: not John, but the Father, according to this explanation. Because if the testimony of Christ as man is not of itself true and productive, much less is the testimony of John. Therefore, the testimony of Christ is not verified by the testimony of John, but by the testimony of the Father. So this someone else who testifies is understood to be the Father. **And I know that the witness he bears on my behalf is true**, for he is truth: "God is light," i.e., truth, "and in him there is no darkness," i.e., lie (1 Jn 1:5).

The first explanation, which is that given by Chrysostom, is nearer to the letter of the text.

806 He also commends the testimony of John by reason of its authority, because it was sought after by the Jews, saying: **You sent [messengers] to John**. As if to say: I know that his testimony is true and you should not reject it, because the great authority John enjoyed among you led you to seek his testimony about me; and you would not have done this if you did not think that he was worthy of belief: "The Jews sent priests and Levites from Jerusalem to him" (above 1:19). And on this occasion, John **bore witness**, not to himself, but **to the truth**, i.e., to me. As a friend of the truth, he bore testimony to the truth, which is Christ: "He declared openly, and did not deny, and stated clearly, 'I am not the Messiah' " (above 1:20).

807 Then (v 34), he gives the reason why an appeal was made to the testimony of John. First, he excludes a supposed reason. Next, he presents the true reason (v 34b).

808   Someone might think that John's testimony was brought in to assure them about Christ, on the ground that Christ's own testimony was not sufficient. He excludes this reason when he says, **I myself do not need proof from men.** Here we should note that sometimes in the sciences a thing is proved by something else which is more evident to us, but which is less evident in itself; and at other times a thing is proved by something else which is more evident in itself and absolutely. Now, in this case, the issue is to prove that Christ is God. And, although the truth of Christ is, in itself and absolutely, more evident, yet it is proved by the testimony of John, which was better known to the Jews. So Christ, of himself, did not have any need of John's testimony; and this is what he says: **I myself do not need proof from men.**

809   But this seems to conflict with: "You are my witnesses, said the Lord" (Is 40:10); and with "You will be my witnesses in Jerusalem and in all of Judea and Samaria, and to the remotest part of the world" (Acts 1:8). So how can he say: **I myself do not need proof from men.**

This can be understood in two ways. In the first way, the sense is: **I myself do not need proof from men,** as relying on it alone; but I have stronger testimony, that is, divine testimony: "For me, it does not matter much if I am judged by you" (1 Cor 4:3); "You know that I have not desired the day of man," i.e., human glory (Jer 17:16).

Another interpretation is: **I myself do not need proof from men,** insofar as the one giving witness is a man, but insofar as he is enlightened by God in order to testify: "There was a man sent by God, whose name was John" (above 1:6); "We did not seek glory from men" (1 Thes 2:6); "I do not seek my own glory" (below 8:50). And so I receive the testimony of John not just as a man, but insofar as he was sent and enlightened by God in order to testify.

A third explanation, and a better one, is: **I myself do not need proof from men,** i.e., human testimony. As far as I am concerned, I receive my authority from no one but God, who proves that I am great.

810   Next (v 34b), he gives the real reason for appealing to John's testimony. First, he states the reason. Secondly, he explains it. The reason for appealing to this testimony was so that the Jews might be saved by believing in Christ, and this because of John's testimony. Thus he says: I do not need John's testimony for my sake, **but I say this in order that you may be saved:** "He desires the salvation of all men" (1 Tim 2:4); "Christ came into this world to save sinners" (1 Tim 1:15).

811 He explains his statement, **in order that you may be saved**: that is, because I am appealing to testimony you have accepted. And so he mentions that John was accepted by them: **He was a lamp, blazing and burning brightly**. First, he states that John was a witness accepted on his own merits. Secondly, he mentions to what degree he was accepted by them (v 35b).

812 Three things perfected John and show that he was a witness accepted in his own right. The first concerns the condition of his nature, and he refers to this when he says, **He was a lamp**. The second concerns the perfection of his love, because he was a **blazing** lamp. The third is related to the perfection of his understanding, because he was a lamp that was **burning brightly**.

John was perfect in his nature because he was a **lamp**, i.e., enriched by grace and illumined by the light of the Word of God. Now a lamp differs from a light: for a light radiates light of itself, but a lamp does not give light of itself, but by participating in the light. Now the true light is Christ: "He was the true light, which enlightens every man coming into this world" (above 1:9). John, however, was not a light, as we read in the same place, but a lamp, because he was enlightened "in order to bear witness to the light" (above 1:8), by leading men to Christ. We read of this lamp: "I have prepared a lamp for my anointed" (Ps 131:17).

Further, he was blazing and impassioned in his affections, so he says, **blazing**. For some people are lamps only as to their office or rank, but they are snuffed out in their affections: for as a lamp cannot give light unless there is a fire blazing within it, so a spiritual lamp does not give any light unless it is first set ablaze and burns with the fire of love. Therefore, to be ablaze comes first, and the giving of light depends on it, because knowledge of the truth is given due to the blazing of love: "If any one loves me, he will keep my word, and my Father will love him, and we will come to him, and make our home with him" (below 14:23); and "I have called you friends, because everything I have heard from my Father I have made known to you" (below 15:15); "You who fear the Lord, love him, and your hearts will be enlightened" (Sir 2:20).

The two characteristics of fire are that it both blazes and shines. Its blazing signifies love for three reasons. First, because fire is the most active of all bodies; so too is the warmth of love (charity), so much so that nothing can withstand its force: "The love of Christ spurs us on" (2 Cor 5:14). Secondly, because just as fire, because it is very volatile, causes great unrest, so also this love of charity makes a person restless until he achieves his objective: "Its light is fire and flame" (Sg 8:6). Thirdly, just as fire is inclined to move upward, so too is charity; so much so that it joins us to God: "He who abides in love abides in God, and God in him" (1 Jn 4:16).

Finally, John had an intellect that was **burning brightly.** First, it was bright within, because of his knowledge of the truth: "The Lord will fill your soul with brightness," i.e., he will make it shine (Is 58:11). Secondly, it was bright without, because of his preaching: "You will shine in the world among them like stars, containing the word of life" (Phil 2:15). Thirdly, it was bright because it manifested good works: "Let your light so shine before men that they may see your good works" (Mt 5:16).

813 And so, because John was of himself so acceptable — for he was a lamp, not smothered out but blazing, not dark but burning brightly — he deserved to be accepted by you, as indeed he was, because **for a time you yourselves exulted in his light.** He fittingly links their exulting or rejoicing with light; because a man rejoices most is that which most pleases him. And among physical things nothing is more pleasant than light, according to: "It is a delight for the eyes to see the sun" (Sir 11:7). He says, **you yourselves exulted in his light,** i.e., you rested in John and put your end in him, thinking that he was the Messiah. But you did this only **for a time,** because you wavered on this; for when you saw that John was leading men to another, and not to himself, you turned away from him. Thus we read in Matthew (21:32) that the Jews did not believe in John. They belonged to that group referred to by Matthew (13:21) as believing "for a while."

814 Then (v 36), he presents the divine testimony. First, he mentions its greatness; and then he continues on to describe it.

815 He says: I do not need proof from men for my sake, but for your sake, for **I have testimony that is greater than that of John,** that is, the testimony of God, which is greater than the testimony of John: "If we receive the testimony of men, the testimony of God is greater" (1 Jn 5:9). It is greater, I say, because of its greater authority, greater knowledge, and infallible truth, for God cannot deceive: "God is not like man, a liar" (Nm 23:19).

816 God bore witness to Christ in three ways: by works, by himself, and by the Scriptures. First, he mentions his witness as given by the working of miracles; secondly, the way God gave witness by himself (v 37); thirdly, the witness given through the Scriptures (v 39).

817 He says first: **I have testimony that is greater than that of John,** that is, my works, i.e., the working of miracles, **the very works which my Father has given me to perform.** We should point out that it is natural for man to learn of the power and natures of things from their actions, and therefore our Lord fittingly says that the

sort of person he is can be learned through the works he does. So, since he performed divine works by his own power, we should believe that he has divine power within him: "If I had not done among them the works which no one else did, they would not have sin," that is, the sin of unbelief (below 15:24). And so he leads them to a knowledge of himself by appealing to his works, saying, **the very works which my Father has given me** in the Word, through an eternal generation, by giving me a power equal to his own. Or we could say, **the very works which my Father has given me**, in my conception, by making me one person who is both God and man, **to perform**, i.e., to perform them by my own power. He says this to distinguish himself from those who do not perform miracles by their own power but have to obtain it as a favor from God; thus Peter says: "In the name of Jesus Christ of Nazareth: stand up" (Acts 3:6). Thus it was God, and not themselves, who accomplished these works; but Christ accomplished them by his own power: "Lazarus, come forth," as John reports below (11:43). Accordingly, **those works that I myself perform — they bear witness to me**; "If you do not believe me, at least believe my works" (below 10:38). We see from Mark (16:20) that God bears witness by the working of miracles: "The Lord worked with them and confirmed the word by the signs that followed."

818   Then (v 37), he presents the second way God bore witness to Christ, namely, by himself. First, he mentions the way; secondly, he shows that they were not able to receive this testimony.

819   He says: It is not only the works which my Father has given me to perform that bear witness to me, but **the Father who sent me has himself given testimony on my behalf**: in the Jordan, when Christ was baptized (Mt 3:17); and on the mountain, when Christ was transfigured (Mt 17:5). For on both these occasions the voice of the Father was heard: "This is my beloved Son." And so they should believe in Christ, as the true and natural Son of God: "This is the testimony of God: he has borne witness to his Son" (1 Jn 5:9). Consequently, anyone who does not believe that he is the Son of God, does not believe in the testimony of God.

820   Someone could say that God also gave testimony to others by himself: for example, to Moses, on the mountain, with whom God spoke while others were present. We, however, never heard his testimony, as the Lord says: **you have neither heard his voice**. On the other hand, we read in Deuteronomy (4:33): Did it ever happen before that the people heard the voice of God speaking from the midst of fire, as you heard, and have lived?" Then how can Christ say: **you have neither heard his voice**?

I reply, according to Chrysostom, that the Lord wishes to show those established in a philosophical frame of mind that God gives testimony to someone in two ways, namely, sensibly and intelligibly. Sensibly, as by a sensible voice only; and in this way he gave witness to Moses on Mount Sinai: "You heard his voice, and saw no form at all" (Dt 4:12). Likewise, he gives testimony by a sensible form, as he appeared to Abraham (Gn 26), and to Isaiah: "I saw the Lord seated on a high and lofty throne" (Is 6:1). However, in these visions, neither the audible voice nor the visible figure were like anything in the animal kingdom, except efficiently, in the sense that these were formed by God. For since God is a spirit, he neither emits audible sounds nor can he be portrayed as a figure. But he does bear testimony in an intelligible manner by inspiring in the hearts of certain persons what they ought to believe and to hold: "I will hear what the Lord God will speak within me" (Ps 84:9); "I will lead her into the wilderness and there I will speak to her heart," as we read in Hosea (2:14).

Now you were able to receive the testimony given in the first of these ways; and this is not surprising, because they were the words and image of God only efficiently, as was said. But they were not able to receive the testimony given in that intelligible voice; so he says: **you have neither heard his voice,** i.e., you were not among those who shared in it. "Everyone who has heard the Father and has learned, comes to me" (below 6:45). But you do not come to me. Therefore, **you have neither heard his voice nor seen his image,** i.e., you do not have his intelligible testimony. Hence he adds: **and you do not have his word abiding in your hearts,** i.e., you do not have his word that is inwardly inspired. And the reason is, **for you do not believe in him whom he,** the Father, **has sent.** For the word of God leads to Christ, since Christ himself is the natural Word of God. But every word inspired by God is a certain participated likeness of that Word. Therefore, since every participated likeness leads to its original, it is clear that every word inspired by God leads to Christ. And so, because you are not led to me, **you do not have his word,** i.e., the inspired word of God, **abiding in your hearts.** "He who does not believe in the Son of God does not have life abiding in him," as it says below (*sic*). He says **abiding,** because although there is no one who does not have some truth from God, they alone have the truth and the word abiding in them whose knowledge has progressed to the point where they have reached a knowledge of the true and natural Word.

821 Or we could say that, **you have neither heard his voice,** can be taken as showing the three ways in which God reveals things. This is done either by a sensible voice, as he bore witness to Christ

in the Jordan and on the mountain, as in 2 Peter (1:16): "We were eyewitnesses of his greatness. For he received honor and glory from God the Father, when a voice came from the heavens." And the Jews did not hear this. Or, God reveals things through a vision of his essence, which he reveals to the blessed. And they did not see this, because "while we are in the body, we are absent from the Lord" (2 Cor 5:6). Thirdly, it is accomplished by an interior word through an inspiration; and the Jews did not have this either.

822   Then when he says, **Search the Scriptures**, he gives the third way in which God bore witness to Christ, through the Scriptures. First, he mentions the testimony of the Scriptures. Secondly, he shows that they were not able to gather the fruit of this testimony (v 40).

823   He says: **Search the Scriptures**. As if to say: You do not have the word of God in your hearts, but in the Scriptures; therefore, you must seek for it elsewhere than in your hearts. Hence, **Search the Scriptures**, that is, the Old Testament, for the faith of Christ was contained in the Old Testament, but not on the surface, for it lay hidden in its depths, under shadowy symbols: "Even to this day, when Moses is read, a veil is over their hearts" (2 Cor 3:15). Thus he significantly says, **Search**, probe into the depths: "If you search for her [wisdom] like money, and dig for her like a treasure, you will understand the fear of the Lord and will find the knowledge of God" (Prv 2:4); "Give me understanding and I will search your commandments" (Ps 118:34).

The reason why you should search them I take from your own opinion, because **you think you have eternal life in them**, since we read in Ezekiel (18:19): "He who has kept my commands will live." But you are mistaken; because although the precepts of the old law are living, they do not contain life in themselves. They are said to be living only to the extent that they lead to me, the Christ. Yet you use them as though they contained life in themselves, and in this you are mistaken, for **they bear witness to me**, i.e., they are living to the extent that they lead to a knowledge of me. And they lead to a knowledge of me either by plain prophecies, as in Isaiah (7:14): "A virgin will conceive." or in Deuteronomy (18:15): "The Lord your God will raise up a prophet for you."; and so Acts (10:43) says: "All the prophets bear witness to him." The Scriptures also lead to a knowledge of Christ through the symbolic actions of the prophets; thus we read: "I have used resemblences in the ministry of the prophets" (Hos 12:10). Knowledge of Christ is also given in their sacraments and figures, as in the immolation of the lamb, and other symbolic sacraments of the law: "The law has only a shadow of the good things to come" (Heb 10:1). And so, because the Scriptures of the Old Testament gave much testimony about Christ, the Apostle says: "He promised the Good News before, through his prophets in the holy Scriptures; the Good News of his Son, a descendant of David in his human nature" (Rom 1:2).

824 The fruit which you think you have in the Scriptures, that is, eternal life, you will not be able to obtain, because in not believing the testimonies of the Scriptures about me, **you are unwilling to come to me,** i.e., you do not wish to believe in me, in whom the fruit of these Scriptures exists, **in order to possess that life** in me, the life which I give to those who believe in me: "I give them eternal life" (below 10:28); "Wisdom infuses life into her children" (Sir 4:12); "He who finds me will find life, and will have salvation from the Lord" (Prv 8:35).

LECTURE 7

41 "Praise from men I do not need,
42 but I know you,
and you do not have the love of God in your hearts.
43 I have come in my Father's name,
and yet you do not accept me.
If someone else came in his own name,
you would be accepting him.
44 How can people like you believe,
when you crave praise from each other,
and yet not even ask for that one praise
which is from God alone?
45 Do not think that I will accuse you
before my Father.
The one who accuses you is Moses,
in whom you place your trust.
46 If you believed Moses,
you would perhaps believe me as well,
for it was about me that he wrote.
47 But if you do not believe in his written statements,
how will you believe in my spoken words?"

825 After God confirmed the greatness of his power by the testimonies of men, of God, and of the Scriptures, he here rebukes the Jews for being slow to believe. Now the Jews persecuted Christ

on two grounds: for breaking the Sabbath, by which he seemed to go against the law, and for saying that he is the Son of God, by which he seemed to go against God. Thus they persecuted him on account of their reverence for God and their zeal for the law. And so our Lord wishes to show that their persecution of him was really inspired not by these motives, but by contrary reasons.

He first shows that the cause of their unbelief was their lack of reverence for God. Secondly, that another cause of their unbelief was their lack of reverence for Moses (v 45). As to the first he does two things. First, he shows their irreverence for God. Secondly, he shows that this is the cause of their unbelief (v 44). Concerning the first he does two things. First, he mentions their lack of reverence for God. Secondly, he makes this obvious by a sign (v 43). With respect to the first he does two things. First, he rejects what they might have assumed to be his intention, from what he had said before. Secondly, he presents his real intention (v 42).

826 The Jews might have assumed that Christ was seeking some kind of praise from men, since he had reminded them of so many witnesses to himself, as John, God, his own works, and the testimony of the Scriptures. Against this thought he says, **Praise from men I do not need**, i.e., I do not seek praise from men; for I have not come to be an example of one seeking human glory: "We did not seek glory from men" (1 Thes 2:6). Or, **Praise from men I do not need**, i.e., I do not need human praise, because from eternity I have glory with the Father: "Glorify me, Father, with the glory I had before the world was made" (below 17:5). For I have not come to be glorified by men, but rather to glorify them, since all glory proceeds from me (Wis 7:25) ["Wisdom is a pure emanation of the glory of the almighty God."] It is through this wisdom that I have glory. God is said to be praised and glorified by men — "Glorify the Lord as much as you are able; he will still surpass even that" (Sir 43:30) — not that he might become by this more glorious, but so that he might appear glorious among us.

827 Thus Christ presented the various testimonies to himself not for the reason they thought, but for another one: because **I know you**, i.e., I have made known about you, that **you do not have the love of God in your hearts**, although you pretend to have it. And so you are not persecuting me because of your love for God. You would be persecuting me for the love of God if God and the Scriptures did not bear witness to me; but God himself bears witness to me by himself, his works and in the Scriptures, as has been said. Consequently, if you truly loved God, then so far from rejecting me, you would come to me. You, therefore, do not love God.

Another interpretation would be this. It is as though he were saying: I have not brought in these witnesses because I wanted your praise; but I know you do not love God and your waywardness makes me sad, and I want to lead you back to the way of truth: "Now they have seen and hated both me and my Father" (below 15:24); "The pride of those who hate you continuously rises," as the Psalm (73:23) says.

828 Here we should point out that God cannot be hated in himself by anyone, nor can he be hated with respect to all his effects, since every good in things comes from God, and it is impossible for anyone to hate all good, for he will at least love existence and life. But someone may hate some effect of God, insofar as this is opposed to what he desires: for example, he might hate punishment, and things of that sort. It is from this point of view that God is said to be hated.

829 Then (v 43), he gives a sign that they do not love God. First, a present sign; secondly, a future sign (v 43b).

830 The present sign concerns his own coming; so he says, **I have come in my Father's name.** As if to say: What I say is obvious, for if one loves his Lord, it is clear that he will honor and receive one who comes from him, and seek to honor him. But **I have come in my Father's name,** and I make his name known to the world: "I have made your name known to those you have given me" (below 17:6), **and yet you do not accept me.** Therefore, you do not love him. The Son is said to make his Father known to men because, although the Father, as God, was known — "God is known in Judah" (Ps 75:1) — yet he was not known as the natural Father of the Son before Christ came. Thus Solomon asked: "What is his name? And what is the name of his son?" Prv 30:4).

831 The future sign concerns the coming of the Antichrist. For the Jews could say: Although you come in his name, we have not accepted you, because we will not accept anyone but God the Father. The Lord speaks against this, and says that it cannot be, because you will accept another, who will come, not in the Father's name, but in his own name; and what is more, he will come, not in the name of the Father, but **in his own name,** precisely because he will not seek the glory of the Father but his own. And whatever he does, he will attribute it, not to the Father, but to himself: "who opposes and is exalted above all that is called God, or is worshipped" (2 Thes 2:4). **You would be accepting him;** and so the Apostle continues in the same letter: "God will send them a misleading influence so that they might believe what is false" (2 Thes 2:11). And this, because they did not accept the true teaching, that they

might be saved. So the Gloss says: "Because the Jews were unwilling to accept Christ, the penalty for this sin will be, fittingly
enough, that they will receive the Antichrist; with the result that
those who were unwilling to believe the truth, will believe a lie."

According to Augustine, however, we can understand this text
as applying to heretics and false teachers: who spread a teaching that
comes from their own hearts and not from the mouth of God, and
who praise themselves and despise the name of God. Of such persons
it is written: "You have heard that the Antichrist is coming; and now
many antichrists have appeared" (1 Jn 2:18). So it is clear that your
persecution of me does not spring from your love for God, but from
your hatred and envy of him. And this was the reason why they did
not believe.

832 He concludes: **How can people like you believe, when you
crave praise from each other,** i.e., human praise, **and yet not even
ask for that one praise which is from God alone?** which is true glory.
The reason they could not believe in Christ was that, since their
proud minds were craving their own glory and praise, they considered themselves superior to others in glory, and regarded it as a
disgrace to believe in Christ, who seemed common and poor. And
this was why they could not believe in him. The one who can believe
in Christ is the person of humble heart, who seeks the glory of God
alone, and who strives to please him. And so we read: "Many of the
leaders believed in him; but they did not admit it because of the
Pharisees, so that they would not be expelled from the synagogue"
(below 12:42). We can see from this just how dangerous vainglory is.
For this reason Cicero says: "Let a man beware of that glory that
robs him of all freedom; that freedom for which a man of great spirit
should risk everything." And the Gloss says: "It is a great vice to
boast and to strive for human praise: to desire that others think you
have what you really do not have."

833 Then (v 45), he shows that they do not have zeal for
Moses. First, how Moses was against them. Secondly, he gives the
reason for this opposition (v 46). As to the first he does two things.
First, he rejects their false zeal; secondly, he shows them true zeal,
The one who accuses you is Moses.

834 As to the first he says: **Do not think that I will accuse
you before my Father.** There are three reasons for his saying this.
First, the Son of God did not come into the world to condemn the
world, but to save it. So he says, **Do not think** that I have come to
condemn; I have come to free: "God did not send his Son into the
world to judge the world," that is, to condemn the world, "but that

the world might be saved through him" (above 3:17). And so the blood of Christ cries out, not to accuse, but to forgive: "We have the blood of Christ, crying out better than that of Abel" (Heb 12:24), whose blood cried out to accuse; "Who will accuse God's elect? It is Christ who justifies. Who is it, then, who will condemn?" (Rom 8:33). As to his second reason for saying this, he says: **Do not think that I will accuse you before my Father**, because I will not be the one to accuse you, but to judge you: "The Father has given all judgment to the Son" (above 5:22). The third reason is: **Do not think that I**, i.e., I alone, **will accuse you before my Father** for what you are doing to me; for even Moses will accuse you for not believing him in the things he said of me.

835 Consequently he adds: **The one who accuses you is Moses, in whom you place your trust**, because you believe you are saved through his precepts. Moses accuses them in two ways. Materially, because they deserved to be accused for transgressing his commands: "Those who have sinned under the law, will be judged by the law" (Rom 2:12). Again, Moses accuses them because he and the other saints will have authority in the judgment: "The two-edged swords will be in their hands" (Ps 149:6).

836 He presents the reason for this opposition when he says: **If you believed Moses, you would perhaps believe me as well**, as is clear from "The Lord your God will raise up a prophet for you, from your nation and your brothers; he will be like me: you will listen to him" (Dt 18:15), and from all the sacrifices, which were a symbol of Christ. He says, **perhaps**, to indicate that their will acts from a free judgment, and not to imply that there is any doubt on the part of God.

837 Then when he says, **But if you do not believe in his written statements, how will you believe in my spoken words?** he gives a sign of this opposition. He does this by comparing two things, and then denying of the lesser of them what is denied of the greater. First, there is a comparison between Moses and Christ: for although Christ, absolutely speaking, is greater than Moses, Moses was the greater in reputation among the Jews. Thus he says: If you do not believe Moses, you will not believe me either. Secondly, he compares the way in which they presented their teaching: Moses gave his precepts in a written form; and so they can be studied for a long time, and are not easily forgotten. Hence they impose a stronger obligation to believe. But Christ presented his teachings in spoken words. Thus he says, **But if you do not believe in his written statements**, which you have preserved in your books, **how will you believe in my spoken words?**

6

1 After this Jesus went across the Sea of Galilee, which is that of Tiberias. 2 And a great multitude followed him because they saw the miracles he worked on those who were sick. 3 Jesus therefore went up a mountain, and there sat down with his disciples. 4 Now the Passover was near, a festival day of the Jews. 5 Then, when Jesus lifted his eyes and saw that a great multitude had come to him, he said to Philip,
"Where shall we buy bread that these may eat?"
6 He said this, however, to test him, for he knew what he would do. 7 Philip replied, "Two hundred denarii worth of bread would not suffice for each to have a little bit." 8 One of his disciples, Andrew, the brother of Simon Peter, said to him, 9 "There is a boy here who has five barley loaves and two fishes, but what are these for so many?" 10 Jesus then said,
"Make the people recline."
There was much grass in the place. Therefore the men reclined, in number about five thousand. 11 Jesus then took the bread, and when he had given thanks, he distributed it to those reclining; he did likewise with the fish, as much as they wanted. 12 When they had their fill, he said to his disciples,
"Gather up the fragments that are left over,
lest they be wasted."
13 They therefore gathered and filled twelve baskets with the leftovers, from the five barley loaves and the two fishes, that remained after all had eaten.

838 The Evangelist has presented the teaching of Christ on the spiritual life, by which he gives life to those who are born again. He now tells us of the spiritual food by which Christ sustains those to whom he has given life. First, he describes a visible miracle, in which Christ furnished bodily food. Secondly, he considers spiritual food (6:26). He does two things about the first. First, he describes the visible miracle. Secondly, he shows the effect this miracle had (6:14). He tells us two things about this miracle. First, its circumstances, secondly, about its actual accomplishment (v 5). As to the first he does three things. First, he describes the crowd that Jesus fed, secondly, the place; thirdly, the time (v 4). As to the first he does three things. First, he identifies the place where the crowd followed Jesus; secondly, the people who followed him; and thirdly, he tells why they followed him.

839   The Evangelist describes the place to which the crowd followed our Lord when he says, **After this Jesus went across the Sea of Galilee**, i.e., after the mysterious words Jesus had spoken concerning his power. This Sea of Galilee is mentioned frequently in various places in Scripture. Luke calls it a lake (Lk 5:1) because its water is not salty, but was formed from the waters flowing in from the Jordan. Yet it is still called a "Sea," because in Hebrew all bodies of water are called "seas": "God called the waters 'seas' " (Gn 1:10). It is also called Gennesaret because of the character of its location: for this water is tossed about a great deal, being buffeted by the winds that come from the vapors rising from its surface. Thus in Greek the word "Gennesaret" means "wind forming." It is called the Sea of Galilee from the province of Galilee in which it is located. Again, it is called the Sea of Tiberias from the city of Tiberias: this city was situated on one side of the sea, facing Capernaum on the opposite side. The city of Tiberias was formerly called Chinnereth, but later, when it was rebuilt by Herod the Tetrarch, it was renamed as Tiberias in honor of Tiberius Caesar.

840   The literal reason why Jesus crossed the sea is given by Chrysostom: to give ground to the anger and agitation which the Jews felt against Christ because of the things he had said about them. As Chrysostom says: just as darts strike a hard object with great force if they meet it, but pass on and soon come to rest if nothing is in their way, so also the anger of defiant men increases when they are resisted, but if we yield a little, it is easy to keep their fury within bounds. So Christ, by going to the other side of the sea, was able to soften the anger of the Jews, caused by what he had said. He thus gives us an example to act in the same way: "Do not be provoked by one who speaks evil of you" (Sir 8:14).

841   In the mystical sense, the sea signifies this present troubled world: "This great sea, stretching wide" (Ps 103:25). Our Lord crossed over this sea when he assumed the sea of punishment and death by being born, trod it under foot by dying, and then crossing over it by his rising, arrived at the glory of his resurrection. We read of this crossing: "Jesus knew that his time had come to leave this world for the Father" (below 13:1). A great crowd, composed of both peoples, has followed him in this crossing, by believing in him and imitating him: "Your heart will be full of wonder and joy, when the riches of the sea will be given to you" (Is 60:5); "Rise up, O Lord, you who demand that justice be done; and the people will gather round you" (Ps 7:7).

842   The crowd that followed him is described as large, **And a great multitude followed him.**

843 The reason why they followed him is because he was performing miracles, hence he says, **because they saw the miracles he worked on those who were sick.** We should point out that some followed Christ because of his teachings, that is, those who were better disposed. But there were others, i.e., those who were less perfect and less perceptive, who followed him because they were attracted by visible miracles; "Signs were given to unbelievers, not to believers" (1 Cor 14:22). Still others followed him out of devotion and faith, those, namely, whom he had cured of some bodily defect: for our Lord had so healed their body that they were also completely healed in soul: "The works of God are perfect" (Dt 32:4). This is clear, because he expressly said to the paralytic, "Do not sin again" (above 5:14), and in Matthew (9:2) he says, "Son, your sins are forgiven"; and these remarks concern the health of the soul rather than that of the body.

844 We might remark that although the Evangelist had mentioned only three miracles (the one at the marriage reception, the son of the official, and the paralytic), he says here in a general way, **the miracles he worked.** He does this to indicate that Christ worked many other miracles that are not mentioned in this book, as he will say below (21:25). For his main object was to present the teaching of Christ.

845 Then he gives the location of the miracle, on a mountain; hence he says: **Jesus therefore went up a mountain,** i.e., privately, **and there sat down with his disciples.** Now a mountain is a place well suited for refreshment, for according to the Psalm a mountain signifies the perfection of justice: "Your justice is like the mountains of God" (Ps 35:7). And so, because we cannot be satisfied by earthly things — indeed, "Whoever drinks this water will be thirsty again" (above 4:13) — but spiritual things will satisfy us, our Lord leads his disciples to a higher place to show that full satisfaction and the perfection of justice are found in spiritual realities. We read of this mountain: "The mountain of God is a rich mountain" (Ps 67:16). Thus he also exercised his office of teacher there, sitting with his disciples; for he is the one who teaches every man.

846 The time is mentioned when he says, **Now the Passover was near.** This time was also well suited for their refreshment, for "Passover" means "passage": "It is the Passover of the Lord, that is, his passage" (Ex 12:11). We understand from this that anyone who desires to be refreshed by the bread of the divine Word and by the body and blood of the Lord, must pass from vices to virtues: "Our Passover, Christ, has been sacrificed, and so let us feast with the

unleavened bread of sincerity and truth" (1 Cor 5:7). And again, divine Wisdom says: "Pass over to me, all who desire me" (Sir 24.26).

This is the second Passover the Evangelist has mentioned. However, our Lord did not go to Jerusalem this time, as the law commanded. The reason for this being that Christ was both God and man: as man he ·was subject to the law, but as God he was above the law. So, he observed the law on certain occasions to show that he was a man, but he also disregarded the law at other times to show that he was God. Further, by not going he indicated that the ceremonies of the law would end gradually and in a short time.

847   Then he considers the miracle itself (v 5). First, why it was needed. Secondly, its accomplishment. We can see the need for this miracle from our Lord's question to his disciple, and the disciple's answer. First, our Lord's question is given; and then the answer of his disciple (v 7). He does three things about the first. First, the occasion for the question is given; secondly, we have the question itself (v 5b); thirdly, we are told why Christ asked this question (v 6).

848   The occasion for Christ's question was his sight of the crowd coming to him. Hence he says, **Then, when Jesus**, on the mountain with his disciples, i.e., with those who were more perfect, **lifted his eyes and saw that a great multitude had come to him**. Here we should note two things about Christ. First, his maturity: for he is not distracted by what does not concern him, but is appropriately concerned with his disciples. He is not like those spoken of in Proverbs (30:13): "A generation whose eyes are proud." And, "A man's dress, and laughter, and his walk, show what he is" (Sir 19:27). Secondly, we should note that Christ did not sit there with his disciples out of laziness; he was looking right at them, teaching them carefully and attracting their hearts to himself: "Then he lifted his eyes to his disciples" (Lk 6:20). Thus we read: **Then, when Jesus lifted his eyes**. In the mystical sense, our Lord's eyes are his spiritual gifts; and he lifts his eyes on the elect, i.e., looks at them with compassion, when he mercifully grants these gifts to them. This is what the Psalm asks for: "Look upon me, O Lord, and have mercy on me" (Ps 85:16).

849   Our Lord's question concerns the feeding of the crowd; so he said to Philip: **Where shall we buy bread that these may eat?** He assumes one thing and asks about another. He assumes their poverty, because they did not have food to offer this great crowd; and he asks how they might obtain it, saying, **Where shall we buy**

bread that these may eat?

Here we should note that every teacher is obliged to possess the means of feeding spiritually the people who come to him. And since no man possesses of himself the resources to feed them, he must acquire them elsewhere by his labor, study, and persistent prayer: "Hurry, you who have no money, and acquire without cost wine and milk" (Is 55:1). And there follows: "Why do you spend your money," i.e., your eloquence, "for what is not bread," i.e., not the true wisdom which refreshes – "Wisdom will feed him with the bread of life and understanding" (Si 15:5) – "and why do you work for what does not satisfy you," i.e., by learning things that drain you instead of filling you?

850 Our Lord's intention is given when he says, **He said this, however, to test him.** Here the Evangelist raises one difficulty in answering another. For we could wonder why our Lord asked Philip what to do, as though our Lord himself did not know. The Evangelist settles this when he says, **for he knew what he would do.** But it seems that the Evangelist raises another difficulty when he says, **to test him.** For to test is to try out; and this seems to imply ignorance.

I answer that one can test another in various ways in order to try him out. One man tests another in order to learn; the devil tests a man in order to ensnare him: "Your enemy, the devil, as a roaring lion, goes about seeking whom he can devour" (1 Pt 5:8). But Christ (and God) does not test us in order to learn, because he sees into our hearts; nor in order to ensnare us, for as we read in James (1:13): "God does not test [i.e., tempt] anyone." But he does test us that others might learn something from the one tested. This is the way God tested Abraham: "God tested Abraham" (Gn 22:1); and then it says (v 12): "Now I know that you fear God," i.e., I have made it known that you fear the Lord. He tests Philip in the same way: so that those who hear his answer might be very certain about the miracle to come.

851 Now we have the answer of the disciples. First, the answer of Philip; then that of Andrew (v 8).

852 With respect to the first, note that Philip was slower in learning than the others, and so he asks our Lord more questions: "Lord, show us the Father, and that will be enough for us" (below 14:8). Here, according to the literal sense, Andrew is better disposed than Philip, for Philip does not seem to have any understanding or anticipation of the coming miracle. And so he suggests that money is the way by which they could feed all the people, saying: **Two hundred denarii worth of bread would not suffice for each to have a**

little bit. And since we do not have that much, we cannot feed them. Here we see the poverty of Christ, for he did not even have two hundred denarii.

853 Andrew, however, seems to sense that a miracle is going to take place. Perhaps he recalled the miracle performed by Elisha with the barley loaves, when he fed a hundred men with twenty loaves (2 Kgs 4:42). And so he says, **There is a boy here who has five barley loaves**. Still, he did not suspect that Christ was going to perform a greater miracle than Elisha: for he thought that fewer loaves would be miraculously produced from fewer, and more from a larger number. But in truth, he who does not need any material to work with could feed a crowd as easily with few or many loaves. So Andrew continues: **but what are these for so many?** As if to say: Even if you increased them in the measure that Elisha did, it still would not be enough.

854 In the mystical sense, widsom is a symbol for spiritual refreshment. One kind of wisdom was taught by Christ, the true wisdom: "Christ is the power of God, and the wisdom of God" (1 Cor 1:24). Before Christ came, there were two other teachings or doctrines: one was the human teachings of the philosophers; the other was the teachings found in the written law. Philip mentions the first of these when he speaks of buying: **Two hundred denarii worth of bread would not suffice**, for human wisdom must be acquired. Now the number one hundred implies perfection. Thus two hundred suggests the twofold perfection necessary for this wisdom: for there are two ways one arrives at the perfection of human wisdom, by experience and by contemplation. So he says, **Two hundred denarii worth of bread would not suffice**, because no matter what human reason can experience and contemplate of the truth, it is not enough to completely satisfy our desire for wisdom: "Let not the wise man glory in his wisdom, nor the strong man in his strength, nor the rich man in his riches. But let him who glories glory in this: that he knows and understands me" (Jer 9:23). For the wisdom of no philosopher has been so great that it could keep men from error; rather, the philosophers have led many into error.

It is Andrew who mentions the second kind of teaching [that of the law]. He does not want to buy other bread, but to feed the crowd with the loaves of bread they had, that is, those contained in the law. And so he was better disposed than Philip. So he says: **There is a boy here who has five barley loaves**. This boy can symbolize Moses, because of the imperfection found in the state of the law: "The law brought nothing to perfection" (Heb 7:19); or the Jewish people, who were serving under the elements of this world (Gal 4:3).

This boy had five loaves, that is, the teaching of the law: either because this teaching was contained in the five books of Moses, "The law was given through Moses" (above 1:17); or because it was given to men absorbed in sensible things, which are made known through the five senses. These loaves were of barley because the law was given in such a way that what was life-giving in it was concealed under physical signs: for the kernel in barley is covered with a very firm husk. Or, the loaves were of barley because the Jewish people had not yet been rubbed free of carnal desire, but it still covered their hearts like a husk: for in the Old Testament they outwardly experienced hardships because of their ceremonial observances: "A yoke, which neither our fathers nor we were able to bear" (Acts 15:10). Further, the Jews were engrossed in material things and did not understand the spiritual meaning of the law: "A veil is over their hearts" (2 Cor 3:15).

The two fishes, which gave a pleasant flavor to the bread, indicate the teachings of the Psalms and the prophets. Thus the old law not only had five loaves, i.e., the five books of Moses, but also two fishes, that is, the Psalms and the prophets. So the Old Testament writings are divided into these three: "The things written about me in the law of Moses, and in the prophets and in the Psalms" (Lk 24:44). Or, according to Augustine, the two fishes signify the priests and kings who ruled the Jews; and they prefigured Christ, who was the true king and priest.

But what are these for so many? for they could not bring man to a complete knowledge of the truth: for although God was known in Judea, the Gentiles did not know him.

855 Next (v 10), the miracle is presented. First, we see the people arranged; secondly, the miracle itself; and thirdly, the gathering of the leftovers. He does two things about the first. First, he shows Christ directing the disciples to have the people recline; secondly, why this was appropriate; and thirdly, he tells us the number of people present.

856 Our Lord told his disciples to arrange the people so that they could eat; thus Jesus says, **Make the people recline**, i.e, to eat. For as mentioned before, in former times people took their meals lying on couches; consequently, it was the custom to say of those who sat down to eat that they were reclining. In the mystical sense, this indicates that rest which is necessary for the perfection of wisdom. Again, the people are prepared by the disciples because it is through the disciples that the knowledge of the truth has come to us: "Let the mountains receive peace for the people" (Ps 71:3).

857 The character of the place shows why it was convenient that they recline, for **There was much grass in the place**. This is the literal meaning. In the mystical sense, grass indicates the flesh: "All flesh is grass" (Is 40:6). In this sense it can refer to two things. First, to the teachings of the Old Testament, which were given to a people resting in things of the flesh and wise according to the flesh: "If you are willing, and listen to me, you will eat the good things of the land" (Is 1:19); "The posterity of Jacob dwells in a land of grain, wine and oil" (Dt 33:28). Or, it can refer to one who perceives true wisdom, which cannot be attained without first abandoning the things of the flesh: "Do not imitate this world" (Rom 12:2).

858 There was a great number of people; thus he says, **the men reclined, in number about five thousand**. The Evangelist counted only the men, according to the custom in the law, for as mentioned in Numbers (1:3), Moses counted the people who were twenty years and older, without including the women. The Evangelist does the same, because only men can be completely instructed: "We speak wisdom to those who are mature" (1 Cor 2:6); "Solid food is for the mature" (Heb 5:14).

859 Then (v 11), the Evangelist presents the feeding of the crowd. First, we see the attitude of Christ; secondly, the food used; thirldy, that the people were satisfied. As to the attitude of Jesus, both his humility and his giving of thanks are mentioned.

860 We see his humility because he took the bread and gave it to the people. Now although in this miracle Christ could have fed the people with bread created from nothing, he chose to do so by multiplying bread that already existed. He did this, first, to show that sensible things do not come from the devil, as the Manichean error maintains. For if this were so, our Lord would not have used sensible things to praise God, especially since "The Son of God appeared to destroy the works of the devil" (1 Jn 3:8). He did it, secondly, to show that they are also wrong in claiming that the teachings of the Old Testament are not from God but from the devil. Thus, to show that the doctrine of the New Testament is none other than that which was prefigured and contained in the teachings of the Old Testament, he multiplied bread that already existed, implying by this that he is the one who fulfills the law and brings it to perfection: "I have not come to destroy the law, but to fulfill it," as we read in Matthew (5:17).

861 We see that he gave thanks, **when he had given thanks**. He did this to show that whatever he had, he had from another, that is, from his Father. This is an example for us to do the same. More particularly, he gave thanks to teach us that we should thank

God when we begin a meal: "Nothing is to be rejected if it is received with thanksgiving" (1 Tim 4:4); "The poor will eat and be satisfied; and they will praise the Lord" (Ps 21:27). Again, he gave thanks to teach us that he was not praying for himself, but for the people who were there, for he had to convince them that he had come from God. Accordingly, he prays before he works this miracle before them, in order to show them that he is not acting against God, but according to God's will.

We read in Mark (6:41) that Christ had the apostles distribute the bread to the people. It says here that he distributed it because in a way he himself does what he does by means of others. In the mystical sense, both statements are true: for Christ alone refreshes from within, and others, as his ministers, refresh from without.

862 Their food was bread and fish, about which enough has been said above.

Finally, those who ate were completely satisfied, because they took **as much as they wanted**. For Christ is the only one who feeds an empty soul and fills a hungry soul with good things: "I will be satisfied when your glory appears" (Ps 16:15). Others perform miracles through having grace in a partial manner; Christ, on the other hand, does so with unlimited power, since he does all things superabundantly. Hence it says that the people **had their fill**.

863 Now we see the leftovers collected (v 12). First, Christ gives the order; secondly, his disciples obey.

864 The Evangelist says that after the people had eaten their fill, Christ said to his disciples: **Gather up the fragments that are left over**. This was not pretentious display on our Lord's part; he did it to show that the miracle he accomplished was not imaginary, since the collected leftovers kept for some time and provided food for others. Again, he wanted to impress this miracle more firmly on the hearts of his disciples, whom he had carry the leftovers: for most of all he wanted to teach his disciples, who were destined to be the teachers of the entire world.

865 His disciples obeyed him faithfully; hence he says, **They therefore gathered and filled twelve baskets with the leftovers**. Here we should note that the amount of food that remained was not left to chance, but was according to plan: for as much as Christ willed was left over, no more and no less. This is shown by the fact that the basket of each apostle was filled. Now a basket is reserved for the work of peasants. Therefore, the twelve baskets signify the twelve apostles and those who imitate them, who, although they are looked down upon in this present life, are nevertheless filled with the riches of spiritual sacraments. There are twelve because they were to preach the faith of the Holy Trinity to the four parts of the world.

14 Now when these people saw that Jesus had worked a miracle, they said: "This is truly the Prophet who is to come into the world." 15 So Jesus, knowing that they would come to seize him and make him king, fled again into the mountains, alone. 16 When evening came, his disciples went down to the sea. 17 After they got into the boat, they set out across the sea to Capernaum. It was already dark, and Jesus had not yet come to them. 18 The sea became rough, agitated by a great wind. 19 After they had rowed twenty-five or thirty stadia [three or four miles], they saw Jesus walking on the water, coming toward the boat, and they were afraid. 20 But he said to them:

"It is I. Do not be afraid."

21 They then wanted to take him into the boat; and suddenly the boat was on the land toward which they were going.

866 Above, the Evangelist told us of the miracle of the loaves and fishes. Now he shows the threefold effect this miracle had on the people. First, its effect on their faith; secondly, on their plans to honor Jesus; thirdly, how it led them (and the disciples) to search for Jesus.

867 With respect to the first, we should note that the Jews said in the Psalm: "We have not seen our signs; there is now no prophet" (Ps 73:9). For it was customary in earlier days for the prophets to work many signs; so, when these signs were absent, prophecy seemed to have ended. But when the Jews see such signs, they believe that prophecy is returning. Accordingly, the people were so impressed by this miracle they just saw that they called our Lord a prophet. Thus we read, **Now when these people**, who had been filled with the five loaves, **saw that Jesus had worked a miracle, they said: This is truly the Prophet**. However, they did not yet have perfect faith, for they believed that Jesus was only a prophet, while he was also the Lord of the prophets. Yet, they were not entirely wrong, because our Lord called himself a prophet.

868 Here we should remark that a prophet is called a seer: "He who is now called a prophet was formerly called a seer" (1 Sm 9:9). Further, seeing pertains to the cognitive power. Now in Christ there were three kinds of knowledge. First of all, there was sense knowledge. And in this respect he had some similarity to the prophets, insofar as sensible species could be formed in the imagination of Christ to present future or hidden events. This was especially due to his passibility, which was appropriate to his state as a "wayfarer."

348

Secondly, Christ had intellectual knowledge; and in this he was not like the prophets, but was even superior to all the angels: for he was a "comprehensor" in a more excellent way than any creature. Again, Christ had divine knowledge, and in this way he was the one who inspired the prophets and the angels, since all knowledge is caused by a participation in the divine Word.

Still, these people seemed to realize that Christ was a superior prophet, for they said: **This is truly the Prophet.** For although there had been many prophets among the Jews, they were waiting for a particular one, according to: "The Lord your God will raise up a prophet for you" (Dt 18:15). This is the one they are speaking of here; thus it continues: **who is to come into the world.**

869 Next, we see the second effect of Christ's miracle: the honor the people planned for Christ, which he refused. First, we have the attempt by the people; secondly, Christ's flight from them.

870 The attempt of the people is mentioned when he says, **they would come to seize him and make him king.** A person or thing is seized if it is taken in a way that one does not will or is not opportune. Now it is true that God's plan from all eternity had been to establish the kingdom of Christ; but the time for this was not then opportune. Christ had come then, but not to reign in the way we ask for his reign when we say, "Your kingdom come" (Mt 6:10); at that time he will reign even as man. Another time was reserved for this: after the judgment of Christ, when the saints will appear in glory. It was about this kingdom the disciples asked when they said: "Lord, will you restore the kingdom to Israel at this time?" (Acts 1:6).

So the people, thinking he had come to reign, wanted to make him their king. The reason for this is that men often want as their ruler someone who will provide them with temporal things. Thus, because our Lord had fed them, they were willing to make him their king: "You have a mantle, be our ruler" (Is 3:6). Chrysostom says: "See the power of gluttony. They are no longer concerned about his breaking the Sabbath; they are no longer zealous for God. All these things are set in the background now that their bellies are full. Now he is regarded as a prophet among them, and they want to set him on the royal throne as their king."

871 We see Christ's flight when he says that he **fled again into the mountains, alone.** We can see from this that when our Lord had first seen the crowd of people he came down from the mountain and fed them in the valley, for we would not read that he went again into the mountains if he had not come down from them.

Why did Christ flee from the people, since he really is a king? There are three reasons for this. First, because it would have detracted from his dignity to have accepted a kingdom from men: for he is so great a king that all other kings are kings by participating in his kingship: "It is by me that kings rule" (Prv 8:15). Another reason is that it would have been harmful to his teaching if he had accepted this dignity and support from men; for he had worked and taught in such a way that everything was attributed to divine power and not to the influence of men: "Praise from men I do not need" (above 5:41). The third reason was to teach us to despise the dignities of this world: "I have given you an example that as I have done to you, so you should do also" (below 13:15); "Do not seek dignity from men" (Sir 7:4). And so, he refused the glory of this world, but still endured its punishment of his own will: "Jesus endured the cross, despising the shame, for the joy set before him" (Heb 12:2).

872   Matthew seems to conflict with this, for he says that "Jesus went up the mountain alone, to pray" (Mt 14:23). However, in the opinion of Augustine, there is no conflict here, because he had reason both to flee and to pray. For our Lord is teaching us that when a reason for flight draws near, there is great reason to pray.

In the mystical sense, Christ went up into the mountain when the people he had fed were ready to subject themselves to him, because he went up into heaven when the people were ready to subject themselves to the truth of the faith, according to: "A congregation of people will surround you. Return above for their sakes," i.e., return on high so a congratation of people may surround you (Ps 7:8).

He says that Christ **fled**, to indicate that the people could not understand his grandeur: for if we do not understand something, we say that it flees or eludes us.

873   Now he considers the third effect of Christ's miracle, the search for Christ. First, by his disciples; secondly, by the people. As to the first, he does two things. First, he tells of the eagerness of the disciples; and secondly, enlarges upon this (v 17b). He does two things about the first. First, he tells that they went down to the shore. Secondly, he tells of their journey across the sea (v 17).

874   Note, about the first, that Christ went up into the mountain without the knowledge of his disciples. So, they waited there until evening came, for they expected that he would come back to them. But their love was so great that when evening came they just had to go looking for him. Thus he says, **When evening came, his disciples went down to the sea**, looking for Jesus.

In the mystical sense, "evening" signifies our Lord's passion or his ascension. For as long as the disciples enjoyed Christ's physical presence, no trouble disturbed them and no bitterness vexed them: "Can the friends of the groom mourn as long as the groom is with them?" (Mt 9:15). But when Christ was away, then they "went down to the sea," to the troubles of this world: "This great sea, stretching wide" (Ps 103:25).

875 He adds that they crossed, saying, **After they got into the boat, they set out across the sea to Capernaum,** for the love that burned within them could not endure our Lord's absence for very long.

876 Now (17b), he enlarges upon what he had already said in summary fashion. First, on their going down to the sea; secondly, on their crossing (v 18).

877 As to the first, he says, **It was already dark, and Jesus had not yet come to them.** The Evangelist does not tell us this without a reason, for it shows the intensity of their love, since not even night or evening could stop them.

In the mystical sense, the "dark" signifies the absence of love; for light is love, according to: "He who loves his brother dwells in the light" (1 Jn 2:10). Accordingly, there is darkness in us when Jesus, "the true light" (above 1:9) does not come to us, because his presence repells all darkness.

Jesus left his disciples alone for this length of time so that they might experience his absence; and they did indeed experience it during the storm at sea: "Know and realize, that it is evil and bitter for you to have left the Lord" (Jer 2:19). He left them, in the second place, so that they might look for him more earnestly: "Where has your beloved gone, most beautiful of women? We will search for him with you" (Sg 5:17).

878 As for their crossing, first we see the storm at sea; then Christ coming to them, and the time; and thirdly, the effect this had.

879 The storm was caused by a rising wind; thus he says: **The sea became rough, agitated by a great wind.** This wind is a symbol for the trials and persecutions which would afflict the Church due to a lack of love. For as Augustine says, when love grows cold, the waves of the sea begin to swell and danger threatens the boat. Still, these winds and the storm, with its waves and darkness, did not stop the progress of the boat or so batter it that it broke apart: "He who perseveres to the end will be saved" (Mt 24:13); and again: "And the rains fell, and the floods came, and the house did not collapse," as we read in Matthew (7:25).

880 Christ did not appear to them when the storm first began, but only some time later; thus he says, **After they had rowed twenty-five or thirty stadia, they saw Jesus**. We see from this that our Lord allows us to be troubled for a while so our virtue may be tested; but he does not desert us in the end, but comes very close to us: "God is faithful, and will not allow you to be tested beyond your strength" (1 Cor 10:13).

According to Augustine, the twenty-five stadia they rowed are the five books of Moses. For twenty-five is the square of five, since five times five is twenty-five. But a number that is multiplied in this way keeps the meaning of its root. Thus, just as five signifies the old law, so twenty-five signifies the perfection of the New Testament. Thirty, however, signifies that perfection of the New Testament which was lacking in the law: for thirty is the result of multiplying five by six, which is a perfect number. So, Jesus comes to those who row twenty-five or thirty stadia, i.e., to those who fulfill the law or the perfection taught by the Gospel; and he comes treading under foot all the waves of pride and the dignities of this present world: "You rule the might of the sea and calm its waves" (Ps 88:10). And then we will see Christ near our boat, because divine help is close: "The Lord is near to all who fear him" (Ps 144:18). Thus it is clear that Christ is near to all those who seek him rightly. Now the Apostles loved Christ very keenly: this is obvious because they tried to go to him despite the darkness, the stormy sea, and the distance to shore. Consequently, Christ was with them.

881 Now we see the effect of Christ's appearance. First, the interior effect; secondly, the exterior effect (v 21b).

882 The interior effect of Christ's appearance was fear; and he mentions the fear of the disciples at the sudden appearance of Christ when he says, **and they were afraid**. This was a good fear, because it was the effect of humility: "Do not be proud; rather fear" (Rom 11:20); or it was an evil fear, because "they thought it was a ghost" (Mk 6:49); "They trembled with fear" (Ps 13:5): for fear is especially appropriate to the carnal, because they are afraid of spiritual things.

Secondly, we see Christ encouraging them against two dangers. First, they are encouraged against the danger to the faith in their intellect when he says, **It is I**, to eliminate their doubts: "Look at my hands and my feet! It is really me" (Lk 24:39). Secondly, Christ encourages them against the danger of fear in their emotions, saying, **Do not be afraid**: "Do not be afraid when they are present" (Jer 1:8); "The Lord is my light and my salvation; whom shall I fear" (Ps 26:1).

Thirdly, we see the reaction of the disciples, for **They then wanted to take him into the boat.** This signifies that we receive Christ by love and contemplation after servile fear has been taken out of our hearts: "I stand at the door and knock. If any one opens it for me, I will enter" (Rv 3:20).

883 There were two exterior effects: the storm abated, and their boat suddenly landed, although it had just been at a distance from the shore, for our Lord gave them a calm journey, without danger. He himself did not enter the boat because he wished to accomplish a greater miracle. So here we have three miracles: the walking on the sea, the quick calming of the storm, and the sudden arrival of the boat on the land although it had been far away. We learn from this that the faithful, in whom Christ is present, put down the swelling pride of this world, tread under their feet its waves of tribulation, and cross quickly to the land of the living: "Your good spirit will lead me to land" (Ps 142:10).

884 There are a number of difficulties here. The first concerns the literal sense: Matthew (14:22) seems to conflict with our present account for he says that the disciples were told by Christ to go the shore, while here it says the disciples went there to search for him. Another difficulty is that Matthew (14:34) says that the disciples crossed over to Gennesaret, while we read here that they came to Capernaum. The third difficulty is that Matthew (14:32) says that Christ got into the boat, but here he did not.

Chrysostom settles these difficulties quite briefly by saying that the two accounts do not deal with the same miracle. For, as he says, Christ frequently miraculously walked upon the sea in front of his disciples, but not for the people, lest they think he did not have a real body. But, according to Augustine, and this is the better opinion, John and Matthew are describing the same miracle. Augustine answers the first difficulty by saying it makes no difference that Matthew says the disciples went down to the shore because our Lord told them to. For it is possible that our Lord did so, and they went believing that he would sail with them. And that is why they waited until night, and when Christ did not come, they crossed by themselves.

There are two answers to the second difficulty. One is that Capernaum and Gennesaret are neighboring towns on the same shore. And perhaps the disciples landed at a place near both, so that Matthew mentions one and John the other. Or, it might be said that Matthew does not say that they came to Gennesaret immediately; they could have come first to Capernaum and then to Gennesaret. [The answer to the third difficulty is not given.]

22 On the next day, the crowd that stood on the other side of the sea saw that there was no second boat there, but only one, and that Jesus had not gone into the boat, but only his disciples had gone. 23 But other boats arrived from Tiberias, near the place where they had eaten the bread, after having given thanks to God. 24 When therefore the people saw that Jesus was not there, nor his disciples, they got into the boats and set off for Capernaum, looking for Jesus. 25 When they found him on the other side of the sea, they said: "Rabbi, when did you come here?" 26 Jesus replied and said:

"Amen, amen, I say to you:
you seek me not because you have seen miracles,
but because you have eaten of the bread
and have been filled.
27 Do not work for the food that perishes,
but for that which endures to eternal life,
which the Son of Man will give you,
for on him has God the Father set his seal."

28 Then they said to him: "What must we do that we may perform the works of God?" 29 Jesus replied and said to them:

"This is the work of God,
that you believe in him whom he sent."

30 They then said to him: "What sign then are you going to give that we may see and believe you? What work do you perform? 31 Our fathers ate manna in the desert, as it is written: 'He gave them bread from heaven to eat.' "

885   After having described how the disciples searched for Christ, the Evangelist now shows the people looking for him. First, he states their motive; secondly, the occasion; and thirdly, the search itself (v 24).

886   The crowd of people was looking for Christ because of the miracle mentioned above, that is, because he had crossed the sea without using any boat. They realized this because the other evening he had not been on the shore near where he had performed the miracle of the bread, and where there had been only one boat which had left for the opposite shore with the disciples, but without Christ. So that morning, when they could not find Christ on this side, since he was already on the other side although there was no other boat he could have used, they suspected that he had crossed by walking upon the sea. And this is what he says: **On the next day**, following the one on which he had worked the miracle of the bread, **the crowd that**

stood on the other side of the sea, where he had performed this miracle, **saw that there was no second boat there, but only one,** because the day before that was the only one there, and they had seen **that Jesus had not gone into the boat, but only his disciples had gone.** This one ship signifies the Church, which is one by its unity of faith and sacraments: "One faith, one baptism" (Eph 4:5). Again, our Lord's absence from his disciples signifies his physical absence from them at the ascension: "After the Lord Jesus spoke to them, he was taken up into heaven" (Mk 16:19).

887 It was the arrival of other boats from the opposite side of the sea that gave the people the opportunity to look for Christ; they could cross on these and search for him. He says: **But other boats arrived,** from the other side, that is, **from Tiberias, near the place where they had eaten the bread, after having given thanks to God.**

These other boats signify the various sects of heretics and of those who seek their own profit, and not the good of Jesus Christ: "You seek me ... because you have eaten of the bread and have been filled" (v 26). These groups are either separated in faith, as are the heretics, or in the love of charity, as are the carnal, who are not properly in the Church, but next to it, insofar as they have a feigned faith and the appearance of holiness: "They have the appearance of devotion, but deny its power" (2 Tim 3:5); "Do not be surprised if the ministers of Satan disguise themselves" (2 Cor 11:14).

888 The people were eager to find Christ. First, he shows how they looked for him; secondly, how they questioned him after they found him (v 25).

889 He says, **When the people saw that Jesus was not there, nor his disciples, they got into the boats,** which had come from Tiberias, **looking for Jesus**; and this is praiseworthy: "Search for the Lord while he can be found" (Is 55:6); "Seek the Lord, and your soul will have life" (Ps 68:33).

890 Once they found him, they questioned him. **When they,** the people, **found him,** Christ, **on the other side of the sea,** they asked him: **Rabbi, when did you come here?** This can be understood in two ways. In the first way, they were asking about the time only. And then, Chrysostom says, they should be rebuked for their rudeness, because, after such a miracle, they did not ask how he crossed without a boat, but only when he did so. Or, it can be said that by asking **when,** they wanted to know not just the time, but the other circumstances connected with this miraculous crossing.

891   Note that now, after they have found Christ, they do not wish do make him their king, while before, after he had fed them, they did. They wanted to make him their king then because they were emotionally excited with the joy of their meal; but such emotions quickly pass. So it is that things that we plan according to our emotions do not last; but matters that we arrange by our reason last longer: "A wise man continues on in his wisdom like the sun; a fool changes like the moon" (Sir 27:12); "The work of the wicked will not last" (Prv 11:18)

892   Then (v 26), our Lord begins to mention a food that is spiritual. First, he states a truth about this spiritual food. In the second place, he clears up a misunderstanding (6:41). As to the first he does three things. First, he presents a truth about this spiritual food; secondly, he mentions its origin; and thirdly, he tells them how this spiritual food is to be acquired (6:34). He does two things about the first. First, he explains this spiritual food and its power; in the second place, he tells what this food is (v 28). As to the first, he does two things. First, he rebukes them for their disordered desires; in the second place, he urges them to accept the truth (v 27).

893   He says, **Amen, amen, I say to you,** that although you seem to be devout, **you seek me not because you have seen miracles, but because you have eaten of the bread and have been filled.** As if to say: You seek me, not for the sake of the spirit, but for the sake of the flesh, because you hope for more food. As Augustine says, these people represent those who seek Jesus not for himself, but in order to gain certain worldly advantages: as those engaged in some business call on clerics and prelates, not for the sake of Christ, but so that through their intervention they might be advanced into the ranks of those who are important; and like those who hurry to the churches, not for Christ, but because they have been urged to do so by those who are more powerful; and like those who approach our Lord for sacred orders not because they desire the merits of the virtues, but because they are looking for the satisfactions of this present life, as wealth and praise, as Gregory says in his *Moralia.* This is obvious: for to perform miracles is a work of divine power, but to eat loaves of bread which have been multiplied is temporal. Accordingly, those who do not come to Christ because of the power they see in him, but because they eat his bread, are not serving Christ but their own stomachs, as we see from Philippians (3:19); and again, "He will praise you when you are good to him," as we read in the Psalm (48:19).

894   He leads them back to the truth by calling their attention to spiritual food, saying, **Do not work for the food that perishes,**

but for that which endures to eternal life. First, he mentions its power; secondly, that it comes from him, **which the Son of Man will give you**.

895 The power of this food is seen in the fact that it does not perish. In this respect we should point out that material things are likenesses of spiritual things, since they are caused and produced by them; and consequently they resemble spiritual things in some way. Now just as the body is sustained by food, so that which sustains the spirit is called its food, whatever it might be. The food that sustains the body is perishable, since it is converted into the nature of the body; but the food that sustains the spirit is not perishable, because it is not converted into the spirit; rather, the spirit is converted into its food. Hence Augustine says in his *Confessions*: "I am the food of the great; grow and you will eat me. But you will not change me into yourself, as you do bodily food, but you will be changed into me."

So our Lord says: **work**, i.e., seek by your work, or merit by your works, **not for the food that perishes**, i.e., bodily food: "Food is for the stomach, and the stomach for food, but God will destroy both" (1 Cor 6:13), because we will not always need food; but **work for that which**, that is, the spiritual food, **endures to eternal life**. This food is God himself, insofar as he is the Truth which is to be contemplated and the Goodness which is to be loved, which nourish the spirit: "Eat my bread" (Prv 9:5); "Wisdom will feed him with the bread of life and understanding" (Sir 15:5). Again, this food is the obedience to the divine commands: "My food is to do the will of him who sent me" (above 4:34). Also, it is Christ himself: "I am the bread of life" (6:35); "My flesh truly is food and my blood truly is drink" (6:56): and this is so insofar as the flesh of Christ is joined to the Word of God, which is the food by which the angels live. The difference between bodily and spiritual food which he gives here, is like the one he gave before between bodily and spiritual drink: "Whoever drinks this water will be thirsty again, but whoever drinks the water that I give, will never be thirsty again" (4:13). The reason for this is that bodily things are perishable, while spiritual things, and especially God, are eternal.

896 We should note that according to Augustine, in his work, *On the Labor of Monks*, that certain monks misunderstood our Lord's saying, **Do not work for the food that perishes**, and claimed that spiritual men should not perform physical work. But this interpretation is false because Paul, who was most spiritual, worked with his hands; as we read in Ephesians, there he says (4:28): "Let him who stole, steal no longer; rather let him work with his hands." The correct interpretation, therefore, is that we should direct our

work, i.e., our main interest and intention, to seeking the food that leads to eternal life, that is, spiritual goods. In regard to temporal goods, they should not be our principal aim but a subordinate one, that is, they are to be acquired only because of our mortal body, which has to be nourished as long as we are living this present life. So the Apostle speaks against this opinion, saying: "If any one will not work, neither let him eat" (2 Thes 3:10); as if to say: those who maintain that physical work is not to be done should not eat, since eating is physical.

897 Next (v 27), he mentions the one who gives this spiritual food. First, we see the author of this food; secondly, the source of his authority to give us this food. Christ is the author of this spiritual food, and the one who gives it to us. Thus he says, **which**, that is, the food that does not perish, **the Son of Man will give you**. If he had said, "the Son of God," it would not have been unexpected; but he captures their attention by saying that **the Son of Man** gives this food. Yet the Son of Man gives this food in a spiritual way, because human nature, weakened by sin, found spiritual food distasteful, and was not able to take it in its spirituality. Thus it was necessary for the Son of Man to assume flesh and nourish us with it: "You have prepared a table before me" (Ps 22:5).

898 He adds the source of his authority to give us this food when he says, **for on him has God the Father set his seal**. As if to say: the Son of Man will give us this food because he surpasses all the sons of men by his unique and preeminent fulness of grace. Thus he says, **on him**, i.e., on the Son of Man, **has God the Father set his seal**, i.e., he has significantly distinguished him from others: "God, your God, has anointed you with the oil of gladness above your fellows" (Ps 44:8).

Hilary explains it this way. **God set his seal**, i.e., impressed with a seal. For when a seal is impressed on wax, the wax retains the entire figure of the seal, just as the Son has received the entire figure of the Father. Now the Son receives from the Father in two ways. One of these ways is eternal, and **set his seal** does not refer to this way, because when something is sealed the nature receiving the seal is not the same as the nature impressing the seal. Rather, these words should be understood as referring to the mystery of the incarnation, because God the Father has impressed his Word on human nature; this Word who is "the brightness of his glory, and the figure of his substance" (Heb 1:3).

Chrysostom explains it this way. God the Father has **set his seal**, i.e., God the Father specifically chose Christ to give eternal life to the world: "I came that they may have life" (below 10:10). For when someone is chosen to perform some great task, he is said to be sealed for that task: "After this, the Lord appointed (*designo*, appoint; *signo*, seal, mark) seventy other disciples" (Lk 10:1).

Or, it could be said that God the Father **set his seal**, i.e., Christ was made known by the Father, by his voice at Christ's baptism, and by his works, as we saw in the fifth chapter.

899 Next (v 28), we see the nature of spiritual food. First, the Jews pose their question; in the second place, we have the answer of Jesus Christ (v 29).

900 Concerning the first, we should note that the Jews, since they had been taught by the law, believed that only God was eternal. So when Christ said that his food would endure to eternal life, they understood that it would be a divine food. Thus when they question Christ, they do not mention this food, but rather the work of God, saying: **What must we do that we may perform the works of God?** Indeed, they were not far from the truth, since spiritual food is nothing else than performing and accomplishing the works of God: "What shall I do to gain eternal life?" (Lk 18:18).

901 The Lord's answer is given when he says: **This is the work of God, that you believe in him whom he sent.** Here we should reflect that in Romans (4:2), the Apostle distinguished faith from works, saying that Abraham was justified by his faith, not by his works. If this is so, why does our Lord say here that to have faith, i.e., to believe, is a work of God? There are two answers to this. One is that the Apostle is not distinguishing faith from absolutely all works, but only from external works. External works, being performed by our body, are more noticeable, and so the word "works" ordinarily refers to them. But there are other works, interior works, performed within the soul, and these are known only to the wise and those converted in heart.

From another point of view, we can say that to believe can be regarded as included in our external works, not in the sense that it is an external work, but because it is the source of these works.

Thus he significantly says: **that you believe in him** (*in illum*). Now it is one thing to say: "I believe in God," (*credere Deum*), for this indicates the object. It is another thing to say: "I believe God," (*credere Deo*), for this indicates the one who testifies. And it is still another thing to say: "I believe in God," (*in Deum*), for this indicates the end. Thus God can be regarded as the object of faith, as the one who testifies, and as the end, but in different ways. For the object of faith can be a creature, as when I believe in the creation of the heavens. Again, a creature can be one who testifies, for I believe

Paul (*credo Paulo*) or any of the saints. But only God can be the end of faith, for our mind is directed to God alone as its end. Now the end, since it has the character of a good, is the object of love. Thus, to believe in God (*in Deum*) as in an end is proper to faith living through the love of charity. Faith, living in this way, is the principle of all our good works; and in this sense to believe is said to be a work of God.

902 But if faith is a work of God, how do men do the works of God? Isaiah (26:12) gives us the answer when he says: "You have accomplished all our works for us." For the fact that we believe, and any good we do, is from God: "It is God who is working in us, both to will and to accomplish" (Phil 2:13). Thus he explicitly says that to believe is a work of God in order to show us that faith is a gift of God, as Ephesians (2:8) maintains.

903 Next, we see the origin of this food. First, we have the question asked by the Jews; secondly, the answer of Christ (v 32). Three things are done about the first: first, the Jews look for a sign; secondly, they decide what it should be; and thirdly, they bring in what is narrated in Scripture.

904 They look for a sign by asking Christ: **What sign then are you going to give that we may see and believe you?** This question is explained differently by Augustine and by Chrysostom. Chrysostom says that our Lord was leading them to the faith. But the evidence that leads one to the faith are miracles: "Signs were given to unbelievers" (1 Cor 14:22). And so the Jews were looking for a sign in order to believe, for it is their custom to seek such signs: "For Jews demand signs" (1 Cor 1:22). So they say: **What sign then are you going to give?**

But it seems foolish to ask for a miracle for this reason, for Christ had just performed some in their presence which could lead them to believe, as multiplying the bread and walking on the water. What they were asking was that our Lord always provide them with food. This is clear because the only sign they mention is the one given by Moses to their ancestors for forty years, and they ask in this way that Christ always provide food for them. Thus they say: **Our fathers ate manna in the desert.** They did not say that God provided their ancestors with the manna, so that they would not seem to be making Christ equal to God. Again, they did not say that Moses fed their ancestors, so they would not seem to be preferring Moses to Christ, trying in this way to influence our Lord. We read of this food: "Man ate the bread of angels" (Ps 77:25).

905 According to Augustine, however, our Lord had said that he would give them food that would endure to eternal life.

Thus, he seemed to put himself above Moses. The Jews, on the other hand, considered Moses greater than Christ; so they said: "We know that God spoke to Moses, but we do not know where this man is from" (below 9:29). Accordingly, they required Christ to accomplish greater things than Moses; and so they recall what Moses did, saying: **Our Fathers ate manna in the desert.** As if to say: What you say about yourself is greater than what Moses did, for you are promising a food that does not perish, while the manna that Moses gave became wormy if saved for the next day. Therefore, if we are to believe you, do something greater than Moses did. Although you have fed five thousand men once with five barley loaves, this is not greater than what Moses did, for he fed all the people with manna from heaven for forty years, and in the desert too: "He gave them the bread of heaven" (Ps 77:24).

LECTURE 4

32 Jesus therefore said to them:
 "Amen, amen, I say to you:
 Moses did not give you bread from heaven,
 but my Father gives you true bread from heaven.
 33 For the true bread is that which descends
 from heaven, and gives life to the world."
34 They then said to him: "Lord, give us this bread always." 35 But Jesus said to them:
 "I am the bread of life.
 Whoever comes to me shall not hunger;
 and whoever believes in me shall never thirst.
 36 But I have told you that you have both seen me
 and do not believe.
 37 All that the Father gives me shall come to me;
 and the one who comes to me I will not cast out,
 38 because I have come down from heaven,
 not to do my own will,
 but the will of him who sent me.
 39 Now it is the will of him who sent me, the Father,
 that of all that he has given me I should lose nothing,
 but raise it up on the last day.
 40 For this is the will of my Father, who sent me,
 that every one who sees the Son and believes in him,
 should have eternal life.
 And I will raise him up on the last day."

906   Having told us the question the Jews had asked Christ, the Evangelist now gives his answer. First, Christ tells us of the origin of this spiritual food; secondly, he proves what he has just said (v 33).

907   Concerning the first, we should note that the Jews had mentioned two things to Christ concerning the bodily food which had been given to their ancestors: the one who gave this food, Moses, and the place, that is, from heaven. Accordingly, when our Lord tells them about the origin of spiritual food, he does not mention these two, for he says that there is another who gives this food and another place. He says: **Amen, amen, I say to you: Moses did not give you bread from heaven.** There is another who gives to you, that is, **my Father**; and he gives, not just bodily bread, but **the true bread from heaven.**

908   But was it not true bread that their ancestors had in the desert? I answer that if you understand "true" as contrasted with "false," then they had true bread, for the miracle of the manna was a true miracle. But if "true" is contrasted with "symbolic," then that bread was not true, but was a symbol of spiritual bread, that is, of our Lord Jesus Christ, whom that manna signified, as the Apostle says: "All ate the same spiritual food" (1 Cor 10:3).

909   When the Psalm (77:24) says, "He gave them the bread of heaven," this seems to conflict with, **Moses did not give you bread from heaven.** I answer that the word "heaven" can be understood in three ways. Sometimes it can mean the air, as in "The birds of heaven ate them" (Mt 13:4); and also in, "The Lord thundered from heaven" (Ps 14:14). Sometimes "heaven" means the starry sky; as in, "The highest heaven is the Lord's" (Ps 113:16), and in, "The stars will fall from heaven" (Mt 24:19). Thirdly, it can signify goods of a spiritual nature, as in "Rejoice and be glad, because your reward is great in heaven" (Mt 5:12). So the manna was from heaven, not the heaven of the stars or of spiritual food, but from the air. Or, the manna was said to be from heaven insofar as it was a symbol of the true bread from heaven, our Lord Jesus Christ.

910   When he says, **For the true bread is that which descends from heaven, and gives life to the world**, he proves that it is from heaven by its effect. For the true heaven is spiritual in nature, and has life by its own essence; therefore, of itself, it gives life: "It is the spirit that gives life" (below 6:64). Now God himself is the author of life. Therefore, we know that this spiritual bread is from heaven when it produces its proper effect, if it gives life. That bodily bread used by the Jews did not give life, since all who ate the manna died. But this [spiritual] bread does give life; so he says: **the true**

bread, not that symbolic bread, **is that which descends from heaven**. This is clear, because it **gives life to the world**: for Christ, who is the true bread, gives life to whom he wills: "I came that they may have life" (below 10:10). He also descended from heaven: "No one has gone up to heaven except the One who came down from heaven" (above 3:13). Thus Christ, the true bread, gives life to the world by reason of his divinity; and he descends from heaven by reason of his human nature, for as we said on the prior text, he came down from heaven by assuming human nature: "He emptied himself, taking the form of a servant" (Phil 2:7).

911 Now he considers the acquisition of this spiritual food. First, we see the Jews asking for it; secondly, he shows the way it is acquired (v 35).

912 We should note with respect to the first, that the Jews understood what Christ said in a material way; and so, because they desired material things, they were looking for material bread from Christ. Hence they said to him, **Lord, give us this bread always**, which physically nourishes us. The Samaritan woman also understood what our Lord said about spiritual water in a material way, and wishing to slake her thirst, said, "Give me this water" (above 4:15). And although these people understood what our Lord said about food in a material way, and asked for it this way, we are expected to ask for it as understood in a spiritual way: "Give us this day our daily bread" (Mt 6:11), because we cannot live without this bread.

913 Then, he shows how this bread is acquired. First, he shows what this bread is; secondly, how to obtain it (v 37). Concerning the first, he does three things. First, he explains what this bread is, **I am the bread of life**; secondly, he gives the reason for this, **Whoever comes to me shall not hunger**; thirdly, he shows why this had to be explained (v 36).

914 Jesus said to them: **I am the bread of life**, for as we saw above, the word of wisdom is the proper food of the mind, because the mind is sustained by it: "He fed him with the bread of life and understanding" (Sir 15:3). Now the bread of wisdom is called the bread of life to distinguish it from material bread, which is the bread of death, and which serves only to restore what has been lost by a mortal organism; hence material bread is necessary only during this mortal life. But the bread of divine wisdom is life-giving of itself, and no death can affect it. Again, material bread does not give life, but only sustains for a time a life that already exists. But spiritual bread actually gives life: for the soul begins to live because it adheres to the word of God: "For with you is the fountain of life," as we

see in the Psalm (35:10). Therefore, since every word of wisdom is derived from the Only Begotten Word of God —"The fountain of wisdom is the Only Begotten of God" (Sir 1:5) — this Word of God is especially called the bread of life. Thus Christ says, **I am the bread of life**. And because the flesh of Christ is united to the Word of God, it also is life-giving. Thus, too, his body, sacramentally received, is life-giving: for Christ gives life to the world through the mysteries which he accomplished in his flesh. Consequently, the flesh of Christ, because of the Word of the Lord, is not the bread of ordinary life, but of that life which does not die. And so the flesh of Christ is called bread: "The bread of Asher is rich" (Gn 49:20).

His flesh was also signified by the manna. "Manna" means "What is this?" because when the Jews saw it they wondered, and asked each other what it was. But nothing is more a source of wonder than the Son of God made man, so that everyone can fittingly ask, "What is this?" That is, how can the Son of God be the Son of Man? How can Christ be one person with two natures? "His name will be called Wonderful" (Is 9:6). It is also a cause for wonder how Christ can be present in the sacrament.

915 Next (v 35), he gives the reason for this from the effect of this [spiritual] bread. When material bread is eaten, it does not permanently take away our hunger, since it must be destroyed in order to build us up; and this is necessary if we are to be nourished. But spiritual bread, which gives life of itself, is never destroyed; consequently, a person who eats it once never hungers again. Thus he says: **Whoever comes to me shall not hunger; and whoever believes in me shall never thirst.**

According to Augustine, it is the same thing to say, **whoever comes**, as to say, **whoever believes**: since it is the same to come to Christ and to believe in him , for we do not come to God with bodily steps, but with those of the mind, the first of which is faith. To eat and to drink are also the same: for each signifies that eternal fulness where there is no want: "Blessed are they who hunger and thirst for what is right, for they will be filled" (Mt 5:6); so that food which sustains and that drink which refreshes are one and the same.

One reason why temporal things do not take away our thirst permanently is that they are not consumed altogether, but only bit by bit, and with motion, so that there is always still more to be consumed. For this reason, just as there is enjoyment and satisfaction from what has been consumed, so there is a desire for what is still to come. Another reason is that they are destroyed; hence the recollection of them remains and generates a repeated longing for those things. Spiritual things, on the other hand, are taken all at once, and they are not destroyed, nor do they run out; and consequently the fulness they produce remains forever: "They will neither hunger nor thirst" (Rv 7:16); "Your face will fill me with joy; the delights in your right hand (i.e., in spiritual goods) will last forever," as the Psalm (16:11) says.

916 Then (v 36), we see why Christ had to explain these things. For someone could say: We asked for bread; but you did not answer, "I will give it to you," or "I will not." Rather, you say, **I am the bread of life**; and so your answer does not seem to be appropriate. But our Lord shows that it is a good answer, saying, **I have told you that you have both seen me and do not believe**. This is the same as a person having bread right in front of him without his knowing it, and then being told: Look! The bread is right before you. And so Christ says: **I have told you (I am the bread of life) that you have both seen me and do not believe**, i.e., you want bread, and it is right before you; and yet you do not take it because you do not believe. In saying this he is censuring them for their unbelief: "They have seen and hated both me and my Father" (below 15:24).

917 Then (v 37), he shows how this bread is acquired. First, he mentions the way to acquire it; secondly, the end attained by those who come to him (v 37b); thirdly, he enlarges on this (v 38).

918 Concerning the first, we should note that the very fact that we believe is a gift of God to us: "You are saved by grace, through faith; and this is not due to yourself, for it is the gift of God" (Eph 2:8); "It has been granted to you not only to believe in him, but also to suffer for him" (Phil 1:29). Sometimes, God the Father is said to give those who believe to the Son, as here: **All that the Father gives me shall come to me**. At other times, the Son is said to give them to the Father, as in 1 Corinthians (15:24): "He will hand over the kingdom to God and the Father." We can see from this that just as the Father does not deprive himself of the kingdom in giving to the Son, neither does the Son in giving to the Father. The Father gives to the Son insofar as the Father makes a person adhere to his Word: "Through whom (that is, the Father) you have been called into the fellowship of his Son" (1 Cor 1:9). The Son, on the other hand, gives to the Father insofar as the Word makes the Father known: "I have made known your name to those you have given me" (below 17:6). Thus Christ says: **All that the Father gives me shall come to me**, i.e., those who believe in me, whom the Father makes adhere to me by his gift.

919 Perhaps some might say that it is not necessary for one to use God's gift: for many receive God's gift and do not use it. So how

can he say: **All that the Father gives me shall come to me?** We must say to this that in tnis giving we have to include not only the habit, which is faith, but also the interior impulse to believe. So, everything which contributes to salvation is a gift of God.

920 There is another question. If everything which the Father gives to Christ comes to him, as he says, then only those come to God whom the Father gives him. Thus, those who do not come are not responsible, since they are not given to him. I answer that they are not responsible if they cannot come to the faith without the help of God. But those who do not come are responsible, because they create an obstacle to their own coming by turning away from salvation, the way to which is of itself open to all.

921 Then (v 37b), the end attained by those who come is mentioned. For some might say, "We will come to you, but you will not receive us." To exclude this he says, **the one who comes to me,** by steps of faith and by good works, **I will not cast out.** By this he lets us understand that he is already within, for one must be within before one can be sent out. Let us consider, therefore, what is interior, and how one is cast out from it.

We should point out that since all visible things are said to be exterior with respect to spiritual things, then the more spiritual something is the more interior it is. What is interior is twofold. The first is the most profound, and is the joy of eternal life. According to Augustine, this is a sweet and most interior retreat, without any weariness, without the bitterness of evil thoughts, and uninterrupted by temptations and sorrows. We read of this: "Share the joy of your Lord" (Mt 25:21); and, "You will hide them in the secret of your face," that is, in the full vision of your essence (Ps 30:21). From this interior no one is cast out: "He who conquers, I will make him a pillar in the temple of the living God; and he will no longer leave it" (Rv 3:12), because "the just will go to everlasting life," as we see from Matthew (25:46). The other interior is that of an upright conscience; and this is a spiritual joy. We read of this: "When I enter into my house I will enjoy repose" (Wis 8:16); and "The king has brought me into his storerooms" (Sg 1:3). It is from this interior that some are cast out.

So, when our Lord says, **the one who comes to me I will not cast out,** we can understand this in two ways. In one way, those who come to him are those who have been given to him by the Father through eternal predestination. Of these he says: **the one who comes to me,** predestined by the Father, **I will not cast out:** "God has not rejected his people, the people he chose" (Rom 11:2). In a second way, those who do go out are not cast out by Christ; rather, they cast themselves out, because through their unbelief and sins they abandon the sanctuary of an upright conscience. Thus we read: **I will not cast out** such; but they do cast themselves out: "You are the burden, and I will cast you aside, says the Lord" (Jer 23:33). It was in this way that the man who came to the wedding feast without wedding clothes was cast out (Mt 22:13).

922 Next (v 38), he gives the reason for what he just said. First, he mentions his intention to accomplish the will of the Father; secondly, he states what the will of the Father is (v 39); and thirdly, he shows the final accomplishment of this will (v 40b).

923 Concerning the first, we should note that this passage can be read in two ways: either as Augustine does, or following the interpretation of Chrysostom. Augustine understands it this way: **the one who comes to me I will not cast out**; and this is because the one who comes to me imitates my humility. In Matthew (11:29), after our Lord said, "Come to me, all you who labor," he added, "Learn from me, for I am gentle and humble of heart." Now the true gentleness of the Son of God consists in the fact that he submitted his will to the will of the Father. Thus he says, **the one who comes to me I will not cast out, because I have come down from heaven, not to do my own will, but the will of him who sent me**. Since a soul abandons God because of its pride, it must return in humility, coming to Christ by imitating his humility; and this humility of Christ was in not doing his own will, but the will of God the Father.

Here we should note that there were two wills in Christ. One pertains to his human nature, and this will is proper to him, both by nature and by the will of the Father. His other will pertains to his divine nature, and this will is the same as the will of the Father. Christ subordinated his own will, that is, his human will, to the divine will, because, wishing to accomplish the will of the Father, he was obedient to the Father's will: "My God, I desired to do your will" (Ps 39:9). We ask that this will be accomplished in our regard when we say, "Your will be done" (Mt 6:10). Thus, those who do the will of God, not their own will, are not cast out. The devil, who wanted to do his own will out of pride, was cast from heaven; and so too the first man was expelled from paradise.

Chrysostom explains the passage this way. The reason I do not cast out one who comes to me is because I have come to accomplish the will of the Father concerning the salvation of men. So, if I have become incarnate for the salvation of men, how can I cast them out? And this is what he says: I will not cast out one who comes, **because I have come down from heaven, not to do my own will**, my human will, so as to obtain my own benefit, **but the will of him who sent**

me, that is, the Father, "He desires the salvation of all men" (1 Tim 2:4). And therefore, so far as I am concerned, I do not cast out any person: "For if, when we were enemies, we were reconciled to God by the death of his Son, now much more, having been reconciled, we will be saved by his life" (Rom 5:10).

924 Then (v 39), he shows what the Father wills; and next, why he wills it (v 40).

925 He says: I will not cast out those who come to me, because I have taken flesh in order to do the will of the Father: **Now it is the will of him who sent me, the Father**, that those who come to me **I will not cast out**; and so I will not cast them out. "This is the will of God, your sanctification" (1 Thes 4:3). Therefore he says that it is the will of the Father **that of all that he**, the Father, **has given me I should lose nothing**, i.e., that I should lose nothing until the time of the resurrection. At this time some will be lost, the wicked; but none of those given to Christ through eternal predestination will be among them: "The way of the wicked will perish" (Ps 1:7). Those, on the other hand, who are preserved until then, will not be lost.

Now when he says, **lose**, we should not understand this as implying that he needs such people or that he is damaged if they perish. Rather, he says this because he desires their salvation and what is good for them, which he regards as his own good.

926 What John later reports Christ as saying seems to conflict with this: "None of them," that is, of those you have given me, "have been lost except the son of perdition" (below 17:12). Thus, some of those given to Christ through eternal predestination are lost. Accordingly, what he says here, **that of all that he has given me I should lose nothing**, is not true. We must say to this that some are lost from among those given to Christ through a present justification; but none are lost from among those given to him through eternal predestination.

927 Now he gives the reason for the divine will (v 40). The reason why the Father wills that I lose nothing of all that he has given me is that the Father wills to bring men to life spiritually, because he is the fountain of life. And since the Father is eternal, he wills, absolutely speaking, that every one who comes to me should have eternal life. And this is what he says: **For this is the will of my Father, who sent me, that every one who sees the Son and believes in him, should have eternal life**. Note that he said above: "Whoever hears my voice and believes in him who sent me, possesses eternal life" (above 5:24), while here he says: **every one who sees the Son**

and believes in him. We can understand from this that the Father and the Son have the same divine nature; and it is the vision of this, through its essence, that is our ultimate end and the object of our faith. When he says here, sees the Son, he is referring to the physical sight of Christ which leads to faith, and not to this vision through essence which faith precedes. Thus he expressly says, every one who sees the Son and believes in him: "Whoever believes in him ... will not encounter judgment, but has passed from death to life" (above 5:24); "These things are written that you may believe that Jesus Christ is the Son of God, and that believing you may have life in his name" (below 20:31).

928   This will of the Father will also be accomplished. So he adds: And I will raise him up on the last day, for he wills that we have eternal life not just in our soul alone, but also in our body, as Christ did at his resurrection: "Many of those who sleep in the dust of the earth will awake: some to an everlasting life, and others to everlasting shame" (Dn 12:2); "Christ, having risen from the dead, will not die again" (Rom 6:9).

LECTURE 5

41 The Jews therefore grumbled about him because he had said, "I am the living bread that has come down from heaven." 42 And they said: "Is he not the son of Joseph? Do we not know his father and mother? How then can he say that he has come down from heaven?" 43 Jesus responded and said to them:
"Stop grumbling among yourselves.
44 No one can come to me
unless the Father, who sent me, draws him.
And I will raise him up on the last day.
45 It is written in the prophets:
'They shall all be taught by God.'
Every one who has heard the Father and has learned,
comes to me.
46 Not that any one has seen the Father,
except the one who is from God –
he has seen the Father."

929   Those opinions that conflict with the above teaching of Christ are now rejected. First, those of the people, who were discontented; secondly, those of the disciples, who were in a state of doubt (v 61).

He does two things about the first. First, we see the people grumble about the origin of this spiritual food; secondly, we see Christ check the dispute which arose over the eating of this spiritual food (v 53). As to the first he does two things. First, he mentions the grumbling of the people; secondly, how it was checked (v 43). As to the first he does two things. First, he shows the occasion for this complaining; secondly, what those complaining said (v 42).

930 He continues that some of the people were grumbling over what Christ had said, that is, because Christ had said, **I am the living bread that has come down from heaven**, a spiritual bread they did not understand or desire. And so they grumbled because their minds were not fixed on spiritual things. They were following in this case the custom of their ancestors: "They grumbled in their tents" (Ps 105:25); "Do not grumble, as some of them did" (1 Cor 10:10). As Chrysostom says, they had not complained till now because they still hoped to obtain material food; but as soon as they lost that hope, they began to grumble, although they pretended that it was for a different reason. Yet they did not contradict him openly due to the respect they had for him arising from his previous miracle.

931 He says those who complained said: **Is he not the son of Joseph?** For since they were earthly minded, they only considered Christ's physical generation, which hindered them from recognizing his spiritual and eternal generation. And so we see them speaking only of earthly things, "He who is of earth is earthly and speaks of earthly things" (above 3:31), and not understanding what is spiritual. Thus they said: **How then can he say that he has come down from heaven?** They called him the son of Joseph as this was the general opinion, for Joseph was his foster father: "the son of Joseph (as was supposed)" (Lk 3:23).

932 Next (v 43), the grumbling of the people is checked. First, Christ stops this complaining; secondly, he clears up their difficulty (v 47). As to the first he does two things. First, he checks their complaining, secondly, he tells why they were doing it (v 44).

933 Jesus noticed that they were grumbling and checked them, saying, **Stop grumbling among yourselves.** This was good advice, for those who complain show that their minds are not firmly fixed on God; and so we read in Wisdom (1:11): "Keep yourselves from grumbling, for it does no good."

934 The reason for their grumbling was their unbelief, and he shows this when he says, **No one can come to me** .... First, he shows that if one is to come to Christ, he has to be drawn by the Father. Secondly, he shows the way one is drawn (v 45). As to the first he does three things. First, he mentions that coming to Christ surpasses

human ability; secondly, the divine help we receive for this; and thirdly, the end or fruit of this help.

That we should come to Christ through faith surpasses our human ability; thus he says, **No one can come to me.** Secondly, divine help is effective in helping us to this; thus he says, **unless the Father, who sent me, draws him.** The end or fruit of this help is the very best, so he adds, **And I will raise him up on the last day.**

935 He says first: It is not unexpected that you are grumbling, because my Father had not yet drawn you to me, for **No one can come to me,** by believing in me, **unless the Father, who sent me, draws him.**

There are three questions here. The first is about his saying: **unless the Father draws him.** For since we come to Christ by believing, then, as we said above, to come to Christ is to believe in him. But no one can believe unless he wills to. Therefore, since to be drawn implies some kind of compulsion, one who comes to Christ by being drawn is compelled.

I answer that what we read here about the Father drawing us does not imply coercion, because there are some ways of being drawn that do not involve compulsion. Consequently, the Father draws men to the Son in many ways, using the different ways in which we can be drawn without compulsion. One person may draw another by persuading him with a reason. The Father draws us to his Son in this way by showing us that he is his Son. He does this in two ways. First, by an interior revelation, as in: "Blessed are you, Simon Bar-Jona, for flesh and blood has not revealed this to you (that is, that Christ is the Son of the living God), but it was done so by my Father" (Mt 16:17). Secondly, it can be done through miracles, which the Son has the power to do from the Father: "The very works which my Father has given me to perform ... they bear witness to me" (above 5:36).

Again, one person draws another by attracting or captivating him: "She captivated him with her flattery" (Prv 7:21). This is the way the Father draws those who are devoted to Jesus on account of the authority of the paternal greatness. For the Father, i.e., the paternal greatness, draws those who believe in Christ because they believe that he is the Son of God. Arius – who did not believe that Christ was the true Son of God, nor begotten of the substance of the Father – was not drawn in this way. Neither was Photinus – who dogmatized that Christ was a mere man. So, this is the way those who are captivated by his greatness are drawn by the Father. But they are also drawn by the Son, through a wonderful joy and love of the truth, which is the very Son of God himself. For if, as Augustine says, each of us is drawn by his own pleasure, how much more strongly ought we to be drawn to Christ if we find our pleasure in truth, happiness, justice, eternal life: all of which Christ is! Therefore, if we would be drawn by him, let us be drawn through love for the truth, according to: "Take delight in the Lord, and he will give you the desires of your heart" (Ps 36:4). And so in the Song of Solomon, the bride says: "Draw me after you, and we will run to the fragrance of your perfume" (1:4).

An external revelation or an object are not the only things that draw us. There is also an interior impulse that incites and moves us to believe. And so the Father draws many to the Son by the impulse of a divine action, moving a person's heart from within to believe: "It is God who is working in us, both to will and to accomplish" (Phil 2:13); "I will draw them with the cords of Adam, with bands of love" (Hos 11:4); "The heart of the king is in the hand of the Lord; he turns it wherever he wills" (Prv 21:1).

936   The second problem is this. We read that it is the Son who draws us to the Father: "No one knows the Father but the Son, and he to whom the Son wishes to reveal him" (Mt 11:26); "I have made your name known to those you have given me" (below 17:6). So how can it say here that it is the Father who draws us to the Son? This can be answered in two ways: for we can speak of Christ either as a man, or as God. As man, Christ is the way: "I am the way" (below 14:6); and as the Christ, he leads us to the Father, as a way or road leads to its end. The Father draws us to Christ as man insofar as he gives us his own power so that we may believe in Christ: "You are saved by grace, through faith; and this is not due to yourself, for it is the gift of God" (Eph 2:8). Insofar as he is Christ, he is the Word of God and manifests the Father. It is in this way that the Son draws us to the Father. But the Father draws us to the Son insofar as he manifests the Son.

937   The third problem concerns his saying that no one can come to Christ unless the Father draws him. For according to this, if one does not come to Christ, it is not because of himself, but is due to the one who does not draw him. I answer and say that, in truth, no one can come unless drawn by the Father. For just as a heavy object by its nature cannot rise up, but has to be lifted by someone else, so the human heart, which tends of itself to lower things, cannot rise to what is above unless it is drawn or lifted. And if it does not rise up, this is not due to the failure of the one lifting it, who, so far as lies in him, fails no one; rather, it is due to an obstacle in the one who is not drawn or lifted up.

In this matter we can distinguish between those in the state of integral nature, and those in the state of fallen nature. In the state of integral nature, there was no obstacle to being drawn up, and thus all could share in it. But in the state of fallen nature, all are equally held back from this drawing by the obstacle of sin; and so, all need to be drawn. God, in so far as it depends on him, extends his hand to every one, to draw every one; and what is more, he not only draws those who receive him by the hand, but even converts those who are turned away from him, according to: "Convert us, O Lord, to yourself, and we will be converted" (Lam 5:21); and "You will turn, O God, and bring us to life," as one version of the Psalm (84:7) puts it. Therefore, since God is ready to give grace to all, and draw them to himself, it is not due to him if someone does not accept; rather, it is due to the person who does not accept.

938 A general reason can be given why God does not draw all who are turned away from him, but certain ones, even though all are equally turned away. The reason is so that the order of divine justice may appear and shine forth in those who are not drawn, while the immensity of the divine mercy may appear and shine in those who are drawn. But as to why in particular he draws this person and does not draw that person, there is no reason except the pleasure of the divine will. So Augustine says: "Whom he draws and whom he does not draw, why he draws one and does not draw another, do not desire to judge if you do not wish to err. But accept and understand: If you are not yet drawn, then pray that you may be drawn." We can illustrate this by an example. One can give as the reason why a builder puts some stones at the bottom, and others at the top and sides, that it is the arrangement of the house, whose completion requires this. But why he puts these particular stones here, and those over there, this depends on his mere will. Thus it is that the prime reason for the arrangement is referred to the will of the builder. So God, for the completion of the universe, draws certain ones in order that his mercy may appear in them; and others he does not draw in order that his justice may be shown in them. But that he draws these and does not draw those, depends on the pleasure of his will. In the same way, the reason why in his Church he made some apostles, some confessors, and others martyrs, is for the beauty and completion of the Church. But why he made Peter an apostle, and Stepehen a martyr, and Nicholas a confessor, the only reason is his will. We are now clear on the limitations of our human ability, and the assistance given to us by divine help.

939 He follows with the end and fruit of this help when he says, **And I will raise him up on the last day**, even as man; for we obtain the fruit of the resurrection through those things which Christ did in his flesh: "For as death came through a man, so the resur-

rection of the dead has come through a man" (1 Cor 15:21). So I, as man, **will raise him up**, not only to a natural life, but even to the life of glory; and this **on the last day**. For the Catholic Faith teaches that the world will be made new: "Then I saw a new heaven and a new earth" (Rv 21:1), and that among the changes accompanying this renewal we believe that the motion of the heavens will stop, and consequently, time. "And the angel I saw standing on the sea and on the land, raised his hand to heaven" (Rv 10:5), and then it says that he swore that "time will be no more" (v 6). Since at the resurrection time will stop, so also will night and day, according to "There will be one day, known to the Lord, not day and night" (Zec 14:7). This is the reason he says, **And I will raise him up on the last day**.

940 As to the question why the motion of the heavens and time itself will continue until then, and not end before or after, we should note that whatever exists for something else is differently disposed according to the different states of that for which it exists. But all physical things have been made for man; consequently, they should be disposed according to the different states of man. So, because the state of incorruptibility will begin in men when they arise — according to "What is mortal will put on incorruption," as it says in 1 Corinthians (15:54) — the corruption of things will also stop then. Consequently, the motion of the heavens, which is the cause of the generation and corruption of material things, will stop. "Creation itself will be set free from its slavery to corruption into the freedom of the children of God" (Rom 8:21).

So, it is clear that the Father must draw us if we are to have faith.

941 Then (v 45), he considers the way we are drawn. First, he states the way; secondly, its effectiveness (v 45b); and thirdly, he excludes a certain way of being drawn (v 46).

942 The manner in which we are drawn is appropriate, for God draws us by revealing and teaching; and this is what he says: **It is written in the prophets: They shall all be taught by God**. Bede says that this comes from Joel. But it does not seem to be there explicitly, although there is something like it in: "O children of Zion, rejoice and be joyful in the Lord your God, because he will give you a teacher of justice" (Jl 2:23). Again, according to Bede, he says, **in the prophets**, so that we might understand that the same meaning can be gathered from various statements of the prophets. But it is Isaiah who seems to state this more explicitly: "All your children will be taught by the Lord" (Is 54:13). We also read: "I will give you shepherds after my own heart, and they will feed you with knowledge and doctrine" (Jer 3:15).

943 **They shall all be taught by God**, can be understood in three ways. In one way, so that **all** stands for all the people in the world; in another way, so that it stands for all who are in the Church of Christ, and in a third way, so it means all who will be in the kingdom of heaven.

If we understand it in the first way, it does not seem to be true, for he immediately adds, **Every one who has heard the Father and has learned, comes to me**. Therefore, if every one in the world is taught [by God], then every one will come to Christ. But this is false, for not every one has faith. There are three answers to this. First, one could say, as Chrysostom does, that he is speaking of the majority: **all**, i.e., very many shall be taught, just as we find in Matthew: "Many will come from the East and the West" (Mt 8:11). Secondly, it could mean, **all**, so far as God is concerned, shall be taught, but if some are not taught, that is due to themselves. For the sun, on its part, shines on all, but some are unable to see it if they close their eyes, or are blind. From this point of view, the Apostle says: "He desires the salvation of all men, and that all come to the knowledge of the truth" (1 Tim 2:4). Thirdly, we could say, with Augustine, that we must make a restricted application, so that **They shall all be taught by God**, means that all who are taught, are taught by God. It is just as we might speak of a teacher of the liberal arts who is working in a city: he alone teaches all the boys of the city, because no one there is taught by anyone else. It is in this sense that it was said above: "He was the true light, which enlightens every man coming into this world" (1:9).

944 If we explain these words as referring to those who are gathered into the Church, it says: **They shall all**, all who are in the Church, **be taught by God**. For we read: "All your children will be taught by the Lord" (Is 54:13). This shows the sublimity of the Christian faith, which does not depend on human teachings, but on the teaching of God. For the teaching of the Old Testament was given through the prophets; but the teaching of the New Testament is given through the Son of God himself. "In many and various ways (i.e., in the Old Testament) God spoke to our fathers through the prophets; in these days he has spoken to us in his Son" (Heb 1:1); and again in (2:3): "It was first announced by the Lord, and was confirmed to us by those who heard him." Thus, all who are in the Church are taught, not by the apostles nor by the prophets, but by God himself. Further, according to Augustine, what we are taught by men is from God, who teaches from within: "You have one teacher, the Christ" (Mt 23:10). For understanding, which we especially need for such teaching, is from God.

945 If we explain these words as applying to those who are in

the kingdom of heaven, then **They shall all be taught by God**, because they will see his essence without any intermediary: "We shall see him as he is" (1 Jn 3:2).

946 This drawing by the Father is most effective, because, **Every one who has heard the Father and has learned, comes to me.** Here he mentions two things: first, what relates to a gift of God, when he says, **has heard**, that is, through God, who reveals; the other relates to a free judgment, when he says, **and has learned**, that is, by an assent. These two are necessary for every teaching of faith. **Every one who has heard the Father**, teaching and making known, **and has learned**, by giving assent, **comes to me.**

He comes in three ways: through a knowledge of the truth; through the affection of love; and through imitative action. And in each way it is necessary that one hear and learn. The one who comes through a knowledge of the truth must hear, when God speaks within: "I will hear what the Lord God will speak within me" (Ps 84:9); and he must learn, through affection, as was said. The one who comes through love and desire – "If any one thirsts, let him come to me and drink" (below 7:37) – must hear the word of the Father and grasp it, in order to learn and be moved in his affections. For that person learns the word who grasps it according to the meaning of the speaker. But the Word of the Father breathes forth love. Therefore, the one who grasps it with eager love, learns. "Wisdom goes into holy souls, and makes them prophets and friends of God" (Wis 7:27). One comes to Christ through imitative action, according to: "Come to me, all you who labor and are burdened, and I will refresh you" (Mt 11:28). And whoever learns even in this way comes to Christ: for as the conclusion is to things knowable, so is action to things performable. Now whoever learns perfectly in the sciences arrives at the conclusion; therefore, as regards things that are performable, whoever learns the words perfectly arrives at the right action: "The Lord has opened my ear; and I do not resist" (Is 50:5).

947 To correct the thought that some might have that every one will hear and learn from the Father through a vision, he adds: **Not that any one has seen the Father**, that is, a person living in this life does not see the Father in his essence, according to: "Man will not see me and live" (Ex 33:20), **except the one**, that is, the Son, **who is from God** – **he has seen the Father**, through his essence. Or, **Not that any one has seen the Father**, with a comprehensive vision: neither man nor angel has ever seen or can see in this way; **except the one who is from God**, i.e., the Son: "No one knows the Father except the Son" (Mt 11:27).

The reason for this, of course, is that all vision or knowledge comes about through a likeness: creatures have a knowledge of God according to the way they have a likeness to him. Thus the philosophers say that the intelligences know the First Cause according to this likeness which they have to it. Now every creature possesses some likeness to God, but it is infinitely distant from a likeness to his nature, and so no creature can know him perfectly and totally, as he is in his own nature. The Son, however, because he has received the entire nature of the Father perfectly, through an eternal generation, sees and comprehends totally.

948 Note how the words used are appropriate: for above, when he was speaking of the knowledge others have, he used the word "heard"; but now, in speaking of the Son's knowledge, he uses the word "seen," for knowledge which comes through seeing is direct and open, while that which comes through hearing comes through one who has seen. And so we have received the knowledge we have about the Father from the Son, who saw him. Thus, no one can know the Father except through Christ, who makes him known; and no one can come to the Son unless he has heard from the Father, who makes the Son known.

LECTURE 6

47 "Amen, amen, I say to you:
Whoever believes in me has eternal life.
48 I am the bread of life.
49 Your fathers ate manna in the desert,
and they are dead.
50 This is the bread that comes down from heaven,
so that if anyone eats of this [bread],
he will not die.
51 I am the living bread
that has come down from heaven.
52 If anyone eats of this bread,
he will live forever.
And the bread which I will give is my flesh,
for the life of the world."

949 After our Lord quieted the grumbling of the Jews, he now clears up the doubt they had because of his saying, "I am the bread that has come down from heaven." He intends to show here that this

is true. This is the way he reasons: The bread which gives life to the world descended from heaven; but I am the bread that gives life to the world: therefore, I am the bread which descended from heaven. He does three things concerning this. First, he presents the minor premise of his reasoning, that is, **I am the bread of life**. In the second place, he gives the major premise, that is, that the bread that descended from heaven ought to give life (v 49). Thirdly, we have the conclusion (v 51). As to the first he does two things. First, he states his point; secondly, he expresses it as practically proved (v 48).

950 His intention is to show that he is the bread of life. Bread is life-giving insofar as it is taken. Now one who believes in Christ takes him within himself, according to: "Christ dwells in our hearts through faith" (Eph 3:17). Therefore, if he who believes in Christ has life, it is clear that he is brought to life by eating this bread. Thus, this bread is the bread of life. And this is what he says: **Amen, amen, I say to you: Whoever believes in me**, with a faith made living by love, which not only perfects the intellect but the affections as well (for we do not tend to the things we believe in unless we love them), **has eternal life.**

Now Christ is within us in two ways: in our intellect through faith, so far as it is faith; and in our affections through love, which informs or gives life to our faith: "He who abides in love, abides in God, and God in him" (1 Jn 4:16). So he who believes in Christ so that he tends to him, possesses Christ in his affections and in his intellect. And if we add that Christ is eternal life, as stated in "that we may be in his true Son, Jesus Christ. This is the true God and eternal life" (1 Jn 5:20), and in "In him was life" (above 1:4), we can infer that whoever believes in Christ has eternal life. He has it, I say, in its cause and in hope, and he will have it at some time in reality.

951 Having stated his position, he expresses it as, **I am the bread of life**, which gives life, as clearly follows from the above. We read of this bread: "The bread of Asher will be rich, he will furnish choice morsels," of eternal life, "to kings" (Gn 49:20).

952 Then when he says, **Your fathers ate manna in the desert, and they are dead**, he gives the major premise, namely, the bread that descended from heaven ought to have the effect of giving life. First, he explains this; secondly, he draws his point (v 50).

953 He explains his meaning through a contrasting situation. It was said above (909) that Moses gave the Jews bread from heaven, in the sense of from the air. But bread that does not come from the true heaven cannot give adequate life. Therefore, it is proper to the heavenly bread to give life. So, the bread given by Moses, in which

you take pride, does not give life. And he proves this when he says, **Your fathers ate manna in the desert, and they are dead.**

In this statement he first reproaches them for their faults, when he says, **Your fathers**, whose sons you are, not only according to the flesh, but also by imitating their actions, because you are grumblers just as "they grumbled in their tents" (Ps 105:25); this was why he said to them: "Fill up, then, the measure of your fathers," as we read in Matthew (23:32). As Augustine says, this people is said to have offended God in no matter more than by grumbling against God. Secondly, he mentions for how short a time this was done, saying, **in the desert**: for they were not given manna for a long period of time; and they had it only while in the desert, and not when they entered the promised land (Jos 5). But the other bread [from the true heaven] preserves and nourishes one forever. Thirdly, he states an inadequacy in that bread, that is, it did not preserve life without end; so he says, **and they are dead.** For we read in Joshua (c 5) that all who grumbled, except Joshua and Caleb, died in the desert. This was the reason for the second circumcision, as we see here, because all who had left Egypt died in the desert.

954 One might wonder what kind of death God is speaking of here. If he is speaking of physical death, there will be no difference between the bread the Jews had in the desert and our bread, which came down from heaven, because even Christians who share the latter bread die physically. But if he is speaking of spiritual death, it is clear that both then among the Jews and now among the Christians, some die spiritually and others do not. For Moses and many others who were pleasing to God did not die, while others did. Also, those who eat this bread [of the Christians] unworthily, die spiritually: "He who eats and drinks unworthily, eats and drinks judgment upon himself" (1 Cor 11:29).

We may answer this by saying that the food of the Jews has some features in common with our spiritual food. They are alike in the fact that each signifies the same thing: for both signify Christ. Thus they are called the same food: "All ate the same spiritual food" (1 Cor 10:3). He calls them the same because each is a symbol of the spiritual food. But they are different because one [the manna] was only a symbol; while the other [the bread of the Christians] contains that of which it is the symbol, that is, Christ himself. Thus we should say that each of these foods can be taken in two ways. First, as a sign only, i.e., so that each is taken as food only, and without understanding what is signified; and taken in this way, they do not take away either physical or spiritual death. Secondly, they may be taken in both ways, i.e., the visible food is taken in such a way that spiritual food is understood and spiritually tasted, in order that it may satisfy spiritually. In this way, those who ate the manna spiritually did not die spiritually. But those who eat the Eucharist spiritually, both live spiritually now without sin, and will live physically forever. Thus, our food is greater than their food, because it contains in itself that of which it is the symbol.

955 Having presented the argument, he draws the conclusion: **This is the bread that comes down from heaven**. He says, **This**, the Gloss says, to indicate himself. But our Lord does not understand it this way as it would be superfluous, since he immediately adds, **I am the living bread that has come down from heaven**. So we should say that our Lord wants to say that the bread which can do this, i.e., give life, comes from heaven; but I am that bread: thus, I am that bread that comes down from heaven. Now the reason why that bread which comes down from heaven gives a life which never ends is that all food nourishes according to the properties of its nature; but heavenly things are incorruptible: consequently, since this food is heavenly, it is not corrupted, and as long as it lasts, it gives life. So, he who eats it, will not die. Just as if there were some bodily food which never corrupted, then in nourishing it would always be life-giving. This bread was signified by the tree of life in the midst of Paradise, which somehow gave life without end: "He must not be allowed to stretch out his hand and take from the tree of life and eat, and live forever" (Gn 3:22). So if the effect of this bread is that anyone who eats it will not die, and I am such, then [anyone who eats of me will not die].

956 He does two things concerning this. First, he speaks of himself in general; secondly, in particular, **And the bread which I will give is my flesh**. In regard to the first, he does two things: first, he mentions his origin; secondly his power (v 52).

957 He said, **I am the living bread**; consequently, I can give life. Material bread does not give life forever, because it does not have life in itself; but it gives life by being changed and converted into nourishment by the energy of a living organism. **That has come down from heaven**: it was explained before [467] how the Word came down. This refuted those heresies which taught that Christ was a mere man, because according to them, he would not have come down from heaven.

958 He has the power to give eternal life; thus he says, **If anyone eats of this bread**, i.e., spiritually, **he will live**, not only in the present through faith and justice, but **forever**. "Everyone who lives and believes in me, will never die" (below 11:26).

959 He then speaks of his body when he says, **And the bread which I will give is my flesh**. For he had said that he was the living

bread; and so that we do not think that he is such so far as he is the Word or in his soul alone, he shows that even his flesh is life-giving, for it is an instrument of his divinity. Thus, since an instrument acts by virtue of the agent, then just as the divinity of Christ is life-giving, so too his flesh gives life (as Damascene says) because of the Word to which it is united. Thus Christ healed the sick by his touch. So what he said above, **I am the living bread**, pertained to the power of the Word; but what he is saying here pertains to the sharing in his body, that is, to the sacrament of the Eucharist.

960 We can consider four things about this sacrament: its species, the authority of the one who instituted it, the truth of this sacrament, and its usefulness.

As to the species of this sacrament: **This is the bread**; "Come, and eat my bread" (Prv 9:5). The reason for this is that this is the sacrament of the body of Christ; but the body of Christ is the Church, which arises out of many believers forming a bodily unity: "We are one body" (Rom 12:5). And so because bread is formed from many grains, it is a fitting species for this sacrament. Hence he says, **And the bread which I will give is my flesh.**

961 The author of this sacrament is Christ: for although the priest confers it, it is Christ himself who gives the power to this sacrament, because the priest consecrates in the person of Christ. Thus in the other sacraments the priest uses his own words or those of the Church, but in this sacrament he uses the words of Christ: because just as Christ gave his body to death by his own will, so it is by his own power that he gives himself as food: "Jesus took bread, he blessed it and broke it, and gave it to his disciples, saying: 'Take and eat it, this is my body' " (Mt 26:26). Thus he says, **which I will give**; and he says, **will give**, because this sacrament had not yet been instituted.

962 The truth of this sacrament is indicated when he says, **is my flesh**. He does not say, "This signifies my flesh," but it **is my flesh**, for in reality that which is taken is truly the body of Christ: "Who will give us his flesh so that we may be satisfied?" as we read in Job (31:31).

Since the whole Christ is contained in this sacrament, why did he just say, this **is my flesh**? To answer this, we should note that in this mystical sacrament the whole Christ is really contained: but his body is there by virtue of the conversion; while his soul and divinity are present by natural concomitance. For if we were to suppose what is really impossible, that is, that the divinity of Christ is separated from his body, then his divinity would not be present in this sacrament. Similarly, if someone had consecrated during the three days Christ was dead, his soul would not have been present there [in the sacrament], but his body would have been, as it was on the cross or in the tomb. Since this sacrament is the commemoration of our Lord's passion – according to "As often as you eat this bread and drink this cup, you proclaim the death of the Lord" (1 Cor 11:26) – and the passion of Christ depended on his weakness – according to "He was crucified through weakness" (2 Cor 13:4) – he rather says, **is my flesh**, to suggest the weakness through which he died, for "flesh" signifies weakness.

963 The usefulness of this sacrament is great and universal. It is great, indeed, because it produces spiritual life within us now, and will later produce eternal life, as was said. For as is clear from what was said, since this is the sacrament of our Lord's passion, it contains in itself the Christ who suffered. Thus, whatever is an effect of our Lord's passion is also an effect of this sacrament. For this sacrament is nothing other than the application of our Lord's passion to us. For it was not fitting for Christ to be always with us in his own presence; and so he wanted to make up for this absence through this sacrament. Hence it is clear that the destruction of death, which Christ accomplished by his death, and the restoration of life, which he accomplished by his resurrection, are effects of this sacrament.

964 The usefulness of this sacrament is universal because the life it gives is not only the life of one person, but, so far as concerns itself, the life of the entire world: and for this the death of Christ is fully sufficient. "He is the offering for our sins; and not for ours only, but also for those of the entire world" (1 Jn 2:2).

We should note that this sacrament is different from the others: for the other sacraments have individual effects: as in baptism, only the one baptized receives grace. But in the immolation of this sacrament, the effect is universal: because it affects not just the priest, but also those for whom he prays, as well as the entire Church, of the living and of the dead. The reason for this is that it contains the universal cause of all the sacraments, Christ. Nevertheless, when a lay person receives this sacrament it does not benefit others *ex opere operato* [by its own power] considered as a receiving. However, due to the intention of the person who is acting and receiving, it can be communicated to all those to whom he directs his intention. It is clear from this that lay persons are mistaken when they receive the Eucharist for those in purgatory.

LECTURE 7

53 The Jews therefore disputed among themselves, saying: "How can this man give us his flesh to eat?" 54 Jesus then said to them: "Amen, amen, I say to you,
unless you eat the flesh of the Son of Man,
and drink his blood,
you will not have life in you.
55 Whoever eats my flesh and drinks my blood
has eternal life;
and I will raise him up on the last day.
56 For my flesh truly is food,
and my blood truly is drink.
57 He who eats my flesh and drinks my blood
abides in me, and I in him.
58 Just as the living Father has sent me,
and I live because of the Father,
so whoever eats me,
he also will live because of me.
59 This is the bread that has come down from heaven.
Unlike your fathers who ate manna and are dead,
whoever eats this bread shall live forever."
60 These things he said teaching in the synagogue at Capernaum.

965 Above, our Lord checked the grumbling of the Jews over the origin of this spiritual food; here, he stops their dispute over the eating of this same food. First, we see their dispute; secondly, our Lord stops it (v 54); thirdly, the Evangelist mentions the place where all this happened (v 60).

966 As to the first, note that the Evangelist brings in the dispute among the Jews in the form of a conclusion, saying, **The Jews therefore disputed among themselves.** And this is fitting: for according to Augustine, our Lord had just spoken to them about the food of unity, which makes into one those who are nourished on it, according to, "Let those who are just feast and rejoice before God," and then it continues, according to one reading, "God makes those who agree to live in one house" (Ps 67:4). And so, because the Jews had not eaten the food of harmony, they argued with each other: "When you fast, you argue and fight" (Is 58:4). Further, their quarreling with others shows that they were carnal: "For while you are envious and quarreling, are you not carnal?" (1 Cor 3:3). Therefore, they understood these words of our Lord in a carnal way, i.e., as meaning that our Lord's flesh would be eaten as

material food. Thus they say, **How can this man give us his flesh
to eat?** As if to say: This is impossible. Here they were speaking
against God just as their fathers did: "We are sick of this useless
food" (Nm 21:5).

967 Our Lord stops this argument. First, he states the power
that comes from taking this food; secondly, he amplifies on it (v 55).
As to the first he does three things. First, he states why it is necessary to eat this flesh; secondly, its usefulness; and thirdly, he adds
something about its truth (v 56).

968 Jesus said: **Amen, amen, I say to you, unless you eat the
flesh of the Son of Man and drink his blood, you will not have life
in you.** As if to say: You think it is impossible and unbecoming to
eat my flesh. But it is not only possible, but very necessary, so much
so that **unless you eat the flesh of the Son of Man and drink his
blood, you will not have,** i.e., you will not be able to have, **life in
you,** that is, spiritual life. For just as material food is so necessary for
bodily life that without it you cannot exist — "They exchanged their
precious belongings for food" (Lam 1:11); "Bread strengthens the
heart of man" (Ps 103:15) — so spiritual food is necessary for the
spiritual life to such an extent that without it the spiritual life cannot
be sustained: "Man does not live by bread alone, but by every word
which comes from the mouth of God" (Dt 8:3).

969 We should note that this statement can refer either to
eating in a spiritual way or in a sacramental way. If we understand
it as referring to a spiritual eating, it does not cause any difficulty.
For that person eats the flesh of Christ and drinks his blood in a
spiritual way who shares in the unity of the Church; and this is
accomplished by the love of charity: "You are one body, in Christ"
(Rom 12:5). Thus, one who does not eat in this way is outside the
Church, and consequently, without the love of charity. Accordingly,
such a one does not have life in himself: "He who does not love,
remains in death" (1 Jn 3:14).

But if we refer this statement to eating in a sacramental way,
a difficulty appears. For we read above: "Unless one is born again
of water and the Holy Spirit, he cannot enter the kingdom of God"
(3:5). Now this statement was given in the same form as the present
one: **Unless you eat the flesh of the Son of Man.** Therefore, since
baptism is a necessary sacrament, it seems that the Eucharist is also.
In fact, the Greeks think it is; and so they give the Eucharist to
newly baptized infants. For this opinion they have in their favor
the rite of Denis, who says that the reception of each sacrament
should culminate in the sharing of the Eucharist, which is the cul-
mination of all the sacraments. This is true in the case of adults,

but it is not so for infants, because receiving the Eucharist should be done with reverence and devotion, and those who do not have the use of reason, as infants and the insane, cannot have this. Consequently, it should not be given to them at all.

We should say, therefore, that the sacrament of baptism is necessary for everyone, and it must be really received, because without it no one is born again into life. And so it is necessary that it be received in reality, or by desire in the case of those who are prevented from the former. For if the contempt within a person excludes a baptism by water, then neither a baptism of desire nor of blood will benefit him for eternal life. However, the sacrament of the Eucharist is necessary for adults only, so that it may be received in reality, or by desire, according to the practices of the Church.

970 But even this causes difficulty: because by these words of our Lord, it is necessary for salvation not only to eat his body, but also to drink his blood, especially since a repast of food is not complete without drink. Therefore, since it is the custom in certain Churches for only the priest to receive Christ's blood, while the rest receive only his body, they would seem to be acting against this.

I answer that it was the custom of the early Church for all to receive both the body and blood of Christ; and certain Churches have still retained this practice, where even those assisting at the altar always receive the body and blood. But in some Churches, due to the danger of spilling the blood, the custom is for it to be received only by the priest, while the rest receive Christ's body. Even so, this is not acting against our Lord's command, because whoever receives Christ's body receives his blood also, since the entire Christ is present under each species, even his body and blood. But under the species of bread, Christ's body is present in virtue of the conversion, and his blood is present by natural concomitance; while under the species of wine, his blood is present in virtue of the conversion, and his body by natural concomitance.

It is now clear why it is necessary to receive this spiritual food.

971 Next, the usefulness of this food is shown: first, for the spirit or soul; secondly, for the body, **and I will raise him up on the last day.**

972 There is great usefulness in eating this sacrament, for it gives eternal life; thus he says, **Whoever eats my flesh and drinks my blood has eternal life.** For this spiritual food is similar to material food in the fact that without it there can be no spiritual life, just as there cannot be bodily life without bodily food, as was said above. But this food has more than the other, because it produces in the one who receives it an unending life, which material food does not do:

for not all who eat material food continue to live. For, as Augustine says, it can happen that many who do take it die because of old age or sickness, or some other reason. But one who takes this food and drink of the body and blood of our Lord **has eternal life**. For this reason it is compared to the tree of life: "She is the tree of life for those who take her" (Prv 3:18); and so it is called the bread of life: "He fed him with the bread of life and understanding" (Sir 15:3). Accordingly, he says, **eternal life**, because one who eats this bread has within himself Christ, who is "the true God and eternal life," as John says (1 Jn 5:20).

Now one has eternal life who eats and drinks, as it is said, not only in a sacramental way, but also in a spiritual way. One eats and drinks sacramentally or in a sacramental way, if he receives the sacrament; and one eats and drinks spiritually or in a spiritual way, if he attains to the reality of the sacrament. This reality of the sacrament is twofold: one is contained and signified, and this is the whole Christ, who is contained under the species of bread and wine. The other reality is signified but not contained, and this is the mystical body of Christ, which is in the predestined, the called, and the justified. Thus, in reference to Christ as contained and signified, one eats his flesh and drinks his blood in a spiritual way if he is united to him through faith and love, so that one is transformed into him and becomes his member: for this food is not changed into the one who eats it, but it turns the one who takes it into itself, as we see in Augustine, when he says: "I am the food of the robust. Grow and you will eat me. Yet you will not change me into yourself, but you will be transformed into me." And so this is a food capable of making man divine and inebriating him with divinity. The same is true in reference to the mystical body of Christ, which is only signified [and not contained], if one shares in the unity of the Church. Therefore, one who eats in these ways **has eternal life**. That this is true of the first way, in reference to Christ, is clear enough. In the same way, in reference to the mystical body of Christ, one will necessarily have eternal life if he perseveres: for the unity of the Church is brought about by the Holy Spirit: "One body, one Spirit ... the pledge of our eternal inheritance" (Eph 4:4; 1:14). So this bread is very profitable, because it gives eternal life to the soul; but it is so also because it gives eternal life to the body.

973   And therefore he adds, **and I will raise him up on the last day**. For as was said, one who eats and drinks in a spiritual way shares in the Holy Spirit, through whom we are united to Christ by a union of faith and love, and through him we become members of the Church. But the Holy Spirit also merits the resurrection: "He who raised Jesus Christ our Lord from the dead, will raise our mortal

bodies because of his Spirit, who dwells in us" (Rom 8:11). And so our Lord says that he will raise up to glory whoever eats and drinks; to glory, and not to condemnation, as this would not be for their benefit. Such an effect is fittingly attributed to this sacrament of the Eucharist because, as Augustine says and as was said above, it is the Word who raises up souls, and it is the Word made flesh who gives life to bodies. Now in this sacrament the Word is present not only in his divinity, but also in the reality of his flesh; and so he is the cause of the resurrection not just of souls, but of bodies as well: "For as death came through a man, so the resurrection of the dead has come through a man" (1 Cor 15:21). It is now clear how profitable it is to take this sacrament.

974 We see its truth when he says, **For my flesh truly is food.** For some might think that what he was saying about his flesh and blood was just an enigma and a parable. So our Lord rejects this, and says, **my flesh truly is food.** As if to say: Do not think that I am speaking metaphorically, for my flesh is truly contained in this food of the faithful, and my blood is truly contained in this sacrament of the altar: "This is my body ... this is my blood of the new covenant," as we read in Matthew (26:26).

Chrysostom explains this statement in the following way. Food and drink are taken for man's refreshment. Now there are two parts in man: the chief part is the soul, and the second is the body. It is the soul which makes man to be man, and not the body; and so that truly is the food of man which is the food of the soul. And this is what our Lord says: **my flesh truly is food,** because it is the food of the soul, not just of the body. The same is true of the blood of Christ. "He has led me to the waters that refresh" (Ps 22:2). As if to say: This refreshment is especially for the soul.

Augustine explains these words this way. A thing is truly said to be such and such a thing if it produces the effect of that thing. Now the effect of food is to fill or satisfy. Therefore, that which truly produces fulness is truly food and drink. But this is produced by the flesh and blood of Christ, who leads us to the state of glory, where there is neither hunger nor thirst: "They will neither hunger nor thirst" (Rv 7:16). And so he says: **For my flesh truly is food, and my blood truly is drink.**

975 Now our Lord proves that this spiritual food has such power, that is, to give eternal life. And he reasons this way: Whoever eats my flesh and drinks my blood is united to me; but whoever is united to me has eternal life: therefore, whoever eats my flesh and drinks my blood has eternal life. Here he does three things: first,

he gives his major premise; secondly, the minor premise, which he proves (v 58); and thirdly, he draws his conclusion: **This is the bread that has come down from heaven.**

976 We should note, with respect to the first, that if his statement, **He who eats my flesh and drinks my blood abides in me, and I in him**, is referred to his flesh and blood in a mystical way, there is no difficulty. For, as was said, that person eats in a spiritual way, in reference to what is signified only, who is incorporated into the mystical body through a union of faith and love. Through love, God is in man, and man is in God: "He who abides in love, abides in God, and God in him" (1 Jn 4:16). And this is what the Holy Spirit does; so it is also said, "We know that we abide in God and God in us, because he has given us his Spirit" (1 Jn 4:13).

If these words are referred to a sacramental reception, then whoever eats this flesh and drinks this blood abides in God. For, as Augustine says, there is one way of eating this flesh and drinking this blood such that he who eats and drinks abides in Christ and Christ in him. This is the way of those who eat the body of Christ and drink his blood not just sacramentally, but really. And there is another way by which those who eat do not abide in Christ nor Christ in them. This is the way of those who approach [the sacrament] with an insincere heart: for this sacrament has no effect in one who is insincere. There is insincerity when the interior state does not agree with what is outwardly signified. In the sacrament of the Eucharist, what is outwardly signified is that Christ is united to the one who receives it, and such a one to Christ. Thus, one who does not desire this union in his heart, or does not try to remove every obstacle to it, is insincere. Consequently, Christ does not abide in him nor he in Christ.

977 Now he presents his minor premise, that is, whoever is united to Christ has life. He mentions this to show the following similarity: the Son, because of the unity he has with the Father, receives life from the Father; therefore one who is united to Christ receives life from Christ. And this is what he says: **Just as the living Father has sent me, and I live because of the Father.** These words can be explained in two ways about Christ: either in reference to his human nature, or in reference to his divine nature.

If they are explained as referring to Christ the Son of God, then the "as" implies a similarity of Christ to creatures in some respect, though not in all respects, which is, that he exists from another. For to be from another is common to Christ the Son of God and to creatures. But they are unlike in another way: the Son has something proper to himself, because he is from the Father in such a way that he receives the entire fulness of the divine nature, so that whatever is natural to the Father is also natural to the Son. Creatures, on the other hand, receive a certain particular perfection and nature. "Just as the Father possesses life in himself, so he has given it to the Son to have life in himself" (above 5:26). He shows this because, when speaking of his procession from the Father, he does not say: "As I eat the Father and I live because of the Father, " as he said, when speaking of sharing in his body and blood, **whoever eats me, he also will live because of me.** This eating makes us better, for eating implies a certain sharing. Rather, Christ says that he lives because of the Father, not as eaten, but as generating, without detriment to his equality.

If we explain this statement as applying to Christ as man, then in some respect the "as" implies a similarity between Christ as man and us: that is, in the fact that as Christ the man receives spiritual life through union with God, so we too receive spiritual life in the communion or sharing in this Sacrament. Still, there is a difference: for Christ as man received life through union with the Word, to whom he is united in person; while we are united to Christ through the sacrament of faith. And so he says two things: **sent me** and **Father.** If we refer these words to the Son of God, then he is saying, **I live because of the Father**, because the Father himself is living. But if they are referred to the Son of Man, then he is saying, **I live because of the Father**, because the Father **has sent me**, i.e., made me incarnate. For the sending of the Son is his incarnation: "God sent his Son, made from a woman" (Gal 4:4).

978 According to Hilary, this is a rejection of the error made by Arius. For if we live because of Christ, because we have something of his nature (as he says, "Whoever eats my flesh and drinks my blood has eternal life"), then Christ too lives because of the Father, because he has in himself the nature of the Father (not a part of it, for it is simple and indivisible). Therefore, Christ has the entire nature of the Father. It is because of the Father, therefore, that the Son lives, because the Son's birth did not involve another and different nature [from that of the Father].

979 Next (v 59), he presents his two conclusions. For they were arguing about two things: the origin of this spiritual food and its power. The first conclusion is about its origin; the second is about its power: **whoever eats this bread shall live forever.**

980 With respect to the first, we should note that the Jews had been troubled because he had said, "I am the living bread that has come down from heaven" (v 51). Therefore, in opposition to them, he arrives at this same conclusion again, from his statement, "I live

because of the Father," when he says, **This is the bread that has come down from heaven**. For to come down from heaven is to have an origin from heaven; but the Son has his origin from heaven, since he lives because of the Father: therefore, Christ is the one who has come down from heaven. And so he says, **This is the bread that has come down from heaven**, i.e., from the life of the Father. **Come down**, in relation to his divinity; or **come down**, even in his body, so far as the power that formed it, the Holy Spirit, was from heaven, a heavenly power. Thus, those who eat this bread do not die; as our fathers died, who ate the manna that was neither from heaven, nor was living bread, as was said above. How those who ate the manna died is clear from what has been mentioned before.

981   The second conclusion, concerning the power of this bread, is given when he says, **whoever eats this bread shall live forever**. This follows from his statement, "He who eats my flesh and drinks my blood abides in me, and I in him" (v 57). For whoever eats this bread abides in me, and I in him. But I am eternal life. Therefore, **whoever eats this bread**, as he ought, **shall live forever**.

982   Jesus said this **in the synagogue**, in which he was teaching at Capernaum. He used to teach in the temple and in the synagogues in order to attract many, so that at least some might benefit: "I have proclaimed your justice in the great assembly" (Ps 39:10).

LECTURE 8

61 On hearing this, many of his disciples said: "This is a hard saying! Who can accept it?" 62 But Jesus, knowing fully that his disciples were grumbling about this, said to them:
"Does this scandalize you?
63 What if you should see the Son of Man
ascending to where he was before?
64 It is the spirit that gives life;
flesh profits nothing.
The words that I have spoken to you
are spirit and life.
65 But there are some of you who do not believe."
For Jesus knew from the beginning those who would believe in him, and who it was that would betray him. 66 And he said:
"This is why I said to you,
that no one can come to me,
unless it be given him by my Father."

67 From this time on, many of his disciples turned back, and no longer walked with him. 68 Jesus then said to the Twelve:
"Do you too wish to leave?"
69 Simon Peter replied: "Lord, to whom shall we go? You have the words of eternal life. 70 We have come to believe and to know that you are the Christ, the Son of God." 71 Jesus answered him:
"Did I not choose you Twelve?
And one of you is a devil."
72 Now he was talking about Judas, son of Simon Iscariot, who would betray him, since he was one of the Twelve.

983 After our Lord put an end to the complaining and arguing among the Jews, he now removes the scandal given to his disciples. First, we see the scandal of those disciples who left him; secondly, the devotion of those who remained with him (v 68). Concerning the first, he does three things: first, we see the scandal given to his disciples; secondly, the kindly way Christ takes it away (v 62); and thirdly, the stubbornness and unbelief of those who leave him (v 67).

984 We should note, with respect to the first, that there were many Jews who adhered to Christ, believed him and followed him. And although they had not left all things as the Twelve did, they were still all called his disciples. It is of these that he says, **many**, that is, many of the people who believed him, **on hearing this**, what he had said above, said, **This is a hard saying!** We read of these: "They believe for a while, and in the time of testing fall away" (Lk 8:13). He says, **many**, because "The number of fools is infinite" (Ecc 1:15); and, "Many are called but few are chosen" (Mt 20:16).

They said: **This is a hard saying!** Now that is said to be hard which is difficult to divide, and which offers resistance. Accordingly, a saying is hard either because it resists the intellect or because it resists the will, that is, when we cannot understand it with our mind, or when it does not please our will. And this saying was hard for them in both ways. It was hard for their intellects because it exceeded the weakness of their intellects: for since they were earthly minded, they were incapable of understanding what he said, namely, that he would give them his flesh to eat. And it was hard for their wills, because he said many things about the power of his divinity: and although they believed him as a prophet, they did not believe that he was God. Consequently, it seemed to them that he was making himself greater than he was. "His letters are strong" (2 Cor 10:10); "Wisdom is exceedingly unpleasant to the unlearned" (Sir 6:21). And so it reads on, **Who can accept it?** They said this as an excuse: for since they had given themselves to him, they should have accepted what he said. But because he was not teaching them things that were pleasing to them, they were waiting for an occasion to leave him: "A fool does not accept words of wisdom unless you tell him what he desires" (Prv 18:2).

985   Next (v 62), we see the kindly way Christ dispelled their difficulty. First, he takes notice of it; secondly, he removes its cause (v 63); and thirdly, he mentions what the cause was (v 65).

986   He had noticed that they were scandalized because they had said, although privately, so he could not hear, **This is a hard saying!** But Christ, who in virtue of his divinity knew that they had said this, mentions it. And this is what he says: **But Jesus, knowing in himself**, what they said within themselves, that is, **that his disciples were grumbling about this** — "He did not need anyone to give him testimony about men. He was well aware of what was in man's heart" (above 2:25); "God searches into the hearts and loins of men" (Ps 7:10) — said to them, **Does this scandalize you?** As if to say: You should not be scandalized at this. Or, it can be understood less strongly, as meaning: I know that you are scandalized at this. "He will be our sanctification," i.e., those who believe in Christ, but "a stumbling-stone to the two houses of Israel," to the grumbling disciples and the crowds (Is 8:4).

987   But since teachers should avoid creating difficulties for those who are listening to them, why did our Lord mention those things that would upset the people and have them leave? I answer that Christ had to mention such things because his teaching required it. For they had pleaded with him for material food, when he had come to strengthen their desire for spiritual food; and so he had to make known to them his teaching on spiritual food.

Nevertheless, their difficulty was not caused by any defect in what Christ was teaching, but by their own unbelief. For if they had not understood what our Lord was saying, because of their own earthly mindedness, they could have questioned him, as the apostles had done in similar circumstances. According to Augustine, however, our Lord purposely permitted this situation, to give teachers a reason for consolation and patience with those who belittle what they say, since even the disciples presumed to disparage what Christ said.

988 Then (v 63), he takes away the occasion of their scandal so far as concerns the person speaking and what he said, as Chrysostom says. First, he deals with the person who was speaking; secondly, with what he said (v 64).

989   The occasion for their scandal was when they heard our Lord say divine things about himself. And so, because they believed that he was the son of Joseph, they were upset at what he said about

himself. God takes away this reason by showing them his divinity more openly, and says: You are upset over the things I have said about myself; **What if you should see the Son of Man ascending to where he was before?** What would you say then? As if to say: You can never deny that I came down from heaven, or that I am the one who gives and teaches eternal life. He did the same thing before with Nathanael. When Nathanael said to him, "You are the King of Israel" our Lord, wanting to lead him to more perfect knowledge, answered him: "You will see greater things than this" (above 1:50). And here too, our Lord reveals to them something greater about himself which would happen in the future, saying, **What if you should see the Son of Man ascending to where he was before?** Indeed, he did ascend into heaven in the sight of his disciples (Acts 1:9). If, therefore, he does ascend to where he was before, then he was in heaven before: "No one has gone up to heaven except the one who came down from heaven" (above 3:13).

990   Let us note that Christ is one person: the person of the Son of God and the person of the Son of Man being the same person. Still, because of his different natures, something belongs to Christ by reason of his human nature, that is, to ascend, which does not belong to him by reason of his divine nature, according to which he does not ascend, since he is eternally at the highest summit of things, that is, in the Father. It is according to his human nature that it belongs to him to ascend **to where he was before**, that is, to heaven, where he had not been in his human nature. (This is in opposition to the teaching of Valentinus, who claimed that Christ had assumed a heavenly body). Thus, Christ ascended in the sight of his apostles to where he was before according to his divinity; and he ascended, by his own power, according to his humanity: "I came forth from the Father, and I have come into the world. Now I am leaving the world and am going to the Father" (below 16:28).

991   Augustine understands this passage differently. He said that the disciples were scandalized when our Lord said that he would give him them his flesh to eat because they understood this in a material minded way, as if they were literally to eat this flesh, just like the flesh of an animal. Our Lord rejected this interpretation and said, **What if you should see the Son of Man ascending**, with his entire body, **to where he was before?** Would you say that I intended to give you my flesh to eat like you do the flesh of an animal?

992   Then (v 64), he settles the offense they took at what he said. And, as Chrysostom says, he distinguished two ways in which his words could be understood. And secondly, he showed which way was appropriate here (v 64b).

With respect to the first, we should note that Christ's words can be understood in two senses: in a spiritual way, and in a material way. Thus he says, **It is the spirit that gives life**, that is, if you understand these words according to the spirit, i.e., according to their spiritual meaning, they will give life. **Flesh profits nothing**, that is, if you understand them in a material way, they will be of no benefit to you, they will, rather, be harmful, for "If you live according to the flesh you will die" (Rom 8:13).

What our Lord said about eating his flesh is interpreted in a material way when it is understood in its superfical meaning, and as pertaining to the nature of flesh. And it was in this way that the Jews understood them. But our Lord said that he would give himself to them as spiritual food, not as though the true flesh of Christ is not present in this sacrament of the altar, but because it is eaten in a certain spiritual and divine way. Thus, the correct meaning of these words is spiritual, not material. So he says, **The words that I have spoken to you**, about eating my flesh, **are spirit and life**, that is, they have a spiritual meaning, and understood in this way they give life. And it is not surprising that they have a spiritual meaning, because they are from the Holy Spirit: "It is the Spirit who tells mysteries" (1 Cor 14:2). And therefore, the mysteries of Christ give life: "I will never forget your justifications, because through them you have brought me to life" (Ps 118:93).

993 Augustine explains this passage in a different way, for he understands the statement, **flesh profits nothing**, as refei ring to the flesh of Christ. It is obvious that the flesh of Christ, as united to the Word and to the Spirit, does profit very much and in every way; otherwise, the Word would have been made flesh in vain, and the Father would have made him known in the flesh in vain, as we see from 1 Timothy (c 4). And so we should say that it is the flesh of Christ, considered in itself, that profits nothing and does not have any more beneficial effect than other flesh. For if his flesh is considered as separated from the divinity and the Holy Spirit, it does not have different power than other flesh. But if it is united to the Spirit and the divinity, it profits many, because it makes those who receive it abide in Christ, for man abides in God through the Spirit of love: "We know that we abide in God and God in us, because he has given us his Spirit" (1 Jn 4:13). And this is what our Lord says: the effect I promise you, that is, eternal life, should not be attributed to my flesh as such, because understood in this way, **flesh profits nothing**. But my flesh does offer eternal life as united to the Spirit and to the divinity. "If we live by the Spirit, let us also walk by the Spirit" "Gal 5:25). And so he adds, **The words that I have spoken to you are spirit and life**, i.e., they must be understood of the Spirit united

to my flesh; and so understood they are life, that is, the life of the soul. For as the body lives its bodily life through a bodily spirit, so the soul lives a spiritual life through the Holy Spirit: "Send forth your Spirit, and they will be created" (Ps 103:30).

994 Then (v 65), he indicates the reason why they were upset, that is, their unbelief. As if to say: the cause of your difficulty is not the hardness of what I have just said, but your own unbelief. And so first, he mentions their unbelief; secondly, he excludes an incorrect interpretation; and thirdly, he gives the reason for their unbelief.

995 Our Lord indicated their unbelief when he said, **But there are some of you who do not believe.** He did not say, "who do not understand." He did more than this, for he gave the reason why they did not understand: they did not understand because they did not believe. "If you do not believe, you will not understand," as we read in another version of Isaiah (7:9). He said, **some,** in order to exclude his disciples: "All do not have faith" (2 Thes 3:2); "All do not obey the Gospel" (Rom 10:16); "They did not believe what he said" (Ps 105:24).

996 The Evangelist then rejects an incorrect interpretation when he adds, **For Jesus knew.** As if to say: Jesus did not say, **there are some of you who do not believe,** because he just recently learned it, but because **Jesus knew from the beginning,** i.e., of the world, **those who would believe in him, and who it was that would betray him.** "All things are naked and open to his eyes" (Heb 4:13); "All things were known to the Lord God before they were created," as we read in Sirach (23:29).

997 Our Lord next mentioned the cause of their unbelief, which was the withdrawal of attracting grace. Thus he said: **This is why I said to you.** As if to say: Thus it was necessary to tell you what I told you before: **that no one can come to me,** i.e., through faith, **unless it be given him by my Father.** It follows from this, according to Augustine, that the act of believing itself is given to us by God. Why it is not given to everyone we discussed above, where our Lord used almost the same words (6:44). They are repeated here for two reasons. First, to show that Christ received them in the faith more for their advantage and benefit than for his own: "It has been granted to you to believe in him" (Phil 1:29). As if to say: It is good for you to believe. Thus Augustine says: "It is a great thing to believe; rejoice, because you have believed." Secondly, to show that Christ was not the son of Joseph, as they thought, but of God; for it is God the Father who draws men to the Son, as is clear from what has been said.

998   Then (v 67), we see the stubbornness of the disciples: for although our Lord had rebuked them and had taken away the cause of their difficulty so far as it concerned himself, they still would not believe. Thus he says, **From this time on, many of his disciples turned back.** He did not say, "they left," but that they **turned back,** i.e., from the faith, which they had in a virtuous way; and cut off from the body of Christ, they lost life, because perhaps they were not in the body, as Augustine says. There are some who turn back in an absolute way, that is, those who follow the devil, to whom our Lord said, "Go back, Satan" (Mt 4:10). We also read of certain women that "Some turned back after Satan" (1 Tim 5:15). But Peter did not turn back in this way; he rather turned after Christ: "Follow after me, Satan" (Mt 16:23). But the others followed after Satan.

Then follows: they **no longer walked with him**, that is, even though we are required to walk with Jesus: "I will show you man what is good," and then it continues on, "to walk attentively with your God" (Mi 6:8).

999   Then (v 68), our Lord examined those disciples who remained with him. First, we see this in the question he asked them; secondly, Peter's answer shows the devotion of those who remained; and thirdly, our Lord corrects Peter's answer (v 71).

1000   Our Lord examined the Twelve who remained as to their willingness to stay on; and so he said **to the Twelve,** that is, to the Apostles, **Do you too wish to leave?** He asked them this for two reasons. First, so that they would not take pride, thinking it was due to their own goodness, in the fact that they stayed on while the others left, and think that they were doing Christ a favor. And so he showed that he did not need them by holding them off, but still giving them strength: "If you live rightly, what do you give him, or what does he receive from your hand?" (Jb 35:7). Secondly, it sometimes happens that a person would really prefer to leave another but is kept from doing so by shame or embarrassment. Our Lord did not want them to stay with him because they were forced to do so out of embarrassment (because to serve unwillingly is not to serve at all), and so he took away any embarrassment in their leaving or necessity for their staying, and left it to their own judgment whether they wanted to stay with him or leave, because "God loves a cheerful giver" (2 Cor 9:7).

1001   Then, from Peter's answer, we see the devotion of those who did not leave. For Peter – who loved the brethren, who guarded his friendships, and had a special affection for Christ – answered for the whole group, and said, **Lord, to whom shall we go? You have the words of eternal life.** Here he did three things. First, he extolled the greatness of Christ; secondly, he praised his teaching; and thirdly, he professed his faith.

1002 He extolled the greatness of Christ when he said, **Lord, to whom shall we go?** As if to say: Are you telling us to leave you? Give us someone better to whom we can go. But then, "There is no one like you among the strong, O Lord" (Ex 15:11); "Who is like God" (Ps 88:7). And so you will not tell us to go. "Where can I go that is away from your spirit?" (Ps 138:7). Further, according to Chrysostom, Peter's words show great friendship; for to him, Christ was more worthy of honor than father or mother.

1003 He praised his teaching when he said, **You have the words of eternal life.** Now Moses, and the prophets, also spoke the words of God; but they rarely had the words of eternal life. But you are promising eternal life. What more can we ask? "Whoever believes in me has eternal life" (above 6:47); "Whoever believes in the Son has eternal life" (above 3:36).

1004 He professed his faith when he said, **We have come to believe and to know that you are the Christ, the Son of God.** For in our faith there are two things above all that must be believed: the mystery of the Trinity, and the Incarnation. And these two Peter professed here. He professed the mystery of the Trinity when he said, **you are the Son of God:** for in calling Christ the Son of God he mentioned the person of the Father and that of the Son, along with the person of the Holy Spirit, who is the love of the Father and of the Son, and the bond or nexus of both. He professed the mystery of the Incarnation when he said, **you are the Christ:** for in Greek, the word "Christ" means "anointed"; anointed, that is, with the invisible oil of the Holy Spirit. He was not anointed according to his divine nature, because one who is anointed by the Holy Spirit is made better by that anointing. But Christ, so far as he is God, is not made better. Thus, Christ was anointed as man.

He said, **We have come to believe and to know,** because believing comes before knowing. And therefore, if we wanted to know before believing, we would neither know nor be able to believe, as Augustine says, and as in that other version of Isaiah: "If you do not believe, you will not understand" (Is 7:9).

1005 Our Lord corrected Peter's answer when he said, **Did I not choose you Twelve? And one of you is a devil.** First, we have our Lord's reply; secondly, the Evangelist's explanation of it (v 72).

1006 Because Peter was great-hearted and included all in his answer, **We have come to believe and to know that you are the**

Christ, the Son of God, it seemed that all of them would arrive at eternal life. And so our Lord excluded Judas from this community of believers. This trust was commendable in Peter, who did not suspect any evil in his companions; but we must also admire the wisdom of our Lord, who saw what was hidden. Thus he says, **Did I not choose you Twelve? And one of you is a devil**; not by nature, but by imitating the devil's malice: "Death came into the world by the envy of the devil; his disciples imitate him" (Wis 2:24); "After the morsel, Satan entered into him" (below 13:27), because Judas became like him in malice.

1007 But if Christ chose Judas, who was later to become evil, it seems that our Lord made a mistake in choosing him. First, we might answer this as Chrysostom does, and say that this choice was not for predestination, but for some task, and in reference to a condition of present justice. Sometimes a person is chosen this way, not in relation to the future, but according to present realities; for being chosen in this way does not destroy one's free choice or the possibility of sinning: hence we read, "Let him who thinks that he stands, take heed so he will not fall" (1 Cor 10:12). And so our Lord did choose Judas, but not as evil at that time; and being so chosen did not take away his possibility of sinning. Secondly, we could answer with Augustine, who said that our Lord did chose Judas as evil. And although he knew that he was evil, because it is characteristic of a good person to use evil for good, God made good use of this evil in allowing himself to be betrayed in order to redeem us. Or, we could say that the choice of the Twelve does not refer here to the persons, but rather to the number; as if to say: I have chosen Twelve. For this number is fittingly set apart for those who would preach the faith of the Holy Trinity to the four corners of the world. And indeed, this number did not pass away, because Matthias was substituted for the traitor. Or, according to Ambrose, Jesus chose Judas as evil so that when we read that our Lord and Master was betrayed by his disciple, we might be consoled if sometimes our friends betray us.

1008 We could ask here why the disciples did not say anything after our Lord said, **one of you is a devil**; for later on, when he says, "One of you will betray me" (below 13:21), they reply, "Is it I, Lord?" (Mt 26:22). I answer that the reason for this is that our Lord was speaking here in a general way when he said that one of them was a devil; for this could mean any kind of malice, and so they were not disturbed. But later on, when they heard of such a great crime, that their Master would be betrayed, they could not keep quiet. Or, we could say that when our Lord said this, each of them had confidence in his own virtue, and so none feared for himself; but after he said to Peter, "Follow after me, Satan" (Mt 16:23), they were afraid, and realized their own weakness. That is why they asked in that indecisive way, "Is it I, Lord?"

1009 Finally, what our Lord had just said privately is explained by the Evangelist when he says, **he was talking about Judas**, as events proved and which will be clear below (c 13).

7

LECTURE 1

1 After this, Jesus walked about in Galilee, for he did not want to walk in Judea because the Jews sought to kill him. 2 Now it was close to the Jewish feast of Tabernacles. 3 So his brethren said to him: "Leave this place, and go to Judea, so that your disciples also may see your works which you perform. 4 Surely, no one works in secret if he wants to be publicly renowned. If you do these things, reveal yourself to the world." 5 For not even his brethren believed in him. 6 Jesus therefore said to them:
> "My time has not yet come,
> but your time is always here.
> 7 The world cannot hate you,
> but me, it hates,
> because I bear witness against it,
> for its works are evil.
> 8 You yourselves go up for this feast.
> I, however, will not go up for this festival,
> because my time is not yet completed."

1010 After our Lord considered the spiritual life and its food, he now treats of his instruction or teaching, which, as mentioned above, is necessary for those who are spiritually reborn. First, he shows the origin of his teaching; secondly, its usefulness (c 8 and onwards). As to the first, he does three things. First, he mentions the place where he revealed the origin of his teaching; secondly, the occasion for revealing this (v 11); and thirdly, his actual statement is given (v 16). Three things are done about the first. First, we see Christ invited to go to the place where he revealed the origin of his teaching; secondly, we see our Lord refuse (v 6); and thirdly, how Jesus finally did go (v 9). As to the first, he does two things. First, he gives the reasons why they encouraged Christ to go to Judea; secondly, he adds their exhortation (v 3). They were influenced by three things to encourage Christ to go to Judea: first, by his lingering on [in Galilee], secondly, by his intention [not to travel in Judea]; and thirdly, by the appropriateness of the time.

1011 They were influenced by Christ's lingering on in Galilee, which showed that he wanted to stay there. Thus he says, **After this**, after teaching in Capernaum, **Jesus walked about in Galilee**, i.e., he set out from Capernaum, a city of Galilee, with the intention to journey throughout this region. Our Lord lingered on so often in

Galilee to show us that we should pass from vices to virtues: "So you, son of man, prepare your belongings for exile, and go during the day in their sight" (Ez 12:13).

1012   Then they were influenced by Christ's intention, which he perhaps told them; hence he says, **for he did not want to walk in Judea,** the reason being, **because the Jews sought to kill him.** "The Jews tried all the harder to kill him, because he not only broke the Sabbath rest, but even called God his own Father, making himself equal to God" (above 5:18).

But could not Christ still have gone among the Jews without being killed by them, as he did after (c 8)? Three answers are given to this question. The first is given by Augustine, who says that Christ did this because the time would come when some Christians would hide from those who were persecuting them. And so they would not be criticized for this, our Lord wanted to console us by setting a precedent himself in this matter. He also taught this in word, saying: "If they persecute you in one town, flee to another" (Mt 10:23). Another answer is that Christ was both God and man. By reason of his divinity, he could prevent his being injured by those persecuting him. Yet, he did not want to do this all the time, for while this would have shown his divinity, it might have cast doubt on his humanity. Therefore, he showed his humanity by sometimes fleeing, as man, those who were persecuting him, to silence all those who would say that he was not a true man. And he showed his divinity by sometimes walking among them unharmed, thus refuting all those who say he was only a man. Thus, Chrysostom has another text, which reads: "He could not, even if he wanted to, walk about Judea." This is expressed in our human way, and is the same as saying: Due to the danger of treachery, a person cannot go anywhere he might wish. The third answer is that it was not yet the time for Christ's passion. The time would come when Christ would suffer, at the feast of the Passover, when the lamb was sacrificed, so that victim would succeed victim: "Jesus knew that his time had come to leave this world for the Father" (below 13:1).

1013   They were also influenced by the suitableness of the time, for it was a time for going to Jerusalem. **Now it was close to the Jewish feast of Tabernacles** (scenopegia). Scenopegia is a Greek word, composed of scenos, which means "shade," or "tent," and phagim, which means "to eat." As if to say: It was the time in which they used to eat in their tents. For our Lord (Lv 23:41) had ordered the children of Israel to stay in their tents for seven days during the seventh month, as a reminder of the forty years they had lived in tents in the desert. This was the feast the Jews were then celebrating.

The Evangelist mentions this in order to show that some time had already passed since the previous teaching about spiritual food. For it was near the Passover when our Lord performed the miracle of the loaves, and this feast of Tabernacles is much later. The Evangelist does not tell us what our Lord did in the intervening five months. We can see from this that although Jesus was always performing miracles, as the last chapter says, the Evangelist was mainly concerned with recording those matters over which the Jews argued and with which they disagreed.

1014 Then (v 3), our Lord is urged on by his brethren. First, we are given their advice; secondly, the reason for it (v 3b); and thirdly, the Evangelist mentions the cause of this reason (v 5).

1015 As to the first, the ones who urge Christ are mentioned; hence he says, **So his brethren said to him.** These were not brothers of the flesh or of the womb, as the blasphemous opinion of Elvidius would have it. It is, indeed, offensive to the Catholic faith that the most holy virginal womb, which bore him who was God and man, should later bear another mortal man. Thus, they were his brothers or brethren in the sense of relatives, because they were related by blood to the Blessed Virgin Mary. For it is the custom in Scripture to call relatives "brothers," as in Genesis (13:8): "Let us not quarrel, for we are brothers," although Lot was the nephew of Abraham. And, as Augustine says, just as in the tomb in which our Lord's body had been placed no other body was placed either before or after, so the womb of Mary conceived no other mortal person either before or after Christ. Although some of the relatives of the Blessed Virgin were apostles, such as the sons of Zebedee, and James of Alpheus, and some others, we should not think that these were among those who were urging Christ; this was done by other relatives who did not love him.

Secondly, we see their advice when they say: **Leave this place,** that is, Galilee, **and go to Judea,** where you will find Jerusalem, a sacred place, well-suited to teachers. "Seer, go, flee to the land of Judah. There eat your bread and there prophesy" (Am 7:12).

1016 They give their reason when they say: **so that your disciples also may see your works which you perform.** Here they show, first, that they are hungry for an empty glory; secondly, that they are suspicious; and thirdly, do not believe [in our Lord].

They show that they are hungry for an empty glory when they say, **so that your disciples also may see your works which you perform.** For they allowed something human to Christ and wanted to share the glory of the human honor that the people would show him.

And so, they urged him to perform his works in public: for it is a characteristic of one who is seeking human glory to want publicly known whatever of his own or of his associates can bring glory. "They like to pray at street corners, so people can see them" (Mt 6:5). We read of such people: "For they loved the glory of men, more than the glory of God" (below 12:43).

They reveal that they themselves are suspicious, and first of all remark on Christ's fear, saying: **Surely, no one works in secret.** As if to say: You say that you are performing miracles. But you are doing them secretly because of fear; otherwise you would go to Jerusalem and do them before the people. Nevertheless, our Lord says below: "I have said nothing secretly" (below 18:20).

Secondly, they refer to his love of glory, saying: **if he wants to be publicly renowned.** As if to say: You want glory because of what you are doing, yet you are hiding because you are afraid. Now this attitude is characteristic of those who are evil: to think that other people are experiencing the same emotions as they are. Notice the disrespect with which the prudence of the flesh reproached the Word made flesh. Job says against them: "You reproach him who is not like you, and say what you should not" (Jb 4:3).

They show they do not believe when they say: **If you do these things, reveal yourself to the world**, doubting whether he did perform miracles. "He who does not believe is unfaithful" (Is 21:2).

1017 The Evangelist tells why they said this when he says, **For not even his brethren believed in him**. For sometimes blood relatives are very hostile to one of their own, and are jealous of his spiritual goods. They may even despise him. Thus Augustine says: "They could have Christ as a relative, but in that very closeness they refused to believe in him." "A man's enemies are in his own house" (Mi 7:6); "He has put my brethren far from me, and my acquaintances, like strangers, have gone from me. My relatives have left me, and those who knew me have forgotten me" (Jb 19:13).

1018 Then (v 6), Christ's answer is given. First, he mentions that the time was not appropriate for going to Jerusalem; secondly, the reason for this (v 7); and thirdly, we see Christ deciding not to go (v 8).

1019 We should note that all of the following text is explained differently by Augustine and by Chrysostom. Augustine says that the brethren of our Lord were urging him to a human glory. Now there is a time, in the future, when the saints do acquire glory; a glory they obtain by their sufferings and troubles. "He has tested them like gold in a furnace, and he accepted them as the victim of a holocaust.

At the time of their visitation they will shine" (Wis 3:6). And there is a time, the present, when the worldly acquire their glory. "Let not the flowers of the time pass us by; let us crown ourselves with roses before they wither" (Wis 2:7). Our Lord, therefore, wanted to show that he was not looking for the glory of this present time, but that he wanted to attain to the height of heavenly glory through his passion and humiliation. "It was necessary for Christ to suffer, and so enter into his glory" (Lk 24:26). So Jesus says to them, i.e., his brethren: **My time**, i.e., the time of my glory, **has not yet come**, because my sorrow must be turned into joy: "The sufferings of this present time are not worthy to be compared with the glory to come, which will be revealed in us" (Rom 8:18); **but your time**, i.e., the time of the glory of this world, **is always here**.

1020 He gives the reason why these times are different when he says, **The world cannot hate you, but me, it hates**. The reason why the time for the glory of the worldly is here is that they love the same things the world loves, and they agree with the world. But the time for the glory of the saints, who are looking for a spiritual glory, is not here, because they want what is displeasing to the world, that is, poverty, afflictions, doing without food, and things like that. They even disparage what the world loves; in fact, they despise the world: "The world has been crucified to me, and I to the world" (Gal 6:14). And so he says, **The world cannot hate you**. As if to say: Thus, the time of your glory is here, because the world does not hate you, who are in agreement with it; and every animal loves its like. **But me, it hates**, and so my time is not always here. And the reason it hates me is **because I bear witness against it**, that is, the world, **for its works are evil**; that is, I do not hesitate to reprimand those who are worldly, even though I know that they will hate me for it and threaten me with death. "They," that is, those who love evil, "hate the one who rebukes at the city gate" (Am 5:10); "Do not rebuke one who mocks, lest he hate you" (Prv 9:8).

1021 But cannot a person of the world be hated by the world, i.e., by another person of the world? I answer that, in a particular case, one worldly person can hate another insofar as the latter has what the first wants, or prevents him from obtaining what relates to the glory of this world. But precisely insofar as a person is of the world, the world does not hate him. The saints, however, are universally hated by the world because they are opposed to it. And if anyone of the world does love them, it is not because he is of the world, but because of something spiritual in him.

1022 Our Lord refuses to go when he says, **You yourselves go up for this feast. I, however, will not go up for this festival**. For just as there are two kinds of glory, so there are two different feasts. Worldly people have temporal feasts, that is, their own enjoyments and banquets and such exterior pleasures. "The Lord called for weeping and mourning ... and look at the rejoicing and gladness" (Is 22:12); "I hate your feasts" (Is 1:14). But the saints have their own spiritual feasts, which consist in the joys of the spirit: "Look upon Zion, the city of your feasts" (Is 33:20). So he says: **You yourselves,** who are looking for the glory of this world, **go up for this feast,** i.e., to the feasts of temporal pleasure; **I, however, will not go up for this festival,** for I will go to the feast of an eternal celebration. I am not going up now **because my time,** that is, the time of my true glory, which will be a joy that lasts forever, an eternity without fatigue, and a brightness without shadow, **is not yet completed.**

1023 Chrysostom keeps the same division of the text, but explains it this way. He says that these brethren of our Lord joined with the Jews in plotting the death of Christ. And so they urged Christ to go to the feast, intending to betray him and hand him over to the Jews. That is why he says: **My time,** that is, the time for my cross and death, **has not yet come,** to go to Judea and be killed. **But your time is always here,** because you can associate with them without danger. And this is because they cannot hate you: you who love and envy the same things they do. **But me, it hates, because I bear witness against it, for its works are evil.** This shows that the Jews hate me, not because I broke the sabbath, but because I denounced them in public. **You yourselves go up for this feast,** that is, for its beginning (for it lasted seven days, as was said), **I, however, will not go up for this festival,** that is, with you,and when it first begins: **because my time is not yet completed,** when I am to suffer, for he was to be crucified at a future Passover. Accordingly, he did not go with them then in order to remain out of sight, and so forth.

LECTURE 2

9 When he had said this, he remained in Galilee. 10 However, after his brethren had gone up, he himself went up for the feast, not publicly, but as it were in secret. 11 The Jews looked for him at the feast, and they asked: "Where is he?" 12 There was much whispering among the people concerning him, for some were saying that he was a good man, while others said, "On the contrary, he leads people astray." 13 Nevertheless, no one spoke openly about him for fear of the Jews. 14 Now when the festival was half over, Jesus went into

the temple, and he taught. 15 The Jews were amazed, saying, "How did this man get his learning, since he never studied?" 16 Jesus answered and said:

"My doctrine is not mine, but his who sent me.
17 If anyone wants to do his will, he will know
whether this doctrine is from God,
or whether I am speaking on my own.
18 Whoever speaks on his own [authority]
seeks his own glory.
But the one who seeks the glory of him who sent him
is truthful, and there is no injustice in him.
19 Did not Moses give you the law?
And yet none of you obey the law.
20 Why do you want to kill me?"

The crowd replied and said: "You have a demon within you! Who wants to kill you?" 21 Jesus answered and said to them:

"I performed one work, and you are all amazed.
22 Therefore, Moses gave you circumcision,
(not that it originated with Moses, but with the patriarchs)
and you circumcise on the sabbath day.
23 If a man receives circumcision on the sabbath day,
so that the law of Moses may not be broken,
why are you indignant with me because I healed
a whole man on the sabbath?
24 Judge not by the appearances, but with a just judgment."

1024   After the Evangelist mentioned how our Lord's relatives urged him to go to Judea, and what Christ replied to them, he then tells us of his journey. First, of his delay in going into Judea; secondly, of the order of the events; and thirdly, the way Christ went up.

1025   He mentions our Lord's delay in going when he says, **When he had said this**, in answer to his relatives, **he remained in Galilee**, and did not go to the feast with them. He did this to keep to his word: "I, however, will not go up for this festival." As we read in Numbers (23:19): "God is not like man, a liar."

1026   He gives the order of events when he says, **However, after his brethren**, that is, his relatives, **had gone up, he himself went up for the feast**. This seems to conflict with what he had said before: "I will not go up", for the Apostle says, "Jesus Christ, whom we preached among you ... was not 'Yes' and 'No,' but only 'Yes.' " (2 Cor 1:19).

I answer, first, that the festival of Tabernacles lasted for seven days, as was mentioned. Now our Lord first stated, "I, however, will not go up for this festival," that is, for its beginning. When it says here that **he himself went up for the feast**, we should understand this to refer to the middle of the feast. This is why we read a little further on: "Now, when the festival was half over" (v 14). So it is clear that Christ was not breaking his word. Secondly, as Augustine says, his relatives wanted him to go to Jerusalem to try for a temporal glory. So he said to them: "I, however, will not go up for this festival," for the purpose you want me to. But he did go to the festival to teach the people and to tell them about an eternal glory. Thirdly, as Chrysostom says, our Lord said, "I, however, will not go up for this festival," to suffer and die, as they wished; but he did go, not in order to suffer, but to teach others.

1027   The way he went was **not publicly, but as it were in secret**. There are three reasons for this. The first, given by Chrysostom, is so that he would not call more attention to his divinity, and so perhaps make his incarnation less certain, as was said above; and so that those who are virtuous would not be ashamed to hide from those who are persecuting them when they cannot openly restrain them. Thus he says, **in secret**, to show that this was done according to plan: "Truly, you are a hidden God" (Is 45:15). Augustine gives us another reason: to teach us that Christ was hidden in the figures of the Old Testament: "I will wait for the Lord, who has hidden his face (i.e., clear knowledge) from the house of Jacob" (Is 8:17); so, "Even to this day ... a veil is over their hearts" (2 Cor 3:15). Thus, everything that was said to this ancient people was a shadow of the good things to come, as we see from Hebrews (10:1). So our Lord went up in secret to show that even this feast was a figure. *Scenopegia*, as we saw, was the feast of Tabernacles; and the one who celebrates this feast is the one who understands that he is a pilgrim in this world. Another reason why our Lord went up in secret was to teach us that we should conceal the good things we do, not looking for human approval or desiring the applause of the crowd: "Take care not to perform your good actions in the sight of men, in order to be seen by them" (Mt 6:1).

1028   Then (v 11), he mentions the opportunity Christ had to show the origin of his spiritual teaching. He mentions two such opportunities: one was due to the disagreement among the people; the other to their amazement (v 15). The people disagreed in what they thought of Christ. He does three things concerning this. First, he shows what they had in common; secondly, how they differed (v 12); and thirldy, whose opinion prevailed (v 13).

1029 What they had in common was that they **looked for him at the feast, and they asked: Where is he?** It is obvious that they did not even want to mention his name because of their hatred and hostility: "They hated him and could not speak civilly to him" (Gn 37:4).

1030 They differed, however, because some looked for him because they wished to learn: "Seek him, and your soul will live" (Ps 68:33); others were looking for him in order to harm him: as in the Psalm (39:15): "They seek my soul to carry it away." And so **There was much whispering among the people concerning him**, because of their disagreements. And although "whispering" (*murmur*) is neuter in gender, Jerome makes it masculine (*murmur multus*) because he was following the custom of the older grammarians, or else to show that divine Scripture is not subject to the rules of Priscian.

There was disagreement: for **some** of the people, that is, those who were right in heart, **were saying**, of Christ, **that he was a good man.** "How good God is to Israel, to those whose heart is right" (Ps 72:1); "The Lord is good to those who hope in him, to the one who seeks him" (Lam 3:25). **While others**, that is, those who were badly disposed, **said: On the contrary**, i.e., he is not a good man. We can see from this that it was the people who thought that he was a good person, while he was considered evil by the chief priests; so they say, **he leads people astray**: "We found this man leading our people astray" (Lk 23:2); "We have remembered that that seducer said ..." (Mt 27:63).

1031 Here we should note that to seduce is to lead away. Now a person can be led away either from what is true or from what is false. And in either way a person can be called a seducer: either because he leads one away from the truth, and in this sense it does not apply to Christ, because he is the truth (below c 8); or because he leads one away from what is false, and in this sense Christ is called a seducer: "You seduced me, O Lord, and I was seduced. You were stronger than I, and you have won" (Jer 20:7). Would that all of us were called and were seducers in this sense, as Augustine says. But we call a person a seducer primarily because he leads others away from the truth and deceives them: because a person is said to be led away if he is drawn from the common way. But the common way is the way of truth; heresies, on the other hand, and the way of the wicked, are detours.

1032 It was the opinion of the evil, that is, of the chief priests, that finally won out. Thus he continues, **Nevertheless, no one spoke openly about him.** This was because the people were held back by their fear of the chief priests, for as stated below (9:22): "If any one should profess him to be the Christ, he would be put out of the synagogue." This reveals the wickedness with which the leaders plotted against Christ; and it shows that those who were subject to them, i.e., the people, were not free to say what they thought.

1033   Next (v 15), we see the second opportunity Christ had to present his teaching, that is, the amazement of the people. First, we see the object of their amazement; secondly, their amazement itself, and thirdly, the reason why they were amazed.
1034   The object of their amazement is the doctrine or teaching of Christ. Both the time and the place of this teaching are given. The time is mentioned when he says, **Now when the festival was half over**, that is, when as many days were left of the feast as had passed. Thus, since the feast lasted some seven days, this took place on the fourth day. As we said, when Christ hid himself, it was a sign of his humanity, and an example of virtue for us. But when he did come before them, and they could not suppress him, this showed his divinity. Further, our Lord went when the feast was half over, because at the beginning everyone would be occupied with matters relating to the feast: the good, with the worship of God, and others with trivialities and financial profit; but when it was half over, and such matters had been settled, the people would be better prepared to receive his teaching. Thus our Lord did not go to the first several days of the feast so that he would find them more attentive and better prepared for his teaching. Similarly, Christ's going to the feast at this time paralled the arrangement of his teaching: for Christ came to teach us about the kingdom of God, not at the beginning of the world, nor at its ending, but during the intervening time. "You will make it known in the intervening years" (Hb 3:2).
The place where our Lord taught is mentioned when he says, **into the temple**. He taught there for two reasons. First, to show that he was teaching the truth, which they could not depricate, and which was necessary for all: "I have said nothing secretly" (below 18:20). Secondly, because the temple, since it was a sacred place, was appropriate for the very holy teaching of Christ: "Come! Let us go up the mountain of the Lord, and to the house of the God of Jacob. And he will teach us his ways, and we will walk in his steps," as we read in Isaiah (2:3).
The Evangelist does not mention what Christ taught, for, as was said, the Evangelists do not report everything our Lord did and said, but those which excited the people or produced some controversy. And so here he mentions the excitement his teaching produced in the people: that is, that those who had said before, "he leads people astray," were now amazed at his teaching.

1035   He mentions this amazement when he says, **The Jews were amazed**. And this is not surprising, for "Your testimony is wonderful" (Ps 118:129). For the words of Christ are the words of divine wisdom.

He adds the reason why they were amazed when he says, **How did this man get his learning, since he never studied?** For they knew that Jesus was the son of a poor woman and he was considered the son of a carpenter; as such, he would be working for a living and devoting his time, not to study, but to physical work, according to "I am poor, and have labored since my youth" (Ps 87:16). And so when they hear him teach and debate, they are amazed, and say, **How did this man get his learning, since he never studied?** Much the same is said in Matthew (13:54): "Where did he acquire this widsom, and these great works? Isn't he the son of the carpenter?"

1036   Having been told of the place and opportunity which Christ had to reveal the origin of his spiritual teaching, we now see the origin of this teaching. First, he shows them that God is the source of this spiritual teaching; secondly, he invites them to accept it (v 37). As to the first, he does two things. First, he shows the origin of this teaching; secondly, the origin of the one teaching it (v 25). He does two things about the first. First, he shows the origin of this teaching; secondly, he answers an objection (v 19). In regard to the first he does two things. First, he shows the origin of this teaching; secondly, he proves that it comes from God (v 17).

1037   He says, **Jesus answered and said**. As if to say: You are wondering where I gained my knowledge; but I say, **My doctrine is not mine**. If he had said: "The doctrine that I am presenting to you is not mine," there would be no problem. But he says: **My doctrine is not mine**; and this seems to be a contradiction. However, this can be explained, for this statement can be understood is several ways. Our Lord's doctrine can in some sense be called his own, and in some sense not his own. First, we can understand Christ as the Son of God. Then, since the doctrine of anyone is nothing else than his word, and the Son of God is the Word of God, it follows that the doctrine of the Father is the Son himself. But this same Word belongs to himself through an identity of substance. "What does belong to you, if not you yourself?" However, he does not belong to himself through his origin. As Augustine says: "If you do not belong to yourself (because you are from another), what does?" This seems to be the meaning, expressed in summary fashion, of: **My doctrine is not mine**. As if to say: I am not of myself. This refutes the Sabellian heresy, which dared to say that the Son is the Father.

Or, we could understand it as meaning that **My doctrine**, which I proclaim with created words, **is not mine, but his who sent me**, i.e., it is the Father's; that is, my doctrine is not mine as from myself, but it is from the Father: because the Son has even his knowledge from the Father through an eternal generation. "All things have been given to me by my Father" (Mt 11:27).

Secondly, we can understand Christ as the Son of Man. Then he is saying: **My doctrine**, which I have in my created soul, and which my lips proclaim, **is not mine**, i.e, it is not mine as from myself, but from God: because every truth, by whomever spoken, is from the Holy Spirit.

Thus, as Augustine says in *The Trinity* (Bk I), our Lord called this doctrine his own from one point of view, and not his own from another point of view. According to his form of God, it was his own; but according to his form of a servant, it was not his own. This is an example for us, that we should realize that all our knowledge is from God, and thank him for it: "What do you have which you have not been given? And if you have been given it, why do you glory as if you have not been given it?" (1 Cor 4:7).

1038   Then (v 17), he proves that his doctrine is from God. And he does this in two ways: first, from the judgment of those who correctly understand such matters; and secondly, from his own intention (v 18).

1039   With respect to the first, we should note that when there is a question whether someone is performing well in some art, this is decided by one who has experience in that art; just as the question whether someone is speaking French well should be decided by one who is well versed in the French language. With this in mind, our Lord is saying: The question whether my doctrine is from God must be decided by one who has experience in divine matters, for such a person can judge correctly about these things. "The sensual man does not perceive those things that pertain to the Spirit of God. The spiritual man judges all things" (1 Cor 2:14). Accordingly, he is saying: Because you are alienated from God, you do not know whether a doctrine is from God. **If anyone wants to do his will**, that is, the will of God, he can know whether this doctrine is from God, **or whether I am speaking on my own** (*a meipso*). Indeed, one who is speaking what is false is speaking on his own, because "When he lies, he speaks on his own," as we read below (8:44).

Chrysostom explains this text in another way. The will of God is our peace, our love, and our humility; thus Matthew (5:9) says: "Happy are the peacemakers, because they will be called sons of God." But the love of controversy often distorts a person's mind to such an extent that he thinks that what is really true is false. Thus, when we abandon the spirit of controversy, we possess more surely the certitude of truth. "Answer, I entreat you, without contention, and judge, speaking what is just" (Jb 6:29). So our Lord is saying: If anyone wishes to judge my doctrine correctly, let him do the will of God, i.e., abandon the anger, the envy and the hatred which he has for me without reason. Then, nothing will prevent him from knowing **whether this doctrine is from God, or whether I am speaking on my own**, i.e., whether I am speaking the words of God.

Augustine explains it this way. It is the will of God that we know his works, just as it is the will of a head of a household that his servants do his works. The work of God is that we believe in him whom he has sent: "This is the work of God, that you believe in him whom he sent" (above 6:29). Thus he says: **If anyone wants to do his will**, that is, God's will, which is to believe in me, **he will know whether this doctrine is from God**: "If you do not believe, you will not understand," as that other version of Isaiah (7:9) says.

1040 Then when he says, **Whoever speaks on his own seeks his own glory**, he proves the same thing from his intention. And he presents two intentions through which we can recognize the two sources of a doctrine. Some are said to speak on their own [*a se*], and others not on their own. Now whoever strives to speak the truth does not speak on his own. All our knowledge of the truth is from another: either from instruction, as from a teacher; or from revelation, as from God; or by a process of discovery, as from things themselves, for "the invisible things of God are clearly known by the things that have been made" (Rom 1:20). Consequently, in whatever way a person acquires his knowledge, he does not acquire it on his own. That person speaks on his own who takes what he says neither from things themselves, nor from any human teaching, but from his own heart: "They proclaim a vision taken out of their own hearts" (Jer 23:16); "Woe to those foolish prophets who prophesy out of their own hearts" (Ez 13:3). Accordingy, when a person devises a doctrine on his own he does it for the sake of human glory: for, as we see from Chrysostom, a person who wishes to present his own private doctrine does so for no other purpose than to acquire glory. And this is what our Lord says, proving that his doctrine is from God: **Whoever speaks on his own**, about a certain knowledge of the truth, which is really from another, **seeks his own glory**. It is for this reason, and because of pride, that various heresies and false opinions have arisen. And this is a characteristic of the antichrist "who opposes and is exalted above all that is called God, or is worshipped" (2 Thes 2:4).

But the one who seeks the glory of him who sent him, as
I do – "I do not seek my own glory" (below 8:50) – **is truthful,
and there is no injustice in him**. I am truthful because my doctrine
contains the truth; there is no injustice in me because I do not
appropriate the glory of another. As Augustine says: "He gave us
a magnificent example of humility when, in the form of a man, he
sought the glory of the Father, and not his own. O man, you should
do the same! When you do something good, you seek your glory;
when you do something evil, you insult God." It is obvious that
he was not looking for his own glory, because if he had not been an
enemy of the chief priests, he would not have been persecuted by
them. So Christ, and everyone who is looking for the glory of God,
has knowledge in his intellect, "Master, we know that you are truthful" (Mt 22:16): thus he says, he **is truthful**. And he has the correct
intention in his will: thus he says, **and there is no injustice in him**.
For a person is unjust when he takes for himself what belongs to
another; but glory is proper to God alone; therefore, he who seeks
glory for himself is unjust.

1041   Then (v 19), he answers an objection. For someone
could tell Christ that his doctrine was not from God because he
broke the sabbath, according to, "This man is not from God, for
he does not keep the sabbath" (below 9:16). This is what he intends
to answer; and he does three things. First, he clears himself, by
arguing from the actions of those who are accusing him; secondly,
we see their vicious reply (v 20); and thirdly, he vindicates himself
with a reasonable explanation (v 21).

1042   He says: Even granting, as you say, that my doctrine is
not from God because I do not keep the law, breaking the sabbath,
nevertheless, you do not have any reason to accuse me since you do
the same thing. Thus he says: **Did not Moses give you the law?** i.e.,
did he not give it to your people? **And yet none of you obey the law**.
"You received the law through the angels, and have not kept it"
(Acts 7:53). This is why Peter says: "A yoke, which neither our
fathers nor we were able to bear" (Acts 15:10). Therefore, if you
do not keep the law, why do you want to kill me for not keeping it?
You are not doing this because of the law, but out of hatred. If you
were acting out of devotion for the law, you would keep it yourselves. "Let us lie in wait for the just man, because he is unfavorable
to us, and against our works, and he reproaches us for breaking the
law" (Wis 2:12); and a little further on we read: "Let us condemn
him to a most shameful death" (Wis 2:20).

Or, it could be explained this way: You do not keep the law
that Moses gave you; and this is obvious from the fact that you want

to kill me, which is against the law: "You shall not kill" (Ex 20:13). Another explanation, following Augustine, is: You do not keep the law because I myself am included in the law: "If you believed Moses, you would perhaps believe me as well, for it was about me that he wrote" (above 5:46). But you want to kill me.

1043 Then we see the vicious reply of the crowd, when he says, **The crowd replied and said: You have a demon within you!** As Augustine says, their reply indicates disorder and confusion, rather than any order: for they are saying that the one who casts out devils has one himself (Mt c 12).

1044 Then when he says, **I performed one work, and you are all amazed**, our Lord, at peace in his own truth, answers them, and justifies himself with a reasonable explanation. First, he recalls the incident that is troubling them; secondly, he shows that this should not bother them (v 22); and thirdly, he shows the way to a judgment that is just (v 24).

1045 Jesus answered them: **I performed one work, and you are all amazed.** He does not trade one insult for another, nor rebuff it, because "When he was derided, he did not deride in return" (1 Pt 2:23). He rather recalls for them his cure of the paralytic, which was the cause of their amazement. But their amazement was not one of devotion, as in "Your heart will be amazed and expanded" (Is 60:5), but a kind of agitation and disturbance, as in "Those who see it will be afflicted with terrible fear, and will be amazed" (Wis 5:2). So, if you are amazed over one of my works, i.e., if you are disturbed and troubled, what would you do if you saw all of my works? For, as Augustine says, his works were those which they saw in the world: even all the sick are healed by him. "He sent his word, and healed them" (Ps 106:20); "It was neither a herb nor a poultice that healed them, but your word, O Lord, which heals all" (Wis 16:12). Thus, the reason why you are disturbed is that you have seen only one of my works, and not all of them.

1046 Then (v 22), he shows that there is no reason why they should be disturbed. First, he recalls the command given to them by Moses; secondly, he states their customary behavior; and thirdly, he presents an argument based on the first two.

1047 The command of Moses was about circumcision; so he says: **Therefore**, i.e., to signify my works, **Moses gave you circumcision.** For circumcision was given as a sign, as we read, "It will be a sign of the covenant between me and you" (Gn 17:11). For it signified Christ. This is the reason why it was always done on the genital organ, because Christ was to descend, in his human nature, from Abraham; and Christ is the one who spiritually circumcises us, i.e., both in mind and body. Or, it was done to the genital organ because it was given in opposition to original sin.

We do not find it explicitly stated that Moses gave circumcision, unless in Exodus (12:44): "Every slave who is bought shall be circumcised." And although Moses did tell them to circumcise, he was not the one who established this practice, because he was not the first one to receive the command to circumcise; this was Abraham, as we see from Genesis (17:10).

1048   Now it was the custom among the Jews to circumcise on the sabbath. And this is what he says: **you circumcise on the sabbath day.** They did this because Abraham was told that a boy should be circumcised on the eighth day: "He circumcised him on the eighth day, as God had commanded him" (Gn 21:4). On the other hand, they were told by Moses not to do any work on the sabbath. But it sometimes happened that the eighth day was a sabbath. And so, in circumcising a boy on that day, they were breaking a command of Moses for a command of the patriarchs.

1049   Our Lord is arguing from those facts when he says: **If a man receives circumcision on the sabbath day, so that the law of Moses may not be broken, why are you indignant with me because I healed a whole man on the sabbath?**

We should note here that three things make this argument effective: two of these are explicit, and the other implied. First, although the command given to Abraham [about circumcision] was the first to be given, it was not canceled by the command given to Moses concerning observing the sabbath. "I say that the covenant, confirmed by God, is not canceled by the law, which came four hundred and thirty years later" (Gal 3:17). And so Christ is arguing from this: Although when dealing with human laws, the later ones cancel the earlier laws, in the case of divine laws, the earlier ones have greater authority. And so the command given to Moses about observing the sabbath does not cancel the command which was given to Abraham concerning circumcision. Therefore, much less does it interfere with me, who am only doing what was decided by God, before the creation of the world, for the salvation of mankind; and this salvation was symbolized by the sabbath.

Another point is that the Jews were commanded not to work on the sabbath; yet they did do things that were related to the salvation of the individual. So Christ is saying: If you people, who were commanded not to work on the sabbath, circumcise on that day (and this concerns the salvation of the individual, and thus it was done to an individual organ) and you do this **so that the law of Moses may not be broken** (from which it is clear that those things that pertain to salvation should not be omitted on the sabbath), it follows with greater reason that a man should do on that day those things that pertain to the salvation of everyone. Therefore, you should not be indignant with me **because I healed a whole man on the sabbath.**

The third point is that each command was a symbol: for "all these things happened to them in symbol" (1 Cor 10:11). Thus, if one symbol, i.e., the command to observe the sabbath, does not cancel the other symbol, i.e., the command to circumcise, much less does it cancel the truth. For circumcision sybolized our Lord, as Augustine says.

Finally, he says, **a whole man,** because, since God's works are perfect, the man was cured so as to be healthy in body, and he believed so as to be healthy in soul.

1050 Then when he says, **Judge not by the appearances, but with a just judgment,** he guides them to a fair consideration of himself, so that they do not judge him according to appearances, but give a judgment which is just. There are two ways in which one is said to judge according to appearances. First, a judge may reach his decision relying on the allegations: "Men see the things that are evident" (1 Kgs 15:7). But this way can lead to error; thus he says, **Judge not by the appearances,** i.e., by what is immediately evident, but examine the matter diligently: "I diligently investigated the strangers cause" (Jb 29:16); "He will not judge by appearances" (Is 11:3). In the second way, **Judge not by the appearances,** i.e., do not show partiality or favoritism in your judgment: for all judges are forbidden to do this. "You will not show favoritism when judging a person who is poor" (Ex 23:6); "You have shown partiality in your judgment" (Mal 2:9). To show partiality in a judgment is not to give a judgment that is just because of love, or deference, or fear, or the status of a person, which things have nothing to do with the case. So he says: **Judge not by the appearances, but with a just judgment,** as if to say: Just because Moses is more honored among you than I am, you should not base your decision on our reputations, but on the nature of the facts: because the things I am doing are greater than what Moses did.

But it should be noted, according to Augustine, that one who loves all equally does not judge with partiality. For when we honor men differently according to their rank, we must beware of showing partiality.

LECTURE 3

25 Some of the inhabitants of Jerusalem then said: "Is he not the man they want to kill? 26 Look, he is speaking publicly, and they say nothing to him! Could it be that the rulers really know that he is the Christ? 27 We know where this man comes from; but when the Christ comes, no one will know where he comes from." 28 So as Jesus was teaching in the temple, he cried out and said:
"You do indeed know me,
and you know where I come from.
And I have not come of my own accord.
But the one who sent me is truthful,
whom you do not know.
29 I know him.
And if I were to say that I do not know him,
I would be like you, a liar.
But I do know him, because I am from him,
and he sent me."
30 They therefore wanted to seize him, but no one laid a hand on him, because his hour had not yet come. 31 Many of the people, however, believed in him, and they said: "When the Christ comes, will he work more wonders than this man has done?" 32 The Pharisees heard the people saying these things about him, so the rulers and Pharisees sent officers to apprehend Jesus.

1051 Having considered the origin of his doctrine, he now tells us about the origin of its teacher. First, Christ shows his source, from which he comes, secondly, he shows his end, to which he goes (v 33). He does three things concerning the first. First, we see the doubt of the people about his origin; secondly, we have Christ's teaching concerning his origin (v 28); and thirdly, we see the effect this teaching had (v 30). He does two things about the first. First, we see the amazement of the people; secondly, their conjecture (v 26). The people were amazed over two things: at the unjust statements of their leaders, and at the public teaching of Christ (v 25).

1052 As we said before, Christ went up to this feast in secret to show the weakness of his human nature; but he publicly taught in the temple, with his enemies being unable to restrain him, to show his divinity. And so, as Augustine remarks, what was thought to be a lack of courage turned out to be strength. Accordingly, **Some of the inhabitants of Jersualem then said**, in amazement, for they knew how fiercely their leaders were looking for him, as they lived with them in Jerusalem. Thus Chrysostom says: "The most pitiable of all were they who saw a very clear sign of his divinity and, leaving everything to the judgment of their corrupt leaders, failed to show Christ reverence." "As the ruler of a city is, so are its inhabitants" (Sir 10:2). Yet they were amazed at the power he had which kept him from being apprehended. So they said: **Is he not the man they,** i.e., their leaders, **want.** This agrees with what was said before: "For reasons like this the Jews began to persecute Jesus, because he performed such works on the sabbath" (above 5:16); "Evil has come out of the elders of the people, who ruled them" (Dn 13:5). This also shows that Christ spoke the truth, while what their leaders said was false. For above, when our Lord asked them: "Why do you want to kill me?" they denied it and said: "You have a demon within you! Who wants to kill you?" But here, what their leaders had denied, these others admit when they say, **Is he not the man they want to kill?** Accordingly, they are amazed, considering the evil intentions of their leaders.

1053 Again, they were amazed that Christ was openly teaching; so they said: **Look, he is speaking publicly,** i.e., Christ was teaching, an indication of the secure possession of the truth, "I have spoken publicly" (below 18:20), **and they say nothing to him,** held back by divine power. For it is a characteristic of God's power that he prevents the hearts of evil men from carrying out their evil plans. "When the Lord is pleased with the way a man is living he will make his enemies be at peace with him" (Ps 16:7); and again, "The heart of the king is in the hand of the Lord; he turns it wherever he wills" (Prv 21:1).

1054 We see their conjecture when he says, **Could it be that the rulers really know that he is the Christ?** As if to say: Before, they sought to kill him; but now that they have found him, they do not say anything to him. Still, the leaders had not changed their opinion about Christ: "If they had known, they would never have crucified the Lord of glory" (1 Cor 2:8), but were restrained by divine power.

1055 Their objection to this conjecture is then added: **We know where this man comes from.** As if to argue: The Christ should have a hidden origin; but the origin of this man is known; therefore, he is not the Christ. This shows their folly, for granted that some of their leaders believed Christ, they did not follow their opinion, but offered another, which was false. "This is Jerusalem; I have set her in the midst of the nations" (Ez 5:5). For they knew that Christ took his origin from Mary, but they did not know the way this came about: "Isn't Joseph his father, and Mary his mother?" as we read in Matthew (13:55).

1056   Why did they say, **when the Christ comes, no one will know where he comes from**, since it says in Micah (5:2): "Out of you [Bethlehem-Ephrathah] will come a leader, who will rule my people Israel."?   I answer that they took this opinion from Isaiah, who said: "Who will make known his origin?" (53:8). Thus, they knew from the prophets where he was from, according to his human origin; and they also knew from them that they did not know it, according to his divine origin.

1057   Then (v 28), he shows his origin. First, he shows in what sense his origin is known, and in what sense it is not know; in the second place, he shows how we can acquire a knowledge of his origin (v 29). He does two things about the first. First, he shows what they knew about his origin; secondly, what they did not know about it (v 28b).

1058   They did know the origin of Jesus; and so he says of Jesus that **he cried out**. Now a cry comes from some great emotion. Sometimes it indicates the upheaval of a soul in interior distress; and in this sense it does not apply to Christ: "He will not cry out" (Is 42:2); "The words of the wise are heard in silence" (Ecc 9:17). Sometimes it implies great devotion, as in, "In my trouble I cried to the Lord" (Ps 119:1). And sometimes, along with this, it signifies that what is to be said is important, as in, "The Seraphim cried to each other and said: 'Holy, holy, holy, is the Lord God of hosts' " (Is 6:3); and in, "Does not wisdom cry out?" (Prv 8:1). This is the way preachers are encouraged to cry out: "Cry out, do not stop! Raise you voice like a trumpet" (Is 58:1). This is the way Christ cried out here, **teaching in the temple**.

And he said: **You do indeed know me**, according to appearances, **and you know where I come from**, that is, as to my bodily existence: "After this he was seen on earth" (Bar 3:38). For they knew that he was born from Mary in Bethlehem, and brought up in Nazareth; but they did not know about the virgin birth, and that he had been conceived through the Holy Spirit, as Augustine says. With the exception of the virgin birth, they knew everything about Jesus that pertained to his humanity.

1059   They did not know his hidden origin; and so he says: **And I have not come of my own accord**. First, he gives his origin; and secondly, he shows that it is hidden from them.

His origin is from the Father, from eternity. And so he says: **I have not come of my own accord**, as if to say: Before I came into the world through my humanity, I existed according to my divinity: "Before Abraham came to be, I am" (below 8:58). For he could not have come unless he already was. And although I have come, **I have not come of my own accord** [*a me ipso*], because the Son is not of himself [*a se*], but from the Father. "I came from the Father and have come into the world" (below 16:28). Indeed, his origin was foretold by the Father, who promised to send him: "I beg you, O Lord, send him whom you are going to send" (Ex 4:13); "I will send them a Savior and a defender, to free them" (Is 19:20). And so he says: **the one who sent me is truthful**, as if to say: I have not come from another but from him who promised and kept his promise, as he is truthful: "God is truthful" (Rom 3:4). Consequently, he teaches me to speak the truth, because I have been sent by one who is truthful. But they do not know this, because they do not know him who sent me; and so he says: **whom you do not know**.

1060 But since every man, although born in a bodily condition, is from God, it seems that Christ could say that he is from God; and consequently, that they do know where he comes from. I answer, according to Hilary, that the Son is *a* (from) God in a different way than others: for he is from God in such a way that he is also God; and so God is his consubstantial principle. But others are *a* (from) God, but in such a way that they are not *ex* (from) him. Thus, it is not known where the Son is from because the nature *ex* (from) which he is , is not known. But where men are from is not unknown: for if something exists *ex* (from) nothing, where it is from cannot be unknown.

1061 Then when he says, **I know him**, he teaches us how to know him from whom he is. For if a thing is to be learned, it must be learned from one who knows it. But only the Son knows the Father. And so he says: If you wish to know him who sent me, you must acquire this knowledge from me, because **I** alone **know him**. First, he shows that he knows him; secondly, he shows the perfection of his knowledge; and thirdly, the nature of his knowledge.

1062 He shows that he knows him when he says, **I know him**. Now it is true that "All men see him" (Jb 36:25), but they do not see him in the same way, for in this life we see him through the intermediary of creatures: "The invisible things of God are clearly known through the things that have been made" (Rom 1:20). Thus we read: "Now we see in a mirror, in an obscure manner" (1 Cor 13:12). But the angels and the blessed in heaven see him through his essence: "Their angels in heaven always see the face of my Father, who is in heaven" (Mt 18:10); "We shall see him as he is" (1 Jn 3:2). The Son of God, on the other hand, sees him in a more excellent way than all, that is, with a comprehensive or all-inclusive vision: "No one has ever seen God," i.e., in a comprehensive way; "it is the Only Begotten Son, who is in the bosom of the Father, who has made him known" (above 1:18); "No one knows the Father but the Son" (Mt 11:27). It is of this vision that he is speaking of here, when he says: **I know him**, with a comprehensive knowledge.

1063 He shows the perfection of his knowledge when he says: **And if I were to say that I do not know him, I would be like you, a liar**. This is mentioned for two reasons. Intellectual creatures do know God, though from a distance and imperfectly, for "All men see him, from a distance" (Jb 36:25). For divine truth transcends all our knowledge: "God is greater than our hearts" (1 Jn 3:20). Therefore, whoever knows God can say without lying: "I do not know him," because he does not know him to the full extent that he is knowable. But the Son knows God the Father most perfectly, just as he knows himself most perfectly. Thus he cannot say: **I do not know him**.

Again, because our knowledge of God, especially that which comes through grace, can be lost – "They forgot God, who saved them" (Ps 105:21) – men can say, **I do not know him**, as long as they are in this present life: because no one knows whether he deserves love or hatred. The Son, on the other hand, has a knowledge of the Father that cannot be lost; so he cannot say: **I do not know him**.

We should understand, **I would be like you**, as a reverse likeness. For they would not be lying if they said they did not know God; but they would be if they said that they did know him, since they did not know him. But if Christ said that he did not know him, he would be lying, since he did know him. So the meaning of this statement is this: **If I were to say that I do not know him**, then since I really do know him, **I would be like you, a liar**, who say that you know him, although you do not.

1064 Could not Christ have said: **I do not know him**? It seems he could, since he could have moved his lips and said the words. And so he could have lied. I reply that Christ did say this and still was not lying. We should explain it this way: If he were to say, **I do not know him**, declaratively, meaning, "I believe in my heart what I profess by my lips," [then he would have been a liar]. Now to say as the truth what is false comes from two defects: from a defect of knowledge in the intellect; and Christ could not have this since he is the wisdom of God (1 Cor 1:30); or it could come from a defect of right will in the affections; and this could not be in Christ either since he is the power of God, according to the same text. Thus he could not say the words **I do not know him**, declaratively. Yet this entire conditional statement is not false, although both its parts are impossible.

1065 The reason for this singular and perfect knowledge of Christ is given when he says: **I do know him, because I am from him, and he sent me.** Now all knowledge comes about through some likeness, since nothing is known except insofar as there is a likeness of the known in the knower. But whatever proceeds from something has a likeness to that from which it proceeds; and so, all who truly know have a varied knowledge of God according to the different degrees of their procession from him. The rational soul has a knowledge of God insofar as it participates in a likeness to him in a more imperfect way than other intellectual creatures. An angel, because it has a more explicit likeness to God, being a stamp of resemblance, knows God more clearly. But the Son has the most perfect likeness to the Father, since he has the same essence and power as he does; and so he knows him most perfectly, as was said. And so he says: **But I do know him,** that is, to the extent that he is knowable. And the reason for this is **because I am from him,** having the same essence with him through consubstantiality. Thus, just as he knows himself perfectly through his essence, so **I do know him** perfectly through the same essence. And so that we do not understand these words as referring to his being sent into this world, he at once adds, **and he sent me.** Consequently, the statement, **I am from him,** refers to his eternal generation, through which he is consubstantial with the Father. But then when he says, **and he sent me,** he is saying that the Father is the author of the incarnation: "God sent his Son, made from a woman, made under the law" (Gal 4:4). Now just as the Son has a perfect knowledge of the Father because he is from the Father, so because the soul of Christ is united to the Word in a unique way, it has a unique and more excellent knowledge of God than other creatures, although it does not comprehend him. And so Christ can say, according to his human nature: I know him in a more excellent way than other creatures do, but without comprehending him.

1066 Then (v 30), he considers the effect of his teaching. First on the people; then on the Pharisees (v 32). He does two things with the first. First, he shows the effect of this teaching on those of the people who were ill-willed; secondly, on those who were favorable (v 31). He does three things concerning the first. First, he mentions the evil intention of the people; secondly, that they were hindered in carrying out their plan; and thirdly, he mentions the reason why they were hindered.

1067 He presents their evil intention when he says, **They therefore wanted to seize him.** Because our Lord said to them, "whom you do not know," they became angry, feigning that they did know him. And so they formed the evil plan of seizing him, so that they could crucify and kill him: "Go after him, and seize him" (Ps 70:11). Yet there are some who have Christ within themselves, and still seek to seize him in a reverent manner: "I will go up into the palm tree and seize its fruit" (Sg 7:8). And so the Apostle says: "I will go after it to seize it" (Phil 3:12).

1068 He mentions that they were hindered in their plans when he says, **but no one laid a hand on him**: for their rage was invisibly checked and restrained. This shows that a person has the will to inflict injury from himself, while the power to inflict injury is from God. This is clear from the first chapters of Job, where Satan was unable to torment Job except to the extent that he was permitted to do so by God.

1069 The reason they were hindered was **because his hour had not yet come**. Here we should note that "There is a time and fitness for everything" (Ecc 8:6). However, the time for anything is determined by its cause. Therefore, because the heavenly bodies are the cause of physical effects, the time for those things that act in a physical way is determined by the heavenly bodies. The soul, on the other hand, since it is not subject to any heavenly body in its intellect and reason (for in this respect it transcends temporal causes) does not have times determined by the heavenly bodies; rather, its times are determined by its cause, that is, God, who decrees what is to be done and at what time: "Why is one day better than another? ... They are differentiated by the knowledge of the Lord" (Si 33:7). Much less, therefore, is Christ's time determined by these bodies. Accordingly, his hour must be regarded as fixed not by fatal necessity, but by the entire Trinity. For as Augustine says: "You should not believe this about yourself; and how much less should you believe it about he who made you? If your hour is his will, that is, God's, what is his hour but his own will? Therefore, he was not speaking here of the hour in which he would be forced to die, but rather of the hour in which he thought it fitting to be killed." "My time has not yet come," as he said before (above 2:4); "Jesus knew that his time had come to leave this world for the Father" (below 13:1).

1070 Then he mentions the effect his teaching had on those who were favorable. First, he shows their faith: **Many of the people, however, believed in him**. He does not say, "of the leaders," because the higher their rank, the further away they were from him. So there was no room in them for wisdom: "Where there is humility, there is wisdom" (Prv 11:2). But the people, because they were quick to see their own sickness, immediately recognized our Lord's medicine: "You have hidden these things from the wise and the prudent, and have revealed them to little ones" (Mt 11:25). This is why in the beginning, it was the poor and the humble who were converted to Christ: "God chose what is lowly and despised in the world, and things that are not, to destroy those things that are" (1 Cor 1:28).

Secondly, he gives the motive for their faith when he says, **When the Christ comes, will he work more wonders than this man has done?** For it had been prophesied that when the Christ came, he would work many miracles: "God himself will come, and save us. Then the eyes of the blind will be opened, and the ears of the deaf will hear" (Is 35:4). And so when they saw the miracles Christ was accomplishing, they were led to believe. Yet their faith was weak, because they were led to believe him not by his teaching, but by his miracles; whereas, since they were already believers, and instructed by the law, they should have been influenced more by his teaching: "Signs were given to unbelievers; while prophecies were given to believers, not to unbelievers" (1 Cor 14:22).

Secondly, their faith was weak because they seemed to be expecting another Christ; thus they say: **When the Christ comes, will he work more wonders than this man has done?** From this it is obvious that they did not believe in Christ as in God, but as in some just man or prophet. Or, according to Augustine, they were reasoning this way: **When the Christ comes, will he work more wonders than this man has done?** As if to say: We were promised that the Christ would come. But he will not work more signs than this man is doing. Therefore, either he is the Christ, or there will be several Christs.

1071 Then when he says, **The Pharisees heard the people saying these things about him**, we see the effect this had on the Pharisees. And as Chrysostom says, Christ said many things, and yet the Pharisees were not aroused against him. But when they saw that the people were accepting him, they were immediately fired up against him; and in their madness they wanted to kill him. This shows that the real reason why they hated him was not that he broke the sabbath; what provoked them the most was the fact that the people were honoring Christ. And this is clear below: "Do you not see that we can do nothing? Look, the entire world has gone after him!" (12:19). Because they were afraid of the danger they did not dare to seize Christ themselves, but they sent their officers, who were used to such things.

33 Jesus then said to them:
> "For still a short time I am with you;
> then I am going to him who sent me.
> 34 You will look for me,
> and you will not find me;
> and where I am, you will not be able to come."

35 The Jews therefore said to one another: "Where is he going that we cannot find him? Is he going to those dispersed among the Gentiles, and teach the Gentiles? 36 What does he mean by saying, 'You will look for me, and you will not find me'; and 'where I am, you will not be able to come'?"

1072 After our Lord told the principle of his origin, he then mentions his end, i.e., where he would go by dying. First, the end of Christ's life is given; secondly, we see that the people are puzzled by what he says (v 35). As to the first he does three things. First, the end of his life is mentioned; secondly, he predicts what they will desire in the future (v 34); and thirdly, he mentions one of their deficiencies (v 34b). He does two things about the first. First, he predicts the delay of his death until later; and secondly, he states where he will go by dying (v 33b). And so, in the first, he shows his power; and in the second, his will to suffer.

1073 Our Lord shows his power by the delaying of his death until later; because, although the Jews wanted to seize him, they could not do this until Christ willed. "No one takes it from me, but I lay it down of myself" (below 10:18). And so Jesus said: **For still a short time I am with you.** As if to say: You want to kill me; but this does not depend on your will, but on my will. And I have decided that **For still a short time I am with you**; so wait a while. You will do what you want to do. These words of our Lord first of all satisfied those people who honored him, and made them more eager to listen to him because there was only a short time left to receive his teaching, as Chrysostom says. "While you have the light, believe in the light" (below 12:36). Secondly, he satisfied those who were persecuting him. As if to say: Your desire for my death will not be delayed long; so be patient, because it is **a short time.** For I must accomplish my mission: to preach, to perform miracles, and then to come to my passion. "Go and tell that fox that I will work today and tomorrow, and on the third day I will finish my course" (Lk 13:32).

1074 There are three reasons why Christ wished to preach for only a short time. First, to show his power, by transforming the entire world in such a brief time: "One day in your courts is better than a thousand elsewhere" (Ps 83:11). Secondly, to arouse the desire of his disciples, i.e., to desire him more (him whose physical presence they would have for only a short time): "The days will come when you will desire to see one day of the Son of Man" (Lk 17:22). Thirdly, to accelerate the spiritual progress of his disciples. For since the humanity of Christ is our way to God, as it says below, "I am the way, and the truth, and the life" (14:6), we should not rest in it as a goal, but through it tend to God. And so that the hearts of his disciples, which were moved by the physical presence of Christ, would not rest in him as man, he quickly took his physical presence from them; thus he said: "It is advantageous for you that I go" (below 16:7); "If we knew Christ according to the flesh (i.e., when he was physically present to us) now we no longer know him in this way" (2 Cor 5:16).

1075 He shows his desire for his passion when he says, **I am going to him who sent me**, that is, willingly, by my passion: "He was offered because it was his own will" (Is 53:7); "He gave himself for us, an offering to God" (Eph 5:2). **I am going**, I say, to the Father, **to him who sent me**. And this is appropriate, for everything naturally returns to its principle: "Rivers return to the place from which they come" (Ecc 1:7); "Jesus ... knowing that he came from God, and was going to God" (below 13:3). And again: "I am going to him vho sent me" (below 16:5).

1076 When he says, **You will look for me, and you will not find me**, he is predicting what the Jews will desire in the times to come. As if to say: You can enjoy my teaching for a short time; but this brief time, which you are now rejecting, you will look for later, and you will not find it: "Search for the Lord while he can be found" (Is 55:6); and "Seek the Lord (at the present time), and your soul will live" (Ps 68:33).

1077 This statement, **You will look for me, and you will not find me**, can be understood either as a physical search for Christ or as a spiritual search. If we understand it as a physical search, then, according to Chrysostom, this is the way he was sought by the daughters of Jerusalem, i.e., the women who cried for him, as Luke (23:27) mentions; and no doubt many others were affected at the same time. It is not unreasonable to think that when trouble was near, especially when their city was being captured, the Jews remembered Christ and his miracles and wished that he were there to free them. And in this way, **You will look for me**, i.e., for me to be physically present, **and you will not find me**.

If we understand this as a spiritual search for Christ, then we should say, as Augustine does, that although they refused to recognize Christ while he was among them, they later looked for him, after they had seen the people believe and had themselves been stung by the crime of his death; and they said to Peter: "Brothers, what shall we do?" (Acts 2:37). In this way, they were looking for Christ (whom they saw die as a result of their crime) when they believed in him who forgave them.

1078 Then when he says, **and where I am, you will not be able to come**, he points out one of their deficiencies. He does not say, "and where I am going," which would be more in keeping with the earlier thought, "I am going," to the Father, "to him who sent me." He says rather, **where I am**, to show that he is both God and man. He is man insofar as he is going: "I am going to him who sent me" (below 16:5). But insofar as Christ had always been where he was about to return, he shows that he is God: "No one has gone up to heaven except the One who came down from heaven" (above 3:13). And so, as Augustine says, just as Christ returned in such a way as not to leave us, so he came down to us, when he assumed visible flesh, but in such a way as still to be in heaven according to his invisible greatness.

He does not say, "You will not find," because some were about to go; but he does say, **you will not be able to come**, i.e., as long as you keep your present attitude; for no one can obtain the eternal inheritance unless he is God's heir. And one becomes an heir of God by faith in Christ: "he gave them power to become the sons of God, to all who believe in his name" (above 1:12). But the Jews did not yet believe in him; and so he says, **you will not be able to come**. In the Psalm it is asked: "Who will ascend the mountain of the Lord?" And the answer given is: "Those whose hands are innocent and whose hearts are clean" (Ps 23:3). But the hearts of the Jews were not clean, nor were their hands innocent, because they wanted to kill Christ. And so he says: you are not able to ascend the mountain of the Lord.

1079 Then (v 35), we see that this was bewildering to the Jews, who, although they thought of Christ in a worldly way, still did believe to a certain extent. And three things happen here. First, they are bewildered; secondly, they form an opinion; and thirdly, they argue against their own opinion.

1080 They are perplexed when they say to each other: **Where** is he going that we cannot find him? For, as was said, they understood this in a physical way: "The sensual man does not perceive those things that pertain to the Spirit of God" (1 Cor 2:14).

1081 And so they came to the opinion that Christ was going to go in a physical way, not by dying, to some place where they would not be permitted to go. Thus they say: **Is he going to those dispersed among the Gentiles, and teach the Gentiles?** For the Gentiles were separated from the way of life of the Jews: "separated from Israel's way of life, strangers to the covenants, without hope in the promise, and without God in this world" (Eph 2:12). And so they said, in a way reproaching him, **to those dispersed among the Gentiles**, who had settled in many different places: "These are the families of Noe ... and they settled among the nations on the earth after the flood" (Gn 10:32). But the Jewish people were united by place, by their worship of the one God, and by the observance of the law: "The Lord builds up Jerusalem, and he will gather the dispersed of Israel" (Ps 146:2).

They did not say that he would go to the Gentiles to become a Gentile himself, but to bring them back; and so they said, **and teach the Gentiles.** They probably took this from Isaiah (49:6): "I have given you to be a light to the Gentiles, to be my salvation to the ends of the earth." However, even though they did not understand what they were saying (just as Caiphas did not understand his own words: "It is expedient for you that one man die for the people, and that the entire nation does not perish"), what they said was true, and they were predicting the salvation of the Gentiles, as Augustine says, for Christ would go to the Gentiles, not in his own body, but by his feet, i.e., his apostles. For he sent his own members to us to make us his members. "And I have other sheep that are not of this fold, and I must bring them also ... and there will be one fold and one shepherd" (below 10:16). And so Isaiah says, speaking for the Gentiles: "He will teach us his ways" (Is 2:3).

1082 Finally, they saw an objection to their own opinion when they said: **What does he mean by saying...?** As if to say: If he had said only, **You will look for me, and you will not find me,** we could think that he was going to the Gentiles. But he seems to exclude this when he adds, **where I am, you will not be able to come,** for we can go to the Gentiles.

LECTURE 5

37 On the last and greatest day of the festival Jesus stood up and cried out, saying:
"If anyone thirsts, let him come to me and drink.
38 Whoever believes in me, as the Scriptures say, out of his heart shall flow rivers of living water."
39 (He said this concerning the Spirit, whom those who believed in him would receive; for as yet the Spirit had not been given, since Jesus had not yet been glorified.) 40 From that moment some of the people, hearing these words of his, said: "Truly, this is the Prophet." 41 Others said: "This is the Christ." But others said: "Would the Christ come from Galilee? 42 Does not Scripture say that the Christ will come from the seed of David, and from David's town of Bethlehem?" 43 And so there was dissension among the people because of him. 44 Although some of them wanted to apprehend him, no one laid a hand on him. 45 So the officers returned to the chief priests and Pharisees, who said to them: "Why have you not brought him?" 46 The officers replied: "Never has any man spoken like this man." 47 The Pharisees then retorted: "Have you too been seduced? 48 Has any one of the rulers believed in him, or any of the Pharisees? 49 But these people, who do not know the law, they are accursed." 50 Nicodemus (the same one who came to him at night, and was one of them) said: 51 "Does our law judge a man without first hearing from him and knowing what he has done?" 52 They answered and said to him: "Are you too a Galilean? Look at the Scriptures and see that the Prophet will not come from Galilee." 53 Then every man returned to his own house.

1083 After our Lord told them about the origin of his doctrine and of the teacher, as well as his end, he now invites them to accept his teaching itself. First, we see Christ's invitation; secondly, the dissension among the people (v 40). He does three things about the first. First, he tells us the manner of this invitation; secondly, we see the invitation itself (v 37); and thirdly, he explains what it means (v 39). The manner of the invitation is described in three ways: by its time; by the posture of the one inviting; and by his efforts.

1084 As to the time, we see that it was **the last and greatest day of the festival**. For as we saw before, this feast was celebrated for seven days, and the first and the last day were the more solemn; just as with us, the first day of a feast and its octave are the more solemn. Therefore, what our Lord did here he did not do on the first day, as he had not yet gone to Jerusalem, nor in the intervening days, but on the last day. And he acted then because there are few who celebrate feasts in a spiritual way. Consequently, he did not invite them to his teaching at the beginning of the festival so that the trifles of the following days would not drive it from their hearts; for we read that the word of the Lord is choked by thorns (Lk 8:7). But he did invite them on the last day so that his teaching would be more deeply impressed on their hearts.

1085 As to his posture, **Jesus stood up.** Here we should note that Christ taught both while sitting and standing. He taught his disciples while sitting (Mt 5:1); while he stood when he taught the people, as he is doing here. It is from this that we get the custom in the Church of standing when preaching to the people, but sitting while preaching to religious and clerics. The reason for this is that since the aim in preaching to the people is to convert them, it takes the form of an exhortation; but when preaching is directed to clergy, already living in the house of God, it takes the form of a reminder.

1086 As to his effort we read that he **cried out**, in order to show his own assurance: "Raise up your voice with strength ... raise it up, and do not be afraid" (Is 40:9); and so that all would be able to hear him: "Cry out, and do not stop; raise your voice like a trumpet" (Is 58:1); and to stress the importance of what he was about to say: "Listen to me, for I will tell you about great things" (Prv 8:6).

1087 Next (v 37b), we see Christ's invitation: first, those who are invited; secondly, the fruit of this invitation.

1088 It is the thirsty who are invited. Thus he says: **If anyone thirsts, let him come to me and drink**; "Come to the waters, all you who thirst" (Is 55:1). He calls the thirsty because such people want to serve God. For God does not accept a forced service: "God loves a cheerful giver" (2 Cor 9:7). So we read: "I will sacrifice freely" (Ps 53:8). And such people are described in Matthew this way: "Blessed are they who hunger and thirst for what is right" (Mt 5:6). Now our Lord calls all of these people, not just some; and so he says: **If anyone thirsts**, as if to say: whoever it is. "Come to me, all you who desire me, and be filled with my fruits" (Sir 24:26); "He desires the salvation of all" (1 Tim 2:4).

Jesus invites them to drink; and so he says, **and drink**. For this drink is spiritual refreshment in the knowledge of divine wisdom and truth, and in the realization of their desires: "My servants will drink, and you will be thirsty" (Is 65:13); "Come and eat my bread, and drink the wine I have mixed for you" (Prv 9:5); "She [wisdom] will give him the water of saving wisdom to drink" (Sir 15:3).

1089 The fruit of this invitation is that good things overflow upon others; thus he says: **Whoever believes in me, as the Scriptures say, out of his heart shall flow rivers of living water.** According to Chrysostom, we should read this as follows: **Whoever believes in me, as the Scriptures say.** And then a new sentence begins: **Out of his heart shall flow rivers of living water.** For if we say: **Whoever believes in me,** and follow this with, **as the Scriptures say, out of his heart shall flow rivers of living water,** it does not seem to be correct, for the statement, **out of his heart shall flow rivers of living water,** is not found in any book of the Old Testament. So we should say: **Whoever believes in me, as the Scriptures say;** that is, according to the teaching of the Scriptures. "Search the Scriptures ... they too bear witness to me" (above 5:39). And then there follows: **Out of his heart shall flow rivers of living water.** He says here, **Whoever believes in me,** while before he said, "He who comes to me," because to believe and to come are the same thing: "Come to him and be enlightened," as we read in the Psalm (33:6).

But Jerome punctuates this in a different way. He says that after **Whoever believes in me,** there follows, **as the Scriptures say, out of his heart shall flow rivers of living water.** And he says that this phrase was taken from Proverbs (5:15): "Drink the water from your own cistern, and from the streams of you own well. Let your fountains flow far and wide."

1090 We should note, with Augustine, that rivers come from fountains as their source. Now one who drinks natural water does not have either a fountain or a river within himself, because he takes only a small portion of water. But one who drinks by believing in Christ draws in a fountain of water; and when he draws it in, his conscience, which is the heart of the inner man, begins to live and it itself becomes a fountain. So we read above: "The water that I give will become a fountain within him" (4:14). This fountain which is taken in is the Holy Spirit, of whom we read: "With you is the fountain of life" (Ps 35:10). Therefore, whoever drinks the the gifts of the graces, which are signified by the rivers, in such a way that he alone benefits, will not have living water flowing from his heart. But whoever acts quickly to help others, and to share with them the various gifts of grace he has received from God, will have living water flowing from his heart. This is why Peter says: "According to the grace each has received, let them use it to benefit one another" (1 Pet 4:10).

He says, **rivers,** to indicate the abundance of the spiritual gifts which were promised to those who believe: "The river of God is full of water" (Ps 64:10); and also their force or onrush: "When they rush to Jacob, Israel will blossom and bud, and they will fill the surface of the earth with fruit" (Is 27:6); and again, "The rush of the rivers gives joy to the city of God" (Ps 45:5). Thus, because the Apostle was governed by the impulsive force and fervor of the Holy Spirit, he said: "The love of Christ spurs us on" (2 Cor 5:14); and "Those who are led by the Spirit of God are the sons of God" (Rom 8:14). The separate distribution of the gifts of the Holy Spirit is also indicated, for we read, "to one the gift of healing ... to another the gift of tongues" (1 Cor 12:10). These gifts are "rivers of living water" because they flow directly from their source, which is the indwelling Holy Spirit.

1091   Then (v 39), he explains what he said. First we see the explanation; secondly, the reason behind this explanation (v 39b).

1092   Christ had said: "out of his heart shall flow rivers of living water." The Evangelist tells us that we should understand this **concerning the Spirit, whom those who believed in him would receive**, because the Spirit is the fountain and river of life. He is the fountain of which we read: "With you is the fountain of life; and in your light we will see light" (Ps 35:10). And the Spirit is a river because he proceeds from the Father and the Son: "The angel then showed me the river of the water of life, clear as crystal, coming from the throne of God and of the Lamb" (Rv 22:1). "He gave the Spirit," that is, to those who obey him (Is 42:1).

1093   He gives the reason behind this explanation, saying, **for as yet the Spirit had not been given**. And he says two things. **as yet the Spirit had not been given**, and that **Jesus had not yet been glorified**.

There are two opinions about the first of these. For Chrysostom says that before the resurrection of Christ the Holy Spirit was not given to the apostles with respect to the gifts of prophecy and miracles. And so this grace, which was given to the prophets, was not to be found on earth until Christ came, and after that it was not given to anyone until the above mentioned time. And if anyone objects that the apostles cast out devils before the resurrection, it should be understood that they were cast out by that power which was from Christ, not by the Spirit; for when he sent them out, we do not read that he gave them the Holy Spirit, but rather that "he gave them power over unclean spirits" (Mt 10:1).

However, this seems to conflict with what our Lord says in the Gospel of Luke: "If I cast out devils by Beelzebub, by whom do your children cast them out?" (Lk 11:19). But it is certain that our Lord cast out devils by the Holy Spirit, as the children did also, that is, the apostles. Therefore, it is clear that they had received the Holy

Spirit. And so we must say, with Augustine, that the apostles had the Holy Spirit before the resurrection, even with respect to the gifts of prophecy and miracles. And when we read here that **as yet the Spirit had not been given**, we should understand this to refer to a more abundant giving, and one with visible signs, as the Spirit was given to them in tongues of fire after the resurrection and ascension.

1094 But since the Holy Spirit sanctifies the Church and is even now received by those who believe, why does no one speak in the languages of all nations as then? My answer is that it is not necessary, as Augustine says. For now the universal Church speaks the languages of all the nations, because the love of charity is given by the Holy Spirit: "The love of God is poured out into our hearts by the Holy Spirit" (Rom 5:5); and this love, making all things common, makes everyone speak to everyone else. As Augustine says: "If you love unity, then you have everything that anyone else has in it (i.e., in the Church). Give up your envy, and what I have is also yours; ill-will divides, the love of charity unites. If you have this love, you will have everything." But at the beginning, before the Church was spread throughout the world, because it had few members, they had to speak the languages of all so that they could establish the Church among all.

1095 With regard to the second point, we should note that Augustine thinks the statement, **Jesus had not yet been glorified**, should be understood as the glory of the resurrection. As if to say: Jesus had not yet risen from the dead or ascended into heaven. We read about this below: "Father, glorify me" (17:5). And the reason why Christ willed to be glorified before he gave the Holy Spirit is that the Holy Spirit is given to us so that we might raise our hearts from the love of this world in a spiritual resurrection, and turn completely to God. To those who are afire with the love of the Holy Spirit, Christ promised eternal life, where we will not die, and where we will have no fear. And for this reason he did not wish to give the Holy Spirit until he was glorified, so that he might show in his body the life for which we hope in the resurrection.

1096 For Chrysostom, however, this statement does not refer to the glory of the resurrection, but to the glorification of the passion. When his passion was near, our Lord said: "Now the Son of Man is glorified" (below 13:31). So, according to this view, the Holy Spirit was first given after the passion, when our Lord said to his apostles: "Receive the Holy Spirit" (below 20:22). The Holy Spirit was not given before the passion because, since it is a gift, it should not be given to enemies, but to friends. But we were enemies. Thus it was necessary that first the victim be offered on the altar of the cross, and enmity be destroyed in his flesh, so that by this we might be reconciled to God by the death of his Son; and then, having been made friends, we could receive the gift of the Holy Spirit.

1097   The Evangelist, having shown us Christ's invitation to a spiritual drink, now presents the disagreement of the people. First, the disagreement among the people themselves; secondly, that of their leaders (v 45). He does two things about the first. First, he states what those who disagreed said; secondly, he states the fact that there was a disagreement (v 43).

What the people said varied according to their different opinions about Christ. And he gives three of their opinions: two of these were the opinions of those who were coming for spiritual drink; and the third was held by those who shrank from it.

1098   The first opinion was that Christ was the Prophet. So he says, **From that moment**, i.e., from the time Christ had spoken on the great day of the feast, **hearing these words of his, some of the people said**, i.e., those who had now begun to drink that water spiritually, **Truly, this is the Prophet.** They did not just call him a prophet, but **the Prophet**, thinking that he was the one about whom Moses foretold: "The Lord your God will raise up a prophet for you from your brothers ... you will listen to him" (Dt 18:15).

1099   Another opinion was of those who said, **This is the Christ.** These people had drawn closer to that [spiritual] drink, and had slaked the thirst of unbelief to a greater extent. This is what Peter himself professed: "You are the Christ, the Son of the living God" (Mt 16:16).

1100   The third opinion conflicts with the other two. First, those who hold this disagree with those who say that Jesus is the Christ; secondly, they support their opinion with an authority. So he says: **But others said**, those remaining in the dryness of unbelief, **Would the Christ come from Galilee?** For they knew that it was not predicted by the prophets that the Christ would come from Galilee. And they said what they did because they thought that Jesus had been born in Nazareth, not knowing that it was really in Bethlehem: for it was well known that he had been brought up in Nazareth, but only a few knew where he was born. Nevertheless, although the Scripture does not say that the Christ would be born in Galilee, it did foretell that he would first start out from there: "The people who walked in darkness saw a great light, and on those who lived in the region of the shadow of death, a light has risen" (Is 9:1). It even foretold that the Christ would come from Nazareth: "A flower will rise up from his roots" (Is 11:1), where the Hebrew version reads: "A Nazarene will rise up from his roots."

1101   They support their objection by the authority of Scripture when they say, **Does not Scripture say that the Christ will come from the seed of David, and from David's town of Bethlehem?** We read in Jeremiah (23:5) that Jesus would come from the seed of David: "I will raise up a just branch for David." And we see that David was "the anointed of God" (2 Sm 23:1). In Micah (5:2) we read that Jesus would come from Bethlehem: "And you, Bethlehem, land of Judah: from you there will come forth, for me, a ruler of Israel."

1102   Then (v 43), the disagreement among the people is mentioned; secondly, the attempt of some of them to seize Christ; and thirdly, the failure of their attempt.

1103   **And so there was dissension among the people because of him**, that is, Christ. For it often happens that when the truth is made known, it causes dissensions and uneasiness in the hearts of the wicked. So Jeremiah says, representing Christ: "Woe is me, my mother! Why did you give birth to me as a man of strife and dissension for all the earth" (Jer 15:10). And our Lord said: "I have not come to send peace, but the sword" (Mt 10:34).

1104   Some of them attempted to seize Christ; so he says, **some of them**, that is, those who had said, "Would the Christ come from Galilee?" **wanted to apprehend him**, to kill him out of hatred: "Pursue and seize him" (Ps 70:11); "The enemy said: 'I will pursue and seize' " (Ex 15:9). On the other hand, those who are good and those who believe want to seize Christ to enjoy him: "I will go up into the palm tree and seize its fruit" (Sg 7.8).

1105   But they were frustrated by the power of Christ. So he says: **no one laid a hand on him**, that is, because Jesus was not willing that they do so, for this depended on his power: "No one takes my soul from me, but I lay it down of myself" (below 10.18). Accordingly, when Christ did will to suffer, he did not wait for them, but he offered himself to them: "Jesus stepped forward and said to them: 'Whom are you looking for?' " (below 18:4).

1106 Then (v 45), we see the dissension of the leaders of the people: first, their disagreement with their officers; and secondly, the disagreement among themselves (v 50). He does three things about the first: first, he shows the leaders rebuking their officers; secondly, the testimony the officers gave about Christ; and thirdly, we see the leaders reprimanding their own officers.

1107   As to the first, let us note the evil of the leaders, that is, the chief priests and Pharisees, when they say to their officers: **Why have you not brought him?** For their evil was so great that their own officers could not please them unless they injured Christ: "They cannot sleep unless they have done something evil" (Prv 4:16).

There is a problem here about the literal meaning of the text. For since it was said before that the officers were sent to apprehend Jesus when the festival was half over (v 32), that is, on the fourth day, and here we read that they returned on the seventh day, "On the last and greatest day of the festival" (v 37), it seems that the Evangelist overlooked the days inbetween. There are two answers to this: either the Evangelist anticipated the disagreement among the people, or the officers had returned before, but it is just mentioned now to show the reason why there was dissension among the leaders.

1108 As to the second point, let us realize how good these officers were in giving this praiseworthy testimony about Christ, saying: **Never has any man spoken like this man**. They deserve our praise for three reasons. First, because of their admiration: for they admired Christ because of his teachings, not his miracles. And this brought them nearer to the truth, and further from the custom of the Jews, who looked for signs, as is said in 1 Corinthians (1:22). Secondly, we should praise them because of the ease with which they were won over: because with just a few words, Christ had captivated them and had drawn their love. Thirdly, because of their confidence: because it was to the Pharisees, who were the enemies of Christ, that they said: **Never has any man spoken like this man**. And these things are to be expected, for Jesus was not just a man, but the Word of God; and so his words had power to affect people. "Are not my words like fire, says the Lord, and like a hammer breaking a rock?" (Jer 23:29). And so Matthew says: "He was teaching them as one who had authority" (Mt 7:29). And his words were sweet to contemplate: "Let your voice sound in my ears, for your voice is sweet" (Sg 2:14); "How sweet are your words to my tongue!" (Ps 118:103). And his words were useful to keep in mind, because they promised eternal life: "Lord, to whom shall we go? You have the words of eternal life" (above 6:69); "I am the Lord, who teaches you things that are useful" (Is 48:17).

1109 As to the third point, see the treachery of the Jews in trying to alienate the officers from Christ; **The Pharisees then retorted**, to the officers, **Have you too been seduced?** Here they do three things. First, they attack what they consider a mistake of their officers; secondly, they hold up their leaders as an example; and in the third place, they reject the example of the people.

1110 They attack the officers when they say, **Have you too been seduced?** As if to say: We see that what he said was pleasing to you. As a matter of fact, they had been seduced, but in an admirable way, because they left the evil of unbelief and were brought to the truth of the faith. We read about this: "You seduced me, O Lord, and I was seduced" (Jer 20:7).

1111 Then they appeal to their rulers as an example, to turn the officers further from Christ, saying: **Has any one of the rulers believed in him, or any of the Pharisees?** There are two reasons why a person should be believed: either because of some authority or because of a religious disposition. And they say that none of these are found with Christ. As if to say: If Christ were worthy to be received, then our rulers, who have authority, would have accepted him; and so would the Pharisees, who have a religious disposition. But none of these believe in him; and so neither should you believe in him. This fulfills the saying: "The stone that the builders (that is, the rulers and the Pharisees) rejected has become the cornerstone (that is, in the hearts of the people). The Lord has done this," because his goodness is greater than man's evil (Ps 117:22).

1112 They reject the statements of the people because they are a rebuke to their own evil. So they say: **But these people, who do not know the law, they are accursed**; therefore, you should not agree with them. This thought was found in Deuteronomy: "Accursed are they who do not live within the law and do not act according to it" (Dt 27:26). But they did not understand this correctly, because even those who do not have a knowledge of the law but act in harmony with it, live more within the law than those who do have a knowledge of the law yet do not keep it. It is said about such people: "This people honors me with their lips, but their heart is far from me" (Mt 15:8); and in James (1:22): "Be a doer of the word, and not just a hearer."

1113 Next, we see the dissension among the rulers. First, the advice of Nicodemus is given; secondly, the opposition of the rulers; and thirdly, the outcome of the whole affair. The Evangelist does two things about the first: first, he tells us something about Nicodemus; secondly, he gives his advice.

1114 He tells us three things about Nicodemus: the first two show us the attitude of Nicodemus himself; and the second reveals the malice of the rulers. The first concerns the faith of Nicodemus, and he says: **Nicodemus, who came to him,** i.e., who believed, for to come to Christ is the same as to believe in him. The second shows the imperfection of his faith, because he came **at night.** For if he had believed perfectly, he would not have been fearful, for as we read below (12:42): "Many of the rulers believed in him; but they did not admit it because of the Pharisees, so that they would not be expelled from the synagogue." And one of these was Nicodemus.

The third thing the Evangelist tells us shows us that the rulers did not speak the truth: for they said that none of the rulers, or of the Pharisees, believed in Christ. And so the Evangelist says about Nicodemus that he **was one of them**: as if to say: If Nicomedus, who was one of the rulers, believed in Christ, then the rulers and Pharisees are speaking falsely when they say that none of the rulers believed in him. "Truly, a lie was spoken" (Jer 16:19).

1115 The advice of Nicodemus is given when he says: **Does our law judge a man without first hearing from him and knowing what he has done?** For according to the civil laws, a judgment was only to be given after a complete investigation. This is why we read: "It is not the custom of the Romans to condemn any man before he has his accusers face him, and can defend himself from the charges" (Acts 25:16). "I diligently investigated the stranger's cause" (Jb 29:16). And so the law of Moses says: "Do not condemn one who is innocent and just, because I hate the wicked" (Ex 23:7).

Nicodemus said what he did because he believed in Christ and wanted to convert them to Christ; yet because he was afraid, he did not act very candidly. He thought that if they would only listen to Christ, the words of Christ would be so effective that perhaps they would be changed like those whom they sent to Jesus, and who, when they heard Christ, were turned aside from the very act for which they had been sent.

1116 We see the opposition of the rulers to Nicodemus when he says, **They answered and said to him.** First, they think that he has been seduced; and secondly, that he does not know the law.

As to the first, they say: **Are you too a Galilean?** that is, one who has been seduced by this Galilean. For they considered Christ a Galilean because he lived in Galilee. And so anyone who followed Christ they derisively called a Galilean. "The girl servant said to Peter: 'You are a Galilean, are you not?' " (Mt 26:69), "Do you also want to become his disciples?" (below 9:27).

About his ignorance of the law, they say: **Look at the Scriptures and see that the Prophet will not come from Galilee.** But since Nicodemus was a teacher of the law, he did not have to look again. It is as if they were saying: Although you are a teacher, you do not know this. Something like this was said before: "You are a teacher in Israel and you do not know these things?" (above 3:10). Now even though the Old Testament does not explicitly say that a prophet will come from Galilee, it does say that the Lord of the prophets would come from there, according to: "A flower (i.e., a Nazarene) will arise from his root ... and the Spirit of the Lord will rest upon him," as we read in Isaiah (11:1).

1117 The outcome of this dissension is seen to be useless. So he says: **Then every man returned**, leaving the matter unfinished, **to his own house**, i.e., to what belonged to him, empty of faith and frustrated in his evil desires. "He frustrates the plans of the wicked" (Jb 5:13); "God destroys the plans of rulers, and frustrates the schemes of the people" (Ps 32:10).

Or, each returned **to his own house**, i.e., to the evil of his unbelief and irreverence. "I know where you live: where the throne of Satan is. You hold to my name, and you have not denied my faith" (Rv 2:13).

NOTES TO THE INTRODUCTION

1. For a fuller documentation of these facts, see James A. Weisheipl, *Friar Thomas d'Aquino: His Life, Thought and Works* (Garden City, N.Y.: Doubleday, 1974), pp. 246-47, 372, and so forth. See also J. A. Weisheipl. "The Johannine Commentary of Friar Thomas," *Church History*, 45 (1976), 185-195.

2. *Ibid.*, pp. 145-46.

3. The full text of this allocution is given in AAS 50 (1958), 150-53.

4. St. Thomas, *Summa theologiae*, I, q.1, a.8, ad 2

5. AAS 35 (1943), 297-325; trans. in *The Catholic Mind* 42 (1944), 257-83.

6. St. Thomas, *Super epistolam ad Hebraeos lectura*, cap.1, lect.4, n.64, *Super Epistolas S. Pauli Lectura*, ed. R. Cai (Turin: Marietti, 1953), I, 350a.

7. *Divino afflante Spiritu*, n.63; trans. *loc. cit.*, p. 280.

8. St. Thomas, *Sum. theol.*, I, q.1, a.10.

9. *Ibid.*

10. See J. A. Weisheipl, "The Meaning of *Sacra Doctrina* in *Summa theologiae* I, q.1," *The Thomist*, 38 (1974), 49-80.

11. Aristotle, *Metaphysics* I, 2, 982a18-19.

12. See *Friar Thomas d'Aquino*, pp. 392-93.

13. Only the second part of this work has been translated into English – J. B. Collins, *Catechetical Instructions of St. Thomas* (New York: Wagner 1939; repr. 1953).

14. St. Thomas, *Catena Aurea*, Epistola dedicatoria (Turin: Marietti, 1925) I, 468.

15. St. Thomas, *Sum. theol.*, I, q.1, a.3; see note 10 above.

16. See Leo XIII, *Providentissimus Deus* (18 Nov. 1893) in *Acta Leonis XIII*, vol. 13, pp. 345-46.

17. See *Friar Thomas d'Aquino*, pp. 164-68.

18. St. Thomas, *Super Evangelium S. Joannis Lectura*, cap.21, lect.6, n.2656, ed. R. Cai (Turin:Marietti 1952), p. 488.

19. Trent. sess. 4, in Denziger–Schönmetzer, *Enchiridion Symbolorum* (1967), n.1501. See the important study of this question in J. R. Geiselmann, *Die Heilige Schrift und die Tradition* (Freiburg i. Br.: Herder 1962), pp. 108-160.

20. Sess. VIII, *Constitutio Dogmatica De divina Revelatione, Dei verbum* (18 Nov. 1965), in *Constitutiones, Decreta, Declarationes* (Vatican 1966), p. 429; see whole of cap. 2.

21. This was the invocation, for example, in the old Dominican rite of the Mass.

APPENDICES OF NOTES HISTORICAL AND THEOLOGICAL

James A. Weisheipl, O.P., S.T.M.

I Brief Note on the Text of Isaiah (6:1) used for the Prologue

II Proofs for God's Existence

III The Concepts of "Nature" and "Person"
"Nature" as a Philosophical Concept
"Person" as a Philosophical Concept

IV The Mystery of the Triune God
A. Consubstantiality of the Son with the Father
B. Three distinct Persons in one Nature

V The Mystery of the Incarnation

VI St. Thomas' doctrine of the Hypostatic Union

I

BRIEF NOTE ON THE TEXT OF ISAIAH (6:1) USED FOR THE PROLOGUE

It was customary for medieval sermons to be based on a special text of Scripture, which would be developed phrase by phrase in the course of the sermon. Naturally, every text was adapted to the ultimate purpose the preacher had in mind. Similarly, every book or important treatise in the Middle Ages would be introduced by a Prologue, which was likewise a development of a text chosen by the author from Scripture. The development of this text was not necessarily an explanation of the literal sense of the passage. It was rather an explanation adapted by the author to prepare the reader for the book about to follow. Usually the text chosen was adapted to cover the special range of material to be discussed, and thus served as a division of the matter about to be treated. There is nothing unusual about this.

Since, as St. Augustine says, St. John's purpose in writing his gospel was "to inform us about the *contemplative life*," St. Thomas chose the text from Isaiah (6:1) to show the reader something about John's own contemplation in that the Lord Jesus is contemplated therein in a threefold fullness: sublime (*alta*), expansive (*ampla*), and perfect (*perfecta*). (See Prologue, n. 1). Hence, St. Thomas adapts the text of Isaiah (6:1) to fit this threefold fullness of John's contemplation revealed in his Gospel. This is a very normal and ordinary procedure. Indeed almost any text is flexible and adaptable in many ways according to the purpose of the preacher or writer.

St. Thomas, in fact, uses the text chosen for two purposes: first, to explain the threefold fullness of John's contemplation; second, to divide the following exposition of John's Prologue into three parts: namely 1 (1—2) concerning the sublimity of the Word, 1 (3-13) concerning the totality of the universe through the Word, and 1 (14a) concerning the Incarnation of the Word. The first division corresponds to Lecture 1, the second to Lectures 2 to 6, and the third to Lecture 7. Consequently, the tripartite reading of the text of Isaiah (6:1) is essential to Thomas' development in the Prologue of his explanation of the Gospel.

The Latin Vulgate that Thomas used had this threefold division of the text of Isaiah (6:1): *Vidi Dominus sedentem super solium excelsum et elevatum, et plena erat domus a maiestate eius, et ea quae sub ipso erant replebant templum.* In the commentary we have translated this literally as, "I saw the Lord seated on a high and lofty throne, and the whole house was full of his majesty, and the things that were under him filled the temple," as required by the exposition of Thomas. Moreover, it is clear from Thomas' running gloss, which he gave in class some time between 1248 and 1252 as a young *cursor biblicus* at Cologne under St. Albert the Great, that this was the actual reading of his personal Bible. (See *Expositio super Isaiam ad Litteram*, in *Opera Omnia*, ed. Leon. 28 [Rome 1974], 6:1, lines 96-103). What is more, St. Albert the Great himself used this full text from Isaiah (6:1), as above, and adapted it for his own purposes for the Prologue to his *Commentary on the Second Book of the Sentences* (ed. Borgnet 27: 1-3), which he wrote when he was already a Master in Sacred Theology at Paris toward the end of 1245 or the beginning of 1246. (See my *Friar Thomas d'Aquino*, Garden City: Doubleday, 1974, p. 45). He too needed all three parts of the text to show the division of Book Two into three parts or three "Treatises."

The historical and textual problem with all of this is that the Latin phrase, *et plena erat domus a maiestate eius*, the second phrase, is not found in the ordinary editions of the Latin Vulgate, neither in the old Clementine version nor in the critical edition prepared by Dom Robert Weber in 1975 (Stuttgart: Württembergische Bibelanstalt, 2 vols.). Nor is this second phrase to be found in the Greek Septuagint nor in the Hebrew Massoretic text of Isaiah. The historical and textual problem is to locate the vulgate tradition to which the Bible of Thomas and Albert belonged; this has not yet been done. The text of Isaiah (6:1) in the critical edition simply reads: *Vidi Dominum sedentem super solium excelsum et elevatum, et ea quae sub eo erant implebant templum.*

The text in Thomas' Bible was somehow a conflation from Isaiah (6:4), *et domus repleta est fumo*, "and the house was filled with smoke," while the reading in the Piana edition of Thomas' works and all subsequent editions, including the Marietti, is a conflation from Isaiah (6:3), *plena est omnis terra gloria eius*, "the whole earth is full of his glory."

The Hebrew author of Isaiah 6 (1-4) wished to say that he saw the splendor of the All High God fill the *temple* (6:1), the whole *earth* (6:3), and the *house* (6:4). This kind of Hebraic development is completely missed in the version Albert and Thomas had before them. But, then, this particular text would not have been suitable for the kind of development Thomas wished to present in his Prologue. Nor would it have been suitable for Albert's purposes either when he commented on Book II of the *Sentences*.

Nothing I have said here makes the slightest difference to our understanding or appreciation of St. Thomas' Prologue. Isaiah 6 (1-4) as St. Thomas had it helps to explicate John's Gospel in a way that the passage as established by biblical criticism does not. Nevertheless, for the study of the Bible in the Middle Ages, the study of medieval exegesis, and a fuller understanding of St. Thomas and his sources, it would be helpful if we could discover St. Thomas' Bible or at least the manuscript tradition to which it belonged. (See the editors of *Expositio super Isaiam, ed. cit.,* Preface, pp. 43-47).

II

PROOFS FOR GOD'S EXISTENCE

Despite the constant teaching of the Catholic Church, many Catholics are surprised to learn that it is reasonable and also a matter of divine revelation that the human mind *can* arrive at a clear and unshakable conviction of the existence of one God as creator of the universe. Many non-Catholics insist that the question of God's existence is strictly a personal matter, and one of faith, not reason. Usually what is meant by "strictly a personal matter" is HANDS OFF! It is a religious question, and of concern only to me! This attitude, however, is not only an insult to God, but also to human reason. Man has an intellect by which he can discover truth, all truth, and even the cause of all truth. By his intellect man knows very few things intuitively and easily; his normal path is one of arduous learning, reasoning, discovering, and problem-solving. This winding path by which he comes to see *why* things are so and not otherwise than they are, is called "proof" or "evidence." On the basis of the proof or evidence the human mind can readily see the truth or falsity of the claim. "Proof" is always our reason for making the claim; that is, the "proof" contains the *cause* of the conclusion we have just drawn. As long as the area of investigation is co-natural to man, i.e., within the ambit of his experience, the "evidence" or "proof" he digs up will very often coincide with the real cause in nature which brought the situation about. That is to say, in all the natural sciences (involving sensible bodies and activities), in the numerous branches of mathematics (involving imagination and consistency), as well as in most human affairs (dealing with right and wrong, responsibility, guilty or not guilty), we can very often amass our evidence from the very causes that produced the situation in question. In that case, the cause of our knowing a truth conclusively coincides with the causes that brought the real situation about. But when, on the other hand, our investigation carries us beyond the realm of human experience, then the only evidence we have is the effects we have in front of us. That is to say, when we raise such basic questions as the efficient designer and creator of our whole being and the totality of the universe, or ask why we ourselves are on this earth, we are asking about causes that transcend all our experience and imagination. But we do have the evidence in front of us all the time that there must *exist* some cause because of the nature of the effects we behold. That is, the totality of the evidence within ourselves and around ourselves is contained *in the effects*. Human footprints in the sand indicate that a man has walked this way before, the evidence is the footprint, an effect. *That* there is a creative God is the most important truth the human mind can reach, because it makes all the difference in our response, our daily lives, our total attitude. To deny human reason the possibility of proving with certitude *that* there is a First Cause of all within range of human experience is to deny our intelligence.

Modern academicians and politicians are all too ready to leave God out of the picture. Rather than say, "He does not exist," as atheists, Marxists, and materialists do say, they would prefer to be skeptical, agnostic, or say it is a matter of religion, not of reason and debate. Because of the prevailing agnosticism, or better, indifference, toward the real existence of a creating God, who is the total efficient, exemplar, and final cause of every single reality outside himself, the First Vatican Council (1870) explicitly declared what was always taught: the human mind can prove with absolute certainty that only one creating God exists, from the evidence of his handiwork, his effects within us and around us. This declaration of the First Vatican Council was not a new truth, but the constant teaching of the Scriptures and the living Church. Time and again the Scriptures declare that the glory and love of the Lord are manifest in his handiwork; and St. Paul insists that even the pagans and irreligious men have no excuse for ignoring God, for "whatever can be known about God is clear to them, as he himself made it so. Since the creation of the world, invisible realities, God's eternal power and divinity, have become visible, *recognized through the things he has made*" (Rom 1:19-20). St. Thomas did not need the First Vatican Council to tell him that the human mind *can* arrive at a firm conviction of the existence (*an sit*) of a First Cause from his effects (*Sum. theol.* I, q.2, a.1-2). As to *what* God is or *who* he is, we can know very little indeed, because his nature has got to be radically different from anything we experience humanly. Even the most sublime terms in the human vocabulary when applied to God pale utterly: terms such as "love," "forgiving," "generous," "all knowing," "all powerful," and the like. It is more honest to say with St. Thomas that we know much more what God *is not* than what he *is* (*Sum. theol.* I, q.3, prol.). Imagination gives an utterly distorted picture of God; this is inevitable. The capacity of the human mind, however, is such that it can not only know *that* God exists, but also a great deal about what he *is not*, and a little bit about what we must say he is, even though human words and experience cannot do justice to the reality, as the prophet Isaiah well understood (Is 64:3; 1 Cor 2:9).

It is particularly important today that all Christians acknowledge the fundamental ability of the human mind *to know* with certitude that God exists. God made man in "his own image and likeness" (Gn 1:26) for this very purpose: that he might know him, love him and serve him on this earth and be happy with him forever in heaven. St. Thomas credits the human mind with far greater potential than would the sceptic and agnostic. What is more, the human mind has every *right to know* about the existence of God, since our whole manner of life depends upon that knowledge. To deny man the right to know God's existence, that is, to prevent him from knowing that God exists, is a far greater crime than a simple denial of man's capacity, for the latter is only an insult, the former adds the perversion of justice. No one today can be complacent about this contemporary insult and injustice presented in the societal game of "important things do not count."

Despite the fact that man can know by reason that God exists, God still chose to reveal his own existence through the Scriptures. For reason is pushed to her greatest efforts when she seeks the highest truth, Truth Itself. Indeed, to Thomas it seemed remarkable that some philosophers, i.e., those gentiles without the Christian revelation, did in fact arrive at the inevitable conclusion that God exists. That is his actual starting point: a few philosophers, highly gifted, using human reason unaided by revelation did, in fact, arrive at the most important issues concerning man: the first of these being that he has a Creator. Thomas, however, was not only a fighting optimist, but also a factual realist. He knew that only a *few* men arrived at the really important truths in human life, and only after a *long time* of persistent struggling against error, and even then, arriving at a few gems of *truth mixed with much dross of falsehood*. These are the three reasons St. Thomas gives *(Sum. theol.* I, q.1, a.1) why God in his infinite mercy felt obliged to reveal even these: so that *all men*, no matter how ungifted, no matter how busy, might know at least the essential truths without any error. In other words, considering the actual condition in this hectic world, God in his infinite goodness revealed even those truths that the human mind can in fact know with its native powers, so that the most important truths of human life "could be known by all men easily, with absolute certitude, and with no admixture of error" (Vat. Council I: sess. 3, cap. 2, Denz 3005). At the same time, that Council condemned as contrary to the true Catholic faith the outright denial that "the one and true God, our Creator and Lord, can be known with certitude from the things he has made, by the natural light of human reason" (Chap. 2, can. 1, Denz. 3026).

In other words, there are two kinds of truths that God has chosen to reveal to mankind: (1) those that we could never know by any amount of human reason, such as man's destiny to eternal beatitude, the Word made flesh for our salvation, the triune nature of God, and the final resurrection of the human body; (2) those that "the human mind" can know, and in fact, that some gifted few have discovered, after a long struggle, and even then with a great admixture of error, such as the existence of one Creator of the universe, his providence over all things, and the immortality of the human soul. The first kind God alone could tells us, and he had to tell us, granting that he freely chose to predestine man to a supernatural end: if God decided to give man a home beyond his nature, then he had to tell us how to get there, namely, by following his Son to Calvary. The second kind, however, God had no need to reveal at all, but he did so that *all men* could come to the essential truths of human life more easily, with absolute certitude, and without any admixture of error. The most important truth in human life is that there is but one God, the Creator and Lord of all.

Thomas always maintained that many philosophers of the past have *in fact* come to know God's existence through his created effects. At the same time, he was well aware how few these highly gifted "philosophers" were compared to the totality of mankind, the length of time they devoted to the search, and the great number of erroneous notions these philosophers had about "God," as they understood him. Nevertheless, Thomas never failed to point out the many different paths philosophers found to God. (See J. A. Baisnée, "St. Thomas Aquinas' Proofs of the Existence of God Presented in Their Chronological Order," *Philosophical Studies in Honor of the Very Reverend Ignatius Smith, O.P.,* ed. J. K. Ryan, Westminster: Newman, 1952, pp. 29-64). In Thomas' own presentation of the various paths the philosophers took, he often simplified, clarified, and strengthened the tortuous paths actually marked out by various philosophers. He often saw more clearly what Plato, Aristotle, Avicenna, or John Damascene wanted to say, and said it with greater precision and less admixture of error. In the *Summa theologiae* I, 2, 3, Thomas gives only five of the simplest and most convincing ways various philosophers actually used. These "five ways," of course, were not the only ways in which philosophers have come to know the one, true God. Thomas himself ennumerated other ways, and in one's own personal experience one can find many other ways to God. So there is nothing exclusive, sacrosanct, or all-inclusive in the "five ways" (*quinque viae*) presented to beginners in the *Summa theologiae*. (See Joseph Owens, "Aquinas and the Five Ways," *The Monist*, 58, 1974, 16-35).

In his Prologue to St. John, Thomas indicates "four" especially selected ways, suitable to his purpose in the commentary, that have brought philosophers to the contemplation of God's existence, and which are most appropriate to point out to the reader of St. John's Gospel. The contemplative is most easily brought to a knowledge of God's creative existence by perceiving his authority, eternity, and incomprehensibility.

(i) Here St. Thomas points out that the "most efficacious way" (*via efficacissima*) for philosophers to know God is through his *authority* over all things. We see things in nature that act for an end they do not and cannot know; such is true of the entire universe with all its stars and galaxies. Since such things lack intelligence, they cannot direct themselves to an end, but must be directed and moved by some Intelligence. Since the whole course of nature is most fittingly ordered to a complexity of ends, there must be something beyond nature with intelligence to direct all things as Lord and Master. In the Prologue, Thomas sees all this expressed by Isaiah in the use of the word "Lord," when he says, "I saw the Lord." And Thomas notes that John reflects the authority of the Incarnate Word when he says, "He came unto his own," that is, into the world that belonged to him. This philosophical argument corresponds to the "fifth" of the famous "five ways" in the *Summa theologiae*. In the *Summa contra gentiles* (I, c. 13, n. 115), written in Paris early in 1259, this argument is attributed to St. John Damascene (*De fide orthodoxa*, I, c. 3) and also associated with Averroes' *In II Phys.*, com. 75. Altogether, St. Thomas uses this argument from "the governance of all things in the world" eight times, and here he calls it the "most efficacious way." (See Baisnée, *loc. cit.,* p. 63). Surely, this way strikes most scientists and those who contemplate the stars and the world of nature. By way of contrast, it might be noted here also, that in the *Summa theologiae* Thomas called the "first" way, the argument from change throughout the universe, the "more manifest " – and so it was for Aristotle.

(ii) Thomas goes on to say that some philosophers come to the knowledge of God through his *eternity*. Many are struck by the constant fluidity, flow, and mutability of everything in our human experience: "Time and tide wait for no man." But some are struck by the fact that certain things are subject to more change than others. The higher a thing is in nature, the less subject to change it seems to be. Thus terrestrial bodies change in every way, and different living things have longer or shorter life-spans, while celestial bodies seem to us only to change their position in the heavens. Nevertheless, all things in the heavens and on the earth are in the constant flow of time. This "historicity" of all things in time and place would lead us to think that the cause of things in time and place must itself be beyond all time. Thus the contemplation of the temporality of every thing we experience has led some philosophers to a God who is eternal and unchanging.

This agrument, it would seem, was never used elsewhere by St. Thomas. It suggests, however, Plato's famous argument that from contemplating "that which is Becoming always and never is Existent" one is led to "that which is Existent always and has no Becoming" (*Timaeus* 27D6-28C4) — an idea Thomas could have read in the translation and commentary by Calcidius (early 4th century). A similar argument from the mutability of all creatures to the absolute immutability of God is also suggested in Malachi (3:6): "I, the Lord, do not change"; while the whole universe constantly changes. The theme of the absolute contingency and temporality of creatures in contrast to the constancy and eternity of God runs throughout all the writings of St. Augustine; it is one of his fundamental themes.

In the Prologue to John, Thomas suggests that Isaiah implies this view when he uses the word "seated," that is, without change and forever. John the Evangelist suggests the same when he says, "In the beginning was the Word." Some contemporary commentators, however, have reduced this argument to the "first" given in the *Summa* (J. A. Baisneé, *op cit.*, p. 63). But this view does not seem tenable, since the argument in the Prologue is cast entirely in terms of temporality and eternity, which is not at all the same as Aristotle's argument from motion (the first way in the *Summa*). For Aristotle, both God and the universe are eternal, yet God is its First Cause and Mover.

(iii) Other philosophers, Thomas continues, come to the knowledge of God from his *dignity*. "And these," he says, "were the Platonists." They saw that everything that *shares* "being" depends on one who has it *essentially*. That is to say, since everything that exists, diverse as things are, shares in the common act of existing (*esse*), there must be a first Being, whose very nature must be *esse* itself (*ipsum esse subsistens*). This same argument is used by Thomas also in *De potentia*, q.3, a.5, and is there attributed to Avicenna (*Metaph.* VIII, c.7; IX, c.4). The underlying principle, however, is fundamental to the whole of Thomas' metaphysics: "Whatever is possessed by participation (*per participationem*) is reduced to one that has it by essence (*per essentiam*)." (Cf. Peter of Bergamo, *Tabula aurea*, s.v. "Participare"). This is the argument Thomas uses to establish the fundamental principle of his existentialist metaphysics: in God alone are *esse* and *quod est* (essence, or nature) identical; in all creatures, even angels, they are truly distinct (cf. *Sum. theol.* I, q.3, a.4). In the Prologue to John, Thomas sees this unique *dignity* of God as expressed in the phrase of Isaiah when he says, "on a high ... throne." John implies the same when he says, "The Word was God, " which brings us back to the very name of God as "I am who am" (Ex 3:14), the source of the name *Jahweh*.

(iv) Finally, there were other philosophers who came to the knowledge of God from the basic *incomprehensibility* of truth. It is obvious to most people that the human mind is limited in its ability to know the truth. Only the most arrogant "rationalist" – usually the very ones who deny the human mind's ability to prove God's existence – would say, "Given time, man will know and be able to explain everything." The reasonable philosopher, as opposed to the "rationalist," is fully aware of the mind's limitations in every sphere of human activity, especially the most important ones. Therefore, those realists have argued there must be some Intellect that not only knows all truth, but is Truth Itself (*ipsa veritas*) and the ultimate cause of all truth. That is to say, if truth exists in the mind, and human minds come and go in the course of human generation and death, and the foundation of our knowledge is a passing world, then there must be some ultimate ground for all truth, even the truth that "two and two are four." In the Prologue, Thomas seems to attribute this way of reasoning to St. Augustine, who is quoted at this point (Prol. n.6). In his careful study, J. A. Baisnée found no other use of this argument by St. Thomas (See *op. cit.*, p. 64). Cornelio Fabro, moreover, sees this as a "refreshing novelty" in Aquinas, carrying expressly the signature of St. Augustine (see C. Fabro, "Sviluppo, Significato, e Valore della *Quarta Via*," *Doctor Communis*, 7, 1954, 82). In any case, Thomas sees this incomprehensibility of God's ways in Isaiah's use of the word "lofty" (*elevatum*), meaning beyond the understanding of every creature. St. John himself intimates this when he says in 1:18: "No one has ever seen God." This reminds one very much of St. Augustine's favorite quotation from St. Paul, "How deep are the riches and the wisdom and the knowledge of God! How incomprehensible are his judgments, and how unsearchable his ways!" (Rom 11:33). Almost anyone who considers even briefly the unfathomable ways of human life and experience comes to one of two conclusions: either there is a God great enough to draw good out of evil or life is "absurd." But even the "absurdity" of life should be enough to lead men to the Lord of the absurd!

These are only four of the many ways Thomas could have chosen to show how serious, contemplative philosophers have come to a knowledge of God's existence and his ways. In the Prologue, St. Thomas uses these four paths by which contemplative philosophers have come in order to expand on only one point: the *sublimity* of St. John's contemplation (*alta*). This, for Thomas, was the first aspect of John's contemplation of the Word that he wished to convey to us in the Gospel. The other aspects of this contemplation — its expansiveness and perfection — are explained and exemplified in the subsequent paragraphs of this Prologue by Thomas.

III

THE CONCEPTS OF "NATURE" AND "PERSON"

The eternal salvation to which God has freely ordained mankind is a blessed, consummate happiness that cannot be attained by the powers of sheer created nature itself — much less by fallen human nature — even though in creating human nature "in his image and likeness" God intended that this nature should partake of the intimate life of his own dynamic being, Life Itself. That such a sublime happiness is in store for those who freely choose to serve the one true God, and him alone, has been *revealed* to mankind by God himself; man could not otherwise conceive even the possibility of such eternal bliss beyond the grave. "No ear has ever heard, no eye ever seen, any God but you doing such deeds for those who wait for him" (Is 64:3, cf. *Sum. theol.* I, q.1, a.1). In order to know that such eternal happiness exists for and can be attained by each individual human being, every person needs the special grace (*gratia*) of God, a purely unmerited "gift" (the meaning of the word *gratia*). Only by grace can man know the wonders of that goal, and the way to the goal, as well as obtain the help (*auxilium*), the actual, daily grace necessary to achieve that goal.

Man receives the message, the "Good News" (*Evangelium*), about this salvation through faith (*fides*) in the God-Man Christ Jesus, "the one mediator between God and men, who gave himself as a ransom for all" (1 Tim 2:5-6). Each person works out his salvation with "fear and trembling" (Phil 2:12), having confidence and hope (*spes*) in God's abundant mercy and power. We achieve this salvation, however, through a total, unconditional affirming love of God and neighbor (*caritas*) exercised daily through all the other virtures required to live a full Christian life as a "pilgrim" passing this way but once to our true home, heaven, "the holy city, the new Jerusalem" (Rv 21:2). "For we do not have here a lasting city; but we are seeking one that is to come" (Heb 13:14). Thus the whole focus of our pilgrim life is the Word-made-flesh, Christ Jesus, who not only merited redemption for us, but is also the true example of the way we must live. He is "the way, the truth, and the life" (Jn 14:6), and only through him can we go to the Father. So, Christian life consists in accepting Jesus as our Lord and Master, and in imitating him, especailly in obedience to the will of the Father.

Since God himself freely chose the ultimate goal for man, he alone is free to determine the means to that goal, the road by which we must travel to attain the destined happiness beyond our dreams. God could have chosen any number of ways, but in fact he chose only one. That one way is the person of Jesus Christ, who within himself unites our human nature with his divine nature. For this reason Jesus said, "I am the way, the truth, and the life; no one comes to the Father except through me" (Jn 14:6). That just happens to be the one and only means set for us before we were born, not by nature, but by the grace of God.

In order that man be saved, he must accept as absolutely certain — through the gift of "faith" — two fundamental mysteries of revelation that defy human language and human comprehension. They are the mysteries of the *Incarnation:* or "the Word became flesh" (Jn 1:14) and of the *Trinity:* or the ultimate mystery of God as three Persons in one nature. These are the two basic mysteries, enigmas, puzzles, incomprehensibles, that every person must take on faith, with love, in order to follow the way of Christ to the Father, by the grace of the Holy Spirit.

The fundamental teaching in this matter is expressed quite simply by St. Thomas:

> *The way for men to arrive at eternal happiness is the mystery of the Incarnation and passion of Christ, for it says: "There is no salvation in any other; for there is no other name under heaven given to men, by which we can be saved" (Acts 4:12). And therefore belief, in some way, in the mystery of the* Incarnation *of Christ was necessary at all times and for all people; but this belief is different according to the different times and persons. (Sum. theol. II-II, q.2, a.7)*

But Thomas goes one step farther:

> *One cannot believe explicitly in the mystery of the Incarnation of Christ without belief in the* Trinity: *because the mystery of the Incarnation of Christ includes that the Son of God* [the Father] *became man; that he renewed the world through the grace of the Holy Spirit; and that he was conceived* [in the womb of Mary] *by the Holy Spirit. (Sum. theol. II-II, q.2, a.8; see also Nicene Creed, Denz. 125, among others)*

Although neither the mystery itself nor anything affirmative and unpuzzling about the mysteries can be proved by human reason, it is a *human intellect* that tries to understand the meaning of the terms used by God in revealing himself to us, and tries also to show what the mystery *is not*, at least by showing that the mystery is not absurd or impossible (See *Sum. theol.* I, q.1, a.8). The English word "mystery" comes from the Greek *mystérion*, meaning what is "secret or hidden from comprehension"; it usually has to do with divine truths, or secrets hidden behind sacred signs and symbols (*sacramenta*). We sometimes speak of the many natural "mysteries" that are around us, in actual fact, the whole of human life is one big "mystery" beyond our comprehension. But there is one big difference: natural mysteries may some day come to be understood, but supernatural mysteries, such as the Trinity, the Incarantion, and God's love, can never be understood, much less comprehended by any created mind. The best the human mind can do is recognize that it is rational for a man to believe in the truth of the mystery.

The special role of theology, as St. Anselm and all the scholastics following Augustine knew, comes from the dynamism of *faith seeking to understand*, insofar as is humanly possible, the revealed word of God: *Fides quaerens intellectum* (Anselm, *Proslogion*, prooem. Opera Omnia, ed. F. S. Schmitt, I, 1938, p. 94. See M.–D. Chenu, *La théologie comme science au XIII siècle*, 2nd ed., Paris: Vrin, 1943, or any of Chenu's works on theology as a science). For St. Augustine, it was not so much a matter of understanding in order to believe, but a matter of believing in order to understand: *Credo ut intelligam*. Quoting the Latin wording from the Septuagint, Augustine based his view on Isaiah (7:9): "Unless you believe, you will not understand" (Aug., *Sermo* 53.7, PL 38:257; *Ennar. in Ps. 118*, serm. 18. 3-4, PL 37:1552-53). What little understanding we are capable of having in this life presupposes two things: a lively faith, and a humble inquisitive mind. To understand as well as possible what faith holds, we must employ every bit of learning, especially philosophical learning, which sheds light on what has been revealed. The words "nature" and "person," each of which has a precise meaning in philosophy, are essential to our understanding of what we believe. For in our Christian faith we assert that Jesus Christ is one *person*, the Son of the eternal Father, and that he has two *natures*, the truly human and the truly divine. The Holy Trinity is three *persons*, and the Father, Son, and Holy Spirit are one in being or *nature*. Our task then throughout the rest of these notes will be to explain as carefully as we can in "the words of men" what we believe, so that through them we might catch some glimmer of the great mystery that is God himself. To accomplish this task we must first examine the words "nature" and "person." In this particular note we shall explain the various meanings these terms have in everyday use, the way they must be understood at the crucial juncture where reason meets faith, where reason surrenders to the mystery of revelation.

"Nature" as a Philosophical Concept

"Nature" is a wider and more comprehensive term than "person," being used of many more things. Thus every person has a nature, but not every nature has or is a person. The various meanings the word "nature" has in common speech and in its philosophical refinements are what concern us here.

The word *nature* in English today is used in all sorts of loose ways. "Nature lovers" think of the great outdoors; "naturalists" usually think of plants and animals, or else of the great variety of "health foods" that help to make one strong physically. Literary people often use the term "nature" in the sense of "the *universe* out there," a meaning more or less synonymous with that of the Greek word *kosmos* (from which we get our English word "cosmetics"). Intellectuals with a deeper understanding of medicine, sociology, or even law, think of nature as a "normal course of events," or "behavior that is found among many," or "laws of behavior" acceptable in civilized society and codifiable. While all these meanings (and many others) can be traced back to ancient usage, none of them focuses fully on the precise philosophical meaning the word had for the ancient Greeks and Latins and on through the Middle Ages as well. Renaissance humanists often distinguished between Nature with a capital *N*, meaning God acting in the universe (*Natura naturans*), and nature with a small *n*, meaning the created universe as an instrument of God (*natura naturata*). This distinction was also utilized by St. Thomas, St. Bonaventure, and many philosophers of the thirteenth century. Even in that context, a certain dynamic character was thought to belong to the universe as God created it. That is to say, in most of these usages the implication is that there is some innate *source within things* for their "normal," "usual," "codifiable" behavior. In all of these usages derived from antiquity, there is implied an inner dynamism that defies our every attempt to turn them into machines.

Our own thoughts about "nature" have to a large extent been molded and influenced by the mechanistic philosophy dominant in academia since the seventeenth century. Today it is hard for us *to avoid* thinking in clear and distinct mechanical terms. We tend to imagine the universe as a big machine, something like a watch, made up of ever smaller and smaller particles that operate according to determined or determinable mathematical laws. All mathematical formulations, even statistical laws of "random probability," are necessarily mechanical, as Leibniz (1646–1716) saw so clearly; but he ended by acknowledging two parallel worlds – the mechanical and mathematical (the phenomenological), and the "real," onto-logical, and metaphysical (the monodological and non-mechanical) world. For Leibniz, the phenomenological world appears to be me-chanical and mathematically determinable, but the real world behind the phenomena consists of monads, each of which is self-contained and non-causal. In order that such a parallelism exist at all and make any sense, Leibniz had to postulate a pre-established harmony deter-mined by God, the Lord of both worlds. It was inevitable that Leib-niz's metaphysics, and even Newton's, passed into oblivion, while their mechanical and mathematically determinable world became the dominant philosophy of modern science.

If we wish, however, to appreciate what the word *nature* meant to the Greek pagans and Christians, to the Middle Ages and the whole history of Christian thought, we must put aside for the moment any mechanistic notions we may have about the universe in which we live, and try to appreciate a philosophical language that expresses what really lies at the foundation of our human experience, a language that describes a world made up of such principles as po-tency and act; the four radically different kinds of causality (formal, material, efficient and final); real substances that are things (*res*); accidental characteristics (nine of them, not counting the post-predicaments and modes), matter and form; essence and actuality of being, or *quod est* and *esse*. This philosophical language is diffi-cult for us moderns to grasp precisely because it is non-mechanistic and apparently foreign to our "scientific" minds and "analytic" philosophy. But in fact, the older, philosophical vocabulary is much less difficult to grasp than are modern "scientific" and "analytic" concepts, contrary to what might have been expected. Therefore it is intelligible to more people and is grounded more securely in human experience. Whatever may be said about the Semitic mind and the picturesque language of the Old Testament, the Christian experience in both East and West, in both Greek and Latin, is more deeply rooted in history and in personal experience than any of the fleeting modern systems of thought. There is indeed a chasm of sorts between the modern "scientific" and "analytic" vocabulary on the one hand and the traditional personalist vocabulary of the ancients. But it is not a chasm between East and West. The clash between the Eastern and Western theologies is not a clash between Greek and Latin mentalities, but a clash between Platonic and Aristotelian phi-losophies – both of which are Greek.

As to the word "nature," there is an important history of Greek and Latin Philosophical usage (see my "Concept of Nature," *The New Scholasticism*, 38, 1954, 377-408; and "Aristotle's Concept of Nature: Avicenna and Aquinas," in press. See also, G. S. Kirk, *Heraclitus: The Cosmic Fragments*, Cambridge, 1954, index).

For our purposes here it is sufficient to note three historical points briefly before zeroing in on the analogical use of the term in Aristotelian and Scholastic philosophy. 1) The Greek seekers of wisdom before Socrates (d. 399 B.C.), the pre-Socratics, are frequently called *physiologoi* because their whole enterprise was a search for the underlying active "source" (*arche*) of all natural processes in the world, including the origin and nature of man. This underlying active source they called *physis* (nature), from which we derive our English words *physics, physical, physician,* and the like. For most of these pre-Socratics, one or other of the basic elements were sought out as the ultimate, active *nature* of things, as though the whole universe had to have been made from one single element; they are commonly called philosophical Monists, from the Greek word *monos*, "single." 2) Socrates and his disciple Plato (427–347 B.C.) gave up the enterprise of the *physiologoi* as hopeless, Socrates establishing a moral or ethical philosophy, and Plato turning from the world of *nature* to the world of separated, subsistent Ideas that defined each thing in itself, and establishing the primacy of *art* over *nature*, and of *mind* or *spirit* over *matter* (See, *Laws* X, 884A–913D). Plato, responding to Parmenides, established a dualism that enticed a host of eminent Fathers of the Church, mystics, separatists, and modern dualists. This is not the Pauline warfare between the "spirit" and the "flesh," but the Cartesian separation of mind and body that overflowed into the pseudo-conflict of faith and reason, Church and science, *sacerdotium* and *regnum*, Church and State. 3) Aristotle (384–322 B.C.), a disciple of Plato, tried to re-instate the quest of the ancient *physiologoi* in order to establish a realist foundation for his metaphysics of being. That Aristotle would have wished to re-establish the investigation of *nature* is not at all surprising, for his father was court physician to Philip of Macedonia and was himself a born naturalist in the pay of Alexander the Great. What is surprising, however, is that he should have found such a simple truth whereby to succeed in his quest. The simple truth was that the word "is" can be used in many different ways, the fundamental distinction being between *actually* and *potentially*. While the *physiologoi* and the Platonists were rightly busy looking for the actual, Aristotle discovered the potential, that is, primary matter (*materia prima*), which was capable of becoming actual. For this simple discovery, the Thomistic commentator Cardinal Thomas de Vio Cajetan called him *Divus Aristoteles, quia invenit materiam* (Divine Aristotle, because he discovered matter).

To *physis* (nature) in the sense of an *active* principle, Aristotle gave the name "form", but to *physis* (nature) in the sense of a *passive* or *potential* principle, he gave the name "matter." Thus Aristotle could say that the word *nature* is analogical, i.e., "equivocal by intent" (*equivocatio a consilio*). For the word *nature* is used in at least two different senses: primarily as "form," and secondarily as "matter" (*Phys.* II, 1). Form as the actual principle is defined as the active "source or cause of being moved and of being at rest in those things to which it belongs primarily (*per se*) and not incidentally" (192-b21– 23). Matter as the potential principle is defined as the passive "source of being moved and of being at rest in those things to which it belongs primarily and not incidentally" (*ibid.*). In either case, nature, strictly speaking, is a principle (*arche, principium*) or a "source" relative to observable and manifest behavior or properties, whether they be movements such as growing or healing, or characteristics more or less static and proper to different kinds of natures, such as size, color, weight, habitat, and anatomy. St. Thomas is very explicit on this very difficult point: "In the definition of *nature*, the term "source" (*principium*) is used as a kind of generic classification rather than a term like "thing" (or any other *quid absolutum*), because the term *nature* bespeaks of a relationship of origin" (St. Thomas, *In II Phys.,* lect.1, n.5). Thomas rejects every attempt to make absolute Aristotle's concept by suggesting that it might be "an innate power within things" (*vis insita rebus*), as some of Aristotle's commentators have attempted to do. In scholastic terms, the noun "nature" is a *nomen relativum*, not a *nomen absolutum*. Thus *nature* is not really a thing, but an origin or "source" from which (*a quo*) other things proceed.

One further, somewhat epistemological or psychological observation ought to be made at this point. To understand the "nature" of anything living or non-living in this universe we must study the *manifestations* or phenomena that are observable to the senses or to the intellect, both static and dynamic. Some manifestations are sensibly observed, as in minerals, plants, and animals; others are only intellectually observed, such as thinking, willing, hating, loving, and other psycho-physical phenomena. In either case, it is the scientific mind that *projects* the notion of "source" as the root and origin of specific or typical diversities. The more a scientist knows about the observed phenomena, the better he understands the *nature* of the thing studied. One should not be misled by the logical or the lexicographical simplification of some definitions. The logical definition of "man" as "a rational animal," while quite good and complete in its way, should not lead us to think we know all there is to know about human nature. The truth is that this marvelous definition of "man," which includes both animality and rationality, is quite elementary and simplistic. It is not likely to carry one very far in understanding "human nature" with all its complexities. While such a definition clearly sets "man" off from "non-thinking animals" and "non-animal thinkers," it has minimal content. This content can come only from patient study, observation, and experience. An understanding of —let us say — "human nature" is directly proportional to the extent and analysis of one's experience, personal or vicarious. While it is easier to understand human nature, mainly because we are *human* and can reflect on ourselves and our inner states with an analytic mind, the same holds true of our understanding of all natures other than man: only through the phenomena can we claim some understanding of the "nature" of anything.

Simply put, therefore, *nature* is that which makes a thing to be *what* it is. It is the response to the question, "What is it?" In other words, the *nature* of a thing is the same as *its definition* (its *quod quid est*, or *ratio*). Aristotle explains that because of this wider meaning of the term, the word *nature* can be applied to things that have no principle of motion, like the "nature" of a triangle, an idea, ideals, and even spiritual things. Thus, "by an extention of meaning from the original sense of *physis*, every essence in general has come to be called a nature" (*Metaph.* V, 4, 1015a11—12). St. Thomas adds that this latter usage is "by way of metaphor" (*In V Metaph.*, lect. 5, n. 823). In this extended sense, the term is understood in a somewhat static fashion as "whatever a thing is." In this sense it is identical with the term *essence*.

Finally, it should be noted that in the technical language of Latin and Greek, nature is not a thing, a *quod est*, but that *by which* a thing is what it is (*quo est*). For this reason, Aristotle can say that "Things 'have a nature' which have a principle of this kind" (*Phys.* II, 192b2—3). It is always an *it* that has a nature, and that *it* must be substantial, an *ousia.*

"Person" as a Philosophical Concept

Since nature is not an *it*, an existing thing, or supposit, it cannot properly be said *to exist*. Existence (*esse*) belongs to things that have a nature, not to nature itself. Aristotle uses two ways to speak of the concrete, existing thing that has a nature. 1) In the *Categories* 5, Aristotle speaks of substance (*ousia*) in the primary and truest sense as "that which is neither predicable of a subject nor present in a subject, whereas substance (*ousia*) in a secondary sense is the apprehended substantial nature or essence of a thing, which, in order to exist, must exist in a subject. This subject necessarily is the concrete, uniquely existing individual, "for instance, the individual man or horse" (2a3). Since the Greek word *ousia* played such an important part in the Christian theology of the fourth century, it is important to remember that for Aristotle, and for all the Greek thinkers, *ousia* in the primary sense is that alone which has existence. It is the ultimate given *suppositum* that has existence, but the kind of existence it has depends upon its *nature* (*physis*). The Latins simply called it a *suppositum*, or first *substantia*, which possessed existence by reason of the "form" making the substance to have the *kind* of nature and existence it has. The scholastic axiom, "Form gives existence" (*Forma dat esse*) simply means that the *kind* of existence a thing has depends on its form, or nature. But ultimately, only the supposit itself can be said "to exist."

2) Frequently Aristotle speaks of this first *ousia* as an *hypostasis*, meaning "that which stands under" all properties and characteristics. Literally, the Greek word was translated as *subsistentia*, but it always had the sense of *substantia* in Latin. The Greeks, however, made a very important distinction between *ousia*, which, in the primary sense, alone had existence (*esse*), and *hypostasis*, which, in Christian thought, played the same role as (*persona*) "person" in Latin. The meaning of these terms must be carefully kept in mind when reading the early Greek and Latin Fathers, as St. Thomas is careful to point out (*Contra errores Graecorum*, prol. *Opera Omnia* ed. Leon. XL A 71, 1-72).

The English word *person* comes from two Latin words, *personare*, "to sound through," as through the mask used in an ancient dramatic performance. Thus we still list the "Dramatis personae" on the program of a play. Because of the influence of the Latin etymology of this word *persona*, some early Roman theologians, such as Sabellius, thought of God as one substance which spoke through three different masks: the Father, Son, and Holy Spirit. More will be said on this subject later.

An important point to establish here is that in Latin philosophy the term *person* was applied only to substances that had a particular kind of *nature*, namely, intellectual. Boethius gave the Latin scholastics the classical definition when he defined a person as "the individual substance of a rational nature" (*Contra Eutychen*, c. 3). Then he goes on immediately to say, "Now by this definition we Latins have described what the Greeks call *hypostasis*." The linguistic difficulty, however, was that the Greeks too had a word they used for the masks placed over the face of the actor playing different roles. As Boethius noted, their word for mask was *prosopon*, which never lost its original meaning. To convery the Greek reality signified by *hypostasis*, the Latins had to adapt their word *persona* to embrace substantial individuals of an intellectual nature. While there is a technical difference between "rational" and "intellectual," the latter being wider in extention, that difference is not the issue here. Only intellectual substances can be *persons*, and these intellectual substances must be individual and unique (See *Sum. theol.*, I, q.29, aa.1-2).

When philosophy demonstrates the existence of a unique First Being, the First Cause of all that exists, it shows him necessarily to be pure spirit, intellect and free volition, the first beginning and last end of all that are created by himself alone. That is to say, philosophy, reasoning from all the effects in the universe, demonstrates that God is a *person*. When philosophers argue about the existence of a "personal" God, they are really asking whether he is an intellectual being, having knowledge and free will. The question has nothing to do with whether or not God has any personal meaning for me as a person, although this question, too, inevitably follows.

Philosophers, Christian or not, also have grounds for acknowledging the existence of pure spirits, both good and evil. Each such spirit, being an individual intellectual substance, is truly a *person*. These are not personifications of subsistent forces of good and evil, but subsistent intelligences, each one unique without the individuality and limitations of material substances. They are spiritual intelligences, created by God, that have certain powers over material things, but belong to a vast world altogether different from our own material universe. Some of these personal spirits are irreparably evil because of a free choice made by each one, and hence are the cause of fiendish evil beyond the comprehension of man. Other personal spirits are pure, having made a free choice by the grace of God, and are now messengers of divine governance in the universe. From a Christian point of view, the world of human beings can be considered a kind of battle ground, a plaything or booty to be won over by the good angels in the name of God, or by evil spirits in the name of Satan, Lucifer (see Is 14:12), or Beelzebub, "the Prince of demons" (Mt 12:24; Mk 3:22). The important point here is that each individual spirit is an intelligence having a will that is either perverted or good. Therefore each "individual substance of an intellectual nature" is to be called a *person*. Each is unique and each has a name, whether we know it or not.

A consequence of what has been said is that each individual substance of an intellectual nature is a *person* even though that nature exists only in an embryonic stage and needs a natural course of development to reach its full potential, which for a Christian is eternal happiness with God. Once an individual substance has been constituted by matter and by a form, namely, the "human soul," it is a true *person* in the strictest sense of the term. It therefore has certain natural "rights" that belong to it not by any human decree, but by the nature of a person being exactly that, a *person*. Any violation of those rights is a crime against humanity, not animality.

From this it also follows that no individual substance of a non-intellectual, non-human nature can possibly be a *person*. Thus a companionate dog, no matter how "loyal" or "intelligent" it may be, is in no way a *person*. Even if that dog responds to a name or its master's presence or absence, it is not a *person*. To use the word *person* of any individual substance of a non-intellectual nature is a misuse of the term, which cannot be tolerated in philosophy. On the other hand, a group of persons may constitute a legal entity known as a corporation or "moral person," which may be the subject of legal rights and obligations before the law. But this is merely a legitimate extention of a basically sound definition of *person*.

Briefly, *nature* is a reply to the question, "*What* is it?" It is the ultimate specific "source" of definite, characteristic phenomena, both static and dynamic. The active, automatic "origin" of these characteristics is the *form* or *species* of the thing, making it to be what it is, the passive, potential "abilities" of such an individual thing are the *matter*. The spiritual forms or species are immaterial natures: these may exist solely in the mind (such as "triangles" and "the square root of two"), or they may exist in physical reality, in which case they are necessarily intellectual substances. *Person*, on the other hand, is a reply to the question, "*Who* is it?" The *person* or "who" is an individual substance (material or immaterial) of an intellectual nature. In all creatures there is a distinction between *person* (as a supposit or *quod*) and *nature*, as that by which (*id quo*) a thing is what it is. That is to say, in all creatures, every person "has" a nature by which he has existence. Thus existence and all actions belong to the *person* or supposit, but *nature* is the means by which the person or supposit has existence and its specific actions.

The importance of all of this will become evident when we consider the two great mysteries of our faith: the Trinity and the Incarnation.

IV

THE MYSTERY OF THE TRIUNE GOD

According to the Creed attributed to St. Athanasius, whoever wishes to be saved must hold to the Catholic faith whole and entire. "The Catholic faith, however, is this: that we adore one God in trinity and trinity in unity, neither mixing the persons nor separating the substance" (Denz. 75). The Athanasian Creed, dating at least to the fourth century, goes on in great detail to profess that "the Father is God, the Son is God, the Holy Spirit is God, but there are not three Gods, but one God." All are equal in immensity, eternity, omnipotence, lordship, and creation. They are all one God. But each Person is really and truly distinct from the other two, and these Persons are only three: Father, Son, and Holy Spirit. This is the incomprehensible mystery that God has revealed to us about his inner dynamic life.

When philosophers prove the existence of one God (cf. Note II above), they prove that in him his very *nature* or essence is to be (*esse*). St. Thomas proves this fundamental truth of his philosophy in many ways (See *Sum. theol.*, I, q.3, a.4 and all parallel places). Simply, in everything that exists, whatever is over and above the essence (*praeter essentiam*) must be caused either by the essence itself (or *nature*), as proper characteristics naturally springing forth from it, like risibility in man, or it must be caused by some extrinsic source, like heat in water being caused by fire. But since the very existence of a thing (*ipsum esse rei*) within our experience is other than its essence, then the thing's existence must be caused either by its essential principles or by some exterior cause. Its own existence cannot in any way be produced by the essential principles of the thing, for then the essence could not but necessarily exist, since whatever is essential necessarily belongs to it. Therefore, the thing whose *esse* is other than its essence must have its existence caused by another — and ultimately by one whose very essence is *to be*. Therefore in God essence and existence (*esse*) are identical. Thus God is his *nature* or essence, and he is his *esse* or existence. Expressed in more Platonic terms, *esse* is a reality in which different things share or participate in varying degrees, but whatever is had by participation (*per participationem*) presupposes one who has it essentially (*per essentiam*).

For St. Thomas the splendor of God's reality is expressed most fully in the identity of his essence and existence. The very *nature* of God is to be *ipsum esse subsistens*, "subsistent being itself." In human history, God, having chosen a special race of people among all those whom he had created, revealed to the Jews his own name, Jahweh, "I AM WHO AM" (Ex 3:14). This truth, as Gilson has constantly emphasized, is the basic principle of the whole of St. Thomas' philosophy. He has also noted that St. Thomas himself referred to this insight as *haec sublimis veritas* (*Sum. c. Gent.*, I, c.32; see E. Gilson, *The Christian Philosophy of St. Thomas Aquinas*, trans. L. K. Shook, New York: Random House, 1956, pp.84-95; *Le Thomisme*, 6th ed., Paris. Vrin, 1965, pp.99-112). It belongs to the *nature* of God necessarily to exist. That is, he cannot not exist.

From this basic truth it follows, first, that God is in every way uniquely and absolutely indivisible, or "simple," as St. Thomas puts it, having no distinctions within his nature whatever (*Sum. theol.*, I, q.3). Thus in God there is no distinction or difference between his intellect and will, truth and love, justice and mercy, and so forth, even though for us each of these words has a real and distinct meaning (*ratio*) that must be retained in our talking about God. In our talking about God, human language does not lose its meaning, but it takes on a subtlety and expansion in which we realize that words are being used differently of God and creatures. The difference is radical and absolute (*per se*), but there is a human reasonableness in using certain words of both God and creatures. This "equivocation by intent," as Aristotle calls it, is more properly called *analogy*, which is quite different from simple metaphorical language, such as God's "walking," or his "coming down" (*Sum. theol.*, I, q.13, etc.). Words such as "good" and "love" can be used properly both of God and man, but in two radically different ways; the reality as it is found in God infinitely transcends our conception of "good" and "love" realizable in man. Thus such statements as "God is love" (1 Jn 4:8), God is truth, God is good, and so forth, are more true and significant than we can possibly realize. The meaning such terms have for us is quite real and proper, but our understanding of those terms is but a shadow of the reality that is in God. Similarly, God's *nature* is *esse* in a way that surpasses our understanding of all the things of our human experience.

The second point is that God has revealed to us through the Law and the Prophets, through Jesus Christ, and through his Church, that he, the Father, "so loved the world that he gave his Only Begotten Son, so that whoever believes in him should not perish, but have eternal life" (Jn 3:16). The Son of God-made-man himself stated time and again that he "was sent by the Father" to do the will of him who sent him, and that all he has is "from the Father." But he also said that he would "ask the Father, and he will give you another Paraclete, to be with you forever – the Spirit of truth" (Jn 14:16-17), "the Paraclete, the Holy Spirit, whom the Father will send in my name, he will teach you all things, and bring to your mind whatever I have said to you" (Jn 14:26). The Son-made-man also said: "When the Paraclete comes, whom I will send you from the Father, the Spirit of truth who comes from the Father, he will give testimony to me" (Jn 15:26). The last injunction of Jesus to his apostles was "go, therefore, and teach all the nations, baptizing them in the name of the Father, and of the Son, and of the Holy Spirit" (Mt 28:19). This baptismal formula reflects the Church's gradual understanding of God as three Persons (See Acts 2:38; 2 Cor 13:13).

The only words God used in revealing himself to us are those of "Father," "Son," and "Holy Spirit" ("Spirit," or "Paraclete," meaning advocate or comforter). And it is only within this context that the theologian must try to understand the inner life of the Godhead. St. John also uses the word *logos, Verbum,* or Word, as synonymous for the Son. St. Paul speaks of Christ as "the image of God" (2 Cor 4:4, Col 1:15). There simply are no other words given to us for theological understanding. These are common enough terms, but how they are to be understood of the one God, whose *nature* is his *esse,* is a difficult problem, where "faith seeks understanding" with the help of philosophy, the age-long "handmaid of theology" (the *ancilla theologiae*) as understood by the Alexandrine theologians, particularly St. Athanasius, and by the Cappadocian Fathers (St. Basil of Caesarea, St. Gregory of Nazianzus, and St. Gregory of Nyssa) in the East, and by St. Augustine in the West.

In this note there are two major points that need clarifying. First, the doctrine of consubstantiality of the Son with the Father, which was the first really crucial development in Christian doctrine. Although the debate over this doctrine reached a climax in the fourth century, still there was the subsequent problem of *Filioque,* which came to a head in the ninth century. The second baffling mystery was how each of the three Persons is identical with the one nature, yet truly distinct from each other.

A. Consubstantiality of the Son with the Father

Frequently in the New Testament Scriptures, Jesus Christ seems to be presented as somehow less than Jahweh, the one true God of the chosen people. He speaks of himself as "sent by the Father" to do not his own will, but "the will of him who sent me."

He always speaks of himself as having only that teaching, that knowledge, that mission, that will, that judgment which has been committed to him by the Father. Throughout the Gospel of St. John, Jesus seems to acknowledge a subservient position to the Father, depending upon the Father's acceptance and glorification of him as a loyal Son. In the Gospel according to St. John, Jesus even declares explicitly that "the Father is greater than I" (Jn 14:28). In the end he commends his spirit to the Father.

One of the prevalent assumptions of such ecclesiastical writers as Origen and Clement of Alexandria was that the Son, Jesus Christ, was *subordinate* to the Father. One form of "subordinationism" insisted that Jesus was no more than a mere man who was "adopted" by God. Other forms, like that held by Arius (*c*.250–*c*.336), maintained that the Person of Jesus was created by the Father from nothing in order to be the instrument of the divine plan; and thus that the Person of Jesus had a substance (*ousia*) different from God's. This was the extreme form of Arianism that developed from the "subordinationism" of the third century. A second party that developed in the early fourth century, called "Homoeans" (from *homoios*, "similar"), tried to avoid the very basic commitment of "What think you of Christ?" by saying that there was much similarity between Father and Son "according to the Scriptures." But the most influential group to emerge was the Semi-Arians, who claimed that the Father and Son were "similar in substance" (*homoiousios*), but not identical. Although the question of the *ousia* of Jesus was the central issue that directly occasioned the synod of Alexandria (*c*.320) in which St. Alexander condemned the teaching of Arius, the Catholic teaching was not universally proclaimed until the Ecumenical Council of Nicaea, convoked by the Emperor Constantine at his summer palace in 325.

At the Council of Nicaea, under the presidency of Hosius of Spain and under the prosecution mainly by Saint Alexander of Alexandria, whose secretary was the deacon St. Athanasius, approximatley 235 bishops (318 according to Athanasius) gathered to consider this crucial dogmatic problem and legislate a number of disciplinary decrees. Basing themselves on the texts "In the beginning was the Word ... and the Word was God" (Jn 1:1), "The Father and I are one" (Jn 10:30), "That they may be one, even as we are one" (Jn 17:11), "That all may be one, as you Father, in me, and I in you" (Jn 17:21) and similar texts, the conciliar Fathers at Nicaea professed the ancient belief that the "Son is of one substance (that is, *homoousion*) with the Father." The Latin rendering is "consubstantial (*consubstantialis*) with the Father." This doctrine was directly opposed by the Semi-Arians under the leadership of Eusebius, bishop of Nicomedia. Eusebius and his many followers insisted on the term *homoiousion*, "of *similar* substance with the Father," in place of the orthodox *homoousion*. Some so-called historians of this controversy of the fourth century have been so insensible and obtuse as to describe it as "a quibble about an *iota*." That *iota* made all the difference in the world between orthodoxy and heresy. As late as 359, St. Jerome could write: "The whole world groaned one day and marvelled to find itself Arian" (*Dial. adv. Lucif.* 19, PL 23, 172C).

The significant point is that the word *homoousion* is nowhere to be found in the Canonical Scriptures, no more than is *homoiusion*. But *homoousion* was a soundly based philosophical term used in response to a Greek philosophical question. Consequently, the crucial question for modern man seeking the Christian truth is not so much "what think you of Christ? Whose Son is he?" (Mt 22:42), but rather, "What think you of *homoousion*? By what authority do you profess it?" In the earliest ages of Christianity, many thought highly of Jesus as the "adopted son of God," and accepted him as the "Christus" of faith giving us hope. But, as we shall see, the fundamental question is about the historical Jesus as "consubstantial with the Father," just as the bishops assembled at Nicaea openly declared to be the true teaching of the Church.

This is one of the earliest examples of the development of Christian doctrine which Cardinal John Henry Newman (1801-90) helped us to understand (See especailly his *Arians of the Fourth Century* (1833), *St. Athanasius*, 2 vols. (1843), *Development of Christian Doctrine* (1845)). The real meaning of the text "The Father and I are one" (Jn 10:30) is that the Son is "consubstantial with the Father" (*homoousion toi patri*). In theological terms, the *ousia* (substance) of the Son is identical to the *ousia* of the Father. From this it is only a short step to the recognition of the Holy Spirit as consubstantial to the Father and Son; that is, the *ousia* of the Holy Spirit is identical to that of the Father and the Son. Moreover, that unique *ousia* is "an individaul substance of an intellectual nature"; that is, God is a "person" or "personal."

B. Three distinct Persons in one Nature

Nevertheless, there are three distinct persons (*hypostases*) identical with the one divine *nature* (*ousia*). Because the divine nature is identical with its existence (*esse*), as explained above, there can be only one God. Thus the *person* of the Father cannot be distinct in any way from the divine nature which is *esse*, or *ipsum*

esse subsistens. (*Sum. theol.* I, q.28, a.2). Although none of the three
Persons is distinct from the one identical nature or *ousia*, each is
really and truly distinct from the other two, as Father is from Son
(*Sum. theol.* I, q.28, a.3). The only meaning open to our appreciation of the mystery is to be found in the terms God himself used
to reveal himself, namely, the relative terms of "Father," "Son," and
"Spirit" (*Sum. theol.* I, q.29, a.4).

The role of a father is "to beget," just as the meaning of sonship
is "to be begotten." The Father, therefore, is unbegotten, but is
origin and progenitor of the Son, who himself does not beget, for
there is no "Son" in the Godhead other than himself. That is to say,
the whole reality of the Father is to beget, to generate, to give all
that he has, namely, his whole divine nature, to the Son. And the
whole reality of the Son is to be begotten, to be generated, to receive
all that he has, namely, his whole divine nature, from the Father.
This relation of Father and Son within the Trinity is clearly expressed throughout the Gospel of John: "All that the Father has are
mine" (Jn 16:15). "Father, glorify your Son, since you have given
him authority over all men" (Jn 17: 1-2); "The teaching you gave
me, I have given to them" (Jn 17:8); and again, "My teaching is not
my own, but of him who sent me" (Jn 7:16). Both St. Augustine and
St. Thomas wax eloquent on the precision of this expression. Jesus'
doctrine does not belong to himself as originating with him. Rather
it belongs to, it is the possession of, the Father (in the genitive case);
it is the Father's doctrine precisely *as received from* him by the Son.
The life of the Father is an eternal *giving* of himself whole and entire
to the Son. The life of the Son is an eternal *receiving* of the Father
whole and entire. The life of the Father and the Son together is an
eternal *breathing* of the Spirit, while the life of the Spirit is an eternal breath, or gift, whole and entire from the Father and the Son
together.

It is obvious that the Spirit must proceed from the Father and
the Son (*Patre Filioque*), and not from the Father alone, for in the
latter case another "son" would be generated and there would be
no distinction between the Son and the Spirit, as Catholic faith
teaches (*Sum. theol.*, I, q.36, a.4; see *Sum. contra Gent.*, IV, cc.1-
26, *Contra errores Graecorum*, etc.). The Holy Spirit thus possesses the identical nature of the Father and of the Son precisely *as
breathed* (*spirata*) by Father and Son. He is the "gift" (*donum*) sent
to the Church and into the hearts of all baptized in the Spirit. He
is the "uncreated grace" (*gratia increata*) by whom all those with
"created grace" (*gratia creata*) live the intimate life of the Godhead.
He is the Spirit that Jesus *breathed* on the disciples that they might
have his Spirit. In other words, the Spirit belongs to the Father and

the Son, just as the Son belongs to the Father. Just as the Son *was sent* into the world at a particular period in human history "when the fullness of time had come" (Gal 4:4), so the Holy Spirit *was sent* in a visible way to men at a special time in human history (*Sum. theol.,* I, q.43, a.2 and a.7).

The precise problem where human understanding must give way to belief in a mystery is how can one personal God, who is *ipsum esse subsistens* and a *person*, be in fact three distinct Persons and not three gods. If there are three Persons, each "an individual substance of an intellectual nature," as Boethius and sound philosophy define "person," then why is not each Person a distinct substance with its own *esse*? That is to say, why are there not three gods, if there are three distinct Persons? Or rather still, why are there not four persons, a quaternity, as Peter of Poitiers seems to have implied, according to Geoffrey of Auxerre, St. Bernard's secretary, in his *Libellus* against the so-called *capitula* (PL 185, 598; cf. *Sum. theol.,* I, q.28, a.2; N. Haring, *The Commentaries on Boethius by Gilbert of Poitiers*, Toronto: PIMS, 1966, 3-13). To put the question in a less philosophical context, how can *one* God be *three* Persons? Or conversely, how can *three* distinct Persons be only *one* subsistent *esse* and not three? At this point no amount of philosophical analysis and explanation can dissolve the real mystery, something transcending mere human intelligence. All we must insist upon is the absolute identity of *person* and *nature* in God, and we must not think of the "person" as "an adjunct, or something extrinsically attached," as Gilbert seems to have suggested (*Sum. theol.,* I, q.28, a.2). Not even when we see God "face to face" and know him as he really is will the mystery dissolve. Only God can comprehend himself. Not even the angels and demons, whose spiritual intelligences far transcend every human intelligence, can understand the mystery.

The importance and sublimity of this mystery of the Trinity becomes more apparent when we prayerfully consider the mystery of the Incarnation: the fact that the Son of God (and only the Son) became true man for our sake, suffered, died, and triumphed over death, that we might have his life. This will be discussed in Note V below.

By way of summary, we can say that the one true God has only one *nature*, which, of itself, is the total actuality of being (*esse*), containing no distinctions, potentiality, temporality, or need, having no beginning or end or mutability. This *ousia* is subsistent truth and love, knowing all things, even what is "future and contingent" *to us*, and loving all those whom he has freely chosen to love and share in his eternal, dynamic bliss. By faith (and faith alone) we are given a glimpse of the dynamic nature of the Godhead in three distinct Persons: the Father, the Son, and the Holy Spirit. Each Person, though identical with the divine nature, is distinct from the other two by the way in which that nature is possessed. The Father is the divine nature precisely as *giving it* whole and entire from all eternity to the Son. The Son is that same divine nature precisely as *being given* it whole and entire from all eternity, himself begotten, but in no way "created." The Holy Spirit is that same divine nature precisely *as breathed* by the Father and the Son, himself unbebotten and ungenerated, but simply the Father's breath of love for the Son and the Son's breath of love for the Father.

In human history the "Only Begotten Son of the Father" *was sent* into the world to become man, suffer under Pontius Pilate, die, and be raised up again on the third day. Also in human history the Spirit of God, the gift of love, *was sent* by the Father and the Son into this temporal world to sanctify and to animate the "people of God" in their pilgrimage to their true home, which is eternal bliss with all the saints in seeing God face to face. "Then I shall know even as I am known" (1 Cor 13:12).

In the prologue to his *Contra errores Graecorum* St. Thomas manifests a fine sense of history, as well as the demands of a good translator. He notes that the writings of our ancient holy Fathers must be seen in their historical context. That is, before the Arian heresy concerning the precise relationship between the person of Jesus and the person of God, ecclesiastical teachers were not as precise in speaking about the unity of the divine essence as were teachers after Arius. Similarly, even St. Augustine, one of the great doctors of the Church, was not as precise about grace and free will when he was writing against the Manicheans in his youth as he was in the face of the heresy of Pelagianism. Thus in his later writings, particularly in his anti-Pelagian works, Augustine speaks most cautiously about man's free will and the primacy of God's free gift of grace and final perseverance. And so, St. Thomas says, it is not surprising if modern doctors of the faith, coming after so many new errors, speak more cautiously and more elaborately concerning the doctrine of faith, so as to avoid all heresies. Hence if some things are found in the writings of the ancient doctors that are not as cautiously expressed as the moderns would like, those writings are not for that reason to be disdained or cast aside. Nor should those statements be expanded but reverently explained.

Coming to the main point in his prologue, St. Thomas notes with sympathy the problems of the translator. What might sound good in Greek may not always sound correct in Latin. For this reason the Latins and Greeks profess the same truth of faith in different words. An important example is the mystery of the Trinity itself. For among the Greeks it is correct and orthodox to say that the Father, the Son, and the Holy Spirit are three *hypostases*. But among the Latins it would not be correct to say that they are three *substances*, even though *hypostasis* for the Greeks is the same as *substantia* for the Latins in literal translation. For among the Latins the term *substantia* is more commonly taken to mean the essence, which both the Greeks and the Latins admit to be only one in God. For this reason, just as the Greeks say there are three *hypostases*, we say there are three *persons*, as even St. Augustine acknowledges in his *De trinitate* (VII, n.7, PL 42, 939).

Therefore, the question of precise language is extremely important for the preservation and development of the true Catholic faith. One of the most important functions of the Catholic theologian is to know exactly what can and what cannot be said consistent with the revealed Christian doctrine. The history of Christian belief or dogma may seem more like a history of heresies. But it is often the case that an outrageous statement or a view that is "offensive to pious ears," *male sonans*, or contrary to the living faith of the Church, occasions a clarification and more exact formulation of the true faith, thus contributing indirectly to the development of Christian doctrine in the history of the Church. Therefore each new formulation, like *homoousion*, must be understood in the historical context of the speculative problem; in this case it was a Greek philosophical problem that needed a Greek theological solution consistent with divine revelation. The true development of Christian doctrine is never a case of abrogating or denying an earlier profession of faith, but always a more explicit profession of the one true faith in the face of given historical obsessions or preoccupations of a certain time in human history. It is only God himself who has no history. Everything created by God and governed by his immutable providence has a very definite history, one that is irreversibly unique and destined to manifest the glory of God.

V

THE MYSTERY OF THE INCARNATION

The Catholic faith professes a firm belief in the divinity of Jesus Christ, the Word Incarnate, in the literal sense of the word "divine," meaning God himself. That is:

> We believe in one Lord, Jesus Christ, the only Son of God, eternally begotten of the Father, God from God (*Deum de Deo*), Light from Light, true God from true God, begotten (*genitum*), not made (*non factum*), one in Being (*consubstantialem*) with the Father. Through him all things were made. For us men and for our salvation (*propter nos homines et propter nostram salutem*) he came down from heaven; by the power of the Holy Spirit he was born of the Virgin Mary, and became man (*et homo factus sit*).

This is the ancient profession of faith approved by the Council of Nicaea (325), more fully formulated by the First Council of Constantinople (381), and recited weekly by the faithful in their Sunday liturgy. It is a belief that Jesus of Nazareth, "born of a woman, under the law" (Gal 4:4), is in his unique personality the Only Begotten Son of the Father, one in nature with him, truly God and at the same time truly man, and born as we are of a woman, "one tempted in all things as we are, yet without sin" (Heb 4:15). Quite simply, it is a belief that the historical Jesus, born of the Virgin Mary, is one divine Person in two natures, one divine, the other human.

For St. Thomas, John the Evangelist proclaims for us in a special way the "mysteries of Christ's divinity." For him, St. John's Prologue is a canticle of the Word become flesh, "full of grace and truth" (Jn 1:14). The reality of *who* he is, therefore, is announced in the first strophe of the Prologue:

> In the beginning was the Word,
> And the Word was with God,
> And the Word was God.
> He was in the beginning with God.

To Thomas' Aristotelian mind, the first two phrases declare the existence (*an est*) of the Word and the other two declare the reality of who he is (*quid est*). The first phrase declares "when" he was, namely, *in the beginning*. The second declares "where" he was, namely, *with the Father*. The third phrase declares *who* he was, namely, *God*. The fourth declares the "manner" so as to exclude the two basic errors concerning the Word: (1) the error of gentiles, such as pagan Greeks and Romans, who thought there were many gods, and the Manichaeans, who thought there were two gods, one good, the other evil; and (2) that of the Arians, who thought that the Word was less than the Father, different in substance, and created by the Father. Both of these errors are excluded by the fourth phrase, that the unique Word *was with the Father from the beginning* and identical with him in nature.

In typical scholastic fashion Thomas sees in these four lines of the first strophe a refutation of *all the errors* of both heretics and philosophers. As for the heretics, there were (1) some like the Ebionites and Cerinthus, who denied the existence of Jesus Christ before his conception in the womb of Mary; that is, they thought Christ to be no more than "a mere man" who later deserved to be called "divine," being "adopted" by the Father and "accepted as the Christ" by his disciples. To this group belong Paul of Samosata (3rd cent.), Photius (9th cent.), Rudolf Bultmann and Hans Kung (20th cent.), and in a certain sense, Nestorius, about whom more will be said later. To all of these the Evangelist says, *In the beginning was the Word*. (2) Then there were those like Sabellius (3rd cent.), who denied the real distinction of Persons, thinking that "Father" and "Word" are two masks for the one true God (see Note III). To these the Evangelist says, *And the Word was with God*, insisting on their distinction in Person. (3) Then there were the heretics like Eunomius (d. 394) and the other extreme Arians, who insisted that Jesus, though pre-existent to his incarnation, was very much unlike (*anomios*) the Father. To them the Evangelist says, *And the Word was God*. (4) Finally, there was Arius himself and all the semi-Arians, who said that the Word was less than the Father and created by him. To all these the Evangelist says, *He was in the beginning with God.*

As to the philosophers, there were (1) the pre-Socratics, who all, except Anaxagoras, were pure materialists, whether they acknowledged one or many elements as "nature," or only atoms in space, for them the universe came about not by Intelligence, but by chance. Against these the Evangelist says, *In the beginning was the Word*; all things come by his agency, not by pure chance. (2) Plato, however, admitted the reality of things immaterial, but for him these were subsistent, immaterial Forms, or Ideas, separate from God as well as from matter. Against this the Evangelist says, *And the Word was with God*. (3) The later Platonists, especially Plotinus (c. 205-270 B.C.), acknowledged the existence of the One, from which proceeded Mind (*Nous*) containing all the Ideas, but who was less than the One. Lest anyone think that the Word was "with God" in this sense of being less than him, the Evangelist says, *And the Word was God.* (4) Finally, Aristotle placed the ideas of all things in God, and acknowledged the identity of intellect, act of intellection, and reality intellected (or known) in God, but he thought that the world was co-eternal with him, that is, created from all eternity by God. For St. Thomas, the word *he* in St. John (*hoc* in Latin; *houtos* in Greek) implies that he "alone" was *in the beginning with God,* excluding not other Persons, but any other co-eternal nature.

This is a typical example of how much a scholastic theologian like St. Thomas could see in a single strophe of John. Everything St. Thomas says in his commentary on the first strophe is entirely true and correct, but he does not mean to imply in any way that St. John had these ideas in his mind when he or his scribe wrote these opening lines of the Prologue. Here is an excellent example of St. Anselm's "Faith seeking understanding," or "an example of meditating on the rationale of the faith."

The climax of the entire Prologue for Thomas is the direct statement, *And the Word was made flesh* (Jn 1:14), because taken literally and strictly it excludes all errors concerning the one *Person* and the two distinct *natures* in Christ, one fully divine, the other as fully human as we are. In this profession of faith lies the mystery of the Incarnation. Everything else in our Christian Belief, that God became man "for us and for our salvation," that "by dying he destroyed our death," that "by rising he restored our life," and that "he will come again in glory to judge the living and the dead," depends upon the basic mystery of the Incarnation, namely, that Jesus of Nazareth, born at a definite time in history of the Jewish Virgin Mary, is *one unique person,* "the Son of the living God," who united in his person *two* wholly complete and distinct *natures*: human and divine.

In this note we will restrict our analysis to the mystery of the union of the human and the divine in the one person of Jesus Christ. Among the many so-called Christological heresies concerning this central mystery of Christianity, we will restrict ourselves to the three most common ones: (a) Christ was not really "divine" either in his person or in nature; (b) Christ was not really "human" like all the rest of mankind, and not "one tempted in all things as we are, yet without sin" (Heb 4:15); (c) there were two persons in Christ, one human, the other divine. But first we must begin with a preliminary note to focus the real problem.

Today it is commmon among historians of Christianity and Scripture scholars, at least since the time of H. S. Reimarus (1694-1768), to distinguish between the Jesus of history and the Christ of faith (see Sebastian Bullough, O.P., "Scripture Survey: From Wrede to the New Quest," *Blackfriars*, 44, 1963, 79-82). Perhaps Rudolf Bultmann more than anyone else today has sharpened the distinction between *Geschichte* (the existential significance of history) and *Historie* (the empirical study of historical facts as objectively real). Although there are no two words in English to convey the difference between *geschichtlich* and *historich*, the whole of Bultmann's work manifests the distinction which is fundamental to modern Christian studies and beliefs (see especially the article of Claude Geffre, "Bultmann on Kerygma and History," *Rudolf Bultmann in Catholic Thought*, ed. T.F. O'Meara, O.P., and D.M. Weisser, O.P., New York: Herder and Herder, 1968, pp. 167-95). Although the bibliography on this important modern distinction is vast, and although there are many ways to exemplify the distinction between "historical science" (*Historie*) and "existential history" (*Geschichte*), we will limit our brief and simple observations to the mystery of the Incarnation.

Simply put, *Historie* deals with what little we can know of the historical Jesus precisely as a human being said to have been born in Bethlehem of Jewish heritage, whose mother's name was Mary, and who was put to death. Many Protestant theologians have given up the quest for the "historical Jesus," claiming that all our knowledge is colored by a *later reaction*, expressed in a kerygmatic manner, by the so-called evangelists and preachers long after the factual historical events, which had by then ceased to be important. *Geschichte*, on the other hand, is the Christ event, the impact on a human being of the escatalogical challenge put to each individual today, as it was at the end of the first century, through the basic kerygma. In other words, many Protestant theologians (and some Catholic ones) do not think that much, if anything, really certain can be known of the historical man known as Jesus of Nazareth. For most of them, the historical Jesus was an ordinary, idealistic Jewish man little different from other Jews at the beginning of the present era; perhaps in his idealism he was a "great man" who came to a tragic death and was buried.

The main thing is that *much was said about him* after his death and burial. And *what was said* is the reaction of living men accepting an eschatalogical challenge. Today the challenge made to the early Christians is made to each of us, the challenge of the existential acceptance of Jesus as "the Christ of faith." Inevitably the *acceptance* of the Christ event by the early Christians expressed itself in a multitude of "myths" that sprang from the believer. The most important of these "myths" was the "deification" or "divinization" of Jesus by the believer. For Bultmann it is the myths alone that are really important. When Christ is "demythologized" there is nothing left but a tragic life of a man called Jesus. Thus the quest for "the historical Jesus" is not only vain and futile, it is also un-Christian and of no salvific value whatever. It is empty *Historie*, having no contemporary existential significance.

Bultmann puts the matter simply when he says: "The saving efficacy of the cross is not derived from the fact that it is the cross of Christ: it is the cross of Christ because it has this saving efficacy. Without that efficacy it is the tragic end of a great man" (quoted by C. Geffré, *op. cit.*, p. 181).

This whole approach to the Jesus of history and the Christ of faith seems to lie at the root of Hans Kung's best seller, *On Being a Christian* (trans. E. Quinn, Garden City: Doubleday, 1976, from *Christ Sein*, Munchen: R. Piper, 1974).

This preliminary note on the contemporary, mainly Protestant, approach to Christology has been introduced here solely to show how radically different is St. Thomas' approach to the mystery of the Incarnation. For St. Thomas (and all those before him in the Catholic faith) it is the historical Jesus who is one divine Person, the Only Begotten Son of the Father, who became man by being conceived of the Holy Spirit in the womb of the Virgin Mary, thereby uniting to himself a truly complete human nature, subject to all the natural ills and pleasures that man is heir to, including suffering and death (but not sin).

(a) The most common error concerning Jesus Christ is the one we have just been talking about, namely, that he was not truly divine in his *Person* as the Only Begotten Son of the Father or in his *nature*, which is consubstantial with the Father and the Holy Spirit. This heresy has assailed the Catholic faith from its very inception, and, as we have seen, some Protestant theologians embrace it today. The mystery of the Incarnation (or "coming in the flesh," *in carne*) does indeed baffle human credulity, and it cannot be accepted without the gift of faith that comes from the Holy Spirit in baptism.

At first, not even the apostles and the immediate disciples of Jesus knew what to make of the Son of Man, the miracles he worked, the doctrine of salvation he preached. Nor did they know what to make of his constant references to God as his Father, to his doing the will of his Father, to the close presence of the Kingdom, to the Father's Kingdom being already at hand, and to the death he was to suffer and to his ultimate victory over death. It was only with the coming of the Holy Spirit that the disciples began to understand the reality of the historical Jesus they had come to know and love. Even after his death and resurrection, Cerinthus and a large Jewish sect called the Ebionites refused to accept Christ as anything more than "a mere man" (*purus homo*). Various theories of "adoptionism" were common throughout the second and third centuries. This was the view that Jesus was born a mere man, but later (some put it at the baptism by John) he deserved to be "adopted" by God, much as parents might adopt an attractive boy as their son. Every form of "adoptionism" implies a "subordinationism" of Jesus, at least as a creature. It was inevitable that Arianism of one kind or another should errupt in the fourth century. Every form of "Arianism" from the extreme "anomeanism" of Eunomius to the semi-Arianism of Eusebius of Caesarea (who baptized Constantine as he lay dying on the battlefield) denied the *identity of nature* in the Father and in the Word, who in the fullness of time became flesh.

It was inevitable that a subdued question raised since the first century should come to a head in the Arians of the fourth century. The question was: What is the relation between Jesus, the Son of Man, and the Father, who is Jahweh? How are Jesus, born of Mary, and the Father "One"? The only possible answer consistent with the biblical writings was the unbiblical term (*homoousion*) "consubstantial." The neo-Platonism of Plotinus unmistakably influenced Origen and many other Greek Christians. For Plotinus the *Logos* or *nous* eminates from the One and is less than the One, just as the Spirit eminates from the Logos and is less than it. Neo-Platonism together with the natural inability to accept any "man" as "God" inevitably resulted in the widespread Arianism of the fourth century. To appreciate even inadequately the threat Arianism posed for the Church even after the Council of Nicaea (325), one might recall how at one time the great St. Athanasius seemed to stand alone (*Athanasius contra mundum*), and how even St. Jerome in the West could say that the whole world woke up one day to find itself Arian. The fourth century, beset as it was by various forms of Arianism and the dubious "freedom" of the Church, was the greatest age of the Fathers, both Greek and Latin, in the history of the Church. It was the "golden age of the Fathers." Through them the Holy Spirit preserved orthodoxy through a development of doctrine and a flowering of heroic sanctity unparalleled since the age of the martyrs.

Possibly the climax of the fourth century came with the Council of Rome in 382 under Pope St. Damasus I, in which the whole development of Christian doctrine up to that date was summarized in the *Tomus Damasi*, and the canonical books of Sacred Scripture were fixed as we have them today (see Denz. 152-180).

The relation of Nestorianism to Arianism will be discussed under heading (c).

(b) The second most common heresy concerning the Incarnation is, in fact, the direct opposite of the first. Just as the first cannot accept a man who is God, so the second cannot accept a God who became man. Just as Arianism (and all forms of adoptionism, subordinationism, and the like) is a kind of *naturalism* that sees Jesus as a creature, so this second heresy (in its many forms) is a kind of *spiritualism* that disdains matter as something unworthy of being a creature of God at all. Basically it is a denial that Jesus had a real human body, and that he really suffered and died. In its earliest form it is called Docetism (from the Greek, *dokeo*, "I seem") and existed as a tendency rather than a formulated and unified doctrine, which considered the humanity and sufferings of the earthly Christ as apparent rather than real. Evidence of its existence in the early Church is to be found in 1 John (4:1-3) and 2 John (v 7); see also Colossians (2:8-9). But it reached its zenith among the Gnostics of the second and third centuries (see G. Bareille, DTC, IV, cols. 1484-1501, s.v. "Docétisme"). Besides Gnostics like Serapion, Bishop of Antioch (190-203), there was Marcion (d. *c.* 160), who claimed that Christ, who was an "emissary" of the Father, suddenly appeared preaching and teaching in the synagogue at Capernaum, and was not born of woman at all, but whose passion and death were the work of the evil Creator God of the Old Testament.

The most complete formulation of this heresy seems to be that of Manichaeism, promulgated by a certain Manes (*c.* 216-276) from Persian Gnostic sources. Its basic principle is that matter is evil and the creature of an Evil God, or Demiurge. Thus the true God could not have assumed a real human body made up of flesh and bones and been born in the manner of men. For them, the body of Jesus was an "apparent body," a "glorified" body. Manichaeism was established in Egypt before the end of the third century, but here its roots were deeply imbedded in the Egyptian Gnosticism of the second century. Early in the fourth century there were sects in Rome, and by the end of that century, Manichaeism spread throughout North Africa. Even St. Augustine himself was a Manichee for nine years before his conversion. Although the details of Manichaeism are complex, as are its subsequent forms as adopted by the Albigensians, Cathari, and Puritans, its basic principle is clear: Jesus Christ could not have been a true man like us. He gave only the "appearance" of joy and tears, suffering and death, since such physical things are unworthy of God. It is fundamentally a dualism unable to reconcile spirit and matter, God and man, divinity and humanity (or even flesh and spirit in man). Together with an irreconcilable dualism in Manichaeian Christology, there is an irreconcilability in its puritanical spirituality, as well as a fundamental inability to accept the human body as a work of God's art, or man as the "image of God." St. Thomas combines all the various sects that deny the full reality of Christ's human body under the heading of "Manichaeian."

The basic point Thomas insists on is the absolute reality of the concrete, individual human nature of Christ that was begotten of the Virgin Mary (*Sum. theol.* III, q.5, a.1). In the words of the *De ecclesiasticis dogmatibus* (c. 2; sometimes attributed to Augustine, but in reality the work of Gennadius), St. Thomas stressed that the "body" (*corpus*) assumed by the Word "was not putative, as though it were something imaginary" (PL 58, 981). For him, the whole significance and purpose of the Incarnation and Redemption of man would have been frustrated unless the "flesh" (Jn 1:14) assumed by the Word were a true physical and organic human body, made of flesh and blood as we are, possessing *all* that is needed to constitute a complete *human nature* without original sin. Apart from Scriptural texts, Thomas relies most heavily on the Council of Ephesus (431), which declared the Virgin Mary to be in truth the "Mother of God, from whom that perfect, holy body, informed with an intellective soul, was taken, to which the Word of God is united in his person (*secundum hypostasim*) and said to be born in the flesh" (Denz. 251; cf. *Sum. theol.* III, q.4, a.3, *Sed contra*, etc.).

Historically there were opinions, later condemned, that denied that Christ had a human soul; such was the position of certain Arians and later of Apollinaris (cf. St. Aug. *De haeres.*, 49. PL 42, 40; St. Athanasius, *Contra Apollinarium*, Lib. II, n. 3. PG 26, 1136; St. Thomas, *Sum. theol.* III, q.5, a.3). For them the place of the human soul was taken by Christ's divinity. Historically there were some, like the Monothelites, who denied that Christ had a human will, its place being taken by the divine will (on this point consult ODCC, 2nd ed. Oxford 1974, 932-33). But most extensive was the view of the Monophysites, whom we shall discuss later, who held that Christ has only *one nature* both divine and human. Such a union, according to St. Thomas, would result in a *tertium quid* that would be less than divine and more than human, which would in effect be a denial of the reality of both Christ's humanity and his divinity (*Sum. theol.* III, q.2, a.1). An extreme form of Monophysitism was condemned in the person of Eutyches (d. 454) at the Council of Chalcedon (451), to which the Monophysites of today have remained implacably opposed (cf. ODCC, 931-32).

The basic view of St. Thomas is that the whole of human nature, past, present, and to come, was united to the divinity in the one, indivisible person of Jesus Christ. In this indivisible unity the eternity of God, which knows no beginning, middle, or end, was joined to the temporality and historicity of man, with all its yesterdays and tomorrows, all its aches and pains, all its grandure and ignominy. How the eternal instant of God felt, thought, willed, grew, and matured, suffered, and died in his human nature is a mystery that is too much for our all-to-temporal being to understand. But we must take consolation in the fact that Jesus fully experienced all the human loves, compassion, loneliness, joys and desires, affection and aspirations that we experience too often in an inhuman and incomplete way. And he endured incredible suffering and death. The same Jesus who could pour out his heart in love for his disciples (Jn 14-17) is the same Jesus who could say, "I am thirsty" (Jn 19:28), and "My God, my God, why have you forsaken me?" (Mt 27:46).

The less we appreciate the true humanity of the historical Jesus, the less we involve ourselves in the divinity that Christ came to give us. One constant theme of all the great Fathers of the Church, especially St. Athanasius and St. Augustine, is that God became a partaker of our humanity that we might become partakers of his divinity. There is only one point in which divinity and humanity meet for all eternity, and that is in the person of the historical Jesus.

(c) The main theological and philosophical difficulty that arises from what has already been said is "Why is the historical Jesus not a human person?" If a *person* is "an individual substance of an intellectual nature," as Boethius had said (see above, Note III), then why is not the individual human nature born of the Virgin Mary not a human person, that is, a "man"? Could a divine Person, the Son of God, assume a human person, in which case there would be *two persons* in Jesus, just as there are *two natures*? As the Greeks put the question, "Why are there not two *hypostases* in Jesus?" We do not say that the Word assumed "a man," but a human nature. Technically, this is a real philosophical problem that has its roots in Aristotelian philosophy. Normally what Mary would have given birth to should have been a human person having an individual human existence (*esse*). But, in fact, she gave birth to a divine Person, the Only Begotten Son of the eternal Father, in human flesh.

Historically, Nestorius, patriarch of Constantinople (428-31), condemned the teaching of some monks concerning the divine maternity of Mary. These monks even went so far as to call Mary, the "Mother of God," *Theotokos* (*deipara*, or *Dei genetrix*), meaning "God-bearer." For Nestorius, God could have no mother, for he existed from all eternity; Nestorius therefore insisted that Mary could only be called *Christotokos*, the mother of Christ, or "Christ-bearer," thus teaching that the hypostasis or person of Christ, born of Mary, was *other than* the divine person begotten of the Father. Thus, while emphasizing the infinite gap between the human nature of Christ and his divine nature as God, Nestorius and his numerous followers (even to this day) also taught that an infinite gap exists between the hypostasis begotten of Mary and the Second Person (*hypostasis*) of the Holy Trinity. In other words, Nestorius taught not only a duality of nature (*physeis*) in Christ, but also a duality of substances (*hypostases*), that is, of persons. We have already touched upon the difficulties of the Greek and Latin terminology in this matter (Notes III and IV above).

The Council of Ephesus was convoked in 431 by Theodosius II at the instigation of St. Cyril, patriarch of Alexandria and representative of Pope Leo I at the Council. Much to the surprise of Nestorius, his views were condemned and the Council declared that the human nature of Christ is united to the divine, not by a fusion of natures (*secundum naturam, kata physin*), but by an identity of person (*kath hypostasin; secundum personam*). In other words, the Council of Ephesus declared as a matter of revealed doctrine that there is only *one person* in Christ — the Divine Word, the Son of the Father, the Second Person of the Blessed Trinity — and a duality of natures that always remain distinct, except by reason of the Divine Person (Denz. 250-264).

One of the monks denounced by Nestorius in his sermons was the archimandrite Eutyches, who taught that in Christ there is an intimate fusion of natures, so that after the Incarnation there was in Jesus only one person and one nature. The Council of Chalcedon was convoked in 541 by the Emperor Marcion under the presidency of St. Flavian to consider the orthodoxy of the extreme view proposed by Eutyches. The Monophysite (one-nature) position held by Eutyches and his followers was condemned outright as contrary to orthodox belief, and the Council declared that Jesus Christ has two distinct natures, in no way "fused or changed into one."

This historical background is necessary in order to understand St. Thomas' commentary on John because he refers to these heresies and their condemnations over and over again. Thomas, in fact, was one of the first scholastics to utilize the Latin translations of the Greek acts, decrees, and canons.

St. Thomas' most important contribution to Christology is his insight into the *manner of the union* between the divine and the human in Christ (see *Friar Thomas d'Aquino*, pp. 307-313). The crux of his profound insight into the fact that the union must be *hypostatic* is most clearly expounded in the two articles on the unity of Christ's *esse* (q.17). To this problem we must now turn briefly

VI

ST. THOMAS' DOCTRINE OF THE HYPOSTATIC UNION

The Council of Ephesus (431) declared against Nestorius that there is only one *hypostasis* in Jesus, and that that *hypostasis* is the eternal Son of the Father, consubstantial with him in nature (that is, *physis*), or substance (*ousia*). The Council of Chalcedon (451) declared against Eutyches that there are two distinct *natures* in Christ in no way "fused or changed into one," but are united *kath hypostasin*, that is, by reason of one person. Since the union cannot be between the two natures, divine and human, for the two would become one nature, and since the union cannot be between the divine Person and the human person, for this could only be a union *secundum quid* and *per accidens*, the union can only be in the unique Person, that is, *secundum hypostasin*. Since, as we have already seen, what the Greeks called *hypostasis*, the Latins called *persona*, the union of the divine and human in Christ is called "personal" or "hypostatic" (see Boethius, *Contra Eutychen et Nestorium*).

But the philosophical clarification and possibility of a theological understanding of the mystery did not come to Thomas until he returned to Naples in 1272 and resumed dictating the *Tertia Pars*. By the time Thomas came to compose question 17 concerning the kind and number of existences (*esse*) in Christ, he saw clearly the mysterious reality of the Incarnation.

We have already explained that for Aristotle *nature* is only a *quo*, that by which a thing is *what* it is. An individual, specific nature is "had by" a concrete *suppositum* or *ousia* (substance) in the primary sense of the term. We also said that existence (*esse*) belongs only to things, substances in the primary sense of *ousia*, that is *esse* belongs to a concrete, individual substance (*ousia*) having a specific kind of nature, by means of which the thing exists as a specific *kind* of thing. A thing is *one* because it has one *esse*.

Regarding the Incarnation the inevitable question arises as to whether Christ is one or many (a.1), and whether in Christ there is only one *esse* or more (a.2). Prior to q.17 in the *Tertia Pars*, for example in the Disputed Question *De unione verbi incarnati*, debated in Paris earlier that year (1272), Thomas thought that the individual human nature begotten of Mary must have some kind of *esse* of its own, even if only "in a certain sense" (*secundum quid*) "as human."

But this would mean that in the strict sense (*simpliciter*) Christ is "one," because he has only one person, namely, the divine; but in another sense Christ is "two" (*secundum quid*), because he has two natures. In the *Summa* (III, q.17, a.2) Thomas in no way allows the human nature of Christ to have an *esse* proper to it. If the concrete, individual human nature that Christ received from Mary had its own *esse* in any way, then the union between it and the Divine Person would be accidental, and Christ would not be absolutely and indivisibly one being, one person. Even if the new manner or mode of God's existence, namely, "as human," had its own *esse secundum quid*, as Thomas earlier thought, then the union would not be absolutely and in every way one, but *secundum quid* many. From this it would follow that the union between the Divine Person and the human nature would be "accidental" like an accident in a substance. But the union between Christ's human nature and his Divine Person cannot be accidental, no more than our human nature can be accidental to our personality. Therefore, St. Thomas concluded, the human nature of Christ and all his natural characteristics and his activities exist by the one *esse* of the Godhead. Thus the special kind of union that exists between the person of Jesus Christ and his human nature is "personal" or "hypostatic," that is, *secundum personam* or *kath hypostasin*.

Thomas' understanding of the hypostatic union rests squarely on his basic principle that in all creatures *esse* is other than *essence*. Only in God are *esse* and his *essence* identical (see *Sum. theol.* I, q.3, a.4, and all parallel places). Fr. Norbert Del Prado, O.P., has called this so-called real distinction between essence and existence in creatures "The Fundamental Truth of Christian Philosophy" (1911). It is only because human nature does not include *esse* in its definition (nature, or essence) that Christ's human nature cannot have an *esse* proper to it as human. It is the real distinction between essence and existence (*esse*) in creatures that underlies Thomas' teaching in III, q.17.

It is clear, therefore, that all other medieval positions that identify essence and *esse* in creatures — such as the Scotists, Nominalists, Suarezians — must face the question of the hypostatic union in another way. This is not the place to discuss those other views.

This then is our faith, that Jesus Christ, born of Mary at a specific time in human history, is in reality God himself; he is the Only Begotten Son of the eternal Father, identical with him in nature and being (*esse*), but distinct from the Father as a Son who *receives* all that he has *from the Father*. As this Only Begotten Son is *identical with his divine nature*, and as he was truly begotten of Mary by the Holy Spirit, Jesus — the historical Jesus — has two

distinct natures, one divine by which he is equal to the Father
(Jn 17:11), the other human by which he is the Son of Mary, less
than the Father (Jn 14:28), a man like us in all things except sin,
in short — our brother in the flesh. Thus our Lord Jesus Christ,
Son of the living God and our brother in the flesh, by the will of
the Father and the work of the Holy Spirit, brought life into the
world by his death and resurrection. By his death on the cross he
destroyed our death of damnation. By his resurrection he restored
our life of grace and glory. And we believe that he will come again
in glory to judge the living and the dead.

The only point that still needs to be mentioned here is that
only the Son, the Word, "became flesh" (Jn 1:14). In the Nicene
Creed we profess our belief in one Lord, Jesus Christ, the only Son
of God, eternally begotten of the Father ... one in being (that is,
homoousion) with the Father. Then we profess our belief in his
Incarnation when we bow our heads as we say: "By the power of
the Holy Spirit he was born of the Virgin Mary, and became man."
That is to say, only the Son of God became man, not the Father, nor
the Holy Spirit. We cannot say that the Father suffered and died for
us; nor can we say that the Holy Spirit became man, suffered under
Pontius Pilate, died and was buried. Only in the heresy of Sabellius
(3rd cent.) where the word *person* is taken to be a "mask" (*persona*, or *prosopon*) through which the one God speaks to us with
different masks, could one say, "the Father suffered and died." This
heresy in the West has also been known as Patripassionism, meaning
that the "passion of Christ" can be attributed to the Father. This
heresy, also known as "Modalism," was condemned in 447 by Pope
Leo I in a letter to Turribius, bishop of Asurias (Denz. 284). It had
long been battled in the East by St. Basil the Great (*c*. 330-379).

Thus Christ alone is the mediator between God and man.
"There is no other name, under heaven, given to men by which we
must be saved" (Acts 4:12). St. Paul expresses the simple truth in
the most direct way when he said (1 Tim 2:5-6):

> There is one God,
> and one mediator between God and man,
> the man Christ Jesus,
> who gave himself as a ransom for all.

INDEX OF PHILOSOPHERS AND THEOLOGIANS*

Alcuin: Word is in the Father by nature, but with him according to person 50. 51; Philip was the companion of Andrew in (1:40) 299.

Ambrose: Brightness is said metaphorically of God 96; Why Christ worked on the Sabbath 721.

Apollinaris: Christ had only a sensitive soul 168; the body of Christ was matter that was inanimate 413.

Aristotle: Exterior sounds are signs of interior affections 25; Ideas of all things are in God, and he is his own intellect, but the world is coeternal with him 65; How our knowledge of complex and simple things differs 603.

Arius (Arians): The Father generates the Son by his will 41; Son is less than the Father 61-64; Christ is God by participation 126; Christ has no soul 167; Word was made and is not coeternal with the Father 198; Refuted by John the Baptist 262; Son of God is a creature 477; Son is generated because of the will of the Father 545; Christ is less than the Father 742; Their arguments for the inferiority of the Son.

Augustine: Gospel of John teaches about the contemplative life 1; Whatever is known is limited by the capacity of the knower 6; On the likeness of the Trinity in our mind when understanding itself 25; The Divine Word is not formable before being formed 26; The Word contains all knowledge 27; Why the Son is said to be a "Word" and not a "notion" 32; *Principium* as indicating the Person of the Father 36; "In the beginning" means before all things 37; Truly to be is not to have a past or a future 39; Word of God is not mutable as our word 55; Word is consubstantial with the Father 71; Sin may be called a "nothing" 87, 88; On "what was made, was life in him" 91; Light is said primarily of spiritual things 96; Man cannot comprehend God 102; Man's lack of wisdom is a darkness 103; On the Word enlightening every man 130; Love of this world hinders our knowledge of God 138; On the sons of God as not being born from the desires of the flesh 160; On "the Word was made flesh" 165; Sometimes seems to have fallen into the error of Pelagius 174; On "we have seen his glory" 182; Christ has all virtues and graces superabundantly 189; Attributes (1:15-18) to John the Evangelist 200; The first grace given is justifying and prevenient grace 206; Wisdom is the knowledge of God, science the knowledge of human things 209; On "there is one standing in your midst" (1:26) 246; Holy Spirit appeared to John as a real dove, newly created 271; *The Christian Combat* 271; Why Holy Spirit appeared in the form of fire 272; Difference between the baptism of John and that of Christ 275; Let our hearts be God's home 294; Symbolism of the tenth hour 297; Why Peter was named such not from birth, but during his life 306; On the

* Major references only.

Manichaeus (Manicheans): There are two principles of things 81; All things have life 89; The Light needs no witnesses or prophets 119; Refutation of his teaching that man was produced by an evil principle 131; The Word did not assume true flesh 169; Christ had only an imaginary body 349; The world is the product of an evil principle, not God 358; God of the Old Testament was not the Father of Christ 389.

Marcionists: World as product of an evil principle, not God 358.

Nestorius: Blessed Virgin is not the Mother of God 170; In Christ, the Word only indwells a human nature 174; Scripture refutes this opinion of his 176; Christ was two persons 400.

Origen: Asks why John speaks of "the Word," rather than the "Word of God" 33; On the meaning of *principium* 34-36; Word was "with God," i.e, always 52; The Word of God is with God and man in different ways 54; Word is not God by essence, but by participation, and so is inferior to the Father 58; On "He was in the beginning with God" 63; On the role of the Word in creation 73; The Holy Spirit was made through the Word 74; Son as inferior to the Father 75; On the phrase "without him nothing was made" 86; "Nothing" may indicate sin 87,88; On "What was made in him was life" 90, 92; The Word as the light of man 98; Only living beings have light; Why God wanted witnesses 119; Christ is God by participation 126; On the Word enlightening all men 130; On the conservation of things 135; On those who believe in the name of Christ 158; "Of his fullness..." was spoken by the Baptist (1:16) 200; John did not have the soul of Elijah 230; On the text: "Are you the Prophet?" (1:21) 233; On "there is one standing in your midst" (1:26) 246; On the confusion between Bethany and Bethabora 251; The Jordan signifies Christ 252; On the animals offered in the Temple 257; Some cannot understand all the teachings of Christ 373; Jesus can calm human emotions 385; The symbolism of Christ's rising in three days 404; Solomon's temple took forty-six years to build 408; On the resurrection of the body of Jesus, i.e., the Church 415; On the unrecorded miracles of Jesus at Jerusalem 419; The soul of Christ pre-existed its union with his body 467; No person with faith is lost 486; The three types of worship: of the Gentiles, the Jews and the Christians 601; "You will worship the Father neither in this mountain nor in Jerusalem," but in heaven 608; On spiritaul and bodily food 635; On the object of our intention when doing good works 642; To harvest is to gather truth into the soul 648; Sowers and reapers are like first principles and their conclusions 651; Even Gentile prophets are without honor in their own country 666.

Paul of Samosata: Christ was a mere man who did not exist before his mother did 64; Refuted by John the Baptist 262; On Christ's power to judge 786.

Pelagius (Pelagians): Augustine seems to have agreed with his error at times 174; On the baptism of children 446.

Photinus: Christ was a mere man and did not exist before his mother 64; Christ took his origin from the Virgin.

INDEX OF SUBJECT MATTER*

* Major references only.

Bethabora: Not the real name for Bethany 251; It means the "house of preparation" 252.

Bethany: Is the name of two different places 251; It means "house of obedience" 252.

Bethsaida: Means "house of hunters," and is appropriate for Philip, Peter and Andrew 314.

brothers: In Scripture this word can mean relatives 370.

Christ: One person with two natures 175-76, 399-400, 479, 990; Has two distinct natures 173; Is one person, one divine *suppositum* 170-72; Is God by nature 742; Is from God in a way different than others 1060; Both divine and human attributes can be attributed to the person 468; The human nature he assumed was without sin, able to suffer, yet incapable of sinning 527; His divine power could influence the condition of his body 563; He was perfect God and perfect man from the moment of his conception 199; He descended from heaven in his divine nature, not as to his human nature 468-470; Yet he "comes from above" both as to his divinity and his humanity 525-529; God dwells in the soul and body of Christ, not just his soul, as with us 399; He is called Only-Begotten in reference to God, and First-born in reference to creatures 187; Existed from eternity 262; His body was perfectly formed, but not of adult size, at the instant of his conception; or formed in 45 days according to Augustine 409-10, Christ has a human soul 167-169; And two wills: divine and human 796, 923; He is superior to Moses in several ways 205; As compared to John the Baptist 196-99, 247-50, 260-62; He knows all things as man, and sees all things by his divine knowledge 462; As God he knew all things from eternity, and as man, he learned from experience 551; His human soul does not comprehend God 219; By reason of his divinity he has perfect knowledge 422; He had three kinds of knowledge: sense, intellectual, and divine 868; As "wayfarer" and as "comprehensor" 667; He comes twice into this world: at his birth and in his glory 673; His office was to bear witness to the truth in a perfect manner 117; He completed and reformed the work of God which had been deformed by man 643; He both taught and accomplished the truth 641; He came to be our example 375; He is the giver of true salvation 663; The source of life 782; His life-giving power extends to souls and bodies 759; He is our bread of life and spiritual food 907-914; He is called the "Anointed," *Unctus*, because he was anointed by the oil of the Holy Spirit 301; Anointed in his human nature 1004; His threefold grace. of union, habitual grace without measure, and the grace of headship 544; His fullness of grace 201; Fully received the Holy Spirit 541; And this without measure, as God and as man 544; He always possessed the power of any virtue and grace 273, Christ's threefold grace 188-90; The various ways he is full of grace and truth 188-190; He is the author of all grace 202; Is head of the Church 190; The Church is his bride 518; He is the source of all virtues found in others 260; The greatness of his power 752; As man he was subject to the law, and as God he was above it 846; And he could use or not use the law as he wished 574; He accomplished miracles by his own power 429; But performed none in his hidden life 263-64.

Christ (*cont.*): Entirely without sin 273; His zeal 392, 395; As prophet 667; Why he is symbolized by a lamb 257-58; And the judgment of believers 485-6, And the judgment of unbelievers 488-89, 490-92; Christ as judge 484-89, His power to judge 763-65, 784-89; God gave him the will to suffer in two different ways 478; Why he willed to die "lifted up" on the cross 474; He rose from the dead by his own power, and was also raised by the Father 403; At death his soul was separated from his body 402; Christ is the cause of the resurrection of men in several ways 791. *See also*: God, Son, Word.

"Christos": A Greek translation of the Hebrew "Messiah" 301.

Church: As the bride of Christ 250, 518; God dwells in the Church by the grace of adoption, but in Christ by the grace of union 404.

circumcision: It signifies our spiritual circumcision by Christ 1047.

contemplation: Can be described as to its height, fullness and perfection 2,7,8.

conservation: God conserves all things in existence 739-40.

creation: To create is to give existence 133; All such things must also be conserved in existence 86; created things are good, and not from an evil source 860; all creation bears witness to God's goodness, especially human beings 116; to create is superior to making something from pre-existent material 358.

darkness: Can be understood as the created intellect itself, or as its lack of wisdom 102-03; or as meaning sufferings, or error 105-07. *See also*: light.

"de": A Latin preposition signifying a material cause, an efficient cause or a consubstantial cause 162; Its three meanings 202.

disciples: Were baptized with the baptsim of Christ, not just with that of John 555; They needed to be taught humility because of their rapid promotion in great honors 570.

Elijah: The Jews thought he would come before the Messiah 228; He was like John the Baptist in three ways 232.

envy: Its conditions and nature 509-511.

esse: All things participate in *esse*, and presuppose something which is *esse* by its essence 5; It is innermost in each thing 133-34.

eternal life: Why it is called a grace 206; It is the same as salvation 482; And the fruit of Christ's passion 475; It is a vision, and the fruit and reward of faith 547; Those who believe in Christ have it in this world in its cause and in hope 950.

Eucharist: In general 954-64; Its necessity 968; Gives eternal life 972-73; Its species, its author, its truth and usefulness 960-63; The whole Christ is contained in both the bread and the wine 962, 970; It can be spiritually or sacramentally received 969, 976.

evil: Its cause is the created will, not the Word, and it is sometimes referred to as a "nothing" 87.

"ex": A Latin preposition signifying an efficient and a material cause, but not a consubstantial cause 162, 448.

faith: How the Father draws us to believe in Christ 935-46; Faith is a gift of God 537, 918-19; Contrasted with vision and science 120, 662; United with charity it is the foundation of salvation 159, 486; It is necessary for wisdom, both natural and supernatural 771; Is induced either by signs or teachings, the second being superior 418; How faith comes to us, its rewards of eternal life, resurrrection and freedom from judgment 773-77; Its fruit and reward is eternal life, a vision 547; Its main tenets are the Trinity and the Incarnation 1004; To be perfect faith should be right, prompt, and certain 662; Three aspect of faith. to believe *in Deum; Deo; Deum* 901

Father: God is the natural Father of one Son; the Father, by adoption, of many 390; Generates the Son by nature, not by will 545. *See also*: God, Son, Word.

fire: Signifies the grace of the Holy Spirit 577.

freedom: Man has free choice 99; This is because he has reason and will 351; Freedom comes from the Holy Spirit 456.

generation: Is of three kinds: one from the flesh, the other from the Spirit, and the third from both 448; The physical generation of men contrasted with their spiritual generation as sons of God 160-63.

God: Proofs for his existence 3-6; Known from his effects 211; And in this life through creatures 1062; May be seen in several ways: by a representation in the imagination; by abstracted intellibible species; through contemplation, etc. 211; God is his own *esse* 211; He is within all things by giving them existence 133; Present in all things by his essence, presence, and power 134-35; He is the cause of the existence of creatures, and of their continuing to exist 739-40; He alone knows himself comprehensively 213; Incomprehensible to every created intellect 6; His essence cannot be known through creatures 211; And he is unknowable to a creature to the extent that he is knowable 213; Though no creature can comprehend God, the Son comprehends the Father 947; He is spirit and truth 615; The term "God" signifies the divinity in a concrete way, unlike "deity," and can apply to a divine Person 44; God cannot be hated in himself, only some effect of his can be hated 828; He is the cause of the goodness in things 753, His great love for us is shown in four ways 477, 480; God is one by essence, but he makes other gods by participation 57, 187.

good: Created substances are good, and thus used by Christ in his miracles 358, All the good we do is from God 496; The difference between material and spiritual goods 915.

grace: Christ is the author of all grace 202; There is a fullness of grace in Christ 201; His grace is of three kinds: of union, habitual, and of headship 188-90, 544. Grace unites us to God 188; It enables us to act well and to attain glory 151, Justifying and prevenient grace is not due to our works 206; Prevenient grace 644; The grace of eternal life 206; Christ always possessed the power of the charismatic graces 273; The grace of union makes Christ the Son of God 327; The Virgin had a fullness of grace 201.

happiness: Can only be perfect with the vision of God 212.

heaven: Can be understood in three ways.

Holy Spirit: Is the same substance and glory as the Father and the Son 74; Is truly God and the source of our rebirth 444; Origin, destination and power of the Spirit 452-56; Holy Spirit and baptism 244; Spirit is given partially with respect to his gifts, but not with respect to his essence or power 542; Spirit is the source of our spiritual regeneration 442, 432; The source of grace 577; Was present at Christ's baptism by John 268; Assumed the form of a dove: how to understand this 270-72; Why he assumed the form of fire 272; The grace of the Spirit is signified by water and fire 577; Spirit as compared to wind 449-51; As present fully in Christ 541; Given to Christ without measure, both as God and as man 543; Spirit was given before the resurrection of Christ 1093; Spirit was given during Christ's life, in his baptism 554; Spirit produces unity in the Church 202.

"in": Latin preposition with various meanings 45.

Incarnation: Three reasons for the incarnation 141; Word assumed human nature to restore it 168-9; Makes it easier for men to see the glory of the Word 181; Its first effect is that men are made sons of God 149, 156; Is a sign of God's great compassion 169; It heals our weakened nature 182; The Word was "made" flesh 165; Word assumed flesh, but did not change into flesh 166; Word assumed flesh with a human soul 167-69.

Intellect: Naturally desires to understand the causes of the effects it knows, including God 212.

Jews: Their respect for John the Baptist 224; Their worship was inferior to that of the Christians in two ways 609; They were chosen by God as his special people, were physically related to him, and the object of his kindness 145.

John, the Baptist: As compared to Christ 196-199, 247-50, 260-62; His qualifications for his ministry 114; His authority, sent by God 111-13; His office is to bear witness 236, 115-18, 192-95, 248, 255, 265, 516-24, 806-13; Compared to Elijah 228-30, 232; The nature of his baptism 244, 266, 501, 505; Why he lived in the wilderness 238; His humility 249; Not the Messiah 225-27; His own disciples tried to turn him against Christ 507-12.

John, the Evangelist: The Order and purpose of his Gospel 10; Lived on close terms with Christ 178; His symbol is an eagle due to the height of his contemplation 11; Characteristics of his contemplation 1-8; How his Gospel differs from the others 66; John considers especially the divinity of Christ 10; He covers matters the other Evangelists omit, i.e., the public life of Christ before John was cast into prison 367, 504, 557; The only Evangelist to make use of two successive "Amens" 430.

judgment: Is of two kinds: of condemnation and of distinction, and at two times 483; Of believers 485-86; Of unbelievers 488-89, 490-92.

justification: What is required for justification 688, 717; Free will is needed, as also is grace 153-54, 578.

lamb: A symbol of Jesus Christ 257-58.

law, old: Could not justify us 190; Promised grace, but did not give it and was insufficient for living well 206; Did not take away sin or reconcile us to God 204; It was perfected, not abolished, by Christ 358; Christ obeyed it to give us an example 375; Yet it was subject to Christ, who could use or not use it as he wished 574.

life: The grades of life 97, 771.

light: Is true, symbolic or participated 125; As applied to the Word 97-101; The Word is light in himself, and the light by which all things are known 118; Son is light by essence; the saints by participation 123; As found in spiritual and material things 96; As object known and as that by which an intellectual creature knows 101.

love: United with faith it is the foundation of salvation 486; Love of neighbor is first in order of doing; love of God is first in order of precept 718; To love is to will good to someone 477; Why it is symbolized by fire 812; The lack of love is symbolized by darkness 877; God's great love for us is shown in four ways 477, 480; In man, good causes love; in God, his love causes good 753; In divine matters it can be understood essentially or notionally 753.

man: His three states: before sin, after sin, in glory 527; Is like God in spirit, not in body 615; The more he is known, the more imperfect he seems; the contrary is the case with God 666; Has free choice 99; Becomes a child of God by grace 150.

marriage: Signifies the union of Christ with his Church 338; Is not evil 341.

Mary, Virgin: She remained a virgin, and Jesus was her only child 370, 1015; Her fullness of grace 201.

Messiah: A Hebrew word, "Christos" in Greek, and "Unctus" in Latin 301.

miracles: Are for unbelievers since they cannot come to Christ through the Scriptures 685.

nothing: Is not a reality, but the absence of reality 79, 83; The word is at times used to indicate evil 87.

participation: What is by participation depends on what is such by essence 127.

Passover: Symbolic of the Christian passover 377; Avarice was frequently found at its celebration 381-82.

"per": Latin preposition indicating causality, but not always the same kind 76.

persecution: Can lawfully be fled from 556.

Pharisees: A sect of which some priests and Levites were members 241; Believed in spirits and in the resurrection of the dead 424; Their attitude toward John the Baptist 242-43; They object to John's baptism 243; They did not recognize Christ from the Old Testament 246.

preachers: Should lead men to Christ and not to themselves 302, 626.

"Principium": It can mean different things in the verse: "In the beginning was the Word" 34-38.

prophets: They have two functions 667; Christ did not denigrate the prophets 237; Why Christ wanted to have the witness of the prophets 119; To predict the future can only be done by divine power 320; The prophets predicted the name of Jesus, his family and native land 317.

regeneration, spiritual: Its necessity 447; Has two causes: the Incarnation and passion of Christ 465; Comes from the Holy Spirit 442; Does not depend on age or size 439; It is to be born again, that is, from above 435; Why water is used 443; The qualities of one who is regenerated by the Holy Spirit 456; Found in the old law in figurative form; and even in the new law it is imperfect because partial 433, 461; It will be perfect in heaven, in a face to face vision 433. *See also*: baptism.

resurrection: Jesus gave two signs of his resurrection: Jonah and the temple 397-98; Christ rose by his own power, and was also raised by the Father 403; Condition of the world after the resurrection 939-40; Its meritorious, exemplary and first cause is Christ 791; Is of two kinds: of the soul and of the body 762, 779.

Sabbath: The Sabbath prohibition was mystical in meaning 723; Its relation to Christ and the law 721; Jesus justified himself and his disciples for breaking the Sabbath 738.

sacraments; Can only be instituted by God, and derive their power from the passion of Christ 276.

Sadducees: Did not believe in spiritual beings or in the resurrection 424.

salvation: There is a true and false salvation 663; Comes from the Jews in two ways 606; Its foundation is faith, united with charity 486; Its only way is the Son of God 489.

sin: Four effects of personal sin which we bring upon ourselves 706; The kinds and degrees of punishment for sin 733-34; symbolized by a fig tree 326; Original sin must be in all descended from Adam 528.

Son: Is consubstantial with the Father 218; Is incomprehensible and invisible 220; Comprehends the divine essence 218, 1062-65; Came as a Savior 270; His competence as a teacher 215-22; His teaching surpasses all others in dignity, authority and usefulness 221; There is only one natural Son of God, the others are adopted 390; Others are made sons by grace 327; One is called a son of God insofar as he is like his natural Son 216. *See also*: Christ, Word, God.

soul: Does not exist before its union with the body 129.

temple: Of Christ's body 399-402; History of Solomon's temple 407-08.

test, temptation: Man tests to learn; the devil to ensnare; and God so others might learn 850; Temptation as a sickness which can lead to death 682.

Testament, Old: Testifies to Christ 822-23.

thanksgiving; Christ gives us an example to give thanks to God 861.

truth: Every truth, by whoever spoken, comes from the Holy Spirit 103, 1037; All our knowledge of the truth is from another 1037, 1040; The true can be contrasted with the false, the symbolic, and the participated 125.

virtue: Christ is the source of virtue 260; Virtue is not the same as a natural disposition 492.

vision, of God: Contrasted with faith 120; presupposes regeneration by the Holy Spirit, and will exist in heaven 432-33; To see God the intellect must be "separated" from the body 213-14; Is had by the angels and the blessed 212; Cannot be attained through any species 211; Is necessary for perfect happiness 212; This vision knows the whole divine essence, but not wholly or comprehensively 213.

wisdom: Consists in the knowledge of God 209; Acquired by experience and contemplation 854; Wisdom as the Son of God 107.

witness: Men bear witness to God by their good actions and by teaching 116, Each creature is a witness to God's goodness 116; Why Christ wanted the witness of the prophets 119.